The Old Man and the Sand Eel

WILL MILLARD

VIKING

an imprint of

PENGUIN BOOKS

VIKING

UK | USA | Canada | Ireland | Australia
India | New Zealand | South Africa

Viking is part of the Penguin Random House group of companies
whose addresses can be found at global.penguinrandomhouse.com.

First published by Viking 2018

001

The publisher is grateful for permission to quote from: *Fishing for a Year* by Jack Hargreaves
(Medlar Press 2011), reproduced by kind permission of Jack Hargreaves's stepson Simon Baddeley,
owner of rights in all Jack Hargreaves's 'Out of Town' films for Southern Television; *John Wilson's
Fishing Encyclopaedia* (Boxtree 1995), reproduced by permission of Pan Macmillan; *The Secret Carp* by
Chris Yates (Merlin Unwin Books 2000), reproduced by permission of Merlin Unwin Books; *Blood
Knots* by Luke Jennings (Atlantic Books 2010), reproduced by permission of Sky Horse Publishing,
Inc and Atlantic Books Ltd; *The Book of Eels* by Tom Fort (HarperCollins 2002), reproduced by
permission of HarperCollins Ltd; *Somewhere Down the Crazy River* by Paul Boote and Jeremy Wade
(Hodder and Stoughton 1994), reproduced by kind permission of Jeremy Wade; *A Game of Thrones*
by George R. R. Martin (HarperCollins 1991), reproduced by permission of HarperCollins Ltd;
'Pike' from *Lupercal* by Ted Hughes (Faber and Faber 1960), reproduced by permission of Faber and
Faber Ltd; *A River Runs Through It* by Norman Maclean (University of Chicago Press 1989), reproduced
by permission of University of Chicago Press; *Fish, Fishing and the Meaning of Life* by Jeremy Paxman
(Penguin 1995), reproduced by permission of David Higham Associates.

Every effort has been made to trace copyright holders and to obtain their permission for the use of
copyright material. The publisher apologizes for any errors or omissions and would be grateful to be
notified of any corrections that should be incorporated in future editions of this book.

Set in 13.5/16 pt Garamond MT Std
Typeset by Jouve (UK), Milton Keynes
Printed in Great Britain by Clays Ltd, St Ives plc

A CIP catalogue record for this book is available from the British Library

ISBN: 978-0-241-27001-1

www.greenpenguin.co.uk

For the great man
who once taught me to fish

Contents

The Greater Sand Eel   1

The Striped Assassin   13

The Water Wolf   81

A Never-Ending Golden Sun   133

The Fish Everyone Hates   191

The Great Game   243

Coming Home   295

Acknowledgements   321

The Greater Sand Eel

What do they know of fishing who know only
one fish and one way to fish for him?
Jack Hargreaves, *Fishing for a Year* (1951)

I depress the playback button on my phone for the fifth
time in five minutes. It's killing me to keep watching,
but I'm desperate to find something, anything, positive
amid this total horror show of a film.

'That is one of the biggest sand eels I've ever seen in
my life!' it begins.

I'm shouting, partly out of excitement, and partly
because the wind is whipping up so hard around
the Dorset coast that it's distorting the sound on the
video.

In one hand I'm trying shakily to film with my mobile
phone, while, in the other, I'm struggling to hold a British record fish. I don't know what else to say. 'It's a

whopper!' I eventually stammer, sniffing back a runny nose and punching the 'stop' button.

I gently place my phone on my table and smash a cushion directly into my face. I've just made the biggest mistake of my entire fishing career, and, worse still, I know I've only got myself to blame.

There are few sensations in life that can match the angler's almost immeasurable sense of loss when a big fish slips from their grasp. It is a poker-hot pain that continues to burn as bright in the memory as it did in the moment itself. Losing the sand eel record set me on a redemptive pathway that spanned the length and breadth of Britain. For over a year of my life I allowed the eel to completely take over, and, in the end, my angling would never be quite the same again. But that was all still to come. For now I was stuck in an angling purgatory, with bent hooks, broken dreams and that video for company. I pressed the playback button once more.

When I was a boy I used to revel in going around my grandparents' home, a small bungalow that for me meant warm milky tea, chocolate sauce on ice cream, well-worn furniture and *John Wilson's Fishing Encyclopedia*. My grandad would take the heavy hardback book in his thick fingers and, when I asked him, rest it on his enormous belly and thumb through the various sections. As far as I was concerned John Wilson was a god. He had a long-running series called *Go Fishing* that used to crop up for a few weeks a year on Anglia Television. It was on pretty late at night so I'd either try and stay up to watch it or get Mum to record it on VHS by laboriously punching the long code printed in the *Radio Times* into our tape player. *Go Fishing* spanned the period of time as a child when I was only ever allowed to catch tiny red-finned roach from the creek directly outside our house, roughly the ages of four to twelve, or 'Argos Introduction to Fishing Kit' through to 'Kingfisher Coarse Supreme Kit', if you prefer. The titles always began with John Wilson's silhouette walking on an animated, but minuscule, planet Earth. He lumbered over the surface of our world as a giant, striding with remarkable ease from continent to continent, passing signs that simply read 'fish' and 'more fish'. Pretty remarkable in itself for an adoring young super-fan from an insular village in the Cambridgeshire Fens, but the best bit about *Go Fishing* is that, despite what you might infer from the titles, Wilson rarely left Britain. His world was the chalk-fed River Wensum in Norfolk, the Royalty stretch of the River Avon, expansive gravel pits, beautiful Irish lochs and picture-postcard-perfect fish. *Go Fishing*'s gift was that it made catching fish, often of a specimen size, seem attainable. By catching well from his own backyard, Wilson made me, a novice angler, believe I too could catch well from mine.

Wilson placed equal value on all species of fish, a sort of 'Martin Luther King' of the fishing world, so it was to be expected that in *John Wilson's Fishing Encyclopedia* no one species, method, bait or habitat was over-represented. From A to Z as much page space was dedicated to boilie baits as bread, carp as catapults, wire traces as wobbling dead baits. This was important because, to juvenile eyes, it presented the world of fishing not as a game to be completed, but as a near infinite set of variables where it was possible to utterly lose yourself in the discovery and mystery of the sport. Anything was plausible, because nothing was predictable.

In the *Go Fishing* era, any catch I deemed to be 'highly unusual' was hastily reported to Grandad with perhaps the same level of enthusiasm as an ecologist might have on discovering a new species after decades of fruitless toil. It mattered not that the fish species were, in reality, just slightly less than common, the days I caught my first zander, ruffe and bleak were moments to be celebrated from the highest platforms possible (from the narrow selection available to me from within my grandparents' bungalow), climaxing with the highly ritualized inspection of the John Wilson *Encyclopedia*. The reason for this was three-fold: first of all, the book allowed me to glean the definitive facts on the 'new' species from the highest authority in the land (John Wilson), secondly it made me feel one step closer to my idol (also John Wilson), and, finally, it was a cast-iron guarantee that I could get the full and unadulterated attention of my grandad, a living breathing angling (demi-)god, of sorts.

I inherited the Wilson *Encyclopedia* when my grandad passed away two years ago. For a few weeks I couldn't even bring myself to open it. It smelt of him and his bungalow; a precious bridge back into those memories before the body and mind of this once strong man gave way to life and death in a nursing home. It just didn't feel right to read it without his permission and his bookstand stomach to open it from. It sat on my shelf untouched, the magic spilling from its pages.

Then the sand eel slithered into my life and changed everything.

I had never caught a sand eel before; let alone one within the 'greater' species definition. I strongly suspected it would be featured in the *Encyclopedia* – pretty much all the common species in the British Isles had made some sort of billing – so, with curiosity eventually getting the better of me, I decided this would be the appropriate time to finally peel open the pages of the formerly forbidden tome.

I found my fish wedged between the obscure Corbin's sand eel and the squid-eating scad. With a supporting image resembling the scabbard of a dagger, the greater sand eel entry read: 'the largest of the sand eel . . . The body is long, thin and smooth with a greeny-blueish back, blending down the sides into lower flanks and a belly of silvery white.' Wilson goes on to say that you can only catch them on exceptionally small feathers armed with tiny hooks. That's funny, I thought to myself. I had mine on the vulgarly named 'Flying Condom', a long hefty lure only really designed for the gaping mouth of the large sea bass or a sea-sprung salmon. The hooks on that lure are massive, thumbnail-sized and thick. Strange I managed to land that sand eel then. I supposed.

For a moment I just let that thought rest on top of my brain. A few more precious seconds of blissful ignorance after what had, up until that point, been a very enjoyable weekend. Inevitably, though, the thought drifted its way into the centre of my skull, fired up the synapses responsible for reasoned thought, and caused the horrifying implications of the Wilson suggested hook size, versus the ones I had used, versus the size of the fish I had managed to land, to dawn on me with force.

I recoiled from the book. What if the reason I landed that fish was that it was, in the modest world of the sand eel, an absolute monster?

The greater sand eel description had taken me onto a second page. I knew the layout of this book as well as if I'd written it myself. At the start of each species section Wilson always details the British record weight, which meant, just one page previously, the auspicious number was lying in wait for me. I felt a tremble somewhere deep within my bowels.

Just close the book, Will.

Close the book, put it back on the shelf and never open it again.

I turned the page back.

Eight and a half ounces. It was staring me right in the face, in black and white, directly below the drawing of the distinctly smug-looking greater sand eel.

Eight and a half ounces. That's a pot of Marmite, a tin of beans, a four-pack of Mars bars, surely not a new British fish record?

I didn't need to review the footage I shot that morning to know with certainty that the fish I had caught was in excess of 8.5oz, but I did it anyway, multiple times, and there it was: as bold as brass, wriggling along the length of almost my entire forearm. A fish clearly over 10oz, possibly even knocking on the door of one pound, a cast-iron miniature record breaker, and I had quite literally thrown it away.

To say I was fuming for the rest of the week would be to put it mildly.

Not only did I not speak for a good few days, but I could hardly even bring myself to look at the offending fishing tackle. I'd had my scales in my bag the whole time, the coastline had been packed with people, including my girlfriend, who had patiently waited for me at the top of the rocks, and I'd even had my camera with me. Getting that sand eel officially registered with the golden trifecta of witness, weight and photo, required by the British Record Fish Committee, would have taken less time than it took me to come up with my stupid little speech on that stupid bloody video. A video, I might add, which now only exists as little more than an everlasting record of my own unbelievable ignorance.

Let's be honest, no one is going to be particularly rushing to break the doors down at the British Record Fish Committee to register a new shore-caught sand eel record; nor are the editors of the national angling press waiting, poised over their typewriters, for the sensational scoop of my 'against the odds' battle with sand eel destiny, but that is precisely the point: no one actually wants the greater sand eel rod-caught record, which means it was the perfect record for me to break.

In truth I am still something of an amateur fisherman. Sure, I know my way around several different styles and techniques, and have had more than my fair share of luck, but realistically that sand eel was absolutely my best chance of making it onto the list of official record breakers, and I had completely blown it.

During the golden years of the John Wilson *Fishing Encyclopedia*, back when I was twelve years old, I would fish only two waters: the Well Creek, outside my childhood home, and Popham's Eau, a vast drain which I would venture to once a week with my grandad. I may have gone to the local school but this was where I truly received my education. More than just the places I caught my first fish, these twin rivers were where I learnt my watercraft and discovered the workings of the natural world, where I made my first real friends, and endured the rain and cold without running home to Mum. Very occasionally they were also the settings of the purest personal triumphs I will ever experience in my life. I would go on to catch much bigger fish from hundreds of different venues with far greater names than Popham's or the Creek, and yet the memories of my time on those banks remains undiminished. I ask myself now, looking back, am I truly more knowledgeable as an angler now than I was then? In my childhood, thanks to the *Encyclopedia*, I knew every single British fish species, and its record weight, by heart.

How could I not have realized I had caught a new record then? The answer was obvious and it was staring me right in the face. On the wall of my study I had pinned two sheets of A4 paper. One is the optimistically titled 'fishing targets', and the other is a list of potential venues and tactics. The list includes king carp, crucian carp, eel, perch, pike, salmon and roach, with ample space for notes.

Many years ago the plan was to work my way through the entire list, breaking my lowly personal bests, and introducing myself to as many new species and varied environments as I possibly could. Just as John Wilson did, and, it pains me to say it, just as my grandad would have liked.

I look up at that list now and know I've badly let him down. The pages next to all the native species are barren, whereas the sections dealing with the introduced and very foreign king carp are absolutely crammed with information: Monument, Linear, Redmire, popped-up plastic corn; 4G squid; the Source, crab-mist, chod, braid and spod. The list goes on and on, years of accumulated information on a single species, from a single type of venue, that has completely suffocated my childhood knowledge of the wider piscatorial world; pushing king carp facts in one ear and everything else I've ever learnt about fish and fishing right out of the other.

That lost greater sand eel was a sign from above. I'd stopped caring about where I fished, as long as there were fish. For two decades straight, the places I fished were near identical commercial ponds and lakes filled to bursting point with artificially reared carp and brought to my net using much the same methods and baits. As a result, I failed to identify the record breaker in my hands and rightfully lost my chance. Now, with the rediscovery of the *Encyclopedia*, I have all the ancient wisdom I could possibly require on virtually every single species and fishing technique within the British Isles, and that sand eel which slipped between my fingers is the kick up the arse I fully deserved and desperately needed.

I prise the list off the wall — it's been up there for a while, the Blu-tack has gone hard and takes a small flake of paint with it — and select the biggest, thickest black marker on my desk. Striking a meaningful cross through the entire king carp section instantly makes me feel better. 'It's catching, not fishing,' Grandad always used to say every time I talked up my latest carp conquest at the local commercial fishery; I'd give him the withering teenage eye roll reserved for uncompromising adults, but it's only now I realize he was bloody right all along. I scribble all over the freshly drawn cross for good measure and focus in on all the other names left on the list, taking delight in rolling my tongue over the names like I'm reading a fairy tale to a child. These are legendary fish, steeped in history, yet bullied to the periphery of most anglers' imaginations by this nationwide king carp obsession. To find the native, truly wild populations of these fish I'm going to have to travel to the sorts of places that exist well beyond the public gaze. Spots where most wouldn't think to cast a line: tangled underworlds, crumbling docks and urban rivers, the dwellings of the truly abandoned, where a unique kind of freedom survives distinct from the regentrified, reimagined and sanitized versions of wilderness that I've just wasted the last twenty years fishing in.

I spread a map of Britain out on the table and am immediately struck by just how well watered this nation really is. The rivers and lakes stretch right across this island like a giant central nervous system, easily dwarfing our roads and motorways through their sheer scale and abundance. Obviously not all these waterways will hold record breakers, and I wouldn't get very far attempting to wet a line in every body of water in Britain, but I know there are definitely ways of shortening the odds in my favour before I set off.

A quick search on the internet finds me the British Record Fish Committee's record-coarse-fish register, which helpfully includes all the places the fish were caught and by whom. That feels as good a place as any to start out, but I know I must avoid becoming completely hamstrung by someone else's list. A lot of these venues will have seen serious angling pressure since they produced their record, and doubtless some of them will also be part of expensive and exclusive clubs that I just won't be able to access. But records are there to be broken and fish die or move on elsewhere. If I'm going to give this a proper crack I need to look to offshoots of pre-established record-breaking waters, speak to local people and be prepared to take seriously the near-mythic stories of park lake monsters and river beasts. After all, just sticking to the beaten track was pretty much what got me into this mess in the first place.

I take a deep breath. It feels like I'm learning how to fish all over again. I know this is going to take patience and extraordinary amounts of luck, but the night before I attempt the first fish is utterly sleepless. I feel like I can actually sense the monsters of my imagination queuing up to be caught, pressing against the inside of my eyelids, willing me on to success.

The Striped Assassin

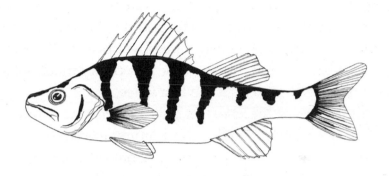

I am haunted by waters.
Norman Maclean, *A River Runs Through It* (1976)

Proper fishermen would never set up their rods before seeing the water they intend to fish, but I'm not a proper fisherman and have learnt the hard way that I make a much more proficient job of putting together my tackle in the dry confines of my kitchen than on the bankside. By the time I've made it out of the door and down to the river, lake or pond, I'm usually far too excited about the prospect of the first cast to concentrate on tying my knots properly, and thus set myself inexorably on the path to experiencing the devastating parting of fish from angler, right at the point of least resistance: my crap knots.

The line peels from the reel's silver barrel with a series of soft clicks and glides over the wooden top of my chair. I plan to keep this set-up extremely straightforward as big perch hate complication.

I squeeze an extra-large shot of weight, the shape and dimension of a rabbit dropping but heavy and hard, on one end of a short, six-inch length of line. That'll keep my bait pinned hard to the lake bottom. To the other end I attach a swivel, a tiny barrel of metal with two small rings at either end, which I then thread onto my main line. The swivel allows the weight to slide sweetly along the length of line without registering any resistance should a big perch pick up my bait. It slides down sweetly; free and smooth, right along the length of the line till it hits the rod's tip with a satisfying 'plink'.

Perfect. Zero resistance. The perch won't even know it's hooked.

My whole life has been one spent surrounded by water and my happiness can be accurately measured by my proximity to it.

I was born in the Cambridgeshire Fens; one of two, five minutes before my twin sister, Anna, with a little brother, Tom, coming along some seven years later. Ours was a house filled with nature, thanks, in no small part, to the unbridled enthusiasm of our dad.

He was a magical figure to me as a scabby-kneed under-five. I didn't really understand why he was so often not around, the demands of his job as the local village doctor frequently taking him away from us for longer than we all would have liked, but when he was there he poured his love of wildlife deep into the souls of his children.

Through him I learnt to seek pleasure in bird-watching walks in fenland waterscapes, or to train my eye onto the very tiniest of life forms, dissecting the underside of a carefully lifted log with forensic preci-sion, in the hope of snaring one of the worms or pungent ground beetles that lived there.

He seemingly hadn't inherited his father's passion for angling, but in those early days he armed me with the essential patience and respect I would require to winkle out fish later in life.

My earliest memories are really just a haphazard collec-tion of senses and emotions, but they all revolve around the natural world brought to my palms by Dad. First there was Norman, the Airedale terrier. Unwisely purchased just before Mum gave birth to us twins, he was a mix of hyperactive, ginger, hard wire wool and smelly wet tongue. Next was the mustiness of Dad's vast butterfly collection, which had a sort of pungent, slightly oppres-sive, perfume-like smell that you might also find around the embalmed corpses in the British Museum. I have always associated that scent with the dark wood and glass that contained his treasures and, if allowed, I would open the drawers with real care and reverence. The resi-dents of these cases were frozen in time. Ossified and rigid, captured and sacrificed, all in the name of science. Even if I removed the glass they were trapped behind they could never grow or float through the sky again. I knew that this was not a time to smile or make jokes as the creatures that lived in there were actually just dead.

Living animals in the house, apart from Norman and the occasional woodlouse that made it (very) briefly into the room I shared with Anna, were accommodated in the circular conservatory at the back of our home. This pleasure dome for captive wildlife all but guaranteed victory for the Millard twins on the Upwell County Primary School 'show and tell' table, something that was of extreme importance to me at that time; plus, it was perfectly placed at the foot of the garden, providing a thrilling portal between the familial and the feral.

Dad would often hatch foreign moths and butterflies in the warmth of the glass house, the death's-head hawk-moths were easily my favourites. With their human skull patterns emblazoned on their thoraxes like bikers' tattoos, I thought they had to be just about the coolest insect that ever lived, but it was in the careful handling of the giant Atlas moths that I learnt the value of being gentle with any living creatures. Even the smallest brush of a wingtip could leave a guilty trace of their dust on my fingers. It was the Atlas depositing tiny scales from their bodies and would dull their colour instantly. Even today, despite having pulled a fish through the water with a hook in its mouth, I chastise myself at the loss of a single scale as a result of any rough handling on the bank.

Dad taught me that it was sometimes okay to catch animals to study and admire, but, as he aged, his focus became less on capture and more on the observation. Photos replaced traps, his butterfly collection waned, and the insect population of the conservatory began to dwindle.

I guess that was where Dad and I differed in our approach to nature. For him it was enough to simply observe and understand from afar; for me, it was necessary to get as close as possible, and, ideally, hold the creature in my hands. It wasn't a case of wanting mastery over the natural world – I wasn't one of those cruel kids who would pick the legs off a daddy-long-legs for a laugh. I just seemed to get infinitely more from something I could actually hold, touch and, years later, catch then release.

One day, a new resident was installed in the conservatory fish tank. It was to be my first close encounter with a fish, and, my goodness, what a fish it was.

In researching for this book I have since learnt from Dad that the brook lamprey was actually with us for only a single night, caught in a willow wicker-work trap by an eel-catcher from our local creek and given to Dad because he was 'into that sort of thing'. Yet I remember it like it was there for the entirety of my early childhood. For the under-fives, time lengthens and memories compress in unusual ways; that one-night stand with the lamprey made a massive impression.

According to the Wilson *Encyclopedia* the brook lamprey 'rarely exceeds an adult length of 10 inches', which is quite extraordinary as I was fairly convinced our specimen was the size and girth of a Burmese python.

Wilson goes on to note that its 'sucker-like mouth is used only for adhering to the undersides of stones'. Now, not that I wish to accuse a fisherman, of all people, of understating the facts somewhat, but at no point does Wilson highlight that this fish has to be one of the most bizarre-looking creatures in Britain, if not the planet Earth. Not only does it have no fewer than seven separate gills, running in a hole-punch-like line right down its body, but he also neglects to mention that its 'sucker-like mouth' is, in fact, a horrific circular suction pad filled with a truly nightmarish series of studded teeth.

For hours my sister and I stared at the curious fish in the tank; utterly transfixed. It didn't seem to move much, preferring instead to spend its time stuck hard to the glass side of the fish tank. Perfect for me, though, as it afforded a close-up view of those extraordinary mouth-parts for the brief period it was in our custody.

It was a highly unusual capture anyway. The brook lamprey is most often found in fast-running streams where it can happily breed on gravel deposits; in the turgid murky waters of the river outside my home it seemed an absolute imposter. That thought delighted me. Out there, beneath a brown theatre curtain of surface water, was a subaquan wonderland just waiting to be discovered: a place where real monsters lived and died, well away from the gaze of us land-dwelling, air-breathing mortals, yet it *could* be accessed briefly; if, and only if, you learnt how.

Dad took its picture, and the next day the lamprey was gone, returned to live out its unlikely, and doubtless quite lonely, life in the water running around our tiny village, and I was left to advance an obsession with what else might be caught from water.

In the ironed-out landscape of the Fens, water is absolutely everywhere and, as a result, I grew up an extremely happy little boy.

I needed guidance to access water for the first time of course, but Mum and Dad were never afraid to let me go near the water's edge, with supervision initially, and later on my own.

I was lucky; lucky to have so much space to play in safely, but also lucky to have parents that understood the importance of allowing me to discover the outdoors and water for myself, by myself.

I'm at that stage of life now where all my friends are starting to have children of their own. It only takes moments in the company of a young person to realize that a fear of water is inherited and not innate. Last week, my two-year-old niece Edie was utterly mesmerized by my fish tank, desperate to dip a net in and learn the names of the fish; her wild eyes reflected in the glass sides as her mind hungrily consumed every new scale pattern and plastic leaf. Eventually she reached out her tiny hand and ran it along the tank corner and on into the wet within, learning, in that moment, the curious interplay between glass and water.

It's fascinating to see, and I believe a vitally important part of development, yet most children these days are absolutely forbidden from taking any interest in water outside of the bathtub. How many times have you seen anxious parents grasping the hands of their children in horror as they approach the six inches of 'deep' water at the edge of the municipal park pond? Or adolescents getting terribly scolded for daring to place their fingers in a perfectly clean town centre stream? Eventually these irrationalities rub off and those children grow up with their own unnatural fear of wild water, and, somewhat inevitably, so do their offspring in turn.

Not all of those fears are completely without foundation. Tragically, the last decade has seen an average of 390 people per year drown in accidents in British inland waters; but look a little closer into the figures and you will see that doesn't automatically mean that the water outside our home is inherently dangerous for young children.

Of those 390 the single largest category is males aged between their mid-teens and mid-twenties. Many instances are alcohol-related, most are avoidable: young people looking to prove themselves by swimming distances beyond their ability or fatal injuries caused by diving head first into surprisingly shallow water, or water that is dangerously fast, or too deep, or just shockingly cold. Instead of teaching young people to be aware of the risks and guiding them towards safer areas to play and wild-swim from an early age, the prevailing attitude seems to favour putting up warning signs, locking gates, building barriers and telling our children that natural water should not be entered under any circumstances, and especially not for your entertainment. Let's face it: since when have any of those sorts of measures stopped your average young person hell-bent on besting his or her peers?

Year on year more obstacles to accessing our waters appear, and year on year the number of deaths stays more or less the same. Surely it is better to invest in teaching our children how to manage risk in water, and thereby avoid tragedy, than to let them stay indoors, where they live their lives vicariously through the internet and television?

There are reams and reams of studies proving the physical and mental health benefits of just being near water. More than that though – perhaps most importantly in fact – our fresh water desperately needs our attention.

Thanks to myopic human development, rampant pollution and climate change, freshwater habitats are now easily the most endangered environments on earth. In the last half-century the doubling of freshwater withdrawals for our own ends has caused 50 per cent of wetlands to vanish altogether, and fewer than seventy of the planet's 177 longest rivers remain free of manmade commercial obstructions.

For freshwater fish, the news is even worse: one third of all species are threatened with extinction today, compared to 21 per cent of mammals and 12 per cent of birds. Yet if you cast a speculative eye on the adverts for all the major wildlife charities, you'd be forgiven for thinking our fishy friends are doing just fine; but if you are beginning to think it's bad for them, you should check how awfully the amphibians and freshwater invertebrates are faring.

You may well like to believe it is in the developing world, in the sorts of places where populations are dependent on harvesting freshwater fish just to survive, that the results would be at their worst, but looking at Europe in isolation we see that the number of fish species facing extinction is nudging up to a shameful 40 per cent, and, according to the European Environment Agency, half of our rivers and lakes are polluted. Things aren't much better in the United States either. Over the pond, the rate of fish extinction is now over 800 times faster than in the fossil record.

We are marching to the brink of a worldwide environmental disaster, and yet there is little more than a whimper of protest.

Of course we should all be up in arms, but how can you reasonably expect people to care about saving an environment that they are preconditioned to believe is irrelevant and dirty at best, or a dangerous menace at worst?

Every garden should have a pond. Ours was oval-shaped and about ten feet wide. At one end there was a neat little shallow area that allowed amphibians to come and go as they pleased and provided a safe nursery area for frogs and toads to spawn. It dropped to a depth of no more than a couple of feet from that shallow point and was stepped in at the edges so Mum and Dad could submerge baskets filled with aquatic plants and water lilies. In the summer the centre was near solid with Canadian pond-weed, an invasive species that shrouded the pond's surface with its green pipe-cleaner-like tendrils while providing oxygen as well as shelter to the host of inverte-brates that lived within its bulk.

It was here I learnt how to hunt frogs, the first living thing I ever knowingly caught from water (the first living thing I caught unknowingly from water was a 'miller's thumb', a three-inch-long micro-fish with a fat head and rounded tail that slipped inside my wellies when I fell into a stream in Yorkshire).

I was appalling at first. My ham-pink hands slapped the water's surface like a drummer's cymbal each time a frog dared to lift its head above the weed. The first rule I learnt then was to be patient and observe.

Soon enough I realized the frogs in the centre of the pond were never to be caught: they always had a couple of feet of water below them to sink down into, whereas I was aiming at only about half an inch of a frog's head. To go for them in the middle was to disturb the whole pond for hours; the best bet was to wait for them to approach the edge, as the shallower water would signifi-cantly narrow the frog's options for escape.

At first I would leap up and try to grab them the moment they came within reach, thus breaking the second rule: keep your profile off the horizon.

Down the frogs would plop en masse. It took me some time to realize that if I stood up, particularly with the sun behind me, the frogs would see my silhouette ten times out of ten and scarper before I could get anything like close enough to catch one. So I took to lying on the grass, obscuring myself with the pond's bordering plants and watching like a tiny blond otter.

It was to be the beginning of a lifelong fixation with peering into water. As a child I couldn't really make out the difference between a natural or a man-made habitat, but that hardly mattered as nor could the wildlife. I remember being amazed to discover that if you left rainwater to puddle in a bucket it would quickly become inhabited all by itself. Usually this just meant a colony of tiny waterbeetles or millions of species of swirling zooplankton, but sometimes I would find mosquito larvae jerking in the water like a tiny hairy finger trapped in a door, and, in bigger, older, water traps, like the defunct water butts or abandoned cattle troughs that got left around farms, it was possible to find small fish, thick black leeches, and, very occasionally, even an eel.

Not all ponds are the same but the best times to observe, and afterwards to fish, were early mornings and later in the afternoon. In most ponds at such times, a background hum of life builds in a crescendo like an orchestra tuning up before the performance begins. This was when our pond was at its most magical. Bright damsels and acrobatic dragonflies, the assassins of the sky, hunted on the wing above my head as fearsome diving beetles plundered the unfortunate larvae living below. I had a soft spot for the alien-faced waterboatmen: they seemed like gentle souls who didn't need to attack anything in the pond, but the pond skaters were always the most impressive. With their fine displays of nimble skills on implausibly long legs, these thumbnail-sized insects comfortably outmanoeuvred the birds and beasts that wanted to eat them by propelling themselves along the pond's meniscus at incredible speed. Dad taught me that everything which lived in the pond relied on the health of its tiniest living organisms, and if I scooped the pond water into my hands and viewed it with my pale palms as a backdrop I could just make out what he was talking about. Hundreds of tiny haphazard dots made up a dense concentration of zooplankton: water fleas, daphnia and the water worms that held this whole environment together. Their presence was why he didn't want to stock our pond with ornamental goldfish or koi carp. Pet fish would soon eat all these miniature friends, as well as the beetle larvae and the frog's tadpoles, until, eventually, the entire system in the pond would stop being able to support itself. Then we would have to buy food to feed the pet fish, food which, I later learnt, was largely made from wild-caught baby sea fish, fish oils and even the krill that provided the foundation of the ocean ecosystem. It all seemed a bit crazy really: damaging one ecosystem to artificially prop up another, so we stuck with the wildlife pond.

If I was really quiet I might be able to see the garden

birds – the song thrushes, blackbirds and sparrows – bathing in the shallow end of the pond. They would do this all year round, even in the middle of winter when the pond had a skin of ice and I could scarcely stand to put my hands in the water, but it seemed to happen most often towards the end of a long hot day. They would shake themselves vigorously afterwards, puffing out their feathers and finery as if they had been placed in front of my mum's hair drier and towelled down. As darkness fell, the pipistrelle bats with their coats coloured like old bricks, their dark ears, faces and wings, would funnel down flying insects by the thousand. I knew I would soon have to go back into the house for tea when that performance began, but not before I checked my surroundings for a repeat appearance from my most exciting discovery of all time: a small shrew that once crawled along the pond's bank and right along my side as I lay there. It sniffed the air with its comically conical nose and screwed up its tiny eyes in disgust. It knew something was up, but I don't believe it ever realized I was there or what I was, before it shuffled its way back into the undergrowth.

The frogs had a curious habit. They would actively hunt and, to my juvenile mind, play in the deeper water, but they tended to come to a standstill when they were submerged in the shallows right in the gaps between the planting baskets. They felt safe there, I guessed, and with that I had cracked my third rule: find the sanctuaries and exploit the routine.

Soon I had my first definite touch of slimy flesh; next I briefly clasped a leg and then, finally, after a summer of study, I proudly held my first frog. I only had it in my hands long enough to splurt out the 'M' of 'Mum', before it released its stripy legs from my clutches and powered its way back into the pond, but it was, in my mind, a massive accomplishment.

I would tell everyone in the family several times of my heroism, establishing a lifelong fourth and final rule: always amplify any special capture, especially if there was no witness.

Finally, with no one else in the house left to tell, and my sister getting visibly irritated by my boorish antics, I made my concluding performance to my grand-parents.

'Impressive, son,' Grandad remarked at the curtain call. Lifting an enquiring white eyebrow from behind his large, wire-framed glasses, he casually dropped an absolute thunderbolt into my life:

'So what would you say to trying to catch a fish?'

A spark flickered into life; somewhere well behind my out-and-proud bellybutton and the small of my back: a truly great journey was about to begin.

I was almost five years old when I caught my first fish but I can't tell you what it looked like. I was so excited by the prospect of catching and holding a real live fish that when my float eventually slid under the water, I struck so hard that I projected my catch directly out of the river, over my head, and deep into a field filled with sugar beet.

'A little too hard perhaps, Will,' said Grandad after a short spell of mutual silence.

He took the rod, freshly baited the hook with a couple of maggots, and re-cast into the middle of the Creek.

Technique wasn't all that important in those seminal days. With Grandad it was all about experiencing the first fish on the bank, by whatever means possible, and enjoying time spent in each other's company. That meant size was an irrelevance also. Our best bet, clearly, was with the vast shoals of roach that teemed within the Well Creek right opposite the house. They never seemed to grow beyond a few inches in length, but that didn't mean they were foolish – far from it in fact.

With the float now bobbing happily in the centre of the Creek once more, I was passed back the rod. It was my first, a bright-red two-piece number with a smooth plastic handle and reel loaded with light monofilament line and I loved it more than anything else I have ever owned.

'I'm just going to feed a few maggots to get them interested,' said Grandad, selecting a pinch of the wriggliest bait tin residents and flicking them around the float with extraordinary accuracy. The float bobbed. 'It's another bite!' I screamed, standing up, blowing our cover, and forgetting to strike. Grandad pulled me back into the seated position via the elasticated waistband of my bright-red shorts.

'You've got to stay calm, Will,' he implored in hushed tones, his eyes sparkling with suppressed laughter tears.

I refocused, pleading with the float and river to give me just one more chance. A couple more maggots flew out and then, finally, mercifully, it happened.

In the photo of that first fish, I am sat next to Grandad with a look of utter disbelief plastered across my face; my eyes are as wide as they could possibly be, gripping a length of line with what can only be described as 'a miracle' on the end of my hook.

Incredibly, given how many roach were in the Creek, my trap had worked its way into the mouth of a small skimmer bream. Like the roach, the skimmer appears to be a silverfish but it is, in fact, the juvenile form of the darker and much larger common bream. It differs from the roach in its elongated, slate-grey anal fin on the underside and its generally much flatter, wider appearance; hence its 'skimmer' name, in homage to a skimming stone.

To be honest, it could have been any fish of any species ever; my reaction would have been just the same. In that moment I was the king; the master and commander of the river; the man who had unlocked the secrets of the deep and tamed the great beasts that lay within. It mattered not that this was, in reality, an extremely small specimen either; in that brief moment I had been handed the keys to a lifetime of pleasure and study, and in Grandad I had a more than willing teacher.

*

The five years I then took to reach the age of adolescence revolved around fishing and an endless supply of fishy stories and patient tuition from Grandad. The pond, the conservatory of animals, my family and, later, school all dissolved into the background. I had a new magic man now, capable of conjuring the most almighty tricks with a dainty flick of his thick wrist.

We float-fished for the Creek's roach at any opportunity. He couldn't say no: I was irrepressible. He would rock up to ours usually on a good sunny day as Grandad really hated being cold, even though he did always like to claim: 'There's no such thing as bad weather, just bad clothes choices.' He would be wearing a floppy sunhat, and a T-shirt usually several times too small for his enormous stomach, and would often have a large pork pie secreted somewhere on his person, wrapped within a capacious handkerchief and brought out well away from the interfering eyes of my grandma.

I had the rod and reel of course, a couple of cheap floats, and a handful of hooks and weights he had given to me himself, but he would always ask: 'Got all your stuff then, Will?' as if my collection of tackle were vastly larger, and not, in fact, comfortably able to fit in his top pocket.

Grandad was both a thrifty man and extremely industrious. His fishing gear was as ancient as it was immaculate and his favourite floats were all handmade from drinking straws. 'McDonald's ones are the best,' he often claimed, usually before adding: 'it's the only time you'll see me in that bloody place.' Repetition and consistency are a key component of any good angler, as well as any good grandparent.

The session would begin with my taking ten times longer than him to prepare my rudimentary tackle. I would first thread a small orange-tipped float onto the line by a tiny hole at one of its ends, and then secure its tip with a small rubber float sleeve, a finely cut piece of tubing that fixed the float to the line. Next I would carefully tie on a hook from Grandad and pinch a small line of lead shots intended to cock the float till just its top half-inch would show above the water. Finally, I was ready for bait. I would take an age to decide which two of the tens of thousands of maggots would be skewered onto my hook, usually drop a couple of hundred on the floor by accident, and then spear the grubs through the wrong end and have to start all over again.

When I was eventually ready to make a cast I would either overdo it and chuck the whole lot straight into a tree, or I would forget to release the line on the reel and tangle my float approximately one million times around the rod tip. Both eventualities took time to fix, and would nearly always result in me having to start the whole process again from scratch.

Grandad would never fish on through my dramas, but he wouldn't just sort it out for me either. I had to learn to do things properly, and, as tackle cost money, it paid to learn quickly.

Time passed and gradually I improved. In the early

days any fish was a real bonus, but several seasons in I was beginning to catch nearly every time we went out. Expectancy is a terrible thing in fishing: it murders the heady rawness of feeling you get from the first few fish you ever caught by suffocating it under a fixation with catching as many fish, or as big a fish, as you possibly can. Sadly, a bit like the first time you ever fell properly in love, or saw a magic trick, or rode on a rollercoaster, that exhilarating feeling of holding one of your earliest fish can never be matched by simply catching more of the same.

With the sheen fading from the silver scales of the roach I began to wonder what other challenges might be living within the depths of the Creek. One day, while quickly retrieving a red-fin roach along the Creek's surface, a massive impact tore my fish clean off the end of the hook. My line fell limp at the rod tip and I turned to Grandad, near rigid with shock.

'Pike, son,' he said, with a solemn and knowing glance at the pathetic remains of my roach, which was now little more than a smattering of tiny silver scales descending to a murky oblivion.

I had just been humbled. That was a man's fish and I knew I wasn't ready to take it on, but luckily there was another, more pocket-sized, predator lingering close to my diminutive grasp.

The temperature gauge on my van tells me it's a dispiriting 4°C outside. I flick the indicator to take a long right-hand turn at the roundabout by the football club, and steam happily away from the commuter traffic trailing into Cardiff for work.

It feels like the wrong day to begin this challenge – the Vale of Glamorgan strikes me as particularly numb and lifeless this morning: lumpen, cold and grey, like the contents of a mortician's drawer. I turn up the fan heater and squeeze the accelerator.

It's overcast too but that doesn't bother me nearly as much. Big perch hate bright conditions. To be fair, even 4°C isn't truly the end of the world – there's plenty of fish willing to feed in those conditions; but this is the first major temperature drop after a sustained period of double digits, which is very bad news indeed as fish really dislike sudden changes in temperature, and, worse still, the opening frost of winter is forecast to arrive tonight. That's an event guaranteed to put every fish in Britain off its food.

After a frost some fish species will remain on the bottom; hidden, in a trance-like torpor, just subsisting off their reserves until the warmer months stir them back to life. Others, like the perch, will adjust to the colder climes after just a few days and will gradually come back on the feed.

The worst possible time you can try and angle for them is just after a frost; the second-worst time is right now: just as it's starting. By rights, I should have stayed under the duvet this morning, but I felt I had one very good reason for wanting it today more than most.

Fishermen are among the worst offenders when it

comes to believing in 'signs'. I've seen the most hardened atheist turn clairvoyant when it comes to the
desperate search for a fish-filled future; scientific anglers
who, no matter what the conditions, will only fish their
lures and flies in a certain order; and those who sincerely
believe that a specific choice of socks or the sudden
appearance of an auspicious bird or favourite mammal
can conjure a fish for the fishless. Even my grandad, a
no-nonsense engineer throughout his working days,
would never fish the river if there was even a hint of a
westerly wind.

What was sticking in my craw that morning was that
it was precisely a year ago to the day that I lost the biggest perch of my life: I simply had to go fishing.

A little perch is almost always every little fisher's first
ever fish. It wasn't quite mine of course, but they were
an ever-present pleasure in the Creek, ready to step in
and save my blushes when a blank day seemed otherwise
inevitable.

'Like a Japanese Warrior in his medieval armour,'
intoned Jack Hargreaves in his 1951 classic book, *Fishing
for a Year*; and what a perfect simile that is for this classy
little predator. With its hard, sharpened gill plates, black
eyes, and spine-tipped and sail-like dorsal fin, the perch
is absolutely built for a fight; but it's a strikingly handsome fish too: its flanks are marked by a series of
immaculate black stripes blended perfectly over a dark
olive backdrop. With striking blood-red fins and a

whitened-cream belly that is wonderfully plump in the bigger specimens, it really is one of the best-looking of all the freshwater fish.

Unsurprisingly, it was one of the most in-demand fish to pass under the taxidermist's scalpel in the Victorian era; but it's the perch's mouth that truly must strike the fear of God into any fish or bait unlucky enough to fit inside, for the perch must be the greediest fish ever to have lived.

Its jutting jaw is specially hinged, allowing its over-sized mouth to engulf surprisingly large prey. As a boy I would often catch them fishing on lures intended for pike ten times larger, such is the perch's capacity to sense weakness and an opportunity. When they are in the mood, they will bully their patch of water and intimidate others with a yobbish enthusiasm.

On the Creek we would catch them near boat moorings, reed-lined banksides or, more often than not, directly beneath wooden jetties: right in among the pilings, where they can leap back and forth from their ambush point. Clearly, they are comfortable in large shoals. I remember one astonishing day with my little brother when we simply could not stop catching them. Like shelling peas, we flicked them out one after the other from an area under a landing stage no bigger than a ping-pong table. Eventually, it got so embarrassing we had to stop and upended a keepnet filled with at least a hundred little stripy fish.

On a clear day I would observe the Creek's vast perch

shoals, tucked tight into the holes and structures they preferred, allowing their zebra stripes and dorsals to fuse with the reeds, wood or each other, till the individuals were near indistinguishable from the shoal. From here they would conduct their remorseless assaults: plundering the roach-fry like a marlin destroys a bait ball, sending their panicked prey scattering on the surface in great shimmering plumes of silver.

On occasion I would spot one or two that were clearly a lot larger than the rest: hump-backed and aloof, these were the adults. These wise old fish were given respectable space by the smaller fish in the shoal, most likely not out of deference, but because big perch have a cannibal's reputation.

They would observe me with an infuriating indifference as I made cast after cast in their direction, never once looking even remotely likely to come to my hook. Eventually they would tire of my intrusion, and would simply disappear with a flick of the tail; leaving a boy with a face redder than his rod, kicking up clods of turf in wretched frustration.

The Wilson *Encyclopedia* describes a 'mega-specimen' as any perch over 3lb, and lists the British record at 5lb 9oz, but, as I write, the current record is now headed by two separate fish caught just a year apart, and which tipped the scales at a whopping 6lb 3oz.

What I wouldn't give to catch such a perch. I can't think of any other species where the gulf in skill between catching the smallest member and the largest is so vast. It has to be one of the biggest challenges available to the British angler. Once hooked the perch is unmistakable. The pugnacious jag-jag-jagging fight, as they repeatedly dive back for their cover, is like having your line attached to the sword of an Olympic fencer. It singles out the striped assassin every single time. In the bigger ones this pulsing motion is only magnified, till the shudders on your rod register with the force of a piledriver.

As a child, having blown my opportunity to snare a big one for just about the millionth time, I consulted Grandad on the appropriate method for snaring the larger of these princely predators. 'The tail of a lobworm, nicked through the bloody stump,' he opined simply, in much the same manner as a witch might recommend a wicked potion for curing warts.

'Is that really all there is to it, Grandad?' I enquired, my heart full of hope.

Grandad was a keen devotee at the church of lobworm; they were the only alternative bait he would consider when his maggots failed to work. He dug his mud snakes, the largest of the British earthworm species, out of the sweet-smelling compost heap he managed out the back of the bungalow. From there, he would roll them tight within long leaves of newspaper and stick them in his large white chest freezer.

I recall the first time he showed me his supply. 'Don't be shy about using a big hook; it'll work, but, look,

Will . . .' He stopped and fixed me with his big brown eyes. '. . . big perch need patience. You can't be jumping about and re-casting all the time. You have to learn to time it right: early mornings or the last hour of light.'

He placed his giant forearms on the chest freezer's top and leant forward. 'You must be prepared to wait for him to make the first mistake. Otherwise,' he added, 'there's not much point in you even trying.'

In much the same way that I discovered collecting conkers was actually more fun than playing with them, I took to collecting worms with more enthusiasm and early success than catching big perch. Of course, Grandad had me pegged. Totally.

I had heard the best time to look for the biggest worms was in the dead of night, just after a summer storm, preferably on the outfield of a cricket pitch. That seemed like a ludicrous number of variables to me, and with night-time cricket matches in the rain particularly thin on the ground in my patch of Cambridgeshire, I took to re-creating a rain storm with a washing-up bowl filled with Fairy Liquid suds, and the tactical deployment of a gently wiggled garden fork. Once I got it right it was like raising Medusa's hair from the turf. Up the worms would pop en masse, no doubt poisoned from their homes by the sudden influx of soap, and I would scoop them up and into my bait tin with unbridled glee.

One week later the largest and juiciest of all my incarcerated lobworms landed within an inch of a big creek perch's mouth with a resounding thump.

It was the stealth equivalent of hiding behind a door for an hour to quietly surprise your mate, and then slapping him round the face with a draught excluder the second he walked into the room. Naturally the big perch flushed immediately from its hole in fright, leaving me sat impotently watching my giant worm squirm its way along the bottom without a single fish anywhere else in sight.

What was it about these cursed bloody worms? Perch holes and playgrounds: lobworms seemed to clear them both with ruthless efficiency.

For thirty seconds I waited, roasting from the inside out with a furious impatience. How did Grandad do it? When I did give up, I made sure I gave the turf the most solid kick I had in me before heading straight home to catch more worms, swearing blind that day I would never bother trying to catch big perch ever again.

After the sand eel was lost and the Wilson *Encyclopedia* found, it made sense to me to start my quest with big perch. Not just because they had such a presence in my childhood, but also because it was the perch that had slowly begun to ease me off my carp addiction in the months before the sand eel hammer blow.

It started with a few speculative casts with a worm a couple of years ago; purely to fill in time when the carp weren't biting. I wasn't expecting anything to happen, but, to my sheer delight, my float zipped away with a familiar jagging riposte and I found the swarms of little perch had been dutifully waiting for me, almost as

if they had been following me around since I was a little boy.

With a bit more managed neglect of my carp rod, a
slightly bigger hook and the careful chumming of the
water with broken lobworm, I soon found I could even
winkle out the odd larger perch in the shoal. Okay, they
weren't that big, perhaps only a pound or so, but I was at
least aware that these were indeed the striped 'monsters'
of my childhood memories and so venerated them
sufficiently.

The following year I made my first concerted effort to
target even bigger perch. I did some research, modified
my tackle, and shipped in 200 live lobworms that I established in a garden shed bucket and fattened up on
vegetable scraps. Within the year I had my first 2lb fish:
a stunning, bristling specimen that scrapped all the way
to my net in a heart-stopping account of itself. As I held
it in my hands I felt a sort of electrical pulse of excitement that I hadn't experienced since I was a boy. Just
why had I wasted the last twenty years fishing almost
exclusively for one species of fish? I slipped her back,
the dorsal slicing the water like a serrated knife through
an apple, and would meet the sand eel on my very next
trip out.

In the past twenty years of fishing almost exclusively
in stocked carp lakes I had inadvertently stumbled across
a very modern phenomenon. With commercial carp
waters sprouting up all over Britain, big perch have
found a habitat where they can absolutely thrive. In

these lakes there are generally no pike present to cull their numbers or compete for the baitfish, and barely any angling pressure from the hordes of Cyclopean fishermen targeting only carp. As a result the perch in these ponds have been allowed to grow to prodigious proportions. Out of the biggest fifty perch caught in Britain nearly half have come from commercially stocked lakes in the last decade; a staggering result that is hardly matched in any other fish species mentioned in this book.

Year on year the established perch records are being pressed and even the 3lb Wilson mega-specimen has seemingly become a happy resident in almost every carp pond you care to mention. You shouldn't be foolish enough to think that means they are easy to catch; big perch will always continue to play their cards very close to their chest, and only the best of anglers will regularly snare the largest specimens. It took me two winters' worth of outings before I had my first decent one, and another year before I had a brush with my very own perch-of-a-lifetime, right here, at the very venue whose gates I was swinging into.

White Springs is pretty much your blueprint for any commercial pond complex you care to pick in the country. It's got a variety of manmade lakes offering everything from pleasure fishing for carp over double figures, right up to a specimen lake with carp over 45lb stirring up the waters. So far, so similar; however, what really set my pulse racing were the reports of the resident perch in one of the ponds: they sounded mega, even by the high standards of this golden age of perch fishing.

I read an article where the author details snaring not one, but three, perch over 3lb in a single session here, which he then topped off with a truly ridiculous fish of over 4lb. Surely, I thought, this had to be one of the greatest big-perch hauls in history, but a few clicks of the mouse proved these ponds had even more to give. A fish of over 5lb is resident here. I've seen its picture. It's a brooding, menacing predator with huge flanks and an appetite to match.

Three-pounders, four-pounders, and even a five: if you were to place that against carp, it would be the equivalent of having a lake holding a fish over 55lb with a head of fish over 40lb as a back-up. It would be among the most celebrated fishing lakes in the country, yet as I roll down the tarmac road and into the complex it becomes apparent that I am going to be fishing the perch ponds almost completely on my own.

I settle right back into the swim where I lost the big one the previous season. It's on a lake known as the Big Pit, an area of water where the White Springs management have fused two lakes together, removing the earthen bank between one lake, which resembled a small canal and held some of the big perch, and another, larger, rounder pond that housed some of the bigger carp.

I have to avoid those carp at all costs now. My perch

tackle is light, so a hook-up with one of the lake's golden mud pigs will necessitate a long and laborious fight which I'm most likely to lose, plus it will certainly scare off any of the big perch that I'm hoping to persuade to my hook.

This cold front will do me a real favour in that respect – carp really don't like the colder months; but there's still a chance I might snare one that's ignoring the forecast, so to boost my chances further I'm avoiding all the baits I would commonly use to target carp (pellets, corn and boilies), and I'm also steering well clear of any parts of the pond where the carp might still be active: the warmer, shallower areas which get more of the limited sunlight, and those fishing platforms which have seen a lot of regular angling activity and feeding. This still might not be enough, though, so I'll also be ready to cut right back on my loose feed of red maggots and broken worms if it looks like I'm attracting the unwanted attention of the *Cyprinus carpio*. Make no mistake, this is a seriously challenging prospect given the intensity of my addiction to that species – a bit like offering a free cigarette to a recently reformed chain smoker – but if I'm going to take this challenge seriously I have to focus my mind solely on the perch.

This corner of the pond absolutely screams 'perch'. It's the area with the thickest banks of marginal reeds, the largest overhanging bushes and, if my depth plummet isn't lying to me, the deepest, darkest holes around.

I can almost feel that big perch's presence; pressed up,

somewhere in the darkness, tight against the sunken tree roots and reeds, perfectly camouflaged, waiting to strike me down with those wild black eyes.

I begin by scooping a dozen red maggots into my catapult. I'm aiming to keep these going in every minute or so. Hopefully the 'little but often' feeding routine will bring into the swim the shoals of little baitfish that the bigger perch like to feed on. If that fails, I've got the crutch of these broken lobworms to rest back on. Chopping them up into pieces will release a slick of worm's blood into the swim: catnip for the big perch. The scent will draw them in, then they'll find all the baitfish, then 'bang': they'll inhale my irresistible bait.

I hook a juicy lobworm through the tail and give it an underhand flick right into the dark shadows at the foot of the reeds. I'll have to be vigilant: any signs of scattering baitfish or big swirls could well be the perch's dinner bell sounding. I may only get one chance to snare a really large one.

Gently, I tighten the line between my hook, the weight and my rod tip, till I can register a bite simply by watching for any minute movement at the end of my rod. Satisfied, I settle back into my chair; and immediately hook into a massive carp.

'For fuck's sake!'

The rod arches down to breaking point and the reel screams in deference as the fish ploughs directly between two small islands. I tighten everything down as much as

I dare, and apply side pressure. My rod forms an almost perfect parabola.

Hold it, Will; just hold it. If it gets behind the islands it's game over.

The line whines in the wind, I'm dancing on the very edge of catastrophe here, but finally I feel the great fish start to turn. Weakness: it's hammer time. I reel down hard and gradually gain ground, steering the carp successfully back through the island maze towards me.

This is a nightmare. The worst possible start. I daren't even begin to think about the damage this carp has already done to my chances with the perch. I prepare my net but the fish is still nowhere near ready; with one giant thump of the tail it cuts its passage straight up the pond, ploughing away from the islands, and my corner, and out into the open water.

That I don't mind at all; it's well away from my traps and there are no obstacles out there. Keep sustaining the pressure and let the rod do all the work. It'll soon start to tire. I'm back in control now. It's just a matter of time.

Actually, this might not be that bad after all. If the grand culture of fishing superstition is to be believed then all that is happening here is that history is repeating itself. This happened last year too. First cast: giant carp. Second cast: giant perch.

The fish reveals itself: it is a stunning ghost carp with golden-white scales and a dark-grey skull pattern framing its head. It's a bit smaller than last year's carp, but for some reason the ghost carp always seem to punch above their weight. I slip it into my landing net first time and walk the fish safely down the pond; as far as possible from my perch spot, and to a place where hopefully it can warn all its carpy mates not to come bothering me up in my corner.

Resettling after such chaos takes time. Lines and bait boxes are strewn everywhere. It's important after any big fish that you don't just cast straight back in. Heart rates and water need time to settle back into a rhythm and hurried casts can result in lost fish and tackle.

After that carp I feel like I'm chasing my shadow, ghosting right back into my mis-steps and mistakes from last year. I remember clearly my next act a year ago: I flung the worm straight back out before I was properly ready and not thirty seconds later the rod tip thumped down hard. I lifted, but I didn't initially feel that familiar perchy fight: I felt a sustained pressure without quite the reel-stripping runs of a truly large carp.

'A small carp,' I supposed then, and bullied it back towards me.

It wasn't till it was almost under the rod that I had the first obvious clue that this was in fact a truly massive perch. The rod suddenly buckled down as the fish dived hard for the wooden posts by my feet. I remember leaving my seat at that point, falling dramatically to one knee and leaning right across the water with my rod outstretched in my hand. The line grated up hard and horrible against the posts and I was convinced I was about to lose it, but, much to my surprise, the perch erupted on the surface right before me.

Time stood still; and, unfortunately, so did I.

I came to my senses at precisely the same time as the giant perch and made a hurried grab for my net just as the perch turned its giant head. It was so large you could have fitted a tangerine in its mouth, and with a single pump of its tail it brought my rod tip back down with tremendous force.

The next scenes unfolded in a bit of a blur. I realized, with sheer horror, that the line had somehow tangled intractably around the arm of the reel. I tried desperately to free it but big fish rarely give second chances and, in that split-second window of weakness, the giant perch freed itself from the hook and was gone. For ever.

It sounds ridiculous, but I bet if I had never seen that perch reveal itself on the surface I would have landed it. The realization that I had my dream fish within touching distance caused me to lose all reason and form. I changed from the confident bully into the horrified victim in an instant. It still makes me shudder at the thought.

'Anyway. You can't let that happen again now, Will,' I tell myself for what feels the millionth time.

I catapult out another pouch of maggots and flick the worm back into the danger zone. Ice cool. I refocus.

Very sadly, history shows no interest in repeating itself. Several hours later, by the time I finally decide to give up and go home, the mercury has plummeted to such an extreme extent that my landing net has frozen solid to the grass. On the drive back, as my fingers come screaming back to life in front of the van's heaters, I swear blind that this will be my last trip to White Springs this winter.

After last year's disaster I have spent a week of my life traipsing up and down the M4 on a hundred-mile round trip, desperately hoping to snare that giant perch again. It has been as torturous as it was futile. I haven't caught a single decent fish.

That all has to stop now. If I am to catch a record, I want it at least to have been fun. Not just me sat static at the most boring end of fishing, freezing cold and achieving absolutely nothing.

It would be all too easy now to simply blame my venue choice for my own shortcomings as an angler. There is nothing actually wrong with White Springs, and those spectacular perch certainly haven't gone anywhere, but it is every inch the commercial fishery. From its sculpted islands to its trimmed shrubs and manicured fishing platforms, it is precisely the sort of place I was supposed to be weaning myself off during this challenge. If I'm going to keep coming to places like this, then I may as well just chuck the Wilson *Encyclopedia* in the lake and carry on catching carp.

I can hear what you are thinking: I bet if you had landed that big perch you wouldn't feel that way. Of course I wouldn't. But I didn't, did I?

*

As the frost settled into something of a rhythm and temperatures stabilized once more, the memory of the various White Springs debacles began to fade. I took up a permit with my local angling club and filled my boots on big perch from a remote farmland pond, finally cracking the 2lb barrier, and snaring more than a dozen fish over 1lb 8oz in one quite remarkable evening. My confidence was restored. I hardly lost a fish that month, and felt far more comfortable with the haphazard rhythm of the big perch's fight. In fact, I can quite honestly say I only broke sweat on a couple of occasions: once, when I accidentally locked the van behind the lake gates, and then lost the key, and then experienced my first serious breakdown; and next, while leaving the lake on another occasion, when I blundered directly into the path of a massive boar badger and almost shit my socks.

I wasn't closing in on that Wilson mega-specimen, though, and knew in my heart of hearts it was probably time to take a long hard look at Grandad's traditional techniques.

Really, as undoubtedly effective as worms clearly still were, I hadn't done anything to update my approach in over twenty-five years; I'd just picked up from where Grandad had left me, rolling his worms into the giant chest freezer.

I began a trawl for new methods and was very surprised to discover that perch fishing was practically everywhere: multiple blogs, on the covers of magazines, all over the internet forums, and in many, many, viral videos. Catching perch seemed suddenly very 'in', and, dare I say, actually, a little bit 'cool'.

Without a doubt, the single greatest piece of public relations to come out of the sport has been the impact of light-rock fishing (LRF) from Japan. In the past, lure-fishing meant shapely chunks of metal, spinners or spoons, and wooden 'plugs', moulded to resemble the features of a wounded baitfish and pulled through the water in a manner designed to fool predatory fish into a take. The trick of LRF is to take these basics and radically lighten the approach. In this way new, infinitesimally small spinners appeared on the market alongside thousands of micro-lures, -jigs and -jerkbaits made of ultra-lightweight rubber and malleable plastics in a bewildering array of colours, shapes and designs.

The masterstroke of LRF is that it has even made fishing for smaller predatory fish really exciting. For fishermen armed with short rods, matched with lightweight reels and hypersensitive braided lines, even the little wasp-like perch are a tantalizing target once again, their attacks registering on the subtle line with an extraordinary jarring force, every run, lunge and headshake transmitted down the rod with surgical precision.

LRF isn't just for small fish though; most of our recent record-breaking perch have been caught using these tactics and, believe me, when you actually do hook into something substantial the feeling of that first heart-stopping run never leaves you.

*

Thanks to LRF, urban fishing is back with a bang, and it was on those previously overlooked waterways that I decided to focus my gaze now.

Armed with a packet of inch-long, rubber, snow-white lures known as 'grass minnows', I scanned through a long list of options for a big-city stripy. The obvious choice would be somewhere on the Thames. The perch-fishing pedigree of this river placed it somewhere among the very best perch rivers in the country, and, according to the perch record list, a 6lb 4oz unclaimed record was landed there just a couple of years ago by a man listed only as 'Bill'. How cool is that? According to reports he had to be forced into declaring any element of his catch at all. I desperately wanted to meet this 'Bill'; a perch-fishing Jedi master to my young Skywalker; but most of all I wanted to meet his perch.

Of course, only a fool would target a river as long as the Thames for just one fish, but Bill's perch was far from the only big one. There's barely a week that passes without a Wilson mega-specimen popping up some-where on that river, either in the press or online, and the overwhelming majority of them are falling to the new LRF techniques.

I had only fished the Thames once before, from a town park in the leafy Berkshire town of Pangbourne, but even then I conspired to lose a very big perch that had engulfed a small roach just as I was about to get it into the net.

That was a 'free-to-fish' spot, and with a little research

I soon found there were actually many more miles of free fishing along other parts of this iconic river. Perfect. It felt too good to be true. I bought a new, ridiculously small rod, coupled with an even smaller reel, and spooled up with braided line. Then I got very over-excited, very prematurely.

Within twenty-four hours Storm Barney had ripped through the nation, bringing gale-force winds and heavy rains in its wake. That rain didn't let up for a week and soon nearly every river in Britain had swelled to bursting point.

I didn't even need to leave the house to know for sure that the Thames would have gone into a serious state of spate; a sort of turbulent chocolate milkshake condition that would need at least another week to settle back down.

The free fishing was irrelevant and my lightweight gear was useless. I chewed my fingers down to stubs.

That's not to say you can't fish flooded rivers – some of the best catches I have ever made have been in the calm areas and eddies where fish are forced to take refuge from the chaos of the main flow during a spate; but LRF fishing in heavy water isn't much fun at all. Even if you do manage to find clean runs away from all the storm detritus, getting the fish to see the lure in heavily coloured water is extremely hard, and getting your light gear to behave in a natural way is nigh on impossible.

*

I had an interview in London coming up that was within a stone's throw of the Grand Union Canal. It wasn't a patch of water I knew very well at all; in fact, I could comfortably count on one hand the amount of times I'd even seen it, but I did know that canals are always a sound bet when the weather is rough.

Canals had to be constructed to allow for the year-round passage of cargo during Britain's industrial heyday. The canal engineers certainly couldn't afford to let a few drops of rain stop traffic, so, with a deliberately even depth and flow provided by numerous manmade gates, locks and drains, you can get far more fishable water in rough conditions; plus, these days, with all the canal boats, low-slung bridges and concrete pilings, there are plenty of features for big perch to hide around and under as well. But the Grand Union Canal? In central London? Really?

The catch reports I read were very mixed, and in some cases downright dangerous. News articles detailed fishermen who were robbed of all of their gear at knifepoint, and others who had actually been pushed in by thugs looking for a laugh. The perch stories ranged from the ludicrous – one man claiming to have landed a seven-pounder from the Paddington area – to the plausible: a head of three-pounders dwelling somewhere within the deeper locks of Camden. But to get anything more specific than that required a more effective knowledge of code-breaking than the employees of Bletchley Park had.

I guess I could understand the need for some secrecy. Having put in so much work to locate a fish you wouldn't then want every jolly perch fisher or poacher from W7 to E6 to descend on your mark and clean up; but some of the anglers had gone to truly ludicrous lengths to hide their knowledge: pictures of giant perch clutched by men who had blurred or blackened the entire background of their image, and others who had even gone so far as to obscure their own faces, as if they were part of a perch-based witness protection programme.

I didn't really get it. If you didn't want people to know where you were fishing then why bother putting up pictures of you with fish on the internet in the first place? Unless, of course, you are just showing off and hyperinflating your own sense of self-importance by blurring your face and background, in which case, why not go the whole hog and come up with an entirely new social-media profile to complete your disguise, instead of posting with your actual name, actual address and actual school leaver's details just one mouse click away?

What really irritated me on all of these blogs, pages and sites was the sheer amount of vitriol reserved for people who did not conform to the rules of the perch-fishing clique. Anglers who posted pictures with specific details of where their fish were caught were slammed for not caring about the welfare of the fish, and those who held their perch with arms outstretched in pride were ridiculed for making their catch appear bigger than it actually was, as if that matters at all at the end of the day.

The worst of the wrath, however, was aimed at those who dared post a picture of their catch with a weight that was not deemed plausible by this, extraordinarily sad, minority of armchair anglers.

I remember one young lad in particular who caught the absolute perch of a lifetime from a town centre pond. It was a fish that looked every inch a record breaker: a glorious, solid-looking perch, which I would happily give away every rod in my household to catch. Doubtless, he was extremely proud of his catch, and, quite reasonably, thought it might be a good idea to post it on the 'Perch Fishing' Facebook group. However, for daring to post the location, weight and method of his catch, he was thrown to the virtual lions and torn to absolute shreds.

Within the hour the picture was gone, as was this boy's Facebook profile, and no doubt any intentions he may have had to learn more about perch fishing from the adults.

If it had happened at that boy's school they would have all been suspended for bullying, but on this platform I'm in no doubt it was pats on the back all round for another job well done. That's what the internet is all about these days though, isn't it?

And so it was as I watched legions of newcomers to the sport turned off for good, derided simply for wanting to publicly celebrate their perch, and feel part of this bizarre little club.

*

It had been a while since I had been in London but I felt I knew the city fairly well, having lived here for a year in my mid-twenties, a piece of my own history I shared with Grandad.

He had actually been part of the engineering team that had helped design the Thames Barrier in the 1970s, a pioneering construction built near Greenwich to stop the city from being flooded in the event of a storm surge or exceptionally high tide; but it's fair to say Grandad revelled in telling anyone and everyone he met about what a truly miserable place he thought our capital city to be.

I remember the first time I visited as a teenager, and, on returning to the village, made the huge mistake of relating to him the following comment by a bus driver: 'In London you are either looking at a shithole or living in one.' Grandad, I recall, nodded along sagely, as if Buddha himself had crafted this singular piece of crude wisdom. 'Well,' he eventually said, 'he's right. Lonely too.'

I swore there and then that I would never go to London through choice, but somewhat inevitably, given the lack of entry-level employment opportunities for a budding Factual Documentarian in the Fens, I ended up in London anyway, and, to my great surprise, absolutely fell in love with the place.

London, despite its faults, is one of the greatest cities on Earth, and don't let anyone tell you otherwise. For me, by day, it may have been: 'I simply can't understand why you're still stood in shot and not bringing our sand-wiches', but by night I was free to enjoy deliberately long strolls home in the darkness, through the buzzing Car-ibbean markets of Shepherds Bush, along the Royal Parklands, and down past the glitzy West London casi-nos where I watched Manny Pacquiao knock out Ricky Hatton live from the MGM Grand, and once lost a month's wages in just twenty minutes.

For a young man from a small village simply living in London was like getting my own star on the Hollywood Boulevard. I could not believe I was living in the capital and seeing instantly familiar sights like Tower Bridge, Big Ben and Piccadilly Circus with my own eyes and not just on TV. It was the sheer scope and cultural diversity of the place that truly blew my socks off though.

'London isn't a place at all. It's a million little places,' commented Bill Bryson, and I have to say I wholeheart-edly agree. I feasted on all the pleasures to be had by throwing myself fully into this city's life and began to wonder if Grandad had simply been overwhelmed by it all.

Of course, it isn't fair to write anywhere off with a sweeping statement, but having now lived in several big cities I have to say they can dish up a very special brand of isolation if you let them.

When faced with such diversity, opportunity and choice, to be incapable of seizing any of it for yourself, through no fault of your own, is to feel like the loneliest leper in the colony. The city then becomes the problem, and will provide evidence for your chosen prejudice wherever you wish to seek it out.

As much as I loved and appreciated all the parklands in London it never once occurred to me that I might be able to fish the canals. In my mind they were irredeemably dirty, the haunts of pimps and muggers and certainly not places to be spending any of my free time in. Whenever I peered into them I saw not near limitless opportunity to fish, but waste and weed, beer bottles and piss; an environment devoid of any life worth looking for.

It's extraordinary looking back to think how easily I turned my back on fishing that year, and so it was that the delights of the Grand Union Canal remained hidden from me, until today.

My alarm sounded at a little past 6 a.m. I was staying with friends right out in East London. Ordinarily this would pose a real barrier to a day's fishing in the city centre, as just the thought of piling on the Underground during rush hour with all my fishing tackle is enough to give me heart palpitations, but that is the beauty of LRF: no one would even have to know.

Just what do you wear for an interview when you know you're going to spend the rest of the day fishing? I suppose the obvious answer would be to favour whichever of the two activities is more important to you and dress accordingly; but that's a dangerous path for me to be walking down and one I suspected wouldn't ever lead to an economically sustainable future, so I had opted for a halfway house: fishing trousers paired with a smart shirt and my fishing jacket to go on top, but within moments of boarding the Tube it becomes apparent that I have got it very wrong indeed.

In the bright light I realize I had been happily spraying Lynx Africa deodorant over what is quite obviously a large circular patch of fish slime on the breast of my jacket: I smell like a teenage boy who has just rolled along the floor in a fishmonger's and then stuck a shirt on.

We pause at Stratford and my aroma wafts in and out of the doors as commuters stream on. A few people scrunch up their noses in disgust, so I do the same, with a shifty sideways glance in an attempt to palm the smell off onto some other unfortunate on the Tube.

Thankfully I'm ignored. Smells on the Tube are simply another inconvenience to add to the thousands of others these Londoners will have to face down today.

I wonder who else here might want to go fishing for a half-hour and what a difference it could make to their day. We pull into Liverpool Street station and dozens of smartphones flicker into life. Emails are coming in. Even down in this hole you can't escape work. These people don't actually have half an hour: they are 24/7 slaves to their emails and work.

I've been in those offices. You procrastinate through half the day but wouldn't dare admit you could get your work done in half the time; you eat your lunch at your desk and then wait to be the last person to leave at the end of the day; you send emails in the middle of the night to give the impression of diligence, when in fact all you're doing is confirming your total servitude to a group of overlords who'll never even notice the extra hours you put in.

We're losing out on our leisure time right across British cities and largely it's a problem of our own making. I moved from this city, worked fewer hours, got out more, and surprisingly got a lot more work done as a result.

Capping the mind-bending and inefficient seventy- to eighty-hour weeks made me much more focused when I was in work, and much happier when I wasn't. I was largely getting to do what I wanted to do outside of work (which was fish) and I slept much better due to the increase in physical activity and fresh air.

I'm determined to prove that it is still possible to go into work, even in our capital city, and find some time to fish somewhere nearby; but it doesn't even need to be fishing – you can do whatever *you* want to do with *your* time as long as it's not illegal and you're back in work on time. The only thing I ask is that if you are a boss employer that you don't read this to mean that I'm promoting the idea of fishing in the lunch break purely to increase productivity for your company: this is about my readers escaping your clutches during the break they richly deserve; it's for them, about them, and your work doesn't come into it – in fact I recommend you try it out for yourself as long as it doesn't become an official 'work outing', 'a team-bonding exercise' or something else as excruciatingly lame.

A man spots my rod so I give him a little smile. He looks at me with large, doleful, baggy eyes: 'Get me out of here,' they plead.

My interview finishes at a very agreeable time. I think it went well: they didn't once mention the smell from my jacket and I reckon they thought the fishing gear was actually pretty charming.

Stepping out of the shiny glass building and onto the Euston Road it's clear I'm not going to get everything my way today. The heavens open and it starts pitching it down hard. Clearly, Storm Barney hasn't let us go yet. I pull my cap over my eyes and head towards King's Cross station.

In keeping with most areas around major train stations the world over, the immediate vicinity of King's Cross is truly one of London's grimmest areas. It really shouldn't be – the station itself is full of Victorian splendour with its neat bricks, grand arches and glass façade, and just down the road is the equally stunning St Pancras Renaissance Hotel and British Library, but the fast-food restaurants, ugly coffee shops, horns, sirens and shouting give it a feel of a place where people would only ever wish to arrive or leave.

Moments later I felt like I was in an entirely new city. The black atmosphere diminished with every squelching step I took down York Way; there was water around here for sure, and it had already cast its comforting net wide down this street.

I pop my head over a low wall, hoping to spot it, but only find rows of parked trains. A little further on I spy the unmistakable shape of a bridge, but it's got traffic piling over it and doesn't look like a particularly inviting spot for my first look at the canal. You can't mess up your first approach to water. It has to feel right; you've got to give your patch space to display itself in its best finery – otherwise you might find yourself writing the water off prematurely and miss out on something truly special.

I take the next right down a narrow alley. I'll catch her out further downstream. Soon I'm passing behind a posh business building, and there, at the alley's end, the world opens out splendidly into wonderful calm water. This is Battlebridge Basin. Victory.

It is hemmed in on all sides by up-market housing developments and the noise from King's Cross is totally suppressed here, leaving this blissful oasis jutting fully 150 metres inwards from the main flow of the canal.

It's wide too, fifty metres across I later learn, and, better yet, it has relatively little weed and no obvious 'no fishing' signs: the perfect place to have my first speculative cast.

I extend my telescopic travel rod and check the sharpness of the hook point by gently pressing it against the cuticle of my thumbnail. There are not many places to actually cast a clean line. The rows of brightly coloured canal boats on the far side look well worth a chuck, but on this bank I've got about fifteen metres of the alley end and a covered walkway leading across a marbled floor at the back of an architectural firm. Still, fifteen metres is better than nothing, and there is at least enough room to put a couple of long casts into the centre of Battlebridge Basin, and probably a couple more along the weeping brickwork running along the water's edge.

I'd better get on with it, at any rate; I'm being eyeballed suspiciously by a security guard with biceps like coiled ropes.

The grass minnow plops into the drink and the time it takes to settle on the bottom tells me that this place is a hell of a lot deeper than it looks. From this point on, I'm fishing on faith and feel.

The braided line and soft rod are incredible; I twitch the minnow through the water and can feel every single bump, nook and cranny, as I make my first retrieve. The rain pours on the surface, flattening it and obscuring any potential signs of schooling baitfish, but I don't mind that at all as the water is painfully clear so a bit of natural cover plays into my hand and obscures my outline.

I'm going to have to box clever today. There's no point taking all my time to cover every single inch of water: the fish are either there or they're not. I need to target specific features: something that casts a shadow and makes its residents feel safe. A couple of tries in each spot and then move on; accuracy, a methodical retrieve and determination are the keys to success here.

I can't be a river snob either; the perch in this canal are just as likely to be living inside a car tyre as in a bank of reeds; it's only us humans who get really fussy about the look of our real estate.

I fish between the canal boats, right along a thick ribbon of duck weed, under my first bridge, round a submerged traffic cone and along the length of a flat-bed trolley. No luck, but I've got to stay confident. Crossing a road out of the Basin I pass a sign giving fishing the thumbs-up and immediately feel buoyed. This place just feels right for a fish.

The next likely feature is another bridge right opposite the King's Cross Theatre. I'm going to be leaping from bridge to bridge like a troll today. The rain clearly isn't going to stop so they'll be my only possible shelter, but the artificial darkness will also appeal greatly to the perch.

A couple of speculative casts into the murk bring my first proper take, but it's short-lived: a single spirited headshake sees the hook easily disgorged. A pity, but a positive sign for sure. I must be doing something right.

I try again, taking care to slow my retrieve right down, and this time the hook finds something far more solid: but this is no fish.

I heave hard and get nothing back bar unyielding resistance. Obviously I've hooked into a heavy piece of solid waste: a trolley, a washing machine or perhaps something more sinister? I try and change my angle but there is still no give. This will have to be my first donation to the canal then. I snap the braided line under the strain.

The very best of fish live in the hardest places to catch them. Of course they do; they've grown in age and weight by being canny feeders, avoiding bigger predators, and picking the best spots to ambush food, but here that doesn't mean supple tree roots or the soft tendrils from an overhanging bush – this is solid city centre litter dumped off the bridges by the lazy and feckless, in short: a tackle graveyard.

Another cast yields another aborted take, but this extra scrap of evidence allows me to narrow down the size and location of the fish.

It's a small perch for sure, hidden somewhere tight against the heavily graffitied far wall. There's no walkway over there so it is clear of human debris, but right in the middle of the canal is a ceiling fan and a billowing white sack. It's a tough cast. I steady myself. I reckon I've got one more crack at this before the little fish spooks for good.

'Any luck, mate?' comes a thick West African accent from over my shoulder. I turn to meet a large man in full train guard uniform, his head topped with an immaculate black cap.

'Not yet, mate, just had a take down here but I missed it, I think.' We both look into the water. 'Ja. There's fish here all right.' He leans over the railing, hoping to spot one on demand, and then gobs into the canal: 'It all depends on the weather.'

I ask about his job and it turns out he isn't a train guard at all.

'It's just a good thick coat and a snappy hat, don't you think?' I nod in approval and smile. I haven't heard the word 'snappy' for over twenty years.

'Plus you get plenty respect on the train.' He laughs heartily.

My new friend and I both agree that there is a little perch under the bridge but, after a couple more casts, we surmise he's probably not going to get caught today.

He shuffles off and so do I, downstream, passing Camley Street Natural Park, which had a couple of volunteers gamely tending to the shrubbery in the torrential rain, and on into my first lock.

St Pancras Lock is really very striking. A cute little white-washed cottage guards the thick oaken lock gates and a string of canal boats line up along my side of the bank.

Each boat is a tiny commercial venture in itself; there are a bookshop, a garden store selling shrubs, even a floating coffee and cake shop and micro-theatre. I feel like I've been transported to the Cotswolds or the Norfolk Broads. The canal boat life looks undeniably quaint and, dare I say, quite attractive. I wish I'd thought of this when I was living here.

Sadly, I have only been on a canal boat once. It was on a stag do along a stretch of this very canal, much further upstream, somewhere between Leighton Buzzard and

Milton Keynes, but, let me tell you, you get a very different experience with thirty drunken blokes dressed as pirates from the one you would onboard the artisan boats of King's Cross.

Still, it was enough to let me know that the canal boat life probably isn't for me after all. It's cramped in there, with or without Long John Silver hogging the toilet, and it gets very cold in the mornings when you wake up at water level.

I forsake the immensely tempting cake and coffee and keep heading downstream in search of the elusive first fish.

Under a large railway bridge I finally get a rattling take that hangs on. After a short fight I've got a spiky London prince in my fingertips: a picture-perfect perch with beautiful markings. It has probably never seen a hook. I gently ease him back and re-cast. Another bite! This could be the mother lode! The next perch is near identical to the first, as is the next, and then I lose my hook on some lumpen piece of sub-aquan detritus.

That's the game: every other cast is a bite and every one in between is a snag. I've got to keep it slow and steady to induce a take, but there's always that risk of snaring up. It's well worth it though: there's a pod of perch hunting in here for sure.

Next cast I hook a much better fish that strips line from the reel, races through the legs of an office chair and manages to transplant my hook into the metalwork.

Bad news. I curse my luck. I've heard it said that big perch are the brainiest of all freshwater fish, and I know a good few anglers who always release them well away from their fishing mark, firm in the belief that a big one can get an entire shoal to back off the feed for the rest of the day, if they so wish.

I rest the swim for five minutes. A couple of long trains shake the thick, grey girders above my head, displacing a shower of pigeon poo into the water. I re-cast and 'bang', the fish are right back on it again.

For a while I'm getting savage bites but I just can't seem to hook up. I try a firmer strike on the next take and the rod buckles down under an immense weight. This time it's animate, and begins to move steadily downstream. There's no jagging fight to be had here; I feel almost certain I've just hooked into a really big pike.

My tackle is light so I've got to be very careful now, but equally I can't just let this fish dictate terms.

I walk downstream and everything goes solid once more. For a moment I think I've been snagged up by the fish again, but then, slowly, carefully, it starts moving upwards, towards me.

Hands shaking with adrenaline, I reach into my pocket and fish out my pike glove. I might only get one crack at this.

'You take it?' An extremely drunk man, who tells me he is from Poland, clutches his can of Tyskie lager and laughs so hard it echoes like thunder around the bridge walls.

I try again to get my hook out of the sleeve of the suit jacket. Some bloody pike that turned out to be.

'Maybe you sell at fishmonger's, get good price!' There are actual tears streaming down the Polish man's face now and he even starts to choke.

For a second I wonder if he's having a heart attack, but he fortifies himself with a generous swig from his can of lager.

'Yeah, very funny, mate.' I try to conceal the rage gnawing my insides and with a hard yank finally free my hook.

I didn't even see this man coming as I was hauling up the coat; it's as if he just materialized from the water like a large, drunken canal spirit.

The jacket slopes back into the murk where I can't retrieve it.

It hangs there with one arm in the air, like a creepy scene from an Asian horror movie: an indistinct demon crawling out of the water ready to feed on livers; mine, obviously, not the Polish man's.

The very next cast brings me another perch. 'I take it.' I turn to see my new friend. He's not laughing any more, in fact he's deadly serious, eyeing me glassily, with one fat red hand outstretched towards me.

'No, mate,' I say casually, 'it really should go back.' I reach under the railing, ready to place it in the water, and feel his hand pressing heavily onto my shoulder.

'No.' He leans in. 'I eat it.'

His hot, drunk breath slaps my face like a bar-room

drip-tray and I realize I'm in a bit of a bind: on the one hand I've got the totally unnecessary and near-certain death of a tiny fish from a recovering canal, and on the other I've got this man bearing down on me with the real possibility of violence should I not concede to his demand.

With little time at my disposal I attempt to make it look like I just dropped the perch back in by accident.

'You fucking English idiot!' The man explodes, screaming with such force I almost jump into the canal in terror.

He throws both hands to the heavens and hurls his can high into the air until it comes crashing down in the middle of the canal with an immense splash.

Fishing's over then, I think to myself, before rationalizing that I'm probably about to get beaten up very badly.

'Look, I'm sorry, mate.' The ability to reason with drunks has long been a skill I admire; my landlord friend tells me the trick is to speak to them like they are three years old: 'I just think the fish should go back, it was only a little one anyway.'

This time round, I place my hand on his shoulder. It was *only* little, I've had bigger fish fingers, yet he looks at me like I've just insulted his wife.

'Pizda!' he screams, inches from my face, before storming off.

Later I check Google Translate and discover he was not actually asking me to buy him an alternative dinner.

I decided it was probably best to head down to the next bridge after that.

Perch after perch come to my line until I've had at least a dozen in ten minutes. Leaning, with my back to an impressive-looking piece of skull graffiti, I attempt a massive cast and watch my lure arch through the air to near certain fish; however, just as the hook strikes the water, I notice two approaching policemen. Instinctively, I just know it's me they're after.

'Any luck so far?' they say in unison.

They look almost identical; with neatly trimmed ginger beards and a slightly unnaturally chummy disposition that makes me feel deeply uncomfortable.

'Er, yeah, quite a few perch,' I stammer, trying to look as 'not guilty' as possible.

I've always been nervous around the police. Not because I've ever done anything really wrong, but because my mum's dad used to find it funny to grab me in a headlock and shout: 'I've got him, officer!' at the top of his voice whenever he saw a police car. That feeling of latent criminality just kind of stuck with me.

'Got your permit then, have you?' they enquire with a well-practised airiness.

I actually do, of course, and happily present my rod licence. If that is all this is about, then I should be back fishing in seconds, I think.

'Nah.' They both look at me sternly.

Oh shit.

'We want your Canal and River Trust permit.'

I don't have one. I don't even know what one is. I had simply assumed it was free fishing on this stretch of canal. The first time I've heard of this permit is right here, right now, in front of the Thompson Twins ginger edition.

I shuffle nervously and think about what prison might be like. 'I'm really sorry, lads, I honestly didn't know. I thought it was free fishing,' I proffer desperately, appealing to their sense of compassion by being completely honest.

They consider my words, obviously sizing up the extent of my law-breaking behaviour, then, without warning, they suddenly change tack: 'Look, we really don't care, mate, between you and me this is a total ball-ache . . .' answers one, looking at his feet sheepishly. '. . . but you've picked the wrong day to try this sort of stunt. The Canal and River Trust are actually here today,' continued the other.

They both then give a worried glance over their shoulders.

Jesus, I think, who are these guys? If they've got the police anxious they must be the canal equivalent of the SAS.

'Okay, guys, I'm not looking for any trouble. I'll sling my hook.'

I hope that little joke at the end there might crack a sympathetic smile, but I'm sadly misguided.

'Good,' they say in harmony, before clicking their heels together and heading back in the opposite direction.

I don't feel much like risking another cast after that and head back to King's Cross with the deeply satisfying smell of perch on my hands: I've already had a brilliant day.

When I eventually made it back home I looked up the Canal & River Trust and discovered, to my eternal shame, that it was only £20 for a permit that covered this section of the Grand Union Canal and a great many other canals right across the UK as well, for an entire year.

They had an email address for contact, so, with a little Dutch courage, I fired off a few words requesting a chat.

I noticed I had another email in my inbox. It was from the interview earlier that morning and it informed me that I hadn't got the gig.

Maybe taking your rods to work isn't always the greatest move after all.

John Ellis had such a nice lilting accent and calm manner that I struggled to associate him with the threat of spectacular violence over the wrong fishing permit, but I thought it was still best to play my cards very carefully.

Whenever I've encountered the people who work the closest with nature they almost always exude a Zen-like sense of eternal perspective. It is as if they have already realized their life's work will last long beyond their graves and 'that's just fine, thanks'.

It is more than just a job to these people, and their knowledge of their area is usually encyclopedic, and so it was with John, the National Fisheries and Angling Manager for the Canal & River Trust: 'We look after every water the CRT owns, that's some two thousand-plus miles of canals and seventy-odd still waters right across the UK,' he effuses. 'Last year there were 61,000 members of our canal clubs, making us the biggest owner of canal-fishing rights in the UK.'

I was far too ashamed to attempt a question about the number of people that fish without permits, plus I didn't want to stop John in full flow. 'The second thing we do is asset management: looking after the fish stocks, the engineering works, repairing riverbeds or draining the locks; right up to fish rescue, when we've had to drain a canal or temporarily relocate fish.'

My ears pricked right up next to the phone receiver: 'Really, John, so it's probably fair to say that if there was, say, a record fish to be had from a canal then you would be the man to ask?' I gently probed.

'Absolutely!' he replied enthusiastically, as I fist-punched the air. 'On the Grand Union Canal for example, just up by the Watford Gap service stations, we found the most massive eel: it was eight pounds, two ounces!'

I was gobsmacked. That is basically an anaconda. I made a note to hit that very spot later in the year for eels.

'It wasn't alone actually,' continued John, perhaps

mistaking the silence on the line for indifference from my end, 'there was another with it, which weighed six pounds, fourteen ounces.'

'Jesus Christ, John!' I exclaimed. 'That's two fish, probably several feet in length, in one stretch of canal!' I was on the verge of losing it, but there was more to come: 'They weren't just in the same stretch of canal, Will! They were both in the same lock together: trapped!' I was basically beside myself; this was a truly astonishing piece of information.

'If you are interested in eels –'

I interrupted him: 'I am, John, VERY interested . . .'

'Well,' he continued, 'then you've just got to try the Monmouth and Brecon Canal, there's plenty of two-pound fish in there; it's practically paved with the things, who knows how big they'll go? But I'll tell you what else, Swansea Canal near to you is absolutely full of brook lamprey as well.'

I could scarcely believe what I was hearing. The brook lamprey from my childhood had returned, thriving in another body of turbid water. Perhaps it wasn't such a rare occurrence as I first thought?

'In September we did some dredging works to remove the silt and caught over a thousand in just one four-hundred-metre stretch. They are thriving, they just love the silt!' John continued with a schoolboy's enthusiasm.

Our chat went on at a feverish pace and by the time we were through his list of potentially record-breaking canals I thought my writing hand was going to fall off:

15lb slab-sided bream from the Regent's Canal, pike over 30lb in the Ashby and Coventry canals, giant perch from the Leeds and Liverpool; it was quite conceivable that I could have attempted this entire challenge from Britain's canal systems alone.

However, there was one irrefutable and unavoidable detail: although the heavy weights in themselves were undeniable, the sheer number of big individual fish coming out of the commercially stocked lakes far outstripped those that came from the canals.

'Well, the management of those commercials is always going to have a big impact on the weight of any fish. What with all those piles of protein-rich baits fed in just to attract the carp.'

There was a pause on the line. I knew what John wanted to say next, it was obvious: 'But ask yourself this, Will, would you feel a greater sense of achievement catching a known giant artificially reared in a pond, or a wild unknown that's built the foundation of its size and strength purely on its own cunning and guile?

'For years the record tench came from a canal,' John lamented. 'It was from the Grand Union Canal's Leicester line. That record stood right through till the 1960s, seven pound something it was, but today the tench record stands at over fifteen pounds; over double the size of the record that once stood for decades.'

Commercials had changed everything. Even I had caught a tench over 7lb from a commercial fishery in the past; a great fish without doubt, but I had no idea it would once have been a new national record. I don't even think I thought to photograph it.

'It's possible that the canals could still turn up a record one day; I don't believe those big eels will find their way out of the canals and back to the sea too easily; and canal catches have never been better, you know; but without doubt the biggest threat to our canals is the lack of anglers,' continued John flatly. 'There are many, many more people choosing to seek their thrills from commercial fisheries, and some of our best canals are falling into a state of serious neglect.'

John believed the mentality of the angler had fundamentally altered. 'We are missing a whole generation of people that learnt to fish on the canals. I grew up on the Llangollen Canal, it cost me my place in medical school,' he quipped, 'but all the kids want is the guarantee of big fish these days.'

I offer my theory that most people, including myself once, didn't actually see the city canal as a place where fish live; that we have this prevailing myth that a lot of them are completely devoid of life.

'Yes,' John agrees, 'then we make these school visits and netting trips and the kids are absolutely amazed!'

It had been fascinating chatting to John, but also really quite sad to think that this iconic natural resource was falling into a state of such serious disrepair through little more than neglect and ignorance. What was for sure, though, was that the Canal & River Trust desperately needed the funds from fishing permits to keep all their important work going; so, feeling like a first-class 'pizda', I sheepishly promised to make a donation to the Trust and swore I would never fish again without double-, triple-, checking I had the right permits.

Sometimes in life it isn't the threat of trouble, or getting caught out, that makes you follow the rules, but actually the idea that you might not be taking your very own opportunity to help preserve something you love.

Storm Barney gave way to Storm Desmond and the rain did not stop until the middle of January.

I had arranged to fish with the wonderful-sounding Perchfishers club on the River Ivel in December, but the weather soon put paid to that, and with John Ellis's ringing endorsement in my ears I decided the time was probably right to try another canal for my next predator.

I had made a start in my quest, but really, in terms of catching a record, my time with the perch had been an absolute failure.

This was obviously going to be a lot harder than I thought, and there are no advancements in fishing tackle or increases in the number of specimen fish that were going to gift me a first-class catch without a great deal of hard graft and sacrifice beforehand. Still, I had made a start and thoroughly enjoyed targeting something new, and that definitely counted for something.

*

My grandma passed away that Christmas. It was heart-breaking, but dementia had taken a hold on her to such an extent that this utterly charming and dignified lady had been reduced to just two sentences: 'I'm managing' and 'Yes, boss.'

Grandma and Grandad had been happily married for over sixty years, the pair of them champions of the life and love that could be extracted from our waterways; him from the end of his rod, her from the tip of her paintbrush.

Twenty years ago Grandad caught a truly big perch. 'You should have seen it, Will! It was massive!'

I remember him splaying out his palms as if he were holding aloft a priceless china plate; re-enacting the precious moment he had held it for the very first time.

I dearly wished I had only been there to witness it. His finest captures always seemed to happen away from me. I wasn't even sure it had actually happened.

I should clarify that Grandad was no liar; he had definitely caught a big perch, but we were both fishermen after all. Memories blur and sometimes the distance between our palms can widen with time.

Grandma left behind an old plastic ice cream tub filled with pictures when she departed, and right there, somewhere in the middle, I found a picture of Grandad with his most magnificent perch.

I hold that image between my fingers as I type this. That picture is more precious to me now than any big perch of my own.

The fish's stripes are a darker shade of green than the stripes on his jumper. He props up the perch's dorsal with the tip of one of his big thumbs and his mouth is wide open in a self-satisfied and slightly stunned grin.

It is a Wilson mega-specimen, and I am in absolutely no doubt he caught it on a lobworm.

The Water Wolf

It was as deep as England. It held
Pike too immense to stir, so immense and old
That past nightfall I dared not cast.
                    Ted Hughes, 'Pike', (1960)

When I was around nine years old I owned one VHS
tape that I kept specifically for Mum to record John Wilson's *Go Fishing* series on direct from the TV. There was
one episode in particular, filmed, I think, somewhere in
the Norfolk Broads, that I had watched so many times
that the tape itself had started to warp and go fuzzy.

I could recall that episode near verbatim. In fact, I'm
pretty sure I still can.

The episode begins with a slightly awkward 'Hello'

from a thick-rimmed-bespectacled gentleman who bore more than a passing resemblance to a giant land tortoise. I didn't realize at the time that this was in fact the legendary Dick Walker, a true fishing icon.

In this film Mr Walker was playing the role of surrogate grandad to the thousands of young fisher folk tuning in across the nation; explaining the rudiments of pike angling and biology in a safe environment, before the hero, John Wilson, took over at the sharper end of the spear.

'Pike are predators, and they're scavengers too,' he begins, with a grim-looking stuffed pike staring on blankly from the wall behind. 'They are very well equipped indeed for both jobs,' he continued, 'they will eat practically anything, dead or alive, that will give them some nutriment.'

A pencil-drawn otter is framed over one of the old man's great oaken shoulders and ancient-looking books surround him. Everything about this office, from the interior to Dick himself, looks like it has been dipped in sepia and warmed up with wood smoke. It was the sort of place where I wanted to be for all time and I poured my consciousness into its cosy security to such an extent that I could well believe Mr Walker was addressing me directly; from right across his well-worn hardwood table to the rug of my parents' lounge, where I would sit cross-legged, inches from the TV screen.

'Now, here you can see what I've been talking about,' continues Mr Walker. He reaches down and produces the giant head of a stuffed pike. The warming atmosphere of

Dick's Den is extinguished in an instant, a brooding malevolence creeps into his office and my sense of longing quietly tiptoes back out.

Mr Walker works the head carefully around his fingers, gradually illuminating the business end in the dull light of his table lamp. He says it is from a 43lb giant caught in Ireland but all I can recall is its enormous jaws. Row upon row of razor-sharp fangs along the jaw-line backed up by hundreds more, pinned hard to the roof of the fish's mouth.

Mr Walker notes how all the teeth angle slightly backwards towards its blackened throat. Whatever goes in there isn't ever coming out, I thought. 'Never put your hand in a pike's mouth,' says Mr Walker, while clearly running his own thumbs and fingers over the teeth. He was my kind of man.

The film cuts to the heroic Wilson rowing his way alongside a tall reed bed. There is a vast expanse of wild-looking fresh water opening out right behind him; it's February, it's bleak, and he even says it's cold, so just what is he doing in that tiny wooden rowing boat with just a tweed hat for company? I grip the remote tightly and pray nothing bad happens to John.

Somewhere along the edge of the deep water he drops anchor and plucks a small live roach out of a bait tin. He says something nonchalant about only using 'small' live baits these days but I can't help noticing that the roach he has selected is actually the same size as my personal best from the creek. A highly unpleasant sense of shame burns at my cheeks, a feeling I later learn to interpret as a sense of inferiority combined with instant emasculation. I remember how it felt to land that best-ever roach, the euphoric 'championship-winning' sensation carried me through the whole summer and the glow stayed with me every night I closed my eyes and thought of that fish. In one swift move by Wilson that feeling had been obliterated: my best was his bait. How, even after a few years of fishing, could it be that the gulf between Wilson and myself, between being a man or just a little boy, was actually widening? He had no idea what he was doing to me of course. Hooking up the roach, he simply swung it out into the water under a large bright-red float and confidently commented: 'When that goes I'm in business.'

The final pike of the programme comes from 'the middle of the hole', which is how Wilson describes the slate-grey no man's land where he has cast his bait. It is, of course, the beast we have all been waiting for, but incredibly, as Wilson battles it to the side of the boat, he describes it as 'only a small one'.

The giant pike writhes on a foam mat after he's got it into the net. It's long – three or maybe even four feet – with a dark, muscular back leading on to a crocodilian head.

'As fat as butter!' exclaims Wilson jubilantly.

He holds his fish up for the camera and I get a good view of its mossy flanks. It is as if an artist had taken the time to delicately flick light-yellow paint along a green pike-shaped canvas, then decided to finish the job by scraping through the lot with a yard brush. The fish's thick, olive sides may be interspersed with pretty blond flecks and subtle vertical stripes, yet the overall look and feel of the fish are of pure brute savagery.

At the rear of the fish a russet-red and black-striped dorsal fin stands erect and rounded. It is set so far back along the body it almost meets the tail fin. This intentional back-loading of the pike's powerhouse affords it all the explosive forward motion it needs to intercept prey from a stationary position. Like the perch, they prefer to ambush their prey, but they can also take fish, frogs and even ducks, well out in open water, such is their confidence in their own turn of speed.

Somewhere towards the end of the programme, Wilson rotates his fish so it is head on to the camera lens. The skull is uniquely flattened in appearance, with large, predatory eyes set unusually high on the sides; perfect for peering up from the depths and selecting its next victim.

The grim jaw of Wilson's fish hisses open like a trapdoor and I can't help but imagine what it must be like to have that as your last view on earth. Horrid, I would expect. 'Absolute magic!' says John victoriously.

When the theme tune kicks in I am left alone with a feeling of raw inadequacy. I was nine, almost ten, and quite desperate for a pike of my own. It represented much more than just another fish. It symbolized growing up, doing something on my own, facing my fears – in short: being a man; but if the fish that Wilson caught in the film really was 'only a small one', and the bait he used as big as my personal best, then how could I ever expect to manage a pike for myself?

The beginning of the winter of '92 saw me fish like I had never fished before. For three months straight I was out almost every single night, drawing a triangular-shaped piece of shiny metal through every inch of the Creek's brown water, but trapped deep in a piker's purgatory.

Spinning for pike was my first major new fishing skill after five years of float-fishing for the Creek's roach and perch. Until that point I had been pretty much sat on my hands waiting for a bite, but spinning required constant movement of both myself and my hook: to animate the spinner – literally, to get it to spin, and make it flash through the water like an injured silverfish.

Winding the spinner in on my line would only last about twenty seconds in the narrow Creek, which meant I was now casting many more times in a day than ever before. Given my earlier problems with this most basic of fishing skills, I felt I was now risking my end tackle almost twice a minute. To make matters significantly worse, I also learnt the most likely pike-holding areas were right under the trees and along the reed beds: the very obstacles I had spent the previous half-decade try-ing to avoid casting towards. The arms of the trees and roots of the reeds might have been tackle thieves, but the shade and shelter they afforded the pike made them the perfect ambush points for any unsuspecting fish. To stand a chance of a pike I had to land my spinner perfectly: firmly in the pike's lair and within an inch of the devastating grasp of the bankside bush.

Grandad wasn't interested in helping at all. 'Pike fishing is too easy,' he would say dismissively. Perhaps he understood this was a fish I needed to meet by myself, but the effect of his words was to heap yet more pressure on my infantile shoulders. If it really was easy, then why couldn't I just catch one?

Looking back, I know precisely what the problem was: my retrieve was always too fast and too uniform. I would never let the spinner drop beneath the top six inches of surface water, meaning any interested pike would have to come right up off the bottom to grab it; nor did I vary the speed of my draw to allow the lure vital space to flit and flutter along like a wounded fish, meaning, in the eyes of a predator, that my spinner was in fact a turbo-charged superfish with a full bill of health.

Zipping my spinner across the Creek's surface merely served to give onlookers the impression I was a man out pike fishing, the man I wanted them to believe I was, while, in reality, I was never really giving myself a chance of hooking my quarry. Effectively, I was a rank boxing amateur dancing round the undefeated prizefighter without ever getting close enough to throw a meaningful punch, or get hit myself. I was simply too terrified of the potential consequences of hooking a pike, and too bloody-minded to just give up.

*

There is a unique existential crisis brought on by anyone seriously into pike fishing.

'Why am I here?' is a question that will inevitably pass the lips of this peculiar breed of angler.

Fish are as much a product of their environment as are the people who angle for them. Carp, with their fat scales, soft mouths and friendly curves, have the look and feel of summer, to be had from lily-strewn ponds and picture-perfect lakes. The typical carp angler prefers fairer weather and appears built for comfort, not speed; paradoxically, though, the fatter the carp, the slimmer and more pathological the bent of the carp fisherman, and no one should doubt that even the laziest-looking carp, and carper, has an extraordinary turn of pace when it is required. The barbel's golden hue is classic autumn; its angular fins are shaped and coloured like an early leaf drop and the torpedo shape marks this fish out as a specimen of fast water. The barbel fisherman, like the fish, is a shrewd and romantic character, a lover of nature and hardy too – easily capable of withstanding stormy weather and early starts – but this angler can't match the pike and pike angler for sheer durability. They are the embodiment of winter and both thrive on a rare form of neglect.

Of course, you can catch pike in the summer, and there are many anglers who fish for all fish species all year round, but the pike are at their largest in mid-winter, and it takes a very special breed of fisherman to convincingly morph their own character to match up to the deep cold their quarry prefers. As a child, I was a pretender, a mere sheep in wolf's clothing, but, unbeknown to me at the time, my dad was about to give me a big helping hand.

On the Creek you know spring is around the corner as soon as the daffodils outnumber the snowdrops. Time was running out for my first pike and me. Soon the water would warm and the river-fishing season would close till 16 June. I lay in my bed near wild with frustration.

I couldn't sleep that particular night for two distinct reasons: firstly, I had discovered Dad had taped over *Flash Gordon* at the precise moment he begins to turn things around in his fight to the death with Barin, and 'Flash! I love you! But we only have fourteen hours to save the Earth!' was now for ever jump-cut with Geoff Hamilton talking about manure on *Gardeners' World*. Naturally I was furious, but the second reason I was counting sheep was considerably more devastating.

Just as Mum and Dad had been going to bed I had overheard them have the following conversation right outside my room:

'Will is spending a lot of his time fishing at the moment, even more than normal,' said Mum, standing on the landing as Dad came up the stairs.

'He's trying to catch a pike,' replied Dad.

'Really?' answered Mum, with audible concern in her voice. 'Isn't that dangerous?'

'Not really,' said Dad, 'but don't worry, he won't get one in. He's not strong enough.'

The words slapped my eardrum and tore straight into my heart. Instantly, I could feel hot tears filling up my face and bee-lining for my tear ducts. It was the first time I had ever heard Dad doubt I could do anything. We had always been brought up on the principle that you can succeed at anything if you just try your best, yet here he was saying that, despite everything I was putting into it, I was never going to be good enough.

I tried to cover my ears with the pillow and will his words to leave my brain. Every fear I had suppressed to that point had been realized in full; the shadow of self-doubt reared up and smothered me in my bedsheets.

Hours later I was still very much awake. I gritted my teeth and thumped my fists on the duvet. Why would he say that? How dare he say that?

I got up and looked at myself in the mirror; my sense of my own shortcomings was quickly being replaced with a wild rage. That was a total betrayal from Dad. I glowered back at myself. I would show him; I would prove I did have the strength.

In its elemental form pike fishing necessitates in an individual a curious brand of madness: crumbling docklands, isolated rivers and windswept reservoirs – the last places your average anglers would choose to spend their time; but the purist piker casts into these locations with a sort of masochistic thrill, fearlessly fishing a fearful landscape for a fish seemingly without fear.

In my late twenties I fished a handful of times for pike

in a long, narrow fenland dyke called the Cuckoo Drain. You could probably spend a lifetime searching through the names of waterways and not find one as ill-fitting as the 'cuckoo' moniker given to this place. The cuckoo throws up more than simply the iconic bird sound of spring; it is the vision of renewal: a glade filled with fresh-sprung wild flowers, an oaken woodland rousing itself after a week of rain, the resurgence and resilience of life – a clarion call to heat the soul, reminding us that winter has passed and the good times are here once more. The Cuckoo Drain in winter was miles of pure brutality. Its near unrelenting misery placed it well among the hardest places I have ever fished. Thus it was near perfect for big pike.

It took some time simply to find the place, tucked, as it was, tight between a pumping station and a dip between two brown fields that stretched ad infinitum. As all fenland drains contain pike of some measure, and with Cuckoo both being deep and sporting a good head of shoaling roach and bream, it seemed fair to assume there might well be some decent-sized resident fish. This assumption was backed up by the only person I ever saw down there besides me: a typical piker, tall and grizzled with a rugged ginger beard and slightly gaunt appearance; he strongly resembled a starving Viking.

Few words were wasted between him and me. 'Anythin' doin'?' he would mumble. I would answer in the negative, and repeat his question back to him. 'Nuffin' doin',' he would respond with a sniff. I was really quite intimidated.

I decided to take a small spinning rod and had huge early success with a trio of fine averagely sized fish on my first outing; but from that moment forward I really struggled. It was as if the drain itself had lured me in with the promise of pike, only so it could then enjoy watching me endure an endlessly barren ice-cold search along its desolate banks.

After a dozen or so visits I began to seriously question whether those early pike had been a mirage. Pike-shaped sprites, kelpies, spirits or sirens? Even the Viking was nowhere to be seen by the bitter end of that bitterest of seasons. A barn owl would usually emerge when there was an hour of daylight remaining. It offered cold comfort, haunting the banks and circling my position like a ghostly vulture, just waiting for me to drop so it could pick apart my frozen carcass.

It would take until my final visit for the drain to yield me another pike. A slamming take and dogged fight marked it out as a decent fish, a good double for sure, but, as I reached down to slip my fingers into its gills, a hard headshake left only the tip of one hook in its stiff upper lip.

I had been fishing with two treble hooks on a wire trace specifically designed for the bony mouth of the pike. The extra hook points (six in this case) should give you a greater chance of landing this hard-mouthed fish, but with just one hook-hold left I now stood a very slim chance of success unless I acted quickly.

I tried to get a solid grip on the fish once more, but another violent headshake brought a tearing sound and the warming feel of fresh blood spilling across my hands. The numbing cold had dampened my pain receptors to such an extent that it took several seconds more than it should for me to realize that all the blood was my own; and several more still to discern that it was not my fingers that had been sliced on the pike's teeth, but that one of the higher treble hooks had torn right through my trouser leg and embedded itself deep within my shin.

Pike fishing leaves scars both real and imagined. I have two you can see: one livid white on my shin, the other, right across the cornea of my right eye, where I almost lost my sight to the hooks of a spinner while pike fishing as a teenager; but these are a small price to pay in the mind of the truly serious piker. I needed to be made of sterner stuff if I was ever to land a monster.

I drew a curtain over my last serious attempt at pike fishing that evening: bum shuffling and whimpering my way back up the bankside of Cuckoo Drain, a hook impaled in my leg, and a 10lb pike dangling around my ankles.

I've heard the pike once described as a 'Gothic' fish, and although I get where this reference is coming from, what with the pike's shadowy behaviour and angular appearance, I think 'prehistoric' is a far fairer depiction of this truly primeval creature.

The earliest British fossils of *Esox lucius*, to give the pike its Latin name, are dated at half a million years old. It is believed the fish first made its way to British shores via the North Sea land bridge, way back when the

River Thames was connected to the River Rhine in the Netherlands, but the latest fossil dating of the *Esox* genus far predates even this, placing the pike in northern America some 80 million years earlier.

The pike's evolutionary masterstroke came sometime during the Cretaceous period when the early *Esox* developed jaws capable of swallowing far greater-sized prey than the other species within the herring–salmon order. From that moment forward the pike had set itself on an extraordinarily durable pathway that would see it survive several Ice Ages and spread its presence from America and right across Europe, eventually spanning almost the entire boreal forest region of the northern hemisphere.

With its elongated body, sharpened head and penchant for aggression, the 'pike' name stuck with the fish from the Middle Ages, aptly chosen for its resemblance to the tall thrusting spear favoured by the infantrymen of the time, and used for taking down knights on horseback with ruthless efficiency and maximum bloodshed; much like the fish might, given the chance among a shoal of roach.

The Wilson *Encyclopedia* describes an average size of between 5 and 12lb, with a mega-specimen topping out at over 30lb. When I was still stuck angling for my first, Roy Lewis shocked the pike-angling world with a whopping 46lb 13oz beast from Llandegfedd Reservoir in South Wales. That record still stands today, taken on little more than a small and humble-looking wooden lure called the 'creek chub pikie'.

There is no other fish species on these shores to have sprung quite the same degree of myth and legend as the pike. The Yorkshire terrier that didn't make it home from its paddle in the park pond, the toothy beast that supposedly went for the ankles of a small swimming boy, the bleached bones of the 90lb fish washed up on the banks of some far-flung Irish loch – all unreliably witnessed, yet all somehow difficult to debunk completely. Just look at that image of the pike caught by Roy Lewis. It is an enormous spawn-filled female fish that appears almost as long as Roy himself. Is it such a leap in imagination to make real the violent water monsters of our childhood then?

The answer is probably 'Yes, it is.' The genuinely big fish have nearly always fallen from the drains and lakes that have seen very little pike-angling pressure or human presence; the pike certainly would not attack a human without any prior provocation. In this day and age the real specimens are to be found lurking safely within trout-fishing-only reservoirs, or concealed somewhere within mile upon mile of undisturbed lake or drain. They prefer the forgotten edges of our nation, you see, the sorts of places where you could still quite easily fish for a lifetime without even laying eyes on a Wilson mega-specimen, and the big old pike can while away their lives well away from our disturbing habits.

Big pike need food though, and lots of it – that's why, I'm told, many of those stocked trout lakes tend to do so well in sustaining monsters – but more than that they require a healthy ecosystem and a relative lack of competition. You should never consider culling pike in order to produce a bigger, better stamp of fish, though, or to protect the other fish in the water, for that matter. Many a world-class pike venue has been destroyed by the unwise attempt to remove its resident predators, and, unless you get them all (and, really, why would you want to do that?), there will inevitably be an explosion of smaller pike that would have otherwise been controlled by the larger, cannibalistic fish. In a pike's world, the only fish that truly controls the pike is the pike.

I first began looking for a big pike for this book in January, but it took until the middle of the month before a sudden break in the rain seemed to offer a true chance of a catch. Overcast, grey, a slight rise in temperature from single to double digits – it wasn't consistent with the forecast at all. I rushed from my desk and straight out to the garden pond to find my goldfish milling around the surface and even feeding. Potentially the biggest catch of the season was on.

Pike feed at ill-defined times. You can convince yourself there are no pike at all in a place and then a small change in atmospherics brings them onto the feed and suddenly you're in. I've heard of anglers catching nearly a hundred pike in just a few hours of ferocious action, then, as quickly as they are turned on, they're all off again, often for hours, sometimes even for days. Of course, the pikers are left scratching their heads and wondering where they're all hiding, but there is a widely held belief that these small rises in temperature can bring the pike out of their stupor. With even the gold-fish showing some signs of life this morning, it was all looking very good indeed.

The problem I faced was that it was now far too late to grab a ticket at any one of the certified big pike venues; and with all the rivers still flooded I needed to think out of the box. John Ellis. The canals, of course.

I flicked the laptop on and used Google Maps to zoom right in on the small network of drains and canals that ran around Cardiff. The one area I was particularly interested in stumbled off a giant space of disused industrial-era docks called the Atlantic Wharf. If big pike thrived on neglect, then this place surely hid a giant. It is only about half a mile from a glitzy shopping centre but it may as well have been on Mars. The blackened remains of rusting high-tower cranes hang over this place, looming large and lifeless over the water like Jurassic-era herons. An unattractive busy main road runs right along one side of the water too, but there were big fish to be had here if you only knew where to look.

I had already started my quest for a big pike there at the year's turn, but I hadn't yet had much luck. I did have some definite follows, though, predatory swirls at the surface, as my lure came back under my rod tip, and, on one occasion, a savage take tore my rubber lure clean in two, narrowly missing the hook, and leaving me with little more than the grinning head of my replica eel.

The other people who fished there tended to be a special breed, but they were friendly enough as long as you didn't ask too many questions about permits or carry on like a member of the Cardiff City Council.

The first time I ventured down there I met an enormous shaven-headed man in a state of some despair: 'Fuckers nicked all my meat and my rods in the night,' he raged – eyes popping from their sockets and his mobile clutched firmly to his ear – I presumed to the police. 'I was a bit pissed up last night to be fair, but they could at least have not cooked up all my fucking meat on my fucking BBQ not ten fucking metres from my fucking tent . . .' He was near apoplectic with rage, which was understandable given he'd just woken to discover nearly everything he owned had been stolen.

There was no fishing club looking after Atlantic Wharf back then, so the fishing was effectively free; but there is always some price to pay.

Some of the local pike fishermen here had an uneasy relationship with both the law and the rules. A few openly admitted to fishing illegally in nature reserves and one even told me he was banned from the local Glamorgan Anglers Club for using live ducklings as bait. Grim, almost beyond belief. Eventually I was trusted enough to be shown the pictures of the pike they had caught: blurry pictures of half-cut anglers with what were quite clearly significantly large fish in their hands.

Some of the pike looked to be over 25lb, perhaps one was even pushing the magic 30lb mark. 'Just beware fishing too long alone after dark . . .' I was warned, '. . . and keep an eye out for the poachers and prostitutes.'

The Royalty stretch of the Hampshire Avon this was not.

Poaching is a growing problem in Britain, particularly in these little-visited urban hinterlands that kiss up against large populations of people. For years I had disregarded those who talked of 'poachers taking all the fish' as just having fishermen's excuses, but John Ellis had been quick to point the finger too, claiming all it takes is a replica lock key to drain an entire stretch of canal in the middle of the night and make off with fish worth upwards of £2,000. In recent times I'd encountered more less-than-formal approaches: gill nets and long-lines dumped on the banks, tragically emptied of their quarry when no one else was around.

Many of my non-fishing friends don't really see the point of the sport if all you are ever doing is catching fish only to put them back. I know plenty of anglers who also believe there is no harm in taking the occasional sample, but the hard reality is that our inland fish stocks would simply collapse if everyone started to take their catches home. The few places where you can do it – trout and salmon fisheries, for example – have very carefully managed and monitored restocking programmes, strict limits on your catch and fastidious attention to the paperwork every angler must complete if he or she intends to take a fish home. Our island nation is too small and too over-populated to expect our recovering fresh water to handle anything other than catch and release, and when it comes to removing pike, the top fish predator, the resultant effect on an ecosystem can be devastating. It was one of the many reasons why predator anglers are so secretive about their catches.

I felt the canals feeding the wharf were easily my best bet for lure-fishing. The wharf was deep enough to take giant coal tankers and industrial container ships in its heyday, so this little spike in temperature wouldn't have even registered in those depths; however, in the relative shallows of the canals, the water would be responding almost instantaneously. I hoped to find the shoals of over-wintering silverfish holed up somewhere in there, which would, in turn, be drawing the big pike up off the wharf and deep into the canal system to feed; like great white sharks on the trail of a great chum-slick of African sardines.

I parked up with just an hour of light remaining in the day, the 'witching hour' for predators the world over, and headed over to a small bridge overlooking a canal. It's hemmed in on all sides by a housing estate; a small ribbon of gently flowing water no more than ten metres in width and a few feet deep. From this point it's only a short walk to where it spills into the vast basin of water that forms the wharf, but upstream from here the canal disappears under the ground, cutting a subterranean path until it pops up behind a posh hotel and meets its maker: the River Taff.

I'd looked into entering those underground canal workings while researching stories for a BBC series on the river, even going so far as to find a local artist who had worked out a plan to sail them on the inflated inner tube of a tractor tyre, but the council had thwarted our plans. The king rats and giant eels of the perpetual dark would have to wait. Still, I peered hopefully off the bridge and into the water below, willing a daylight giant to materialize somewhere in the void below.

Superficially, it couldn't be less welcoming. Hard slabs of concrete encase this narrow patch, and the water is clogged hard with storm-swept branches that reach to the heavens with their long skeletal fingers.

The litter here is far worse than the stuff on the Grand Union Canal, and there's certainly no caring edge or quirky canal culture to be found in this forgotten space. The slack water teems with beer bottles, cans and plastics, and as the streetlights flickered into life, a grimy orange hue was cast right across the scene, lighting up the canal like some bargain basement red-light district.

A series of gently expanding rings appear suddenly on the water's surface. Even here, there are signs of wildlife. It is a shoal of feeding fish, moving around in the upper layers of water, just as I'd hoped; basking in the relative warmth, and snatching the very occasional fly or grub ensnared in the surface film. Perhaps I can dare to dream?

Removing the four-inch rubber lure from the end of my line, I quickly switch to a tiny spinner. These topping fish are small; I don't want to stand out too much from the crowd. I make my first cast and the water stirs with mass movement. Clearly there are a lot more silverfish here than I'd first thought. Seconds later a pluck on the line is converted into a jarring take. It feels small and awkward, possibly a perch, but more likely just a foulhooked fish.

Yes. I've accidentally punctured a pristine roach right through its silvery side. I've massively underestimated this place – there are quite literally thousands of fish holed up in here; there's barely room in the water to work my spinner without risking hooking one in error.

Another cast sees me lodged into something solid and inanimate on the canal bottom. I yank hard in an attempt to free the hooks and spook something very large to the left of my tightened line. It sends a V-shaped bow wave down the water and scatters hundreds of frightened roach across the surface in its wake.

It just has to be a pike.

A man with a pram filled with plastic bags wanders past, eyes down, followed by a jogger whose music is cranked up so loud I can almost hear the lyrics of the R&B song blasting from his headphones. I re-cast and immediately hook into a tiny pike. It writhes on the line as I ease it in to the canal's side, splashing the surface and disturbing the water. That was a very bad move on this little pike's part: with little warning the V-shaped wave is back; but this time it's coming straight for us.

Time slows and my heart rolls up towards my gullet. A monstrous pike emerges right beneath its victim. The little pike, the big pike and I, we all know what is coming next. In a flash the larger has ingested the smaller, spinner and all, without any of it needing to touch the sides.

As my line is still attached to the small pike, we both now have quite a problem. Realizing it is tethered the monster projects itself clean out of the water in fright, using the power of its tail alone to skip impressively along the surface before crashing back into the pool with a thunderclap. I receive a full view of its extraordinary length during these acrobatics; it is in excess of 10lb, perhaps not a big fish in terms of big pike, but a true giant for such a tiny canal.

I try to keep tension on the line but a microsecond of slack sees the hook dislodged and, as the fish belly-flops its way back into the water, I realize we are sadly no longer in contact.

A steady rain blisters the water as night falls hard and cold. The supreme power of the pike's re-entry has sent shock waves slapping into the canal's concrete sides. Briefly, a single tennis ball is projected up onto the walkway. It rolls a wet trail for a few feet before landing back into the murk with a 'plop'.

I walk downstream towards the wharf breathing heavily. I need to pull myself together, fast. There is still a chance that the fish hasn't yet felt the steel of my hooks – it might just take another bait, but I know I must rest the swim before attempting anything else. Both the pike and I need time to consider our next moves.

Clearly, I'm on edge. A grey heron explodes from a thicket at my ankles and I momentarily leave my body in fright. Come on, Will, it's only a fish. Except it wasn't, that fish was a miracle out in that squash-court-sized patch of water, and right now, in this very moment, I'm probably the only person in the world that even knows it exists.

In the desolate car park just before the wharf, a fight between two drug dealers breaks out. I try not to catch their eye as they scream each other down about some aborted deal. With their identical enamel-white parka jackets and fur-lined hoods they look like a pair of duelling swans, puffing out their chests and jostling for territory. I duck down and take a couple of speculative casts into the darkness of the wharf, snagging some weed and finding a sense of calm just in the process of removing the soft green matting from the trio of hooks at the end of my spinner. It's soon time to go back and try again.

I underhand-cast the spinner back into the same spot and get an instant slamming response from the monster. He's ready, and this time so am I. I heave hard against its bulk, in my mind setting the hooks securely into its fang-filled mouth, but, again, I feel the gut-wrenching give of a slack, fish-free line.

I don't understand. Under a downstream bridge a pair of boys smoke marijuana from a roll-up they're sharing. Its sweet smell drifts on the night air right down to my latest disaster. Edgily, they flick their lighter on and off. They haven't noticed my fish, my crisis or me. I reel up and to my surprise discover that yet another small roach has found its way onto the hooks.

This roach is in a truly sorry state: heavily lacerated with a severed spinal cord and a frozen expression. It has been thoroughly mangled by the pike. Stone dead on arrival. Gently, I place a hook through its lower lip and flick it back in. This is now my last chance.

Almost imperceptibly the line starts to shudder and slide. Unbelievable luck. I wait, imagining the giant pike first taking the roach sideways in its mouth before turning it slowly towards its final journey on this earth. I take a deep, deep breath, wind down, and lift into the fish as hard as I dare.

Massive resistance gives way to a thunderous charge towards the bridge. The pot-smokers have gone now and my reel screams as line escapes the spool at speed. There's no acrobatics to be had this time around: just dour, dogged confrontation.

The pike steams right through the bridge and out the other side. I didn't think I was going to be able to stop it from rounding a bend in the canal at first, but, at last, it starts to yield to pressure.

As the great pike inches to the surface I drop to my knees. Here she comes, like a thick, green submarine. I steady myself as the head presents itself. There is only one spot on a pike where you can grasp it by hand without lacerating your fingers or hurting the fish: it's inside the mouth, right underneath the lower jaw by way of its hardened gill plates. With no time to put on a glove I slide my hand into the cavity and lift.

She's beautiful. A spawn-filled female, thick and so darkly marked that you could easily be staring right at her without ever realizing she's there; a metaphor for this canal system if ever there was one.

I roll out a soft mat to safely remove the hooks without causing any more disruption to her day, and spend a few moments on my knees simply gazing at this precious sword from the stone.

A man in a suit walks right past me without even acknowledging our presence. Even with the fish out of water the canal's secrets remain invisible to those incapable of belief.

I lie down on my chest and attempt to self-take a photo at arm's length, but I'm interrupted. 'Jesus Christ, mate!' It's one of the boys from beneath the bridge, back with the remains of his spliff hanging at a comedic angle from his trembling lower lip. 'What dafuk is that!?'

He pulls down the hood on his black Adidas tracksuit to reveal a tightly dreadlocked scalp. He attempts to take a photo with his phone, but his hands are shaking uncontrollably.

'Oh my days,' said the lad, wiping his brow at the sheer intensity of the experience, 'I'm not going to lie,

I've seen some crazy shit down here but I ain't never seen anything like that.'

Together, we sat down next to the great fish. Paying gentle homage as I showed him its mouthparts, fins and armour, before sliding her carefully back into the canal.

Momentarily the pike just sat on the shallow bottom glowering right back up at us.

'That's crazy,' he said.

'I know,' I replied.

It really was.

A waft of her tail eventually sent her back to a life of obscurity beneath a floating mat of litter, and my partner decided it was also time to make his own way back into darkness.

I watched him as he went, pulling his hood back over his head and sparking up the biggest spliff this side of Jamaica.

If Grandad had been around today we would've talked about that capture for weeks, but all I had was the Wilson *Encyclopedia* to pour my experience into, and all that came back was the cold hard fact that my fish wasn't a record breaker. In fact, it wasn't even anywhere close to being a Wilson mega-specimen.

A 30lb pike is a very rare beast in itself, but a forty-pounder capable of threatening Roy Lewis's 46lb 13oz record is almost beyond the realms of possibility. Scanning the list of the fifty biggest pike ever caught, and immediately discounting the sketchy records, repeat captures or those that are likely to now be deceased, I felt it was probably realistic to say there were fewer than twenty known 40lb pike alive in Britain today; most of which were highly nomadic individuals living within immense expanses of water.

Llandegfedd, the water that provided Roy with his record back in 1992, would have seemed the obvious place to start, but by the turn of the century the water had headed into such a state of pike-fishing decline that a five-year hiatus on predator angling was called in 2010.

By the time it reopened in 2015 there was already a new contender firmly on the block. Fifty kilometres to the south-east, Somerset's Chew Valley Lake, or 'Chew' as it is affectionately known by pike anglers, was crushing all comers. 2015 saw an astonishing trio of pike over 40lb grace Chew's banks, and with a further seventeen fish of over 30lb falling in just the first week of the pike season, it was no longer a question of whether Chew was the No. 1 pike water in the UK, but whether it could actually be one of the greatest of all time.

From the moment Chew's super-sized pike started hitting the angling press I was quite literally desperate to fish there. If I was going to stand any realistic chance of catching a record-breaking pike, then clearly Chew was the place to go, but simply getting tickets to pike fish the place represented an immense challenge of will and patience.

There are only two periods in a year you can actually

fish for pike on Chew: one two-week spell in February, and a second, longer spell, running through October and November. These are known as the 'pike trials', and the only way of getting tickets is to call the Lodge land-line on the first Saturday after the Christmas and New Year holidays. With every serious pike angler in Britain jamming up the line, for the strict limit of twenty-five boats and twenty bank tickets, the odds of getting a result are extremely slim. No one could say it wasn't fair: everyone is equally unlikely to win this lottery.

It endeared Chew to me no end. Predominately it was a trout-fishing water that happened to contain mon-strous pike. No one wanted to outright deny pike anglers the opportunity to catch the fish of a lifetime, but equally the owners felt they had a duty of care to their bread-and-butter trout anglers, and, as we already know, big pike hate attention.

As if the odds weren't already stacked against me, the great Chew phone-in landed on 9 January: the morning after the World Darts quarter-finals at the Lakeside. It took the most almighty effort just to find my phone that morning, but I was present and correct at 9 a.m., albeit barefoot and surrounded by pizza boxes and screwed-up tickets from the night before (our hero, 'Scotty-Dog' Mitchell, had been knocked out). I took a deep, fortifying breath, and began punching in the number.

An hour passed as I notched up my first hundred unsuccessful calls. I was then joined by my bleary-eyed mate Stuart, who deployed both his landline and his mobile phone, effectively tripling my chances, but it was all to be in vain.

We ceremoniously called it a day once we had heard the engaged tone for the 1,000th time. 'I guess that's why they call it the pike "trials", mate,' said Stuart while looking for his van keys. He could see how much it meant to me, I appreciated that. We sloped off to the semi-finals and I tried my best to thoroughly drown my sorrows.

I eventually got through three days later. The polite West Country man on the phone told me all the spots for 2016 were long since gone. The horse had not only bolted before the stable door was closed, he was in the next town and midway through a national lecture tour on farm security. The man told me there were now a raffle and an auction to try for. I failed in the former and the latter topped out at an extraordinary £880 for a single day on a boat. There was nothing more I could do. I was just going to have to look elsewhere for my chance.

With Chew gone and Llandegfedd out of the running, I had to find another big trout water fast. Closer to my childhood home there were the Graffham and Rutland reservoirs, but the really big pike had been curiously absent there for the last few seasons; over in the Brecon Beacons there was Llangorse Lake, famously referenced in *The Domesday Book of Mammoth Pike* for producing the world's biggest-ever pike (in 1846 to the rod of a Mr Owen, a giant fish weighing an alleged 68lb), but that was unsubstantiated, and would have been dead for well over a hundred years. I called up the kindly owner anyway, and he readily admitted that, although the lake certainly had potential, it realistically couldn't ever compete with Chew for the sheer size of pike. The last big fish there was a thirty-two-pounder in 2007. It wasn't looking good. I had one last avenue to try, but I knew this was an even longer shot than Chew.

Scarborough's Wykeham Lakes had a lot going for them on paper. Currently the biggest known living pike in Britain, a giant 46lb 11oz fish, was resident in their waters, and at only seven acres (to Chew's 1,000-plus) the odds of a record-breaking hook-up were dramatically reduced. However, access to pike fish the water was strictly restricted to members of an exclusive syndicate. I fired off a hopeful email and was extremely surprised to get a quick response inviting me to speak to Jake Finnigan, the fisheries manager.

Jake was a politely spoken and articulate northerner who clearly cared deeply about the fish in his lake. I wanted to get a feeling of what it must be like to look after a water with such a legendary fish, a real-life Loch Ness monster, a proper, tangible lake beast; and then I wanted to nonchalantly request special permission to have a crack at it.

I was going to have to play my cards very carefully indeed, but Jake tripped me up within moments of answering my call.

'She's been out on six occasions over the last five years,' he began. 'First she was thirty-nine pounds, fifteen ounces back in November 2010 . . .' He paused. 'It was me that caught her then actually.'

'Sorry, Jake, can I stop you there?' I presumed I'd misheard. 'You just said you caught the pike first?'

This was an absolute bombshell. I stammered on but my carefully loaded questions on fish care, leading up to a request to fish the lake, had just flown clean out of the window.

'Tell me exactly how it happened.' I leant into the phone and tore a fresh sheet of paper from my notebook.

'It was just a trout lake back then and this fish was a total unknown. People aren't totally sure how she even got in there. Some think she was placed in, but I reckon she most likely travelled up the becks and streams that flow to the River Derwent; right back when this whole place was flooded some years ago. From that point, she's obviously just gotten bigger and bigger.'

It was more than plausible that a small pike had made its way into this trout lake, and with rich pickings and freshly stocked trout, she would have piled on the poundage: up to 4lb a year for the best weight-gaining predators.

'The water here is deep,' Jake continued, 'twenty-eight foot in places, and has been stocked with trout for some thirty-odd years. It wasn't hard for it to hide, I guess, but the occasional trout angler talked of seeing a really big fish chasing their trout on the retrieve.' He took a deep breath. 'Honestly though, Will, we all thought the most it could be was thirty pounds.'

I had seen a few photos of this pike from its most recent captures. It was incomprehensibly enormous: a long, fat, female fish, with a back so wide you could fit it with a saddle.

My personal best pike was a 22lb fish caught from the depths of the Fens when I was twenty-five years old. I couldn't reasonably imagine tackling a pike nearly twice that size, and nor, it turned out, could Jake.

'A couple of trout anglers had returned their boat early one evening, so I just hopped in for nothing more than a twenty-minute mess about.' I liked that: a 'mess about' that led to the biggest single pike discovery since the turn of the century. 'I went out in the boat around the edge of the lake. It was right at the end of the day and I was on my last couple of casts, making my way back to where the boats were all kept, when suddenly the big girl took my spinner.

'At first I thought it was just a trout of a couple of pounds; she didn't really do that much, just headed straight in towards me. Then I saw it for the first time. That's where the fight truly began. I couldn't believe it.'

I couldn't believe it either. What a story. He went on to say that by the time he had the fish under control he realized the net he had with him wasn't anywhere near large enough to fit her in, and that he had then been forced to use the electric motor on board to get within shouting range of the shore. By a supreme stroke of good fortune a colleague eventually managed to net her tail first before the fish could free itself from the tether.

He had just landed the fish that would go on to become both the English record and the largest known living pike in the United Kingdom today. His previous personal best was just 14lb. It was, and still is, a fishing miracle.

'You just don't know how to feel when it happens. You're gobsmacked.'

That was where the good times ended for Jake and the pike. News of the giant fish travelled fast and Wykeham had to immediately limit the number of pike anglers allowed on the water. She next came out just four months after Jake had first caught her, but, astonishingly, the fish was some 6lb heavier. Now, with her just one meal away from being the next British record, interest in the fishery reached fever pitch. Jake was soon bombarded with requests to fish the lake for the pike.

'Look, it's a trout lake at the end of the day,' he said, with more than a touch of exasperation. 'Trout fishing was getting compromised. I had guys ringing up to enquire about trout fishing that couldn't get through because of all the interest from pike anglers. The syndicate seemed the best way to go then: limit it to ten anglers with a maximum of four a day on the water. I know it's very exclusive, but I prefer this run as a trout lake with the pike as something of a bonus. The amount of pressure she'll get is overwhelming if I don't do something. At least on Chew they've got more than one forty-pound fish and over a thousand acres for them to disappear into: here she's on her own with just seven.'

That last comment struck me hard. I started to feel a sense of real guilt. This wasn't what fishing should be about.

'Pike groups are getting more and more abrasive, just like the carp groups in fact,' continued Jake, 'you can't post a photo anywhere without someone tearing into someone over something. Every time our fish gets caught you've got one big group of people saying we're running it like an exclusive club and then another big group of people saying it's going to be a dead fish within a year. We've had one guy who said this time around: "I know I said last time it'll be a dead fish next year, but this time I really mean it: next year it will be dead." What are we supposed to do? We just can't win.'

Clearly Jake had a point: you've got to really look after these big individual fish. I started to wonder if this pike was more of a curse than a blessing.

'If only I could turn back the clock, I would make this lake invitation only for pike fishing and that's it,' he said, with finality.

For the first time in my entire fishing life I didn't want to catch a fish. Jake was right, pike fishing was going the same way as carp fishing and chasing named and known fish into potential oblivion on small waters was not cool at all. It was actually quite disturbing.

By the end of our conversation I no longer wanted to ask him for permission to fish; in fact, I was quite embarrassed at myself. I wondered what Grandad would make of it all. I knew what he would think actually: he'd laugh at me and question why anyone would ever place value on such a shortsighted pursuit.

Without me needing to say, Jake offered to set me up with a couple of the guys on the syndicate, and potentially, with their permission, have a little fish for the big one.

I told him how grateful I was for the offer, and really meant it, but there was no real mystery around this pike any more. It was still a challenge of sorts, but Jake's original discovery and capture were the real purist piece of angling. That's what was really impressive. That's what I wanted for myself.

Barring a miracle, any hopes I now had of angling for a record pike were fundamentally over. There wasn't much more I could do. Jake was spot on for trying to keep his fish safe in a small water and Chew were doing the same by massively limiting their numbers and restricting the pike-fishing windows.

The start of Chew's February pike trials saw bad weather and a few blowouts. The £880 angler didn't get his day out due to high winds and I managed a couple more sessions down the wharf and canals, but returned empty-handed.

One afternoon I went to Garry Evans Tackle, my local Cardiff shop and a tackle enthusiast's haven, and chatted to my friends Rich and Andrew about pike. 'I reckon there's a chance of a big one in the bay,' suggested Andrew, 'we've all been catching big perch down there all year.'

I told them about the fishing I'd been doing on the canal and down the wharf, and Andrew showed me a picture of a young bloke with a huge 16lb sea trout from one of the feeder streams. 'Yeah, the docklands are doing really well,' continued Andrew, stowing his phone back in his pocket, 'I've had loads of small pike down there, but the carp fishermen reckon they keep seeing really big pike battling it out with the rats.'

That sounded pretty much in keeping with that particular set of docks. It's a pike-eat-rat world down there. 'I've had a really big pike, and I mean a really big one, chasing my floating frog lures down there on several occasions,' Andrew continued, 'but there is something about that lure that the big pike really doesn't like. He keeps turning away right at the last minute . . .' He looked to his fingernails with a touch of embarrassment. '. . . So I've bought a lure shaped like a rat.'

I didn't even know there was such a thing, but Andrew knew everything that was worth knowing about lure-fishing, and, besides, it wasn't like I didn't get it; I'd once spent an entire afternoon fishing with a Pot Noodle on a whim.

'I'm going to be trying that soon,' he said, suddenly far surer of himself, before a ringing phone took him back to his work.

I left the tackle shop wondering about making a proper effort on the wider docks, as well as the wharf, or at least buying myself a rat lure and joining Andrew. In my heart, though, I couldn't help but think that this was feeling very much like needle-in-a-haystack time, or at least floating-rat-in-giant-rat-infested-dock time.

I went home feeling a little defeated, but on the journey back my phone pinged to life with an email. It was from a man named John Horsey, a legendary fishing guide who led trips to Chew during the pike trials, if you had already been lucky enough to snare a ticket of course.

I had contacted him a few weeks before the great phone-in but there didn't seem any point following up, given I hadn't managed to get a ticket. The email read:

Hi Will

Just to let you know there are guided boats available on 5, 7 and 16 Feb with me as the guide. This is a new initiative by Bristol Water.

If you want one of these boats then ring Chew ASAP.

Kind regards
John Horsey

Frantically, I hammered the now very familiar number for the Lodge. No answer. I left a voicemail, wrote an email, and tried to get through four more times, before finally, mercifully, I heard that glorious West Country accent once more: 'Hello, Chew Lakes.'

The words of my request spilled from my mouth at such a pace I was surprised the man on the end of the receiver could even figure out what I was trying to say.

'Ooh, I'm not sure.' I could hear some riffling of papers in the background. 'Possibly they are all booked out, possibly there is one left.'

I tried to sound cool, but it was pretty difficult given how badly I wanted this to work out. My heart was firmly in my mouth as the riffling continued, back-dropped with the occasional 'hmm'.

Eventually he answered.

'Yep, one left.'

16 February 2016. My date with pike-fishing destiny.

It was more money than I'd spent on a single day's fishing in my entire life, but I was over the moon. I had my ticket and I was absolutely determined to make the very most of it. All my ethics about chasing pounds and ounces and being part of a pike-fishing circus were firmly buried; I was boarding the clown car with a front-row seat for the big top and the undisputed ringmaster for hire. I just prayed we had a run of good weather.

The days quickly passed and I started to feel increasingly nervous. A feeling of inadequacy I hadn't felt since I was listening to Dad in the stairwell started to creep into the back of my mind. Am I actually up to these fish? I opted to spend yet more of my dwindling savings on tackle: bigger lures and a beefy braided line that felt like woven rope.

Extraordinary reports from Chew began to filter in. By all accounts this was shaping up to be one of the best February pike trials of all time. By the time my big day eventually came around, twenty pike over the 30lb barrier had already been snared, with two truly enormous fish topping out the scales at 41lb. To give that some sort of perspective, Martin Bowler, one of the best all-round anglers in Britain (who also just happens to be John Wilson's nephew), landed a 34lb 12oz fish and commented to the *Angling Times*: 'If I'd caught that fish at any other venue it would be a safe bet that it would be the best of the day, but I think the day I was fishing it was only third-biggest.' One man even commented on Chew's pike-fishing Facebook group that he wasn't sure it was even worth him posting a picture of his fish as 'it was only 28lb'.

Twenty-eight pounds. Six pounds bigger than my biggest all-time pike. Not even worth posting. I spooled up my strongest reel with my all-new braided line and selected the three most powerful rods I owned from the garden shed.

'I remember a fisheries scientist saying to me, "A pike doesn't know how big he is." I thought that was a silly thing to say, but actually it isn't, is it? It's not like they've got a mirror to look in, is it?'

I liked John Horsey immediately. He was a bright, liberal man, with an exceptional knowledge and enthusiasm for his sport. His heart lay with fly-fishing, particularly in competitions where he had captained England at world and European levels, and had even won the World Championships back in 2009; however, unlike many professional fly-fishermen, he wasn't the sort of person who would turn his nose up at coarse fishermen purely on principle. Plus he had a 40lb pike to his boat, caught, remarkably, on a fly. For all of that, I was extremely grateful.

His point, regarding the pike and the mirror, was that big fish don't necessarily change their feeding habits just because they are big fish. They are able to take bigger baits of course, but it is prudent not to assume their diet exclusively matches their size. Almost every animal is still partial to the food it grew up on, and therefore you shouldn't be surprised if, every once in a while, you encounter a fish of far greater size than your diminutive bait would expect; the biggest carp I've ever caught simply swallowed a single kernel of sweetcorn.

'Everyone always says it has to be a heavily stocked trout water to break a record, where there's plenty of big trout for the big pike to eat, but I don't believe that's strictly true,' explained John.

With his shock of white hair hidden beneath a baseball cap and neatly trimmed goatee beard, he had an air of the 'rock star' about him. 'Chew is the best pike fishery in Britain today because the levels of biodiversity here are exceptional. It's not just the pike; everything in this water is big: big trout, big tench, big eels, big roach; it's all thanks to the rich aquatic insect life that lives and breeds here' – he cast out an arm across the water in front of us – 'especially the black chironomids. The pike here are full of them.'

I had to look up 'chironomid' later. Essentially they are a variety of midge and closely resemble small mosquitoes, but don't let that put you off; this species is non-biting and, according to the Natural History Museum, they are a vitally important indicator species of the health of any water. They are extremely sensitive to any kind of pollutant or acidity in water, so their presence in numbers is a good sign of a first-rate environment; fantastic news to fish of all sizes, from giant pike to minute stickleback, which readily gorge on the flies and their larvae. John mentioned an autopsy on a mid-sized dead pike that revealed a stomach literally crammed with these small, jet-black insects, and my friends, who had fly-fished Chew in the past, claimed to have actually seen the pike scooping the insects right out of the lake, breaching the surface like packs of dolphins.

Chew is just that sort of place – where accepted logic is warped to such a degree that you genuinely start to believe in miracles. The lake looked truly serene at first light and sight. A clear, deep-blue morning had left a light ripple, and a blanket of wispy fog was playing on the water's surface. Chew dwarfed the Cardiff docks, of course. It appeared oceanic in comparison, but it wasn't as intimidating as I'd thought it might be.

As I perused the map on the back of my fishing permit I noted it resembled a hen's chick in profile, albeit with a slightly oversized head. There were a few attractive-looking bays, a pair of trench-like 'legs', and a large island, placed somewhere around the eye of the bird: lots of potential fish-holding areas that broke up the immensity of the venue then.

With John I was far from fishing blind at any rate. He purposefully hung back to see where all the other boats would go. 'Pike fishermen can be a bit like sheep,' he declared, placing his tackle in the bottom of the boat, 'they all tend to go where big fish have been caught that week and will follow each other around throughout the day. It's always best to give them all a wide berth and find your own place to start. There's no rush anyway; the best time on this lake is often the late afternoon to the sunset.'

John elected to start just left of Wick Green Point, a slight protrusion on the far bank from the Lodge, some-where around the centre of the chick's back. It was lined with a thick growth of reeds that had been bleached a starchy white in the winter air. Instinctively, I would have taken our boat right in among those reeds, looking for a take from a pike hidden up against the beds. This, I learnt, would not have found me a record.

'These are big open-water fish,' explained John, 'they don't even know the meaning of the word ambush. The average depth here is only about thirteen feet, so quite shallow, but you've got to get the bait down there to catch the really big ones. They won't come up to get it, especially not when it is cold like this. They are immensely fat, and immensely lazy.'

I picked up the pair of lures that I'd bought brand new for this trip and handed them over to John for inspection.

They felt sticky, like they were fresh out of the mould, and were utterly free of blemishes or experience; I was like a young boy on his first day at secondary school, conscious that my sparkling-new pencil case was missing the requisite band insignias, amorous messages or pictures of cocks, which all the older, far cooler boys seemed to have.

One of the lures was the perfect replica of a small trout. I thought, given this was a trout lake, that was a fair choice. The second was a luminescent-looking perch, like the fish had spent its days swimming around nuclear fallout before finally making its way to my tackle box. I couldn't imagine what had drawn me towards that one; it looked hideous.

John eyed them both up before giving something of a damning verdict: 'Well, I wouldn't go with that perch, Will, not right away anyway, and the pike won't recognize that as a rainbow trout either. They've never seen a rainbow trout under two pounds in this place.'

I hadn't even made my first cast and I was already on the back foot. John, perhaps sensing I felt a little downcast, revisited the trout. 'They might just take it thinking it's a roach though; it is very white and, after all, all you need in this lake is just one take.'

That was good enough for me. I hooked it up to a strong wire trace and took a deep breath. It had taken an awful lot just to get to this point. I cast out well away from the reeds, watched my braided line snake out a little before feeling the lure strike the lake's bottom. John was right; it really was shallow. I began my retrieve, keeping it slow, steady and tight to the bed, as instructed. This was it. I was finally fishing Chew.

Five minutes later I felt the telltale thump and head-shake of a predator. A brief but solid fight brought an impeccable little pike of about 4lb to the edge of the boat. It was a nerve settler, the piscatorial equivalent of a pre-match pep talk, and there was even a small, but satisfactory, tear in the side of my new trout now. Perhaps I was worthy after all?

Soon afterwards a spiteful wind picked up off the Mendip Hills, rocking our boat and biting sharply into my bare hands. Of course, Chew wasn't going to let me have it all my own way. We pulled up our anchor and headed for shelter behind a large, semi-flooded island. 'Blimey, John, there's plenty of boats down here.' A quick head count revealed well over half of all the boats on the lake were also taking refuge, strung out in a long line like the floating buoys of a giant gill net.

I blew some hot air into my hands. 'Don't be fooled. They're not down here just to stay warm,' said John, with a quiet intensity, 'this was where that forty-one-pound giant was caught last week.' He selected a very, very large, fresh-looking mackerel from his bait box and fixed it firmly to a treble hook. 'I know, because I was here.' He cast the mackerel right out into the middle of the channel and tightened down his line till his fat, red-topped float could be seen bouncing happily along the surface.

I settled into a trance-like state: casting my lure, retrieving, focusing in on the play of the line through the water, and arching my neck occasionally to check our floats were still in place. A curious sensation came over me. It was a feeling that comes along with such infrequency that it feels like a sort of temporary psychosis, yet it strikes with such undeniable force that it is impossible to ignore.

As sure as King Canute knew he could not really turn the tides, I became convinced the pike were coming on to feed.

'We're going to get a fish here, John,' I said, venturing to vocalize my forecast, in spite of the lack of any discernible evidence. It was a gut instinct, a primeval intuition long since buried beneath several thousand generations of comfortable living and comfort eating, but I was utterly convinced I was right.

One of the men on the string of boats suddenly stood bolt upright with a rod buckling in his hand. I knew it.

We watched as his boat partner threw a massive black net from port to starboard, like a man wrestling with some giant sail on an ocean-going clipper. The angler started to pump the fish towards him; the tide was turning against this pike; soon it was subdued somewhere down by the engine block. They shook hands. It was a good one, at least 20lb in weight.

'My float is doing something funny.' Instantly, I snapped my gaze from the drama unfolding in the other boat. John was staring out at his float, which was now beginning to wheel.

When I was sixteen I learnt how big pike can often feed in spells. I remember that day clearly, my legs whirring as I ran away from the riverbank and back towards Grandad's bungalow. Behind me, submerged in a net, I had left a pike. A proper one, not a small jack or an emaciated summer fish, but a fat female that almost tore my rod into the deep alongside my smelt dead bait. The fish in itself was remarkable, but of far greater significance was the other, even bigger, pike that lay in the net right beside it.

In just ten minutes I had smashed my personal best, twice. I was in pike-fishing nirvana and I prayed Grandma had film in her camera as I exploded into the kitchen.

Grandma took my photo with both fish. 'Well done, boy!' shouted Grandad, giving me the thumbs-up I'd hoped for. He was off to play carpet bowls, he said; fishing in the bleak mid-winter wasn't really his thing.

I knew that was a special day. Over 30lb of pike in just two casts. Sometimes I feel I've been paying for that piece of good fortune ever since.

John's float started kiting hard to the left. This really was it.

'You take it . . .' John pulled the rod from its rest and handed it down to me in an act of extraordinary generosity. 'Really, are you sure?' I stuttered, and we had a brief and ridiculously British standoff, at the absolutely critical moment.

'Yes! Go for it, Will!' he eventually shouted, imploring me to take up the rod.

I didn't need to be asked for a third time. I reeled up the slack line, sank the tip and swept the rod upwards.

But there was nothing. No riposte. No bone-churning heavyweight thump. Just air and slack. I reeled down once more and gave it another slam, but it was useless. The pike had already let go.

'That was the big mackerel bait, wasn't it?' I asked, half hoping John might answer in the negative, or just assure me it was possible a trout could have chewed the bait from the hook. 'Yes, Will.'

My chance had been and gone. As plausible as it is that a 40lb pike might feed on a tiny chironomid, there was no way a small fish was ever squeezing a 1lb mackerel bait down its gullet. As quickly as the feeding spell had been triggered, the big pike turned themselves off once more.

There was excited chatter among the boats as we pulled into the docks that sunset. A Chew employee placed a thick boot on the side of our boat as we drifted into the melee. 'There were seven thirties out today, lads!' he revealed gleefully. 'How did you guys get on?'

The van's windscreen wipers squealed as I fought with the drizzle on the drive back home. I wonder how big that fish really was? I'll never know now of course, but I felt oddly calm.

When I was a boy I recall Grandad telling me a story about a great fish he once hooked that ran with an unstoppable force until it emptied his reel of a hundred metres of line and eventually broke free, leaving his rod hanging limp like a washing line cracked in a storm.

I asked him to recall this anecdote many times, both because I loved the idea of the mysterious giant in our waters, but also because I was unable to process how he could recall such a tale of calamity and yet appear so at peace. Perhaps in the retelling his demeanour would one day buckle, betraying his true feelings of raw hurt and resentment; but, of course, it never did.

Grandad, I realize now, was simply enriched by the experience of angling. His inner tranquillity came from a confidence emboldened by the knowledge that when it comes to hooking a big fish, a degree of loss is simply inevitable. It was not something to resent or regret; it was simply an acceptable part of what it meant to be a true fisherman, and a better person.

I would return to Chew if I ever get the chance again, but for all the ticketing process, the beefed-up tackle, circumstance and ceremony, could I reasonably say my day today had brought me more pleasure than the pike I had caught in the canal? Perhaps anglers' success is not determined only by the sheer size of the fish they catch, but the manner of, and pleasure to be had from, the pursuit and chase.

It had taken me over twenty years to learn the wisdom Grandad was once trying to impart, but I'd understood in the end. I would turn my attentions to fish of smaller proportions for the rest of this fishing year, and leave the giants for another time and place.

It was almost the close of the winter of '92 before I caught my first pike. As is often the way with these things, the fight of my fears was over before it began.

My spinner approached a hole within a cluster of reeds and a small pike materialized hot on its heels. I hastened my retrieve, and the fish, believing its meal was about to escape, near launched itself out of the water to engulf the lure.

Of all the pike I have caught, it was by far the easiest to land. I hooked it less than a foot from the bank and simply sprinted backwards, tearing the fish clean from the water and almost getting run over by a passing car in the process.

Unfortunately, behind the wheel was my Year Four primary school teacher, Mrs Hills. I could tell I was in for a massive rollicking by the steam coming from her brakes and ears, so I quickly scooped up my pike and sprinted off before she could even lay a hand on her car door handle.

It didn't occur to me then that this fish was merely a juvenile, or that I had been extremely lucky not to lose it or snap my line with my terrible antics. As far as I was concerned I now had living, breathing proof that Dad and Grandad were not always right. Pike were extremely hard to catch but I did have the strength to do it on my own.

In a quiet, teacher-free corner of the Creek I slipped my little pike back into the shallows. I couldn't possibly have realized it at the time, but, as it kicked its tail to disappear once and for all, it was taking a vital piece of my childhood down into the murk with it.

A Never-Ending Golden Sun

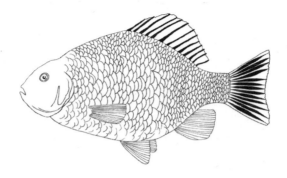

Summer will end soon enough,
and childhood as well.
George R. R. Martin, *A Game of Thrones* (1996)

Early June in Britain has a definite smell. It's not quite
the sharp relief that you might associate with the first
shoots of spring; a sliced crab apple that's fallen straight
off the tree, maybe, or a sudden rain shower on crisp
grass, perhaps. But it isn't anything like the sweaty
oppression of a hot summer's day either, which hovers
somewhere between a damp gym sock and an overripe
banana.

Early June is much more subtle than that. It's a gradual sweetening of the air, an almost honey-like scent

that creeps out across the land and rolls out a yellowing haze in its wake. It is experienced especially well at dawn by the side of a pond, when it can feel like the whole country is being gently dusted with a caramelized sugar crust simply for your pleasure, or that you've been viewing the land through a pair of ginger-coloured stockings that are pulled tight right across the balls of your eyes.

When early June is on form it brings the humans warily to their gardens, to cook meat and attempt some ice in their drinks, and also calls bees out of their hives to gather and discuss making a move. Don't be fooled, though – early June brings a sense of threat too. It is not yet summer, and all that has built since winter could quite easily be swept aside in a solitary night of single-digit temperatures, or a week of sullen rain. It is a risk that only doubles if someone is foolish enough to remark: 'What wonderful weather we've been having recently.'

For me, and anglers like me, early June exists as a hidden fifth season. It's not always found in early June; it can actually be any time from May, or even as early as late April, if we have had an exceptionally warm spring. Throwing our increasingly irrelevant Gregorian calendar aside, it is more accurate to place this season somewhere between the point the bluebells pass their best, and the seven days of proper sun we call summer. It brings trout to the surface to feed voraciously on the first of the serious fly hatches, a time known as 'duffer's fortnight', where even the most novice of anglers could seemingly catch a fish with a bent pin, but it is early morning on a certain type of water targeting a certain type of fish that defines the hidden season for some of us.

If you are lucky enough to catch this bridging spell at its climax then it is as close to climatic perfection as I think it is possible to experience as a fisherman. To achieve true flawlessness, though, is to time these rarefied atmospherics with your presence beside a lily-choked and tree-lined pool, at the exact point of sunrise. Obviously you will need a rod, loaded with light line and a bright float. Preferably there will also be a billowing steam peeling off the water's surface, and, once you have made your first cast, great plumes of pinhead-sized bubbles will surround your patch of water in a fizzing carpet.

If there is an angling scene that better represents the quintessence of this unsung time of year then I am yet to see it, but the fish that leads the charge doesn't just show itself to anyone. You have to be willing to search.

It was the start of the summer holidays from school, my first in secondary education, and Grandad was searching furiously at the back end of his living room. His arse had just nearly knocked the television over.

'Yes! I've got it!' he shouted in triumph. While lifting an old Polaroid cleanly from the labyrinth of VHS cassettes and family albums, he resembled an immense old walrus emerging from the water with a fresh fish in its teeth.

It was a black-and-white photo showing a solid-looking young man kicking a rugby ball. His shoulders are leaning back, his spine is straight, and the ball has just been thumped so hard it is leaving his toe as nothing more than an egg-shaped blur.

Grandad restored his breath. 'There, Will.' He presents me with the image while inhaling, this time for dramatic effect. 'The perfect kick. You'll never see it done better than that.' He thumbs the photo to make his point. 'That. Is how you do it, my boy.'

I grip it in my hands.

It's him in the picture, isn't it? Of course it's him.

Things hadn't gone too well at my new school. The endless evenings of fishing after lessons were over for a start – homework and a long journey to and from the gates had made sure of that – plus, after seven years of climbing the year groups at the local village primary school, I had found myself unceremoniously dumped back at the very bottom of the pecking order. It wasn't like Wisbech Grammar was all that bad. I was bullied, but not terribly so; it was the brand of schoolboy cruelty that had you tying a coin into the knot of your tie, to stop it being pulled so tight it was impossible to undo, rather than the threat of actual bodily harm. But having any sort of fear of attending school was new to me, and I didn't like it at all.

This was the start of adult life, though, where the first lesson you learn is that your free time will be leased back to you only once you've earned it, and that your future now depends on your ranking within an extremely narrow field of disciplines.

In lieu of stellar grades – I was no academic – I was to be judged by my ability to hit a cricket ball and take a full-contact rugby tackle. The problem was I was terrible at both rugby and cricket. We had played neither at my primary school, bar the very occasional game with a soft ball, or tag rugby, where the worst thing that could happen is that your mate grabs your shorts, and not your tag, and you end up exposing yourself to the class.

Unfortunately there really isn't much room for fishing in the arena of competitive team sports, especially those played by adolescent boys. Sure, there is a match-angling scene, but mostly this still boils down to individuals performing against other individuals, and no one – I repeat, no one – has pictures of the latest match-angling stars plastered across their bedroom walls. Anglers just aren't idols or icons for your normal teenager. My obsession with John Wilson suddenly seemed very childish and, to be frank, a bit embarrassing.

My recent progression as an angler was an irrelevance to my new classmates, of course. No one cared how good my casting was getting or that I had recently broken my perch personal best. Instead, my fishing became my escape route, the secret place I could vanish into to hide from my struggles at school. Later angling would actually offer me something of a pathway out of my problems, but that was all to come and in the first year of the new school I simply had no choice but to play the sports they instructed me to play.

I couldn't even catch a cricket ball, let alone throw it. They were rock-hard and frightening, much like the teachers and older kids who pushed past me in the corridor, and, as such, I tried to avoid them, all of them, at any cost.

'You're a bit of a loner, aren't you?' remarked one of my peers, after yet another lunchtime of dodging the other pupils in the first year. I felt hot tears puddling in my eyes and quickly looked away. 'No.' You're just all dickheads, I wish I could've said.

Dad and I were sat together in the Rose Tavern pub at the end of the school year. He was a massive real-ale nerd so going to pubs was hardly something new. Even as a twelve-year-old I had seen the inside of most of the decent pubs in our area, especially if they graced the hallowed pages of the *CAMRA Good Beer Guide*, but it was a rare occurrence to be alone with him and without the rest of the family. I was finally sat in the inner sanctum, the actual bar and not just the 'Family Fun Zone'. In with the real men, who drank by the pint, smoked and swore, I thought for a moment that Dad might even buy me a beer, but really I knew the real reason why I was here. I had just experienced the sporting equivalent of being tarred, feathered and marched around the market square naked. It was time for a fatherly pep talk. He slid an orange juice across the table towards me. 'It will get better, give it time, Will.' I felt too sick to even drink it. He had to 'give it time' at his school, he explained, and it wasn't easy for him either, at first.

'It actually took me right till sixth form before I really started enjoying it,' he attempted, jovially. Sixth form! Was Dad absolutely out of his mind? That was six years away! I looked at the orange juice in front of me and wished my whole life would go away.

My first rugby season had been a complete and utter disaster. It began with quite possibly the most anonymous performance in rugby union history, where the one touch of the ball I had was the moment it collided with my face, and split open my nose, and ended, even more dramatically, when one of the teachers used my limp form to demonstrate the dump tackle and shattered my collarbone in the process.

Sadly, my collarbone had re-fused just in time for the cricket season, but, unlike the X-Men, it had not mutated into anything that might have given me superpowers or even just a better throw. The year's crowning glory, truly the fly on this absolute turd of a term, had occurred just an hour before Dad's morale-boosting speech in the pub.

The Under-12 first-team cricketers were a man down, and as I had volunteered to do the scoring in the ludicrously misguided parental belief that 'it's all about taking part', I was drafted in as the eleventh player.

I spent our opponents' innings just trying to avoid the ball, a feat I achieved well by virtue of the fact my team wanted me nowhere near the ball either, but when it came to our turn to bat my luck ran clean out.

Wickets tumbled with regularity from almost the moment our batsmen began their run chase. They had a bowler with an arm like Hercules, who, quite remarkably, also appeared to have grown some facial hair. I could only assume this man-boy was part of some witness protection programme, sent to terrorize the Under-12 cricket scene in relative anonymity.

Stumps exploded into puffs of sawdust and all too soon I found I was strapping myself into every single piece of protective equipment the school owned. I was sure I was going to die at the crease, and, ten minutes later, I realized I had.

All I needed to do for our team to escape the debacle with a draw was to bat for three balls. Three balls. The first fizzed past my head. I didn't even see it. Hercules glowered at me. 'He isn't moving,' I heard an ignoramus shout from within my own team, who, I noted, had helpfully gathered in a ten-man semi-circle around the boundary rope, as if they were witnessing an execution by stoning.

The second ball swung away, just inches from shattering my fingers or, worse, my stumps. Everyone groaned. Hands were placed on heads on both sides. Just one more left, I thought to myself. I looked to my dad, off work for the game, but never really a sporting man either. He tried to give me an encouraging thumb's-up look from behind his glasses and improbably thick hair, but his face betrayed his true feelings: I was in deep shit. With sad inevitability, the third and final ball crumpled my wicket.

You could've heard my teammates on Mars as I trudged off the pitch. 'Fucking useless Millard, we should never have sent him out there.' A darkness descended. I scooped up my bag and headed for Dad's car and the Rose Tavern pub, without speaking a single word till I was wedged in the triple sanctuary of a Toby mug, a fruit machine and my dad.

'They totally blamed me, Dad. You heard what they said. How can I show my face in school after that?' I was ranting at my juice. 'I hate this place. I hate this school. I hate everything about it. All of my primary school friends went to Downham, I just don't understand why I'm here in this place with these blazers and rules and teachers and tests . . . and terrible sports . . . and not . . . not with all my friends.' I started to cry, properly this time.

Dad put a hand on my shoulder. 'If you still hate it at the end of next year we'll move you out. I promise.' I sniffed hard and plunged my wet face into his shirt. 'Give it time,' he said again. I could tell it was hurting him too, but I didn't care.

'But what about rugby season next year, Dad?' I shouted. 'They'll kill me!'

He looked at me with glassy brown eyes, and said nothing.

The reason for Grandad's sudden expedition to the land that time forgot was that he had spoken to my dad and believed the solution to all of my problems was behind his television set.

'All you need to do is study this picture and you'll be able to kick penalties from the centre spot.' He slapped me so forcefully between the shoulder blades I felt the tremor in my stick-thin legs, like two albino chipolatas.

There was no way that this was what Dad had advised Grandad to do. He had come up with this solution all on his own.

'You've got all summer before the start of the rugby season. Just give it some beef, boy!'

I looked up at him, hoping he could see through to the lost child within. There was a pause as he stooped to meet my gaze, understanding dawning perhaps?

'You can even take it home and study it if you like?' He gave me a chummy wink and another slap on the back.

I didn't take it home. I had eight weeks before I had to be back at that school and I intended to spend it all forgetting the place ever existed. That meant two things: fishing, and really big carp.

By my final year of primary school the memory of the first pike had faded. I had a clutch of close friends from the village whom I fished with and, together with our bikes and the timetable of the Norfolk Green bus, we were pushing further than ever before. Bigger drains for bigger fish, stronger rods, thicker lines and the greater levels of patience required to sit through the shoals of roach and perch for something really special.

With them I caught my first zander, our first proper pike, my first ever chub, all by strapping rods to the crossbars of our bikes and pedalling as far as our legs could carry us in a single day. We were the kings of the Fens, bound only by the parental rule that we must be home by nightfall, and by the end of our time together in school our angling ambitions were inevitably extending beyond what we could feasibly catch from our home waters. We wanted more, and we weren't alone.

From the late 1970s onwards anglers nationwide were draining from Britain's rivers and canals and taking their tackle to well-stocked and exceptionally well-polished commercially motivated fisheries. Overwhelmingly, the explosive popularity of one single species had driven the change: the king carp. It had first been introduced from Asia as food for monks during the Middle Ages, and selective breeding had seen the proliferation of a heavier, hardier and highly varied cyprinid species that combined a readiness to feed with a heart-stoppingly powerful fight from even the smallest specimens. There was hardly a pond in the UK that they couldn't be stocked in, and, with astronomic annual weight gain possible from a new wave of protein-rich baits, targeting the species passed from the specialist and into the hands of the everyman.

Images of these giant fish, with their magnificent scale patterns, implausibly broad guts and thick, rounded mouths, screamed from the front page of every fishing magazine and tackle shop in the country. Even John Wilson was far from immune to carp fever: he built a carp lake in his own back garden, and soon released a video titled *Oliver's First Carp*, in which a boy exactly our age caught a single fish that weighed more than our entire annual catch from the Creek.

That was enough for us; and what remained of that summer was spent begging our parents to drive us out to our closest commercial carp lake.

I have hardly ever felt as ill-prepared as the day we

eventually arrived on the banks at Wood Lakes in Stow-bridge. This wasn't fishing as we knew it: it was war. Row upon row of stiff, carbon-fibre rods sat on tripods backed onto hi-tech bite alarms, like a battery of anti-aircraft missiles, and behind each rig sat a grizzled-looking angler dressed head to toe in camouflage gear. Even the baits were unrecognizable: brightly coloured balls called boilies that looked more like sweets than an edible fish attractant, but, my God, these set-ups were effective. Every so often a bite alarm would scream off and one of the men would lift nonchalantly into the sort of fish that would have had us talking for months.

We stood in silence and watched the carnage. It was all we could do. Our rods, cobbled-together collection of tackle and Mum-made foil-wrapped sandwiches were pathetic in comparison.

When we eventually did attempt to fish we hid away in the far corner of the lake, and took to plundering our way through the shoal of tiny perch that lived there. It had to be tiny perch, didn't it? Despite all the fish we had caught together in months past we were now thrown to the minnows of our adolescence. That one morning in the company of the kings of carp had proven we were still just little boys after all, and I wasn't actually the king of anything. Things just got worse from that point. I would be even more aware of my shortcomings the following summer, thanks to cricket at my new school, but of even greater concern that year was the discovery that I was no longer surrounded by my friends. In big boys' school I was just another fluff-faced squeaky-voiced competitor lining up in a bizarre, hormone-driven race without rules or a discernible finishing line. Quite quickly, catching a big carp became the embodiment of my teenage frustrations. It was my fantasy fish, the one creature capable of bridging the gap between my short-comings as an angler and my teenage aspirations, and meant so much more than just ticking off another species in the Wilson *Encyclopedia*. For me, it *was* puberty.

If only I knew then what I know now I might not have been so eager to commit myself fully to commercial carp fishing at such a young age.

My friends and I were very late to the party. It was the early 1990s by the time we graced the banks of Wood Lakes, by which point the nature of commercial carp fishing had been refined to such an extent that it felt like the whole fishscape might well have spilled off the back of the same truck.

Identikit lakes, fish and fishermen spread out across the land, reducing the sport to catching as big, or as much, with as little effort as humanly possible. Well-maintained fishing platforms replaced wild holes in the reeds, flattened roads led direct to well-manicured banks, and, in many places, fishing swims were dragged entirely clean of debris, detritus or any other snags that could result in a lost carp, and a spoiled day.

For the most part, any native wildlife that could be seen to have any detrimental impact on carp growth in the carp pond was actively discouraged or ruthlessly controlled. At the fisheries that could afford them otter-proof fences were erected, cormorants – 'the black death' – were managed, or just shot, and so-called 'nuis-ance' fish species – bream, roach, rudd and tench – were netted en masse and removed altogether. The key to success is to ensure the customer's hook baits always have the very best chance of working their way to the lips of a specimen carp, and specimen carp only.

Chris Yates, an angling legend and staunch tradition-alist, who famously broke the British carp record in 1980 on an antique rod and single grain of corn, wrote a scathing attack on the direction of the sport in his bril-liant 1997 book *The Secret Carp*: 'this standardization has gone beyond a joke. Not only do the majority of carp anglers have to fish with at least three identical rods and reels, they must also have the complete product range of whoever happens to be the most fashionable tackle and bait manufacturers of the day. And of course they also require waters that can accommodate this multi-rodded, heavily equipped regimental approach. So the lakes have become standardized as well. Ultimately even the fish have become standardized with all specimens entered onto graphs which show growth ratios, condition fac-tors, identification marks, colour variations, dietary habits, intelligence ratings, dress sense, musical appre-ciation and knowledge of world history.'

He's being disingenuous of course, but only slightly. Carp fishing today has arguably gone even further down the standardization road. On one side are the big fish venues with lightly stocked, but named and well-known, carp giants that might grace the bank several times in a season, and on the other are fish-filled carp factories that provide constant rod-bending action all year round.

Thirty years ago a fishing catch totalling 100lb or more would have been big news, but this season a six-hour match was won by an angler who banked an astonishing 1,500lb of carp. His haul amounted to 350 fish at a catch rate of one carp a minute. With the top three competitors also catching in excess of 1,000lb of fish each as well, it amounted to over 1,900 carp out of that one lake in a single August afternoon.

Given the Environment Agency recommends that natural fisheries can only hold 200 pounds of fish per acre to remain healthy, it is clear something is very definitely, very seriously, wrong. No fisherman is that good. Fishing in this way places fish, and fish welfare, as firmly secondary to the demands of the angler. In the worst-case scenario, the fish in these oxygen-depleted and unnatural environments must eat the food we offer them just to survive. It's little more than *Battle Royale* or *The Hunger Games* of carp, fishing reduced to a game of numbers based wholly on a single species.

It sounds awful, it really does, but for the past twenty years I've absolutely lapped it up. This is, in part, because not all commercial fisheries are quite that bad, but also because they can be an enormous amount of fun. I get the attraction, I really do. When you haven't got much spare time to indulge in a hobby that has a tendency to be a slow burn on the best of days, sometimes you just want to catch, but this overpowering magnetism of the commercial lake has fundamentally altered fishing as we know it, and not for the better: for the majority of anglers today, there is simply no longer any alternative to the commercial.

I had learnt from the Canal & River Trust that many of our once great waterways have fallen into a state of neglect purely through a total lack of angling interest, but I also recalled John Ellis's comment that all the youth seek these days are thrills from bigger and bigger carp; and this, I discovered, doesn't necessarily keep them in our sport for life.

This season's rod licence sales show there is a huge lack of young people coming to fishing; worse yet, junior licences are down a massive 50 per cent in just the last five years. The only growing branch of the sport today is among pensioners, the sorts of people who had grown up around massive canal matches and the understated pleasures to be had from dangling a worm in wild rivers and streams.

In building up to the carp lakes through the small perch, roach and pike of my local river, I had already received a gradual apprenticeship in the essential techniques I needed, but I also formed a critically important, and deeply intense, connection to my natural environment. It just isn't the same if you jump straight into the sport and catch a big lump from a stocked pit at the very first time of asking. There's no question that carp fishing is extremely exciting, but the buzz wears thin if that's all you ever experience and catching something is guaranteed. It's hard to imagine many young people sticking with fishing once that box has been ticked multiple times, and I can't see them reverting to the subtle pleasures to be had from plundering small fry from a river either, especially once they've been hooked on the power of the carp.

You can't blame the owners of the commercial fisheries. It's just business after all, and many have since taken serious steps to set up in a manner that is better for the carp, but these waters shouldn't be to the exclusion of all other fishing styles and species. It is down to us, as a fishing community, to take responsibility for protecting the integrity of our sport by choosing to be more diverse with our angling. After all, shouldn't fishing represent the exception, the foil, the buffer, to a modern world already filled with uniformity, instant gratification, clickbait buzzes and shrinking attention spans? Angling, by its very nature, is a random, often chaotic, collection of environments, species, methods and possibilities that afford the fisherman the opportunity to get utterly lost for a lifetime or more. You can't always win, but that doesn't mean you necessarily lose.

'Whatever next? Rods that reel the fish in for you, or devices that cast your bait into the perfect spot?' I didn't want to tell Grandad about the electronic bait boat I'd seen during my latest trip to Wood Lakes – it quite literally did cast that man's bait into the perfect spot. 'It's taking the skill out of fishing,' he droned on and on.

By the end of the summer after that fateful first year at secondary school my fishing friends from the village had drifted away. We had caught a handful of small carp between us, and had swapped our river tackle and maggots for our own series of identical rods and bags of boilies, but the polarizing demands of our new schools in different towns had come between us in the end. We were all on different paths now, and I missed them a great deal.

The biggest new challenge on my horizon was found within the new commercial carp fishery that had just opened, ironically, at the end of Grandad's garden. I knew beyond doubt that I needed those carp more than ever now. Besides, it seemed more than just mere coincidence that big carp were available a stone's throw from Grandad's lobelias. This was my chance to fill the void left by friends and sporting failures, and it felt like it was being handed to me on a plate. I told Grandad we had to go. He just laughed. So I went on my own.

It took a couple of weeks down there before it happened. I was fishing a bunch of maggots tight to the back of a purpose-built island feature when my rod was, quite literally, ripped clean off its rests and into the lake.

I picked it up by its disappearing butt and began a fight like no other. The reel screamed and the rod hooped to breaking point as it tried in vain to cushion a thunderous opening run. It was far and away the biggest fish I had ever been connected to at the time, a fish I had long dreamt of and a fight I had spent long hours practising for and considering. But now it was all happening I felt a sense of near-paralysing fear, both at what the fish might do to my tackle and what it would do to my vulnerable emotional state if it managed to escape.

Eventually the great carp wallowed, hippo-like, directly under the rod tip. It was as if I was watching Wilson on a video of my childhood, laughing along and reaching for the net, but it wasn't him, it was me. I leant forward, waist-high in the lake with water seeping down deep into the fibres of my Umbro tracksuit bottoms, and folded the fish deep into my memory for all time.

I had caught a mirror carp, so named after the set of shining reflective scales that adorn its flanks. It tipped my scales at a hefty 12lb, not massive by carp standards, but the restorative properties that fish had for my self-belief were worth a thousand centuries in cricket or a winning goal in the ninety-third minute. If I could emulate my fishing hero, then what else couldn't I achieve? I was euphoric that night and, in a rush of blood to the head, asked Mum, our household's cricketing impresario, if I could join the village cricket club.

From now on I would seek only bigger and bigger challenges, and I would take them head-on. The capture of the mirror carp had bolstered my sense of self-belief to such an extent that I could almost imagine its immaculate scales were to be worn as plates in my own suit of armour. No one was going to make me feel scared or hopeless ever again; and I was going to get better at sport, even if it did kill me.

In spring, I returned from a long period of filming in the jungles of New Guinea to find blissful sunshine bathing the nation. Finally, the horror rains of the endless winter had passed and the new season had brought some superb fishing weather.

I had wanted to catch crucians from the outset of this challenge. Mostly because I thought they were among the most beautiful fish swimming in our waters – I still do – but I also hoped it would be a really good way of exploring the unsung traditional still waters of the nation. The sorts of places you might see in the paintings of the English Romantics, very Constable-esque, I imagined, but I also felt, after the drubbing at the hands of both the pike and the perch, that this was a fish I actually had a fairly good chance with. I had caught a fair few crucians while out carp fishing, including one real beauty almost 3lb in weight, so surely with just a few tweaks to my tactics, and perhaps a bit of research, a whopper was well within my reach?

I, along with many others, believed that the crucian was native to Britain. Its pocket-sized and dignified appearance was surely more in keeping with these fair isles than the brutish king carp? However, I soon discovered that was not the case at all. The most recent DNA analysis of a sample in Norfolk can only place the crucian here in the medieval period, around the same time as all the other carp species. I forgave myself for my mistake – the analysis was only a couple of years old and was hardly official. Even Alwyne Wheeler, fish expert and former curator of the Natural History Museum's fish department, had believed they were native, stating as much in his paper published in the year 2000, but there was still no way of getting round the cold, hard, present-day facts: this fish was introduced.

Its being so much smaller than the king carp has led to suggestions that the crucian might have been brought here from the east as something of an ornamental species, a splash of colour in the noble's pond, but it is hard to find precise references to support the supposition. What we do know is that carp as a whole were a much sought-after food item in the Middle Ages: perhaps a multitude of carp species were actually ordered to create something of a smorgasbord for those with a piscatorial palate? Carp was no food for the peasantry though – maintained by monks and consumed by monarchs, carp were both luxury food items and status enhancers, favoured, in particular, by the House of Tudor. Who knows? Perhaps the rotund King Henry VIII was chewing down on his umpteenth crucian while considering executing another wife? He certainly had a partiality for the carp species, and practically every other freshwater fish in Britain. Susanne Groom, in her book *At the King's Table: Royal Dining through the Ages*, describes a magnificent starter course served to Henry

VIII that naturally included carp, but also herring, cod, lampreys, pike, salmon, whiting, haddock, plaice, bream, porpoise, seal, trout, crabs, lobsters, custard, tart, fritters and fruit, and that doesn't even touch on the man's penchant for whale meat, black pudding and swans. It was curious, I thought, how all the other fish species to grace the tables and plates of the palace were so well distinguished and explicitly referenced, yet when it came to the carp, everything from goldfish, to commons, to crucians, fell under the same generic 'carp' banner. I glossed over this detail at the time, but it was actually a sign of things to come.

I thumbed through the Wilson *Encyclopedia* to the crucian section. I noted his description of the unusual 'upturned mouth (without barbels)' and tendency to 'shoal according to their size'; but it wasn't until I came to cast my eye on the listed British record size that I stopped in my tracks. Something wasn't right.

5lb 10.5oz.

There was no way that could possibly be accurate. I knew for a fact that there was no verified crucian catch in Britain in excess of 5lb as, after I caught my three-pounder, I had checked the record books and discovered that the record back then was only around 4.5lb, but I just couldn't imagine Wilson making such an elementary mistake either. I was going to need some help.

Peter Rolfe runs a wonderful website dedicated wholly to the species (http://www.crucians.org) and after a friendly exchange of emails I tapped the digits of his number into the receiver and a gravelly, almost Shake-spearean voice soon answered the phone.

'The sooner we drop "carp" from "crucian carp" the better,' he growled.

Peter Rolfe has been dedicated to the preservation of the crucian for the past forty years. He is a bona fide hero for the species (even receiving the Fred J. Taylor Award for Environmental Stewardship in acknowledge-ment of his work), but I doubt he'd ever wear such a title.

'People think the fish is related to the king carp, when they hear that "carp" moniker, when of course it isn't. It's related to the goldfish.' I scribbled furiously as he spoke. It was all news to me. 'The bigger carp species out-compete crucians for territory and food, so that's bad for one, but also they interbreed with them with tre-mendous ease, as does the very similar brown goldfish. As commercial fisheries and the stocking of king carp became popular everywhere, well, the humble crucian didn't really stand much of a chance.'

In my twelve-year-old haste to pivot on the scaly backs of king carp and hop into the world of 'real' men, I didn't once stop to consider what the consequences of such a wholesale stocking programme might be. By the end of the 1990s it had become abundantly clear that the crucian was actually in very real trouble indeed. 'It hadn't seemed so bad at first, I suppose it was just that they had become less popular,' continued Peter, 'but once we realized just how many fish that we thought were crucians were in fact cross-breeds with goldfish or common carp, well, we realized the situation was somewhat dire.'

Peter was putting it delicately. If the crucian wasn't marching to the brink of extinction in this country, it was certainly gearing up for the walk. It was a paradox of sorts, our obsession with the king carp speeding the decline of a different species of carp, but it was pretty easy to see why things had gone so wrong for the crucian: it was small enough to be ignored. Little wonder it preferred the hidden season: as a fish of Britain it was once dangerously close to vanishing altogether.

The Wilson *Encyclopedia* puts a crucian mega-specimen at over 3lb: that is chump change for the king carp, really, a very average-sized fish; and with an angling population hooked on the bigger-is-better mantra the crucian was almost predestined for trouble. The odds were stacked further against the fish as their traditional habitat – small, rural pools – began to disappear nationwide through drought, pollution and shifting agricultural practices. The crucians might have stood something of a chance in an environment where a disappearing waterway would at least make local news – in small pools in our parks or urban ponds, for instance – but unfortunately the well-intentioned communities here have a tendency to unwittingly liberate their pet goldfish directly into the crucian gene pool. With that, it seemed, to Peter and his friends at least, the crucians' fate was sealed.

Then came a quite unexpected turn in their fortunes.

In 1997 the British Record Fish Committee hit the 'reset' button on the whole crucian record list. Following the cross-breeding revelations it was felt the record as it stood was essentially redundant: no one could be sure if the leading fish were pure crucians or just cross-breed hybrids with goldfish and common carp. Clear rules were set out to help the layperson identify the fish – between thirty-two and thirty-four scales along the lateral line, a lack of barbels around the mouth, a large convex dorsal fin – and a new fishing challenge was laid down to an army of anglers apparently itching for something new.

One year later, the capture of a truly enormous 4lb 2oz pure crucian lit up the angling press, and the wider fishing public, surprisingly, switched on to this diminutive fish wholesale. Perhaps the king-carp-shaped blinkers were gradually being lifted as the new millennium approached, but, either way, as the tragic plight of the fish made the national press, the call to do much more to save the crucian reached an unprecedented level.

'Things were quite suddenly much more optimistic for the crucian.' Peter warmed at the thought. 'The word has since spread and many more people are interested in fishing for them these days. Really, I'm chuffed it's all happening.'

The Wilson *Encyclopedia* had hit the shelves, and my Grandad's own Henry VIII-esque stomach, in 1995. Wilson, like the rest of us, simply didn't realize these 'carp' were all separate species with a truly extraordinary ability to cross-breed.

'There is a lot of misinformation out there about the fish still. Ponds and fisheries claiming to hold the crucian when really they don't, and also fish breeders who think they are selling pure crucians when in fact they are goldfish or common-carp hybrids. You can see online, people still think they are catching near-record crucians when, in fact, they are all just cross-breeds. The problem is, as soon as you've unwittingly stocked these hybridized fish you stand no chance of maintaining a healthy pure-crucian population.'

I put down the receiver and immediately ordered a copy of Peter's superb book *Crock of Gold*, which is, to date, the only book dedicated solely to the crucian carp, but I had an awful feeling. If the entire nation, and many of our top anglers, had been so easily duped with cross-bred fish, then what was to say every crucian I'd ever caught was not an imposter too?

Days later, with Peter's book spread across my thighs, my fingers hovered nervously over several digital folders filled with photos of fish. Gradually, I began clicking my way through my catches past.

The princely brace from a recent visit to a farm pond were clearly just brown goldfish; they looked like crucians but the scale count was way over. I went back further. The surprise two-pounder from a Newport commercial in the depths of winter. Urgh. It was glaringly obvious now: the dorsal was the wrong shape and the – almost grossly – disproportionate fantail marked it out clearly as another goldfish cross. This was looking bad. Armed with the truth in Peter's book I was starting to feel pretty foolish. I clicked through to the folder containing my personal-best crucian, the 3lb fish, a real beauty: a Wilson mega-specimen none the less. Staring proudly down the lens in the twilight, I'm holding what I knew now could only be a clear crucian–common-carp cross. I even sent the image to Peter Rolfe to be sure. His capitalization of the word 'not' before the words 'a crucian' was the final thumping nail in my specimen-crucian-carp coffin.

I continued, searching, almost desperately, for something to cling to, but as fish after fish failed to make the grade it slowly became clear that in all my years of carp fishing there was probably only one occasion when I caught a pure crucian. I was eleven years old, fishing a holiday pond somewhere in the rolling farmland of the south-west because I had been told by the owner that it held a mirror carp. The surprise crucian had taken a fancy to the piece of sunken bread flake I had freelined unwittingly into its path, but, back then, I couldn't have been more underwhelmed.

I can remember it now, this little golden fish in my palm, all friendly curves and smoothened fins, that I decided couldn't possibly be a proper carp. It was small and somehow fraudulent, more suited to a goldfish bowl than a fishing pond. Mutton dressed as mutton. I plopped it back in and re-cast, harder and further, hoping pure brute power would bring me closer to my own Shangri-La: my first king carp, just like the ones in all the magazines.

I hadn't even bothered to photograph that fish, and here I was, over twenty years later, pleading the details of that distant memory to materialize into a barbel-less fish, with a convex dorsal fin, and thirty-two to thirty-four scales along its lateral line. It probably only weighed around 6oz, but that crucian, I realized now, was my new personal best.

In that moment my whole record-breaking challenge had been turned right on its head. It was like someone had fired a rocket into my front room. I slapped the laptop closed, more astonished than disappointed. This was absolutely extraordinary. All this time. All those carp. Not one of them actually a crucian. I laughed out loud and sent Lottie, my cat, charging out of the catflap in fright.

This was far bigger than me and some record chase. Not for one moment did I actually ever think I would end up chasing a species with the pure objective of simply catching one for potentially the very first time as an adult, let alone a fish that had survived such an epic threat to its very existence.

I fell in love with the thought.

As I type, the crucian record at 4lb 10oz is held jointly by two anglers: Stephen Frapwell and Michael James, who caught the same fish in early May 2015 from the crucian mecca, Johnson's Lake in Surrey. I had been very kindly invited by Peter to fish the crucian ponds he had developed with his own hands, but they observed the close season until 16 June. I couldn't wait till then. It wasn't simply just aesthetically pleasing to be bankside at this time of year: all my research pointed to the fact that the bigger crucians came out then too. They were fit to burst with spawn by early June, preferring to deposit their loads before the king carp, and, according to Peter, just after the roach, perch and rudd. This year June had arrived with unseasonably high temperatures, and the king carp in my local lakes were already beginning to splash the shallows and deposit their loads; if I was going to smash my personal best I needed to act right now.

Utilizing the fisheries database on Peter's crucian website I narrowed down the potential waters to those that had either recently broken records or had only just been pipped at the post, then I hit the phones. Back in May 2003, Little Moulsham Pit near Yateley had given up a 4lb 9oz fish to Martin Bowler. It was tricky to get a ticket and there were few details online. A call to the Yateley angling centre revealed it was now a syndicate carp lake owned by a man named Alan Cooper, who ran a groundbait company. Eventually I got through to Alan, but the news was bad. 'They've all been eaten by cormorants, mate,' came his flat reply, 'it's too expensive to restock them and it'll take twenty years before a crucian ever gets to that size again. That's twenty years of running the gauntlet with the cormorants and even at record size they can still be eaten. Big carp are a much better bet for me, everyone is a carp fisherman these days. I'm afraid it's where the sensible money is.' Over in Pembrokeshire, I was very excited to learn that Holgan's Farm claimed to house potential record-breaking crucians, in a bespoke crucian lake, but a phone call there brought another rebuff. They had opted to stock brown goldfish and the resultant 'crucians' today were almost certainly hybrids. Realistically that only left me with two other places: one a real wild card, the Leather Lake, on the Verulam Angling Club ticket, which had produced a – at the time – record-equalling fish of 4lb 9oz five years previously; and the other the home of the current record, Johnson's Lake, which is looked after by Godalming Angling Society.

I was in a very tight spot. Membership to both those clubs would set me back over £200. Perhaps if I lived closer it might be worth considering at a real stretch, but just for a day's fishing out of my home in South Wales it was, quite simply, an insane amount to spend. I'd learnt my lesson the hard way that winter on Chew and my funds just weren't going to stretch.

I emailed both clubs and explained my case. A week later the wonderful people at Verulam got in touch to grant me permission to fish the Leather Lake, asking only that I let the bailiff know when I intended to fish, but sadly I didn't hear anything back from Godalming. Life at the top of the crucian tree is probably tough – you can't be granting permission to every Tom, Dick and Harry with a hard-luck story. There was some very good news though. Johnson's Lake was actually closed till 16 June anyway, to give the fish a deserved break, but right next door was Harris Lake, which was available to the public on a day ticket and stocked with the same group of crucians as Johnson's (which I later discovered, to my immense surprise, were all originally taken from the monsters past of Little Moulsham, an afterlife of sorts for this exceptionally strong strain of fish). A call to the on-site tackle shop revealed the lake had emerged, perhaps unsurprisingly, as the odds-on favourite to best the fish in Johnson's, and with favourable conditions and a larger stamp of crucians coming out earlier in the week I needed to get down there sharpish. I cancelled all my work plans for the next day and set the alarm for 2 a.m.

I had a chance.

Just before 5 a.m. the sun was rising on the most beautiful lake I have ever had the fortune to visit. Found the other side of a glistening trout stream seemingly fit to burst with Canada geese and their young, the Leather Lake unfolded from a thicket like something out of a dream.

It looked almost like the water had been poured into a divot in a fantasy forest, such was the density of the trees and greenery pressing into the water and spilling out of the sides of the small, shrub-tufted islands. It felt to me that if you simply were to pull the plug and drain the lake water, the rest of that forest would still be there underneath, just waiting to heave up from the lakebed.

The dawn added to the whimsy. Reflected in the gin-clear water it cast something of a week-old-bruise purplish haze across the place, and one inviting-looking corner was so choked with lily-pads that it wouldn't have felt out of place in a Beatrix Potter book. Indeed, I could very well imagine the hapless frog, Jeremy Fisher, punting his way through the whole scene in search of his next minnow.

But it was the noise of the birdlife that set this place apart from anything else I'd ever experienced. There was a riotous, cacophonous clamour coming from all sides of this avian amphitheatre. I don't think it was simply that I was up at a ridiculous hour – I have been fishing at silly-o'clock many times in the past, but I have never ever heard birdsong quite like this in Britain. For at least an hour it was absolutely astonishing and caused the whole lake to crackle with the sort of electricity usually reserved for major sporting events. This was a gathering of feathered souls participating in a massive collective experience, and I felt utterly privileged to witness it. This was their performance though – I was merely an uninvited audience member, and shuffled round the junglified banks with my head down in deferential silence.

I settled myself into a spot hemmed in by a weeping willow and a semi-submerged tree branch. I had seen a few bubbles, not a mass of action by any means, but certainly better than nothing. Plumbing the depth revealed it was significantly deep at the margins, a healthy five foot or so, but also that the entire swim was chock full of weed. A long tendril of green blanket snared on my line as I retrieved, like the clasping arm of a mighty kraken or sea serpent. On inspection, the tendril was erupting with tiny bloodworm that leapt from the fresh air and back into their lake water home as I tried to free it. It was a wonderful sign of the health of the place, but not so good for my chances of catching. These were naturally fed fish that didn't need the carpet of synthetic bait I was proffering. Here the ethos seems to be to stock light and let nature do the rest. There was no question it had worked, as, alongside the record crucian, the lake had once housed a legendary leather carp, a variant on the mirror that has hardly any scales, which had risen to be among the largest leathers in the UK.

I put down a couple of doormat-sized patches of freebies to try and tempt the crucians in for breakfast – a few halibut pellets, some sweetcorn, maggot and casters – and float-fished over the top with the lightest kit I dared. Crucians are renowned for being delicate feeders, taking small baits and giving only the slightest indications of their presence – a murmur on the float and tiny plumes of bubbles, so I had heard – but my presumptive experiences with the crucian had taken such a battering recently I had elected to start from the standpoint that I effectively knew nothing.

Great spirals of buzzers and nymphs drifted like

wood smoke across the lake. As the night gave over its hold and allowed day to break, a regal-looking pair of great-crested grebes hunted in the depths beyond my float. Their wonderful russet-coloured plumage fanned water droplets from the upper reaches of their slender white necks every time they emerged from the drink, resembling snowflakes cascading from a furry bordering around the hood of a winter jacket. Clearly, they were having significantly more success with the fish than me.

The birdcalls faded as the dog walkers arrived. All too soon I could hear the M25 droning in the background and all the magic that had briefly held the lake in suspense had gone. It was midnight and Cinderella was back to being a maid with a pumpkin and I was back in the world of man. Nature was supposed to take its rightful place on the seats at the back of the theatre.

It was weird. Like the compression of our natural and wild spaces in this phenomenally over-cultivated and over-populated island had caused the most intensely compacted expression of the resident wildlife in the space of that single hour. I began to pack up my gear.

When I was a child, my favourite joke was:

'Knock-knock.'

'Who's there?'

'Cook.'

'Cook who?'

'That's the first one I've heard this year.'

If I'm blessed with children, the amount of explanation required to describe why that joke is funny will be as tragic as it is pointless. I remember reading recently that one in five birds in Britain are now on the Royal Society for the Protection of Birds Red List. Just in my lifetime the majority of those have had their natural habitat reduced by half.

By mid-day I had successfully negotiated my way around the massive single-storey, three-lane car park that is the M25 at rush hour, and arrived at a very different place entirely.

Images of crucians adorned the sign to the Marsh Farm complex that housed the Harris Lake, as if I were in any doubt that in the small world of crucian fishing this place was the celebrity venue.

At first glance, it felt every inch the comfortable commercial: cut grass, a huge on-site tackle shop, neat gravel paths, and clean toilet blocks with hot water and hand towels, but down at water level there was more than a nod to wildlife. Thick flag iris and reeds smothered the banks between fishing pegs, lending the place an air of seclusion once you had settled into your spot lakeside. Numerous mallards cruised the water alongside diving tufted ducks, and, most wonderfully of all, a breeding pair of Arctic terns had taken up residence for the summer. With their long, brilliant-white starburst tail feathers, black caps and bright-red bills, they danced like sprites over the water all day long, remarkably fresh from their recent migration from the Arctic.

All the other anglers had stationed themselves in the deeper water that ran along the opposite bank next to a trainline. The tackle shop had advised that these were very much the hot swims, but, as I'd turned up late, I was going to have to look elsewhere.

I wandered around the lake perimeter before eventually settling into an overgrown corner fed by a stiff breeze. I was feeling confident despite the slim pickings. I quite liked the look of my corner. In truth, I probably would have picked it regardless – it put more space between me and the other anglers on the complex, which I always liked – and within seconds of placing my bag a large fish rolled right at my feet. If that wasn't a good omen, then I didn't know what was.

I had some fairly hi-tech gear with me – flavoured fish pellets and syrupy liquid attractants – but I decided to leave them all in the bag. Instead I mixed up a bucket of blended breadcrumbs, which I balled into the deeper water about three rod lengths out, and fixed up a simple float rod with half a worm as hook bait. This was fishing just as Grandad had taught me: traditional and simple.

I had been forewarned that though the king carp might rock up to your bait and sucker-punch you like a heavyweight champion, the crucian tends to dance around it like a featherweight, throwing the occasional jab, that might just quiver your line, without actually taking the hook. That means you need to be prepared to spend time sat on your hands with your heart in your mouth: waiting for a positive indication that something has happened down there.

Half an hour in, my float tip wobbled. It was so gentle, like a divination rod in the presence of a spirit. The crucians had arrived and were transmitting their presence. Gently, oh so gently. The float tip lifted.

The fight of the crucian isn't anything like the smash-and-grab of the king carp; nor is it jagged like the perch or a sustained pressure like a tench. In the words of the Supremes: it's a game of give and take; a tug of war where your opponent gets randomly weaker and stronger, leaving the hook free to be pulled out at any time.

Gradually I stole line from the fish till I had it in the net.

It was breathtaking. I wrapped my hand around its golden form. The crucian was exactly 2lb, a phenomenal start, and everything about it – scale counts, fin shape, mouth – matched up precisely, but I just couldn't believe the size. It was well above the average for this fish. I had crushed my personal best with my first fish. I looked up to see an even larger crucian roll on the surface above my groundbait. The plan, unbelievably, was working.

I slipped the 2lb fish right back and re-cast feverishly. This place was extraordinary; by rights these are fish that should be the sole preserve of the dedicated specimen fishermen, yet here I was fluking one out after an absence of over twenty years. I felt as cheeky as if I'd borrowed the rod of a proper crucian carper, caught his fish, and then nicked his wallet.

Almost immediately I hooked and landed a second fish. Slightly smaller this time at 1lb 8oz. These crucians are deep-bodied, high-backed fish. They had a totally different feel to the so-called crucians I had caught before. Of course, that is understandable, given what I now know, but holding that first brace of fish, with their wonderfully curved underbellies that so elegantly filled the palm of my hand, it felt as rarefied an experience as cradling a newborn baby. In fact, the Harris crucians were so utterly distinct in feel (and, I realize now, I did need to 'feel' the fish, as photographs simply don't cut it) that it is hard to believe I could ever have mistaken those hybrids of my past for the real thing. The crucian is one of those very few fish that doesn't seem to lose its sheen after capture. If anything, the shape and golden hue are so satisfying, you could fool yourself into thinking the crucian was crafted purely to be held in the human hand.

Other anglers approached. No one else on the lake was catching anything. My late coming had put me right on the fish. Another huge crucian flopped over my carpet of breadcrumbs. 'They are really taking the piss,' laughed an elderly angler, albeit through gritted teeth.

As the afternoon wore on into evening I felt I was going crazy. Not only was my swim fizzing like a jacuzzi, but also massive crucians just kept rolling, one after the other, right next to my float. If that wasn't enough, one specific fish kept swimming forward, projecting its body clean out of the water, and tail walking like a dolphin in repeated nail-straight assaults on my float. To be perfectly honest, it made me feel so self-conscious I started to look over my shoulder to check no one could see what was going on. (Later I read a chapter in Peter's book by a very experienced crucian angler called Peter Wheat. He too had witnessed the performance, and attributes it to one individual fish, commenting: 'I have never known another crucian to activate itself in this way.' I was just glad I hadn't completely lost my marbles.)

My float bobbed and weaved like a crochet needle. The bites were near imperceptible and almost impossible to hit. I was missing twenty indications for every hook-up, and lost several crucians to hook pulls in the fight. It was frustrating, and not purely down to having had just three hours' sleep the previous night. These fish were living up to their reputation of being extremely cute feeders. I took a risk and upscaled the size of my hook and immediately snared another brace of fish, breaking my personal best for the second time that day.

As the evening came on, the intense exhaustion I was feeling, combined with the insane levels of concentration it took to just watch a flickering float in windy conditions, started to puddle my mind. Everything was exacerbated by the total lack of activity elsewhere on the lake, and the constant heady presence of those giant acrobatic crucians, every one a fish of a lifetime, crammed en masse into my corner. It began to have me wondering whether really I was just asleep at my seat and dreaming it all: giant golden hubcaps bouncing around the lake like fluffy sheep over a gate. I would have started counting the fish if I hadn't been sure I'd end up falling in, but, then, was it possible to fall asleep while still in a dream? A mallard croaked to the right of me. I considered striking up a conversation, but then my float started to tremble.

Grandad, truly, would have loved this place. Perhaps I had honoured him in some small way by fishing the lake in the same style I knew he would have adopted had he been here in my stead, but I also knew that, in spite of all the advances in fishing techniques, tackle and bait, I had caught today because I had simply been in the right place at the right time. Sometimes that is all it takes.

The big one dropped at 2lb 5oz. It was like holding on to the moon.

After a not inconsiderable amount of sleep the next day, I rationalized my crucian was no record shaker. It wasn't even a Wilson mega-specimen and, in reality, the British record is exactly double the size of the fish I caught. All sobering food for thought, but, quite honestly, I didn't care. It was still a very good fish and one to be proud of. Besides, how often do you break your personal best three times in a day?

At last light the biggest crucian of the lot had rolled over my float. It was as deep as a breezeblock, dark and ancient-looking, like it had been cut out of a piece of pure teak. It looked to be well in excess of 4lb, perhaps even a five-pounder at a push, but I couldn't be sure. Moments later, the great fish rolled again, this time right next to a particularly nervous-looking tufted duck. It really was huge. I peered on from behind the reeds with an intense longing, a neurotic dog trapped behind a window as a cat plays freely in the front garden. Some fish are just not meant to be caught.

Mum took me to almost every match and training session throughout the first summer of carp. In the company of men I grew up fast and their patience allowed me to learn the game properly and in my own time. By the end of the next summer I had banked numerous double-figure carp and had developed a competitive, aggressive streak that saw me take over as captain of the school cricket team the year after my humiliation.

I hated losing, but I hated cowardice in myself even more, and would absolutely insist I faced the first ball of our innings when the opposition bowlers were at their freshest and the ball was at its hardest.

Grandad came to my match in Upwell one summer's evening. I was annoyed because, being only thirteen years old and playing in a team filled with men, I had been put down at the end of the batting order.

When it was my time to bat, I remember the bowler being told to come off a shorter run and bowl slower. 'Not a chance,' he spat, 'if he wants to play in a men's league he'd better be ready to take it like a man.' Good, I thought. I took my guard, and chinned his first delivery straight back over his head for four runs.

'You little twat.' The bowler strode right into the middle of the wicket with his hands on his hips. I stepped forward too and stared right back at him. Over his shoulder, back on the boundary, I could see Grandad stood up, and the rest of my team going ballistic. I knew that the next ball was going to be short and aimed at my throat, so when it came I made sure I was well on my back foot and hooked him right into the cow field down at deep fine leg.

The only time I have ever seen steam come out of a man's ears is in cartoons and that evening. The next ball was full, straight and right on middle stump. I should have defended it but the adrenaline was coursing through my veins and I knew I was better than him, so I swung at it with everything I had.

The ball hit the meat of my bat and just kept going and going. It bounced only once before it hit the pavilion filled with my teammates, who were, it is fair to say, absolutely losing the plot. I was out caught on the boundary in the very next over, but they all gave me a standing ovation as I walked off.

'They were banging on the windows, son,' said Grandad, his face still bright red with pride. It was an hour later and we were all crammed into the Red Lion pub down the road. The team were spread out across the bar, hammering the fruities and swearing, but Grandad and I were sat alone and quiet at a corner table.

Grandad slid a frothing pint of beer my way. He didn't need to know that it was the capture of that big carp, and not the picture of him kicking the perfect rugby penalty, that had turned things around for me. In fact, nothing more needed to be said. In his eyes, I had made it.

'The fish in this pond all came from just seventeen crucians I purchased from a fish farm over in Essex. They sat them down on the platform at Gillingham station and called me up: "Mr Rolfe, we have your fish."'

Finally, I was putting a face to the gravelly voice of crucian authority. It was late summer by the time I had picked my way to Peter's ponds. I rolled the van through Dorset, over the chalk beds of the River Frome and Nadder, and on into the leafy borders of Wiltshire. There is something of the fairytale about this whole part of the country. The map reveals charmingly titled hamlets – Milkwell, Birdbush, Hammoon, Bugley – and by the time I made it to my eventual destination at Donhead, it felt infinitely more plausible that it would be twinned with Hobbiton of Middle Earth, than in any way conjoined to the same land mass that belches the Regent's Canal out at King's Cross. I should have been arriving on horseback with a staff, not in a van with rods, but none the less I can't tell you the precise location of these ponds. Even if Peter had sworn me to secrecy, which he hadn't, after a couple of blissful hours floating through this landscape I was wonderfully lost.

Peter runs a large tanned hand over a clear plastic box filled with floats. Here was a man who spent most of his summer days outside. Methodically, he tackled up his rod and traditional centre-pin reel; you could tell he had done it so many times before that he didn't really need to think about it any more, so we chatted about his past instead.

He had always fitted his work as an English teacher around his fishing, and had thus been able to spend his spare time visiting a vast roll call of big fish rivers across the south. 'After the big-roach fishing in the Stour turned sour I decided to look into wild-pond fishing, but really there was virtually none to choose from back then.' Peter slid his float to the appropriate depth. The country was being swept by a commercial-fishery fever by the late seventies; the sea-change had been so great that by the time I was wetting a line, the thought that there was once an alternative to the commercial lake hadn't ever really occurred to me. Peter, faced with the same issue but armed with memories of catching crucians from secluded sand pits in Essex in the 1950s, took matters into his own hands. 'I spread out an Ordnance Survey map and saw all of these wonderful blue specks. Forgotten ponds, hidden away on farmland and in remote woods, some of them really ancient too. After that it was just a case of going from farm to farm and asking for permission to stock a few fish.'

I was quite surprised. Throughout my youth I had feared farmers and the way they aggressively defended their rights to their territory. All of my friends had stories of being chased from fields by the shotgun-wielding 'geroff-my-feckin-landers', so the thought of door knocking with a request to fish seemed suicidal. Mind you, I was a BMX-wielding oik, and not a Cambridge University-educated grammar school teacher.

'How do you convince a farmer then, Peter?'

'Light pressure, Will,' he replied, his eyes twinkling. 'Most farmers are conservation-minded at heart. The idea of saving a species has a lot of appeal, and besides . . .' He paused for a moment as he fixed his hook. '. . . I always explained that there was a market for the crucian, if they multiply.'

Peter was almost ready to fish whereas I was still sat on my chair scribbling notes with my pencil. I had instantly recognized him at his door from the warm and wide smile he shared with the man on the jacket of his book, but I had been expecting a schoolmasterly presence, a fiercely intense man who might dole out fifty licks across the back of a chair for a wayward cast. In reality Peter exuded a benevolent brand of charisma, a gentle soul armed with the infinite patience you need to be a really good fisherman, and, I suspect, a thoughtful and caring teacher. With trousers tucked into socks, flat cap and long, playful white hair flowing out the back, there was more than a sense of a man refusing to slow down in his senior years. Peter was clearly exceptionally fit; we couldn't travel together in his car as he had a large, double-handed scythe and a pair of anvil loppers filling the boot, 'just in case we need to do some work on the banks later on'. It was, in fact, while he was swinging his heavy scythe into a rampant mass of brambles that he revealed he was eighty-two years old. I was gob-smacked, and felt guilty for leaning on a fence post prattling on while this octogenarian beat out the earth in front of me. Clearly crucian rearing is something of an elixir of youth, and my goodness was it worth the sweat and blood. Peter's ponds were stunning.

The waterways in the south-west bleed with a life you rarely see elsewhere in Britain, but there was a palpable intensification of nature around Peter's ponds. Tucked away in a patch of trees on a dairy farm, these twin ponds acted like a pair of lungs, heaving their influence from the water and into the trees and fields that framed their banks. Kingfishers, ducks, clusters of lilies, sedges, iris, even an otter were all drawn to the restored water, and it was occasionally hard to focus just on the fishing.

Peter tapped his float, loaded with a chunk of bread-flake for bait, a rod's length out and near a fringing bush. 'I limit it to only about fifteen anglers on these ponds, but most of the time you've pretty much got it to your-self.' He flicked a few tiny fish pellets around his float to draw the crucians in. 'Once I feel we have a surplus of crucians in these ponds, I try to sell them off for around £5 or £6 a pound. It's less than the going rate, but I just want to get the crucians out there.'

I finally got my own rod in, carefully shot down so the float was merely an ultra-sensitive pinprick, and plumbed the depth to perfection to ensure my bait just about kissed the sediment on the pond's bottom. My float immediately dipped and I turned out a tiny thumb-sized perch. I laughed. I was ten years old and back at Wood Lakes again. The next cast brought another, and then another. 'Try some of my bread, Will, it'll keep those pesky perch away.' Peter leant over to reach for a fluffy white roll and his float dipped purposefully, proving conclusively my long-held belief that certain fish will only ever bite when you are distracted.

'Oh! Huh oh!' A youthful delight creased Peter's face as his rod tip danced to the fish's tune. 'I've got one!'

A short fight delivered a perfect little crucian, like a small gold medallion. 'What a lovely little fella,' said Peter, admiring his work before underarming me the bread roll. His float dipped again before I could re-bait. 'I can't believe it!' he laughed as I reached once more for the landing net. 'I promise I put you in the better swim!'

I managed to get my own piece of bread out in the water in front of me and, incredibly, caught a perch on bread. This was something I had previously considered to be impossible, but there was little time for contemplation: Peter was bent into his third and, all too soon, his fourth crucian.

'I really don't understand.' I could sense a tinge of embarrassment in his voice. 'I usually fish your swim. I promise I gave you the more favourable area.' I slipped the net under his fifth. I really didn't mind; in fact, this moment in time meant far more to me than simply a few hours studying this crucian-whisperer.

I was far too shy to say so at the time, but I was right back with Grandad, decades earlier, stood at the Creek, devouring every movement of skilled operation, trying to learn, not simply catch. The student with the master. 'Right,' announced Peter, snapping me out of it, 'you must come here and use my rod.' I settled into his cushioned seat, desperate not to make a mistake or miss my chance, but moments later I was up netting his sixth fish, this time on my rod, in the swim I had only just that moment vacated. 'Oh, I'm so so sorry about this, Will.' Peter's voice trembled with something approaching remorse as I near shook with laughter. His metamorphosis into my grandfather was truly complete. It was destiny, of course. Just as there was never an evening, no matter how shot Grandad's eyesight or reactions became, when he didn't catch more than me, there was never a family cricket match where my dad, who really couldn't play cricket, failed to clean bowl me while I was batting. Some men are simply meant to always be your better, and it is much easier to take their lessons squarely on the chin than ever try to fight it.

The fish were all quite small and Peter was keen to place them in the other pond to improve the stock. Together we carried a white, plastic-handled bucket through a small thicket and over a stile towards the dammed end of the second pond. 'I liked the line in your book, Peter,' I began, hitching up the bucket as Peter gently waded into the shallows, 'that read: "The only unsuccessful fisherman is the one who is not enjoying what he's doing."'

'Ha! Oh yes! I think I may have been making a comment about those that obsess over the weight of their catch, the commercial carp fishers' mentality.' He began to gently hand-place each crucian into the new pond. 'Fishing is a ridiculous pastime anyway of course: "A worm at one end and a fool at the other", as the great essayist Samuel Johnson once wrote, but there has to be so much more interest to it if your enjoyment is going to last through the decades. It's being in beautiful places, like this, and probing the mystery of the depths not for what is, but what might be. If you already know what's in there the catching can simply become a bit, well, stale.' Peter's bucket was empty of fish now, so he upended the remains into the pond with a 'splosh'. '. . . But each to their own.'

That afternoon I spotted a water vole scurrying along the banksides. It was the first I'd seen in over twenty years. It took me a while to place the location of the last one, but on the drive home I nailed down the memory. I was eleven years old, fishing a farm pond near identical to Peter's, also somewhere in the rolling farmland of the south-west. It was when I had caught my very first crucian. Sometimes in fishing, the stars can align in quite curious ways.

'I'm a crucian carp madman.' It was impossible not to like the crucian scientist Dr Carl Sayer. He possessed a wonderful Norfolk twang to his accent, placing him as more combine harvester than petri dish, and spoke of

the halcyon days of his youth, rods across the handle-
bars, with a melancholic nostalgia I could instantly relate
to. If fifty-odd miles of dykes and drains hadn't separated us, I'm sure we would have been good friends
when we were tearing around Norfolk in the 1980s.

Dr Sayer and his colleagues have been busy rein-
troducing crucians and restoring ponds in remote
farmlands across Norfolk from their Norwich head-
quarters. He has kept his work largely secret, in part to
keep the landowners onside – 'in case they think we're
planning on starting a fishery' – but also because their
success in breeding the crucian means theirs are now
worth a small fortune. There are some 23,000 ponds on
Norfolk farmlands, but the vast majority of them have
grown over, dried up, or been smeared into new fields
for crops. '"Ghost ponds" is what we call them,' chirped
Carl, 'we've actually found beer cans on some of the old
sites that date from the 1960s and '70s, clearly the last
time there was anyone actually sat there fishing!' The
seeds of waterside plants can actually exist in a dormant
state for centuries, which means, even if several feet of
soil and corn crop have been layered on top of an old
pond, a bit of an uncovering job, fresh water and fresh
fish can see a 'ghost pond' brimming with wild plant and
animal life once more. Isn't nature brilliant when it's
given a chance?

'But why should we care about saving the crucian in
Britain if it was never a native species?' I asked, somewhat pointedly.

'Who is to say it isn't native, Will?' shot back Carl, bluntly. I stammered something about the DNA analysis that had placed them here somewhere in the Middle Ages. 'True, it did, but that work was based on just one tiny sample of fish.' Carl pressed. 'Since then we've found so many more ponds with crucian populations. We should be pushing for a much wider study of all these newly discovered populations. You can't tell me you can take one study, from one population, and just say: "Well, that's it, the crucian isn't native then."'

He certainly had a point. Carl went on to describe a remarkable theory that hinged on how ancient waterway management during the Roman era, which saw many ancient ponds and oxbow lakes drained to irrigate lands for agriculture, could easily have wiped out the crucian, only for them to be reintroduced at a much later date. 'But that's the problem, isn't it?' he concluded. 'You can't prove absence, can you? You can only prove presence, and it is impossible to get grants to fund these sorts of studies.'

I could see where he was coming from. All that DNA results can really confirm is that that particular sample set were introduced during the Middle Ages, but there was nothing to say that other populations from other ponds might have been here much earlier than that. Dr Sayer's theory jogged my memory of the extraordinary story of the British pool frog. Right through until the 1990s it was generally accepted that the pool frog was native only to mainland Europe (in fact, until the 1970s it was incorrectly classified as merely a subspecies of the edible frog, when in actuality it transpired that it was the edible that was a hybrid of the pool and marsh frog); then, in the Norfolk town of Thetford, a colony of pool frogs was discovered that would electrify amphibian science.

Found in a 'pingo', an ancient pool formed by the melting of subterranean swellings of ice at the end of the last Ice Age, the small colony appeared darker and browner than the classic livid greens sported by the pool frogs of France. That couldn't be, though; the accepted wisdom read that our climate was far too cold for the pool frog to establish itself here naturally. Bone analysis of the Thetford frogs was conducted and, sensationally, it was discovered that these frogs had in fact been here since before the last Ice Age, making their own way from Europe before the close of everyone's favourite fresh-water species superhighway: the Doggerland land bridge, which delivered us the pike all those centuries ago. The pool frog was hastily reclassified and, almost overnight, we gained a second native frog species to call our own.

For the crucian, though, until the 'smoking gun' of some conclusive DNA evidence can be unearthed, its plight in Britain remains precarious. 'Why should we care?' might seem a narrow-minded question, but a lot rests on the indigenous status of our wildlife. The classification of what is and what isn't a native may seem ambiguous to say the least. As Richard Kerridge states in his superb book on reptiles and amphibians, *Cold*

Blood, qualification only hinges on proving whether a species 'established itself in a country independent of any human activity, no matter how long ago the arrival occurred', but without it, it is virtually impossible to gain access to government funding and practical protective legislation for a species.

For the pool frog it all came too late. In 1999, the year before the startling results of the bone analysis were published, the last of the Thetford population died in captivity; an avoidable tragedy caused by our somewhat over-zealous ranking of wildlife based on arbitrary status and public popularity.

Whether we like to admit it or not, we inflate the importance of certain species over others all the time. The face has to fit. It has to penetrate the public consciousness and pull at the heartstrings for virtually anything to be done. Take the otter, for example. I love otters, and unlike most fishermen would dearly love to see one in the wild, but their celebrity status and cute looks have seen them garner a massively disproportionate amount of public sympathy and a hugely successful reintroduction, whereas other, less desirable, freshwater species have slid to virtual, or even actual, extinction with little or no protest whatsoever. The pool frog is one example, but what of the orache moth or the large copper butterfly? The slimy burbot fish? The Davall's sedge plant? Or my water vole, with its yellow teeth and *Wind in the Willows* fame, whose numbers have plummeted by 90 per cent in the last twenty years?

I could go on, but my point is that we quite clearly have much bigger environmental issues to worry about than simply whether a species is definitely native. As I write, one in ten of the UK's wildlife species are threatened with extinction and the numbers of our most endangered animals have crashed by two thirds since 1970. I don't mean to unduly anger those specialists who work tirelessly to curb the catastrophic damage caused by invasive species (see the grey squirrel, signal crayfish, American mink and oak processionary moth for further details), but there is absolutely no evidence to suggest that the presence of crucians affects our freshwater environment negatively in any way. According to Dr Sayer and Peter Rolfe, they cause no harm, and coexist with other species in just about the most high-quality environment you can imagine, so can we just get on with protecting them properly, please?

We can be in no doubt today that our crucian populations are absolutely vital to the survival of the wider European crucian species. Over in Europe the aggressive-feeding and exceptionally well-travelled gibel carp, an interloper from Asia, has spread its seed into virtually every major watercourse on the Continent, even making it to the remote eastern reaches of the Baltic Sea. Of course, the gibel can cross-breed with the extraordinarily licentious crucian, and, with that, the purity of the entire continental species is now seriously under threat. However, we have no gibel here and, thanks to the unheralded (as well as unfunded) dedication of Marsh

Farm, Peter Rolfe, Dr Sayer and all their friends, the British crucian has a fighting chance once more, and for that, I believe, we should all be very grateful.

The years passed. I got the knack for carp fishing and fished almost exclusively in commercials until I left school at eighteen. Largely, I fished alone. I was pushing the envelope, fishing for hours and hours in conditions that a man in his late seventies just couldn't take, but even when some of my friends showed an interest in joining me, I largely shunned them. I fully accepted I was obsessed, and that they would just hold me back from my ultimate ambition to catch bigger and, in my eyes, better carp. I would fish on through anything: terrible weather, hunger, tiredness, it just didn't matter to me; there was almost nothing I wouldn't put myself through to get in front of a fish.

Dad had ultimately been right to persuade me to stick with school that afternoon in the pub. I made friends for life there and received grades that I just wouldn't have managed anywhere else. Academically, I realized I needed to be sat on and chained to a desk to achieve, and my ability at sport had improved exponentially. I was extremely fortunate to be in a place where if you showed potential you had all the facilities you needed to improve, and, more than anything, to have loving parents who would do anything they could to nurture an interest in any of their children.

Looking back, though, I just wish the by-product of

all of it hadn't been the development of a competitive, win-at-all-costs impudence that bordered on over-confidence. I realize now it wasn't in fact the winning or the competition I had enjoyed at all, it was the feeling that I belonged somewhere, but in defining success purely through the rigid prism of personal triumph I had totally lost touch with any of the pleasures to be had just from being part of something. The same had become true of my fishing, and as I got older it was inevitable my interest began to wane. After I left school I never played a competitive game of cricket or rugby again.

Perhaps, in its own way that is what crucian fishing is all about. The fish is small and challenging in its own way, but it is the subtle pleasures to be found in the sort of environments it inhabits that bring such a unique joy to this style of fishing. I am indebted to the fish for my having found the traditional British pond before it fully faded from my consciousness. It feels like the blinkers have been lifted from my eyes, but with so many fish records to chase I'm not entirely sure what to do with the rest of my year. Am I really saying that the thought of continuing for something really big is now a pointless endeavour? Of course I'm not, but the spirit of crucian fishing can only influence me to look for more than just a big fish as I continue this quest. Like my grandad before me, I'm a fisherman for life now, and have learnt those who pursue size, and size alone, can never expect their interest in this pastime to see them all the way to the grave.

Early June came and went with no record-shaking fish. Then, utterly against the grain, the biggest crucian of the year was landed from a secret pond hidden away somewhere in leafy Shropshire in the middle of August. It weighed almost 4lb and was accompanied by another brace of fish of over 3lb. Ed Matthews, a hooded chap with a broad smile, had hand-stocked and reared the fish just seven years earlier. 'I was overwhelmed,' he gushed in the pages of the *Angling Times*, 'I stocked these crucians when they were around one inch long and cared for them for so many years, just hoping one day that they'd weigh over 3lbs . . . now it's got me wondering just how big they could go.' Perhaps the hidden season is no longer the time to target the record shakers, or perhaps it is just that the hidden season means much more. I'll leave it to you to find out.

The Fish Everyone Hates

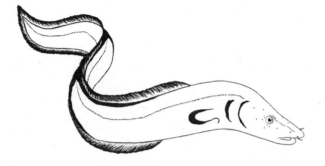

It is easy to see, in the mind's eye, a salmon
resting behind a rock, a trout sipping down an
insect between two trails of green weed, a
chub or barbel swaying in the current where
the willow branches dip. With the eel, the best
I could do was say to myself, 'I know you're
down there somewhere.'
Tom Fort, *The Book of Eels* (2002)

The world lacks love for eels.

The bed of the Creek was absolutely paved with them.
It didn't seem to matter if you tried a big bunch of lobworms or the tiniest of maggots from the tub, if you
rested any bait on the deck for any stretch of time it

wouldn't be long before the float started to give you the telltale tap-tap-tap of an eel making its enquiries.

Such a subtle touch for such a grotesquely powerful fish, but the twisting, pounding fight was not an event to be celebrated; in fact, hooking an eel was categorically, unequivocally and absolutely – a disaster.

If you managed to get it out of the water before it severed your nylon with its teeth it would reward your effort by quickly coiling itself up in a ball against your line, creating a tangle of Rubik's cube difficulty and thoroughly coating you, your tackle, your net and anything else in your proximity in a thick layer of ectoplasmic snot that would linger for days. To actually unhook and release the eel, which has long since taken your bait, hook and half a foot of your line into the depths of its tubular intestinal tract, took such an extreme level of luck and skill it was nearly always better for everyone to just snap the line and hope the hook worked its way out of the fish by itself. A thoroughly upsetting and dispiriting event that left us fishing almost exclusively in the upper layers of the river as children on the Creek.

The eel, like the perch, had a funny habit of following me around throughout my childhood. I continued to catch them in the Creek in spite of my best efforts, and even managed to catch a freshwater eel while out sea fishing off a set of rocks in West Wales. It was my first-ever fish from the sea but it was not a sea fish. I was furious, and quite ignorant of just how unusual a catch that was.

The eels were all the same size: never longer than a bootlace or in excess of 1lb in weight. Small, rapacious creatures that my friends and I didn't really even count as fish. Then, one sultry summer afternoon in the heart of the school holidays, my fishing friend Paul Woods screamed his BMX into my backyard and announced there were eels the 'size of snakes' in his neighbour's back garden, and that they were 'feeding on cat food'.

Paul had a wonderful gift for telling tall tales and attracting trouble. There was the 20lb carp he caught at Wood Lakes when none of us were around, the rope bungee jump in his back garden that nearly killed us all, and then his extraordinary pyrotechnic skills that saw a home-made rocket simultaneously blast all the glass clean out of a neighbouring greenhouse and kill every single fish in their koi carp pond. I didn't know whether to expect nothing or everything, but I jumped on my bike all the same, picking up the third of our angling triumvirate, Lee Wales, from his house on the way back over to Paul's.

We threw a handful of cat food into the Creek and watched. 'That's it, young man,' croaked Paul's elderly neighbour, 'they'll all come out now.' Lee made a highly exaggerated and very sarcastic eye roll and I had to pinch the inside of my arm to stop myself from laughing out loud, but just minutes later all three of us were stood in stupefied silence.

They were everywhere. I looked at Paul. Paul looked at Lee. Lee looked at me. Like those twenty-foot-long handkerchiefs produced from a magician's sleeve, the eels had kept going and going until the mud was simply alive with writhing bodies. It was the snakepit in *Raiders of the Lost Ark*, plenty enough to turn the stomach of lesser mortals, but we were the fishing gods and these creatures were desecrating our temple. We sprinted for the rods, fixed the biggest hook we owned on the strongest line we had, and deployed a single piece of cat food deep into the centre of the twisted masses.

A darkly marked python bee-lined for my bait, angled its neck, and swallowed. As I struck, the shoal scattered to the darkness and my serpent hauled back hard on the hook. Any thoughts of a prolonged fight were banished: I was using my sea rod with a line like steel-wire and my reel drag was bolted down so tightly it would take a spanner to loosen. In short, this fish was coming out by hook or by crook.

The beast landed on the grass and we leapt on it with all three pairs of our hands. We were never going to keep this eel, but since we had now caught and subdued it, it seemed somehow wasteful to just put it back straight away. It was magnificent. Thick and black as the ace of spades, it probably only weighed 2lb but it was double the size of any eel we had ever seen before. We needed to at least try to do something different to celebrate the catch.

For some inexplicable reason I decided to place my thumb in the eel's mouth.

I remember being momentarily surprised to learn the

eel's teeth felt a bit like sandpaper before a brand of pure, crushing pain consumed my digit. It pulsated from my thumb, travelled up my arm, and exploded out of the roof of my skull with a scream.

Lee and Paul jumped back in fright and the eel, realizing it was partially free, went into something of a crocodilian death roll, comfortably twisting my arm around in its socket and leaving me with the very real fear that it would soon tear my thumb clean off. As its tail met water it showed mercy to me, released its teeth and back-paddled into the murk to tell all its friends about the idiot boy it had just encountered.

Eels are the absolute opposite of the carp, in physicality, feeding habits, popularity, everything, and now I hated them more than ever, but then, one day, I baited the bottom of the river and didn't catch one. I tried the next day and failed again. I spoke to my friends; no one had caught one in weeks. It was utterly bizarre, but the eels of the Fens seemingly disappeared overnight.

There's something about the shape of the snake that makes us stand up and take notice. We are actually hardwired to pay greater attention to the snake than the frame of any other animal. Surprisingly, the fear of snakes is not actually innate. According to findings published in the *Journal of Experimental Child Psychology* we are only born with the ability to quickly detect, and immediately respond to, the serpentine form, but the phobia itself is a culturally conditioned response. The two aren't mutually exclusive of course: the fact that we are so reactive to snakes makes the adoption of a negative emotional response so much easier, regardless of whether the animal in question is actually dangerous or not. Bad news for the eel then.

The eel does itself no further favours in the public-relations department by conjoining its superficial likeness to the snake with what Wilson describes as a 'slippery body . . . covered in a heavy coating of protective mucus . . . and strong jaws lined with microscopic whisker-like teeth'.

It is unfortunate that the eel's appearance has brought it such loathing. If you can look beyond its aesthetics there is truly a wondrous fish in waiting. The eel can live comfortably for over eighty years, with some reports of fish passing over a hundred; they can also increase or decrease the size of their eyes, jaw and head, and change colour, to suit their surroundings; and, when required, the eel can even survive out of water by absorbing all the oxygen it requires through its skin. The dorsal and anal fins are fused seamlessly with the caudal fin, framing the eel's entire body in one continuous paddle, which allows the eel to swim backwards just as strongly as it can forwards; plus they are born as hermaphrodites with the ability to adjust their sexual organs to suit the demands of their locale. Impressive stuff in itself, but none of this can come even close to matching the greatest feat of the eel.

Most eel species live entirely at sea – giant congers

with breezeblock heads, and colourful and sharp-
toothed morays that slither across tropical reefs – but
there are also sixteen freshwater species to be discovered right across Europe, southern and eastern Africa,
North America, parts of Asia, and the South Pacific.
Every year, hundreds of thousands of these freshwater
eels undertake an extraordinarily perilous quest to reach
their breeding grounds, with the most obscure, and certainly the most remote, reserved for our own eel species:
Anguilla anguilla, the European eel. If the following tale
of endurance doesn't make your eyes glisten and chest
swell with new respect for the eel, then truly: you have
no heart.

When the time is right, nothing can get between the
adult European eel and its desire to reproduce. Wilson
notes, in a rare moment of encyclopedic ebullience, that
the eel's snout 'becomes more pointed, the eyes glass
over, and the body's fat content increases in readiness
for the monumental journey ahead . . . Even eels living
in tiny ponds or pits miles from the nearest river system
find running water and travel downstream.' Their determination to breed is the stuff of legend. Fishing author
Fred Buller writes of a night in Cumbria when he witnessed 'a stream of eels' that 'were not halted by my
walking among them'. I too remember once encountering an eel in the middle of a cricket pitch just after
rainfall, head down and thrusting forward to flowing
water some half a mile away. I wanted to pop him in my
worm bucket and take him there myself, but this fish

needed no help, and was soon gone, at a far greater pace than your average outfielding farmer might make in pursuit of a cricket ball.

It quickly became clear, to those who cared to look, that the freshwater eels were all heading out to sea. Even the philosopher Aristotle was moved to record in the fourth century BC how the eel would suddenly become hell-bent on making it to salt water, but for centuries no one had a clue where they went once they were there, or, indeed, why.

Tom Fort superbly breaks down the origins of the eel in what is surely the seminal eel text of our time: *The Book of Eels*. He highlights how it was actually not until the seventeenth century that an Italian naturalist, Francesco Redi, correctly hypothesized that the eggs of the eel were laid at sea; before that, the best guess was that eels were formed from mud, but Francesco was a long time dead before any evidence was unearthed to support his theory. In 1897, another Italian, the celebrated biologist Giovanni Grassi, was the first ever to net a sperm-carrying eel and then went one better by capturing and identifying the youngest eels ever recorded: gentle, transparent fish only a few centimetres long, known henceforth as 'thin-heads'.

Grassi's seminal capture was made off the coast of Sicily in the Strait of Messina, a turbulent spot where giant tides and severe up-swelling currents frequently dragged unusual deep-sea creatures towards the clutches of man. It might have seemed a leap of faith to then assume that the breeding place of European eels had been found along with the thin-heads, but Grassi had the weight of Italian pride bearing down on his shoulders, and as he watched his captive samples metamorphosize into elvers, the final juvenile stage of the eel before adulthood, he rushed to announce that he had dispelled 'the great mystery which has hitherto surrounded the reproduction and development of the Common eel', and claimed *Anguilla anguilla* for his country. That's where the case could have been closed; then a young Dane rocked up and spoiled everything.

Sadly for Grassi, and the people of Italy, it transpired that the young eels of Messina were actually fully grown thin-heads. He couldn't possibly have known at the time – these were still the first correctly identified thin-heads after all – but the thin-head only metamorphosizes into the elver after up to three years of drifting eastwards on the Atlantic Gulf Stream. The results in Grassi's aquarium had been such an instant success because he had collected his thin-heads right on their home straight: they were absolutely primed to begin their new lives in fresh water.

In 1904 the Great Dane, Johannes Schmidt, a botanist by trade, was merely expanding his knowledge of land plants and researching the spawning grounds of cod, when a young-fish trawl happened to bring a 7.5cm thin-head to the net. The problem for Grassi was that Schmidt and his Danish research vessel weren't in Messina; in fact, they were nowhere near. Schmidt was

2,000 miles away, trawling a net off the North Atlantic's Faroe Islands.

By 1922, Schmidt had declared in a Royal Society paper that 'all the eels of Western Europe come from the Atlantic', having successfully, and somewhat sensationally, narrowed his search down to a 700-mile-wide patch of sea located off the eastern coasts of Florida and Bermuda. Simply, Schmidt had gathered along a southern line that produced gradually smaller thin-heads until he captured the smallest thin-heads ever recorded, a positively larval five millimetres in length.

Grassi was blown clean out of the water. Schmidt's research vessel was hovering above the abyssal recesses of the Sargasso Sea when it snared its minute prize. Could there be a more fitting circle of ocean to untangle the enigmatic web that surrounded the origin story of the eel? Perhaps only the Bermuda Triangle can conjure up a greater sense of mystery; little wonder then that the borders of these twin obscurities overlap. Contrary to popular belief the Sargasso is not chock-full of the brand of tentacular monster that once dragged pioneering explorers and their boats to a grisly oblivion. Sargassum weed might occasionally exhibit itself on the surface in vast golden clods but the sea itself is relatively benign, fenced in on all sides by currents that swirl in perpetual motion around its great oval perimeter, as waves of long-distance runners might around an athletics track. It leaves the centre of the sea calm, quiet and, relative to the rest of the Atlantic, quite devoid of life.

Quite why every eel from across Europe, North Africa and America chooses this spot to spawn is anyone's guess, but that is merely the tip of the iceberg when it comes to what we are still waiting to discover about the eel.

After the adult eels have mated, the baby eels hatch from fertilized eggs as the tiny, willow-leaf-shaped thin-head larvae of Schmidt and Grassi's obsession. The second wave of the eel's mass migration can then begin again, as the adults, finally relieved of their life's burdens, pass away into a three-mile abyss, where their bodies are gratefully feasted on by the type of globular scavengers that lie in the endless black.

I wish I'd known about all of this when I was a child. That each eel I held in my hand had virtually no peer in the whole world of freshwater fish. I would have shown them the deference and respect they deserved. I'm pretty sure I could even have grown to love them.

We might not always have had a grip on the specifics of the eel's life cycle, but humans have certainly tracked their movements for about as long as we've been hunter-gatherers. Eels have been harvested in their masses as far back as 6000 BC and eel traps and spears have been discovered on the banks of Northern Ireland's Lough Neagh that date right back to the Stone Age. There was scarcely a watercourse in the UK where eels couldn't be found in plentiful supply. From the River Thames to the Scottish lochs, the major drawcard of the eel was simply its pure unadulterated abundance.

The eel was the fish of the everyman, as, unlike the carp, anyone could employ virtually any method to catch it and near guarantee protein for the table. Izaak Walton wrote in his 1653 *magnum opus, The Compleat Angler,* that in one Staffordshire pond he noticed: 'such small eels abound so much, that many of the poorer sort of people that inhabit near to it, take such Eels out of this mere with sieves or sheets; and make a kind of eel-cake with them, and eat it like as bread'. They were so plentiful you didn't even need to worry about salting their meat for another day: simply re-cast the lines or reload the traps and haul in all the eels you need afresh. In October 1257 Henry III celebrated St Edward's Day with 15,000 eels, and in 1697 the north-eastern Italian fishery of Comacchio took three quarters of a million fish in a single night; earlier still, the annual tithe of eels paid under the terms of King Edgar's charter of 970 saw just twenty fishermen hand over some 60,000 eels every year; a truly mind-boggling figure from a time before the deployment of industrial fishing techniques.

The fact is, eels were available in serious numbers for a very long time, and there was real money to be made, especially from elvers. This immature adolescent eel is a thing of real beauty. Its translucence makes its dark eyes and black spinal column stand out against the rest of its body, almost as if it has been comically electrocuted as part of a child's cartoon, but when a mass of elvers are held together in your hand their bodies blend collectively into piles of immaculate silver-white threads, as if pulled from a royal wedding dress. Given their appearance it is perhaps little surprise they were termed 'white gold', especially when elver prices can peak at as much as £500 per kilo on the French and Japanese markets. I once met an elver fisherman who used to illegally fish the estuary of the River Taff, 'before they put the barrage over the river and ruined it', who claimed he could make £5,000 in half an hour of work back in the 1970s. He was hardly an exception though: around the corner in the prolific Severn estuary it was apparently possible to make as much as £100,000 in a season; in fact the head of running elvers in the Severn was once so great they held an annual competition to eat a pint of elvers in the quickest time, and would regularly spread any surplus catch right across the fields to fertilize the soil.

The value of the eel had something of a role to play in the life of my grandad too. He might have lived out his senior years in the Fens but he was a Bedford boy born and bred, and plundered the rivers around his home with great proficiency. He hadn't been called up to the frontline during the Second World War owing to his skill as an engineer, but it can hardly be said that the threat of imminent invasion by the Nazis softened his ability to recognize a clear economic opportunity.

Grandad wrote a self-published book detailing many of his exploits, but sadly there is only one copy of *Bedford, My Bedford* by Ken Millard in circulation. He hadn't quite mastered the art of saving his work to the computer, so he'd just type out a page of memoirs and then print it straight away. This is a great shame as I think it is only myself, Dad and his second cousin Christine (whom he press-ganged into editing his material) who have actually been able to read his masterpiece, and thus the world will never know of the time he once watched the town brass band sink into the river during an ill-advised attempt at a floating bandstand, or the time his father forced the local school to promote him up the classes with the wonder-fully illiterate and vaguely threatening: 'just because this boy has a hole in his pants, he is still going to get an edu-cation', or even how he narrowly avoided being court-martialled for what I can only gather from the chapter marked 'Home Guard' was a heady mixture of utter fecklessness, heavy drinking and a total disregard for any figure of authority. The end of that section cli-maxes in a particularly entertaining story that involves a pub, a dentist's chair, a narrowly avoided night-long exer-cise in a ditch, and the revealing, yet clearly quite accurate, words: 'we were very poor soldiers'.

The chapter marked 'Fishing' recounts a story I had heard many times before. Wartime restrictions around the coasts meant fresh fish were extremely scarce, so when Grandad approached the local fishmonger to ask if he would like some eels, it came as no surprise that the answer came back: 'As many as you can supply.' Every Friday night thenceforth Grandad and his mates were to be seen creeping off around the local gardens in search of lobworms before fixing up to six rods behind the Clapham Club in the dark.

'Many a night the six rods would be dipping in the river,' he writes, 'making a very hectic time difficult because the hooks had to be removed under a covering blanket and in a black-out as any flashing light would bring the local copper.' Yes. My grandad was out fishing during the Blitz, a period of time when virtually every other person in Britain was hiding in the darkness within sprinting distance of the local air-raid shelter due to the very real fear of German planes bombing anything illuminated. 'Our best haul was twenty-two fish,' he proudly recounts, 'which to us at one and ninepence a pound was very acceptable.' Sadly his days of illicit eeling were to come to a premature end, not at the hands of the police, the Home Guard or, dare I say, the Nazis. No, much worse than that. 'A number of the local ladies soon discovered that if they waited in Clapham Road they could stop us and buy our eels before we got to the fishmonger's. It became so bad that the competition between these ladies meant that they would wait nearer and nearer to Clapham, so in the end we had to stop', presumably before he started Bedford's first eel riot. 'Enterprise is very difficult,' he laments, at the chapter's close.

Comfortably the largest of the freshwater eel species are the longfins found in Australia and New Zealand. Some specimens Down Under have been reliably recorded at almost five feet in length, and with other, less reliable accounts of eight-feet-long 100lb eels seen dragging cows into the depths, it is fair to say the crown for the world's biggest eel is unlikely to ever leave the southern hemisphere. Meanwhile, here in the UK, the long-standing eel record stands at a comparatively small, but none the less very impressive, 11lb 2oz. It was caught by Steve Terry in 1978 from a lake in Hampshire, but there have long been rumours of unclaimed record breakers which have enough clout behind them to very reasonably suggest that Terry's record is breakable.

In 2013 an 11lb 8oz beast snared on sausage meat failed its verification checks for not having an independent witness; three years prior to that, a purported 13lb 10oz record fish also slipped through its angler's hands for the same reason, but the most famous close call arose in 2005, when another 13lb monster was caught by a man known as 'Norman the plumber'. His bait might have been intended for a big carp, but the rules and regulations of his fishery guaranteed a lifetime ban for anyone seen to be publicizing record breakers from any species. Despite a number of witnesses to the fish, and its immense weight, no photos were ever released to the public and the giant eel was not mentioned again.

I was heartened to learn that my childhood home had turned up some of the most legendary eels in British history. The Fens are rightfully steeped in eel folklore, as, prior to the drainage work beginning in 1630, the entire landscape was flooded bar a couple of hillocks occupied by small hamlets, and eel fishing was a massive part of the economy. Indeed, so esteemed was the eel, our local city, Ely, took its name from them, and to this very day it holds an annual festival dedicated purely to the fish. The eel-hunting market was monopolized by a band of lawless hunter-gatherers known as the Fen Tigers, who ruthlessly opposed the drainage schemes and took to destroying the newly constructed sluices, justifiably concluding that they would devastate their eel-catching, reed-cutting and duck-hunting practices.

I was fortunate enough to once meet the last of the Fen Tigers. Ernie James lived with his wife in a house right out on the Welney Washes, nestled in a remote spot between the prolific Delph and Old Bedford rivers. He trapped eels well into his nineties and built the most amazing willow eel traps with his hands, one of which he gave to my dad, who was his doctor right until the day he passed away at the princely age of ninety-nine. I was only a child when I met Ernie, and, sadly, I never had the chance to ask him about really big fenland eels. If I had I would've asked him if it really could've been possible that the River Ouse once produced a 36lb giant, or if Izaak Walton's Peterborough eel of almost two yards in length was plausible, but, most of all, I'd want to ask him about an immense eel supposedly caught from a dyke not two miles from my house back in the nineteenth century. Witnessed by a man of the cloth and reputed to be some six feet in length, it seems from the realms of pure fantasy, but then what would a man of God stand to gain from lying about such things? Stranger things have happened in these parts, after all.

Ernie and his friends once trapped a 34lb sturgeon in the Welmore Sluice, a critically endangered armour-plated fish that numbers fewer than 1,000 in Europe and which has long since been extinct in the United Kingdom. Unfortunately, for the fish at least, it was taken to the markets of London and fetched such a good price that the men of the village all skipped out of work and went on the beers for a week. You'd now have a better chance of harvesting poo from a rocking horse than ever seeing a repeat capture of such a fish in the wild.

Okay, so I might not be able to conclusively prove there were once record breakers in the Fens, but one thing I do know beyond doubt is that there were very big eels to be found here, as, against all the odds, the fenscape had already gifted me my own giant.

I was nine years old when I had my first afternoon fishing with Grandad and Dad on the big river. Popham's Eau flowed sluggishly down to the tidal Ouse and out towards the sea at King's Lynn. It was the river where Grandad spent most of his time; it was close to his bungalow and contained large heads of bream and massive roach, if you knew how to catch them. I was keen to impress, but having been used to fishing the Creek, at no more than ten metres across and a few feet in depth, I was really struggling to cast my heavier, deeper tackle without help from Dad. Late in the day I managed one serviceable cast on my own and the float dipped with purpose.

The fight tested my tackle to its absolute limit. I knew nothing of playing big fish, and this was far and away the biggest fish I'd ever hooked, so I simply wrenched as hard as I could and refused to give the fish any chance of running. The eel eventually erupted on the surface, projecting its long, muscular body out of the water like the arm of a giant octopus. We struggled to get it into the net as the eel was thicker than my wrist and as long as my arms, and when we tried to weigh it the fish thrashed so violently we were forced to take pity on it and quickly release it back to its domain.

Grandad estimated it was around 5lb in weight, which made it my first bona-fide Wilson mega-specimen. I smelt my net afterwards; the eel slime resembled freshly sliced cucumbers. I didn't wash it out for weeks, and carried the webbing as a badge of honour.

As Wilson had prescribed, this eel had packed on the last of its weight and was on its great journey out to the sea. It didn't have far to go at least: Popham's Eau spewed out into the great estuarine mudflats of the Wash not fifteen miles from where we were sat. It's a memory I haven't considered in a very long time indeed. It was well over twenty years ago now and an absolute one-off, a shock that only fishing can produce, but as is customary with such moments in life they either stick with you for ever or they lose their momentum and fade into the background. I soon went back to deriding eels.

I could consider heading back to the rivers of my youth in search of that eel – it is possible it's still alive and it would've accrued a great weight in such a time – but realistically there would not be a repeat capture of that fish; what's left of him was probably digested and excreted somewhere in the Sargasso many, many years ago. Catching another big one was going to be a tough undertaking. I had been warned that serious eeling took a lifetime of study. This was a marginal branch of fishing where only the utterly committed found success. I joined the 'Eel fishing' Facebook group and found one expert advising an enthusiast not to give up on his potential water 'till you've fished at least 10 nights without a fish, and even then don't totally discount it'.

I could've been in real trouble, but I had an ace hidden up my sleeve: I knew exactly where I was going to look for my big eel.

I flicked back through my notebook, right back to when this all began at the start of last winter. There, scrawled in my shorthand, were the following words: 'Leicester Line. Roadside service station. 8lb 2oz, 6lb 14oz'. I knew that would come in useful, I just knew it.

I emailed John Ellis of the Canal & River Trust for more information and he graciously returned my message with specifics. It still wasn't going to be easy: the Leicester Line Canal is some thirty-five miles long, and it spills into the Grand Union Canal and the River Soar at either end, but the numerous locks offered a real chance of eel entrapment at least, and the massive weights of those two fish suggested they may have gone sedentary in that patch for a number of years.

The key to finding any record-breaking eel in the

United Kingdom is the discovery of a landlocked fish. The sorts of water where either escape to the Sargasso is impossible or the supply of food is so undeniably consistent that the eel decides to hunker down for an extended stay. Most specimen-eel hunters head to large commercial lakes, where carp fishermen have piled in baits and unknowingly supplemented the growth of a giant; in fact, out of the fifty biggest eels of all time only two have come from canals. I wasn't going to let that put me off though; after all, the larger of the captured eel pair was only 3lb off the British record. When it came to canals I strongly suspected it was the lack of anglers that had failed to deliver a record, and not the lack of potentially record-breaking fish.

In truth, though, I knew my focus had shifted from the pursuit of rod-caught records. I just didn't have that burning desire any more. Don't get me wrong, it would still have been very nice, but I felt that I was finally in a place where the experience of fishing meant more to me than anything else and I didn't want to spoil that by now tearing off to the nearest big-water commercial to fish for eels with a legion of carp anglers. The canal eels felt like a gift, an opportunity to fish somewhere unusual, where I knew the chance of encountering another angler was virtually zero; pure guerrilla fishing for a pair of fish who have almost certainly never been caught on rod or line. Either one would be a massive achievement, comfortably smashing my personal best right out of the water: really, what wasn't there to get very excited about?

I began to make plans. This was uncharted territory for me: to say I was a novice big-eel angler was a gross understatement – I didn't have the first idea what I was doing and scoured internet forums, books and specialist websites for the best advice on tackle, location, bait and fish care. Wilson writes that 'thundery weather finds them particularly active', a fact borne out by almost every single expert on the subject. I needed a serious downpour, preferably a storm, right now, in the middle of summer.

It felt weird hoping for rain, especially since I had been so comfortably outmanoeuvred by bad weather earlier in the year. We were experiencing the most extraordinary period of good weather as summer heaved on in its finery, a few days of sprinkling showers here and there, but nothing more than a blessing, and the whole nation was basking in a sort of collective euphoria.

I felt a little guilty, but these big eels demanded a near biblical event: Old Testament rain of the sort that brings the pagans to the hills and leaves a disgustingly sticky night in its tail. Weeks dragged into months and I began to worry that it might not actually happen at all, then one day I woke up, checked the forecast and saw cloud icons blacker than Satan's arsehole spreading right out across Britain.

I should have been delighted but I had one very serious problem: the storm was due to hit the Leicester Line the day before my twin sister's wedding. I spread out the map. It wasn't all bad: the fishing spot was pretty much slap bang in the centre of the country, and as Anna was getting wed out east I could just about justify the diversion. However, this was no daytime sortie. There was absolutely no question but that the big eels were at their most voracious in darkness – why else would Grandad have risked arrest? But I absolutely had to be at the wedding venue the following afternoon for a family barbecue, which meant leaving bright-eyed and bushy-tailed first thing in the morning and not turning up looking like I'd been on a night-long eel-bender the day before the seminal event of my beloved sister's life.

There was another major consideration: the stench. If I caught a giant eel I knew I was going to end up looking like the Creature from the Black Lagoon, and even if by some miracle I didn't, the bait I intended to use was firmly from the drawer marked 'stinkiest imaginable'.

Specimen-eel fisherman Matt Johnson in *Eel Fishing for Beginners* makes the case quite clear: 'I will prebait for several weeks, on a regular basis, using a mixture of old fish, maggots, chopped worms and, if allowed, chicken offal,' he notes, before coming to his senses and adding the following caveat: 'Please check with your fishing club before baiting up with chicken intestines, as I do not want to be held responsible for your expulsion from the club for breaking the rules.'

If I had been able to act alone I might just have got away with it, made up some excuse about getting a last-minute job in a sewerage system, and palmed it all off as an unavoidable inconvenience, with: 'Hey, guys! I'm at the wedding now so just direct me to the showers and I'll be down in a jiffy!' However, for a couple of years now my life has been intractably intertwined with another. I didn't quite know how I was going to tell my girlfriend, Emma, that we had to leave for Anna's wedding a day early so I could fish for giant eels, but I knew how it was going to go down.

I did some more virtual pre-baiting of my own and quickly discovered there was some sort of hotel located in the very set of roadside services I needed to be at to fish for the eel. Perfect. I could just imagine Emma having a bit of a pampering session there before the eve of the wedding as, Lord knows, she wasn't going to be interested in the eeling. If I played my cards correctly I might even be able to convince her that this was actually a really great idea, a way of breaking up the long journey ahead of the weekend's festivities.

An internet search revealed a very reasonable early-bird price of just £46.75 for a room, but just as I was about to punch my credit card number into the booking form I foolishly read a couple of reviews on the establishment. One, on motorwayservices.com, gave the hotel a two-burger rating out of a possible five, worrying both for being a low score and for the fact that the place couldn't even score well on a rating system inspired by fast food.

I wish I could tell you I closed the computer down and saved my money. I wish I could tell you I picked a different, more reasonable fish from my list of options. I wish I could tell you I didn't check that the lorry park was actually right next to the canal, so ideally located for the fishing, but the memory of *Bedford, My Bedford* by Ken Millard burnt brightly. I asked myself, quite honestly, what would Grandad do?

And then I booked the hotel.

All I can think about is eels and all I can see is eels.

The storm hits on the drive over and the lightning streaks across the sky like livid white eels. Small seathrough eels streak in watery lines down my windscreen before the giant pair of rubber eels sweep them aside. I follow a thin white eel on my satnav and funnel my car along the thickest and greatest eel in the land: the M1.

The services turned out to be the wrong side of the motorway, but I discovered a little flyover behind the hotel that led into the sort of seedy-looking darkened layby where you wouldn't want to inadvertently flash your lights around. A squeeze under a fence line, a scramble through a furrow fit for a badger, and I'm shipped onto thick grass and the water's side.

My London perch water stretched all the way from King's Cross to Birmingham on the Grand Union Canal, a distance of some 137 miles, but shortly after leaving Northampton a single arm separates from the main route and heads in a new direction up through

Leicester. It was along here that I'd found myself, in the dusk, somewhere below the Watford Gap locks.

Down by the canal all was calm. Nightfall was approaching fast and the tiny pipistrelle bats had taken to the Persian blue skies to hunt insects. They danced silently like blackened flakes of ash during a forest fire, their calm animation serving only to emphasize just how quiet the canal actually was. The water, frankly, was disturbingly still.

It couldn't be more different to the section of the Grand Union I experienced in London. There the banks were filled with people and commerce and the clear water revealed a sub-aquan dumping ground jostling for space among the city's waste. It wasn't pretty, but there was an elemental honesty to the place. Here, there was something of an unsettling air.

Two rows of hazel and sycamore trees, and a heavily grassed towpath with blackthorn, elderberry and patches of giant hogweed, were all lovely enough, but the driving rush of the M1 in the background, the white lights from the cars and screeching brake pads, the constant pounding of air, like herds of wildebeest trapped in a ravine, stopped it from truly feeling like a breathing space.

When you encounter green patches in densely populated areas there is something exciting about it, like you've discovered a small and unlikely victory for nature, a place where urban tension can be released, where the citified world can take stock and just 'be' for a little while. But when the scenario is reversed, when human waste collides with the countryside, it feels like an assault. Human hands built this canal, but the presence of water is usually good company for the wild, however it is formed. The M1, however, struck right through this place like a great grey spear.

The whole place felt as if it was in a state of limbo, like this pair of opposing forces were simply getting through the uncomfortable pleasantries before each moved on with its life, two manmade cousins forced together for Christmas, one brash, right on and relevant, the other sloping towards retirement with stories to tell if the other would only listen. I'm sure if I had walked a mile up- or downstream I would have reached a point where the M1 curled a satisfactory distance from the water and the atmosphere would instantly have lifted, but then the monster eels wouldn't be there, would they?

Bricked on either bank and filled with a fudgy brown water that resembled something the greedy Augustus Gloop may have entered in the children's book *Charlie and the Chocolate Factory*, the canal possessed a regimented symmetry that made it quite hard to find features where my water serpent might actually feed. Eventually I identified two potential areas that differed from the rest. One was a step into the canal on the opposite bank, cut deliberately to about the size of half a tennis court. It was designed to allow boats to pass each other, but its position off the main flow, and the accompaniment of overhanging trees, made it prime real estate for an ambush, or, failing that, at least the sort of area where I could imagine insects or carrion would get held up for the eel to feast upon. The second spot was further along and on my bank. It was a small instep in the brick-work about thirty metres from the first lock gate for the Watford Gap, where a series of seven gates have lifted canal boats over the sixteen metres of elevation known as the 'Leicester summit' from as far back as 1814. I couldn't fish any closer to the gates of the locks as, understandably, the Canal & River Trust didn't want anglers getting themselves or their tackle in the way of the working machinery. Still, I could imagine an eel might patrol out from those giant wooden doors, mould-ing its body tight to the canal walls till it found that little deviation in the brick, and then hopefully landed upon my feed.

The shade came on fast and the recce drew to its natural close. I cursed myself for not bringing a few bits of bait to drop into my spots to tempt some fish in early. A single white security light flickered into life above the locks. It cast an uneasy paleness over the place, like pallor mortis shortly after death; just per-fect, I felt, for those that slither from their holes to gorge on the dead. I returned to the van as a plume of silver fish scattered across the canal's surface like shards of broken glass from a mirror. The predators had arrived.

*

The more I learnt of the eels' plight the more I grew to respect their resilience. Given the sort of dark and nasty places they turn up in, it's all too easy to transfer the characteristics of their bleak dwellings onto the animal itself. To do so is an injustice. When an eel appears in a storm drain, sewer or horse trough, it is a display of its extraordinary tenacity and iron will to survive and not necessarily an indication of preference. Never judge an animal purely by where it is forced to rest its head.

'So, I erm.'

I haven't felt this guilty in a very long time. Probably not since I grassed my sister up to my parents for putting orange juice in my shoes when we were ten.

The hotel where I'm going to have to leave Emma is too depressing for words. It's the sort of place you would come to cheat on your partner, not turn up together for a romantic overnight stay. If anything, the reviews on TripAdvisor were generous. Quite what levels of depravity you would have to reach to get less than a two-burger rating doesn't bear thinking about.

Nicotine-coloured walls blend seamlessly with a floor that's more stain than carpet. The whole place smells like the smoking area in a factory and it appears that the last guests had opted to have a massive fight with a full cafetière right before they left.

Emma peels the net curtains back from the glass. 'So this is my view for the night.' We gaze silently at the petrol station forecourt out front. A large man fills his lorry with one hand and inhales a Ginsters Cornish pasty into his face with the other.

'I feel, to be honest with you, like the biggest bastard in the world.' I look earnestly into Emma's eyes.

If I'd thought this ham-fisted attempt at emotional revelation might elicit some sympathy then I was barking up the wrong tree entirely. 'There's probably a dead body in here,' she says bluntly, flicking the blind shut and turning sharply, which is lucky as she doesn't notice the enormous black blowfly wafting up from the window frame. I attempt a stiff grin and widen my body frame out to conceal the uninvited guest.

'Come on, it isn't so bad,' I proffer, knowing it's actually worse than bad.

'Will. This is the sort of place in the films where women get murdered while they are left alone in a motel.' She climbed onto the bed.

'What, while their boyfriends are all off eel fishing?' I retort, while dying a little inside. 'Don't be so ridiculous.'

I consider, very seriously, just jacking the whole night in and heading off. But where could we possibly go now? The wedding doesn't start till lunchtime tomorrow and we are hours from home.

Liminality. 'The quality of ambiguity or disorientation that occurs in the middle stage of rituals, when participants no longer hold their pre-ritual status but have not yet begun the transition to the status they will hold when the ritual is complete.' It feels quite fitting that I am attempting this feat from a service station, the symbol of being neither here nor there, where no one wants to be, but a stop you simply have to take if you want to make it to your destination eventually. In the services we are a metaphorical stream of eels, pausing to sniff the water, to feed, confirm the direction of our target and leave at the earliest available opportunity. I have extended our stay here purely for my own purposes; what, I wonder, does that say about me? I sensibly opt to keep my navel-gazing to myself.

'Look, love, why don't you just come out with me?' I try, as a last resort, while knowing really how reluctant Emma is to fish at the best of times, and that a canal towpath at night could well be the final nail in the coffin of the chances of me ever luring her into my hobby. 'It'll be fun!' I add, somewhat weakly.

'No.'

She thumps the remote and sends the television crackling into life. 'I'm just going to sit here and do a facemask for tomorrow. See, I told you there were flies.'

The giant fly settles above the head of the bed as I creep out of the door and accede to Emma's demand to lock it securely behind me.

I left school, went to university and entered the real world with little idea of how I was going to pay for the ticket on the door. I wanted to travel, so I worked as a barman and slept on a mattress before getting one of those month-long English language teaching qualifications that gives you access to the planet and a classroom of people who are sadly expecting an actual teacher. That introduced me to a small school in the Indonesian half of New Guinea and from that moment forward something of a spell was cast over me and my future. Nothing was ever really the same again.

This wild, natural fortress had repelled outsiders like me for centuries, but in recent decades a gradual easing of borders had revealed some of the most fascinating tribal communities on earth. Spread out across the most bizarre set of geographical extremes that included the largest mountain range in Oceania, Asia's most intact primary rainforest, and the largest swamplands south of Borneo, I discovered that these people had maintained pathways and networks of intertribal trade for almost the entirety of their 45,000-year history. These were the longest-running trade routes in human history and they were virtually unreported, but as the modern world pressed into New Guinea at pace they were in danger of fading into the background without record.

I took it on myself to try and walk as many of these routes as I could, documenting the experiences of those local people who could still remember them, and then released my evidence onto the world, evidence, I felt, that elevated these people beyond the stereotype of them as backward, cannibalistic savages and firmly into the realms of what they deserved: recognition as a highly functioning, highly complex, co-operative society.

The world wasn't really interested though. I spent the best part of the next decade of my life applying for small grants, researching, and going on ever more dangerous expeditions on the island. I had some successes, making the first record of the foot-only salt trade in the far west of the island and mapping almost the entire length of a 1,000-kilometre section of trade route stretching out to the southern coasts, and for many years that was just enough. I was living my dream and felt uniquely privileged to be following my own path in life. Sure, I had no money, and my work only interested the most fanatical of geographers, but I had enough to get by and, besides, I passionately believed in what I was doing. I supplemented my income away from the island by slowly going up the rungs in the world of documentary television, flitting from being a runner in London to working as a researcher in Cardiff, and generally felt quite happy with my lot, but as the years passed a creeping anxiety began to seep into my soul.

In the beginning it felt a bit like the first time you get scared climbing trees as a child. You've done it hundreds and hundreds of times without a care in the world and then suddenly the fear grips you, usually when you are right at the top of some oaken giant with no obvious safe path back down. You realize you are mortal, that what you are doing is reckless, that if you fall you could seriously hurt yourself, or even die, but you are hopelessly addicted to the buzz and thrill of pushing forever forward so you don't get down, you just sort of sit there, helplessly.

My moment came when I was lost somewhere deep in West Papua, the Indonesian side of New Guinea. I had dragged my friend and medic Callum with me and we were now without food having barely escaped a maiden white-water descent with our lives. I had made a terrible error of judgement that had led us not onto an ancient trade route, but down into a vast, uninhabited, 400-mile square of thick forest that it would take us weeks to escape from. I lost two and a half stone, and we walked out with our lives, but Callum and I would never work together again and I left behind something vital of myself that I never quite recovered.

I had gone almost as far as I could with my expeditionary career, probing towards my own breaking point and plumbing the pits of a very real, very visceral, fear of death, but I couldn't seem to escape my hard-wired desire to push even further. Leading expeditions was my full-time job by the end of my twenties, and I didn't feel qualified to do anything else. I pressed onwards and downwards into ever more dangerous territory: the Pennine Way alone in a tent in minus 10°C temperatures, the first solo descent of the river that marks the war-torn border of Sierra Leone and Liberia, alone and afraid, but blinkered to the damage I was doing to myself and everyone who cared about me. I had a recurring nightmare during that time in which I was an animal being hunted by an unseen but very deadly predator. I would put distance between me and my pursuer and almost slip free, only to suddenly discover I didn't know how to run any more and instantly find myself back in front of its fangs. Its hot, smelly breath would pound the backs of my calves and I knew I was seconds from death, and then I would awake covered in my own sweat.

A hundred million years ago the first freshwater eels left their sea home and were also settling in to a new way of life somewhere off the coast of Indonesia.

We still don't know exactly how the eel reproduces and an eel egg has still never been found. We don't know the nature of the adult eel's extraordinary navigational skills or why the European eel doesn't just join the American eel in making the much shorter hop to the American continent from their shared breeding sea. We have yet to witness an adult eel actually die from the exertion of spawning, and, despite thousands of assaults on the Sargasso, a breeding adult eel is yet to be recovered. According to Tom Fort, there has only ever been one record of an adult eel being found in the open Atlantic: it was semi-digested and in the stomach of a sperm whale somewhere off the Azores. We may not know any of these things for sure, but there is one thing we do know: during my twenties the eel experienced a catastrophic decline in its numbers.

By 2010 the Environment Agency had recorded a 95 per cent decline in the European eel. In keeping with the astonishingly one-sided ratio of questions over answers whenever the eel is involved, it still isn't clear precisely what is driving eels towards early extinction. One factor could be illegal fishing and the over-exploitation of the elvers; the eel, after all, is one of the only fish to face such abuse of their young; but another possibility involves the spread of a particularly nasty nemotode worm that feeds parasitically on their swim-bladders. Then there is the increased use of hydroelectric dams and their thwarting of eel migration, and surely there can be no question that climate change, which has warmed the Arctic ice cap and slowed the Gulf Stream, has hampered the procession of thin-heads to these shores. The truth is, it is probably a mixture of all of these factors, but actually getting a firm grip on how to reverse the crash is proving extremely difficult.

Export bans and tighter restrictions on fishing have helped, as have restocking programmes, but the benefits are only found locally in those places that care enough about the eel to invest in its future; elsewhere, the out-look is still very bleak indeed. My entire childhood was spent trying to avoid the attentions of the eel; then, for almost twenty years, I didn't catch a single one. I felt deep shame at having taken this fish for granted.

I shuffle along the towpath in the pitch black, glad of the half-light recce. Everything changes after dark. Things move around and obstacles emerge from nowhere. I want to limit the use of my torch, to allow my eyes the time to adjust naturally, but also to slip through here without disturbing the eels, or any other animals that could be watching from the shadows for that matter.

The elemental vulnerability of spending time in the dark alone can quickly bring a deep sense of paranoia with it. A fear of the dark is something we dismiss as adults as being somehow childish, but ask yourself this: how much time do you actually spend in the true dark? When the light switch isn't within reach and you have only your own mind for company? Total darkness was for a long time a CIA-approved 'enhanced interrogation technique', and those who have experienced interrogation in Guantánamo Bay claimed it to be the most feared torture method; proof that there is not much worse than being forced to retreat into your own mind to find out what fears feed down there.

I was used to hiding in the dark. On expeditions, especially as I started to go solo, I would pride myself on my ability to conceal my camp. I felt far more fear of the random acts of people than I ever did of the more predictable behaviours of the wild animals that roam the forest floor. When night fell I would retreat well away from any paths or watercourses and pull myself into the densest foliage I could find. One night in West Africa I remember being near paralysed with fear as a pair of poachers hunted the banks of the river I was following. I could see their torches, scanning the bushes like a searchlight from a prison, and was absolutely convinced they were about to discover me. They came so close I could see the whites of their eyes and teeth and smell the pile of dead and dying primates they had gathered in a sack, but I remained undiscovered.

This canal might not be Conrad's 'heart of darkness' – it's just a towpath in the Midlands after all – but it still has the ability to really scare. Here I have nowhere to go and nowhere to hide. There is no shelter, just one way in and one way out, and I'm perching myself right on the main thoroughfare, where anything could pass: a person, a badger, a fox, perhaps even a ghost.

I'm glad of the moon then. It is almost full. So bright and lumpen in appearance, like it has been drawn by a child or moulded out of porridge, but it means my way is lit comfortably enough, and I'm able to shuffle my feet along the path to my chosen spot without too much emotional upset.

I take a deep restorative breath and my heart rate starts to drop. A beautifully soft ethereal smoke drifts off the fields and a pair of spectral-looking moths flutter past, using the canal's unnatural break in the treeline as an unencumbered passage. I wonder if they will make it past the squadron of pipistrelle bats though.

In West Papua and West Africa, any break in the wilderness provided by rivers was always a relief from the intense claustrophobia of the forest. If I could, I would always use them to expedite my passage on a particular bearing, and many of the coolest things I've ever seen have been thanks to them. Rivers have a mag-netism for people and wildlife – it was one of the reasons I continued to love them so much – but if you were potential prey you knew your life was out of your hands every time you opted for this clear path through the forest. It was why I spent so much of my projects hiding.

I peel the lid off my bait bucket. In keeping with all

I've learnt about the particularities of the eel's nose a putrid cloud fills the air with the smell of microwaved vomit. The bait is suitably horrendous then, pellets soaked in fish oils for over a year and dead fish from the depths of the freezer: a lamprey, a smelt, a small joey mackerel. I'll fix their heads to large single hooks and throw a generous handful of dead maggots over the top. I set up two bite alarms paired with stiff carp rods and strong lines. Who really is to say what could come to my baits out here in these under-fished passages? Whispered rumours of giant catfish, hulking canal pike and record-shaking perch brush shoulders with monstrous eels, snapping turtles and at least one truly massive python. The canal systems of Britain might have been made by man but they have long since been reclaimed by nature, both natural and discarded, so it pays to be prepared for anything.

It is surprisingly hard to sever the head of the lamprey from its body. I use a knife and the plastic top of the bait bucket and stick to my dour butchery till I have successfully parted tendons and spine. It oozes blood and oil, the perfect chum for the eel, a connoisseur of the gruesome. The dark feels right for this work, but I try and keep my mind focused on the task at hand and steer well away from the grim acts that may, or may not, take place in these hedged lands after dark.

I underarm the lamprey head out into the dark and listen as the line fizzes satisfactorily from my reel. By some miracle it lands with a splash somewhere in the far bank hole and I feel the lead meet a solid bed. It is sat right on the fringe of the bushes. Perfect.

Ten minutes later, with both traps laid, I flick my bite alarms on. Momentarily they light up, just to let me know the battery is charged and they are ready to go, before settling into the night's watch. I too settle. Keeping my profile low to the moonlight, I pull the hood of my sweater over my head and hunch forward over the water like a gargoyle.

When I was a child I was warned that the eel was known as 'the Devil's fish' and that if you lay them out in a cross shape they will remain that way until they die. Later in life I learnt that they are actually just an unusually sensitive fish. They are armed with thousands of sensors along their bodies that aid them when hunting in the murk, and I discovered it was actually possible to crash their nervous system by simply tipping them up and running a finger along their lengths. It made unhooking them a much more straightforward task, as they simply fell into something of a trance. The crucifix stuff was a nonsense, of course. The eels had simply been subdued, and stupid people had just seen what they had always wanted to see, but the power of suggestion can't be underestimated. Night fishing to exorcise freshwater snakes from brown water certainly sounds like fiendish work.

The alarm on the lamprey lets out a single bleep and my adrenal glands eject their load. Something is out there. Something is stirring in the dark. I hover over the rod. 'Do it again,' I whisper, and the alarm obliges with another bleep. Do I strike? Do I not strike? The mind swims with what it could be: something with a pulse for certain – the canal is far too still and the lamprey far too dead for it to be anything else.

It bleeps again. One more time and I'm definitely going to hit it. The giant could be out there right now, just mouthing the bait. I don't want to snatch it from its jaws before the hook is in place. Perhaps it's just a small perch though? Pulled in by the fishy scent. Or maybe it's a crayfish gently stripping the severed head from the hook? I wouldn't be too surprised if they were in here – they seem to be everywhere else – in which case I should definitely reel in and check the head.

The rod settles again, and this is where madness lies. Do I reel up and check the bait is still there or leave it out in what I know is the perfect spot? Do I risk disturbing a swim with a feeding fish for an unnecessary investigation? What if I can't cast it back into that perfect spot again? But what if I'm now fishing on a bare hook? I'll never ever catch and all this time is wasted. I sit back down and reposition my hood. 'What the hell am I doing down here?' I say, to no one in particular, suddenly feeling very restless and quite scared. An intense feeling of disquiet enters the pit of my stomach. 'I don't like it here,' I whisper through gritted teeth. In fact, I don't like it here at all.

When I was younger I used to believe in ghosts. In fact, I was so convinced the house I grew up in was haunted I once persuaded Paul and Lee to come over and stake the place out for a night. It was a disaster though, and the worst thing we captured was Anna smashing our carefully laid cotton trip lines and shouting 'woooooo' down my tape recorder at the top of her voice in the middle of the night. I did have one very odd experience when I was twelve though. The family were all staying in an old fisherman's cottage in Little Haven and my brother Tom and I were sharing a bunkbed in one of the back rooms. In the middle of the night I woke to see the shadow of a boy hanging over me on the top bunk. I assumed it was Tom and told him to go straight back to bed, slightly surprised he had managed to climb the ladder without me waking, especially since he was only five years old and pretty clumsy on his feet. The shadow simply waved at me, before noiselessly drifting away from view. Shaken up a little I flicked on the light switch and discovered Tom was sleeping soundly and I had been staring at a wall no more than a foot from my face the entire time.

Weird things seem to happen around water and those associated with it, but in all the years I've spent fishing in the dark alone I've only experienced a handful of occasions when I've felt genuinely unsettled. Certainly this night eel fishing on the canal is one of them, but there is also one pond in the Vale of Glamorgan that I simply will not fish in the dark no matter how much you pay me – as soon as the sun falls behind the trees I am out of there like a whippet from a trap and so is almost every other angler I know.

The best, and certainly the most convincing, of all stories of the paranormal are the ones where 'the weird' catches you utterly unaware though, when you aren't already in an anxious state and primed to elevate a suggestion into a full-blown apparition. One autumnal evening I was walking home along a stretch of Cardiff's River Taff with Emma when we both heard the distinct sound of a cycle bell right behind us. It was no great surprise given we were on a route frequently taken by cyclists, so without even breaking our conversation, we took to walking in single file as the bike rushed past. Except there was no bike. Just the hair-raising sensation of having something pass right through your body that isn't really there at all. We stopped, looked up and down both banks, waited for a few moments, and concluded there was not another single living soul for hundreds of metres.

As I said, though, I don't believe in ghosts. The inner machinations of our complex brains and their multitude of ways of interpreting the world on our behalf seem to me to be both deeply fallible and something that we are only just beginning to understand. However, I do absolutely believe people who say they have seen ghosts. In their mind's eye they definitely have, in which case they are telling the truth. I just don't necessarily think what they believe they've seen is evidence of the undead.

Still, the paranormal naturally appeals to the fisherman in me. Not necessarily the idea of things that go bump in the night per se, but more the idea that if anyone spends enough time really focusing on the world, and I mean really intensely focusing, they will naturally begin to notice things that deviate from the norm. Fishing by its very nature is prying into the unknown, dropping a line into a largely unseen world and trying to make a connection. Certainly, the best fishermen I know have something of a supernatural instinct about them. They can literally feel the presence of a fish and will go on to catch with such an enviable sense of inevitability it is almost as if they have arrived from a realm in the future where they have already seen the precise location of every fish on earth. It must be sublime.

Yes, if pressed, I would say I am an open-minded sceptic, but I recognize we are still a very long way from fully understanding ourselves, and nearly completely ignorant of that mysterious other part of the world that operates all around us, in spite of us, and not because of us.

The red light on the alarm lights up once more in the black. It is like something from a fantasy novel, the crimson eye of a demon approaching me in a tunnel. So I can conclude that the head of the lamprey is definitely intact then, unless a fish has simply swum into my line. One more bleep, but still no full-blooded run. The first hour alone on the canal has been a bit like being buried alive in a coffin, a sensory deprivation chamber that has left my nerves shredded and my wits screaming at me to switch on my torch, but once I committed to denying myself that indulgence my body tapped back into a set of skills deep within us all.

The animals start to creep out of their holes since it has become clear I am not a threat. The featherweight rustles of rodents disturb the leaf litter, those miniature tigers emerging to hunt the night-crawling insects, worms, bugs and spiders, followed up by larger crashes and intermittent barks and moans from the brush behind me. Disturbing, but actually just a family of foxes burrowing their way through the thin wooded strip between this canal and the M1. The fox is one of the great mammals of our time. Adaptive and loathed, just like the eel. I didn't see an urban fox till I first moved to London, and could scarcely reconcile the mange-filled and greying creature before me with the snatched glimpses I had had of the fenland fox, back implausibly arched as it leapt over another fence line and vanished. The mammalian expression of the wild as we know it today is a plucky *Vulpes vulpes* strolling through the Marble Arch with an entire KFC chicken carcass trapped between its teeth.

Every sound is amplified when your eyesight is dimmed. The movement of mammals is thunderous, like pressing your ear to a metallic track as a train approaches, and the rolling fish of the canal resemble a whale breaching right at my toes. I know that can't be, that this is just my body over-compensating for the loss of one of its primary senses and that the still water itself is acting as an amplifier, but it's a compelling idea. This is precisely where monster legends originate from of course: I see an eel and report a Nessie, I hear a tabby cat and report a panther, I smell a badger and report Big Foot.

A large rat slips into the canal and sends shockwaves out across the water's surface. They detonate on the brickwork bank like a bouncing bomb so I use a finger-tip to check the line is still running under tension to the bait. I can feel the pulse of my heart and the gentle give and take of the water. All is in place still. The torch stays off, the baits remain out, and I keep still.

Another hour passes and I realize my eyesight has not departed me: it has just taken longer than my other senses to come to the party. As brain and eye eventually pull together I am prised from the blanket of pure dark-ness and into the multi-textured world of the colour black. Against the bushes on my bank the coal black is so uniform it lends the whole scene a one-dimensional effect, as if the bushes are simply the stuck-on backdrop to a shadow puppet theatre, but where the moonlight casts a silver-tipped black on the scene my adjusted eye is able to pick out textures: the outline of the branches, the frame of a crow's nest, the denser hollows in the shrubbery that taper into a fine inky black at the water's edge.

One of the hollows pierces right through the bush and into a wide field behind. It billows with mist and stirs in a playful candyfloss fashion, as if the whole scene were being whipped up with a giant invisible spoon. A large ancient oak tree stands out proud and solid in the field's centre and its long, loving arms reach out to offer shelter to several dozen sheep. As the traffic on the motorway fades I begin to hear their bleats offering both them and me reassurance. The championship rounds of the night are pulling in. This is real darkness.

My most recent trip to the forests of New Guinea was just one month before. I had been living with a remote forest people known as the Korowai, as part of a series for the BBC. The Korowai are rightfully famed for their abilities as hunter-gatherers but also for their extraordinary houses, built high on stilts, clear of the forest floor, well away from the floods, mosquitoes and white devils that live down there. It was my second trip out in a long-running project that intends to follow their turbulent lives over the course of a year. The old men I befriended requested I bring a lamp on my return. Instantaneous light. After food security, shelter and clothes it is the next thing on the list before money. I lay in that treehouse every night, silently watching as the lamp I had brought was switched on and off, on and off, and on, again.

Having light at the flick of a switch is such a luxury that denying yourself it when you do have it feels quite self-indulgent; however, I know that one press of that button will expunge all I can see now in an instant. It will leave me in a puddle of artificial light with the pitch black waiting just outside the reach of the bulb. It's actually far more frightening than just being in the dark, where I can at least see the shadows. It will take another hour of waiting for my night vision to be restored if I turn on my torch now.

The bleep of the alarm thumps through the night air like a lump hammer through a breezeblock. My soul leaps clear of my body in fright and I have to race it to the far rod, but just as my world is about to conjoin into one clean strike the line, once again, falls dead. I curse the black as my striking hand shakes. I'm being taunted by unseen forces.

I remember from my research that the best of the big-eel fishing is to be had two hours before midnight, and two hours after dawn. I check my watch and note that this last take has happened on the stroke of the witching hour and decide that if nothing happens on the lamprey line in another half an hour then I must reel it in. Having not given the crayfish a single thought prior to nightfall, I have long since convinced myself that the canal is absolutely crawling with them and that they've definitely relieved me of at least one bait. By the time the half-hour is up I've descended further into my own mind and reel in both my lines, fully expecting to find them utterly barren at the hands of the thieving crustacean.

The baits on both are unmolested. It was the wrong call. I re-bait and re-cast, but I suspect I may well have blown it now.

After 1 a.m. there is a palpable shift in atmosphere. It feels like someone has drawn a shroud over the entire canal, that a switch has been flicked and all of the life that was, no longer is. The foxes have gone with the rodents, splashes, moths and bats and in their stead the dank smell of the canal fills my nostrils. It is a stagnant aroma, like an old fishtank long after the death of its residents. Even the grass beneath my feet has expelled the last heat from the day now and I begin to feel a creeping chill through the rubber soles of my boots. It is definitely a lot colder and I know the time for catching has passed. My lines hang still and limp, the water makes no noise. I close my eyes and can feel sleep trying to take me.

I don't know if I've got what you need to take up solo night fishing. In my heart I know I'm just not hardcore enough. There have been other times on the bank when I have thought of going home late at night, but I've always eked every last moment of fishing out of an experience, no matter how cold, wet, hungry or uncomfortable I might feel. There is always the chance of that one take which turns around a session, and the list of last-gasp fish I've caught in the dead of night stand as a testament to the lingering angler.

However, it was precisely that 'never say die' attitude that eventually led me into so much trouble as an expedition leader. Sometimes my determination tips over into blind stupidity. There is nothing to catch here now and I know it.

Robert Macfarlane once drew the conclusion that 'those who travel to mountain tops are half in love with themselves, and half in love with oblivion'. The same is probably true of most modern-day adventurers.

By the end of my twenties I had taken things to the point where I had burnt through relationships, jobs, finances and expedition partners with frightening efficiency. My last girlfriend had walked out on me with the epitaph that I had taken my life to the point 'that no one can ever reasonably go with you'. She was right. My myopic desire to confirm my theories thinly masked a burning desire to prove myself. To whom, I'm still not even sure.

I eventually found rock bottom on the jungle-choked river that splits Sierra Leone and Liberia. My hammock was laid in the leaf litter, enveloping me, entombing me, as *Plasmodium falciparum* malaria pumped its way around my bloodstream and into my cerebral cortex.

My parents and close friends had all been to great lengths to vocalize their fears for my well-being throughout that decade. I remembered then how Grandad had been the only person who said I would be all right, but years later Grandma told me that he too was terrified. He just hadn't wanted to say it to my face.

I fished much less through that decade, but Grandad had persevered in going out to the bank. He started missing takes as he moved into his mid-eighties and all too soon his eyesight began to seriously trouble him. However, he did manage to snare another giant eel from Popham's Eau. Later he reported back to me how his line had been halfway across the river before he had even noticed the float was missing. It became a serious worry for us all. He was slowing down on a big river that was no place for an old man to fish alone. Dad was convinced he would fall in and drown one day, but he absolutely would not be stopped.

The last time we fished Popham's Eau together he fell three times, once on the way to the bank and twice on the way home. The final time he fell I remember shouldering his great weight and how he had looked at me with these great sad brown eyes that I had never seen on him before. The legendary Irish boxer Barry McGuigan, a man whom I knew Grandad admired, once remarked how '*boxers* are the *first to know* when to quit and the *last to admit it*'. That was the moment we both knew the game was up. Wordlessly I carried on home, and didn't speak a word about what had happened to anyone, least of all to Grandad. He never returned to Popham's Eau, and I never wanted to see the place again either.

Grandad, the greatest of all the great eels in my life, was sliding towards the abyss of the Sargasso, having lived a fantastic and full life. Whereas I was simply at risk of ending mine prematurely, an adolescent elver who had chosen a stupidly dangerous path that would consume him without hesitation unless something changed.

I crawled out of the West African forest on my hands and knees and came home. With little idea of what I would do next I quit solo expeditions and moved in with Anna and her boyfriend, James, back in the Fens, back where I needed to be. I picked up my rods and started fishing again, targeting the only fish I could remember how to.

It was while carp fishing that I found eels again. The familiar tap-tap-tap and back-winding resistance in the fight, the struggle to net and unhook, were throwbacks to times past, but for the first time in my angling life I felt the utter euphoria of being covered in their slime. The eel was back and now so was I.

A spring of clear water had opened up ahead of me as I pulled into my thirties. It was leading me towards the coast and I knew what I needed to do.

I pick the reel off the rests and wind both rods in. I don't need to be like this any more. I shouldn't have allowed the old selfish me to bring Emma out here but I'm so grateful to the eel for the lesson. Everyone is allowed a relapse.

We made it to Anna and James's wedding the very next afternoon and I don't believe I smelt too bad. Maybe I had had a chance on the canal that night, but I doubted I would ever return to test the theory.

The Great Game

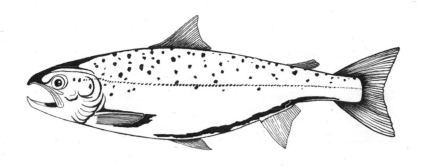

Home is a trial, domestic chores a torment, life
is dust and ashes until you take up a fishing rod.
Wales was my answer to this problem.
Paul Boote and Jeremy Wade, *Somewhere
Down the Crazy River* (1992)

I never really liked autumn when I was a child. It was
always a tense time. The year was running out, the
fishing was getting harder, and September always meant
back to school.

When I was inside, staring at the white iron bars that
framed the school radiators, I used to wonder what on
earth had just happened to August. It was the only
month of the year when we weren't interned for at least

some of the time in classrooms and when it started it felt like it would go on for ever. Then the last Bank Holiday weekend would flash past and I was back here, locked in until Christmas with only the prospect of a few fireworks in November to get me through.

I felt the days shorten with quiet inevitability; nature's way of telling us that our time on earth is limited, another circuit around the sun. I would blow hot air onto my chilly fingers, stare at those radiators, and feel a sense of real disquiet.

These days I feel neither the sense of desperation to catch nor the feeling of entrapment of autumns past. The river crackles with tension, and the fish can feed exceptionally hard during this period if you can get a break in the weather. After a long, late summer, and the blank night with the eel, I started to catch really well again. For two nights running I ended up in the water in my pants: the first instance was on a remote Forestry Commission lake where a robust, double-figure wild carp snagged me up in a rotting bed of lilies, and I had to fetch it, and the second was a tussle with a big barbel which ran my line into a rocky snare and refused to lift its head until I had made my way downstream of its lie. I fished the magisterial River Wye with Dad, getting him onto his first big brace of chub, as happy for him as if I had caught the fish myself, and landed a pair of picture-perfect grayling trotting a fat float loaded with maggots through fast water above Cardiff.

My slate is wiped clean in August and it has long since

become my second spring, responsible for delivering me more fresh starts than any other time of the year; and some of the biggest fish of my life.

The week after I had wrestled with my first eel for twenty years my life took a major turn. I had been visiting my friend, and occasional boss, Steve at his cottage down on the Gower coast in South Wales. We had supposed to go on a fishing trip, but, having nearly lost the family car in the turning tides around Port Eynon, we wisely decided to call it a day. I thought that was pretty much it in terms of the weekend's dramas, but then he slid a large manila envelope my way across his garden table.

In it was a thick document with a colourful picture of a mask-wearing man stood waist deep in azure blue seas on the cover. The photo caption told me this was an indigenous shark caller from the island of New Britain in Papua New Guinea, and the title told me this was a pitching document for a new BBC series.

While I had been embroiled in my existential (and malarial) crisis in Sierra Leone, Steve, who runs an independent documentary company in Cardiff, together with my director friends Jamie and Will, had pitched me as a presenter to BBC Two. *Hunters of the South Seas* was set in the South Pacific and would see me live cheek by jowl with the last subsistence hunter-gatherers of the sea. Sensationally, BBC Two had agreed to let us all make it together.

'Is this for real, mate?' I asked nervously. He laughed,

and forced a beer into my hand. Not one season after I had quit expeditions, and just two years after I had sworn I would never work another day in the world of television, I was sat, in Cardiff, penning my name against a primetime project. After a decade of juggling my careers in both adventure and television it seemed the hand of fate had finally found a way of meeting my passions in the middle. I couldn't have been happier.

Well, actually, I probably could have. I needed to move back to Cardiff immediately to start researching potential communities and locations, and, in my haste to get settled, I signed for quite possibly the loneliest single man's flat in history.

The hallway was unlit, the windows were cracked, and every appliance, from the fridge to the oven, had a major fault. When I flicked on the lights for my first evening alone the switch simply crumbled backwards into a giant cavity in the wall. I called the landlord immediately but found his mobile to be strangely 'out of service' since the rapid collection of my deposit and non-refundable two months' advance rent.

Fishing provided a release. My new place was in a supposedly rough part of town known as Riverside, but if you can look beyond the concrete, graffiti and grit, there was a wonderful stretch of the River Taff to discover.

The Taff flows for just forty-five miles from its high source in the Brecon Beacons to the sea at Cardiff's Tiger Bay. It is one of the steepest and shortest descents of any river in Wales but it packs in the features along its length. There's world-class trout fishing in its upper reaches and some of the biggest chub and barbel in Britain towards its mouth, but hardly anyone ever seems to fish it.

I had lived in Cardiff for a couple of years before but had only thought to fish the Taff once. I found it a difficult and wild river, met at a time when I was interested in neither. I caught one stringy roach and turned my gaze back to the carp ponds, but now I was back, and, living alone, it felt like the time was right to give the river more effort.

The Taff was nothing like the rivers and drains of the Fens. My home waters were slow and sluggish, man-made receptors used to keep the fields from sinking under water. The Creek was almost completely static and the only times the big drains ever moved were if someone had cranked open the sluice gates at Denver. The Taff stirred under its own immense gravitational pull. When it rained on the hills the water would flow with a rabid intention towards the coasts, swelling and raging with an angry brown foam that boiled with litter, streamer weed and sometimes even entire trees.

Thinking I could rock up and fish this river effectively because I had experience in the Fens was like believing I could look after a wild wolf because I had once owned an Airedale terrier. It took many weeks just to learn the basics, and months more before I would even come close to catching a reasonable fish.

The first lesson was that using the same tackle and tactics every day was a definite no-no. Different fish came on in different conditions, and the River Taff was a living, breathing ecosystem that changed its moods continually. Sometimes you would need a heavy single bait rolling along the deck and other days you could get away with light float tackle and a steady trickle of grubs. There were days you could wade out across crystal-clear waters and trundle a bait right along the middle of the river, and others when one misplaced foot would see you swept to the north coast of Somerset. Through trial and error I eventually discovered there was nearly always somewhere you could cast a line, though, and, in spite of the Taff's reputation for being devoid of life after decades of industrial punishment, I found there were some fantastic fish just waiting to be caught.

I can pinpoint the precise moment fishing the Taff became more than just a distraction from my hovel of a flat. It was early autumn, but the river's water was still warm and I was able to wade in barefoot. I cast a large golden spinner towards a weeping willow tree on the far bank. My mind was utterly blank, locked in the trance-like state that only spinning produces, when an explosion, something like a silvery pipe-bomb, bowed my rod and electro-shocked my soul.

I heard it once said by a crinkly old angler that just as a watched kettle never boils, an over-considered fish never bites. I didn't even realize there were salmon in the Taff, but by the time my brain had processed the cause of the assault the fish had thrown the hook and vanished. I cast again, and again, and again, till my arms ached and darkness fell all around me, but I couldn't seem to raise the fish for another round.

It was a big salmon, of that I was in no doubt: returned from the sea to spawn and recovering its strength somewhere out in a hidden hole just off the main flow. My spinner had invaded its personal space. It hadn't snapped at my spinner to feed on it, like a pike or a perch might – the take had been violent, GBH on the line. I just hadn't been prepared.

I was back every night through that season but the salmon proved to be exceptionally elusive. My lack of success wasn't down to an absence of fish: every time the river rose a conveyor belt of fresh sea-run salmon moved upstream and into the holes outside the city park. I knew they were there because they always declared their position in the last hour of light, leaping clean of the river and flaying their silver sides with water. Perhaps it was just an effort to blast irritating sea lice from their bodies, but it was hard not to feel like I was being ridiculed.

Carp fishing had made me soft. After weeks of effort my fingers and thumbs had blistered and calloused into layers of hardened skin on my casting hand. I hadn't wanted to catch a fish this badly since the winter of '92 and that first pike. This was way beyond a simple distraction now. I had to catch that fish.

*

The American humorist Ian Frazier noted how 'casting for steelhead is like calling God on the telephone, and it rings and rings and rings, hundreds of rings, a thousand rings, and you listen to each ring as if an answer might come at any moment, but no answer comes, and no answer comes, and then on the 1,001st ring, or the 1,047th ring, God loses his patience and picks up the phone and yells, "WHAT THE HELL ARE YOU CALLING ME FOR?" in a voice the size of the canyon.'

It took me until the final week of the game-fishing season to finally make the salmon's acquaintance. The trees had turned a golden brown and the horse chestnuts had swelled and dropped their load, but my reel roared forward once again. I was up to my knees in water, my rod bowed to the river king.

The take had come from nowhere. Salmon have this ability to materialize, not like eels from the mud, but like some shape-shifting spirit blessed with the ability to metamorphosize from mineral to animal at will. The salmon may happily take the form of a rock for hours, even days, before deciding to emerge as a mighty fish and collide with your world with all the brute force of an articulated lorry meeting a wall.

On a city canal you will be noticed – runners have to go around you and pedestrians will take a passing interest in you as a curio – but in a big city river anglers are absorbed within its width like just another shopping trolley or abandoned car. As I fought tooth and nail with the fish the urban world swirled all around me like flakes in a snow-globe. A family chatted above the banks, a man threw a dog a stick, an ambulance screamed over a distant bridge and no one noticed my salmon pounding the rod and rocking the world beneath my feet. It isn't that city folk don't care, they just don't believe in their wildlife.

Eventually I beached the fish and placed my hands across its sides. When you have to wait for something you really want, and have fantasized about it each day to such an extent that you feel like you must have experienced it in a previous life, sometimes when it happens for real it can all feel a little anticlimactic, that the thrill of the chase was truly greater than the capture itself. That was never the case with my first salmon: it was like I had been trapped in a dream where I had been reaching and reaching for something that I could almost touch, only for it to slip from my grasp at the last moment, but here, now, I had woken to discover the very object of my desires had been lying in my hands all along.

The fish was beautiful. I cradled it in my arms and took in its thickened, muscular body, its dark, paddle-like tail and its kype, an elongated and upturned lower jaw that resembles the tip of a billhook. It was a mature male fish, a 'cock', but it wasn't the brilliant silver of an adult salmon just hours out of the sea. It had quite some colour to it: a hood of brown along its top and black spots that met with a dark silvery side. I had almost mistaken it for a giant brown trout at first glance.

Its smoked appearance was a sure sign that this fish

had spent some weeks waiting to move upstream. I didn't mind that at all. I was new to the salmon game and immune to the strange angler's belief that a fish progressively loses its value with each day spent away from salt water. This was my fish, my first salmon, and I gripped it tenderly as it recovered in the shallows.

My friend Fred had been with me that day and took a couple of pictures on his phone, and so it was, later that evening, that I was able to post the picture on Facebook and change the trajectory of my life for the second time that season.

As was standard with my Facebook friends the typical commentary sidestepped the magnificence of the fish and focused entirely on some irrelevant detail, in this case the shortness of the pair of shorts I was wearing, but the picture did catch the eye of a girl I had long admired but hadn't dared approach.

Emma and I had been friends since we worked together the last time I lived in the city. She was beautiful, smart and funny, and lived in the most delightful pool imaginable. But it was an impossibly difficult cast away, tangled right up in the complex branches of other relationships with far cooler guys who probably thought fishing was for nerds. I didn't think I stood a chance.

She messaged me saying it was good to see that I was back in Cardiff, and that the fish was pretty great, but advising me I needed to purchase some new shorts. Then she asked me out for a drink. I overcast my finest lure right into the trees in my excitement to reply. Far too much punctuation and an over-liberal use of the caps lock button made me appear more than a little desperate in my message, and then I foolishly gushed: 'I live in a right dump in Riverside these days so any excuse to get out of the flat is gratefully received.'

Incredibly, she considered my lure anyway. I mean, it was my finest, after all.

Sixty-five years earlier the life of a young man with a shock of black hair was slowing to a standstill. The other figures grinding and spinning in the dance hall were blending gently into the background, leaving behind just one striking, confident young lady.

Ken Millard was aware that this was like a moment in a romantic film, so it was possible it couldn't actually be real. He straightened his tie, turned to his mates, and announced: 'That's the girl I'm going to marry.'

Dad recently found Grandad's diary from that year. It was a small, pocket-sized book with a black leather cover that detailed his everyday comings and goings. He was hardly going to pour his emotions into his prose, Grandad wasn't that kind of man, but it was clear the shift in his behaviour after he met Grandma was seismic. The heavy-drinking, rugby-playing, cinema-going dance hall wag all but disappeared overnight, to be replaced by a man wholly and fully dedicated to his new relationship.

Nadine. He wrote her name in excitable large lettering with a dramatic use of space on the page; hers was a name that mattered. He eased right off the fishing as the diary filled up with the details of their various dates and trips out on his motorcycle. This was more than just a man in love; Grandad had found a new way of life through Grandma and it was obvious he was fantastically happy.

Grandma squeezed a teabag with her fingers and topped up my mug with a more than generous measure of milk. 'I had lost my previous boyfriend in World War Two. He was a pilot returning to the airbase near Ripon when his aircraft became lost up in the mist on the Yorkshire Moors. I found out about the accident through the matron; it was all in the papers before anyone had told me. She just asked: "Have you read the news?"' Grandma placed my tea on her coffee table. She still had the newspaper clipping somewhere, she said. Grandma was extraordinarily resilient. Years passed, the pain eased, and then Grandad swept her off her feet in the dance hall.

'They were wonderful times,' she smiled.

I had seen pictures of Grandma when she was young. She had striking dark hair, hazel eyes and an impish grin that stuck with her for life. 'I was training to be a nurse and living in the nurses' lodgings. The girls would all watch for him out of the window and shout: "He's here!" Then in he would sweep on his bike with his long coat and black helmet. I would wear a canary-yellow swimming cap, just in case any rain would spoil my hair, and off we would go on all kinds of adventures.'

Grandad's trips out with Grandma became fewer and

further between as their relationship became increasingly more serious. They were saving coins for the day Grandad could write in his diary with the biggest letters he dared: 'Got Engaged!'

They were soon married, but it was fair to say that some members of Grandma's family were unsure about the suitability of my grandad for her hand. He was considered a coarse fish, as well as a coarse fisherman.

For 200 years fishing books had been written with a wonderful breadth and simplicity: no class divide, no alienating language, no suggestion of a hierarchy of rank, just the idea that angling involved a set of skills that anyone could learn to catch all species of fish. There were no discernible divisions in angling literature, and as a result very few obvious divisions in angling.

Things changed dramatically with the arrival of the twentieth century. As the fishing author Jack Hargreaves notes: 'The salmon and trout were raised to piscine peerage and the rest were called by the new name of "coarse fish". By the years between the wars the assumption that gentlemen went fly-fishing while ordinary men confined themselves to cork and quill was so well established that nobody would have believed the idea to be scarcely more than a generation old. The two tribes developed their separate private mysteries, and fishing books were pretty well divided into two classes – *Where My Fly Has Fallen* (cream-laid in handsome boards), and *Gentles and Groundbait* (paperbacked).'

The prevailing wisdom dictated that 'coarse' fish were rougher, dirtier and easier to catch, to be targeted by the great unwashed public using their crude tactics, whereas the 'game' fish, by contrast, were much more exclusive. It all came down to little more than the presence of a small rayless fin found behind the dorsal. This, the 'adipose' fin, carried the weight of an elitist fantasy on its fleshy form, marking these fish, the salmon, the sea trout, the grayling, as the target of the more distinguished sportsmen. The sheer volume of writing since the world wars has only served to progress this prejudice. Quite honestly, I can count on one hand how many recent fishing books care to mention the fallacy behind the origins of the 'coarse' and 'game' classification. An utterly standard reading occurs in the opening pages of Jeremy Paxman's *Fish, Fishing and the Meaning of Life*, where he highlights the sense of superiority of 'the grander British rivers and clubs' in describing the game fish as 'wilder, freer and harder to catch', before touting 'fly fishing' as the advanced version of the sport because it is 'more dainty, more predicated upon observation of the natural world, requiring greater precision and skill'. Warming to his theme Paxman concludes: 'The numinous properties of fly fishing are held to embody some Platonic ideal of fishing.'

Paxman, I believe, must have his tongue slightly in his cheek, but, really, the 'Platonic ideal of fishing'? As any serious angler of any discipline will tell you, there is just as much skill and precision required in any aspect of fishing you choose to master. The lure anglers who can flick their trap to within an inch of an overhanging branch have equivalent finesse to the fly casters who can drop a fly on a handkerchief; the pole fishermen, who tie their rig to such a level of precision that it becomes virtually invisible to its quarry, pay the same attention to detail as the fastidious fly tier; and the trotting specialists, who can weave their float perfectly around obstacles and catch fish from a hundred feet away, utilize the same watercraft as the very best of the crack fly-anglers. In actuality, I have yet to meet any successful angler, of any discipline, who has not spent some several thousand hours reading the water and learning to interpret the habits and routines of whichever fish they hope to trap. As far as I can tell this game vs coarse snobbery is designed to catch the fisherman and not the fish: a carefully crafted sales pitch to boost egos and lighten wallets, as, make absolutely no mistake, when it comes to freshwater angling there is no division of the sport that can end up costing you more money than a few weeks on the fly.

Fish don't recognize the size of your bank balance; nor do they care who you are or where you're from, a fact borne out by the vast numbers of celebrities who go fishing precisely to feel a sense of anonymity. Just as game fishing does indeed attract a high percentage of the more well-heeled members of society, there is nothing to stop that very same class of person enjoying an afternoon drowning maggots down the local carp pond.

Equally, for every salmon fisher dropping a rapper's bankroll on a helicopter fishing trip to Russia's Kamchatka peninsula, or a weekend fishing the Junction pool at Kelso, there are hundreds more catching salmon on cheap season tickets up and down the country, especially on urban rivers like the Clyde and my own Taff in Wales. We are all equal before the fish and yet this sense of a divide has successfully bored its way deep into our collective angling consciousness. It serves to do our sport absolutely no favours.

Of course, I was immune to all this nonsense as a child. I just did whatever Grandad told me to do, and as the only exposure I had to angling literature was the inclusively penned Wilson *Encyclopedia*, I had no reason to suspect there was any sort of divide in the sport. Age and experience narrow the mind. It wasn't long into my teenage years when I began to notice a divide between 'us and them'. None of the magazines I ever bought (*Angler's Mail*, *Angling Times*, *Improve Your Coarse Fishing*, *Carp Talk*, etc.) ever mentioned fly-fishing, and when I did eventually locate the game-fishing publications I discovered they were in a different part of the newsagent's altogether, apparently more comfortable rubbing shoulders with copies of *Tatler* and *Horse and Hound* than they were *Auto Trader* and *Guns and Ammo*.

Against my better judgement I began to buy into the prejudice. Fly-fishing and fly-fishermen really were fundamentally different to Grandad and me and, as we had no real chance to fly-fish in the Fens anyway, it wasn't exactly hard to buy in to the idea. On the one occasion we did actually try it, during a family holiday to Scotland, it became pretty clear that we were both spectacularly awful at it anyway, and when you've spent most of your life getting good at one particular aspect of fishing it is extremely hard to go back to being terrible again. To our great discredit, the fly rods were quickly binned.

My dad, however, did have what it took to stick at it. His work had mostly kept him away from the bank with Grandad and me, but fishing wasn't really his thing when I was a child anyway. By the time I was able to take myself fishing Dad had extended his hobbies beyond birdwatching and butterfly collecting to include scuba diving, a sport where he really could enter the fishes' world and examine them at first hand. He loved to dive, and gave me a great many tips on finding fish, particularly the specific sorts of structure favoured by the perch, but around the same time my carp fishing was at its peak he had been forced to hang up his tanks. A fish-shaped void was left behind, and given he had recently moved north to the trout rivers of the Yorkshire Dales, it made sense that he finally learnt how to fly-fish properly.

Fly-fishing made sense to Dad. He understood a lot more than most about the trout's invertebrate prey, and there was something about the surgical accuracy of the cast and meticulous preparation of the artificial fly that I think appealed to his diligence as a doctor, but the fact that game fishing was never taken seriously by Grandad would definitely have appealed too. Grandad was impossible to beat at any of the sports he played or followed. Even if you weren't interested in having a competition with him, from dominoes to bowls, to rugby union and Test match cricket, or the FA cup draw on the television, you could not avoid being dragged into some sort of gentleman's wager, which he would, with unerring inevitability, win.

Dad had tried to distinguish himself before. Grandma once told me he had taken up table tennis at school purely because it was a sport Grandad didn't play. Grandad, who was also in the room at the time, laughed so hard that you could see his great golden molars shaking in their root canals, before regaling us both with a protracted and highly detailed story of a table tennis triumph that had seen him smoke the entire opposition in a county-wide Bedfordshire tournament. Grandad had, at least, the self-awareness not to let on to his teenage son about his latent talents at the time. Fly-fishing, though, was something he had genuinely shied away from. I am certain if I had ever pressed him for a reason he would have trotted out the idea of fly-fishing being a sport for a certain type of person, from a certain type of background, but I knew from our Scotland trip that in reality Grandad simply wasn't very good at it. In our family, Dad became the master of the fly.

It feels right to me to have the salmon making its appearance in these pages after the eel. Both of them are undeniably magnificent travellers, but, I'm afraid to say, in terms of raw underdog spirit the eel has to trump the salmon. However, the eel will simply never move people in the same way as the salmon. The 'King of Fish' has achieved an enduring status in our collective imaginations, spawning hundreds of pieces of literature and featuring in innumerable documentaries, films, poems and folk stories. There is scarcely another freshwater creature on earth that has had such an impact on world culture: the salmon, quite simply, is one of the most instantly recognizable and well-known fish that ever there was.

Most have heard of the legendary Pacific salmon run of North America, where millions of returning chum, pink, chinook and coho salmon come back from the sea to spawn in salmon 'redds', those small nests dug by female fish into pebbly patches of gravel; but few realize this mass replenishment of salmon numbers also feeds thousands of bears, wolves and birds, and that, in death, the release of nitrogen from the salmon's rotting body is so great that it sustains some 12,000 square miles of Canada's Great Bear Forest. Indeed, in the peak years of the run, when numbers of salmon are at their highest, scientists have found spruce trees where 80 per cent of their nitrogen is provided by the fish alone.

In the UK, if you head to a weir on any of our Atlantic salmon rivers in early autumn, you stand a very good chance of experiencing the seminal salmonoid event of our own returning running fish. It was this season at the

Blackweir on the River Taff where it last happened for me, and, although it might have lacked the sheer strength in numbers of a Pacific run, at least the action didn't take place deep in some montane wilderness; in fact I was staring at the turbulent waters on the corner of Bute Park with a mother and child, a city boy in a suit, a cyclist in lycra and a man in a turban.

Such is the wonder of urban wildlife. We were bound not by action on a silver screen taking place hundreds of miles from home, but by the silvery flash we all witnessed just minutes from our own doors and offices. The salmon's task was formidable, seemingly impossible, but this fish had already fought ridiculous odds just to make it back here. It leapt forward and we started to cheer.

Attacking the fast water head on it slid down the weir's face again and again. We counted over a dozen fails. The Blackweir is a horrible obstacle, a steep tongue of smoothened concrete, a hangover from an age when we needed to harness our waters for industrial production, and with the river nearly in spate the sheer volume of water spilling down the ramp threatened to utterly overwhelm this fish.

Surely the salmon was running out of steam on its umpteenth attempt? Human naivety. The fish had simply been plotting its course, working out the weaknesses, the faults and lines of least resistance. With each move calculated and carefully tested, it was time for the final push.

Once more it emerged and our excitement threatened to overspill. Fists, palms and brollies belted the iron bridge we had gathered upon. A mighty leap brought a skittering zig-zag run that closed the distance to the top lip of the weir. An arching sweep, so uniform it could've been drawn with a compass, placed our fish directly below the top pool, and a simple dip and flick of the tail propelled it neatly up and over the lip. Noiselessly it continued into the next stage of its life. We let out a collective sigh of relief and drifted our separate ways.

As Michael Wigan describes in his 2013 book *The Salmon*, both the Pacific and Atlantic salmon are facing multi-pronged threats today. Man's lack of foresight in the construction of weirs and, in particular, monstrous dams, as well as unregulated salmon netting, poaching, pollution, and the same manmade climate change that thwarts the eel's navigation, is overpowering the salmon species. On the West Coast of the States, the *Scientific American* claims, salmon numbers are down by as much as 99.9 per cent since European settlement began, and, industrial pollution had all but wiped out the salmon on Britain's Taff, Tyne and Clyde rivers by the 1980s. If you thought that farming salmon in pens might provide an easy solution to the industrial-scale harvest of the wild population, then I am afraid the unfortunate plague of parasitic sea lice released as a by-product of that practice has put paid to that. In 2012 the Royal Society estimated that a shocking 39 per cent of wild Atlantic salmon were dying from this parasite alone. They simply attach themselves to the wild fish as they pass the pens, tear into their flesh, and slaughter them in their thousands.

It might seem yet another boorish example of man's commercial ambition trumping that of a lowly fish, but it is worth bearing in mind that the value of recreational salmon fishing to the economy is hardly chump change. In Canada every single freshwater rod-caught salmon is estimated to be worth over £700, and in Scotland salmon fishing represents almost 3,000 local jobs and generates some £120 million a year. Big money by any marker, but when you also consider that salmon fishing is taking place in some of the most remote and rural areas on earth, where money and secure local employment are increasingly hard to come by, then the value of this fish really cannot be overstated. For many, salmon fishing is a vital lifeline in a world of diminishing opportunities.

Without question, commercial salmon harvesting and intensive salmon farming practices need to be curbed and regulated. New dams and weirs should have fish ladders built into their designs as a mandatory part of any construction agreement, or, better yet, they should be torn down altogether. The United States has dismantled over 150 dams since the turn of the century, to no small benefit for the salmon, and on my home river the simple acts of deconstructing weirs and thoughtful restocking have made the Taff salmon the most resurgent population in England and Wales put together. The banks of Scotland's River Tweed, which contains the largest salmon population in Europe, have been protected from cattle and sheep overgrazing by fencing along the river's length. This has allowed the river to mature more naturally and has resulted in some of the largest catch returns in recent history. Even in the absolute worst-case scenarios nature has an unerring way of filling a vacuum when it is given the chance. In my lifetime the salmon of both the Tyne and the Clyde have also made a comeback on rivers that were salmon-free deserts in their industrial heyday.

Having hatched and successfully completed the transformation from small salmon parr to finger-sized salmon smolt (a feat that is only achieved by one fish in every ten), the young fish then enters salt water for the first time. Here it must avoid a phalanx of marine predators, everything from grey seals to skates, sharks and seabirds, while making its way north to the great pelagic feeding grounds off Greenland and the Faroe Islands. If the smolt successfully runs the 3,000-kilometre gauntlet, without being killed, then it can expect to seriously pile on the pounds. Protein banquets of shrimps, sand eels, fish fry and krill funnel into the extreme parts of the northern Atlantic, allowing the salmon to fatten up over a period of up to four years. They can reach weights in excess of 50lb, several hundred times bigger than their size on leaving the rivers, but eventually a hormonal release will call them back across the ocean. All the way home to the very rivers that once gave them life.

Scientists believe that the remarkable journey could

involve a mix of celestial navigation, magnetic fields, ocean currents and even chemical memory. Some salmon have even been known to locate the precise pool they were birthed in. Truly extraordinary behaviour that is without parallel in the animal kingdom; just last week I couldn't even find my way back to a house I'd lived in for over a year.

The sheer bloody-mindedness of the breeding salmon cannot be underestimated. Not only will they surmount all manner of obstacles to achieve their goal, but once they return to fresh water they will not eat another thing. The homecoming adult salmon is entirely reliant on the seafood reserves it built up in the north, so much so that the stomach actually begins to disintegrate to allow the fish to pack in more eggs or sperm for breeding. The suicide pact has been made: from that point on it's breed and die. Which prompts the question: if they don't feed, just how do you convince them to take a bait?

Wilson comments in the *Encyclopedia* that a salmon 'instinctively' snaps at 'worms, spinners and particularly shrimps', but when it comes to the purist, tactics begin and end with the artificial fly.

There is a blistering array of painstakingly designed and hand-tied flies, crafted from natural furs, silks and cottons to imitate everything from tiny nymphs right up to palm-sized baitfish, but, whatever you choose, fly-fishing is unique in that the weight of the cast comes from your line and not your end tackle. It means your chance of catching a fish of any description relies heavily on your ability to cast well.

The perfect fly cast begins with you gradually releasing line from a reel while making false casts overhead, extending the line, and your fly, out across the river incrementally, without ever losing a metronomic rhythm to your casting arm. Sounds hard, but all being well, you release your line in the final cast and watch it unfurl like the striking arm of a darts player, hitting a bull's-eye on the far bank and sweeping your fly upstream towards the fish in a single, beautiful arc.

In other forms of fishing you may well be able to glean a lot from the armchair, but the fly cast is so much more about 'the feel' than it is about careful study. The best fly casters I've ever met struggle to articulate what makes them so good at the sport: they sort of stammer through a few platitudes, and might even offer to cradle your arms from behind as you try, but it never really works. The fact is that, much like throwing a dart at a board, when you are learning to cast and finally get it right, it feels so fluid and natural that you will wonder just how you managed to get it so badly wrong for the previous 4,000 attempts. That's the thing with fly-fishing. It feels utterly improbable, from the weird casting technique to the fact that you are trying to convince a fish that a piece of fluff is worth having, but when it all comes together, the thrill is almost without parallel in angling.

I could cast well enough on a short rod and had spent some time fly-fishing with Dad on several occasions. My best trout on the fly might have been a 6lb humpbacked Franken-fish from a stocked pond, but I had experienced what it was like to 'get it right' on a river on a couple of occasions. An evening fly-fishing above the town bridge at Pontypridd allowed me to borrow the feeling of what it must be like to actually be quite good at fly-fishing, when your cast and choice of fly come together at just the time the fish really decide to feed en masse, and earlier that same season, while I was flicking a fly armed with a small golden bead, a large brown trout had done me a huge favour from deep within a concrete pipe nestled in front of Merthyr Tydfil's central bus station. In both instances I had been fishing under the wing of truly skilled operators, though, lifelong fly-fishermen who instinctively knew the habits of the trout. When it came to casting for salmon I was completely in the dark.

Bill Currie notes in *Days and Nights of Game Fishing* that 'trout fishing is much more reasonable, more logical and in every way a more delicate art . . . It would perhaps be better if I gave no explanation for wanting so much to fish for salmon.' Although trout fishing might sometimes be very hard, at least you know the fish must eventually come on to feed. Salmon fishing is absolutely ridiculous from the outset, so when Dad called to invite me onto his annual trip to Scotland, that gave me pause for thought, but, then, I've never turned down a fishing trip, so . . .

There are over 300 salmon rivers to discover in Scotland and my dad, alongside a small group of his fly-fishing friends, had visited a fair few of the most legendary rivers. Lately, however, they had gone fairly static at one location, the River Findhorn, where, if they were to be believed, they had discovered something of a sweet spot, at which the quality of fishing, natural surroundings and après-fishing verged on perfection.

My salmon from the Taff was caught on coarse tactics, and although I was mightily pleased with the capture, I had to admit I was curious to try and catch one as a purist would. More than anything, though, I wanted to learn why my dad was so enthused about salmon fishing in particular. Whatever it was, it went far beyond an adolescent desire to find something other than table tennis that Grandad couldn't do; the way he spoke of the Findhorn was as if he had had some sort of a spiritual awakening. Believe me, from a man armed with the brand of analytical mind that my dad had it was quite something to hear.

For the last couple of years he had returned from the Findhorn with beautiful stories and pictures, and although he would be the first to admit that salmon fishing could never fill the void in his life left by scuba diving, it was clear that in the Findhorn he had found something which ran it pretty close.

With no spinning tackle, no coarse tactics – in fact, no rod, line or tackle to call my own – I hopped into the van and began the very long journey towards salmon fishing's tweed-covered heart. I considered the chances of a record-breaking salmon as I made my way north.

Wilson notes the salmon-fishing record stands at a whopping 64lb, but this entry in the *Encyclopedia* does little to conjure up any of the sentiment or the story behind this remarkable fish or the woman who landed it.

Etched into my memory is a faded sepia image of Miss Georgina Ballantine. She is wearing all tweed, a wrap-round jacket partnered with a long woollen skirt, and is leaning up against her rods with what might appear to be a practised nonchalance. Her spare hand is casually placed in a pocket, but her expression, the slight angle inwards of her head, her lips, pressed together but almost upturned, in something of a Mona Lisa smile, seem to me to be screaming: 'Go on then, lads, come and have a go if you think you're hard enough.' Lying on the floor, just in front of her, is the longest-standing record in British angling history.

The image was taken on 7 October 1922, the date she landed the 64lb fish from the Glendelvine stretch of the River Tay. Georgina was simply the gillie's daughter, drafted into the trip at short notice as the local laird had pulled out with a headache, but that trip was to be life-changing.

She later gave a wonderful account of the fish's capture in a letter to her rod builder and friend, Mick Glover, in which she describes the 'Homeric battle', where her reel 'screeched as it had never screeched before', and mentions how at one stage she became so desperate she suggested pelting the fish with stones to get it to move closer to her boat. Her father, one of the finest rods in

Scotland, gave her a stiff rebuke: 'Na, na, will try nane o' thae capers.'

After two hours and five minutes she finally landed the fish, feverishly recalling: 'What eloquence could do justice to such a moment in one's life, better left to be imagined ... two hours and five minutes of nerve-wracking anxiety, thrilling excitement and good stiff work.' Her arms were so swollen afterwards that they took two weeks to recover.

Of all the things written about this fish, Bruce Sandison, a writer and longtime contributor to *Trout and Salmon* and *The Scotsman*, reveals perhaps the most telling story of the woman. 'When Georgina's salmon was displayed in the window of P. D. Malloch's shop in Perth, she stood at the back of the crowd who had gathered to admire it. Two elderly men were particularly overawed by the size of the salmon and Georgina heard them talking: one said to the other, "A woman? Nae woman ever took a fish like that oot of the water, mon. I would need a horse, a block and tackle, tae tak a fish like that oot. A woman. That's a lee anyway." She said, "I had a quiet chuckle up my sleeve and ran to catch the bus."'

How cool is she? What strength of character! What modesty! What reticence and patience, in the face of such intolerance. Female anglers are just as good as men – many are far better – yet fewer than a quarter of licences purchased each year are bought by women, and I can count on one hand the women I see regularly on the banks I fish.

Of course, attitudes have progressed markedly since Georgina's time, but I still believe there is a lingering prejudice that angling is a man's game. This falsehood, based on much the same narrow-minded thinking that led to the game and coarse divide, seems to play to the idea that as fishing requires countless hours in the cold, handling smelly baits, and, very occasionally, smellier fish, it is not something that would be attractive to women. Well, let me be the first to say that if this is all fishing boiled down to then it wouldn't be attractive to me either. I don't actually like having hands and fingernails that stink like the Seven Seas, nor do I enjoy being frozen solid to my fishing seat, and I'm not exactly 'loving it' when a bream or eel decides to coat me in its mucus, but have you ever stopped to consider that perhaps the barrier to more women in the sport, as well as young people and anyone else who might like to try one day, is the appalling job we do of presenting fishing as an appealing way to spend your time? Perhaps instead of allowing the focus to settle on the aspects of fishing that even we don't enjoy, we should be promoting what it is we all love about getting outside with a rod and reel. Better still, take a friend fishing, get them onto a fish, and then see how they feel. More than that, even if fishing is occasionally cold, smelly and boring, who is anyone to tell someone else what they can or can't do, or what they are supposed, or supposed not, to like? I do believe there are some male anglers still out there who place an unhealthy amount of their ego and, dare I say, manhood, on their ability to catch fish. This minority, and they are a minority, might very well be threatened by the idea that a woman could come along and catch a bigger fish than them, but ultimately it is of far greater importance that fishing as a sport is allowed to progress in spite of these Neanderthals and their opinions; the very future of angling could very well depend on it.

Long before I had reached the Scottish Borders I had deduced the chances of me breaking Georgina's British Atlantic salmon record were practically zero. Even if I overlook my novice's knowledge of salmon fishing, and that is a very big 'if' indeed, the Findhorn has never really been a renowned big-fish river. The Scottish crown probably still rests with the Tay, with the very occasional big fish cropping up on the Tweed, but there has been nothing substantiated on any British river that has ever come close to touching that fantastic 1922 fish.

I was easy with that, though: some records are not meant to be broken.

I left my vehicle at Mum and Dad's place in the York-shire Dales so Dad and I could make our way up into Scotland together. We were travelling on a Sunday, which Dad explained was the traditional 'no-fishing day' as it was when all the anglers turned around from the fishing marks, or 'beats'. There really was no rush then, which was fortunate as the A9 above Perth is a treat to savour, or, as Dad put it: 'This is where it starts to get really good.'

The further you press up into Scotland's far north the more you feel you are shedding the trappings of the rest of our densely populated island. It was cold and dry as the snow-dusted Cairngorms loomed large over our car. The hilltops had a scrubby, stripped look to them: iced at their summits, with bilberry, heather and sheep clinging to the slopes. The valleys were cut by clear rivers, the flow hefting hard over clean stones and exposing gravel beds. They looked low. 'Ignore that, just enjoy the scenery,' scolded Dad. It was like being thirteen years old again. We plunged on into a large forest and a trio of plump-looking red deer scattered behind a curtain of Scots pines.

The fishing cottage finally emerged after a final eighteen miles of real wilderness. A classic highland landscape strewn with lochs, lavender, gorse, more pine, larch, and a patch of birch trees with blistering white trunks. The satnav simply read 'road'.

I had it in my head that Dad's trips up here were something of a wilderness survival epic. That the lodgings would be one-roomed, mud-earth-floored, bothy-cum-bunkhouse affairs, where they were probably forced to forage to survive. In fact, the multi-roomed house contained several bathrooms and bedrooms, a large kitchen, an expertly tended garden and no fewer than three boxes of luxury Scottish shortbread awaiting our arrival. Dad's friend Dave had arrived ahead of us and was already in the process of unloading enough rations to last us for several weeks more than required. Dad, misinterpreting my wide-eyed astonishment as one of concern, sought to comfort me: 'Don't worry, Will. We will have food in the pub on at least one of the nights and Nigel will soon be here with his wife's homemade lasagne.' I wondered, seriously, whether I would still fit in my waders at the end of my time in Scotland.

Dave was far and away the most experienced salmon angler I had ever met. He organized the trips to Scotland and had a wealth of knowledge; as such, I hung on his words, and his words weren't that great. 'They took seventy-seven fish last April, a new Findhorn record,' he began positively.

'So where were they when we were here in March?' chirped in Dad with a chuckle.

'Still all at sea,' answered Dave solemnly, 'but the conditions are even worse for us now. We are going to have to work really hard for our fish.'

I couldn't quite believe it; having begun this adventure with it absolutely shelling it down and facing up to flooded rivers, it was now too dry.

'They just can't move. The salmon are either waiting to enter the river or they are stuck in the pools and going into a dormant state.' Dave glanced outside at the crisp weather and clear skies with more than just a furrow in his brow. 'We need two foot of water from somewhere.' Praying for rain in Scotland. I'd seen it all.

At daybreak I shuffled my feet through leaves that crunched as if they had been baked in salt overnight. It hadn't rained but I did have a raging headache. Nigel had arrived after dark, barrelling through the doors with irrepressible energy, his wife's lasagne and a fantastically rural Lincolnshire accent on hand. As is typical on virtually any holiday exclusively for adults, we got over-excited at the prospect of the coming days, overdid it on the wine, and then decided an impromptu blind tasting of all the single malts we had brought with us was a brilliant idea. I had comfortably lost the game to my more experienced company and was now feeling decidedly rough. Luckily, though, the Findhorn was poised to provide perfect distraction. In front of a fishing hut that wouldn't have looked out of place in backwoods Alaska, the river swept my hangover away with all her majesty.

I'm not basing this on any knowledge of course, but the Tweed always sounded a bit twee to me. Prolific for sure, and very pretty, but its Borders location made it all feel a little too accessible and easy. The Findhorn, however, purely by name alone, conjured up images of a craggy and mysterious waterway, a place frequented by trolls and witches, where you might even still find an army of Iron Age Picts, casually barbecuing a deer and entirely unaware that Hadrian's Wall had been turned into a tourist attraction.

In actuality the Findhorn was all of these things and more. It cut a deep cleft in the side of a heavily forested ravine and the size of the stones scattered on the outside of the bend acted as a testament to the sheer violence the river could wreak. The carpet of moss and lichen on practically every tree in view lent the place a magical green hue. It hummed with wildlife, and confident-looking chaffinch and robin took scraps of bread practically from our fingertips. I sipped at a fortifying cup of tea and noted a community of toads swirling in the pools below my feet. Further down, mustelid prints on virtually every exposed patch of sand signalled that there was a very healthy population of otters in residence.

The river was impossible to ignore. It meandered under a compelling black-tea curtain of colour in the deeper pools and broke into a forceful white in the shallows and rapid tops, clattering over the rocks with a hollow, rolling sound like a bottle of champagne might, if you threw it down a flight of stairs. I shuddered at the thought of what it must look like in high water and was warned to be very careful if I headed upstream into the gorge – downpours brought instant changes to the Findhorn's water levels, blasting the gorge with water and claiming the lives of unsuspecting wading anglers in times past.

Our gillie, George, a very friendly old Scotsman who wore a traditional tweed cap and smart-looking tie, had offered to help me learn to Spey cast. It was a new but necessary discipline. The salmon rod required the use of two hands on the cork grip and was much longer and heavier than I was used to. The lines were much thicker too, and, as I would have to cast some distance at times, it was best that I learn how to execute the cast correctly.

The Spey cast, so named after the wide Scottish river, provided the salmon angler with a far more powerful cast than what could be achieved on standard trout-fishing gear; critically, the method also kept most of your line in motion in front of you, meaning that you could cast a considerable distance even with obstacles, such as trees and bushes, directly over your shoulders.

I carefully taped up the joints of the rod Dad had lent me for the trip – apparently the jolting shock of the Spey cast had enough beef to occasionally rip rod sections apart. I doubted I'd generate enough power to achieve that feat, but I enjoyed playing along as if I could. I had tried to Spey cast once before, on the River Wye. A friend of a friend had a regular rod up there, and, unable to make it one evening, it got offered out to us. I leapt at the chance, but, unfortunately, I found Spey casting about as subtle as fishing with a giant broom handle and ship's rope. Angling success revolves around confidence, and, as I had none, we quickly gave up and went to the pub.

'Lift up the rod tip, roll to your right, arch the tip down and cast in a D-shaped motion aiming the fly for the far bank.' Poor George must have said it a hundred times, patiently showing me again and again how to do it, as my brow beaded with anxious sweat. 'Keep that fly away!' implored George. 'You were looking good till you collapsed at the end, and that brings the fly closer into you.' He wasn't kidding. We spent a good few minutes extracting the salmon fly from deep within the neoprene that covered my rear end.

We were attempting to fish the very top of a milk-bottle-shaped stretch of water. The far bank was severely undercut by the flow of the Findhorn, red stone warped into attractive-looking coves and flat platforms, good fish-holding areas if only I could reach them. Eventually I learnt to keep the fly away from my underpants but I just couldn't get the distance no matter how hard I punched the rod out. 'You need to relax and feel for a rhythm,' said George. 'The best casters are the lady fishers,' he continued, reaching gently for my wrist. 'Relax your grip.' I did, and a couple of hours later my casting had improved markedly.

'Let me have a look at that fly,' George said after a time. I swung it in towards George's fingers. 'Blimey, it's as bare as a baby's behind!' he exclaimed. He was right — my fly was ruined from the constant whipping through the air and contact with objects other than the water. He flicked open a box of flies as colourful as a tub of Quality Street chocolates and selected a double-hooked and bright-blue number. 'Let's try that all again from the top of the beat.'

Almost immediately a shuddering take developed into a short but firm fight. I landed a fin-perfect brown trout just shy of the bottle's neck, and consecutive casts brought me two more fish: tiny salmon parr this time, my first Scottish salmon, of sorts. 'I think I'll celebrate with my disgusting habit,' George laughed, and sparked up a cigarette.

Clearly Spey casting wasn't supposed to be as brutal

as I had thought, and even with a stiff thirteen-foot rod, 15lb leader and enormous fly I had really felt the bites I'd had. Even those salmon parr, fish of no more than a couple of ounces each, had given a satisfying thump. Goodness knows what a fully fledged salmon must feel like then. 'Just make sure you get through the first line of the national anthem before lifting into it,' advised Nigel at lunchtime. 'The absolute worst thing you can do is strike,' added Dave, 'just tighten down on the fish gradually and you'll soon find it's on.'

The first day closed out with a single small salmon taking a swish at my fly. 'They are in there if we can just find a way to switch them on,' remarked Dave as we packed up the gear. 'I saw one of about five pounds up the top. She was bootiful,' purred Nigel, 'scarpered as soon as she saw me, mind.'

That evening Dad told me how Grandad had taken him to fish Ireland's Blackwater River. 'It was one of the best day's fishing Grandad had ever had.' I could tell by the way Dad began the story it was far from his best day. He took a sip of his beer and continued. 'We fished at the mouth of a waste pipe flowing from an abattoir. The anglers lined up and waited for the squeal from the pigs inside, then the pipe would churn out enough blood to turn a whole section of the river red. "Quick, son. Get the net and hook out all the blood clots," he'd say; stringy, worm-like, woollen lengths of clotted blood which he'd hook and trot downstream in the hope of big bream.'

It was a horrific tale and I could palpably feel Dad's sense of revulsion in the retelling. 'I remember catching a massive dace that day.' He indicated the fish's considerable size between his palms, but his tone was one of disgust. 'It was horrible. Its gills poured with pig's blood. I put it straight back in.'

The next morning we all stood outside in the mist as Dad diligently checked the moth traps he had set up overnight, his friends indulging him as he gleefully called out the names of each species: 'Red and green carpet! Hebrew character! Oh! Wonderful! A nut-tree tussock!'

It was hard to reconcile Dad's character with that of his father. Grandad was simply a product of a very different era. Dad was all peace and love, punk and revolution, tight trousers, big hair and open-minded, blue-sky thinking. Grandad, in spite of his rebellious, anti-authoritarian streak, was still operating within the confines of an ultra-conservative world that had just survived one of the most severe wartime periods ever. Back then animal welfare and ethical considerations were the indulgence of those who lived in lands of plenty and peacetime. Any small edge offered was exploited to its maximum advantage at a time when the screws were really being twisted. You simply never knew when, or if, any edge might be offered again.

Perhaps catching fish on pig's blood wasn't the end of the world. You could argue it wasn't exactly adding to the harm of the slaughterhouse, simply by using its waste product, but that day at the Blackwater the war had finished a very long time ago, and, clearly, Grandad's actions were upsetting his young son.

Grandad remained tough and uncompromising throughout his life. He never seemed to take a backward step over anything; I can't even recall him ever apologizing. I used to admire his doggedness, his ability to laugh off almost anything, and interpreted his stubbornness as strength. To no little extent, I modelled myself on him when I was a young man. Only now it seems a little excessive, inconsiderate even.

The moth collection was so much fun we lost track of ourselves and turned up quite late at the river. Grandad would never have done that, I thought, he would've fished a burning ghat on the Ganges with a human head for bait if he'd thought it would have put him onto a monster. For Dad, though, the Findhorn was more than just the sum of its fish.

'Dad . . .' We sat together on a rock promontory looking directly down into a pool. '. . . this is as close to perfect as I think it's possible for a salmon run to be.'

We had headed further up into the gorge than I had been before, scrambling over rocks and occasionally pulling ourselves along the smooth, rock-slab sides by rope to get right to the very top of the beat. It was steep and tight but there was still a prevailing quality to the air of a sort of breathy alpine atmosphere that is only really felt in the bands of forest at the extreme ends of the globe. It didn't feel claustrophobic in there in the slightest. Pungent pine and birch forests stood tall above a maze of warped and twisted boulders, the largest of which tapered high above me as if dropped from a giant Mr Whippy ice cream machine. In spite of the lack of water, the pools in the gorge still looked very deep and alluring.

'I'm sorry, Dad.' I picked myself off the stone and reached for my rod. 'I can't wait any longer, I've got to have a cast.'

The water cascaded down in great steps of a dozen or more. At points the entry to a pool was little more than a foot or two wide, the full force of the Findhorn's flow channelled through a natural gap you could quite easily hop across. It seemed highly improbable that any living creature could be able to swim against such power, but clearly the salmon here had found a way; of greater concern, then, was what might happen if I hooked a fish in one of these pools and it decided to exit via such an opening? Surely it would be impossible to stay in touch with a fish if that was its will? It was a prospect that was both inviting and intimidating in equal measure.

We took the pools on methodically, covering the water twice over before moving on down the staircase. I came nose to nose with a deer at one point and we both watched a goosander chase, then swallow whole, a trout. The salmon, though, continued to evade us.

We headed ever deeper into the gorge. Our nets and rods slung over our shoulders or held in our teeth as we were forced to rock-climb with greater regularity. 'It's guerrilla fishing, Dad!' I called out, as he swung on a rope. Finally, I was about as far from the commercial fishery as it was possible to be. The sense of relief was palpable and, to no small degree, I felt I had achieved one of the major ambitions I had set myself at the outset of this journey. Unquestionably, I had dipped a line in some wonderful places before coming here, but the Findhorn was in a different class of magnificence; a big fish now would be very nice indeed.

In the last pool of the beat Dad makes a long cast and lets his fly drift along the edge of some rocks and out across the deeper water. It sinks into the depths and he begins a jerking retrieve, lifting the fly, which I notice looks very much like a small carrot, up through the water column and towards the surface.

I'm sat high above the pool so I get a very clear view of what happens next. Just as the fly looks like it might break the surface, right at the edge of the deeper water, a salmon resembling a silver submarine emerges directly underneath the carrot, swims to within an inch of the hooks, and then drifts back into the shadows.

I am utterly stunned, but I know I can't exactly start shouting down to Dad and risk scaring the fish. I stare at his head. Trying to project the scene into his brain, or at least get some sort of telepathic communication going where he might think to look up at me. It's pointless though; he's locked within his own little world and definitely did not see the fish. He re-casts and nothing happens. Maybe I imagined it? He casts again and up it floats once again. It really is huge, comfortably the big-gest salmon I've ever seen, clearly over 15lb, at a push possibly even 20lb.

'Dad!' I can't help myself. 'Dad!' I try again in my best shout-whisper. I can see he's considering changing his fly. Bollocks to it. 'Dad!' I really shout it this time. He looks straight up at me, smiling. 'There is a massive salmon in that pool! He's gone for that fly twice!' He wasn't smiling any more. The fly was cast and re-cast, right back into the hole.

How many times has that happened when I've been fishing, I wonder? How close have I been to my own levia-than and not even realized it was there? Surely that fish is going to go for it this time though. I watch on, holding my breath, and Dad gets that great fish to rise up again.

Many months later I read the following words by Michael Wigan: 'A salmon that has dwelt in one place for a month may have watched innumerable flies swing-ing over it and pays them no greater attention than the man on the park bench does who subconsciously watches buses looping their circuit.'

I wish I had known that then. The fish, like a jealous boyfriend removing his girlfriend from a club, nosed right up to Dad's fly and chaperoned it from the pool. We tried every fly in the box after that, but only Dave man-aged to get that great fish to move again. However, it was not going to make a mistake for any of us. That salmon wasn't interested in anything other than rain and spawn.

*

The story of Dad fishing with the blood clots hadn't actually been news to me. Grandad had told me about that treasured memory before – of course he had, he broke his bream record twice that day. It was the other fishing memories that spilled from Dad's head, mundane stories when records weren't on the menu, that were much more telling about their relationship.

'I would have to trudge behind him for miles carrying his gear,' recalled Dad, 'off to some distant swim where we would sit in the cold for hours and if I tangled my line that was it. I was on my own. It would reduce me to tears trying to unknot those bird's nest tangles as he just carried on fishing.'

Grandad was extraordinarily blinkered when it came to his determination to catch for himself, and even when Dad did manage to cast a line and hook into something it was hardly a cause for celebration. 'I remember him putting a huge lobworm on my hook and me then landing this really big perch. You'd think he'd be pleased, but he was absolutely green with envy!'

We both laughed. I could picture it perfectly.

It was all beginning to add up. It had never been about sharing his world with others, it was about catching well and winning. It felt obviously and immediately familiar. It was me.

I was strangely relieved. All this time I had been chasing Grandad's higher wisdom it had never actually occurred to me that he had been bound by exactly the same failings as me when he was on the banks as a younger man; but he must have changed at some point later in his life. Grandad may have resembled his younger self at times, but he was undoubtedly a lot more relaxed on the banks we had shared. I wondered when the transformation in him had occurred, and why?

When he taught me to fish he spent far more time paying me close attention than he did actually fishing himself. If I tangled my lines he would make me untangle them, but he would always help; he would never have fished on. Two stories stuck in my mind as Dad recounted his experiences: the first was an evening when Grandad and Grandma were babysitting us and Grandad spent the entire night carefully untangling one of my rods for me; the second was the absolute pleasure he took in seeing me catch a big fish. When I was eight years old he helped me land a thuggish and powerful tench, scooping it out of the river with handfuls of lily stems, embracing me and cheering with joy.

The late, great fishing godfather Bernard Venables famously noted the three stages of an angler's evolution, summarized by Luke Jennings in the excellent *Blood Knots*: 'To begin with, as a child, you just want to catch fish, any fish. Then you move to the stage where you want to catch big fish. And finally, with nothing left to prove, you reach a place where it's the manner of the catch that counts, the rigour and challenge of it, at which point the whole thing takes on an intellectual and perhaps even a philosophical cast.'

Fishermen reflect their life in their fishing. Grandad

just didn't have anything left to prove, to himself, to the world of man, fish or his son, by the time I turned up with my 'Argos Introduction to Fishing Kit'. Grandparents often become second parents, but they get second chances too.

'I make a very close link between our belonging here and the will to fish,' Bernard Venables said towards the latter stages of his own career. 'Most of the things which are least pleasant about life now are the things which are most antithetical to fishing.' Fishing, he believed, was sullied by competition, by men taking on other men, by obsessing over size and records, by inviting self-promotion and all the jealousy that came with it. It took my Grandad a long time, but as we headed towards our last casts together he cared for nothing more than company.

There was more to Grandad curbing his enthusiasm for competition than simply a mellowing with age, however; if he really had always been obsessed with just catching, then the commercial carp fishery would have represented the absolute zenith of his angling ambitions, and the modernization of the sport, the carbon elasticated poles, the baitrunners on reels, the bite alarms and synthetic baits, would all have been must-haves in the decades before his epiphany. Yet, even when he was at his most addicted to the sport, his methods barely changed from when he was a child.

Grandad despised the commercial carp fishery as it suppressed the wild and precarious element for which he fished. Fishing rivers was a distillation of his character: unpredictable and bold. He felt changes in fishing eviscerated the sport of its elemental sense of fairness and dulled the angler's wits and skill. On that, he had common ground with his son; plus, they were both fantastic observers of the natural world.

Fairness and a keen eye for nature. For all Grandad's faults, they were two great traits to pass on to his son. Dad had just applied their uses to different ends and standards, but he was still his father's son.

Stepping out of your dad's shadow can be hard. Grandad had been a legend in his own lifetime, and my dad, the local doctor, was known by everyone in my area. I occasionally found it hard too. A lot of people really looked up to my dad and I felt, as the doctor's son, that I was expected to behave in a certain way. People knew who I was, and even though it wasn't ever said, I felt whatever I did would be held up for extra scrutiny as a result of my dad.

I wonder whether that influenced me in my determination to plough my own furrow later in life. I knew my expeditions were something that Dad could and would never do. They were dangerous and risky, and they had no obvious outcomes, pay cheques or prospects. He made it very clear he didn't approve of me leaving steady jobs to pursue those dreams, and that served to spur me on even more to make a success of what I was trying to do.

It was hardly a wholesale rejection of him, though. I

massively coveted my dad's attention and approval, more than anything else in fact, and when he showed any interest in what I was doing I gratefully embraced him within my world.

It's the curious dichotomy of growing up, the desperate rejection of figureheads while secretly wanting to imitate them at almost every stage of our lives. For most of us a predictable pattern inevitably follows that sees us steadily morphing into a version of the very role models we spent so much of our energy and time denigrating. In that, I was no exception.

More and more I see my own father in me. Not just a zero-tolerance attitude for lateness at airports, but an appreciation of life's details and an interest in how the world ticks, for both good and bad. I don't feel like I am in such an enormous rush any more, that it's me versus the world, or that I'm constantly having to prove myself to other people, but I haven't quite abandoned Venables' second stage of the angler's evolution either. So I still occasionally seek big fish and big challenges, but at least I know enough now to try to live and fish for the things that make me, and the people closest to me, happiest. I have always loved my dad, and only hope I might be half the man he is one day.

I was alone in the gorge as my fly descended neatly into the mouth of a salmon. It rose up from behind a rock and sucked it right in. It was so close I could see the sun reflecting off the white on the roof of its mouth. Indeed,

I was so close I was also able to perfectly track the frame of the fly leaving the fish's mouth and disappearing around the bend.

The old suck and blow. It had done me in.

It was as close as I got to snaring my first salmon on the fly but I wasn't too disheartened. As Dad, Nigel and I made to leave, Dave stayed on with his new recruit, another superb salmon fisherman named Jon. 'We used to fish all the time with a friend who once went thirteen years without a salmon,' Jon began. 'He'd come with us and we would always let him take the first cast in the top pools or the water that was easier to fish but he just caught nothing. It must've been so disheartening, especially when we would catch on a pool he had just left. Then, one day on the Dee, he caught two grilse to start, then a springer salmon. It was like a curse was lifted, he didn't stop catching after that.' I just needed some more time.

Nothing was caught for the rest of the week but I emerged from my time on the Findhorn deeply satisfied in a way I hadn't been for years. If I had already been surprised to learn that it doesn't matter if you don't catch anything big, I was quite shocked to realize that it actually doesn't matter if sometimes you don't catch anything at all.

'Grandad, I've got someone I would like you to meet.'

I had seen Grandad almost every day when I lived with my sister and James back in the Fens, but since I'd moved back to Cardiff to work on the BBC series my visits to his home had become inevitably more infrequent. His dementia had been steadily worsening over the last year, but in the last few months it had become really quite severe. He was living in a residential care home away from Grandma and spent the greater part of his days asleep in a chair, not really aware of where or who he was most of the time, and barely speaking at all.

I squeezed his hand and repeated my words. I had warned Emma about his state, but I had wanted him to meet her anyway, even if it was only to be a token gesture.

She took his hand tenderly and, quite suddenly, some light penetrated the dark clouds that had previously been puddling his mind. He woke up, and in that moment seemed to return to the saddle of his motorbike. Screaming into the nurses' quarters with his shock of black hair and that 'devil may care' attitude.

'Grandad, this is Emma.'

He took her in through his big brown eyes and flashed her a handsome grin.

'Hello, Ken,' Emma blushed, 'is Will a good fisherman?'

'He thinks he is,' he replied.

The cheeky bugger.

I held his other hand. They were the last words we would share together.

Three years after I caught that first Taff salmon, Emma and I returned to the very spot where the fish was caught. It was cold and the River Taff was in a foul mood. I had a couple of casts but sometimes there is no serendipity to fishing. I knew I didn't need that fish any more. Perhaps the river knew it too.

That weekend we were married.

Coming Home

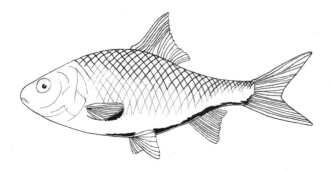

For all our time together in the Fens the thick-lipped and fat-chested chub was very much Grandad's fish. He talked about catching them from the running water around Bedfordshire with relish: 'Large lumps of bread crust or a plump slug, that's all you need for a whackin' great chub, my boy.' I caught my first one on a metal spinner and wisely elected not to tell him anything about it; my second came twenty years later and told me with certainty that he was finally on his way out.

Dad took him out fishing just one more time. It was to a local pond in the centre of a town park, and, despite a cancer beneath his right eye and floating blobs that cruelly obscured his vision, he still managed to winkle out a tiny perch or two: the tiny perch, the fisherman's escort in and out of the sport. On the front cover of the order of service at his funeral was a picture of him holding the monster perch caught from our favourite swim at Popham's Eau. I felt my chest heave and eyes fill with tears as I looked at it. He had been on his way for a long time, so there was no sense of robbery at his loss, but time did little to dull the impact of actually losing him for good.

The gathering of friends and family brought out many of the old stories. Some were familiar, such as the time his friend was so thoroughly depressed at being out-fished by him they swapped rods, only for Grandad to continue to catch more; other stories were new even to me, including one outrageous tale involving Grandad's knowledge of the Russian word for 'ice cream' and an interrogation at the hands of the KGB. I made a small speech about what he meant to us grandchildren, but I struggled to talk about his relationship with his son. It felt uncomfortable, as if all the awkwardness of his alpha-male posturing and the resultant shunning of real emotions had been transferred directly onto me for the day. Grandad was very different to Dad, but he was none the less extraordinarily proud of his son and loved him deeply. He just couldn't bring himself to publicly show it. If I had my time again I would say what he once told me on the riverbank. The banks always were his confessional box. 'Just aim to be like your dad, Will,' he said. 'Aim to be like your dad.'

I wanted to end this journey back where it began. I wanted to come home. I wanted to see the Creek again and fish Popham's Eau. I needed to see the Fens. I hadn't been back since his funeral over two years ago, and I hadn't fished Popham's Eau since I carried Grandad off the banks on our last fishing trip together. Almost every fish I've tried to catch from when this challenge began has been influenced by what he tried to teach me there. I need to go back now to really see what else I have learnt. Going full circle, right back to where in effect it all began, is the only way I will know if I've really changed at all.

It was the week before Christmas when I began the long drive cross-country from South Wales to fenland. I had returned from a honeymoon in Zambia and headed straight back out to New Guinea for more filming with BBC Two, so I really wasn't ready for the cold on my return, and nor was the van. Strong cross-winds and exposure made it a bit like steering a sail between the great concrete pillars that hold up the M4 bridge into Wales, fittingly rising up like giant rugby posts in this rugby-mad nation. I love crossing the River Severn in bad weather, though; just so I can see the bleak savagery of the wind-whipped tidal currents, the coal-black exposed rock at low tide. The fish are probably impossible to catch in conditions like this. I gaze into the turbid waters and imagine the advancing squadrons of bass as the tide changes, the flatfish and the elver eels on their way up on the ride. I've rarely seen it worse than this down there but the fish are just fine; humans, though, would stand no chance. Stripped down and bare, without technology or clothing, the far bank would hang tantalizingly in view but your body would slide away on the savage current long before you froze to death. I sail over the bridge and on into England.

There is great value to keeping an eye out for wildlife, even on motorways as barren in feel as the M4. There are always red kites to be spotted, cutting through the sky and seeking roadkill, and a great many deer species hang on the fringes of the woodland set aside at the road's edge, staring forward with their twitching ears and glassy, doll-like eyes. Everything drops away as the sun fades. Three hours in and the earth is flattening around me, an indication I am entering the far east of the country.

By the time I finally reach the outskirts of the Fens it is already pitch black. Fen black. It should be its own colour. The density of the darkness on the long roads between communities here is something you can only fully experience on a clear winter's night like this. It feels like I've been ejected into deep space, ploughing my van on through some infinite void. Wispy, frozen mist envelops me as I head out onto the fields; but I am calm. I learnt to drive in these conditions and am far more fearful of driving in big cities than I ever will be driving out here.

A buzzard rests near the royal-purple sign that welcomes me back into fenland proper. I catch its feathers in the headlight beam of my car. Its wings are angled down and flattened by the moisture in the air. It looks like the large, leathery hood of an axe-wielding executioner from the Middle Ages when it hangs in the trees like that. The bird is waiting until first light to hunt. We both are.

This darkness, especially nightfall, had a big role to play during my childhood. It was the time all activity, fishing and war games must come to an end. No matter how far from home we were, we all knew the consequences of arriving back through the front door in the Fen black. My life was one without mobile phones, or even clocks, we ate when we were hungry and used the passage of the sun across the sky to dictate what we would do next. Everything else could be pushed to the limits, but there was no justification for a post-dusk homecoming; besides, we respected our parents and valued our liberty far too much to ever push our luck too far.

It was only when I left this area and met people from outside that I began to realize how different my childhood had been to most. As long as we were home before dark, and didn't speak to strangers, my friends and I pretty much did as we pleased. We looked after each other and stuck together. As long as we kept to the basic rules, we had the chance to be free. Really free.

Although the draining of the Fens began in 1630 it would take right through till the 1850s for the fertile farmland to be effectively free of water. The introduction of Victorian engineering and the first steam-powered pumps saw the land increase in value some four times over; the Fens would become the vegetable basket of

Britain, and people flocked to help with the massive harvests on the exposed blackened peat.

Soon the sense of familiarity is so intense I feel I can almost close my eyes and drive the rest of the way home: Ring's End, Guyhirn, Wisbech St Mary, Leverington, Wisbech and the spectral glow of the old factory site I used to work on; all so well-known yet so distant, as if they were locations cast off from another life I had once led.

The A47 leads me on down to the roundabout by the Elm Hall Hotel. This is the place where I turn towards my village, but I always knew it for the little roadside fishing pond stocked for the workers in the local canning factory. My friends fished it once and spoke of catching dozens of little common carp on sweetcorn. I was much older when I eventually made it there to fish, but it was already long barren of its anglers and carp. At one end the wind was corralling hundreds of super-strength cans of Polish beer on the water's surface. When change came here, it came quickly.

The modern-day mechanization of farming practices after the Second World War both dramatically reduced the number of labourers needed and boosted the land's productivity to stratospheric proportions. By the late 1980s the Fens were accounting for more than one third of the national output of vegetables, and the supermarkets' use of new computer technology meant orders could be placed the moment a product had been purchased. With the scan of a barcode and click of a mouse, the supply chain was essentially streamlined and retro-fitted around the exact buying habits of the consumer. Massive orders of fruit and vegetables were now capable of doubling or halving overnight, so farms and their fac-tories took to calling in their workers to pick, pack and process at the shortest notice possible, but supermarket competition and customer expectation demanded the product price was still kept as low as possible. There was no real rise in wages for the legions of workers who had survived when the machines replaced people, but the uncertain shifts, unpredictable hours and now the crap wages on top meant many locals finally felt that enough was enough. There were still many jobs that needed the human hand, though; the farmers and factory owners were going to have to look elsewhere.

I was sheltered from these monumental changes as a child, particularly as I was still able to find local work fruit picking as a teenager well into the 1990s, but in the time it took me to leave school and finish my degree I went from being able to walk onto a factory line any-where to finding it virtually impossible to get a job at all.

Many of my friends in the fields and factories blamed the migrant workers for 'coming over here and taking all the work', but this was as far from the mark as those that pointed fingers at the 'lazy benefit-scrounging' local population who were 'all just racist'.

When the locals had started to refuse to meet the new demands, farms and factories simply turned to foreign gangmasters and agencies to pick up the shortfall.

Eastern European workers from the poorest parts of the former Soviet bloc, Poland at first, but latterly Latvians, Lithuanians and Russians, flooded to the area on the false promise of good wages and regular jobs, but when they arrived they discovered that the meagre wages they were to be paid were largely siphoned into the hands of criminal gangmasters under the guise of being 'back payments' on transportation costs, or taken as outlandish rental rates for the overcrowded houses they were placed in. Away from the houses, I began to notice tents cropping up, concealed deep within hedges and patches of trees. Out on the banks, fyke nets and long lines turned up for the first time in my lifetime. People were desperate. Desperate enough to spend winter in a tent, desperate enough to risk a criminal record for poaching fish; accruing debts with terrible people and sinking into a worse state of poverty than the one they had left behind.

The rate of new migrants coming into the area was higher than anywhere else in the UK – it had to be, no one else would tolerate that sort of treatment longer than they had to. Soon, some of the worst examples of poverty in the country were to be seen right on my doorstep, but that should hardly be surprising, should it? When we demand our food is available at bargain prices, around the clock and throughout the seasons, there was always going to be someone paying the cost somewhere.

There were times I felt like we were still all cast adrift

in flooded Fens. I grew up in a Bermuda Triangle of land where the county borders of Lincolnshire, Norfolk and Cambridgeshire all meet. We had one train line a half an hour's drive away, a scattering of main roads and definitely no motorways, and our nearest McDonald's took two bus journeys and a change at Wisbech. In the Norfolk Broads or on the north Norfolk coast it is all part of the charm, but visitors rarely came to my neighbourhood through choice, and yet I still love it here. There is a sense of the truly mystical to the big skies and open fields, and the greatest sunsets and starry nights I will ever see have always been here. A comic once said if you stand on a milk crate you can see the curvature of the earth. As a child I would sneak out the back of the house in the depths of winter and climb the last apple tree in the orchard. From my vantage point I could see across the earthen sugar beet fields, stripped bare of their crop and frozen solid like the sea. I used to imagine it was the point where the world was stitched together, an elongated patch atop the earth's surface sewn in the same way my school trousers were when I holed the kneecap.

Fenland people are mocked, of course. We are the uneducated, slack-jawed inbreds. 'NFN' – 'Normal for Norfolk' – the outsiders like to joke. Folk-of-the-flat interned in a land where people go mad because of the lack of hills. Later the madness was actually attributed to malaria from the swamps, but we never shed the rest of the character stains, and everywhere I go people like to poke fun about where I'm from. It doesn't bother me, though. I liked the people I grew up with here, and I actually felt sorry for people that took the piss out of us, as I knew they had missed out. Most of all, I liked the adult contentment of feeling small in a vast, unbroken landscape. I am grateful to this land: for the respect and interest in water it has given me, the lack of fear and sense of control I have in the wild. I now realize that it is something special, and not something simply innate in everyone.

Perhaps I am indulging my nostalgia now I no longer live here. I couldn't wait to leave this place when I did. I felt a sense of suffocation as I grew older, that the whole place was getting perversely smaller and more inward-looking with each year of my life that passed. New Year's Eve and when Glastonbury was on as a teenager were always the worst. Watching mass celebrations on the television I would feel frustrated and jealous of everyone else. Worse still I couldn't shake the feeling that we were the sorts of people that would never be invited to the party. However, a decade after all of my friends and I had been released from the Fens and headed to jobs in the big cities of Britain, I realized that it was now that we were actually trapped for real and that what we had as kids would never be ours again. I never really felt at home in cities, and thought that any day soon someone in a suit would tap me on the shoulder and remind me where I was from, that I was wearing the emperor's new clothes, that it was time to go home now and that my performance was over. It took another ten years before I realized everyone else working in the city feels exactly the same.

According to the Wilson *Encyclopedia*, the 'Roach is the most commonly caught British freshwater shoal fish.' It was the footsoldier of the Creek, the fish that made up the bulk of my keepnet as a child, but, as a result of their sheer volume and small size, I feel they never really received the respect they deserve. Coming home, it had to be the roach I went for.

The eyes are a virulent, violent red in colour, but there is something of the underdog spirit in the way the rest of its curved and downward-facing mouth appears. Its neat head fronts a classically fish-shaped body, and with white-silver sides and orange-red fins it is, unfortunately, the prime target for live-baiting for pike. A Finnish friend of mine even uses their eyeballs to catch perch: 'But they shimmer with an animation you just can't get from any bait,' he said, in response to my disgust at his practice. As I said, the roach deserves more respect.

Before the opening day of the coarse season on 16 June I would walk the Creek and look under the bridges at Popham's Eau. Thousands of roach in great shoals were to be seen basking in the sunshine together and the day couldn't come quick enough when we could try and catch them. The greatest catch I ever made came in that opening week. I was on the River Delph at Welney with Grandad, Dad and my friend Lee. We had happened upon a truly vast shoal of roach that would not stop bit-ing. We baited with maggots and threw in breadcrumbs by the handful till we had precipitated a feeding frenzy so great that even when we ran out of free-feed they still just kept on coming. They continued to bite through pike attacks, they even continued to bite when I fell in. It was simply an incredible day's fishing, and when it came to tip our keepnets up and return the roach to the river I can still remember that feeling of amazement that such a great quantity of fish could be living in such a small patch of river.

Numbers, though, are one thing. There were other days when the roach came on strong for a time, but, out of the thousands and thousands that came to my hook, the biggest I ever landed was well under the 2lb mark. Jack Hargreaves writes: 'It took me thirty years to catch a two-pound roach, even fishing in the best southern roach-waters.' The current record roach, standing at 4lb 4oz, was caught from a lake in Northern Ireland, and the only river to feature any fish in the current top ten record roach list is the Stour in Dorset. Truly, the Fens were never likely to trouble the roach record books then, but some very fine roach have been landed here, many fish over 2lb, and I even once heard of a fish in excess of 3lb coming from the Great Ouse near Ely. In angling, there is always a chance, but, really, how much did I actually care by this stage?

I approached the outskirts of my village a little be-fore dawn. My entire childhood world had just been compressed into a little under an hour in the car, but fifteen years after I had left it was heartening to discover my village had hardly changed.

I chose to drive the long way to Popham's Eau so I could pass both houses we had lived in. The first, a beautiful Georgian doctor's house in the middle of the village, had electronic Christmas candles in the window; the second, on the outskirts, had a new shed on one side, and that seemed to be the sum of the modifications. I drove beside the Creek, noting the nonsensical new sign that declared it the 'Nene–Ouse Navigation Link', then on past the butcher's, the hairdresser's, the corner shop and Navrady's, which still sells the best fish and chips in Britain. Out towards the end of the village I closed in on Grandad's place but flicked the indicator to signal right, just before I made it to his bungalow. Following the nail-straight road towards the Sixteen Foot Bank I headed instead towards his spiritual home, travelling just a few hundred metres before pulling into a small lay-by beside a field.

You wouldn't know the river was here in light or dark. The pancake-flat landscape creates an optical illusion that hides Popham's Eau perfectly in its dip, but I knew it was there. I opened the boot and lifted out a large bucket filled with groundbait and a couple of tubs of maggots and casters. It was cold but not as cold as it used to be at this time of year. When I was a child the winters here could be savage, days of sub-zero temperatures would freeze the fields solid and turn the flooded

Welney Washes into a giant ice rink that produced many a champion speed skater, but the walk along the edge of the field towards our spot was still just as long as I remember.

The fen drains intimidate some anglers. They appear as a blank canvas, miles of unrelenting uniformity in both directions with very few obvious fish-holding features to cast at. When Grandad came here he would walk from his bungalow, across the road and alongside a small orchard between the field and the river. He followed a fence line to a concrete post at its end. Here he would tie off a length of rope for safety and, effectively, abseil his way down the bank to the water's edge. That was where I needed to be and I did eventually find the post, still standing proud; but it would take till the sun was fully up for me to realize the fence and the entire orchard were all long gone. One solitary old apple tree remained, surrounded by long grass.

I grip the cold concrete post and feel an overwhelming sense of belonging. I used to sit right here when I was old enough to come to the Eau on my own. I would wait for him, his heavy steps along the bank, his 'all right, my beaut' greeting. It would never come again now, but I can still feel his presence here, far more than I could at his funeral service, or by holding his rods or reading his books. This is where we both once belonged. Wet mist soaks the banks. I had been nervous walking here, warning myself repeatedly to take my time and watch my step, that one slip in the darkness could see me plummet from height and into the drain, but the post makes me feel secure and the banks are nothing like as steep as I found them as a child. I move down easily and quickly towards the water's side.

I doubt many people have been here since I last fished this spot with Grandad all those years ago. The bed of common reeds on this bank stand some eight foot high, forming a caramel-yellow fence between me and the water, but there is still a gap just big enough for me to squeeze into my seat and cast my roach tackle. I begin rolling apple-sized balls of groundbait laced with maggots and casters. The sluice gates are open downstream at Denver so the water is pushing through at a real clip, plus there is twelve foot of deep water in front of me: if I want to guarantee the balls make it to the bottom of the river I will have to squeeze them really tight. This is where I want the roach shoals to find them, and then, once the shoals are here and feeding confidently, I'll flick out a hook. I must remember to keep the bait going in, though – it won't last long in this flow and I'll want to hold the fish here for as long as I possibly can. 'It's not little and often, it's a lot and often, Will', that's what Grandad would have said had he been next to me now; then he would have told his old story about the fishing match he once lost because he only brought ten kilos of groundbait with him. 'Don't be afraid to keep it going in, as once the roach are gone you'll never get them back.' I throw the bait in as accurately as I can and return to the car for the rods.

Two hours slide by and the sun gently rises without bringing much warmth. The river elects to retain its misty coat and small jenny wrens buzz around in the reeds like hummingbirds. On the far bank a pair of swans dance neck to neck out across the water, but mostly it is very quiet. I didn't realize how much I miss the silence. The real fenlands personify a rare brand of solitude. Many can't hack it. I can understand that and I've always felt for the occupants of the remote farmhouses out here, miles from people and each other. Clumps of rotting water lily leaves float past on the flow. The living plant that formed them is firmly on the retreat now, back towards the silty riverbed where it will safely wait until the weather warms once more. In the spring the lily beds are dense and sometimes many metres thick. I used to love fishing off these lilies. It produced some of our finest fish, but a monster lived in there too, a fish that contained unstoppable power. It was our Moby-Dick. I hooked it just once; Grandad managed it several times, of course, but neither of us ever saw that beast – it simply tore the line from our reels and straightened our hooks right out. Looking back, we never once scaled our gear up to actually attempt to land the creature; we simply tolerated its occasional intrusion, probably in much the same way as it tolerated us. Many years later a young lad from the neighbouring village of Three Holes landed a carp well in excess of 20lb from this very stretch of water; perhaps that was all the legend had ever amounted to, but we never liked to think so.

I have set up for the roach exactly as Grandad taught me, with one of his handsome handmade floats, thick and well weighted, set at twelve feet in depth with the bulk of my shot strung out close to a small hook. I want to get the bait right down in the river, but if I don't get a bite down on the river bed that doesn't mean the roach are definitely not present. I'll just have to adjust the float and bring my bait off the bottom a little, an inch or two every ten minutes or so, just to check that they aren't shoaling a little higher up and intercepting all my groundbait as it sinks through the water column. Even with the heavy float and weights, I still have to steady the tackle in the flow, mending the line almost as if I were float-fishing the River Taff. I keep the bait trickling in with one hand and fix my eye firmly on the bright-red tip of the float for any possible indication of arriving roach.

Roach can be extraordinarily cute when they take the bait and sometimes a gentle bite might only register as a tickle on the float tip. In his prime Grandad could seemingly catch roach without any indication whatsoever, though: he would give a sudden crack of his wrist and there the roach would be, writhing on his hook as if spirited there by some unseen force. When the poet Ted Hughes wrote of float-fishing in 1967 he commented that 'your whole being rests lightly on the float'. That's the state you must look to achieve to be a truly success-ful float-fisher like Grandad, a condition of such intense concentration that there is nothing more in life than you and your float; when a pulse, a flick, a tremble on that tip will register in your body as if an earthquake has struck under your tackle box. It sounds tense – it really isn't, and, even if you fall short of such a lofty goal, float-fishing still offers its junior practitioners a shot at pure escapism. Staring at a float erodes stress at a far greater rate than any trip to the gym, pub or psychiatrist's couch ever will. It alleviates anxiety and leaves the angler fixed within a world where there are no bills to pay, no pieces of work to deliver and no problems at home. Time both slows down and speeds up. You can spot micro-details like how a cloud of nymphs expands and contracts on a river's surface, or how a kingfisher dramatically throws its neck forward as it strikes the water, but while observing the translucence on the wing of some damsel, or watching a toad crawl in animated slow motion, you suddenly realize it is getting dark and that you didn't even touch your lunchtime sandwiches.

I always feel better after a day's float-fishing, even when I miss all my bites, and if I were allowed to fish only one method for the rest of my life then the float would be it.

I tried to settle into the rhythm of my float that morning but it was impossible to get over the piece of my personal history I was sat in. Why did Grandad fish here almost exclusively for the last twenty years of his life? I had always put it down to the Eau's close proximity to his bungalow, but he really could have lived just about anywhere in the village. I blew some hot air and life back into my fingers. Popham's Eau didn't have the obvious aesthetics of the Creek even; you had to look hard for both the beauty and the fish down here. Maybe that was part of it, the idea that it was a bigger challenge. The fish here were definitely bigger if you did find them but I knew there was more at play here too.

I flicked a lily pad off the float. I never want to return to fishing just one set of venues for just one fish, but the immense enjoyment to be had at seeing a river change its shape and character from just one vantage point seemed pretty clear. Only by returning to the same place over and over can you see that no one day is ever the same as the next. Watching a river change its character through the seasons somehow ballasts us as anglers and people. It reminds us of our own mortality in the face of natural forces that are out of our control. It should not be an intimidating or frightening prospect. There is great comfort to be found in the discovery of something larger than your life. I can very well imagine that bearing witness to the changes in your grandchildren has a similar effect. Eventually we all get left behind, of course, but at least we can take steps to make sure that when we do go the things we love continue to grow without us around. Grandad kept his grandchildren, and this place, close. I know he was proud of us all, and now, against all odds, I've found my way right back here to check all is well on his behalf. I bet he always knew I would as well, the silly old sod.

Jiang Taigong was a statesman and strategist who lived in ancient China in the second millennium before

Christ. According to legend, he had served the tyrannical Zhouwang, the last king of the Shang Dynasty. Zhouwang was a debauched slave owner who took enormous pleasure in torturing, then executing, anyone who objected to his rule. Jiang Taigong hated him with every inch of his being and was desperate to overthrow the despot. However, despite being an expert in military strategy, Jiang Taigong was old and had no army to call on.

Jiang Taigong left his position with the king, but knew that one day his special talents would be needed to defeat him. He took to fishing and lived in seclusion for many years. As time slipped by it became clear to those who lived around the riverbank where he fished that Jiang Taigong never actually seemed to catch anything; in fact, on closer inspection, they discovered he wasn't actually fishing with a hook at all. Jiang Taigong believed that the fish, when they were ready, would come to him of their own volition. And so it was that King Wen of the powerful Zhou state found Jiang Taigong, at the ripe old age of eighty, fishing without his hook and, through pure curiosity alone, engaged this peculiar man in conversation. The king soon realized that Jiang Taigong was a uniquely gifted person, as well as a military expert, and hired him as his mentor. Together they would go on to overthrow Zhouwang and eventually establish the legendary Zhou dynasty throughout China, the longest dynasty in Chinese history.

Jiang Taigong gave out the image of a man fishing, when in fact he was waiting for an army to overthrow

King Zhou. It was a cunning piece of sleight of hand: he had a hidden purpose that was heavily masked by an obvious one, but it took him time. The morals of the story: good things come to those who wait, and things aren't always as they seem.

My bite alarm has just gone off.

Gently, I place my roach rod down on its rests, leaving my seat behind as the bleeps start to sing out in a string. Forgive me, readers, for slightly pulling the wool over your eyes with the roach-fishing lark, and forgive me, Grandad, for the blatant use of technology in your treasured spot, but hidden at the end of the reed bed a heavy rod baited with a single smelt has been lying in wait this entire time.

I scoop that rod off its rests. Its feels like gripping the trunk of a tree in comparison to the roach rod but this is no time for clever comparisons: the line is pulling alarmingly taut, signalling that it is high time to strike, and strike hard I do.

At first I feel solid resistance and the line grinds horribly. It is locked up against something but I sense instinctively that now is not the time to ease off on the pressure. Suddenly the line pings free and I can tell from the opening, steaming, pile-driving run which follows that this is going to be the biggest fish of my journey by an absolute fucking mile.

Despite the mammoth run I feel strangely in control. Don't let the fish bully you. I pile on strain when I feel it is trying to rest and give it line and space to run when it decides to assert itself. After ten minutes I get my first glimpse of the fish and it is, as expected, a very big pike. It shakes its head angrily at me, like a bullock caught in an electric fence, and, to my absolute horror, I notice that there is only a single, barbless, hookpoint left in the fish's mouth, sat right between its bony teeth like an after-dinner toothpick. It is, as they say, brown-trouser time.

The pike steamrollers towards the dead lilies and reeds on my side of the bank so I apply as much side-strain as I dare; if it goes in there I know I'm done for. Mercifully, she turns her head at the last moment and drives back into open water. It's definitely a female pike: the solid belly, shoulders and head are unmistakable. The reel whines and my hands and knees begin to rattle with adrenaline. I know now that this is not just the biggest fish of the journey, it is the biggest fish I have ever seen in Popham's Eau. It is the beast.

In front of me, in a flash of a second, I swear blind that a giant shoal of roach rolls on the surface of the river, momentarily rippling the place with a life I haven't seen in a hundred winter visits here. In the middle of them all is my great fish, wallowing like a hippo just out of reach of the net. I hold the rod up to its maximum extent and slowly win back the line, gently heaving the magnificent animal back towards me. The weight of the fish leaves my rod the moment it hits the base of my net; at the same time another, unseen, weight slides right off my shoulders. I stare up to the sky and feel my eyes heave with tears.

Thank you, Grandad. Thank you for teaching me how to fish and thank you for everything else. Thank you for just being there.

I didn't break any angling records during this journey and, in reality, I was always quite some considerable distance off the mark. That greater sand eel is still as close as I've been to a submission to the hallowed British Record Fish Committee and its list, but, still, I had a lot of fun and did break several personal bests. In my own way, I did at least avenge the memory of that greater sand eel.

The fact is, you just can't drop into any old swim and hope to catch a record on wild water. Yes, the chances are significantly narrowed when you know there is a record fish trapped within a lake, or even behind a lock gate, but you still need to learn that creature's habits and harmonize yourself to the natural rhythm of a place. That all takes more time than I had, and yet I still wouldn't have changed how I approached this challenge one bit.

I realized ultimately that I'd had infinitely more pleasure catching fish from ridiculously unlikely spots, meeting new people and discovering new places to try, than I ever did from actually chasing a record fish. The sand eel was beautiful not because it was a record on some other man's list but because it was a total surprise and the first I had ever caught. What is fishing without the element of surprise?

There have been many failures in this book and plenty of days when I caught absolutely nothing at all. In the past this would have been a major problem, rectified quickly with a trip to my nearest carp stew pond to confirm I hadn't lost the magic. In fact, this very act confirmed I *had* already lost the magic. Fishing is our way of tapping back into something we have lost in our comfortable and cosseted lives, a throwback to a time when we did need to catch to survive; it should not ever be reduced to purely a competition to catch the biggest fish. The baited line is our link to the secret underwater world and it reconnects us with nature in an immensely powerful way that few other pastimes ever could. We are a part of a much wider, wilder system, and not simply above it. Failure to catch demonstrates we do not have full dominion over nature all of the time and plugs us back into the notion that we, as humans, should only ever be participating in a mutual and fair exchange with the natural world, one where we can't always guarantee a win.

At the end of it all I have discovered that I am still at my most relaxed when I am by water, but I am also at my happiest when I'm fishing a river. My river fishing, like my family, has always been there for me, and I've been at my lowest when I've abandoned them both. I now realize that it is the fishing, and not actually the fish, that has provided the levelling presence throughout my life. Even when I've neglected it, river fishing has waited for me. I promise I'll never leave the rivers again.

My hero, John Wilson, made 160 television programmes in a career spanning over twenty-five years. In
2009 he justifiably received an MBE for services to
angling and eventually retired to Thailand, where he
runs a fishing lake with his brother, Dave. I spent a wonderful evening drinking beers in the bath while watching
episodes of *Go Fishing* back to back for hours on end,
drunkenly raising a glass to the man who inspired a
legion of young fishermen just like me. Thanks, John.

My grandad was not a second father. I already had
one of those and never needed another, so what was he
to me? He was my older best friend. He would do anything for me (as long as it didn't cost too much money!)
and I would do anything for him. There was nothing
I wouldn't tell him, and no judgement he would ever
pass. He was a superficially hard and competitive man
to his death, but his core held an utter softness. He
brimmed with absolute and unwavering love for his son,
his family, his grandchildren, and for me.

Grandad and I kept the secrets we shared with each
other on the banks, but there was one of his musings
that I knew I would eventually have to tell Dad about
when the time came. I was ten years old and we were
fishing Popham's Eau side by side. He was sat there with
his floppy white hat on, watching his float while absent-
mindedly moulding breadcrumb groundbait all around
the cork handle of his rod. It was a fairly typical summer
afternoon. Then he leant towards me and said: 'When I
go don't put me in the ground with the rest of the silly

buggers. Put me in the river, back where I was a boy, my boy.'

Dad found the exact spot he spoke of in words Grandad had written in *Bedford, My Bedford*, and one crisp spring afternoon my dad, my brother and I carried him back home: up the River Great Ouse above Bedford, below a bridge, across a field, and into a break in the eight-foot-high common reeds.

Grandad finished his journey where his passion began. Gently we eased his ashes between our fingers and let him slip into his infinite water.

Acknowledgements

This book has focused far too much on men at times. I would like to thank three of the most important women in my life: my loving mum, for everything she did for me growing up, giving me my self-belief and providing an environment for all her children to flourish; my brilliant twin, Anna, for being there for me and having my back for, quite literally, my entire life; and, most of all, thank you to my wonderful wife, Emma, for always believing in me, for keeping me going, and for putting up with me heading off to catch fish in the same year we got married.

Grandparents are quite often the unsung heroes of any family. Thank you to both sets of mine for the unconditional love they always gave. I wish you were all still with us, and that you can forgive my occasional swearword in this book; I don't really mean it. I'm blessed with some really awesome friends and a fantastic wider family. I won't turn this into a mammoth love-in as I hope they already know how much they've helped shape me and my writing, but I would like to single out my brother Tom for special praise. Thanks, Tom, both for putting up with a brother who was as obsessed with fishing as I was as a child, and for giving me the metaphorical boot-up-the-arse I needed when I was spending too much time watching fishing on satellite TV and not enough time writing about it.

I am very grateful to the Society of Authors for their generous grant for yet more tackle and miles more in the petrol tank. Huge thanks to everyone who has helped along the way at Viking, Anna-Sophia Watts for her beautiful illustrations, John Hamilton for his superb cover art, Mark Handsley for his copy-editing patience, and to Emma Brown for handling the latter stages of the book edit. Emily Robertson has been the best editorial partner I could have ever hoped for. Without your guidance and encouragement this book would never have happened. Thanks for convincing me this would work, Emily, and for understanding what I was struggling to commit to words.

On the banks, my thanks go to the Canal and River Trust and especially John Ellis for switching me on to the wonders of our canals, Jake Finnegan at Wykeham Lakes for relating the story of his monstrous pike, John Horsey for his exceptional knowledge of Chew, and for letting me blow his chance at a big pike, Peter Rolfe and Pam for their incredible hospitality and introduction to all things crucian, Verulam Fishing Club for being so kind in letting me fish their pond, Dr Carl Sayer for his patience in explaining his research to a dullard like me, Glamorgan Anglers Club for the access to all the excellent fishing to be had in South Wales, the guys at Garry Evans Tackle Shop, especially Rich and Andrew, for all of their advice and help, and to Dad's salmon mates, Dave, Nigel and John, for letting me gatecrash their trip. Thanks also to my childhood friends Lee Wales and Paul Woods, who picked up where Grandad left off, and helped create some of my fondest fishing memories.

The final word of thanks must go to Dad, Grandad and John Wilson. Thanks for the inspiration, guys. May your lines be for ever tight.

Feminist Interpretations and Political Theory

*To Kate and Anthony Chromey
and the memory of
Harry Pateman*

Feminist Interpretations
and Political Theory

Edited by Mary Lyndon Shanley
and Carole Pateman

Polity Press

Copyright individual essays: 1 © 1977 Princeton University Press;
2 © 1985 Praeger Publishers; 3 © 1989 Carole Pateman;
4 © 1978 American Political Science Association; 5 © 1981 *Social Theory
and Practice*; 6 © 1991 Moira Gatens; 7 © 1991 Seyla Benhabib;
8 © 1991 Christine Di Stefano; 9 © 1981 Sage Publications, Inc.;
10 © 1989 Basic Books, Inc.; 11 © 1988 Elizabeth V. Spelman;
12 © 1986 Hypatia, Inc.; 13 © 1991 Mary G. Dietz; 14 © 1989 The
Regents of the University of Minnesota.
This collection and the introduction © 1991 Mary Lyndon Shanley and
Carole Pateman

First published 1991 by Polity Press
in association with Basil Blackwell

Editorial office:
Polity Press, 65 Bridge Street,
Cambridge CB2 1UR, UK

Marketing and production:
Basil Blackwell Ltd
108 Cowley Road, Oxford, OX4 1JF, UK

British Library Cataloguing in Publication Data

A CIP catalogue record for this book is available
from the British Library.

ISBN 0 7456 0704 7
ISBN 0 7456 0705 5 (pbk)

Typeset in 10 on 12pt Baskerville
by Hope Services (Abingdon) Ltd.
Printed in Great Britain by
T. J. Press Ltd., Padstow, Cornwall

Contents

Contributors   vii

Acknowledgments   ix

Introduction
Carole Pateman and Mary Lyndon Shanley   1

1   Philosopher Queens and Private Wives: Plato on Women
    and the Family
    Susan Moller Okin   11

2   Aristotle: Defective Males, Hierarchy, and the Limits
    of Politics
    Arlene Saxonhouse   32

3   "God Hath Ordained to Man a Helper": Hobbes,
    Patriarchy and Conjugal Right
    Carole Pateman   53

4   Early Liberal Roots of Feminism: John Locke and the
    Attack on Patriarchy
    Melissa A. Butler   74

5   Rousseau and Modern Feminism
    Lynda Lange   95

6   "The Oppressed State of My Sex": Wollstonecraft on
    Reason, Feeling and Equality
    Moira Gatens   112

7   On Hegel, Women and Irony
    Seyla Benhabib   129

8   Masculine Marx
    Christine Di Stefano   146

9   Marital Slavery and Friendship: John Stuart Mill's
    The Subjection of Women
    Mary Lyndon Shanley   164

10 John Rawls: Justice as Fairness – For Whom?
    Susan Moller Okin   181

11 Simone de Beauvoir and Women: Just Who Does She
    Think "We" Is?
    Elizabeth V. Spelman   199

12 Foucault and Feminism: Toward a Politics of Difference
    Jana Sawicki   217

13 Hannah Arendt and Feminist Politics
    Mary G. Dietz   232

14 What's Critical about Critical Theory? The Case of
    Habermas and Gender
    Nancy Fraser   253

Index   277

Contributors

Seyla Benhabib is associate professor of philosophy and women's studies at the State University of New York at Stony Brook. She is the author of *Critique, Norm and Utopia* (Columbia University Press, 1986) and co-editor with D. Cornell of *Feminism as Critique: On the Politics of Gender* (University of Minnesota Press and Polity Press, 1987). She is currently working on a reinterpretation of Hannah Arendt's political philosophy from a feminist perspective.

Melissa Butler is associate professor of political science at Wabash College. She is currently completing a book on Jean-Jacques Rousseau and the idea of self-love.

Mary G. Dietz is associate professor of political science at the University of Minnesota. She is author of *Between the Human and the Divine: The Political Thought of Simone Weil* (Rowman and Littlefield, 1988), and editor of *Thomas Hobbes and Political Theory* (University of Kansas Press, 1990) as well as articles on the history of ideas and feminist political theory.

Christine Di Stefano teaches political theory at the University of Washington in Seattle. She is currently at work on a study of "Autonomy: The Fate of an Ideal." Her forthcoming book, *Configurations of Masculinity: A Feminist Rereading in Modern Political Theory*, offers gender-inflected readings of Hobbes, Marx and J. S. Mill.

Nancy Fraser teaches philosophy at Northwestern University. She is the author of *Unruly Practices: Power, Discourse, and Gender in Contemporary Social Theory* (University of Minnesota Press and Polity Press, 1989). She is currently at work on a new book, *Keywords of the Welfare State*, which she will co-author with Linda Gordon.

Moira Gatens lectures in philosophy at the Australian National University. She is author of *Feminism and Philosophy* (Polity Press, 1990). Her current research concerns philosophies of the body (Spinoza, Nietzsche, and Freud) and their relations to theories of ethics.

Lynda Lange teaches feminist philosophy at the University of Toronto, Scarborough campus. She has published articles on Rousseau and feminist theory, and is co-editor (with L. Clark) of *The Sexism of Social and Political Theory: Women and Reproduction from Plato to Nietzsche* (University of Toronto Press, 1979). Her current research is mainly on the development of democratic feminist thought.

Susan M. Okin is professor of political science at Stanford University. She is the author of *Women in Western Political Thought* (Princeton University Press, 1979) and *Justice, Gender, and the Family* (Basic Books, 1989).

Carole Pateman is professor of political science at the University of California, Los Angeles. Her most recent books are *The Sexual Contract* and *The Disorder of Women: Democracy, Feminism and Political Theory* (both Polity Press and Stanford University Press, 1988 and 1990). She is currently continuing her research on women and democratic citizenship.

Jana Sawicki is associate professor of philosophy at the University of Maine. She has published many articles on Foucault and feminism which address issues in the philosophy of desire, motherhood, and technology. A collection of her essays on sexuality and reproduction will be published by Routledge Press in 1991.

Arlene Saxonhouse is professor of political science at the University of Michigan. She is author of *Women in the History of Political Thought: Ancient Greece to Machiavelli* (Praeger, 1985). She has published widely in the area of ancient political theory, and is currently working on a book, *The Fear of Diversity in Greek Thought*.

Mary Lyndon Shanley is professor of political science at Vassar College. She is the author of *Feminism, Marriage and the Law in Victorian England, 1850–1895* (Princeton University Press, 1989) and many articles on the history of political theory. She is currently working on a book on liberal theory, feminism, and contemporary family law.

Elizabeth V. Spelman teaches in the philosophy department at Smith College, and is the author of *Inessential Woman: Problems of Exclusion in Feminist Thought* (Beacon, 1988). Her writings have focused on the mutual construction of gender, race and class and the implications of their interconnections for feminist theory and politics. Her next long-term project is an examination of the treatment of suffering in Western philosophy.

Acknowledgments

The editors and publishers are grateful for permission to reproduce the following:

Susan Moller Okin, "Philosopher Queens and Private Wives: Plato on Women and the Family," first published in *Philosophy and Public Affairs*, 6(4), Summer 1977, pp. 345–69. Reprinted with permission of Princeton University Press. The essay has also appeared in Jean Elshtain (ed.), *The Family in Political Thought* (Amherst: University of Massachusetts Press, 1982), pp. 31–50.

Arlene Saxonhouse, "Aristotle: Defective Males, Hierarchy and the Limits of Politics," abridged from the original published in Arlene Saxonhouse, *Women in the History of Political Thought: Ancient Greece to Machiavelli* (New York: Praeger, 1985). Abridged and reprinted with permission of the author and Praeger Publishers, a division of Greenwood Press, Inc.

Melissa Butler, "Early Liberal Roots of Feminism: John Locke and the Attack on Patriarchy," first published in the *American Political Science Review*, 72, 1978, pp. 135–50. Reprinted by permission of the American Political Science Association. It appears here in a shortened version.

Lynda Lange, "Rousseau and Modern Feminism," which originally appeared, in a longer version, in *Social Theory and Practice*, 7, 1981, pp. 245–77; by permission of the editorial board of *Social Theory and Practice*, Florida State University.

Mary Lyndon Shanley, "Marital Slavery and Friendship: John Stuart Mill's *The Subjection of Women*," first published in *Political Theory*, 9(2), May 1981, pp. 229–47. Reprinted by permission of Sage Publications, Inc.

Susan Moller Okin, "John Rawls: Justice as Fairness – For Whom?" which is drawn from "Justice and Gender," *Philosophy and Public Affairs*, 16(1), Winter 1987, pp. 42–72, copyright © 1987 by Princeton University Press, excerpt adapted with permission of Princeton University Press; and "Reason and Feeling in Thinking about Justice," *Ethics*, 99(2), January 1989, pp. 229–49, by permission of University of Chicago Press. This version is adapted from that in Susan Moller Okin, *Justice, Gender, and the Family* (New York: Basic Books, 1989) and is reprinted by permission of Basic Books, Inc., Publishers, New York.

Elizabeth V. Spelman, "Simone de Beauvoir and Women: Just Who Does She Think 'We' Is?" abridged from the original published in Elizabeth V. Spelman, *Inessential Woman* (Boston: Beacon Press, 1988). Copyright © 1988 by Elizabeth V. Spelman. Reprinted by permission of Beacon Press.

Jana Sawicki, "Foucault and Feminism: Toward a Politics of Difference," which originally appeared in *Hypatia: A Journal of Feminist Philosophy*, 1 (2), Fall 1986, pp. 23–36.

Nancy Fraser, "What's Critical about Critical Theory: The Case of Habermas and Gender": a longer version of this essay was published in *New German Critique*, 35, Spring/Summer 1985, pp. 97–131, and in Nancy Fraser, *Unruly Practices: Power, Discourse and Gender in Contemporary Social Theory* (Minneapolis: University of Minnesota Press; Cambridge: Polity, 1989). Reprinted by permission of the University of Minnesota Press.

Introduction

Carole Pateman and
Mary Lyndon Shanley

Since the early 1970s, feminist theorists have been examining the familiar, and some not so familiar, texts of political theory. Their rereadings and reinterpretations have revolutionary implications for an understanding not only of the books themselves, but also of such central political categories as citizenship, equality, freedom, justice, the public, the private, and democracy. Despite the importance of the new feminist scholarship, it has developed for the most part alongside rather than as part of "mainstream" political theory. Remarkably little attention has been paid to the implications of feminist arguments in the ever-increasing volume of commentary on the famous texts, or in discussions of contemporary political problems.

This volume illustrates the range and depth of feminist studies of the texts and, by collecting the essays together, we hope that their significance for political theory and practice will be more readily acknowledged. Some contributions have been published before, the earliest in 1977 and the most recent in 1989; others have been specially commissioned for this collection. The interpretations presented here could be challenged by other feminist readings of each of the texts, but we are not aiming to collect together a set of definitive accounts. Rather, our aim is to make a reasonably wide selection of feminist scholarship more easily accessible to political theorists and to the general reader.

Each of the chapters raises the question of how useful the texts of political theory are or can be to feminist theorists. The standard commentaries on the texts invariably either ignore or merely mention in passing the arguments of the great writers about sexual difference. These essays show, on the contrary, that arguments about the characters and attributes of men and women are fundamental to political theory. As

Susan Okin commented in *Women in Western Political Thought*, "it is by no means a simple matter to integrate the female half of the human race into [the Western] tradition of political theory."[1]

When feminists first turned to the classic texts they were mainly concerned with exposing the misogyny of many famous theorists and the way in which virtually every writer assumed that women's stunted rationality and moral and political capacities made them unfit for citizenship and political life. Indeed, one initial reaction was to reject the whole tradition of political theory and to call for feminists to begin again on completely new terrain. Thus, Lorenne Clark and Lynda Lange announced that "traditional political theory is utterly bankrupt in the light of present [feminist] perspectives . . . [It] is up to us to remedy this by providing new theories which reflect a deeper understanding of our historical position."[2] Most of the authors in this volume (including Lange) now suggest that the theorists whom they discuss do have something valuable to offer to feminist political theory. For example, Butler sees Locke as an embryonic "equal rights" feminist; Lange presents Rousseau as providing insights into the problems for women if social life is based on generalized competition between individuals; Okin argues that Rawls's theory has subversive potential for reconceptualizing familial as well as political justice; Dietz suggests that Arendt's notion of the *vita activa* should be incorporated into any feminist vision of the good life; and Sawicki claims that Foucault offers feminists a critical method and a "set of recommendations" about how to assess feminist theories.

The order of the chapters follows the conventional manner of discussing political thinkers and there is a rough thematic pairing throughout; Plato and Aristotle come first and we conclude with Mill and Rawls, de Beauvoir and Foucault, and Arendt and Habermas. The volume is not entirely conventional, however; two theorists included here, Mary Wollstonecraft and Simone de Beauvoir, do not usually make an appearance in the canon of texts that make up the standard curriculum of "political theory." Feminist scholarship has raised some awkward questions about the construction of this canon. Why, for example, are Mary Wollstonecraft and Simone de Beauvoir so rarely studied in courses on political theory? William Godwin (Wollstonecraft's husband) and Jean-Paul Sartre (de Beauvoir's companion) are much more likely to be read, and many more obscure, minor male authors of both the eighteenth and twentieth centuries are discussed.

Both Wollstonecraft and de Beauvoir were the friends of the leading radicals of their time, led unconventional lives and wrote novels as well as books of political theory and philosophy. Their major feminist works, *A Vindication of the Rights of Woman* and *The Second Sex*, are important works in the history of political thought, raising questions that other advocates of the "rights of men and citizens," and existentialist and individualist philosophers, repressed and ignored. The neglect of both writers appears to be because they were feminists writing about the relation between the sexes, a matter treated by contemporary political theorists as outside their subject matter. John Stuart Mill wrote on the same issue from a feminist perspective, and, until very recently, his feminist writings have also been largely ignored by political theorists, despite the very extensive discussion of his other work.

The authors of these chapters write from a variety of perspectives from within political theory and feminism; there is no single "feminist view" of the texts, nor is there a feminist conclusion about the theoretical way forward. Rather, this volume reflects the great diversity of both feminist argument in general and feminist approaches to the history of political thought. Nonetheless, despite the varied approaches of the contributors, the chapters are related because these scholars have approached the texts with specifically feminist questions in mind. The questions concern the political significance of sexual difference and men's power over women; the patriarchal construction of central categories of political thought; the relation between nature, the sexes, reason and politics; the relation between the private (in the sense of the domestic, the familial, the intimate) and the public (in the sense of the economy and the state); and the political importance of differences among women.

Notwithstanding all the differences between theorists from Plato to Habermas, the tradition of Western political thought rests on a conception of the "political" that is constructed through the exclusion of women and all that is represented by femininity and women's bodies. Sexual difference and sexuality are usually treated as marginal to or outside of the subject matter of political theory, but the different attributes, capacities and characteristics ascribed to men and women by political theorists are central to the way in which each has defined the "political." Manhood and politics go hand in hand, and everything that stands in contrast to and opposed to political life and the political virtues has been represented by women, their capacities and the tasks seen as natural to their sex, especially motherhood. Many political theorists have seen women as having a vital part to play in social life – but not as citizens and political actors. Rather, women have been designated as the upholders of the private foundation of the political world of men; or, as Saxonhouse argues of Aristotle, femininity symbolizes the private ties, restraint and stability that support the *polis*.

The question of sexual difference, that is to say, is inseparable from the question of the relationship between the "private" and the "public," which also runs through this volume. Mainstream political theory takes for granted, but generally ignores, a major distinguishing feature of modern

Western societies: the fact that they are divided into two spheres, only one of which, the public sphere, is seen to be of political relevance. Long before the separation of the world of women and the household from the masculine realm of politics and citizenship took its peculiarly modern form, political theorists had set the "political" in opposition to "private" concerns. On the face of it, this may seem untrue of Plato, who, in Book V of the *Republic*, had included women among his guardian class. Okin argues that although Plato's view that the most able upper-class women could share in political rule was "more revolutionary than [that] of any other major political philosopher," whether or not women ruled depended on Plato's willingness to abolish the private family and with it women's subordination as wives and their consequent exclusion from political activity. In the *Laws*, Plato demonstrated his unwillingness to undermine the patriarchal household, and so inaugurated a tradition in which the political and women were seen as incompatible.

For Aristotle there was no question about women's exclusion from the reasoned discourse and activities of the *polis*. Aristotle insisted that the natural order prescribed that the superior must govern the inferior. Saxonhouse stresses that, although Aristotle did not believe that all males were naturally superior to all females, even those women who might be fit for political life were precluded from it; in nourishing the young with their bodies and preserving the household, women lacked the necessary leisure to engage in politics. Nonetheless, Saxonhouse argues, women performed a vital political role in sustaining the life of the *polis*. The view that women must remain outside the public world of politics, even though they have a fundamentally important political task to perform, recurs in many of the classic texts.

In the modern period, however, the idea that women, by virtue of their natural capacities, had a distinctive political part to play gave rise to a problem that still remains unresolved. Before the proclamation of the revolutionary modern doctrine that all men were by nature, or by birthright, free and equal to each other, the exclusion of women from political life was unremarkable; many other categories of the population (such as the poor, the propertyless, or slaves) were deemed unfit by nature for citizenship. But once the "rights of man" became the currency of modern political argument, women posed a special problem – precisely because they are not the same as men. Standard accounts of the history of political theory assume that the statement that "all men" are born free and equal should be read as "all humankind"; that is, the doctrine of individual freedom and equality is assumed to be universal, to apply to everyone. On this reading, the incorporation of women into citizenship poses exactly the same problem in principle as the inclusion of, say, propertyless men or men of racial minorities. The only difficulty is putting theory into practice.

Such a view is shared by contemporary feminists who press for equal rights for women and men and for all differences between the sexes as citizens to be swept away through the enactment of gender-neutral laws and policies.

At this point textual interpretation becomes important. The standard commentaries pay virtually no attention to the fact that almost all the famous modern political theorists agree that "human nature" is sexually differentiated; womanhood and manhood do not have the same political meaning. But now the crucial question arises: what exactly is the significance of sexual difference? Do the different natures and capacities of women and men mean that women cannot be citizens? Or does it mean that, if women are citizens, their citizenship will differ in some ways from that of men? Feminists have recently been conducting a vigorous debate about equality, difference and citizenship, and some contemporary feminists argue that women can make a distinctive and valuable contribution to political life. Sexual difference (women's specific attributes, capacities and tasks), they claim, should be acknowledged in law and public policy.

The readings of the modern texts in these chapters reflect the wide difference of opinion over sexual difference and equality, and also illustrate the complexity of the relationship between masculinity and femininity, and the political and the private, equality, freedom and citizenship. The modern construction of separate public and private spheres was developed in the seventeenth century, and two contrasting interpretations are offered here of texts from that period. Hobbes stands alone in the tradition of political thought, although his singularity receives little attention from mainstream theorists. Hobbes is the only writer received into the "tradition" who assumed that the same human nature is common to women and men. Hobbes's theory begins from the premise that women, like men, are born free and are men's equals. Why, then, did he endorse the dominion of men over women in civil society, and how does he make the theoretical move from sexual equality in the state of nature to patriarchal rule in civil society? Pateman's reading of Hobbes is that all the women in the state of nature are conquered by men and so incorporated as servants into "families." Having lost their status as free and equal "individuals," women lack the standing to participate in the original contract. Men thus make a contract that creates modern patriarchal marriage and the private sphere and that legitimates men's jurisdiction over women in civil society.

Locke did not share Hobbes's view that the state of nature was a condition of sexual equality. Butler's reading of Locke, however, is that his theory has the potential to be expanded to allow the incorporation of women into political life on the same basis as men. The crucial factor is that Locke argued that women, like men, could be educated; thus women's political fate was not determined by their nature. Women, Butler states, are capable "of satisfying Locke's requirements for political life." Moreover, Locke stands at the beginning of liberal individualism, a doctrine with universal implications. Locke's legacy, Butler argues, meant that "liberals would be forced to bring their views on women into line with their theory of human nature."

The feminist John Stuart Mill was one liberal who saw the subjection of women as a glaring anomaly in the modern world. Mill tried (albeit without success) to bring the relation between the sexes into line with his wider liberal principles, which meant that he had to attempt to bridge the divide between public and private. The tenets of liberalism, Mill argued, applied to marriage as well as political life. Shanley interprets Mill as arguing for friendship, not domination, in marriage and she sees Mill's demand for equal opportunity for women as a means to marital friendship rather than an end in itself. But Mill's attempt to universalize liberal principles remains an exception in political theory. Other writers, including twentieth-century theorists who figure prominently in the canon of modern political theory, construct their arguments around the separation between public and private.

For example, Hannah Arendt's examination of labor, work and action assumes a strict division between the worlds of productive (male) and reproductive (female) work and labor. As Dietz points out, "the fundamental activities Arendt designates have actually been lived out as either male or female *identities. Animal laborans*, 'the reproducer,' has been structured and experienced as if it were natural to the female, and *homo faber*, 'the fabricator,' has been constructed as if it were appropriate to the male," rather than taken as irreducible dimensions of humanness itself. As Fraser shows, Habermas's extremely elaborate and sophisticated analysis, with his distinctions between material and symbolic reproduction and between socially integrated and system integrated action contexts, similarly maintains the patriarchal division between private and public. Habermas's theory has an implicit "gender subtext," and, because he fails to investigate how the public – the (masculine) worker and the workplace – are linked to the private – the family – his theory defends "an institutional arrangement which is widely held to be one, if not the, linchpin of modern women's subordination."

The example of Habermas illustrates how even radical theorists are oblivious to the problem of sexual difference and sexual subordination. Thus they rarely ask any questions about Rousseau's credentials as the father of radical democracy. Yet Rousseau could not be more explicit in his exclusion of women, whom he sees as natural political subversives, from citizenship. Many feminists have seen Rousseau as merely inconsistent in his argument about the sexes, but Lange argues against this reading.

Within the structure of Rousseau's theory, political order requires that the public world reflect the sexual order of nature. The education of men and women must be different and women must maintain the family, the foundation of the state. If both men and women acted as competitors, making decisions on the basis of private advantage and subjective interest – that is to say, if both sexes acted in the manner seen as properly masculine – then, Rousseau believed, women would always lose because men already have an advantage in the competition. The lesson to be learnt from Rousseau, Lange argues, is that women should be cautious about equality with men; "meaningful equality of right, or privilege, or social consideration, may have to be based on an accommodation of sexual differences."

Like Rousseau, Hegel made his views on men's and women's political place clear enough; indeed, Hegel not only confined women to the private family but even excluded them from history. Yet Hegel, as Benhabib emphasizes, was an Enlightenment thinker who upheld the transformation begun in the French Revolution – at least, where the freedom of the male subject of the modern state is concerned. He drew back when faced with the emancipated women of his day; his "views on love and sexuality . . . reveal him to be a counter-Enlightenment thinker." Benhabib states that Hegel is "women's grave digger"; he confines women to a doomed phase of the dialectic. Hegel called women "an everlasting irony" in the life of the community, and Benhabib urges the restoration of irony and the "otherness of the other" – that is, the difference of women – that Hegel sought to expunge from political theory.

The pervasive and protracted unwillingness of political theorists to examine and question the arguments of theorists such as Rousseau and Hegel about sexual difference and the public and private is exacerbated by the exclusion of feminist works from the canon of texts. Mary Wollstonecraft, for instance, insisted that public and private, and, hence, the characters of men and women, could only be understood in relation to each other. Wollstonecraft is especially interesting, too, because two different arguments can be found in her writings, an argument for women's political equality with men and an argument that motherhood, women's special capacity or what she called their "peculiar destination," meant that women's citizenship must differ from that of men. Wollstonecraft was by no means alone in this mixture of arguments. In the late nineteenth and early twentieth centuries, the suffragists also argued, on the one hand, that (political) virtue had no sex, and that justice demanded that women should have the same political rights and be enfranchised on the same basis as men; on the other hand, they argued that women had a unique contribution to make (and so had a different claim to the vote than men) because of their special responsibilities as mothers.

In many of her comments on motherhood, Wollstonecraft sounds like the precursor of contemporary feminist thinkers who advocate bringing the traditionally female practices and values associated with motherhood into the public realm. In this volume, such arguments are represented by Di Stefano's discussion of Marx. Di Stefano makes the sweeping charge against Marx that – regardless of or despite what he said explicitly about women – the very structure and style of his thought is masculinist and denies the importance, and even the existence, of mothers, mothering activity and maternal labor. "Marx has essentially denied and then reappropriated the labor of the mother in his historical and labor-based account of self-created man." The denial of the mother, in Di Stefano's view, maintains the domination of women and nature, and "the case of the missing (m)other in western political theory," not unique to Marx, supports a deep misogyny in the tradition of political thought.

Wollstonecraft provides a necessary counter to this aspect of the tradition, but one problem in her arguments, Gatens states, is that she treats women's tasks as mothers as necessarily following from women's embodiment and biology; a political division of labor between women and men is then justified as natural. Wollstonecraft agreed with Rousseau that the family was the foundation of the state, but sharply disagreed that women could be good mothers in conditions of marital despotism or without public standing as citizens. Yet their duties as citizens coincided with their duties as mothers. At the same time, Gatens stresses, Wollstonecraft also insisted that reason had no sex. Women's apparent incapacity was due to lack of education, and their natures were corrupted by passion – the passion of men. Thus Wollstonecraft argues simultaneously that the bodily difference between the sexes is crucial for their citizenship, and appeals to a disembodied reason, or what Gatens calls "the essential sexual neutrality of the rational agent," in her defence of the rights of woman.

A defence of the rational agent is presented by Dietz and Okin in their analyses of Arendt and Rawls. They argue that to pay attention to sexual difference in policy and public law is not only detrimental to women but wrongly conceptualizes the nature and purpose of political life. Dietz recoils from the strand of contemporary feminist theory that shares "an emancipatory vision that defends the moral (or subversive) possibilities of women's role as reproducer, nurturer, and preserver of vulnerable human life." Okin takes Rawls to task for failing to see the need to apply liberal principles of justice to the private sphere, and thus for not considering how his acceptance of the conventional sexual division of labor excludes women from public life and relieves men of domestic burdens. While both Dietz and Okin argue that in the past the concept of the "universal citizen," or neutral rational agent, has not been universal or neutral but masculine, they think that one should be able to discern, and articulate and act according to, universal, gender-neutral standards of justice.

In contrast, Spelman and Sawicki reject a unitary model of citizenship. In their discussions of the works of de Beauvoir and Foucault they defend difference and also go further by emphasizing that, if women differ from men, so women also differ from each other. Spelman and Sawicki acknowledge the danger that to sweep away universally applicable rules and precepts may put women back into a position where they have different, but also lesser and secondary, obligations and rights from men. However, they see the possibility of second-class citizenship as less of a problem than the failure to recognize that "equality" (at least as presently conceived) rests on binary oppositions – such as private/public, feminine/masculine, citizen/woman – and denies the myriad and crosscutting differentiations between individuals and groups.

De Beauvoir's famous observation that "one is not born, but rather becomes, a woman" may undermine notions that biology determines women's destiny, but it also suggests to Spelman that there is no single, prototypical "woman" whose interests can shape a single feminist agenda. The lesson we must learn from the fact that, as Spelman argues, de Beauvoir implicitly wrote from the perspective of a middle-class white woman, is not simply that political theory has ignored or not adequately accounted for women's political position, but that there is no "woman's place" unmediated by class, race, ethnicity, religion, sexual orientation and other factors. Similarly, Sawicki argues that Foucault's theory helps feminists to see that it is not necessary for all differences between women to be obliterated if women are to be able to resist male domination. She argues that difference theory puts the "sexuality debate" that has polarized American feminists into a new perspective. It becomes possible to see that the two sides share common conceptions of power, freedom and sexuality that obscure and deny the historical character and diversity of women's sexual experiences. Unless the multiplicity of women's voices and interests are taken into account, women in dominant groups are likely to neglect or silence other women just as they have been neglected or silenced by most political theorists.

Political theory is often taught as if reading (selected) classic texts – the "history of political thought" – can be kept separate from pressing, current political problems. Feminist interpretations of the texts show that this is far from the case. This volume illustrates that one of the major tasks facing feminist theorists is to develop democratic theory into a theory of political and civil equality that encompasses the differences between the sexes and among women so that full citizenship for varied women can be secured. Despite the disagreements among the authors, they agree that among the greatest wrongs done to women has been their exclusion from taking part as full members and citizens of the polity in political debate, deliberation and contest. The classic theorists, and the construction of the academic canon of political theory, have been instrumental in achieving and maintaining this exclusion. We hope that the very diversity of feminist perspectives that follow will encourage many others to join in reinterpretating the texts, and so in the reconstruction of the discipline of political theory itself. To join in the theoretical dialogue is to participate in the vital argument over the purposes and goals of our common life which lies at the heart of politics.

Notes

1 Susan Okin, *Women in Western Political Thought* (Princeton, NJ: Princeton University Press, 1979), p. 286.
2 Lorenne M. G. Clark and Lynda Lange, *The Sexism of Social and Political Theory* (Toronto: University of Toronto Press, 1979), p. xvii.

1

Philosopher Queens and Private Wives: Plato on Women and the Family

Susan Moller Okin

Plato's ideas about women have attracted considerable attention in recent years.[1] This is not surprising, since his proposals for the education and role of the female guardians in Book V of the *Republic* are more revolutionary than those of any other major political philosopher, not excluding John Stuart Mill. However, Plato on the subject of women appears at first to present his reader with an unresolvable enigma, especially when his other dialogues are taken into account. One might well ask how the same, generally consistent philosopher can assert, on the one hand, that the female sex was created from the souls of the most wicked and irrational men and can argue, on the other hand, that if young girls and boys were trained identically, their abilities as adults would be practically the same. How can the claim that women are "by nature" twice as bad as men be reconciled with the radical idea that they should be included among the exalted philosophic rulers of the ideal state?

While I cannot here discuss all the relevant dialogues, the following paper attempts, through analysis of Plato's arguments about private property and the family in relation to the *polis*, to explain why he appears so inconsistent about the nature and the proper role of women. I contend that when one compares the arguments and proposals of the *Republic* with those of the *Laws*, it becomes clear that the absence or presence of the private family determines whether Plato advocates putting into practice his increasingly radical beliefs about the potential of women. Only by examining the proposals of *Republic* V in the context of the overall aims and structure of the ideal society, and by doing likewise with the contrasting proposals regarding women in the *Laws*, will we find the differences intelligible.

The aim of the true art of ruling, as Plato conceives of it, is not the welfare of any single class or section, but the greatest possible happiness of the entire community.[2] "Happiness," however, can be a misleading word, for if it leads us to thoughts of freedom, individual rights, or equality of opportunity, we are far from Plato's idea of happiness (*eudaimonia*). Neither equality nor liberty nor justice in the sense of fairness were values for Plato. The three values on which both his ideal and his second-best cities are based are, rather, harmony, efficiency, and moral goodness; the last is the key to his entire political philosophy. Because of his belief in the intrinsic value of the soul and the consequent importance of its health, Plato does not think that happiness results from the freedom to behave just as one wants; it is in no way attainable independently of virtue. Statesmen, therefore, should "not only preserve the lives of their subjects but reform their characters too, so far as human nature permits of this."[3] Though the ultimate aim of the true ruler is the happiness of all his subjects, the only way he can attain this is by raising them all, by means of education and law, to the highest possible level of wisdom and virtue.

The gravest of all human faults, however, one considered by Plato to be inborn in most people is that "excessive love of self" which is "the cause of all sins in every case."[4] Worse still, whereas the soul and next the body should take priority, man's all too prevalent tendency is to give his property – in truth the least valuable of his possessions – his greatest attention. Thus, in the *Laws* the currency and system of production, while allowing for private property, are so designed as to ensure that "a man by his money-making [will not] neglect the objects for which money exists: . . . the soul and the body . . . Wherefore we have asserted (and that not once only) that the pursuit of money is to be honoured last of all."[5] Clearly Plato's citizens were never to forget that material possessions were but means to far more important ends.

The ruler's task in promoting his subjects' virtue is therefore two-fold. He must aim to overcome their extremes of self-love and their fatal preference for material possessions over the welfare of their souls. A man who is to be virtuous and great must be able to transcend his own interests and, above all, to detach himself from the passion to acquire. As Glenn Morrow has noted, there is abundant evidence in both the *Republic* and the *Laws* that Plato regarded the maintenance of a temperate attitude towards property as essential for the security and well-being of the state.[6] It was acquisitiveness, after all, that had led the first city Socrates depicted – the simple, "true" and "healthy" city – into war with its neighbors and all the complications that this entailed. Again, corruption that results from increasing possessiveness is the recurrent theme of *Republic* VIII, which analyzes the process of political degeneration.[7]

The *Republic* is an extremely radical dialogue. In his formulation of the ideal state, Plato questions and challenges the most sacred contemporary conventions. The solution he proposes for the problem of selfishness and divisive interests is that private property and hence private interests be abolished to the greatest possible extent. For in this city, not just harmony but unity of interests is the objective. "Have we any greater evil for a city," asks Socrates, "than what splits it and makes it many instead of one? Or a greater good than what binds it together and makes it one?" He concludes that the best governed city is that "which is most like a single human being."[8] Nothing can dissolve the unity of a city more readily than for some of its citizens to be glad and others to grieve over the same thing, so that all do not work or even wish in concert. The highest possible degree of unity is achieved if all citizens feel pleasure and pain on the same occasions, and this "community of pleasure and pain" will occur only if all goods are possessed in common. The best governed city will be that "in which most say 'my own' and 'not my own' about the same thing, and in the same way."[9]

If he had thought it possible, Plato would certainly have extended the communal ownership of property to all the classes of his ideal city. The first of the "noble lies," according to which all citizens are told that they are one big family, can be read as the complete expression of an ideal which can be realized only in part. Because he believes in the tendency of most human beings to selfishness, Plato considers the renunciation of private property to be something that can be attained only by the best of persons. This is made clear in the *Laws*, where he rejects the possibility of eliminating ownership for the citizens of his projected "second-best" city, since tilling the soil in common is "beyond the capacity of people with the birth, rearing and training we assume."[10] What is impossible for the citizens of the second-best city, with all their carefully planned education, must regretfully be regarded as beyond the capacity of the inferior classes in the ideal city. Thus it is the guardian class alone which is to live up to the ideal of community of property and unity of interests.[11]

The overcoming of selfish interests is regarded as most necessary for those who are to have charge of the welfare and governance of all the other citizens – quite apart from their greater capacity for it. Since a person will always take care of what he loves, the guardians, especially, must love the whole community, and have no interests other than its welfare. Above all, then, the permitted property arrangements for them must be "such as not to prevent them from being the best possible guardians and not to rouse them up to do harm to the other citizens."[12] Plato argues that the possession by the rulers of private lands and wealth would inevitably lead to their formation into a faction, whereupon they would consitute "masters and enemies instead of allies of the other citizens."[13] The combination of wealth and private interests with political power can lead only to the destruction of the city.

Plato's ideal for the guardians is expressed by the proverb, "friends have all things in common."[14] But if communal ownership of inanimate property is a great aid to the unity of the city, it appears to him to follow that communal ownership of women and children will conduce to even greater unity. It is clear from the way Plato argues that he thinks the communalization of property leads directly to the abolition of the family. He does not regard them as distinct innovations requiring separate justifications. In fact, he slides over the first mention of the abolition of the family, almost as a parenthesis,[15] and in both the *Republic* and the brief summary of this aspect of it presented in the *Laws*, the two proposals are justified by the same arguments and often at the same time. In the *Laws* especially, when Plato looks back to the institutions of the ideal city, the classification of women and children with other possessions occurs frequently. Thus he talks of "community of wives, children, and all chattels," and later, by contrast, of that less desirable state of affairs in which "women and children and houses remain private, and all these things are established as the private property of individuals."[16]

Women are classified by Plato, as they were by the culture in which he lived, as an important subsection of property.[17] The very expression "community (or common having) of women and children," which he uses to denote his proposed system of temporary matings, is a further indication of this, since it could just as accurately be described as "the community of men," were it not for its inventor's customary way of thinking about such matters.[18]

Just as other forms of private property were seen as destructive of society's unity, so "private wives" are viewed by Plato as diverse and subversive in the same way. Thus, in contrast to the unified city he is proposing, he points to those institutional arrangements that foster the ascendance of particularism and factionalism, with "one man dragging off to his own house whatever he can get his hands on apart from the others, another being separate in his own house with separate women and children, introducing private pleasures and griefs of things that are private."[19] Again, in the *Laws*, he strikes simultaneously against contemporary Athenian practices with regard both to private property and to women: "we huddle all our goods together, as the saying goes, within four walls, and then hand over the dispensing of them to the women . . ."[20] It is clear that conventional marriage and woman in her traditional role as guardian of the private household were seen by Plato as intimately bound up with that system of private possessions which was the greatest impediment to the unity and well-being of the city.

In *Republic* VIII, however, as Plato reviews the successively degenerate forms of the political order, we can see his association of private women with corruption at its most graphic. Just as women were communalized at the same time as other property, so are they now, without separate explanation, made private at the same time as other property, as the course of the city's degeneration is described. Once private, moreover, women are depicted as hastening the course of the decline, due to their exclusive concern with the particular interests of their families. First, when the rulers begin to want to own land, houses, and money, and to set up domestic treasuries and private love-nests, they will begin to fail as guardians of the people, and the city will start to degenerate.[21] Thereafter, private possession of women is depicted as a major cause of further corruption. The mother's complaints that her husband's lack of concern for wealth and public prestige disadvantages her among the other women make the timocratic youth begin to despise his worthy father and to feel challenged into showing that he is more of a man. The wife with her selfish concerns, who "chants all the other refrains such as women are likely to do in cases of this sort," is, like Pandora, the real originator of the evils that follow.[22]

The fact that Plato identifies the abolition of the family so closely with the communalization of property, and does not appear to regard the former as a more severe emotional deprivation than the latter, must be understood in the context of the functions and status of women and the family in contemporary upper-class Athenian life. In view of the chattel status of Athenian women and the "peculiarly close relation thought to hold between a family and its landed property," Plato's blending of two issues, which to us appear to be much more distinct, is far from inexplicable.[23] There is abundant evidence in classical Greek literature that the women who were eligible to become the wives of Plato's contemporaries were valued for silence, hard work, domestic frugality, and, above all, marital fidelity. Confined to the functions of household management and the bearing of heirs, they were neither educated nor permitted to experience the culture and intellectual stimulation of life outside their secluded quarters in the house. Accordingly, it was almost impossible for husbands and wives to be either day-to-day companions or emotional and intellectual intimates.[24] Consequently, as recent scholars of Greek life agree, "the family does not bulk large in most Greek writing, its affective and psychological sides hardly at all," and "family life, as we understand it, hardly existed" in late fifth-century Athens.[25] The prevailing bisexuality meant that "two complementary institutions coexisted, the family taking care of

what we may call the material side, pederasty (and the courtesan) the
affective, and to a degree the intellectual, side of a man's intimate life."[26]

On the other hand, while the family was certainly no center of the
upper-class Greek's emotional life, it did function in ways that the modern
family does not – ways which rendered it potentially far more socially
divisive. The single-family household had emerged from the clan in comparatively recent times, and only gradually did the *polis* gain the loyalty
that had once belonged to the autonomous clan. Antigone represents the
paradigm example of this conflict of loyalties; there were, in fact, various
areas of life where it had not yet become clear whether family or civic
obligations should prevail. The extent to which the victim's kin, rather
than the rulers, were responsible for ensuring that crime was properly
avenged is well documented in the *Laws*.[27] Again, the predominance of
duties to parents over any notion of legal justice is clearly indicated in the
Euthyphro, where Socrates is incredulous that a man could even think of
prosecuting his own father for the murder of anyone who was not a
relative.[28] Despite its minimal functioning as an emotional base, then, the
Athenian family of the early fourth century, as a firm economic entity and
the focus of important duties, constituted an obviously divisive force and
potential threat to civic loyalty.

Those Plato scholars who have expressed profound horror at the idea
that the family be abolished and replaced by those mating arrangements
designed to produce the best offspring seem to have treated the issue
anachronistically, by neglecting the function of the family in Athenian life.
When G. M. A. Grube, for example, objects to the system of temporary
matings advocated for the guardians as "undesirable because it does
violence to the deepest human emotions" and "entirely ignores the love
element between the 'married' pair,"[29] he seems to be forgetting that at
the time, the family was simply not the locus for the expression of the
deepest human emotions. Even a cursory knowledge of the *Symposium*,
with its deprecating comparison of those who turn their love towards
women and raise families with those whose superior, spiritual love is
turned towards boys and philosophy, reveals that Plato and his audience
would not have regarded the abolition of the family as a severe limitation
of their intimate lives. Stranger still is the attitude taken by Leo Strauss,
who not only assumes that the family is "natural" and any move to
abolish it "convention," but makes the issue of whether the abolition of
the family is possible or not into an acid test for determining the feasibility
of the entire ideal state.[30] Those passages of the *Republic* to which he refers
in order to demonstrate the supposed "fact that men seem to desire
naturally to have children of their own" are remarkably inadequate to
prove his point. Moreover, his objection that Plato's controls on heterosexual behaviour mean that "the claims of *eros* are simply silenced"

implies a complete denial of the prevailing homosexual *eros* of the time. It is very probable that Plato's listeners would have regarded the ideal state's restrictions on their homosexual behavior as more repressive of their sexual feelings than the abolition of the family and the controls placed on heterosexual intercourse.

The same scholars – Grube, Taylor, and Strauss – who reject the abolition of the family as impossible, are those most intolerant of the proposed alternative, in which partners are chosen for each other, supposedly by lot but, in fact, for eugenic purposes. Those who reject such proposals as quite impracticable, given human nature, because of their "intolerable severity"[31] would do well to consider the position of respectable Greek women. For they were just as controlled and deprived in their sexual lives as both sexes of guardians were to be in the ideal city, and without having available to them the compensations of any participation in life outside the domestic sphere. The Greek woman was not permitted to choose her sexual partner, any more than Plato's guardians were. Moreover, in her case the partner had not only the absolute right to copulate with and reproduce via her for the rest of her life, but also all the powers which her father had previously wielded over her. Once married, a woman had no condoned alternative sexual outlets, but was entirely dependent on a husband, who might have any number of approved hetero- or homosexual alternatives, for any satisfaction that he might choose to give her. The extent of the double standard is brought clearly into relief by the fact that the Greek word for adultery *meant* nothing but sexual intercourse between a married woman and a man who was not her husband. Needless to say, the punishments were very severe. Even if her husband died, a woman had no control over her life or her body, since she was returned to the custody of her father or guardian, who could remarry her at his pleasure. Alternatively, a citizen could give his sister or daughter into concubinage, from which she could be sent to a brothel without any reproach to her owner.[32]

If Athenian women of the highest class, living in one of the most highly cultured societies the world has known, could be controlled and deprived to this extent, it is hardly arguable that the exigencies of human nature render the Platonic mating system, with its requirement of supposedly "unnatural continence,"[33] impossible to enact. Women's sexual lives have been restricted throughout the greater part of world history, just as rigidly as Plato proposes to control the intimate lives of his guardians. "The claims of *eros*" have been "simply silenced" in women with considerable success. It is apparent from much of the history of the female sex that, with suitable indoctrination and strong sanctions, human beings can be conditioned to accept virtually any extent of control on their sexual and emotional lives. The point is, of course, that the scholars concerned have used the terms "human emotions" and "human nature" to refer only to men. What seems really horrific to Grube, Taylor, and Strauss is that whereas the Greeks, like many other peoples, merely reserved women for the production of legitimate issue and controlled their lives accordingly, Plato has dared to suggest that the sexual lives of both male and female guardians should be controlled for the purpose of producing the best possible offspring for the community.

The significance of Plato's abolition of the family is profound; the proposal has been echoed by a number of subsequent theorists or rulers of utopian societies that depend to a very high degree on cohesion and unity. As Stanley Diamond has asserted, in an illuminating essay which analyzes the significance of Plato's treatment of the family, "The obvious aim is to disengage [the guardians] from all connections and motives which might diminish their dedication to the state . . . Plato clearly sensed the antagonism between state and family, and in order to guarantee total loyalty to the former, he simply abolished the latter."[34] It is important to notice that Plato's revolutionary solution to the conflict was not to obliterate the primary ties of kinship, but to extend them throughout the entire ruling class. The guardians were in fact "to imagine that they were all one family,"[35] and it is stressed in many ways that the formation of the rulers into one family is to be no mere formality. They are required not only to address but to behave towards each other as brother, parent, and so on. "It would be ridiculous," Glaucon agrees, "if they only mouthed, without deeds, the names of kinship."[36] Thus, the fear and shame associated with violence towards a parent will operate as an unusually strong sanction against attack on anyone at all of the older generation. Likewise, lawsuits and factional disputes will be no more common than they would be within a family, and the city's success in war will be in large part due to the fact that soldiers will be no more likely to desert their comrades than to abandon members of their own families.[37] Indeed, as Gregory Vlastos has concisely stated, "The ideal society of the *Republic* is a political community held together by bonds of fraternal love."[38]

The most radical implication of Plato's transforming the guardian class into a single family concerns the role of women. Rousseau, in the course of a bitter attack on Plato both for doing away with the family and for giving equal opportunities to women, nevertheless reveals a perceptive understanding of the connection between the two innovations. "I am well aware that in the *Republic* Plato prescribes the same exercises for women as for men," he says. "Having dispensed with the individual family in his system of government, and not knowing any longer what to do with women, he finds himself forced to turn them into men."[39] It appears that he is correct, except that in place of "men" we should substitute "people," since for Rousseau in many important respects only men were people. Scholars who have considered the connection between the first two "waves of paradox" of Book V – the granting of equal opportunities to women and the abolition of the family – do not, however, agree. Some have stressed the independence of the two proposals, some have maintained that there is probably a causal link between them but have not committed themselves on its direction, and at least one has asserted, without giving any reasons, that it is the emancipation of women which renders necessary the abolition of the family.[40] For a number of reasons, however, it seems that any causal connection that exists between the two paradoxes goes the other way, as Rousseau claims.

In the ideal city, since there is no private wealth or marriage for those in the guardian class and since their living arrangements are to be communal, there is no domestic role such as that of the traditional housewife. Since planned breeding and communal childrearing minimize the unpredict-ability of pregnancy and the time demanded of mothers, maternity is no longer anything approaching a full-time occupation. Thus, women can no longer be defined by their traditional roles. However, every person in the ideal city is defined by his or her function; the education and working life of each citizen are to be dedicated to the optimal performance of a single craft.[41] If the female guardians were no longer to be defined in relation to particular men, children, and households, it seems that Plato had no alternative but to consider them persons in their own right. If they were to take their place as members of the guardian class, each must share in the functions of that class. Thus Plato had to convince his skeptical audience that women were able to perform tasks very different from those customarily assigned to them.

Socrates first reminds his audience that they have all agreed that each individual should be assigned work that is suited to his or her nature. But, he says, since none of them will claim that there is no difference of nature between the male and the female, they are in danger of contradicting themselves if they argue that the female guardians should do the same work as the male. However, there are many ways in which human beings can differ, and we do not regard all of them as relevant in assigning different functions to different persons. Socrates asserts that we have not yet considered "what form of different and same nature, and applying to what, we were distinguishing when we assigned different practices to a different nature and the same ones to the same."[42] But, he continues, is it not reasonable to consider only those differences and similarities that have some bearing on the activity in question? We do not worry about whether a man is bald or longhaired when assessing his capacity to be a good shoemaker. There is, therefore, no reason to consider the difference in procreative function between the sexes – "that the female bears and the male mounts" – as relevant in deciding whether they should play equal roles in the ruling class. Socrates lays the burden of proof firmly on whoever should claim that it is. He argues, rather, that since the characteristics of the soul determine whether a person is capable of a certain pursuit, and since sex is no more related to the soul than the presence or absence of hair, members of both sexes will be skilled in all the arts, depending on the nature of their individual souls. Thus, though he asserts that women in general are not as capable as men in general, especially in physical strength, individual members of both sexes will be capable of performing all the functions needed by the city, including guardianship and philosophy. The only way to ensure that persons are assigned the jobs for which they are best suited is to assess the merits of each, independently of sex.

This argument, simple as it seems, is unique in the treatment of women by political philosophers, and has revolutionary implications for the female sex. Plato's bold suggestion that perhaps there is no difference between the sexes, apart from their roles in procreation, is possible only because the requirement of unity among the ruling class, and the consequent abolition of private property and the family, entail the abolition of wifehood and the absolute minimization of motherhood. Once the door is open, the possibilities for women are boundless. The annihilation of traditional sex roles among the guardians is total – even the earliest childcare is to be shared by men and women.[43] Plato concludes that, though females as a class are less able, the best of women can share with the best of men in the highest functions involved in ruling the city. The "philosopher monarchs," as they should always have been called, were to include both sexes.[44]

The overwhelming hostility from male scholars to Plato's first wave of paradox is fascinating in its own right, but this is not the place to discuss it. However, one charge that has been laid against him must be dealt with here. Leo Strauss and Allan Bloom have claimed that Plato's arguments for the equality of women depend on his "abstracting from" or "forgetting" the body, and particularly his "abstracting from the difference between the sexes with regard to procreation."[45] Clearly they do not. Plato is very careful to take into account those differences between the sexes that are palpably biological and therefore inevitable – pregnancy, lactation, and a degree of difference in physical strength. These scholars, in the company of millions of other people, mistakenly assume, as Plato very rationally does not, that the entire conventional female sex role follows logically from the single fact that women bear children. The real significance of the treatment of the women question in *Republic* V is that it is one of the very few instances in the history of thought when the biological implications of femaleness have been clearly separated from all the conventional, institutional, and emotional baggage that has usually been identified with them. Plato's elimination of a private sphere from the guardians' lives entailed the radical questioning of all the institutionalized differences between the sexes.

During the argument about the proper education and role of women, Socrates twice indicates directly that these and the abolition of the family are really parts of the same issue. He talks, first, of the "right acquisition and use of children and women" and later of "the law concerning the possession and rearing of the women and children."[46] In addition, the way he introduces the emancipation of the female guardians is in itself significant. Having dropped in an aside the proposal that the guardians will have women and children as well as their other possessions in common, Socrates is challenged, at the beginning of Book V, to justify this important decision. In answer to this challenge, he embarks on his discussion, first, of the equal education and treatment of women and, second, of the communal breeding and rearing arrangements. It seems, then, that having decided to do away with the conventional role of women by doing away with the family, he feels impelled to support this proposal by demonstrating that women are capable of filling many roles outside of their traditional sphere. A brief passage from the *Laws* shows how aware Plato was of the danger of freeing women from their confined, domestic role without giving them an alternative function. He thought the example of the Spartans should be enough to discourage any legislator from "letting the female sex indulge in luxury and expense and disorderly ways of life, while supervising the male sex."[47] Thus it was his dismantling of the family which not only enabled Plato to rethink the question of women and their potential abilities but forced him to do so.

Two additional arguments show clearly that it is the abolition of the family that leads Plato into emancipating the female guardians rather than vice versa. First, no mention is made of the women of the inferior classes. We are told that among these householders and farmers, private land, houses, and other property are to be preserved. The close connection between these things and the private ownership of women and children implies, though we are not specifically told this, that the family too is preserved among the lower classes.[48] Efficiency is no doubt one of Plato's primary aims in the organization of the artisans. But although the argument in Book V about women's talents is just as applicable to the other crafts as to that of governing the city, there is no suggestion of applying it to the women of any class but the guardians. The only possible explanation seems to be that where the family is retained, women continue to be private wives and functional mothers, so that their equality with men in other roles is not considered an open issue.[49]

Second, what happens to women in Plato's second-best city – that depicted in the *Laws* – overwhelmingly confirms our hypothesis. On the subject of women, Plato in the *Laws* is a study in ambivalence. He is caught in a dilemma caused by the impossibility of reconciling his increasingly firm beliefs about the potential of the female sex with the reintroduction of private property and the family into the social structure of his city. On the one hand, having thought about women as individuals with vast unused talents, Plato seems to have been more convinced than ever, by the time he wrote the *Laws*, that existing practice with regard to women was foolish and that they should be educated and used to their greatest capacity. In theory, the radical statements about women from *Republic* V are carried in the *Laws* to new extremes. On the other hand, the *Laws* is a considerably less revolutionary document than the *Republic*; far from being "a pattern laid up in heaven," the second-best city is put forward as a far less utopian construct.[50] The very title of the dialogue, usually translated "Laws," is in fact more accurately rendered as "Tradition." A significant casualty of this "realism" is Plato's conception of the role of women. What is proposed for them in general terms is simply not fulfilled by the details of the society, in which they are again private wives and the functioning mothers of particular children.

Plato's arguments and conclusions in the *Laws* about the natural potential of women are far more radical than those of the *Republic*. He appears to attribute to the different rearing and education of the two sexes practically all differences in their subsequent abilities and achievements. Pointing to the example of the Sarmatian women, who participate in warfare equally with the men, as proof of the potential of the female sex, he argues that the Athenian practice of maintaining rigid sex roles is absurd. Only a legislator's "surprising blunder" could allow the waste of half the state's available resources, by prescribing the "most irrational" practice – "that men and women should not all follow the same pursuits with one accord and with all their might."[51] In addition, a few speeches before these striking assertions are made, Plato prepares the way for them by means of an elaborate metaphor about ambidexterity – a lightly veiled allusion to his belief that men and women, like right and left hands, would be far more equal in ability if they received equal training.[52]

By the time he wrote the *Laws*, then, Plato had clearly come to recognize that female human nature was not fairly represented by the deprived and stunted women of his own society. Indeed, it was as yet unknown, although one could derive some impression of what women were capable of achieving from the example of the female warriors who in other societies held their own with the men in battle. However, in the *Laws*, the statements of general principle about women are far more radical than the actual details of the society as it is drawn up. Having made the general proclamation that the law should prescribe the same education and training for girls as it does for boys and that "the female sex must share with the male, to the greatest extent possible, both in education and in all else" – should "share with men in the whole of their mode of life"[53] – Plato's Athenian legislator fails to apply these precepts, in many of the most crucial instances. In order to understand the inconsistency between the general statements about women and the detailed specifications given for the most important of civic duties, we must turn to the effects on women of the reintroduction of private property and the family.

Though it is clearly a source of regret to Plato, he concedes that the citizens of the second-best city, not being gods or sons of gods, are not capable of holding their property in common. The reinstatement of private property, one of the most far-reaching differences between the *Laws* and the *Republic*, brings with it in the same paragraph the reintroduction of marriage and the family.[54] It is clear from the context that the need for a property-holding man to have an heir requires the disappearance of the communal ownership of women and children simultaneously with that of other property. However, the identification of women and children together with other possessions was so automatic to the Greek mind that, again, no separate justification is felt to be necessary. The failure to achieve communism of property, it seems, entails the private possession of women.

The family, moreover, is the basis of the polity planned in the *Laws*. As Glenn Morrow has noted, "the state is a union of households or families, not a collection of detached citizens," and "the vitality of the family in Plato's state is evident at many points in his legislation."[55] The existence of family shrines, the complexity of marriage and inheritance laws, the family's crucial role in the prosecution of criminal justice, and the denial to sons of the right to defend themselves against their fathers – all these provisions indicate the central and authoritative position of the family.[56] The marriage laws are the first to be drawn up, and their repercussions for the position of women are immediate and extensive. In contrast to the temporary mating system of the *Republic*, in which neither sex had more freedom to choose or refuse a mate than the other, the reintroduction of permanent marriage seems to involve, without any explanation, a very different degree of choice of spouse for women and men. Marriage is to be compulsory for all, since procreation is regarded as a universal duty. But whereas a man, subject to the provision that he seek a partnership that will result in the best offspring for his society, decides whom he will marry, a woman is "given" in marriage.[57] The "right of valid betrothal" of a woman belongs in turn to a long succession of male kindred, and only if she has no close male relatives at all can she have any say in choosing her husband. Ironically, considering this preemption of women's choice, Plato refuses to enforce legally the prohibition of unsuitable marriages, since he considers that to do so, "besides being ridiculous, would cause widespread resentment."[58] Apparently what was to be customary for women was considered intolerable control if applied to men.

The treatment of women by the marriage laws is closely related to the fact that they are virtually excluded from property ownership. Even if she has no brothers, a daughter can participate in the inheritance of the family estate only by serving as the instrument through which the husband her father chooses for her can become her father's heir, if she has no brothers.[59] The *Laws* documents the essential connection of property and inheritance to the marriage system and position of women. When a man owns inheritable property, he must own a wife too, in order to ensure a legitimate heir. The fact that women are private wives entails that in many ways they are treated as property rather than as persons. They themselves cannot inherit real property, which to a large extent defines personhood within the society (a disinherited son must leave the city unless another citizen adopts him as his heir);[60] and they are treated as commodities to be given away by their male relatives. Given these basic features of the social structure of the city, it is not surprising that Plato, in spite of general pronouncements to the contrary, is not able to treat women as the equals of his male citizens. Their status as property seems to prevent the execution of his declared intentions.

Although the legal status of women in Plato's second-best city is an improvement on that in contemporary Athens, it is not one of equality with men. Glenn Morrow has said that "it is certainly Plato's expressed intention (though not fully carried out) to give women a more equal status under the law . . ."[61] The proposed divorce laws, unlike the marriage laws, do treat women considerably more equally than did those of contemporary Athens; the criminal statutes enforce the same punishments for the wounding or murder of wives as of husbands, and they are generally applied without discrimination according to the sex of either plantiff or defendant.[62] The most striking instance of equal treatment before the law is in the case of extramarital intercourse, where the same penalties are extended to offenders of both sexes.[63] This unusual departure from the double standard that one might expect to find in a society so firmly based on monogamy and inheritance can probably be explained by Plato's wish to make all the members of his city as virtuous and temperate as possible. After all, the standards are not relaxed for women, but they are considerably tightened up for men. However, the Athenian concept of women as legal minors is still present in significant ways in the *Laws*. Besides not being eligible to own property, they are not allowed until the age of forty to give evidence in a court of law or to support a plea, and only if unmarried are they allowed to bring an action.[64] Women, especially if married, are still to a large extent *femmes couvertes*.

What begins to be revealed through the denial of important civil and legal rights to women is strongly confirmed by the roles allotted them within the official governmental sphere. In the *Republic*, once we have been told that women of the guardian class are to share with men in every aspect of ruling and guarding, they are not specifically assigned to any particular offices, and there is no implication that they are ineligible for any. The only case where women are specifically mentioned as being eligible for office is at the end of Socrates' account of the philosophers' education. Here, presumably because the very idea must have seemed so outrageous, Plato feels it necessary to remind his audience that everything he has been saying applies equally to all women with the necessary abilities.[65] It is most unlikely that the women guardians, if allowed to compete for the highest rank of all, would have been excluded from any other office.

In the *Laws*, by contrast, in spite of the general pronouncements cited above, Plato both specifies when a certain function, such as the priesthood, is to be performed by persons of both sexes, and makes particular mention of women's holding certain offices, frequently with the strong implication that only women are eligible for them.[66] Thus, it is women who supervise married couples, who look after infants, whose role in the educational system is to provide the children's meals and oversee their games – in short, who perform, in positions not of the highest rank, all those domestic, nurturing, child-oriented tasks to which women have traditionally been assigned. On the other hand, there is no hint of women's participation in the magistracy, or the "divine nocturnal synod," whose role parallels that of the philosophers in the *Republic*.[67] The children are given their lessons by male educational officers; the post of supervisor of education is "by far the most important . . . of the highest offices of State" and must be filled by "that one of the citizens who is in every way the most excellent," and it is explicitly laid down that its occupant be male, for he must be "the father of legitimate children."[68] This qualification adds weight to what is implied throughout the work – that in the second-best city, unless the eligibility of women is plainly mentioned, most offices, and especially high ones, are reserved for men.[69] Even for those in which she can share, a women is not eligible until age 40, whereas a man is eligible from the age of 30.[70]

In spite of his controversial proposal in the *Laws* that, in the interests of order and discipline, even married women should take their meals communally, though segregated from the men, it is clear that Plato was ambivalent about the wisdom, or perhaps the feasibility, of bringing wives out of their domestic seclusion. Thus when he describes the funeral processions for distinguished citizens, women of childbearing age are noticeably omitted from a list in which every other class of citizen has its place. They are similarly omitted from the choral competitions.[71] Most remarkable, however, given his previous insistence that neither gymnastics nor riding are improper for women, and that trained women can perform in the military sphere equally as well as men,[72] is the fact that, once the detailed regulations are being made, he exempts women almost entirely from military service. Young girls are to learn the military arts only "if they agree to it," whereas they are obligatory for the boys.[73] Then, although he makes the general provision that men, women, and children are all to participate in military training at least one day a month, when the details are given, women after the age of marriage (20 at the latest) are again noticeably absent. They are not included either in races or in wrestling, both of which are integral parts of the training. As for horsemanship, it is decreed that "it is not worthwhile to make compulsory laws and rules about their taking part in such sports," but that they may do so "without blame," if they like.[74] It should be noted that Plato was not in the habit of making aspects of his educational systems optional – particularly those relating to the defense of the state.

Finally, whereas the term of military service for men is from the ages of 20 to 60, "for women they shall ordain what is possible and fitting in each case, after they have finished bearing children, and up to the age of fifty, in whatever kind of military work it may be thought right to employ their services."[75] This means that for all the grand assertions about the necessity and rationality of women's being trained equally with men to share in the defense of the state, they are in fact allowed, not compelled, to train up to the age of, at latest, 20, they are then excluded from most military activity until they are past childbearing, and they are subsequently exempted again at 50. In a society in which men had no other condoned sexual outlet than their wives, and contraception was hardly in an advanced state, this could well mean an expectation of five years of military service from adult women. Surely this was no way to produce Amazons.

Despite Plato's professed intention to have the women of the second-best city share equally with the men in all the duties of citizenship, the fact that they are private wives curtails their participation in public life for three reasons. The first is pregnancy and lactation, which is not controlled and predictable as it was in the *Republic*, where the guardians were to mate only at the behest of the rulers. In the *Laws*, since women are permanent wives, they are far less able to time or limit their pregnancies and cannot be held continuously liable for public and, especially, military duties. Second, the reinstitution of the private household makes each wife into the mistress responsible for its welfare, and it is clear that in the *Laws* a mother is to participate far more in early childcare than did the female guardian, who was not even to know which child was hers.[76]

The third reason is that Plato found it inconceivable that women who are "private wives" – the private property of the male citizens – should play the same kind of public and, especially, military roles as the female guardians, who were not defined in terms of a traditional relationship to a man. Whereas the female guardians, like their male counterparts, could exercise naked, the young girls in the *Laws* must be "clad in decent apparel," as if a maiden who was shortly to become the respectable wife and private property of a citizen could hardly be seen naked by the world at large.[77] Plato expresses as much expectation of ridicule for his suggestion in the *Laws* that wives should dine at public, though segregated, tables as he had expressed in the *Republic* for his proposal that all the guardians of both sexes should exercise together naked.[78] Although he thought it even more dangerous to leave women undisciplined than to neglect men and insisted that women too should dine in public, he was well aware that, in the kind of society he was planning, there would be enormous resistance to such an idea. Consequently, although he deplored the fact that even the supposedly trained women of Sparta had panicked and run when an enemy invaded their city, and thought it folly that so important a potential for defense as the entire female sex should be neglected, he seems to have found it impossible to hold to his original proposal that women should participate in military activities equally with men. If the segregated public dining of private wives could cause a general outcry, there was no knowing what revolutions might be provoked by the proposal that men should mingle with other men's private wives on the battlefield. Despite all his professed intentions in the *Laws* to emancipate women and make full use of the talents that he was now convinced they had, Plato's reintroduction of the family has the direct effect of putting them firmly back into their traditional place.

In the *Republic*, because the abolition of property and the family for the guardian class entails the abolition of woman's traditional sphere, the difference between the sexes is reduced to that of their roles in procreation. Since the nature of the women of this class is declared to be the same as that of the men, the radical proposal that their educations and lifestyles are to be identical follows accordingly. Plato has prescribed an androgynous character for all the guardians; both male and female are to be courageous and gentle, and both, because of their education and continued fellowship, will hold precious the good of the entire community. For the purposes of this society, therefore, the abolition of traditional sex roles is declared to be far more in accordance with nature than is the conventional adherence to them.

In the *Laws*, by contrast, the reinstatement of property requires monogamy and private households, and thus restores women to their role of "private wives" with all that this entails. Although his general statements about women's potential are considerably stronger here than in the *Re-*

public, Plato *cannot*, because of the economic and social structure he has prescribed, carry out to any significant extent the revolution in woman's role that would seem to follow from such beliefs. In this society, the "nature" of woman must be different from the "nature" of man. She must be pure and respectable, as befits a private wife who is to ensure the legitimacy of the property owner's heir, while he is to retain the noble and courageous qualities which resemble those of the ideal guardian.

The striking difference between the roles of women in the *Republic* and the *Laws*, then, is not due to a change in Plato's beliefs about the nature and capacities of women. On the contrary, his convictions appear to have changed in exactly the opposite way. The difference is due to the abolition of private property and the family, in the interest of unity, in the former dialogue, and their reinstatement in the latter. When a woman is once again perceived as the privately owned appendage of a man, when the family and its needs define her function, the socialization and regulation prescribed for her must ensure that her "nature" is formed and preserved in accordance with this role.

Notes

1 See, for example, Christine Pierce, "Equality: *Republic* V," *Monist*, 57 (1), January 1973; Anne Dickason, "Anatomy and Destiny: The Role of Biology in Plato's Views of Women," *Philosophical Forum*, 5, (1–2), 1973–4; and, since this paper was written, Arlene Saxonhouse, "The Philosopher and the Female in the Political Thought of Plato," *Political Theory*, 4, (2), May 1976.

2 *The Republic of Plato*, trans. Allan Bloom (New York, 1968), 420b.

3 *Statesman*, trans. H. B. Skemp, in *The Collected Dialogues of Plato*, ed. Edith Hamilton and Huntington Cairns (New York, 1961), 297b. Cf. *Laws*, trans. R. G. Bury (Cambridge, Mass., 1926), 630c, 644–5, 705d–6a, 707d; *Euthydemus*, trans. W. H. D. Rouse, in *Collected Dialogues*, 292b–c; and cf. Sheldon Wolin, *Politics and Vision* (London, 1961), pp. 34–6.

4 *Laws*, 731e.

5 Ibid., 743d–e.

6 Glenn R. Morrow, *Plato's Cretan City* (Princeton, 1960), p. 101; cf. *Laws*, 736e.

7 *Republic*, 372e–3e, and VIII passim.

8 Ibid., 462a–e.

9 Ibid., 462a–e.

10 *Laws*, 739c–40a.

11 *Republic*, 416c–17b.

12 Ibid., 416c–d.

13 Ibid., 417a–b.

14 Ibid., 423e; *Laws*, 739c.

15 *Republic*, 423e.

16 Ibid., 423e, 462, 464; *Laws*, 739c, 807b.

17 The Greeks' basically proprietary attitude towards women is well illustrated by the following statement from Demosthenes' account of the lawsuit, *Against Naera*: "For this is what living with a woman as one's wife means – to have children by her and to introduce the sons to the members of the clan and of the deme, and to betroth the daughters to husbands as one's own. Mistresses we keep for the sake of pleasure, concubines for the daily care of our persons, but wives to bear us legitimate children and to be faithful guardians of our households." Demosthenes, *Private Orations*, Loeb edn, trans. A. T. Murray (Cambridge, Mass., 1939), III: 122. For confirmation that this was a prevalent attitude see Victor Ehrenberg, *Society and Civilization in Greece and Rome* (Cambridge, Mass., 1964), p. 26.

18 Cf. G. M. A. Grube, *Plato's Thought* (London, 1935), p. 89.

19 *Republic*, 464c–d.

20 *Laws*, 805e.

21 *Republic*, 547b, 548a.

22 Ibid., 549c–e.

23 Morrow, *Plato's Cretan City*, n. 13 on p. 102, in which he notes that in Athens custom forbade the alienation of family land. The connection in classical Greek thought and practice between the wife and custody of the household property is amply confirmed in the descriptions of household management given by Xenophon and Aristotle.

24 See, for example, Thucydides, *The Peloponnesian War*, 46; Sophocles, *Ajax*, Loeb edn, trans. F. Storr (Cambridge, Mass., 1913), 291–3; Xenophon, *Oeconomicus*, in *Xenophon's Socratic Discourse*, trans. Carnes Lord, ed. Leo Strauss (Ithaca, 1970), p. 29 and cf. pp. 30–3; Aristotle, *The Politics*, I, xiii, II; Victor Ehrenberg, *The People of Aristophanes*, 2nd rev. edn (Oxford, 1951), pp. 202, 295.

25 M. I. Finley, *The Ancient Greeks* (New York, 1963), pp. 123–4; Ehrenberg, *Society and Civilization*, p. 59.

26 Finley, *Ancient Greeks*, p. 124.

27 *Laws*, for example, 866 and 873e.

28 *Euthyphro*, 4a–b.

29 Grube, *Plato's Thought*, p. 270; cf. A. E. Taylor, *Plato: The Man and His Work* (London, 1926; 7th edn, 1960), p. 278.

30 Leo Strauss, "On Plato's Republic," in *The City and Man* (Chicago, 1964), p. 117.

31 Taylor, *Plato*, p. 278; see also Grube, *Plato's Thought*, p. 270, and Strauss, "On Plato's Republic," p. 117.

32 Jean Ithurriague, *Les idées de Platon sur la condition de la femme* (Paris, 1931), p. 53.

33 Grube, *Plato's Thought*, p. 270.

34 Stanley Diamond, "Plato and the Definition of the Primitive," in *Culture in History*, ed. Diamond (New York, 1960), p. 126.

35 *Timaeus*, trans. Benjamin Jowett (Oxford, 1871), 18c–d.

36 *Republic*, 463c–e.

37 Ibid., 464d–e, 465a–b, 471c–d.

38 Gregory Vlastos, *Platonic Studies* (Princeton, 1973), p. 11.

39 Rousseau, *Emile*, Pléiade edn (Paris, 1914), 4: 699–700 (my translation).

40 For examples of these three positions, see Pierce, "Equality," p. 6; Strauss, "On Plato's Republic," p. 116; Taylor, *Plato*, p. 278.

41 *Republic*, 370; this is graphically illustrated by the assertion at 406d–7a that if one can no longer perform one's task, it is worthless to go on living.

42 Ibid., 454b; cf. 454–6 in general for source of this paragraph.

43 Ibid., 460b.

44 Ibid., 540c.

45 Strauss, "On Plato's Republic," pp. 116–17; Allan Bloom, "Interpretive Essay," in *Republic of Plato*, trans. Bloom, pp. 382–383.

46 *Republic*, 451c, 453d.

47 *Laws*, 806a–c.

48 *Republic*, 417a–b.

49 It is illuminating that in Aristotle's response to the proposals of Book V, once the issue of the family is settled, that of the role of women is not considered an independent one. It is clear that, since Aristotle considers himself to have refuted the proposal for the community of women and children, he does not deem it necessary to argue against Plato's wild ideas about women and their potential as individual persons. Given the family and the private household, women are private wives with domestic duties, and further discussion of the subject would be superfluous. *Politics*, II: 1264b.

50 *Republic*, 592b; *Laws*, 739.

51 *Laws*, 805a–b.

52 Ibid., 794c–d; see also Morrow, *Plato's Cretan City*, p. 329.

53 *Laws*, 805c–d.

54 Ibid., 740a–c.

55 Morrow, *Plato's Cretan City*, pp. 118–19.

56 *Laws*, 866a, 868b–c, 871b, 879c; cf. Morrow, *Plato's Cretan City*, pp. 120–1.

57 *Laws*, 772d–3e, 774e.

58 Ibid., 773c.

59 Ibid., 923e.

60 Ibid., 928e–9a.

61 Morrow, *Plato's Cretan City*, n. 55 on p. 113.

62 *Laws*, 784b, 929e, 930b, 882c; cf. Morrow, *Plato's Cretan City*, p. 121.

63 *Laws*, 784d–e.

64 Ibid., 937a–b.

65 *Republic*, 540c. The fact that Plato's rulers have always been referred to as philosopher kings suggests that the reminder was, and still is, necessary.

66 *Laws*, 741c, 759b, 764c–d, 800b, 813c, 828b, 784a–c, 790a, 794a–b, 795d, 930.

67 Ibid., 961.

68 Ibid., 765d–6b.

69 Ronald Levinson agrees with this conclusion – see *In Defense of Plato* (Cambridge, Mass., 1953), p. 133 – and Morrow notes that Plato gives no hint that women should perform the basic civic function of attending the assembly of the people. See *Plato's Cretan City*, pp. 157–8.

70 *Laws*, 785b.

71 Ibid., 947b–d, 764e.

72 Ibid., 804e–5a, 806b.

73 Ibid., 794c–d.
74 Ibid., 833c–d, 834a, 834d.
75 Ibid., 785b.
76 Ibid., 808a, 808e.
77 Ibid., 833d.
78 Compare *Laws*, 781c–d with *Republic*, 452a–b.

2

Aristotle: Defective Males, Hierarchy and the Limits of Politics

Arlene Saxonhouse

Teleology and Nature

Aristotle was the son of a Greek physician serving at the court of the Macedonian king. Whether or not Aristotle's interest in scientific questions can be traced to the influence of his father, the study of the natural world plays a central role in the development of his thought. The study of the physical world, of which animals are a part, is for Aristotle the study of nature, *physis*; and for him the study of nature is the study of how things grow. The Greek term *physis* derives from the verb *phueo*, which means "to grow." The questions which Aristotle asks as he analyzes the natural world have to do with growth and change over time, according to set patterns of development. We understand living things, according to him, by understanding their patterns of development, whether we are talking about a flower, an earthworm, a woman, a family, or a political community. Growth as we see it in the natural world is not indiscriminate. There are certain patterns of growth in nature for each class of things. A maple sapling does not suddenly become an elephant: if the maple sapling follows the course prescribed by nature, it becomes a maple tree. Every living thing, including ourselves, possesses a certain potential. We have the capacity to grow into something, and it is that something at the end of our growing process that defines what we are – for instance, a human being or a tree.

Aristotle's study of living things is based on the apprehension of the end toward which each thing directs itself. The sapling has the potential to become a maple tree when it has come to the conclusion of its growing process. This process may not be the usual or normal pattern followed by all maple saplings. Indeed, most die. But, according to Aristotle, in order to fulfill its nature, the maple sapling *should* become a maple tree. It is this focus on the normative end that defines Aristotle's work as teleological. Each plant and animal, including the human being, has an end, a *telos*, a point at which it attains its final form, toward which it is directed from the moment of generation – that is, from the moment it is put into motion. If it fails to reach that end, it has not fulfilled its potential, and it has not become what it can become under normal conditions.

There is an end toward which each must aspire by nature. This "must" is implanted by nature, and with the acceptance of nature as an end becomes a moral "must." In order to be good, that end must be pursued. Not to attain that end is a deformity, a deviation from natural patterns of growth. For the human being, that completion is attained when, as a fully grown person, one exercises one's reason to make the right choices concerning good and bad, right and wrong actions. The end for the human being is not a static condition but one of activity, specifically the activity of choices according to reason, which, for Aristotle, is the source of human happiness.

In order to attain this end, the human being must live in the *polis* – that is, the human being is a political animal. The individual must associate with others in the political realm and benefit from the educative processes of the *polis* and its laws. The natural end of the human thus does not come simply from nature. For other animals, the end, their perfection, is determined by nature; if they arrive at the perfection of their nature, they do so whether they chose to or not. If nature succeeds, they reach that point. If nature fails, which is often the case (the sapling dies, the acorns rot), then they do not. But for humans this is not the case. Human actions work with nature. The human being must employ convention, the laws of the city, in order to reach a condition of completion. Life must be ordered through the creation of the *polis* and its law. There must be human activity directed specifically to the creation and preservation of the realm of the city, the realm of reasoned choice, speech, and education.

The human being is different from other living creatures because of the possession of reason (*logos*), a term that in the Greek also entails speech. To exercise our reason-speech is the fulfillment of our natures, but in exercising our reason we must engage in discourse with others, must make choices, and must be able to explain to others the choices we have made. These choices and the grounds we have for making them determine the kinds of lives we shall lead. The difference between the maple sapling and the human being is that the human engages in choice; the maple sapling is influenced by external factors: the weather, the gardener, the soil conditions. The human is self-moving, making decisions and choices concerning how to live. These choices allow for a certain openness, but they also allow for mistakes. The plant does not make mistakes.

All natural phenomena can be studied according to Aristotle's model of growth and teleology. In his biological works he applies this mode of analysis to the female. When we look at his analysis of the female as a natural biological creature, however, what we find is not particularly congenial to our notions of equality. For Aristotle the biologist studying the generation and the growth of living things, the female of the species, human or otherwise, is the defective male. She arises when the growth process is not completed according to its natural pattern.

The duality of the sexes, Aristotle explains, is necessary: "To be is better than not to be and to live is better than not to live: on account of these causes there is the generation of animals. Since it is impossible that the nature of one born is to be everlasting, it is everlasting according to the way open to it, that is, generation."[1] In order that there be this generation that keeps specific classes of beings in existence, it is necessary that there be both the male and the female principle.[2] However, though both are necessary for generation, Aristotle continues, it is also necessary that the male and the female be kept separate, "for the better and the stronger are to be kept apart from that which is inferior."[3]

The male is better in this context because he gives to that which is generated both the final cause, the *telos*, the reason for existence, and the form, the shape that being will take when it has reached its completed state. The female provides only the matter. Aristotle offers an elaborate comparative analysis of semen and menstrual fluids to support his observations, which include the notion that the female's body is incapable of concocting the necessary heat, the "pneuma," which transfers to the generated being both reason and form.[4] He does not deny the necessity of the female's participation in this process. Both male and female contribute "residues," the difference being that the male's residue is "concocted" through the presence of heat, while the female's is not.[5]

Behind his attempts to offer scientific presentations of the processes of generation lie Aristotle's biological assumptions concerning the physical inferiority of the female because she cannot "concoct" the "pneuma" that gives form to matter. This failure on the part of the female comes from a disruption at the point of conception. Aristotle begins Book IV of *The Generation of Animals* by noting that the distinctions between male and female arise while the animals are still incomplete: the female arises when the male principle, the semen, fails to gain mastery over the female principle. The case for the weakness of the male principle is the absence of heat. Aristotle then proceeds to support these speculations with evidence: young parents produce more female offspring, and more female offspring are conceived when the wind is in the north or when the moon is waning. All these conditions are characterized by reduced heat and lead to the birth of females and deformed children.[6] The growth pattern of the human being normally leads to the full-grown male; the existence of the female suggests that the pattern was not fully followed. Throughout his work on the generation of animals, Aristotle compares the female to a child or a boy. The female is understood as an infertile male, but whereas the child has the potential to continue to grow and to become the fertile male, the female's growth has already been diverted and she retains no such potential. With analyses such as these from his biological works, Aristotle has easily become the *bête noire* of ancient philosophy, the classic male chauvinist who assumes the natural inferiority of the female, she who failed to become male.

Hierarchy and the Limits of Observation

The world for Aristotle is hierarchically structured. Aristotle's teleology entails an orderly, structured perspective on the universe, and part of this order is the relation of things to one another, specifically in terms of better and worse. For the human being this hierarchy begins on the most basic level: the soul is superior to the body. In an ordered individual, living according to his nature, the soul rules the body. This hierarchy is crucial if life on earth is to continue. The mind must rule the body, or the body could not be fed and clothed and housed. Similarly, according to Aristotle's analysis of the generation of the female as the defective, incomplete male, the male is superior to and should have authority over the female – *if* all works according to nature *and if* the intentions of nature are clearly understood and capable of being implemented.

Reading Aristotle's comments concerning teleology and the processes of generation, and his justification of hierarchy, might easily lead (and has led) to a view of him as a simple supporter of the society of ancient Athens, where the female was indeed considered an inferior being entirely subject to the males around her, incapable of making appropriate choices in marriage or in monetary affairs. But all this would assume that the society of ancient Athens is the society that comes from the natural growth processes that Aristotle emphasized elsewhere in his works, that nothing similar to the absence of heat in the generation of the female hindered Athens's growth, that all the choices entailed in the "growth" of Athens were correctly directed not to the apparent but to the true good.

This was not the case. Athens is not the regime according to nature. At the very end of Book III of the *Politics*, Aristotle tells us that the regime according to nature is that in which the best rules; he who is most able by nature must be left to rule over those who by nature are inferior.[7] However, after ending Book III on this note, Aristotle turns in Book IV to the cities that are possible – especially those he finds in his own time, such as the democracy at Athens or the oligarchy at Chalcis in Euboea; there the best do not rule. Athens as a democracy is one of the defective regimes. It makes equal those who are not and acts in the self-interest of the many against the interest of the rich. Along with the oligarchies found elsewhere, it does not allow for the rule of the best. Indeed, Athens has even instituted ostracism to remove the best from the city.[8]

The disjunction between what is and what should be in a world organized around the principle of the superior having authority over the inferior is particularly apparent in Aristotle's discussion of the problems presented for Greek society by slavery. He begins by noting that the slave is an animate piece of property; the problem, however, occurs when the question is asked as to who is to be this piece of animate property and who is to control it. Can such a relationship between human beings be based on nature? Immediately, what is not sufficient for the subordination of one individual to another is clear: "It is necessary to look to that by nature which obtains according to nature rather than to those [relations] which have been corrupted."[9] In the corruption of Aristotle's society we find slaves who exist in such a condition according to the laws of the society but not necessarily according to nature.

The slaves in Athens are those whose cities have been conquered by the stronger forces of the Athenians. Though some would argue that such strength would justify the enslaving of those conquered, since the stronger are the better by nature, Aristotle does not agree. Nevertheless, even if one were to grant *this* position, Aristotle further argues that we cannot take the children of slaves as slaves as well. The enslaving of the children of slaves assumes that "just as humans are born from humans, and beasts are born from beasts, so too the good are born from the good." Aristotle demurs: "But while nature may wish to do this often, it is not, however, always able to do so."[10]

As a consequence, Aristotle suggests, those who are not worthy by nature to rule over others remain masters while those not worthy by nature to be subjected remain slaves. Force rather than friendship, therefore, is necessary to preserve the hierarchical structure of slavery.[11] The pattern of growth within the city has been perverted, and slavery is but one example of this problem.

What holds for the master–slave relationship may also be true in the case of the male–female relationship. According to nature the male is superior to the female, but in the cases where nature has not fulfilled itself, which are outside or against *physis*, the female may be superior to the male; and when she is, then it is against the natural hierarchy that the male rule over the female. In this case, the inferior rules over the superior. Aristotle does not state that all males are better than all females, only that this is natural. We cannot be assured that nature is in control at all times.

At the end of the first book of his *Politics*, Aristotle discusses fleetingly the relationships within the family. He distinguishes between the rule of the master over the slave and that of the husband and father over the wife and children. The latter two forms of rule he defines as political, while the former is despotic. Rule over the child and the wife is rule over free individuals, though in the case of the child it is rule over one who has not yet reached a condition of completion – that is, the reasoning powers have not matured.

In other words, wife and child are free and to be treated as one treats fellow citizens – or potential fellow citizens. Aristotle's understanding of the political relationships that he attributes to the husband–wife relationship entails the process of a rule among equals, those who are equal in taking their turns to rule. In the case of the wife, though, what he sees around him is that the rule of the male is permanent, whereas in other political relationships the process is one of taking turns to rule and be ruled. Later, he will say of political relationships: "In the largest number of states the ruler and the ruled exchange positions, wishing to be equal in nature and differing in nothing."[12]

Aristotle brings home the ambiguity of the ascription of power according to sex or birth with an allusion to a play by Sophocles. Concerned with the problem of whether the virtues of the ruler and the ruled are the same, he turns to the question of the unity or multiplicity of virtues: is virtue the same for all, ruler and ruled, master and slave, male and female? Aristotle quotes Sophocles to show the common assumption concerning the virtue of the female: "Silence brings orderliness to a woman."[13] These words are spoken by Ajax to his wife Tecmessa in Sophocles' tragedy the *Ajax*. Ajax is angered that Achilles' shield has been given to Odysseus rather than to himself. This brings on his madness, his slaughter of the cattle of the Greeks, which he mistakes for the heroes of the Greek army. Tecmessa tries to calm him, urging him not to put on his armor in his rage.

It is in this context that Ajax speaks the words concerning the appropriateness of silence for women. In this context they are entirely inappropriate, an indication of his madness and failure to see the truth in what she says. Had he listened to her words, he would not have acted so destructively. He would have maintained the order that he claims Tecmessa's silence would preserve. The natural hierarchy of the male over the female has been reversed, and it is the failure of Ajax to recognize this aberration in the natural way of things that leads to disaster. Virtues are not easily assigned to a class of people or things. The context and the particularity of the situation must be taken into account if what is natural is to be preserved. To treat all those who lived in conquered cities as slaves, or all those born female as lacking sense, is to fail to recognize the diversity of nature and to limit oneself to a functionalist perspective.

The problems for women in Aristotle's model of society and sexual relations do not come from their reproductive role, as some have suggested,[14] but from the perception of women as controlled by their emotions rather than their reason (*logos*). In the story of Tecmessa and Ajax, however, it is the male who lets his emotions and his anger rule, while the female retains perspective on the situation. The subordinate position of women comes from their being inferior by nature, but the problem with society – and precisely where Aristotle is critical of the hierarchical relations in the society in which he lived – arises when it is unable to determine when the female, and which females, may have something to offer to the males to whom society has given authority. The failure to recognize such times and such women is a sign of the defects of the society, a sign that it is not ruled by the best.

At the end of Book I, when Aristotle is trying to clarify the differing relationships within the family, he does so at one point with reference to the deliberative power (*to bouleutikon*) of each member of the family. The deliberative power gives each individual the capacity to choose actions and to be able to express in words the justifications for such choices. The activity of the city is deliberative – that is, it debates courses of action as participants justify to each other one policy or another. Therefore, it is in their interest to be the subjects of those who can choose. In a child the deliberative capacity is not yet fully developed, and thus the child must be educated so as to mature into an individual who can make the appropriate choices and be able to justify his actions to others. In the female, the deliberative power, Aristotle maintains, is *akuron*, without authority.

Here there is a problem with translation: often *akuron* is translated as "inferior" and *kuros* as "superior." In the Greek, though, *kuros* is associated with the possession of authority or the right to rule over another. When the male is described as being *kuros* over the female, Aristotle is not saying that he is superior, only that he has authority. Thus, the deliberative power in the female lacks authority. The problem of translation goes further, though: does Aristotle mean authority within the soul, or in the female's relationships with others? If we are meant to take this only as referring to relationships within, then women would appear to be emotional cripples, unable to control their desires through rational choice. On the other hand, if we see *akuron* as referring to relations between people, we can see that Aristotle is suggesting that the female lacks authority with the males around her, who would refuse to listen to the advice of a woman just as Ajax refused to listen to the advice of Tecmessa. The actual meaning of *akuron* here is ambiguous, but this ambiguity is crucial because it leads to an ambiguity concerning who should rule and who should have authority in situations that arise in opposition to nature, such as those in which the female may be more "deliberative" than the passionate male.

The failure of Athenian society to understand when the female *bouleutikon* should and should not have authority leads to the indiscriminate exclusion of the female from all deliberations, and thus fails to take account of the natural (rather than the conventional) hierarchy. The city has had to rely on an inadequate criterion, sex, in order to determine that hierarchy, and thus the actual regimes give precedence to those who are inferior (the many) rather than the superior, just as within the family the Athenians always give authority to the male rather than the female.

The problem arises because the city needs some external standard by which to distinguish between people, by which to decide who shall rule and who shall be ruled, who shall participate in government and who shall not. But a problem arises: virtue resides in the soul, which we cannot see, and thus it is difficult to recognize the goodness of one individual in contrast with another. The problem is particularly acute for Aristotle in the case of the slave.

> Nature wishes to make the bodies of free men and of slaves different, the latter strong for the sake of life's necessities, the former straight and useless for such work, but useful for the political life. . . . but often the opposite happens and slaves have the bodies and souls of free men. Since this is clear, if in body alone men would differ so much as the statues of the gods, then all would agree that those who are inferior are worthy of being enslaved to them. And if this holds concerning the body, then by so much more justly is this said with regard to the soul. But it is not entirely easy to see the beauty of the soul as of the body.[15]

We can't see the souls of the individuals who are placed in a position of authority because nature does not always relate the beauty of the soul to the beauty of the body. The problem of political life, for Aristotle, is how to discover superior and inferior, who should rule and who should be ruled. Nature has not made it easy for us to answer this question, since observations of what exists do not give us information about the worth of the individuals who have power.

The task of politics, for Aristotle, is how to deal with this problem of distortion. The answer is not to install the best in positions of power, since we cannot know the best. Therefore, observing the problems in the society in which he lives – the instability of the political regimes in which men disagree about who should have power, since they cannot see the best – Aristotle turns to the question of stability: "For the good of each thing preserves that thing."[16] It is not simply preservation for preservation's sake, but that stability ensures the leisure that is necessary to pursue the

higher things in life. In Book VII he elaborately develops the point that
war is for the sake of peace and that the polity, giving us leisure to become
full human beings exercising our capacity to make reasoned choices, must
be preserved. But how can the political system that is not directed by the
best preserve itself? Although much of Book V, on revolutions, is devoted
to this question, it is in Book II that we learn how women specifically help
or hinder the preservation of order and stability in the political realm.

The Family, the Female, and the Problem of Political Stability

At the beginning of Book I of the *Politics*, Aristotle explains the genesis of
the political community and expresses the view that the growth of the city
entails the transformation of the human concern with mere life into a
concern with the good life. The *polis* provides the condition for the good
life, the life of moral choice; but before we can live the good life, the
necessities of the body must engage us. We must live in order to live well.
Thus, Book I of the *Politics* quickly becomes a compendium of ways to ensure
life itself on the most basic levels of reproduction, manual labor, and food
gathering. Even on this level, Aristotle assumes social interaction, cooperation between individuals to draw forth from nature that which creates and
supports life. He presupposes that there must be families. They exist by
nature and are the expression of our most fundamental drives. Even more
basic than our life in the *polis* is our life in the family. The move toward the
family comes initially from an inclination no different from animals'
inclinations to reproduce themselves. There is no choice for animals but,
according to Aristotle's conception of the development of human reason,
the human being moves beyond simple inclination, to choice.

The attempts of philosophers and lawgivers to envision and create the
best political regimes evidence a deep concern with the family. The social
organization of the family, unlike the social organization of the ancient
city, includes both the female and the male, the slave and the master, the
child and the parent. How does the female fit into the society dedicated to
the preservation of life, and how does the organization of this association
affect the *polis*' problems of stability? If the barbarians ordered their
private life incorrectly, what is the right way to order private life?

The answer is clearly not just submission to the husband's authority.
Even as defective male, the female is not a slave, nor is the difference
between male and female so great as to lead to slavery for women.[17] But
where does the difference that does exist lead? What solution is possible?
In Book II Aristotle discusses several very different solutions, two of
which are presented below. On the one hand, he explains the Spartan
answer, license for women of the city: freedom from laws and constraints,

and little contact with their husbands. On the other hand, he offers for consideration the solution that Socrates in Plato's *Republic* proposes: a community of wives and children in which anything that is private is destroyed among those, including women, who are to be the rulers in his city.

Freedom for women: the case of Sparta

> The freedom given women [in Sparta] is harmful concerning the aims of the regime and the happiness of the city. Just as the man and the woman are a part of the household so it is clear that it is necessary to think of the city as divided into almost two equal parts, that of men and that of women, so that in existing regimes which hold as trifling matters the affairs having to do with women, it is necessary to think of one half of the city as being without laws and legislation. This is what has happened [in Sparta] for the lawgiver wishing to make the entire city strong, has done so clearly among the men, but was unconcerned with the women.[18]

The result in Sparta, according to Aristotle, has been a regime that, though directed toward military superiority, the expression of virile power, is in fact ruled by women. The women, uncontrolled by the traditions and the laws of the society, live a life showing no restraint, dedicated to the pursuit of luxuries. Thus, the regime from which we get our term "spartan" is one that honored wealth. The principles of the Spartan regime had not been directed toward women, and thus the *polis* was divided within itself – on the one hand ascetic and martial in its aims; on the other, luxurious and effete. When Sparta was attacked, Aristotle notes, the women offered no help: they had not been trained in the art of courage, and thus they created more commotion than the enemy did.

In this brief analysis of the Spartan constitution, Aristotle goes against the conventional wisdom of his time, which had commended that constitution for its good laws, its *eunomia*. Tradition had it that these laws had survived 700 years. They had provided for a strong military city considered the model of orderly existence for the Greek world.[19] Aristotle here does not criticize the aim of the regime[20] but, rather, its failure to recognize the distinction it unwittingly made between male and female. The men of the city came to understand the demands of a social life from their experience on military campaigns. There they had learned to submit to the discipline required in a political community. They had thus been willing to submit to the authority of the laws that governed their lives off the battlefield as well as on it. But the women, having been left at home to do as they liked, were free from the exigencies of the military life and did not learn the art of submission to authority. They resisted the restraints of political authority even within the city, and pursued private rather than communal aims.

In his critique of the Spartan regime and its failure to take seriously the political education of women, whether it be through military campaigns or otherwise, Aristotle recognizes the importance of the female in the political life of Greece. Precisely because he recognizes her importance, he rejects the common opinions of the Greeks concerning the virtue of the Spartan regime, a regime not attendant to its women. In the *Rhetoric* he also criticizes the Spartans: "Whoever treats the affairs of women as worthless, as the Spartans do, lacks one half of happiness."[21] He sees not only the license and lack of courage that came from the failure to deal appropriately with the women, but also the avarice of the society as a whole. The women are greedy and, as rulers over their men, they make the city as a whole one that is governed by greed: even as success greeted the male warriors, the seeds of internal decay were growing.

The passage cited at length above, taken out of context, might lead to the view that Aristotle saw women as naturally weak and licentious. Nevertheless, there are two important points to note here: the men were not as weak or as lascivious as the women because they were taken out on military campaigns and thus learned the art of submission, while the women were left free at home; and the problem is not insoluble, for since men had learned to submit to political and military authority, so could the women. The latter were lacking in discipline because the male lawgiver had forgotten them. The female must be part of the city, part of its educative process. The city is to train men to make them part of the community, to make choices that correspond to the needs and the interests of that community; and if it forgets about the education of women, it creates within itself a destabilizing force.

Political life must attend to the problem of stability because it cannot discern who is best; thus, such a disregard for the education of the females in the city undermines the entire political endeavor. Socrates' city in the *Republic*, with its education for women and its inclusion of the female in the city's army, seems to answer Aristotle'a reservations about the Spartan regime. But Socrates adds a community of wives and children, which in Aristotle's mind undermines Socrates' whole endeavor and becomes a destabilizing force.

The community of women: the case of Socrates' city

When a modern reader turns to Plato's *Republic* and the utopian scheme therein, the most striking suggestion for many is the proposal that women be allowed to participate along with men of equal talents in the political and military life of the city. Aristotle, when he evaluates Socrates' proposals, ignores the issue of sexual equality. Rather, he finds the most novel proposal to be the community of wives; the question of equality would arise only if there were such a community. For Aristotle the community of wives assumes the equality of the sexes, while the preservation of the family entails the maintenance of sexual inequality. So long as there continue to be females to keep the race in existence, there will be, for Aristotle, hierarchy, authority, and inequality – the family.

The problem that Aristotle poses for himself as he begins to consider Socrates' city is how much should be held in common in the political association: some, all, or none? Clearly some, since without something held in common there is no city. At the most basic level the land on which the city is located must be shared. But Socrates goes to the other extreme and says that all must be held in common. His arguments for this communism are varied, but behind them all lies the concern with the stability of the political system that comes from unity.

The female and the family exist within a private realm that focuses on what is particular rather than on what is universal; thus they work, as Socrates presents it, in opposition to the interests of the community, which must emphasize a devotion to the universal. By destroying the private realm through the destruction of the family and its particularistic orientation, Socrates aims to leave the self open to the complete devotion to the public.

This had been possible in Socrates' city because Socrates had abstracted from the body, which ties one to the procreative and nutritive aspects of the family. He had worked through education in poetry to train his warriors to scorn their bodies and their bodily needs. The abstraction from the body had removed a concern with the private and the particular. The bodies of Socrates' citizens did not define who they were, and thus the female body could be ignored in the communism of the city and the equality of the sexes introduced at the beginning of Book V.

Aristotle does not abstract from the body; instead, he emphasizes how the body works against Socrates' proposals, how nature turns our attention to our bodies, what is particular about them, and how, by nature, we love our own bodies. Socrates abstracts from difference by avoiding bodies. Aristotle emphasizes bodies and, thus, difference. For instance, he finds support for the ties between children and specific parents in the natural physical resemblances between parent and child. He suggests that the people in Socrates' city would be driven to discover their own relations. "Furthermore, it is not possible to escape some form of guessing about who are brothers, and children, and fathers and mothers."[22] Socrates' citizens will engage in this guessing precisely because it is possible to recognize similarities between children and parents. Our bodies indicate these connections.

Bodies, by revealing these connections, accomplish what intellects, particularly Socrates' intellect, may wish to ignore. Denying such connections, as Socrates tries to do in the *Republic*, is, according to Aristotle, to act against nature. Acting against nature leads to unholy and impious deeds that are offensive even in the contemplation of them. In referring to such deeds, Aristotle moves from violent acts against one's parents to the sexual liaisons that would occur between the members of one's own natural family: fathers with daughters and even, what he considers the most horrendous and unnatural of all, brothers with brothers. The anonymity imposed by Socrates' scheme, and thus the lack of shame to restrain human actions, opens the door for all these acts against nature.

Aristotle finds further problems with Socrates' city, for it fails to take account of the natural love of oneself and of what is one's own. "Not in vain," he says, "does each have a love of oneself. This is according to nature."[23] We love ourselves and we love what we create. We exist through activity, and since we love our existence, we love what that existence has brought into being, be it our children, our handiwork, our writings. We act in accordance with a love of ourselves and of what we have created.[24] Socrates' community eliminated that natural love of oneself and one's creative activity. This distortion of our natural drives, Aristotle claims, will cause instability and lead to the demise of the city. He uses the example of household slaves to support this point: if too many slaves are assigned a particular task and no one feels that the accomplishment of that task entails his or her creative activity, the task will not be performed. The many, having no particular attachments to the task, having no sense of seeing themselves in the accomplishment of that task, will leave the work to others. "There is the least concern for what is common, but the most care for what is private."[25]

The female, as the symbol of what is private, of the home and what is particular, as the source of children who are one's own and recognized as such by the city at large, is a vivid expression of the need all humans have to tie themselves to that which is particular and one's own. To communalize the female is to destroy the private and to overemphasize the public and its universalistic aims; for Aristotle this is the same as destroying the moral and psychological bases of the city. The community of women, so opposed to the demands of nature, cannot support the city as an institution arising from the natural drive of men to perfect themselves.

There are other problems with Socrates' city. By removing the family and ignoring the difference between male and female, Socrates destroys the diversity, multiplicity, and interdependence at the core of the city. Aristotle argues that diversity is essential for the city; we need cobblers as well as doctors. To make the cobblers and the doctors the same, to ignore what is different about them, and to expect the same expertise from each is to change the city into an individual. By nature we are different and have different abilities. Socrates himself had stressed this as he began to found his city in the city of pigs.

By nature the male is not the same as the female. Though in Aristotle's biological works these differences are often expressed in terms of defects, in the "practical" pieces he focuses on the differences in virtues. "The virtues of a youth are moderation and courage in the soul. . . . The virtue of a girl is beauty and greatness of body, and in the soul moderation and a love of work without slavishness."[26] That diversity must be retained on the private level, or the city – lacking cobblers and doctors, men and women – will die. Socrates' abstraction from the private realm casts doubt on the survival of his city. In contrast, on the public level, the realm of political life, there must be an equality, a focus on what unites through similarity. All are citizens, all are capable of ruling and being ruled. The particular differences between individuals defined as equal become irrelevant. But we can reach this state of equality only when the necessities that demand differentiation have been met.

The problem with Socrates' model, as Aristotle sees it, is that Socrates, in proposing sexual equality in the political realm, had done so through ignoring the diversity demanded in the private realm, through ignoring that the public must build up from the private. As shown in Book I of the *Politics*, Aristotle cannot discuss the good life until he has discussed life itself. In Book V of the *Republic*, Socrates tries to ignore life in order to jump headlong into the good life. As a result, as Aristotle understands it, Socrates destroys the potential for both.

Aristotle on the family and the female in the polity

There seems to be a friendship between man and woman by nature. For the human being by nature is more disposed to live in pairs than in the polis, insomuch as the household is prior in time and more necessary than the polis, and the creation of children is more common with other animals. Among other animals, the community extends only this far [to the creation of children], but for the human being, living together is not only for the sake of reproduction, but also for various aspects of their lives. Immediately, the work is divided, and there is one task for men and another for women. So they assist one another, putting their individual talents into the common good. On account of these things, there seems to be both usefulness and pleasure in this sort of friendship. This friendship also exists in accordance with virtue, if they are both good. For there is a virtue of each, and they are pleased by this. . . . It seems that children are a bond, wherefore marriages without children dissolve more quickly. For children are a common good for both and what is common holds them together.[27]

This passage offers a picture of human involvement in the family often forgotten as one turns to the Aristotle of the famed "man is a political animal" quote. Here he portrays the human being as an economic being, in the true sense of the term. We see in this passage a concern with the community that is the family, the pleasure that both members, male and female, derive from a friendship devoted to what is common and their individual talents exercised in their attention to what unites them. The family here is not a dark recess of subordination and domination, but a prepolitical condition incorporating into itself many of the elements of unity and friendship that the actual cities of Greece in Aristotle's time failed to exhibit.

Neither the Spartan lawgiver nor Socrates recognized the special value that Aristotle attributes to the family, a value that takes it far beyond the process of reproduction that ties the human species to other animals. The Spartans with their men at war all the time and Socrates with his communism ignored the family and the female who was a part of it. Aristotle wants to reassess the stature of the family, and his criticism of the utopian and the practical regimes is a major part of that reassessment.

In Socrates' city Aristotle had found a community with no family to educate in a love that goes beyond the self, a community where the door had been opened for the common practice of impiety. Socrates' city left no room for liberality. If one identified the city as being the same as oneself, to act for the city could not be called a liberal act. Thus, the communism of his city destroyed all the potential for virtue. The Spartan regime had failed to educate women in the art of submission to authority that all regimes must entail. The failures of others are captured in Aristotle's attempt to justify and resuscitate the family. The *polis* arises, in his view, to help complete what the family ultimately cannot do successfully: educate the young. It is to continue the process begun in the family, not to make the family irrelevant, as the others had tried to do.

Throughout all the criticisms of Socrates' city and the Spartan regime, Aristotle never focuses on the inherent deformity of the female that had been a part of his work on the biology of animals. His arguments against communism do not come from arguments about the inequality of women, that women need supervision, as does the natural slave. The value of the family for Aristotle is not that it brings about subordination, but that it provides the orderly community of love and friendship, the natural hierarchy whose stability offers the preconditions for the pursuit of virtue. Though the family may not always conform perfectly to the rule of superior over inferior, it appears to order itself naturally, to be founded on a natural hierarchy that the city composed of supposed equals can only pretend to approximate.

Because of the problems with observation noted above, it is difficult within the context of the city to determine who is equal, who should rule, and who should be subject. The justice of the city in distributing offices is artificial rather than complete. It is dependent on an inequality that cannot be secure. All polities depend on this justice. Within the family the hierarchy in operation is closer to the natural way of things. The family is the model of the natural aristocracy. By this Aristotle means an association in which the man rules according to his worth "and about those things that it is necessary for a man to rule, but whatever fits well with a woman, he hands over to her."

If the man chooses to rule in those areas where he is not suited by nature to rule, he transforms the aristocratic relationship into one that is oligarchic, one in which he rules in his own self-interest and not in the interests of the community. A few lines before the passage just cited, Aristotle had suggested that an oligarchy is a regime in which the rulers do not distribute the affairs of the city according to worth, but give all the good things to themselves.[28] The well-structured family recognizes the differences between the members and takes these differences into account as they all work toward the common good. Within the city that is based on equality and a sharing in the process of rule, the differences between those who are citizens must be ignored and each has the same tasks as everyone else. With all citizens determined by artificial criteria of equality, there can be no distribution of offices or tasks according to worth, since all must share in the activities of the political community.

When cities are threatened with revolution and instability, it is because there is disagreement about the meaning of equality, who is to be equal and who is to be subject. In Book V of the *Politics*, Aristotle notes that in all cases, "on account of inequality, there is internal conflict."[29] While men agree that justice is simply distribution according to worth, "they differ nevertheless with some saying that if they are equal according to one attribute, then they are completely equal, while others claim that if they are unequal in one attribute, then they are worthy of unequal treatment."[30] In families in which the difference between the sexes and the generations at the base of the distribution of tasks is more readily observed, the distribution of tasks and authority is more easily accepted.

The city's inequality and equality are not precise. They therefore remain constantly subject to debate and are an incentive for internal strife. The city becomes, in a sense, only an imperfect reflection of the natural hierarchy of the family, and the order of the family is only inadequately captured by men's attempts to set up barriers among themselves, barriers for which nature has offered no clear signposts. Even within the patriarchal household, where differences are more subject to observation, mistakes can occur, as in the case of Ajax and Tecmessa. Thus, even within the smaller unit of the family, true justice is not always at work, because the criterion of differentiation is not always adequate to justify differential treatment.

The portrait of the female within the family may not earn much admiration from contemporary students of women in the social sphere, but Aristotle's analysis of the family, as a cooperative adventure in which the friendship between the members comes from a common concern for the welfare of the unit, goes far beyond the view of the family in ancient Greek society that many have offered to us. Students of the Greek legal system trace a set of relationships in which the female is little more than the instrument for transferring property from one family to another and for giving birth to future protectors of the religious rites of a particular family. Aristotle's understanding of the family goes beyond such "uses" for women and suggests that the family must be understood as a set of associations and relationships from which the grander and more important *polis* derives.

Within the family, the role of the female, that task assigned to her because of her special abilities, is the same one taken up by the statesman within the city – preserving what has been acquired, providing for stability. Nevertheless, however important the female may be in the family, Aristotle never envisions her as part of the public realm of the city. Again this view derives from his understanding of the notions of equality and inequality. The family as a realm of hierarchy stands in contrast with the city as a realm of equality. Within the family the male retains authority over the female, the father over the son, the master over the slave. Inequality of authority or power derives from differences with regard to sex, age, ability.

The family, unlike the city, is characterized by its differences; and in order for it to continue over time, it must incorporate these differences. The male must be different from the female if there is to be sexual reproduction. The master must have the intelligence that the slave lacks, and the slave must have the physical capacity that the master need not develop. The relations of difference within the family maintain the unit. Within the *polis*, the criterion must be one of equality: citizens must be equal in their possession and exercise of reasoned speech, of discourse about the just and the unjust, and they must be equal in their leisure to engage in such speech. Thus, as workers captured by the necessities of existence, lacking the leisure to participate in such discourse, cannot be part of the citizen body, neither can the female, who, because she is nourishing the young with her body, lacks such leisure.

For Aristotle, then, the exclusion of women is based in part on their unequal leisure time, their role as the preservers of the household and the bearers of the young. However, more significant for Aristotle's exclusion of the female from the public realm is the lack of authority of her reasoned discourse. Since the *polis* is to be a realm of activity for the *logos*, the female, in whom that *logos* is not predominant, cannot participate fully.

In being so excluded, women are not alone. Slaves obviously are excluded, but so are workers, not because Aristotle the aristocrat rejects the lower classes, but because his conception of political life requires the participation of those who engage in the reasoned discourse of the complete human being. Workers lack the leisure for this engagement. In contemporary society, where political participation is not defined by the activity of reasoned discourse, the restrictions that Aristotle established appear meaningless or downright unjust, but his concern that the public realm serve as the arena for the highest human activities (after philosophy) led to his demand for such an intellectual engagement.[31]

In the last two books of the *Politics*, Aristotle discusses the city of his dreams.[32] Women figure here only very briefly as he considers the issues of reproduction and the earliest stages of the child's life. The legislator must have the best material with which to work, and that means the healthiest population. To ensure this health, he must attend to the laws governing matrimony and reproduction. Aristotle is particularly concerned that reproduction not begin at too young an age, when deformed offspring (including women) are likely to be born.

But Aristotle slips from these biological considerations to psychological ones. Picking up on the themes in the *Ethics*, he maintains that the legislator must also be concerned with the community that is created within the family and must ensure that there is a compatibility of sexual life for the married couple. This means that the ages of husband and wife must match, so that one will not be able to be reproductively active when the other can no longer function in this capacity. Thus, since he sees 70 as the age for men's declining sexual potency and 50 for women, he suggests that the man be 20 years older at the time of marriage.[33]

Once conception has taken place, the female is to exercise her body, but not her mind, for her body must be strong in order to give strength to the growing child, just as something growing draws from the earth.[34] If we look only at these last words comparing the female to the soil, Aristotle could justly be accused of seeing only the material role of the female. She is the matter out of which the citizens grow, but the earlier comments expressing concern for the compatibility within marriage suggest that Aristotle has a deeper understanding of the female's place in the polity. Though she is not a part of the public community, the private community depends on a nonexploitive, communal relationship between the male and female.

Again, however, the student of Aristotle must go further to understand fully the place of the female in his analyses of the best city. Specifically, one must note the persistent hostility to the city as an armed camp composed of virile warriors, spirited in their desires to acquire dominion. As Aristotle expresses it at the beginning of Book VII, the best city, the one that need not worry about stability, is the one that promotes the individual happiness of its citizens. The task for Aristotle is to explain the conditions that would provide this happiness. The mistake of the many, according to him, is that they equate happiness with what is external, with the excessive accumulation of goods. For these men conquest, war as the means to acquire goods, becomes the source of happiness. Aristotle argues that the city must not be structured to facilitate the continual pursuit of goods, but the limitless pursuit of virtue. And how does one pursue virtue? Not through conquest, but through education, through attention to the arts.

In chapter 7 of Book VII, Aristotle attacks regimes dominated by a spirited love of war. He associates such regimes with the cannibalism practiced by the Cyclops. The most choiceworthy life, with which Aristotle's investigation into the best regime began, is not one of domination – one country over another, the male over the female, the master over the slave, all of which are based ultimately on war and inequality – but one of the processes of ruling over men who are equals.

Thus, Aristotle's analysis of the best regime focuses on the processes of education in moderation, the characteristic that he had previously ascribed to the good woman. The cities of Aristotle's time that catered to a concern with material wealth emphasized the virility that was necessary to pursue domination. The city of Aristotle's dreams exalts the feminine virtue of restraint. While the female herself appears only in her reproductive capacity in these last two books, the feminine, as opposed to the masculine, virtue provides the foundation for the city that offers human beings the truly happy life. The body of the female is not the same as the female soul; and just as those who attend exclusively to what is external are mistaken in their evaluations of the source of happiness, so are those who attend exclusively to the body of the female. Aristotle's books on the best city are incomplete, but in what remains, little is actually said about the public life of the citizen; the focus is on education in moderation. The female is part of that education, and thus part of the true life of the city.

Conclusion

Aristotle is well known in the literature today as the classic misogynist, and his words have often been used to support misogyny throughout the ages.[35] The accusation of misogyny today can condemn an author and relegate him to the scrap heap. In Aristotle's writing there is no hatred of women; rather, there is the attempt, from the perspective of the male, to understand the origins of the female and her role in the male city. The female is a defective male, but so are most of the males whom Aristotle sees around him. Seldom is the true man found, one who combines the physical, intellectual, and moral qualities of the individual who has reached the completion of his growing process.

Aristotle's understanding of the female in the political world leads to a vision of hierarchy, but not submission on all levels. The woman, he steadfastly maintains, is not a slave. Thus he must understand her distinct role in society, and he finds it in her capacity within the structure of the family – a realm in which she not only gives birth but also gives stability, preserves and educates the young of the city. It is a realm in which she can demonstrate her unique virtue.

The Socratic vision in the *Republic* had excluded the private realm. All virtue was public. Aristotle retains the private and encourages the pursuit of excellence and community there. Without that excellence on the part of both the male and the female, there can be excellence nowhere in the life of the city. Cities that ignore the female and her potential for excellence, such as Sparta or Socrates' city, Aristotle warns, are placing themselves in jeopardy of internal conflict, dissolution, and chaos. In no way can we pretend that the female is the central issue in Aristotle's writings, but she raises for him a variety of questions and alternative perspectives with which he must deal before he can complete his presentation of the full political life for the human being.

Notes

1 Aristotle, *The Generation of Animals*, 731b30–33.
2 Ibid., 767b8ff.
3 Ibid., 732a6–7.
4 Ibid., 765b10ff., 766a30ff., and passim.
5 *Aristotle's Generation of Animals*, ed. and trans. A. L. Peck, (Cambridge, Mass.: Harvard University Press, 1943), p. xiv.
6 Aristotle, *Politics*, VII.16 (1335a11–13, 1335a39–1335b2).
7 Ibid., III.17 (1288a26–29); see also I.5 (1254b33–1255a2).
8 Aristotle describes the institution of ostracism in his *Constitution of Athens*, XXII.
9 *Politics*, I.5 (1254a36–37).
10 Ibid., I.6 (1255b1–4).
11 Ibid., (1255b12–15).
12 Ibid., I.12 (1259b4–6).
13 Ibid., I.13 (1260a30).
14 Susan Moller Okin, *Women in Western Political Thought* (Princeton: Princeton University Press, 1979), chapter 4, argues from this perspective.
15 *Politics*, I.5 (1254b27–1255a1).
16 Ibid., II.2 (1261b9).
17 In the *Nicomachean Ethics*, V.6 (1134b8–18), Aristotle distinguishes paternal

and despotic relationships from the marital relationship with regard to justice. There can be no injustice to things that are one's own possessions (slaves) or to children (up to a certain age), since no one can wish to harm oneself. "Wherefore there is more justice towards a wife than towards children and possessions." This he calls household justice in the *Ethics*. Justice is not part of one's relationship with slaves.

18 *Politics*, II.9 (1269b12–22).

19 J. Peter Euben, "Political Equality and the Greek Polis," in *Liberalism and the Modern Polity*, ed. Michael J. Gargas McGrath (New York and Basel: Marcel Dekker, 1978), p. 210.

20 However, see the discussion in Book VII of the *Politics*, where Aristotle explicitly rejects a focus on military achievements as the aim of his best regime, especially chapter 2.

21 *Rhetoric*, I.5 (1361a9–11).

22 *Politics*, II.3 (1262a14–16).

23 Ibid., II.5 (1263a41–1263b1).

24 In the *Nicomachean Ethics*, IX.7 (1168a24–26), Aristotle comments: "On account of these things mothers love their off-spring more [than fathers do]. They suffer in childbirth and know with greater certainty that they [the children] are their own."

25 *Politics*, II.3 (1261b36).

26 *Rhetoric*, I.5 (1361a2–7).

27 *Nicomachean Ethics*, VIII.12 (1162a16–29).

28 Ibid., VIII.10 (1160b35–36).

29 *Politics*, V.1 (1301b26–27).

30 Ibid. (1301b35–39).

31 We might, nevertheless, see in Aristotle's framework a greater potential for an egalitarian, nonhierarchical relationship between males and females than emerges from Plato's thought. If the female could be shown to be the intellectual equal, if her reason could be shown to have authority, and if leisure were hers, participation in the political community could follow. Plato, in contrast, in his works sees the potential for such intellectual capacity, but because of the female's ties to the processes of reproduction, she cannot participate fully. Plato's equality depends on advances in reproductive technology, while the Aristotelian model could incorporate women once their capacity was acknowledged and women were not denied the leisure to engage in the deliberative life.

32 Questions have been raised about the order of these books. For the most recent assessment that would place them after Book III, see Carnes Lord, "The Character and Composition of Aristotle's *Politics*," *Political Theory*, 9, November 1981, pp. 459–78.

33 *Politics*, VII.16 (1335a7–10).

34 Ibid., (1334b19).

35 See Maryanne Cline Horowitz, "Aristotle and Woman," *Journal of the History of Biology*, 9, Fall 1976, pp. 183–213: she traces some of the uses to which Aristotelian quotes about women were put in the Middle Ages.

3

"God Hath Ordained to Man a Helper": Hobbes, Patriarchy and Conjugal Right

Carole Pateman

The decisive moment in the conjuring trick has been made, and it was the very one we thought quite innocent.

L. *Wittgenstein*, Philosophical Investigations

Most studies of Hobbes have nothing to say about the relation of his political theory to seventeenth-century patriarchalism. Writers who have thought it worthwhile to consider the question have almost all agreed that Hobbes's argument is patriarchal, although more recently the claim has been made that, for example, Hobbes's views were subversive of "patriarchal attitudes," or that his theory is free from patriarchal assumptions.[1] More strongly, in a rational choice interpretation of Hobbes (which shares Hobbes's radical individualism) the implicit assumption is that Hobbes's theory is so far opposed to patriarchalism that his sovereign can be referred to as "she."[2] Despite such differences, political theorists are united on one point; they agree that to argue about patriarchy is to argue about the family and paternal power. Hobbes is assumed to be a patriarchal theorist in the same sense that his adversary Sir Robert Filmer is a patriarchalist; or, conversely, Hobbes is assumed to be opposed to patriarchalism because his theory is antithetical to Filmer's on some crucial issues.

The major debates about patriarchy over the past two decades have been conducted by feminists, not mainstream political theorists, but feminists have paid remarkably little attention to political theory in the controversy over the meaning and usefulness of the term "patriarchy." The predominant assumption among feminists, or, at least, among those engaged in the theoretically informed controversies over patriarchy, is also that patriarchal relations are familial relations and that patriarchal political right is paternal right.[3] To be sure, many feminists also use "patriarchy" to mean the power that men exercise over women more generally – what I shall call masculine right – but, notwithstanding the copious empirical evidence available to support this interpretation, the usage has not yet been given a great deal of theoretical substance. A major reason for this lack of theoretical robustness is feminist neglect of the arguments among political theorists about patriarchy in the seventeenth century. Feminist scholars have undertaken some very revealing and exciting work on the classic texts of political theory, but little attention has been paid to Hobbes, whose writings are of fundamental importance for an understanding of patriarchy as masculine right. Hobbes is a patriarchal theorist – but the possibility that is considered by neither conventional political theorists nor feminists is that he is a patriarchalist who rejects paternal right.

Both feminism and political theory are dogged by a anachronistic, although literal, interpretation of patriarchy as father-right. Patriarchy is assumed to be about fathers and mothers. For example, Di Stefano has argued that Hobbes is a masculinist theorist, but her reading of Hobbes is that his arguments rest on a denial of the mother. His picture of natural, atomized individuals, who spring up like mushrooms – "consider men as if but even now sprung out of the earth, and suddenly, like mushrooms, come to full maturity, without all kind of engagement to each other"[4] – denies any significance to the mother–child relationship and the dependence on the mother that provides the first intersubjective context for the development of human capacities. Di Stefano claims that there is no room for nurture within the family in Hobbes's state of nature; "men are not born of, much less nurtured by, women, or anyone else for that matter."[5] Hobbes's family is certainly very peculiar, but the problem with Di Stefano's argument is that, in the state of nature, mothers, far from being denied, are enthroned. For Hobbes, political right in the natural condition is mother-right. Hobbes goes to great lengths to deny that father-right is the origin of political right, yet he is still seen as a patriarchalist in the same sense as Filmer for whom political and paternal power were one and the same.

A different problem confronts the writers who argue that Hobbes subverts patriarchalism, or merely tacitly assume that the terms "men" and "individual" in Hobbes's texts are used generically; they fail to explain why Hobbes's writings contain so many references to the rightful power of fathers – or why he endorses the subjection of wives to husbands. Commentators on Hobbes, like almost all political theorists of the recent past, see no problems of political interest arising from the subordination of wives to husbands. Conjugal right, the right exercised by men, as husbands, over their wives, is not a matter that falls within their scholarly purview. The standard interpretations of the theoretical battle between the classic contract theorists, including Hobbes, and the patriarchalists of the seventeenth century is that the engagement concerned the political right of fathers and the natural liberty of sons. That the father was a master, exercising jurisdiction over servants and apprentices, is acknowledged, but another inhabitant of the family is usually ignored. The father is also a husband, and as a husband is a master over his wife. In discussions of Hobbes and patriarchy, the position of the *wife* in the family is rarely mentioned. She appears, if at all, in another capacity, as a *mother*. When a problem about women is admitted to exist, it is taken to be that of maternal jurisdiction over children.

The failure to distinguish marriage from the family and to recognize the existence of conjugal right means that the most distinctive aspect of Hobbes's political theory is disregarded. Hobbes is the only contract theorist (and almost the only writer admitted into the "tradition" of Western political theory) who begins from the premise that there is no natural dominion of men over women. In his natural condition female individuals are as free as, and equal to, male individuals. The remarkable starting point of his political theory is usually passed over extremely quickly. Even in discussions that focus on patriarchy no questions are asked or explanations offered about why and how it is, in the absence of sexual dominion in the state of nature, that marriage and the famly take a patriarchal form. Nor is anything odd seen in the fact that Hobbes argues both that women are naturally free and always subject to men through (the marriage) contract.

There are also other problems about Hobbes, patriarchy and contract when "patriarchy" is interpreted literally. Some commentators have noted certain tensions in Hobbes's arguments between contract and patriarchy; one earlier scholar, for instance, took the logical position that if Hobbes is interpreted as a patriarchalist then the original contract is superfluous.[6] Another commentator has attributed a consensual form of patriarchy to Hobbes and argued that his patriarchalism is, therefore, the strongest form – and even a more typically English variety.[7] Hobbes took contract much further than most other classic contract theorists and claimed that even infants (could be said to have) contracted themselves into subjection to mothers. To posit a contract by an infant is to reject outright any suggestion that political subjection is natural and to confirm in the most emphatic possible manner that all dominion is conventional in origin. Yet it was precisely the doctrine of the natural freedom of mankind and its corollary, contract and consent, that Sir Robert Filmer saw as the major cause of sedition and political disorder. Why, then, should a purported advocate of patriarchy as paternal right, and a writer who, in his own way, was as absolutist as his opponent, take so many pains to deny the assumptions of Filmer's theory? More generally, if political right has a natural origin in fatherhood and contract is thus superfluous – and, according to Filmer, politically dangerous – why should Hobbes argue that civil society was created through an original contract?

To remain within the standard, patriarchal interpretation of "patriarchy" as fatherly power is to remain within a patriarchal reading of Hobbes's texts, a reading that ignores the subjection of women. Hobbes's patri-archalism is a new, *specifically modern* form, that is conventional, contractual and originates in conjugal right, or, more accurately, sex-right; that is, in men's right of sexual access to women, which, in its major institutional form in modern society, is exercised as conjugal right (a term also pro-viding a polite locution in, say, a discussion of Adam and Eve). To appreciate the character of Hobbes's patriarchal theory the distinctive features of his natural condition – mother-right and the absence of natural dominion of male over female individuals – have to be taken seriously as fundamental premises of his political theory. In addition, Hobbes's extra-ordinary conception of the "family" needs to be emphasized. Hobbes did not merely leave no room for nurture or argue that the family was conventional, a political rather than a natural social form. For Hobbes, a "family" was solely composed of a master and servants of various kinds and had its origins in conquest.

I

Before looking in greater detail at Hobbes's arguments it is necessary to say something more about patriarchy and to look again at Filmer's patri-archalism.[8] A good deal of confusion over the term "patriarchy" has arisen because of the failure to distinguish between three different historical forms of patriarchal theory: traditional, classic and modern. Traditional patriarchal argument assimilates all power relations to paternal rule. For centuries the family and the authority of the father at its head provided the model and metaphor for political society and political right. The traditional form is also full of stories, of conjectural histories, about the emergence or creation of political society from the family or the coming together of many families. Such stories are also to be found in the writings of the classic contract theorists, even though they defeated and eliminated the second, shortlived form of classic patriarchalism. Classic patriarchy was formulated and died in the seventeenth century and is exemplified by Sir Robert Filmer's arguments. Schochet shows in *Patriarchalism in Political Thought* that Sir Robert broke with the traditional form by insisting that paternal and political rule were not merely analogous but identical. In the 1680s and 1690s, "the Filmerian position very nearly became the official state ideology."[9] The classic form was a fully developed theory of political right and political obedience and was the first of its kind; "there was no patriarchal theory of obligation prior to 1603."[10] The standard claim in political theory is that patriarchalism was dead and buried by 1700 – but the form that passed away was Filmer's classic patriarchy.

Filmer wrote in response to the challenge posed by the doctrine of the natural freedom of mankind. If men were born free and equal then, necessarily, political right or the dominion of one man over another could be established in one way only; through an agreement (contract) between those concerned that such a relation should be brought into being. According to Filmer, acknowledgement that Adam had been granted monarchical power by God by virtue of his fatherhood cut the ground from under the feet of the contract theorists. At the birth of his first son, Adam became the first king and his political right passed to all subsequent fathers and kings, who were one and the same: all kings ruled as fathers in consequence of their procreative power, and all fathers were monarchs in their families. Sons were born into political subjection to their fathers and hence to the monarch: no such political nonsense as talk of contracts was required to justify political subjection. Filmer's account of the natural origin of political right appears straightforward enough, and no hint is given in discussions of the relation between the theories of Hobbes and Filmer that patriarchy is more complicated.

Paternal right is only one dimension of patriarchy – as Filmer himself reveals. Filmer's apparently straightforward statements obscure the original foundation of political right. Paternal power is not the origin of political right. Father-right is established only after political right has been brought into being. Another act of political genesis is required before a man can acquire the natural right of fatherhood. Sons do not spring up like mushrooms, as Filmer was quick to remind Hobbes. Adam's political title is granted *before* he becomes a father. If he is to be a father, Eve has to become a mother. In other words, *sex-right or conjugal right must necessarily precede the right of fatherhood*. The genesis of political dominion lies in Adam's sex-right, *not* in his fatherhood.

Filmer makes clear that Adam's political right is originally established in his right as a husband over Eve: "God gave to Adam . . . the dominion over the woman," and, citing Genesis 3:16, "God ordained Adam to rule over his wife, and her desires were to be subject to his."[11] (Genesis states that Eve's "desire shall be to thy husband, and he shall rule over thee".)

Adam's desire is to become a father, but in no ordinary sense of "father."
He desires to obtain the remarkable powers of a patriarchal father. Filmer
briefly mentions Adam's original, divine grant of political right over Eve
at various points, but it has a shadowy presence in his writings. In recent
(patriarchal) commentaries on his texts, sex-right has completely disappeared. And, to be sure, when reading Filmer from the perspective of
only one dimension of patriarchalism, conjugal right is not easy to discern
under the cloak of Adam's fatherhood.

The biblical patriarchal image (here in Locke's words) is of "nursing
Fathers tender and carefull of the publick weale."[12] The patriarchal story
is about the procreative power of a father who is complete in himself, who
embodies the creative power of both female and male. His procreative
power both gives and animates physical life and creates and maintains
political right. Filmer is able to refer to Adam's power over Eve so
casually because classic patriarchalism declares women to be procreatively
and politically irrelevant. The reason that Adam has dominion over "the
woman" is, according to Filmer (here following the patriarchal idea of
fatherhood, which is very ancient), that "the man . . . [is] the nobler and
principal agent in generation."[13] Women are merely empty vessels for the
exercise of men's sexual and procreative power. The original political
right that God gives to Adam is the right, so to speak, to fill the empty
vessel. Adam, and all men, must do this if they are to become fathers. But
men's generative power has a dual aspect. The genesis of new physical life
belongs in their hands, not in the empty vessel. Men are the "principal
agents in generation," and "generation" includes political creativity. Men's
generative power includes the ability to create new political life, or to give
birth to political right.

In view of the character of the extraordinary powers that classic patriarchalism arrogates to men, it is appropriate that the powers are contained
in the name of "father" and encompassed under the writ of "fatherhood."
The presence of conjugal right is very faint in Filmer's writings because
(although at one level he must acknowledge it) Adam's original political
right is subsumed under the power of fatherhood. For instance, after
stating that Eve and her desires are subject to Adam, Filmer continues in
the next sentence, "here we have the original grant of government, and the
fountain of all power placed in the Father of all mankind." Moreover,
Adam is also Eve's father. In the story of the Book of Genesis, Eve is
created only after Adam and the animals have been placed on earth. God
creates and names the animals and Adam but, we are told in Genesis 2:20,
"for Adam there was not found an help meet for him." Eve is then
created, but she is not created *ab initio* but *from* Adam, who is, in a sense,
her parent, and Adam, not God, gives Eve her name. Filmer is therefore
able to treat all political right as the right of a father. Eve is not only under

the dominion of Adam, but he is (with God's help) the "principal agent" in her generation. The father in classic patriarchal theory is not just one of two parents – he is *the* parent, and the being able to generate political right.

The greatest story of masculine political birth is the story of an original contract that creates civil freedom and civil society. The classic patriarchalists lost the battle over fathers and sons and the natural origin of political right. Patriarchalism, in the sense of paternal right, ceased to be politically relevant by the end of the seventeenth century. Civil society is constituted by the (ostensibly) universal, conventional bonds of contract not the particular, natural bonds of kinship and fatherhood. However, the standard account of the defeat of patriarchy ignores the fact that the contract theorists had no quarrel with classic patriarchalism over the true origin of political right; they fought against paternal right but had no wish to disturb the other dimension of patriarchy, conjugal right.

The "freedom of mankind" in contract argument means what it says, the freedom of *men*. The victory of contract doctrine over the classic form of patriarchal argument was, rather, the *transformation* of classic patriarchy into a new form. The contract theorists constructed their own, modern patriarchal argument – the third of the historical forms. Modern patriarchy is contractual not natural and embodies masculine right not the right of fatherhood. Hobbes, the most brilliant and bold of contract theorists, is a patriarchal theorist in the modern sense, but his arguments differ in some significant respects from those of his fellow contract theorists and, in the end, it was they, not Hobbes, who provided the necessary theoretical framework for patriarchal civil society.

II

On the face of it, Hobbes's writings seem unequivocally opposed to both dimensions of classic patriarchy. Hobbes's theory rests on mother-right and the absence of natural sexual dominion; how, then, does Hobbes transform natural maternal power and women's natural freedom into patriarchal right, and why have scholars been able to identify so many passages in Hobbes's writings where he apparently falls back on the traditional form of patriarchal argument? The appropriate place to begin to consider the conjuring tricks is with Hobbes's picture of the natural condition. Hobbes's imaginative resolution of civil society into its most fundamental ("natural") parts was much more rigorous than the similar undertakings of the other contract theorists. Hobbes was willing to take the logic of individualism to its most radical conclusions in this as in other respects. When Hobbes reconstitutes natural entities in perpetual motion into something recognizably human, the result is that humans interact in a natural condition that can barely be recognized as social. Hobbes's state of nature is the famous war of all against all, and, in a statement which is rarely seen as of political significance, Hobbes writes that in the natural condition there are "no matrimonial laws."[14] Marriage – that is to say, a long-term relation between the sexes – must be brought about in exactly the same way as any other relation between the inhabitants of the state of nature where there is no natural order of dominion, and no politically significant difference in strength or prudence between individuals. Relations can arise in two ways only: either individuals contract themselves into a given relationship; or one, by some stratagem, is able to coerce another into the desired arrangement. This is also true of relations between a man and a woman. In the natural condition women face men as free equals; Hobbes writes that "whereas some have attributed the dominion to the man only, as being of the more excellent sex; they misreckon in it. For there is not always that difference of strength or prudence between the man and the woman, as that the right can be determined without war."[15]

In the state of nature there is no law to regulate marriage – and no marriage. Marriage does not exist because marriage is a long-term arrangement, and long-term sexual relationships, like other such relationships, are very difficult to establish and maintain in Hobbes's natural condition. The boundaries separating the inhabitants one from another are so tightly drawn by Hobbes that each one can judge the rest only from a subjective perspective, or from the perspective of pure self-interest. Natural individuals will, therefore, always break an agreement, or refuse to play their part in a contract, if it appears in their interest to do so. To enter a contract or to signify agreement to do so is to leave oneself open to betrayal. Hobbes's natural state suffers from an endemic problem of keeping contracts and of "performing second"; "If a covenant be made, wherein neither of the parties perform presently, but trust one another; . . . upon any reasonable suspicion, it is void: . . . And . . . he which performeth first, does but betray himself to his enemy."[16] The only contract that an individual, of his or her own volition, can enter into in safety is one in which agreement and performance take place at the same time. An agreement to perform an act of coitus provides an example of a contract that comes close to meeting this criterion, but an agreement to marry, to enter into a long-term sexual relationship, would founder in the same manner as contracts to create other relations that endure over time.

The women and men in Hobbes's state of nature can engage in sexual intercourse and, therefore, children can be born. A child, however, is born a long time after any act of intercourse. As Hobbes notes, in the absence of matrimonial laws proof of fatherhood rests on the testimony of the mother. Since there is no way of establishing paternity with any certainty, the child belongs to the mother. Hobbes's argument is all the more striking since he, too, suggests that men are the "principal agents" in generation. Echoing the classic patriarchal view of fatherhood, Hobbes writes that "as to the generation, God hath ordained to man a helper"[17] – but the female "helper" in the state of nature becomes much more than an auxiliary once the birth takes place. Hobbes insists that no man can have two masters and so only one parent can have dominion over the child. In the natural condition the mother, not the father, enjoys this right. In direct contradiction of Sir Robert Filmer and the patriarchal doctrine that political right originates in the father's generative power, Hobbes proclaims that "every woman that bears children, becomes both a *mother* and a *lord*."[18] At birth, the infant is in the mother's power. She makes the decision whether to expose or to nourish the child. To have the power to preserve life is, according to Hobbes, to exercise rightful dominion, whether the subject is a newly born infant or a vanquished adult. If the mother preserves the infant, she thereby becomes a lord; "because preservation of life being the end, for which one man [or infant] becomes subject to another, every man is supposed to promise obedience, to him [or her], in whose power it is to save, or destroy him."[19]

From 1861 for a half century or more (following the publication of Sir Henry Maine's *Ancient Law* and Johann Bachofen's *Mother Right*) another controversy raged about political origins, matriarchy and patriarchy. The proponents were all reluctant to admit that matriarchy in the literal sense – rule by women as mothers – ever existed, even hypothetically.[20] Similarly, some contemporary theorists still find it necessary to take issue with Hobbes's logic on mother-right. The rather amusing objection has been raised that Hobbes is mistaken; a mother "simply does not wield" the power Hobbes ascribes to her.[21] The "helper" herself always requires another helper. In Hobbes's day, the objection continues, the mother was attended by a midwife or male physician, and it is the latter who, at the moment of birth, has power over the child in her or his hands. Hobbes should have concluded that neither fathers nor mothers possessed an original political power in the natural condition, but then his argument against natural paternal right would have been "more absurd still." In his eagerness to combat Filmer, Hobbes "overlooked the defects attached to an argument which would transfer this power to a party – the mother– whom no one supposed ever had a proper right or even opportunity to exercise it (given the establishment of a civil society)."[22] Precisely; in patriarchal civil society, past or present, political theorists rarely are willing to contemplate that mothers (women) could legitimately exercise political right, even in an hypothetical state of nature or as a matter of mere logic. The other social contract theorists, unlike Hobbes, built masculine sexual dominion as a natural fact of human existence into their political theories and so demonstrated in a straightforward fashion that, for all that their arguments are couched in universal terms, equality, freedom and contract are a male privilege – although contemporary political theorists still manage to avoid noticing the fact.[23] Hobbes's logic is impeccable. In his natural condition (whatever the facts of childbirth in the seventeenth century) a pregnant woman would not give herself up as a hostage to fortune by enlisting helpers in her labors; no free, strong woman would place her right of dominion at risk with such assistance.

By nature, a mother is a lord who can do as she wills with her infant. If she decides to "breed him," the condition on which she does so, Hobbes states, is that "being grown to full age he become not her enemy."[24] That is to say, the infant must contract to obey her. The mother's political right over her child originates in contract, and gives her absolute power. A woman can contract away her right over her child to the father, but, when the premise of Hobbes's argument is that women naturally stand as equals to men, there is no reason why a woman should do this, and, least of all, why she should *always* do so. To argue that a tiny infant can contract, or should be regarded as if it had contracted, with its mother is, as Filmer insisted, anthropological nonsense. In terms of Hobbes's understanding of "contract," however, this agreement is as convincing an example of a contract as any other in Hobbes's writings. Scholars have drawn attention to Hobbes's claim that the reasons and circumstances under which agreement are given are irrelevant to the validity of the contract; for Hobbes, it makes no difference whether a contract is entered into after due deliberation or with the conqueror's sword at one's breast. Submission to overwhelming power in return for protection, whether the power is that of the conqueror's sword or the mother's power over her newly born infant, is always a valid sign of agreement for Hobbes. Hobbes's assimilation of conquest to contract, enforced submission to consent, is often remarked upon, but the political significance of his peculiar notion of contract for the origin of the family in the state of nature and for the making of the original pact is less often appreciated.

III

The logical conclusion of Hobbes's resolution of civil society into its natural parts of rational entities in motion, and his reconstitution of the natural condition, is that the sexes come together only fleetingly and that the original political right is mother-right. Yet Hobbes also writes in a passage (cited by Richard Chapman and Gordon Schochet, for example), "that the beginning of all dominion amongst men was in families. In which, . . . the father of the family by the law of nature was absolute lord of his wife and children: [and] made what laws amongst them he pleased."[25] And he also refers to familial government or a "patrimonial kingdom" in which the family:

> if it grow by multiplication of children, either by generation, or adoption; or of servants, either by generation, conquest, or voluntary submission, to be so great and numerous, as in probability it may protect itself, then is that family called a *patrimonial kingdom*, or monarchy by acquisition, wherein the sovereignty is in one man, as it is in a monarch made by *political institution*. So that whatsoever rights be in the one, the same also be in the other.[26]

Moreover, Hobbes also makes statements such as "cities and kingdoms . . . are but greater families,"[27] and "a great family is a kingdom, and a little kingdom a family."[28] He also remarks that Germany, like other countries "in their beginnings," was divided between a number of masters of families, all at war with each other.[29] Such statements have been treated as evidence that Hobbes was a patriarchalist like Filmer and that his natural condition was composed of families not individuals. Such an interpretation leaves unanswered the questions of how the transformation comes about from mother-right to the patriarchal family in the state of nature and how the family is generated.

Chapman has stressed that Hobbes's family is an artificial, political institution rather than a natural social form, but its extraordinary character consists in more than a conventional, political origin. No attention is paid to the most bizarre aspect of Hobbes's account of the family because conjugal right and the position of a wife are ignored. Indeed, the scholars involved in the debate about Hobbes and the family have not paused to wonder how there can be wives in the state of nature where there is no law of matrimony. Nor have they asked how families can come into existence when marriage does not exist and yet marriage is the "origin" of the family. Hobbes's "family" is very curious and has nothing in common with the families of Filmer's pages, the family as found in the writings of the other classical social contract theorists, or as popularly understood today. Consider Hobbes's definition: in *Leviathan* he states that a family "consist[s] of a man and his children; or of a man and his servants; or of a man, and his children, and servants together; wherein the father or master is the sovereign."[30] In *De Cive* we find "a *father* with his *sons* and *servants*, grown into a civil person by virtue of his paternal jurisdiction, is called a *family*."[31] What has happened to the wife and mother? Only in *Elements of Law* does he write that "the father or mother of the family is sovereign of the same."[32] But the sovereign cannot be the mother, given the conjectural history of the origin of the family implicit in Hobbes's argument.

The "natural" characteristics postulated by Hobbes mean that long-term relationships are very unlikely in his state of nature. However,

Hobbes states in *Leviathan* that, in the war of all against all, "there is no man who can hope by his own strength, or wit, to defend himself from destruction, without the help of confederates."[33] But how can such a protective confederation be formed in the natural condition when there is an acute problem of keeping agreements? The answer is that confederations are formed by conquest. If one male individual manages to conquer another in the state of nature the conqueror will have obtained a servant. Hobbes assumes that no one would willfully give up his life, so, faced with the conqueror's sword, the defeated man will make a (valid) contract to obey his victor. Hobbes defines dominion or political right acquired through force as "the dominion of the master over his servant."[34] Conqueror and conquered then constitute "a little body politic, which consisteth of two persons, the one sovereign, which is called the *master*, or lord; the other subject, which is called the *servant*."[35] Hobbes distinguishes a servant from a slave, but his definition of a servant makes it hard to maintain the distinction: "the master of the servant, is master also of all he hath: and may exact the use thereof; that is to say, of his goods, of his labour, of his servants, and of his children, as often as he shall think fit."[36]

The master and his slave-servant form the little body politic of a defensive confederation against the rest of the inhabitants of the state of nature. That is to say, according to Hobbes's definition of a "family," the master and his servant form a family. For Hobbes, the origin of the family is entirely conventional. A "family" is created not through procreation but by conquest, and a family consists of a master and his servants; that is, all those, whatever their age or sex, who fall under his absolute jurisdiction. A "family" composed only of a master and his male servants is a singular institution and it becomes more singular still if this male household contains children. Hobbes remarks at one point that sovereignty can be established "by natural force; as when a man maketh his children, to submit themselves, and their children to his government."[37] Children have again sprung up like mushrooms, ready to submit to (contract with) their fathers. And what of their mothers; how are they included in the "family"? In the natural condition there are two ways only in which sexual relations between free, equal women and men can take place. Either a woman freely contracts to engage in intercourse or she is outwitted and taken by force. There is no reason why a woman should contract of her own free will to enter into a long-term sexual relationship and become a "wife," that is, to be in servitude to – to become the servant (slave) of – a man. In the state of nature a woman is as able as a man to defend herself or to conquer another to form a protective confederation of master and servant. Why then does Hobbes assume that only men become masters of servants?

The answer is that, by the time the original contract is entered into, *all* the women in the natural condition have been conquered by men and become servants. Hobbes is explicit that "dominion amongst men" begins in the defensive confederation or small body politic he calls a family, but he does not spell out that men also gain dominion over women by creating "families." A conjectural history of how this comes about might run as follows. At first, women, who are as strong and as capable as men, are able to ensure that sexual relations are consensual. When a woman becomes a mother and decides to become a lord and raise her child, her position changes; she is put at a slight disadvantage against men, since now she has her infant to defend too. Conversely, a man obtains a slight advantage over her and is then able to defeat the woman he had initially to treat with as an equal. Mothers are lords in Hobbes's state of nature, but, paradoxically, for a woman to become a mother and a lord is her downfall. She has then given an opening for a male enemy to outwit and vanquish her in the ceaseless natural conflict. Mother-right can never be more than fleeting.

The original political dominion of maternal lordship is quickly over-come and replaced by masculine right. Each man can obtain a "family" of a woman servant and her child. Thus mother-right is overturned and the state of nature becomes filled with patriarchal "families." All the women in the natural condition are forcibly incorporated (which for Hobbes, is to say contract themselves) into "families" and become the permanent ser-vants of male masters. The "help" given by women to men in procreation then becomes the unending help of domestic servitude. The "wife" is relegated to the status of a helper too politically insignificant to be worthy of listing as a member of this peculiar protective association. A story along these lines is necessary to explain the existence of patriarchal "families" in the state of nature, and also to explain why a patriarchal law of matrimony is instituted through the original contract.

But it is hard to tell a consistent and convincing story about women's subjection when beginning from the postulate of natural freedom and equality between women and men.[38] The conquest of women would surely take more than one generation. Some women, either by choice or the accident of nature, would be childless and so would remain free. Indeed, once childless women saw the fate of women who decided to exercise maternal lordship they would, as rational beings, choose to remain child-less and conserve their natural freedom. Free women would, however, be found only in the first generation in the natural condition. Childless women would die, and all subsequent generations of women would be born into servitude (and so, according to Hobbes's definition of servitude, would be under the jurisdiction of the master). The problem with this version of the conjectural history is that, if there are free childless women in the first generation in the natural condition, there is no reason why they should not form protective confederations of their own by conquering men, or each other, and so obtaining servants. Women and men would then wage the war of all against all as masters of "families" – and who knows who might win in the end? But in Hobbes's theory we do know who wins, and thus there is only one story that can be told. Women must all be conquered in the first generation; there can be no female masters in the state of nature or there will be no original contract and no law of matrimony.

IV

The method through which Hobbes constructed his picture of the state of nature meant that, as a ruthlessly consistent theorist, he had to begin from the logical but shocking premise of an absence of sexual dominion and original mother-right. But Hobbes was well aware, as indicated in the passages that I cited above, that, historically, paternal right and the subjection of wives was the established custom. In the *logical* beginning, all political right is maternal right. In the *historical* beginning, masculine or "paternal" right holds sway. The story of the defeat of women in the state of nature explains how patriarchal "families," incorporating all the women, are formed through conquest and ruled by "fathers." This stage of the history of the natural condition must be reached if men are to enter the original contract, exercise their political creativity and create a new phase of history in the form of modern patriarchal society. Commentators on contract theory generally take it for granted that there are no problems in referring to "individuals" entering into the original contract, so implying that any or all of the inhabitants of the state of nature can participate. Some commentators are more careful, and Schochet, for example, notes that in the seventeenth century fathers of families were assumed to have sealed the original pact. He argues that Hobbes shared this assumption. Despite Hobbes's use of traditional patriarchal language, his "families" are not ruled by men as fathers but by men as masters. Masters of families rule by virtue of contract (conquest) not their paternal, procreative capacity. Men as masters – or as free and equal men – enter into the original contract that constitutes civil society. Women, now in subjection, no longer have the necessary standing (they are no longer free and equal or "individuals") to take part in creating a new civil society.

The civil law of matrimony, which upholds conjugal right, is created through the original pact. Political theorists consistently omit to mention one of the most remarkable features of Hobbes's political theory. Hobbes makes it quite clear that conjugal right is not natural. Conjugal right is created through the original contract and so is a *political* right. The right is deliberately created by the men who bring civil society into being. The other classic contract theorists presuppose that the institution of marriage exists naturally and that conjugal relations are nonpolitical relations, carried over into civil society. In Hobbes's theory, the law of matrimony is created as part of the civil law. Contemporary political theorists, too, take for granted that the structure of the institution of marriage is nonpolitical and so they pay no attention to conjugal right. Hobbes's political theory makes clear what the other classic contract stories, and contemporary commentaries on contract theory, leave implicit: that the original contract is not only a *social* contract that constitutes the civil law and political right in the sense of (state) government; it is also a *sexual* contract that institutes political right in the form of patriarchal – masculine – power, or government by men, a power exercised in large part as conjugal right.

Hobbes states that in civil society the husband has dominion "because for the most part commonwealths have been erected by the fathers, not by the mothers of families."[39] Or again, "in all cities . . . constituted of *fathers*, not *mothers* governing their families, the domestical command belongs to the man; and such a contract, if it be made according to the civil laws, is called matrimony."[40] If free and equal women could enter the original contract there is no reason whatsoever why they would agree to create a civil law that secures their permanent subjection as wives. Matrimonial law takes a patriarchal form because *men* have made the original contract. The fact that the law of matrimony is part of the civil law provides another reason for self-interested individual men to make a collective agreement. In addition to securing their natural liberty, *men as a sex* have an interest in a political mechanism which secures for them collectively the fruits of the conquests made severally by each man in the natural condition. Through the civil institution of marriage they can all lawfully obtain the familiar "helpmeet" and gain the sexual and domestic services of a wife, whose permanent servitude is now guaranteed by the law and sword of Leviathan.

Hobbes had no wish to challenge the law of matrimony of his own day, embodied in the common law doctrine of coverture. The law of coverture was given classic expression by Sir William Blackstone in his *Commentaries on the Laws of England* in the eighteenth century. Under coverture, a wife had no independent juridical existence; she was a civilly dead being, absorbed into the person of her husband. No one, it would seem, could fail to be struck by the legal powers given to husbands, whether in Blackstone's gloss on the law or in marital practice – powers that can only be compared, as they were regularly compared by feminists in the nineteenth century, to those of slave-masters.[41] Yet patriarchy runs so deeply in the contemporary theoretical consciousness that Chapman comments (echoing Blackstone) that "the most striking feature of the common law family is the liabilities attached to the man, particularly regarding the acts of his wife and servants."[42] Now, if women had made the original contract, civil law might well reflect the fact and attach all manner of "liabilities" to men. But we did not make it, and could not have made it, and so "the most striking feature" of coverture is the juridical nonexistence of a wife (just as she disappears in Hobbes's definition of the "family" in the state of nature). The liabilities of the husband that impress Chapman are the other side of the wife's subjection. "Liabilities" are the price the husband pays for being a master, that is, a protector. The most fundamental premise of Hobbes's political theory is that no individual will give up the right of self-protection.[43] In the state of nature women too have this right, but in civil society women as wives have given up (been forced to give up) this right in favour of the "protection" of their husband – and husbands are now protected by the sword of Leviathan.

Students of Hobbes do not usually make a connection between the original overthrow of mother-right and the establishment of Leviathan. The crucial political significance of the conquest of women in the natural condition is that, unless the defeat occurs, Leviathan is impossible to envisage. The conjuror Hobbes is far too clever a wizard for his patriarchal successors and the trick is never remarked on in discussions of his theory. If women took part in the original contract the awesome figure of the mortal god Leviathan could not be created. Leviathan can be brought into being only if participation in his generation is confined to men. The creation of civil society is an act of masculine political birth; men have no need of a "helper" in *political* generation. In the state of nature, individuals are differentiated only by their sex; that is to say, by their bodily form (in strength, rationality and prudence there is no politically significant difference between individuals with female bodies and individuals with male bodies). Hobbes's account of the institution of Leviathan makes sense only if the participants in the original contract all have the same bodily form.

The creation of Leviathan, Hobbes tells us, involves "more than consent, or concord; it is a real unity of them all, in one and the same person."[44] When men cease to be a mere natural multitude and transform themselves through the act of contract into a unified body, or body politic, bound together through the conventional bonds of contract and civil law, their unity is represented in a very literal sense by the person of their (absolute) master and ruler, Leviathan. They create him "to bear their person," and, Hobbes states, "it is the *unity* of the representer, not the *unity* of the represented, that maketh the person *one*."[45] No such unity would be possible if both sexes took part in the constitution of Leviathan – there could be no representative figure who could represent the "person," the bodily form, of both sexes. Men must be represented and their civil unity given literal symbolic personification by one of their own kind. Similarly, "private bodies" are also represented by one person, and Hobbes uses the example of "all families, in which the father, or master ordereth the whole family." Husband and wife cannot govern jointly in the family; there can be one master only, and the husband is the necessary "one person representative" of the family in civil society.[46] An act of masculine political birth creates civil beings and their sovereign in the image of their makers (only Adam, the first man, through the hand of God, could generate a woman). If the representer is to be unified, he must be *he*. To attempt to represent both sexes within the figure of one master would be to dissolve his unity and oneness and to shatter political order.

V

Hobbes turned classic into modern patriarchy but several features of his argument worked against him becoming a founding father of modern patriarchal theory. For example, Hobbes negated Filmer's arguments but that was not sufficient to create the theory required for civil patriarchy. Hobbes turned Filmer's social bonds into their opposite. Filmer saw families and kingdoms as homologous and bound together through the natural, procreative power of the father. Hobbes saw families and kingdoms as homologous, but as bound together through the conventional tie of contract, or, what for Hobbes is the same thing, the force of the sword. Hobbes also agreed with Filmer that sovereignty must be absolute – but sovereignty in the state, not in private bodies. Civil fathers and masters are not miniature Leviathans. Their powers run only so far as permitted by Leviathan's laws and his sword. Leviathan thus enabled Hobbes to offer a solution to the problem that dogged Filmer's classic patriarchalism. Hinton has noted that if fathers were kings then there could be no king with true monarchical power.[47] Hobbes's civil masters cannot detract from the absolute mastery of Leviathan. Hobbes's solution, however, retained absolutism in the state, the form of political right that, as Locke argued, had to be replaced by limited, constitutional government in a properly *civil* order.

The absolute power of Leviathan's sword was not the only problem with Hobbes's patriarchalism. Hobbes was too revealing about civil society. The political character of conjugal right was expertly concealed in Locke's separation of what he called "paternal" power from political power and, ever since, most political theorists, whatever their views about other forms of subordination, have accepted that the powers of husbands derive from nature and, hence, are not political. Not only are a range of important questions about domination and subjection in our own society thus suppressed, but some other important questions about the "origin" of civil society are also neatly avoided. In the past two decades, individualism of a radical, Hobbesian kind has become very influential, although the absolutist conclusions that Hobbes drew from his individualist premises are rejected in favour of a view of the state as a minimal, protective association.[48] The association is held to have a legitimate origin in voluntary transactions between individuals in the state of nature. In the final chapter of *Leviathan*, Hobbes writes that "there is scarce a commonwealth in the world, whose beginnings can in conscience be justified."[49] Hobbes's "beginning" of the original contract between men can only be justified if, as he believed, political order depended on the erection of Leviathan. Without Leviathan, and from Hobbes's starting point of free and equal women and men, a voluntary beginning might be possible. Such a story could not be told by political theorists who acknowledge only half the original contract (the social contract) and thus endorse patriarchal right. The origin of the patriarchal protective state in Hobbes's theory lies in the conquest and servitude of women in the state of nature and in their civil subjection and domestication as wives.

Hobbes's theory is an early version of the argument, presented in the later nineteenth and early twentieth centuries in elaborate detail and with reference to much ethnographic data, that civilization and political society resulted from the overthrow of mother-right and the triumph of patriarchy. The silences and omissions of contemporary political theory and the standard readings of Hobbes's texts do nothing to question that argument. Scholars do not mention the problems about women and the civil order arising from Hobbes's theory and the subsequent development of contract theory. For example, why has conjugal right never been seen as political when every other form of power has been subjected to the closest scrutiny and judgment? Why is women's exclusion from the original pact not mentioned in most discussions of contract theory? If women can take no part in the original contract what is their status as parties to the marriage contract? Has Hobbes's identification of enforced submission with consent (contract) any relevance to present-day sexual relations? By the beginning of the eighteenth century, when, according to political theorists today, patriarchalism had come to an end, Mary Astell asked, "if *all Men are born Free*, how is it that all Women are born Slaves?"[50] Most political theorists have yet to recognize the existence or relevance of Astell's question – or the political significance of the fact that Hobbes did not think that we were so born.

Notes

1 The arguments are those, respectively, of Richard A. Chapman, "*Leviathan Writ Small: Thomas Hobbes on the Family,*" *American Political Science Review*, 69, 1975, p. 77; and John Zvesper, "Hobbes' Individualistic Analysis of the Family," *Politics*, 5, 1985, p. 33. For references to other discussions of Hobbes and patriarchy see Chapman, nn. 2–14 on p. 76.

2 Jean Hampton, *Hobbes and the Social Contract Tradition* (Cambridge: Cambridge University Press, 1986).

3 Contemporary feminist arguments about patriarchy are discussed in Carole Pateman, *The Sexual Contract* (Cambridge: Polity; Stanford: Stanford University Press, 1988), ch. 2.

4 Thomas Hobbes, *Philosophical Rudiments Concerning Government and Society*, the English version of *De Cive*, in *The English Works of Thomas Hobbes of Malmesbury* (London: John Bohn, 1841), vol. 2, ch. 8, p. 109.

5 Christine Di Stefano, "Masculinity as Ideology in Political Theory: Hobbesian Man Considered," *Women's Studies International Forum*, 6, 1983, p. 638.

6 Leslie Stephen in 1904; cited by Gordon Schochet, *Patriarchalism in Political Thought* (Oxford: Basil Blackwell, 1975), p. 234.

7 R. W. K. Hinton, "Husbands, Fathers and Conquerors," *Political Studies*, 16, 1968, p. 57.

8 This section draws on Pateman, *Sexual Contract*, ch. 4.

9 Schochet, *Patriarchalism*, p. 193.

10 Ibid., p. 16.

11 Sir Robert Filmer, *Patriarcha or the Natural Powers of the Kings of England Asserted and Other Political Works*, ed. Peter Laslett (Oxford: Basil Blackwell, 1949), pp. 241, 283. Genesis, too, can be interpreted in more than one way, and equality of men and women in the sight of God is not incompatible with male supremacy in human affairs; e.g. Calvin argued from both the perspective of *cognitio dei* (the eternal, divine perspective in which all things are equal) and the perspective of *cognitio hominis* (the wordly perspective in which humans are hierarchically ordered). See Mary Potter, "Gender Equality and Gender Hierarchy in Calvin's Theology," *Signs*, 11, 1986, pp. 725–39.

12 John Locke, *Two Treatises of Government*, 2nd edn, ed. Peter Laslett (Cambridge: Cambridge University Press, 1967), II, §2.

13 Filmer, *Patriarcha*, p. 245.

14 Hobbes, *Leviathan*, in *English Works*, vol. 3, ch. 20, p. 187.

15 Ibid., pp. 186–7.

16 Ibid., ch. 14, pp. 124–5.

17 Ibid., ch. 20, p. 186.

18 Hobbes, *Philosophical Rudiments*, ch. 9, p. 116.

19 Hobbes, *Leviathan*, p. 188.

20 For an account of the controversy, see Rosalind Coward, *Patriarchal Precedents* (London: Routledge and Kegan Paul, 1983), ch. 2. See also Pateman, *Sexual Contract*, ch. 2.

21 Preston King, *The Ideology of Order* (London: Allen and Unwin, 1974), p. 203.

22 King, *Ideology of Order*, pp. 205, 206. Hobbes's most recent biographer suggests that his argument about mother-right derives from his own experience as a child. Hobbes's views perhaps "owed much to that occasion during those years when the curate [Hobbes's father], possibly long before his disappearance, was forced by his character and circumstances to yield the government to Hobbes' mother." Arnold A. Rogow, *Thomas Hobbes: Radical in the Service of Reaction* (New York and London: W. W. Norton, 1986), p. 132. Hobbes's father, rather fond of drink and neglectful of his parish, fled after being accused of assaulting a rector of a neighboring parish. Ironically Rogow was unable to find any new information about Hobbes's mother. Even her maiden name remains uncertain.

23 The other classic contract theorists are discussed in Pateman, *Sexual Contract*, chs 3 and 4.

24 Hobbes, *Philosophical Rudiments*, ch. 9, p. 116.

25 Thomas Hobbes, *A Dialogue between a Philosopher and a Student of the Common Laws of England*, in *English Works*, vol. 6, p. 147.

26 Thomas Hobbes, *De Corpore Politico, or The Elements of Law*, in *English Works*, vol. 4, ch. 4, pp. 158–9 (Hobbes's emphasis here and below).

27 Hobbes, *Leviathan*, ch. 17, p. 154.

28 Hobbes, *Philosophical Rudiments*, ch. 8, p. 108.

29 Hobbes, *Leviathan*, ch. 10, p. 82.

30 Ibid., ch. 20, p. 191.

31 Hobbes, *Philosophical Rudiments*, ch. 9, p. 121.

32 Hobbes, *De Corpore Politico*, ch. 4, p. 158.

33 Hobbes, *Leviathan*, ch. 15, p. 133.

34 Ibid., ch. 20, p. 189.

35 Hobbes, *De Corpore Politico*, ch. 3, pp. 149–50.

36 Hobbes, *Leviathan*, ch. 20, p. 190.

37 Ibid., ch. 17, p. 159.

38 I am grateful to Peter Morriss for raising the question of generations and for other helpful criticisms.

39 Hobbes, *Leviathan*, ch. 15, p. 187.

40 Hobbes, *Philosophical Rudiments*, ch. 9, p. 118.

41 On the implications of coverture, see Pateman, *Sexual Contract*, chs 5 and 6.

42 Chapman, "*Leviathan* Writ Small," n. 90 on p. 84.

43 Hampton, *Hobbes*, pp. 197–207, argues that his deduction of absolute sovereignty fails precisely because Hobbes makes self-protection an absolute right. But because she takes no account of Hobbes's patriarchalism, she fails to mention that, if the argument about sovereignty in the state is correct, then conjugal sovereignty fails too.

44 Hobbes, *Leviathan*, ch. 17, p. 158.

45 Ibid., ch. 16, p. 151.

46 Ibid., ch. 22, pp. 221–2.

47 R. W. K. Hinton, "Husbands, Fathers and Conquerors," *Political Studies*, 15, 1967, pp. 294, 299.

48 For an argument that absolutist conclusions are ultimately unavoidable, see Carole Pateman, *The Problem of Political Obligation*, 2nd edn (Cambridge: Polity;

Berkeley and Los Angeles: University of California Press, 1985), ch. 3. Hampton, *Hobbes*, interprets Hobbes's commonwealth as a union of slaves within the will of a master.

49 Hobbes, *Leviathan*, part IV, p. 706.

50 Mary Astell, *Some Reflections Upon Marriage*, from the 4th edn of 1730 (New York: Source Book Press, 1970), p. 107 (emphasis in the original).

4

Early Liberal Roots of Feminism: John Locke and the Attack on Patriarchy

Melissa A. Butler

In early seventeenth-century England, patriarchalism was a dominant world view.[1] It was a fully articulated theory which expressly accounted for all social relations – king–subject, father–child, master–servant, etc. – in patriarchal terms. Sir Robert Filmer and other patriarchal writers insisted that the king ruled absolutely, the divinely ordained father of his people. No one was born free; everyone was born in subjection to some patriarchal superior. Each individual human being could find his or her proper place by consulting patriarchal theory. Places were not matters of individual choice but were assigned according to a divinely ordained pattern set down at the Creation.

By the end of the seventeenth century, the patriarchal world view had crumbled. It was replaced by a new understanding of human nature and of social and political organization. Whigs such as Sidney, Tyrrell and Locke grounded political power in acts of consent made by free-born individuals. Contract and individual choice supplanted birth and divine designation as crucial factors in social and political analysis. These changes raised problems concerning the status of women in the new order. At first, liberal theorists resisted the suggestion that the old assigned position of women might have to be abandoned. The champions of consent theory saw no need to secure the consent of women. Yet their critics insisted that excluding women violated the very theory of human nature on which liberalism was based. Eventually, liberals would be forced to bring their views on women into line with their theory of human nature. This changing image of women certainly played a part in that shift in consciousness which paved the way for the sexual revolution.

The Statement of Patriarchy: Sir Robert Filmer

Full-blown patriarchal political theory was occasioned primarily by the turbulence of seventeenth-century English politics, but patriarchal ideas and intimations could be found in political writings long before they received more systematic theoretical expression in the writings of Sir Robert Filmer.[2]

In that era of "divine right kings," the legitimacy of a monarch's claim to absolute rule could be proved if the source of a divine grant of power could be found. Patriarchal political theory satisfied this need. It offered an explanation of the historical origins of the king's political power and of the subject's political obligation. By tracing the king's power back to Adam, the theory provided more than mere historical justification; it provided divine sanction.

The explanation derived its effectiveness from a general awareness of the obvious truth which patriarchalism told.[3] The patriarchal family experience was universal. The family patriarch was a universally-acknowledged authority figure with immense power. By linking the authority of the king with the authority of the father, a theorist could immediately clarify the nature of a subject's political obligations. Moreover, monarchical power grounded in patriarchal power took on the legitimacy of that least challengeable social institution, the family. The linkage of paternal and monarchical power provided a means for transcending any intermediate loyalties a subject might have. Absolute, patriarchal, monarchical power was vested in the king. It was to the king, not to the local nobility, that loyalty and obedience were rightfully owed.

Patriarchalists insisted that God, nature and history were on their side. For proof, one need only consult the Book of Genesis. Not only was Genesis divinely inspired, it was also the oldest possible historical source and the best guide to man's nature.[4] There, in the Genesis account, was the evidence that God had created Adam in His image – patriarch and monarch He created him.

The gradual unfolding of biblical history showed that the basic institution of patriarchy, the patriarchal family, had always been a fundamental feature of society. Throughout Judeo-Christian society, family life, bolstered by marriage and divorce laws, primogeniture and property rules, continued thoroughly patriarchal down to the seventeenth century.[5]

During the English Civil War, both divine right monarchy and the patriarchal theory which helped support it were severely challenged. In reaction to new and dangerous doctrines, Sir Robert Filmer penned the best-known treatises in defense of the patriarchal position, including *The Anarchy of a Limited or Mixed Monarchy* (1648), *The Freeholder's Grand Inquest*

(1648), and *Observations upon Aristotle, Touching Forms of Government* (1652). The work for which he is most remembered, *Patriarcha*, was begun around 1640, but was published posthumously in 1680.[6]

To elaborate his patriarchal theory of politics, Filmer turned to both classical and constitutional sources. But Filmer's most important, most authoritative source was always scripture. The scriptural arguments for monarchy illustratę the most literally patriarchal aspects of Filmer's thought. In brief, his account of the biblical origins and justifications of patriarchy was as follows:

> God created only Adam, and of a piece of him made the woman; and if by generation from them two as parts of them, all mankind be propagated: if also God gave to Adam not only the dominion over the woman and the children that should issue from them, but also over the whole earth to subdue it, and over all the creatures on it, so that as long as Adam lived no man could claim or enjoy anything but by donation, assignation, or permission from him.[7]

Again and again throughout his works Filmer recalled the divine grant of paternal, monarchical power to Adam. Filmer drew upon the Book of Genesis, specifically Genesis 1:28, when he claimed that "the first government in the world was monarchical in the father of all flesh."[8]

As critics from Filmer's own century were only too happy to observe, Sir Robert had erred in his biblical analysis. Filmer had assigned all power to Adam, but God had given dominion to Adam *and* Eve. The divine grant of power in Genesis 1:28 was made to "them," ostensibly the male and female whose creation had been announced in the preceding verse. Sir Robert had to tamper with the text because the original grant of power detailed in Genesis 1:28 was not, as he maintained, an exclusive grant of private monarchical dominion given to Adam, the patriarch. On the contrary, the blessing was given to both the male and the female.

If evidence for the patriarchal theory could not be found in God's blessing, perhaps it could be found in His curse. Filmer could have maintained that the lines of patriarchal authority were established after the Fall. Genesis 3:16 could have been offered as proof: "Thy desire shall be to thy husband, he shall rule over thee."

Indeed, in the *Anarchy*, Filmer did refer to these lines as proof that "God ordained Adam to rule over his wife . . . and as hers so all theirs that should come of her."[9] Nevertheless, Sir Robert preferred the Genesis 1:28 passage. By using that text, he could show that patriarchal order was in accord with man's original nature, not simply with his fallen nature. Filmer hoped to show that the human hierarchy was established in the *very* beginning. Each passing second made monarchical power appear less natural, and shared dominion more legitimate. Consequently, Filmer preferred to insist that Adam was monarch of the world from the very first moment of creation: "By the appointment of God, as soon as Adam was created he was monarch of the world, though he had no subjects; . . . Adam was a King from his creation . . . Eve was subject to Adam before he sinned; the angels who are of a pure nature, are subject to God."[10]

Genesis was not the only biblical source of patriarchal theory. The Decalogue, too, served to support patriarchal political authority, according to Filmer: "The power of the government is settled and fixed by the commandment of 'honour thy father'; if there were a higher power than the fatherly, then this command could not stand and be observed."[11] Filmer's omission is obvious. In service of political patriarchalism, the last half of the fifth commandment was dropped. All honor due to mother was forgotten.

Filmer and the Contract Theorists

Filmer's selective quotation was not overlooked by his critics. In the 1680s Whigs severely attacked *Patriarcha* by dredging up one biblical reference after another to prove Sir Robert had flagrantly abused scriptural texts to support his theory.[12] In the eyes of his fellow Englishmen who shared his world view, the only way Sir Robert could be refuted was by destroying his scriptural base.[13]

In the course of the seventeenth century, standards of evidence and styles of argument changed dramatically. Forms of argument which had been perfectly acceptable in earlier political discourse were rejected in favor of newer "rational" arguments. Although John Locke would champion the new mode of thought, the old form still had a hold on him. Locke took Filmer's biblical arguments seriously, as challenges to be met and overcome. Locke's attack on Filmer, though incomplete, gives the impression that once the biblical criticism was finished, he believed Filmer stood refuted and the attack on contract theory rebutted. This was not necessarily true.[14]

Filmer staunchly insisted that man was not by nature free. Rather, man was born to subjection: "Every man that is born is so far from being free-born that by his very birth he becomes a subject to him that begets him."[15]

By looking to the Garden of Eden, Filmer thought he could demonstrate the truth about natural man and his natural forms of association, but his assertion did not receive its force solely from the scriptural account. Sir Robert also relied on constitutional and classical sources to complement his biblical evidence. More importantly, however, his claims were strengthened by their apparent empirical relevance. The paternal power of the father and of the king was evident to all who would but look about them. So too, paternal power in a kingdom would remain constant: "There is and always shall be continued to the end of the world, a natural right of a supreme Father over every multitude."[16]

There was absolutely no room in patriarchal theory for free-born individuals. Government could not begin with an act of consent made by free and equal individuals in a state of nature. Filmer insisted that such government could be based on no more than myth. Furthermore, he insisted that contract theories which advanced such a myth would be replete with contradictions and logical fallacies.

Filmer offered a theory which was truly comprehensive and coherent, one which provided a place for every individual in society. His opponents, on the other hand, were far less able to provide a satisfactory accommodation for all the individuals and groups which made up seventeenth-century English society. They wished to destroy the patriarchal base of monarchy, and sever the connection between patriarchalism and divine-right politics, yet they were unable to reject less comprehensive forms of patriarchalism as basic organizing principles of government and society. They developed a new theory of human nature, but did not forsee or develop the implications of that theory.

Despite their criticisms of patriarchalism and their arguments based on consent, neither Edward Gee nor Algernon Sidney nor James Tyrrell, nor his friend, John Locke, were willing to allow participation to all comers. Tyrrell, for example, wished to limit participation to male property owners. Locke, as MacPherson argues, would have limited participation to the demonstrably rational (read "acquisitive") classes.[17] But these limitations were swept away by historical actualities over the next two centuries. Rights to political participation were gradually extended to all men and subsequently to all women. Indeed, Filmer rather than Locke or Tyrrell, proved the better predictor of the historical course plotted by the liberal logic when he wrote of government by the people:

> If but one man be excluded, the same reason that excludes one man, may exclude many hundreds, and many thousands, yea, and the major part itself; if it be admitted, that the people are or ever were free by nature, and not to be governed, but by their own consent, it is most unjust to exclude any one man from his right in government.[18]

No one could be excluded from political participation if contract theorists were to remain true to their principles. Filmer understood that in speaking of "the people" and their natural liberty, one had to talk about all mankind.

Though contract theorists came to consider their theories as logical or moral rather than as historical, Filmer used the historical problems of the social contract in an attempt to undermine the logical and moral status of the theory. Filmer insisted that the state of nature and the social contract became logically and historically unacceptable doctrines if "the people" were to be equated with "all mankind." Furthermore, he believed that contract theorists themselves would recoil when faced with the full implications of their theory.

Filmer demanded to know the details of the great meeting where the contract was approved. When did the meeting occur? Who decided the time and place? More importantly, he wanted to know who was invited. Filmer saw these as serious problems for consent theorists since:

> Mankind is like the sea, ever ebbing and flowing every minute one is born another dies; those that are the people this minute are not the people the next minute, in every instant and point of time there is a variation: no one time can be indifferent for all of mankind to assemble; it cannot but be mischevious always at least to all infants and others under the age of discretion; not to speak of women, especially virgins, who by birth have as much natural freedom as any other and therefore ought not to lose their liberty without their consent.[19]

Filmer's attack was no longer simply historical; it was now logical and moral as well. It was clear to him that if the "natural freedom" of mankind was to be taken seriously, obviously the natural freedom of women and children would have to be considered. If women and children were free, they would have to be included in any sort of compact. "Tacit consent" was an impossibility, and was rejected by Filmer as "unreasonable" and "unnatural." Simply to "conclude" the votes of children, for example, in the votes of parents would not be adequate:

> This remedy may cure some part of the mischief, but it destroys the whole cause, and at last stumbles upon the true original of government. For if it be allowed that the acts of the parents bind the children, then farewell the doctrine of the natural freedom of mankind; where subjection of children to parents is natural there can be no natural freedom.[20]

Filmer would probably have agreed that the same line of reasoning could be used to analyze the relationship of women to the social contract.

Filmer's technique in this instance was one of his favorites – *reductio ad absurdum*. His aim was to show the absurdity of the concept "consent of all the people." He insisted that "all the people" must be taken at face value. It must include groups of people generally accounted unfit for such decision making, that is, children, servants and *women*. Each of these groups had been accorded a place within the social and political theory of patriarchy. Each group's place was in accord with a traditional evaluation of its status.

Those who asserted the natural freedom of all mankind upset the applecart. If men were born free and equal, status could not be ascribed at birth, but would have to be achieved in life. If Filmer's opponents were to be consistent, new political roles would have to be opened up for those previously judged politically incompetent. This consequence was never fully clear to Filmer's critics. Though Tyrrell and Sidney criticized Filmer's patriarchalism, they were not ready to break with all the trappings of patriarchy. Consequently, they faced additional difficulties when they tried to account for the political obligation of the politically incompetent.

They maintained that the obligation of disenfranchised groups stemmed from their nurture, from the debt of gratitude owed to the government for their upbringing and education. Members of these groups had no actual voice and were themselves never expected to give free consent to their government. Yet still they were held to be obliged – out of gratitude.

This sort of obligation theory is not far removed from Filmer's. The natural duties of Filmer's king were "summed up in a universal fatherly care of his people."[21] The king preserved, fed, clothed, instructed, and defended the whole commonwealth. Government by contract would do the same things for those who were not part of the contract. In return for these services alone, political nonparticipants owed "a higher Obligation in conscience and gratitude." No participation, no express consent was necessary to put an end to their natural freedom.

A third problem was created for both Filmer and his critics when the questions of participation and monarchical succession were considered together. Filmer did not use patriarchal theory to challenge women's claims to the throne. His critics, especially Sidney, seized upon his silence, protesting that Filmer would allow even women and children to rule as patriarchs. Patriarchal theory enthroned "the next in Blood, without any regard to Age, Sex or other Qualities of the Mind or Body."[22]

Whig theorists did not render Filmer's arguments less damaging to their cause, but they did turn them back on patriarchal theory. To Filmer, contract theory was absurd because it entailed the participation of politically unfit groups in the formation of government and society. To Whigs, the patriarchal position was outrageous because it risked giving a single, similarly incompetent individual absolute unchecked dominion.

To summarize, both Whig and patriarchal theorists used the position of women as a critical tool in evaluating competing theories. Both Whig and patriarchal theorists had to find places for women in their theories. Each criticized the other for the role and status eventually assigned to women.

In effect, Whigs substituted a community of many patriarchs for Filmer's supreme patriarch. Filmer, the patriarch, realized immediately that this simple substitution alone was much less than was required by the doctrine of natural freedom of all mankind. Slowly, over the next two centuries, even liberal thinkers would be drawn to the same conclusion.

Locke's Attack on Patriarchy

While other Whig writers simply declared that their theories necessitated no new roles for women, John Locke treated the problem somewhat differently. He was among the first to sense the inherent contradiction in a "liberalism" based on the natural freedom of mankind, which accorded women no greater freedom than allowed by patriarchalism. New places had to be opened to women. This is not to claim that John Locke planned or even foresaw the feminist movement. It does seem true, however, that Locke took his individualist principles very seriously, even when they entailed an admission that women, too, might have to be considered "individuals."

Clearly Locke was not interested in creating a world in which all were equal; in his view, there would always be differences among individuals. The key question here concerns the extent to which a Lockean society would discriminate on the basis of sex. Would the fact that some are more equal than others necessarily be determined by traditionally assigned sex roles?

Filmer's patriarchal theory included a particular view of the status of women, based on biblical arguments, so Locke's refutation had to deal with that view. Concerning the benediction of Genesis 1:28, Locke noted that it was bestowed on "more than one, for it was spoken in the Plural Number, God blessed *them* and said unto *them*, Have Dominion. God says unto *Adam* and *Eve*, Have Dominion."[23] This argument introduced the possibility that Adam's dominion was not exclusive but was shared with Eve. Further, Eve's subjection to Adam need not have prevented her from exercising dominion over the things of the Earth. Eve, too, might have had property rights.

In the fifth chapter of the *First Treatise*, Locke argued against "Adam's title to Sovereignty by the Subjection of Eve." He took issue with Filmer's use of Genesis 3:16 ("And thy desire shall be to thy Husband and he shall rule over thee"). Those words, Locke objected, were a "punishment laid upon Eve." Furthermore, these words were not even spoken to Adam. The moment after the great transgression, Locke noted, "was not a time when Adam could expect any Favours, any grant of Priviledges from his offended Maker." At most, the curse would "concern the Female Sex only," through Eve, its representative.[24]

Here, Locke argued that Genesis 3:16 offered no evidence of a general grant of power to Adam over all mankind. By limiting the curse to Eve and to women, Locke effectively removed males from the sway of the patriarchal monarch. But he went even further, and suggested that the arguments for the subjection of women based on the Genesis 3:16 passage could be faulty.

First, the subjection of women carried no political import. The curse imposed "no more [than] that Subjection they [women] should ordinarily be in to their Husbands." But even this limit on women's freedom was not immutable and could be overcome:

> There is here no more Law to oblige a Woman to such a Subjection, if the Circumstances either of her Condition or Contract with her Husband should exempt her from it, then there is, that she should bring forth her Children in Sorrow and Pain, if there could be found a remedy for it, which is also part of the same Curse upon her.[25]

Nevertheless, Locke largely accepted the empirical fact of women's inferiority and saw it grounded in nature as ordered by God. He attempted to avoid the conclusion that Adam became Eve's superior or that husbands became their wives' superiors, yet his effort is fairly weak:

> God, in this Text, gives not, that I see, any Authority to Adam over Eve, or to Men over their Wives, but only foretells what should be the Woman's Lot, how by his Providence he would order it so, that she should be subject to her husband as we see that generally the Laws of Mankind and customs of Nations have ordered it so; and there is, I grant, a Foundation in Nature for it.[26]

Locke was principally interested in refuting the idea of a divine grant of authority to Adam. He lived in a world in which the subjection of women was an empirical fact and he willingly yielded to the contemporary view that this fact had some foundation in nature. His tone was hesitant, though. Locke seemed to wish that God had not been responsible for women's inferior status. He tried to cast God in the role of prophet rather than creator. God merely "foretold" what women's lot would be. Locke found it difficult to keep God in the role of innocent bystander, however. Where Locke admitted the use of divine power, he tried to remain tentative: God, in his Providence, "would order" social relations so that wives would be subject to their husbands. But God did not give men any kind of rightful authority over women. Locke implied that God merely suggested one empirical relationship which was subsequently adopted by mankind and reinforced by the laws and customs of nations. That these laws and customs were largely established by males did not, in Locke's opinion, damage the case. It did not seem to bother him that such laws and customs offered proof of the authority which men exercised over women.

Locke simply wished to deny that male authority was exercised by virtue of some divine grant. At this point, he had no need to reject the customary exercise of such authority. It was enough to show only that it was human and not divine in origin.

Peter Laslett notes that "Locke's attitude towards the curse on women in childbearing is typical of his progressive, humanitarian rationalism."[27] But Locke's views on women were also evidence of his individualism. Though Locke believed there was a "foundation in nature" for the limitations on women, he remained faithful to the individualist principles which underlay his theory. In his view, women were free to overcome their natural limitations; each woman was permitted to strike a better deal for herself whenever possible.

In conjunction with his attack on Filmer's use of Genesis 3:16, Locke touched another of patriarchy's soft spots. He sensed the weakness of Filmer's insistence on women's inferiority in a nation where women had worn the crown. Locke made no sustained analysis of this point, but remarked, instead, "[will anyone say] that either of our Queens *Mary* or *Elizabeth* had they Married any of their Subjects, had been by this Text put into a Political Subjection to him? or that he thereby should have had Monarchical Rule over her?"[28]

Locke also accused Sir Robert of performing procrustean mutilations of "words and senses of Authors".[29] This tendency was most evident in Filmer's abbreviation of the fifth commandment. Filmer cited the command throughout his works, always in the same terms, "Honour thy Father." Locke noted this and complained that "and Mother, as Apocriphal Words, are always left out." Filmer had overlooked the "constant Tenor of the Scripture," Locke maintained. To bolster his position, Locke produced over a dozen scriptural citations showing the child's duty to father *and* mother. A mother's title to honor from her children was independent of the will of her husband. This independent right, he argued, was totally inconsistent with the existence of absolute monarchical power vested in the father.[30] Ultimately, Locke denied that the fifth commandment had any political implications at all.[31]

In this analysis, Locke broke with one of patriarchy's strongest traditions. Political obligation had been justified through the fifth commandment. In seventeenth-century sermon literature and catechism texts, the subject's duty of obedience was firmly rooted in this command. Locke refuted these arguments, not by rejecting scriptural evidence, but by analyzing the interpretations supposedly based on that source.

This completed the destructive part of Locke's case. His attack rent the fabric of Filmer's theory. Since patriarchalism represented a complete, integrated theory of society, an adequate successor theory would have to replace all its shattered parts. If all social relations could no longer be understood through the patriarchal paradigm, how could they be understood? Locke's answer came in the *Second Treatise*. There he made his positive contribution to the understanding of social relations.

Social Relations in the *Second Treatise*

For Filmer and his sympathizers there was only one type of power: paternal power. This power was, by its nature, absolute. Filmer's simplistic, uncluttered view of power fits in perfectly with his analysis of social relations. Filmer admitted only one kind of social relationship: the paternal relationship. Each member of society was defined by his or her relation to the patriarchs of the family and of the nation.

Locke, however, maintained that there were many kinds of power and many types of social relations. He analyzed several nonpolitical relationships including those of master–servant, master–slave, parent–child, and husband–wife.[32] Each of these forms of association was carefully distinguished from the political relationship of ruler–subject. Two of the nonpolitical relationships, namely the parental and the conjugal, reveal a great deal about the status of women in Lockean theory.

From the very outset of the discussion of the parent–child relation, Locke rejected the terminology of patriarchy, claiming that "[paternal power] seems so to place the Power of Parents over their Children wholly in the Father, as if the Mother had no share in it, whereas if we consult Reason or Revelation, we shall find she hath an equal Title. . . . For whatever obligation Nature and the right of Generation lays on Children, it must certainly bind them equal to both the concurrent Causes of it."[33]

The basic argument at the root of his terminological objection was one familiar from the *First Treatise*. Patriarchal theory could not stand if power were shared by husband and wife. As Locke argued in the *Second Treatise*, "it will but very ill serve the turn of those Men who contend so much for the Absolute Power and Authority of the *Fatherhood*, as they call it, that the *Mother* should have any share in it."[34]

Locke's examination of the conjugal relationship demanded a more extensive analysis of the roles and status of women in society. He described conjugal society as follows:

> *Conjugal Society* is made by a voluntary Compact between Man and Woman: tho' it consist chiefly in such a Communion and Right in one another's Bodies, as is necessary to its chief End, Procreation; yet it draws with it mutual Support and Assistance, and a Communion of Interest too, as necessary not only to unite their Care, and Affection, but also necessary to their common Off-spring, who have a Right to be nourished and maintained by them, till they are able to provide for themselves.[35]

Conjugal society existed among human beings as a persistent social relationship because of the long term of dependency of the offspring and further because of the dependency of the woman who "is capable of conceiving, and *de facto* is commonly with Child again, and Brings forth too a new Birth long before the former is out of a dependency."[36] Thus the father is obliged to care for his children and is also "under an Obligation to continue in Conjugal Society with the same Woman longer than other creatures."[37]

Though the conjugal relationship began for the sake of procreation, it continued for the sake of property. After praising God's wisdom for combining in man an acquisitive nature and a slow maturing process, Locke noted that a departure from monogamy would complicate the simple natural economics of the conjugal system.[38] Though conjugal society among human beings would be more persistent than among other species, this did not mean that marriage would be indissoluble. Indeed, Locke wondered "why this *Compact*, where Procreation and Education are secured, and Inheritance taken care for, may not be made determinable, either by consent, or at a certain time, or upon certain Conditions, as well as any other voluntary Compacts, there being no necessity in the nature of the thing, nor to the ends of it, that it shall always be for life."[39]

Locke's tentative acceptance of divorce brought him criticism over 100 years later. Thomas Elrington commented that "to make the conjugal union determinable by consent, is to introduce a promiscuous concubinage." Laslett notes that Locke was prepared to go even further and suggested the possibilities of lefthand marriage.[40] In Locke's view, the actual terms of the conjugal contract were not fixed and immutable: "Community of Goods and the Power over them, mutual Assistance and Maintenance, and other things belonging to *Conjugal Society*, might be varied and regulated by that Contract, which unites Man and Wife in that Society as far as may consist with Procreation and the bringing up of Children."[41] Nevertheless, Locke described what he took to be the normal distribution of power in marital relationships: "The Husband and Wife, though they have but one common Concern, yet having different understandings will unavoidably sometimes have different wills, too; it therefore being necessary, that the last Determination, *ie.* the Rule, should be placed somewhere, it naturally falls to the Man's share, as the abler and the stronger."[42] Clearly all forms of patriarchalism did not die with Filmer and his fellows. Here, the subjection of women is not based on Genesis, but on natural qualifications. Nature had shown man to be the "abler and stronger." Locke's patriarchy was limited, though. The husband's power of decision extended only to those interests and properties held in common by husband and wife. Locke spelled out the limits on the husband's power:

> [His power] leaves the Wife in the full and free possession of what by
> Contract is her Peculiar Right, and gives the Husband no more power over
> her Life, than she has over his. The *Power of the Husband* being so far from
> that of an absolute monarch that the *Wife* has, in many cases, a Liberty to
> *separate* from him; where natural Right or their Contract allows it, whether
> that Contract be made by themselves in the state of Nature or by the
> Customs or Laws of the Country they live in; and the Children upon such
> Separation fall to the Father or Mother's lot, as such contract does deter-
> mine.[43]

In addition, Locke distinguished between the property rights of husband
and wife. All property in conjugal society was not automatically the
husband's. A wife could have property rights not subject to her husband's
control. Locke indicated this in a passage on conquest: "For as to the
Wife's share, whether her own Labour or Compact gave her a Title to it,
'tis plain, her Husband could not forfeit what was hers."[44]

There were several similarities between the conjugal and the political
relationship. Both were grounded in consent. Both existed for the preservation of property. Yet conjugal society was not political society because it
conferred no power over the life and death of its members. In addition,
political society could intervene in the affairs of conjugal society. Men and
women in the state of nature were free to determine the terms of the
conjugal contract. But in civil society these terms could be limited or
dictated by the "Customs or Laws of the Country."

The extent to which the participants in the parental and conjugal
relationships could also participate in political relationships remains to be
considered. We may gain some insight into the matter by following
Locke's route, that is, by tracing the origins of political power from the
state of nature.

To Locke, the state of nature was a "state of perfect Freedom" for
individuals "to order Actions and dispose of their Possessions, and Persons,
as they think fit." Furthermore, Locke also described the state of nature
as:

> A *State* also of Equality, wherein all the Power and Jurisdiction is reciprocal,
> no one having more than another: there being nothing more evident, than
> that Creatures of the same species and rank promiscuously born to all the
> same advantages of Nature and the use of the same faculties should also be
> equal one amongst another without Subordination or Subjection, unless the
> Lord and Master of them all should by any manifest Declaration of his Will
> set one above another.[45]

Because of certain inconveniences, men quit the state of nature to form
civil society through an act of consent. It was in criticizing the formation
of society by consent that Filmer's theory was most effective. Indeed,

Locke found it difficult to show how free and equal individuals actually formed civil society. Ultimately he was forced to admit that the first political societies in history were probably patriarchal monarchies. He described the historic origins as follows:

> As it often happens, where there is much Land and few People, the Government commonly began in the Father. For the Father having by the Law of Nature, the same Power with every Man else to punish his transgressing Children even when they were Men, and out of their Pupilage; and they were very likely to submit to his punishment, and all joyn with him against the Offender in their turns, giving him thereby power to Execute his Sentence against any transgression . . . [the] Custom of obeying him, in their Childhood made it easier to submit to him rather than to any other.[46]

In this passage, Locke lumped paternal power and natural power together, allowed for the slightest nod of consent, and – presto – civil society emerged. Even in a Lockean state of nature, paternal (parental?) power could be effective. Children growing up in the state of nature were under the same obligations to their parents as children reared in civil society. What of natural freedom and equality? Locke confessed:

> *Children* are not born in this full state of *Equality*, though they are born to it. Their parents have a sort of Rule and Jurisdiction over them when they come into the World, and for some time after, but 'tis but a temporary one. The Bonds of this Subjection are like Swadling Cloths they are wrapt up in and supported by in the weakness of their Infancy. Age and Reason as they grow up, loosen them till at length they drop quite off, and leave a Man at his own free Disposal.[47]

Of course, once children reached maturity in the state of nature they no longer owed obedience to their parents, but were merely required to honor them out of simple gratitude. At this stage, however, Locke introduced another sort of power to support the father's claim to his child's obedience – namely that power which accrued to every man in the state of nature, the power to punish the transgressions of others against him. But the father's power was reinforced by his children's longstanding habit of obedience to him. In the state of nature, the father's commands to his mature children received added weight and legitimacy because he *was* their father. His children would recognize this legitimacy and would join their power to his to make him lawmaker. At this point, it seems, the father's former paternal power and his existing natural power were transformed by consent into political power.

In this discussion, Locke was willing to concede the historical or anthropological case for patriarchalism. He was not ready to concede the moral case, however. Filmer had tied his moral and historical arguments together by using the Book of Genesis as the source of both. Locke split the two cases apart. Locke's biblical criticisms were intended to demonstrate the weakness of the moral conclusions which Filmer had drawn from the Genesis creation account. Thus, at best, Filmer was left with only an historical case. But, Locke insisted, history was not the source of morality. He wrote that "an Argument from what has been, to what should of right be, has no great force."[48] Instead, he broke with history and based his moral theory on a new understanding of human nature. In doing so, however, he reopened questions closed by Filmer's theory. Locke had to deal with the political roles and status of women, children and servants. He was somewhat sensitive to Filmer's criticisms concerning the place of these politically unfit groups within contract theory. He certainly tried to make a consistent explanation of the relationship of children to civil society; "We are *born Free*, as we are born Rational; not that we have actually the Exercise of either: Age that brings one brings with it the other too. And thus we see how natural *Freedom and Subjection to Parents* may consist together and are both founded on the same Principle."[49] No immature child could be expected to take part in the social compact. Yet children's inability to participate in politics would not preclude their right to consent to government when they reached adulthood. Locke indicated the necessity of each person giving consent as a condition of full political rights and full political obligation. Grown sons were free to make their own contract as were their fathers before them. An individual could not be bound by the consent of others but had to make a personal commitment through some separate act of consent.

But what of women? Unlike Tyrrell and Sidney, Locke remained silent on the specific question of their participation in the founding of political society. Of course, it is possible Locke referred to the role of women in the lost section of the *Treatises*. Or, perhaps Locke understood that explicit exclusion of women seriously weakened a theory grounded in the natural freedom of mankind. Yet Locke was also a good enough propagandist to have realized how deeply ingrained patriarchalism was in everyday life. Locke had criticized Filmer's use of the fifth commandment – "Honor thy father" – as a basis for political obligation. If the command were taken seriously, he charged, then "every Father must necessarily have Political Dominion, and there will be as many Sovereigns as there are Fathers."[50] But the audience Locke was addressing was essentially an audience of fathers, household heads and family sovereigns. Locke had freed them from political subjection to a patriarchal superior – the king. He did not risk alienating his audience by clearly conferring a new political status on their subordinates under the patriarchal system, that is, on women. Nevertheless, despite the absence of any sustained analysis of the problem of women, we may draw some conclusions from an examination of Locke's scattered thoughts on women.

Though Locke gave the husband ultimate authority within conjugal society, this authority was limited and nonpolitical. Yet when Locke's account of the husband's conjugal authority was combined with his account of the historical development of political society, several questions occur which were never adequately resolved in Locke's moral theory. Did not the award of final decision-making power to the father and husband (in conjugal society) transform "parental power" into "paternal power"? Was the subsequent development of political power based on paternal power a result of that transformation? What was woman's role in the establishment of the first political society? Since her husband was to be permitted final decisions in matters of their common interest and property, and since political society, obviously, was a matter of common interest, would her voice simply be "concluded" in that of her husband? If so, then Filmer's question recurs – what became of her rights as a free individual? Did she lose her political potential because she was deemed not as "able and strong" as her husband? If this were the case, Locke would have had to introduce new qualifications for political life.

Locke portrayed political society as an association of free, equal, rational individuals who were capable of owning property.[51] These individuals came together freely, since none had any power or jurisdiction over others. They agreed to form a civil society vested with power to legislate over life and death, and to execute its decisions in order to protect the vital interests of its members, that is, their lives, liberties and estates. Yet John Locke was certainly no believer in the absolute equality of human beings. Indeed, on that score, he was emphatic:

> Though I have said . . . *That all Men by Nature are equal*, I cannot be supposed to understand all sorts of *Equality; Age* or *Virtue* may give Men a just Precedency: *Excellence of Parts and Merit* may place others above the Common Level; *Birth* may subject some and *Alliance* or *Benefits* others, to pay an Observance to those whom Nature, Gratitude, or other Respects may have made it due.[52]

But these inequalities in no way affect an individual's basic freedom or political capacity, for Locke continued in the same passage:

> yet all this consists with the *Equality* which all Men are in, in respect of Jurisdiction or Dominion one over another, which was the *Equality* I there spoke of, as proper to the Business in hand, being that *equal Right* every Man hath, *to his Natural Freedom*, without being subjected to the Will or Authority of any other Man.[53]

If "Man" is used as a generic term, then woman's natural freedom and equality could not be alienated without her consent. Perhaps a marriage contract might be taken for consent, but this is a dubious proposition. Locke had indicated that a marriage contract in no way altered the political capacity of a queen regnant.[54] While decision-making power over the common interests of a conjugal unit belonged to the husband, Locke admitted that the wife might have interests apart from their shared interests. Women could own separate property not subject to their husbands' control. If a husband forfeited his life or property as a result of conquest, his conquerors acquired no title to his wife's life or property.

Did these capacities entitle women to a political role? Locke never directly confronted the question; nevertheless, it is possible to compare Locke's qualifications for political life with his views of women. Locke used the Genesis account to show that women possessed the same natural freedom and equality as men. Whatever limitations had been placed on women after the Fall could conceivably be overcome through individual effort or scientific advance. Furthermore, women were capable of earning through their own labor, of owning property and of making contracts.

Locke and the Rational Woman

The one remaining qualification for political life is rationality. For Locke's views on the rationality of women it will be necessary to turn to his other writings, notably his *Thoughts on Education*.

In the published version of his advice on education, Locke mentioned that the work had been originally intended for the education of boys; but he added that it could be used as a guide for raising children of either sex. He noted that "where difference of sex requires different Treatment, 'twill be no hard Matter to distinguish."[55]

Locke felt that his advice concerning a gentleman's education would have to be changed only slightly to fit the needs of girls. However, in a letter to a friend, Mrs Edward Clarke, Locke tried to show that his prescriptions were appropriate for her daughter and not unnecessarily harsh.[56] On the whole, Locke believed that except for "making a little allowance for beauty and some few other considerations of the s[ex], the manner of breeding of boys and girls, especially in the younger years, I imagine, should be the same."[57]

The differences which Locke thought should obtain in the education of men and women amounted to slight differences in physical training. While Locke thought that "meat, drink and lodging and clothing should be ordered after the same manner for the girls as for the boys," he did introduce a few caveats aimed at protecting the girls' complexions.[58]

Locke introduced far fewer restrictions in his plan for a young lady's mental development. In a letter to Mrs Clarke he wrote: "Since, therefore I acknowledge no difference of sex in your mind relating . . . to truth, virtue, and obedience, I think well to have no thing altered in it from what is [writ for the son]."[59]

Far from advocating a special, separate and distinct form of education for girls, Locke proposed that the gentleman's education should more closely resemble that of young ladies. For example, he favored the education of children at home by tutors. Modern languages learned through conversation should replace rote memorization of classical grammars. In addition, Locke suggested that young gentlemen as well as young ladies might profit from a dancing master's instruction.

Taken as a whole, Locke's thoughts on education clearly suggest a belief that men and women could be schooled in the use of reason. The minds of both men and women were blank slates to be written on by experience. Women had intellectual potential which could be developed to a high level.

Locke's educational process was designed to equip young men for lives as gentlemen. Since the gentleman's life certainly included political activity, a young man's education had to prepare him for political life. If a young lady were to receive the same education, it should be expected that she, too, would be capable of political activity.

Finally, 300 years ago, Locke offered a "liberated" solution to a controversy which still rages in religious circles – the question of the fitness of women to act as ministers. In 1696 Locke, together with King William, attended a service led by a Quaker preacher, Rebecca Collier. He praised her work and encouraged her to continue in it, writing, "Women, indeed, had the honour first to publish the resurrection of the Lord of Love; why not again the resurrection of the Spirit of Love?"[60] It is interesting to compare Locke's attitude here with the famous remark made by Samuel Johnson on the same subject in the next century: "Sir, a woman's preaching is like a dog's walking on his hindlegs. It is not done well; but you are surprized to find it done at all."[61]

Perhaps a similar conclusion might be reached about the roots of feminism in Lockean liberalism. In a world where political antipatriarchalism was still somewhat revolutionary, explicit statements of more far-reaching forms of antipatriarchalism were almost unthinkable. Indeed, they would have been considered absurdities. Thus, while Filmer had presented a comprehensive and consistent patriarchal theory, many of his liberal opponents rejected political patriarchalism by insisting on the need for individual consent in political affairs but shied away from tampering with patriarchal attitudes where women were concerned. John Locke was something of an exception to this rule. Though his feminist sympathies certainly did not approach the feminism of Mill writing nearly two centuries later, in view of the intense patriarchalism of seventeenth-century England, it should be surprising to find such views expressed at all.

Notes

1 On patriarchalism as a world view, see Gordon J. Schochet, *Patriarchalism and Political Thought* (New York: Basic Books, 1975); also, W. H. Greenleaf, *Order, Empiricism, and Politics* (London: Oxford University Press, 1964)‚ chs 1–5; Peter Laslett's introduction to Sir Robert Filmer, *Patriarcha and other Political Works of Sir Robert Filmer*, ed. Peter Laslett (Oxford: Basil Blackwell, 1949), p. 26; and John W. Robbins, "The Political Thought of Sir Robert Filmer," Ph.D. dissertation, The Johns Hopkins University, 1973.

2 Patriarchal strains may be found in the literature of the sixteenth century including John Knox, *First Blast of the Trumpet Against the Monstrous Regiment of Women* (Geneva, 1558); James I in *The Trew Law of Free Monarchies* (1598); Richard Field, *Of the Church* (1606). Patriarchal theorists among Filmer's contemporaries included John Maxwell who wrote *Sacro-Sancta Regum Majestas or the Sacred and Royal Prerogative of Christian Kings* (Oxford, 1644); and James Ussher, *The Power Communicated by God to the Prince, and the Obedience Required of the Subject* (written ca. 1644, first published 1661, 2nd edn, London, 1683); and Robert Sanderson, in his preface to Ussher's work.

3 Peter Laslett, *The World We Have Lost* (New York: Scribner's, 1965), passim; Greenleaf, *Order, Empiricism and Politics*, pp. 80–94; Peter Zagorin, *A History of Political Thought in the English Revolution* (New York: Humanities, 1966), pp. 198–9.

4 On the use of scripture in historical argument see J. G. A. Pocock, *The Ancient Constitution and the Feudal Law* (Cambridge: Cambridge University Press, 1967), pp. 188–9.

5 See especially Greenleaf, *Order, Empiricism and Politics*, p. 89; also Julia O'Faolain and Lauro Martines, eds, *Not in God's Image* (New York: Harper Torchbooks, 1973), pp. 179–207; and Schochet, *Patriarchalism*, p. 16.

6 See Filmer, *Patriarcha and Other Political Works*, ed. Laslett.

7 Ibid., 241.

8 Ibid., 187.

9 Ibid., 283.

10 Ibid., 289.

11 Ibid., 188.

12 See, for example, Edward Gee, *The Divine Right and Original of the Civil Magistrate from God* (London, 1658); [James Tyrrell], *Patriarcha Non Monarcha* (London: Richard Janeway, 1681); and Algernon Sidney, *Discourses Concerning Government* (London, 1698).

13 Arguments had to be structured to persuade the widest possible audience. For an exploration of this general problem, see Mark Gavre, "Hobbes and his Audience," *American Political Science Review*, 68, December 1974, pp. 1542–56.

14 Laslett concluded that "neither Locke nor Sidney nor any of a host of others who attacked *Patriarcha* ever attempted to meet the force of [Filmer's] criticisms [about political obligation], and that none of them ever realized what he meant by his naturalism." Filmer, *Patriarcha and Other Political Works*, introduction, p. 21.
15 Ibid., 232.
16 Ibid., 62.
17 C. B. MacPherson, *The Political Theory of Possessive Individualism* (London: Oxford University Press, 1962), ch. 5; and MacPherson, "The Social Bearing of Locke's Political Theory," *Western Political Quarterly*, 7 March 1954, pp. 1–22.
18 Filmer, *Patriarcha and Other Political Works*, 211.
19 Ibid., 287.
20 Ibid., 225, 287.
21 Ibid., 63.
22 Algernon Sidney, *Discourses Concerning Government* (London, 1698), p. 4.
23 John Locke, *Two Treatises of Government*, ed. Peter Laslett (Cambridge: Cambridge University Press, 1960), p. 29.
24 *Two Treatises*, I, 45–7.
25 Ibid., I, 47.
26 Ibid.
27 Ibid., ed. Laslett, p. 210n.
28 Ibid., I, 47.
29 Ibid., I, 60.
30 Ibid., I, 63.
31 Ibid., I, 65.
32 See especially R. W. K. Hinton, "Husbands, Fathers, and Conquerors," *Political Studies*, 16 February 1968, pp. 55–67; Geraint Parry, "Individuality, Politics and the Critique of Paternalism in John Locke," *Political Studies*, 12 June 1964, pp. 163–77; and MacPherson, *Possessive Individualism*.
33 Locke, *Two Treatises*, II, 52.
34 Ibid., II, 53.
35 Ibid., II, 78.
36 Ibid., II, 80.
37 Ibid.
38 Ibid.
39 Ibid., II, 81.
40 Ibid., ed. Laslett, p. 364n.
41 Ibid., II, 83.
42 Ibid., II, 82.
43 Ibid.
44 Ibid., II, 183.
45 Ibid., II, 4.
46 Ibid., II, 105.
47 Ibid., II, 55.
48 Ibid., II, 103.
49 Ibid., II, 61.
50 Ibid., I, 65.

51. See MacPherson, *Possessive Individualism*, ch. 5. MacPherson argues that Locke assumed a class differential in the distribution of these qualities. Full membership in political society would be limited to those who fully demonstrated them. The question under consideration here is the extent to which this class differential might also be a sex differential.

52 Locke, *Two Treatises*, II, 54.

53 Ibid.

54 Ibid., I, 47.

55 John Locke, *Some Thoughts Concerning Education*, section 6; also, see Locke to Mrs Clarke, Jan. 7, 1683/4, in *The Correspondence of John Locke and Edward Clarke*, ed. Benjamin Rand (Cambridge: Harvard University Press, 1927).

56 Locke to Mrs Clarke, Jan. 7, 1683/4, in *Correspondence*, ed. Rand, p. 121.

57 Locke to Mrs Clarke, Jan. 1, 1685, in ibid.

58 Locke to Mrs Clarke, in ibid., p. 103.

59 Locke to Mrs Clarke, in ibid., pp. 102–3.

60 Locke to Rebecca Collier, Nov. 21, 1696, reprinted in H. R. Fox Bourne, *The Life of John Locke*, vol. 2 (New York: Harper and Row, 1876), p. 453.

61 E. L. McAdam and George Milne, eds, *A Johnson Reader* (New York: Pantheon Books, 1964), p. 464.

5

Rousseau and Modern Feminism

Lynda Lange

Introduction

Jean-Jacques Rousseau has often been charged with inconsistency, despite his own assertion that all his writing is informed by the same principles.[1] Recently, however, there has been a different sort of charge of inconsistency. It is claimed that his spirited opposition to sexual equality is grossly inconsistent with his defence of equality for all citizens.[2] On the other hand, the conservative Allan Bloom, who claims to detect consistency in his approach to women and men, finds him a stay of contemporary antifeminism.[3] I propose an interpretation of Rousseau which is different from both of these perspectives. In my view, Rousseau is basically consistent in his treatment of men and women, despite a few discrepancies. However, writing as a feminist, I believe his views can be studied to advantage by feminists. Rousseau addresses almost every social issue that contemporary feminism is concerned with, and he does this in a manner which proves on examination to be surprisingly relevant to present problems, whether one agrees with his precise conclusions or not. With regard to sexual equality, it is possible to "turn Rousseau on his head," in a manner of speaking.

The theory of women's nature and their role in society which I shall present has been developed on the basis of ideas and insights found in many works of Rousseau. The years 1756 to 1759, immediately following the writing of the First and Second Discourses, saw Rousseau's production of a large body of work devoted to a great extent to the relations of the sexes and the nature and role of women. His major work on the subject is found in *Julie ou la nouvelle Héloïse*, the *Lettre à M. D'Alembert sur les spectacles*, and *Emile ou de l'éducation,* all written during this period. Book V of *Emile,* on the education of women, was written before the other books of that work, immediately after the *Lettre à M. d'Alembert.* Prior to this period, some footnotes in the Second Discourse, as well as the philosophical anthropology concerning the origin of the family in that work, show that this subject had earlier been of interest to Rousseau as well. In other words, it is not peripheral to his central work as a political philosopher, even from his own point of view.

Rousseau was a severe critic of what he regularly referred to as *la société civile.* It is my view that *la société civile,* as Rousseau pictures it, has the main features of capitalism, or "possessive market society," as it is modelled by C. B. Macpherson.[4] Just as Macpherson demonstrated that the work of Hobbes, Locke, and others had the effect of justifying the crucial features of "possessive market society" by showing that their assumptions and conclusions conformed to that model of society, and not by showing that they had a concept of "possessive market society," I believe that Rousseau's criticism applies to that model, but not that he actually perceived the emergence of capitalism out of feudalism. The view that Rousseau's criticisms are applicable to a certain form of civil society, and not to civil society *per se,* bridges the gap between the vitriolic criticism of "civil society" in the early discourses, and the ideal of a good and legitimate society present later in *Du Contrat Social.*

All the evils of modern civil society, according to Rousseau, are derived ultimately from the fact that personal or particular interest (*l'intérêt personnel, l'intérêt particulier*) is the dominant rationale for action. What is worse, according to Rousseau, is that society is structured in such a way as to make this type of behavior rational in the circumstances. For Rousseau, the incompatibility of this with our authentic interests, and its deeply corrupting effect on our moral character, only appear after a thorough study of nature and history.

Feminist ideas were widely discussed in prerevolutionary France, but Rousseau thought that the idea that the sexes might *both* operate on these modern principles and that women should not be denied the right to advance their particular interests as men do was one of the most absurd and lamentable consequences of this modern philosophy. It is in this area that I find his views insightful and potentially instructive. It has been a theme of feminist criticism that the opposition of interests, exploitation, competition, and so on, endemic to our social and economic system, are, in some sense, male values. Yet because these values *are* endemic, they tend to shape feminism in their mold, and may be perfectly compatible with a lack of social discrimination between the sexes. It is another question, however, whether these individualist principles are ultimately useful to *democratic* feminism. This essay addresses these concerns through an examination of Rousseau's works.

Origins and Foundations of Sexual Inequality

According to Rousseau, and contrary to contractarian theory, the innate drive for self-preservation (*amour de soi*) does not, in itself, suggest any necessary opposition of interests. The gradual development of interdependence and entrenched inequality of power and wealth transform the expression of the drive for self-preservation into rational egoism, or *amour propre*. Since all develop these same concerns, their interests are necessarily in constant opposition. It is frequently apparent that Rousseau's views on women are a response to feminist arguments, and he was a severe critic of these arguments, in a manner which was consistent with his general criticism of individualist thought.[5]

In Book V of *Emile*, Rousseau states the following essential difference between the moral potential of men and women:

> The Supreme Being wanted to do honour to the human species in everything. While giving man inclinations without limit, He gives him at the same time the law which regulates them, in order that he may be free and in command of himself. While abandoning man to immoderate passions, He joins reason [*la raison*] to these passions in order to govern them. While abandoning woman to unlimited desires, He joins modesty [*la pudeur*] to these desires in order to constrain them.[6]

The functions of these virtues, it may be noted, have a difference that corresponds to the difference in their character. The man "controls" or "governs" (*gouverner*) his own behavior with the use of reason; the woman merely "restrains" hers (*contenir*).[7]

While the man under the sway of *amour propre* may be thought to display his human potential for rationality in a corrupted form, the woman so swayed is sharply deflected from her unique human virtue of modesty. How has Rousseau concluded that there are such great differences between the sexes? It is done, surprisingly enough, in a manner which appears on analysis to be determinedly empiricist. Contrary to expectation, Rousseau does not rely on custom, prejudice, or God's will in the course of his attempt to justify a unique and inferior feminine role for women. It is probably because he uses these modern methods that Rousseau's theories of feminine and masculine social roles have remained influential even to the present.

In the *Discours sur l'origine et les fondements de l'inégalité* (Second Discourse), and in *Emile*, Rousseau's method is that of philosophical anthropology, and he even uses a type of argument found in contemporary evolutionary biology. This putatively scientific approach seems to him to justify the quick inference of a principle with vast consequences. It is one which is only too familiar to the contemporary reader, but by no means evidently true: "the man should be strong and active; the women should be weak and passive."[8] The different biological contributions of the sexes to their common aim (*l'objet commun*) of reproduction dictates this principle, according to Rousseau. Equal strength and self-assertion are inconsistent with the reproductive biology of each sex. This argument concerns *homo sapiens* in the pure state of nature, prior to the development of any specifically human culture or society. From a biological point of view, for procreation to occur, Rousseau writes, "One must necessarily will and be able; it suffices that the other put up little resistance."[9]

In another direct response to feminist debate, he argues that it is scarcely natural that men and women should enter with equal boldness on a course of action that has such very different consequences for each of them.[10] This response, however, presumes that the woman in the state of nature knows the consequences of sexual interaction for herself, which is at least debatable given what Rousseau says about the total inability of *homo sapiens* to formulate ideas or project expectations in the pure state of nature.[11]

Is sheer physical domination of women by men then natural? No. In the pure state of nature men are not very aggressive about anything, including sex, and natural compassion (*pitié*) is undiminished. We may suppose that a rebuff, or flight, or even a display of fear on the part of a woman would probably be sufficient to discourage an unwanted partner in the pure state of nature. Most importantly, honor is not at stake for men. According to Rousseau, the violence and incessant competition commonly attributed to male sexuality are a result of the knowledge and pride of *amour propre* developed in social relations. They are not "natural."

The timidity and weakness of the woman, according to Rousseau, inspire her to be pleasing to a man out of the basic impulse of self-preservation, that is if she is pleasing he is less likely to be violent. Rousseau thinks this behaviour simultaneously makes the man more inclined to remain with her (an important consideration if one has given up one's autonomy). These are the means she is given to supplement her weakness, and therefore, to act to please men is a quality of women directly derivable from nature. Rousseau writes:

> If woman is made to please and to be subjugated, she ought to make herself agreeable to man instead of arousing him. Her own violence is in her charms. . . . From this there arises attack and defence, the audacity of one

sex and the timidity of the other, and finally the modesty and the shame
with which nature armed the weak in order to enslave the strong.[12]

However, as we have seen, these responses, based on natural compassion
(*pitié*), are corrupted by the individualistic society of *amour propre*. If within
civil society the man is stronger and dependent on the women only
through desire, as Rousseau claims, whereas she depends on him through
desire and need,[13] why should he bother to please her, and refrain from
simply exercising his will? Rousseau has provided two answers to this
question in *Emile*, concerning women and men in what Rousseau considers
a good society.

The first argument is that real violence in sexual relations is contrary to
its own ends since it is a declaration of war which may result in death,
whereas the goal of sexual relations is the perpetuation of the species. This
is clearly a restraint which is based on sophisticated rationality. Rousseau
believes that it is reason that restrains masculine sexuality, and it is
noteworthy that it is not the mode of rational egoism which is said to be
the restraint in question. The goal of sexual relations is here defined as a
collective goal of the species, rather than in terms of individual self
interest.

The other argument is related to the ultimately conventional character
of paternity. It is that "a child would have no father if any man might
usurp a father's rights."[14] This is meant to be a consideration that a *man*
might use to govern his own behavior, and is once again a collective,
rather than a purely individual, motive. However, from a feminist perspective, this is a surprisingly explicit admission of male solidarity opposed
to women, rather than of fully social motivation.[15] Here Rousseau tips on
his head quite easily!

As we have seen, the male-dominated family is not a purely natural
phenomenon for Rousseau, inasmuch as he does not suppose it to be
present in the pure state of nature. In the speculative history of the Second
Discourse, women are depicted in the state of nature as able to provide for
themselves and their dependent children. It is a momentous development
for humanity when increasing population drives some to less balmy climates
where they are motivated to learn to build permanent shelters. Rousseau
writes:

> The habit of living together gave rise to the sweetest sentiments known to
> men: conjugal love and paternal love. Each family became a little society all
> the better united because reciprocal affection and freedom were its only
> bonds; and it was then that the first difference was established in the way of
> life of the two sexes, which until this time had had but one. Women became
> more sedentary, and grew accustomed to tend the hut and the children,
> while the men went to seek their common subsistence.[16]

Though able to meet her own needs when solitary, the woman is assumed to be weaker than the man, so that living together is assumed to result in a division of labor.[17] It also results in more frequent pregnancy, which is thought to entrench the dependence of the woman on the man. The man, though quite insensible to love in the state of nature and utterly ignorant of his connection to children, is thought to become attached to both woman and children through constant association. This response is similar to that of the woman in the state of nature, who is thought to care for her offspring because she grows fond of them "through habit."[18] However, there is a crucial philosophic difference, which is a good example of the way in which thought may be shaped by male bias. The woman's attachment to her dependent offspring is "natural" in the fullest sense of the word: it could be said to be merely instinctive, since it is presumed to occur when human beings live exactly like animals. Paternal affection, however, is said to be a significant development, the result of socialization, and based on a rather abstract knowledge.

As such, paternity is a product of human artifice, based on knowledge and custom, and therefore, according to this philosophy, specifically human in a way that maternal love is not thought to be. Because of this, paternity will not be treated as a disqualification for the highest forms of human artifice, namely, political life and rational discourse. Allegedly natural maternity, on the other hand, is typically treated as such by political theorists, including Rousseau. This difference has important implications for the structure of Rousseau's political philsophy. For the moment, however, we will confine our discussion of this issue to the terms of Rousseau's own theory.

The sexual division of labor which appears as a result of the association of the sexes is not simply the result of practical cooperation for Rousseau, but a reflection of the essential difference between the sexes. The woman is so constituted that passivity and timidity are assets to her "proper purpose" (*leur destination propre*) once social relations have developed. This purpose is to reproduce within a family whose unity depends entirely on her behavior. Natural passivity and timidity in sexual relations, according to Rousseau, form the natural base for modesty (*la pudeur*) which is the specifically feminine virtue in civil society.

Modesty is the virtue which may ensure biological paternity of the children to the man she lives with, and the necessity Rousseau sees for this dictates the retiring and wholly domestic life of good women. "She serves as the link between them and their father; she alone makes him love them and gives him the confidence to call them his own."[19] On account of the artificiality and apparent fragility of the bond of the father to his children, the woman is required to live a life dictated by the necessity to appear respectable, that is, to convince her husband and everyone else that she is sexually monogamous. Nothing less than this degree of certitude, bolstered by public opinion, is thought to be sufficient to induce him to remain attached to that particular family and provide for its support.

> By the very law of nature women are at the mercy of men's judgments, as much for their own sake as for that of their children. It is not enough that they be estimable; they must be esteemed. It is not enough for them to be pretty; they must please. It is not enough for them to be temperate; they must be recognized as such. Their honor is not only in their conduct but in their reputation; and it is not possible that a woman who consents to be regarded as disreputable can ever be decent.[20]

The wholly incompatible bases of masculine and feminine virtue are summed up in the following sentence from *Emile*: "Opinion is the grave of virtue among men and its throne among women."[21]

This abandonment of moral autonomy for women is particularly damning from Rousseau, who considers such autonomy essential not only for citizenship, but even for true humanity.[22] That the male-headed family requires women to abandon moral autonomy functions without alteration as a severe criticism of that institution.

Rousseau does not leave himself completely exposed to empirical refutation concerning the nature of women. In the *Lettre à M. d'Alembert sur les spectacles*, he writes:

> Even if it could be denied that a special sentiment of chasteness was natural to women, would it be any the less true that in society their lot ought to be a domestic and retired life, and that they ought to be raised in principles appropriate to it? If the timidity, chasteness, and modesty which are proper to them are social inventions, it is in society's interest that women acquire these qualities.[23]

Thus although Rousseau does not argue that the male-headed biological family is natural and unaffected by history, he does argue that it is nevertheless a social institution that may be grounded on nature by reason. He writes: "When woman complains on this score about unjust man-made inequality, she is wrong. This inequality is not a human institution – or at least, it is the work not of prejudice but of reason."[24] This type of willingness to come to grips with a "tough necessity" still seems to be bracing to conservative antifeminists!

It is of philosophic significance that virtuous women in civil society are characterized as closer to "nature" than virtuous men. The men must be transformed and denatured in a good society, according to Rousseau.[25] The modest woman appears still as little more than uncorrupted. As such she will form a necessary link between the supreme artifice of the good society on the one hand, and nature, on the other.

The Problem of Female Power

According to Rousseau, the social equality of the sexes poses a serious danger to civic virtue. His view of this danger is based on the critical analysis of modern "civil society," especially the concept of *amour propre*. It is Rousseau's belief that if women attempt to act in society according to the norms of *amour propre*, engaging in constant competition to further their "particular interest," they will inevitably be bested by the men. But this does not signify his admiration for the success of the male within that mode of social interaction.

The basic inequality of Rousseau's approach appears, however, in his belief that the woman who enters public life on the terms of *amour propre* does even more violence to her nature than the man caught up in that mode of interraction.

In the *Lettre à M. d'Alembert*, Rousseau argues at great length that one of the major reasons why there ought not to be a theatre established at Geneva is that this will result in women going out in public in company with men. Because of the very nature of sexual relations, according to Rousseau, the presence of women in public life undermines masculine excellence and exacerbates *amour propre*. The frequent attendance of men and women at public entertainments will focus attention on the natural impulses of the sexes to be pleasing to one another. While this is an expansion of the domain of women, since love is their "empire," it diminishes men. This occurs because the standards of behavior appropriate to love and courtship are inevitably feminine standards, given Rousseau's view of female power. According to Rousseau, men who lead a life of constant association with women become enervated and weak.[26] Such men will be far more prone to turn their learning or talent to the pleasing performance arising from *amour propre*, rather than to the rigorous, or morally challenging, pursuit of truth, since they will inevitably compete with one another for feminine approbation. He writes: "By themselves, the men, exempted from having to lower their ideas to the range of women and to clothe reason in gallantry, can devote themselves to grave and serious discourse without fear of ridicule."[27] Why these "grave and serious" intellectuals should be such an easy prey to ridicule is probably a question best answered by feminists over a few drinks at the faculty club. It does not seem to occur to Rousseau that the importance of the feminine role for the good society is rather dicey if there is this degree of tension between the masculine and feminine spheres. From the perspective he presents, a presumed seductive power of women to impose their standards, on account of the nature of sexual relations, enables women to dominate even in areas which are thought to be ultimately beyond their competence. It appears in the Second Discourse, and in *Emile*, that "love" may have been the original stimulus to the appearance of *amour propre*, even though it quickly lost sight of its origin. At the beginning of the "state of savagery," when people first settled in shelters of their own making, they were soon seduced by the pleasures of social life:

> People grew accustomed to assembling in front of the huts or around a large tree; song and dance, true children of love and leisure, became the amusement or rather the occupation of idle and assembled men and women. Each one began to look at the others and to want to be looked at himself, and public esteem had a value . . . that was the first step toward inequality and, at the same time, toward vice. From these first preferences were born on one hand vanity (*la vanité*)[28] and contempt, on the other shame and envy; and the fermentation caused by these new leavens eventually produced compounds fatal to happiness and innocence.[29]

In civil society, according to Rousseau, the consequences of the combination of *amour propre* and "love" as a value in itself (that is, unconnected to duty) are morally disastrous. According to him, this is an important reason why women should be confined to the sphere of their true competence: childcare, household tasks, and "rest and recreation" for men. Regarding the actual mental capacity of women, Rousseau does what is rare for him – he confuses a social artifact with a natural quality, a lack of education and opportunity for development, with an inherent deficiency.

Much of what Rousseau writes concerning the desirability of a separate feminine sphere centers around the evils to be thus avoided, and the harshness of his strictures are no doubt partly constructed out of his fear of female power. There is, however, a substantive contribution which can be made to the good of society by women, according to Rousseau, one which is an essential feature of a truly legitimate society governed by the general will.

The Foundation of the Good Society is Built out of Women

The contribution women make to a good society by playing a feminine role has ramifications for virtually every issue in moral and political life, according to Rousseau. The scheme he presents also includes a fully developed romantic ideal of the relations of the sexes, presented in a very complete form in *Julie ou la Nouvelle Héloïse,* and to a lesser extent in *Emile* in Book V dealing with the education of women. Nevertheless, the place of the feminine role in Rousseau's political philosophy may be focused around two basic themes. These are:

1   The need for the family and its particular attachments as a natural
    base for patriotism (*amour de la patrie*), and hence as a nursery for good
    citizens; and,
2   The need for certainty of paternity in connection with the requirements
    of the institution of private property.

Regarding the first of these themes, it is apparent that it concerns
education in the widest sense of the term, which is to say, the whole
socialization of citizens. It is not surprising, therefore, that Rousseau
addresses this issue most directly in his work on education, *Emile*. Like
Plato, he puts correct education at the very foundation of the good society.
The contractarian solution to the conflict between individual self-interest
and the existence of the civil state, which is to attempt a logical identification
of the two in the terms of enlightened self-interest, was rejected by Rousseau
as an inadequate foundation of political right.[30]

Rousseau fields a third alternative in which he attempts to sustain the
materialist epistemology which was a philosophically progressive element
in early contractarian theory. It is the injunction not to obey the law
because it is rational (though it ought to be in fact rational), but to love it,
and thus bring into harmony particular and public interest. This emotional
leap is what makes possible the transcendence of *amour propre* required for
the determination of the general will.

It is Rousseau's belief that those who are incapable of loving those near
to them and who have no particular attachments will be even less capable
of the love of their country and its laws or of any sacrifice for the common
good. Particular affective relationships are an essential part of the personal
development of the citizen for Rousseau, and play a foundational role in
civil society. Although the virtue of citizens consists in a conformity of the
individual will to the general will, which may in principle be justified by
reason, Rousseau places a great deal of emphasis on the necessity for
appropriate feeling to make such a civil state possible in fact. Mere
abstract principles, he argues, even if backed by force, will never be
enough to prevent individual self-interest from undermining the state. He
recommends patriotism (*amour de la patrie*) as the most efficacious means of
raising the sights of individuals from self-interest to the good of the state,
for "we willingly want what is wanted by the people we love."[31] Patriotism,
therefore, is not an abstract principle for Rousseau, but an active sentiment which promotes the type of personal development needed to create
citizens.

Even supposing the average citizen were a philosopher, according to
Rousseau, this would not solve the problem of sustaining the general will
in a good state. Reason, because of what it is, is cosmopolitan in its
outlook. Patriotism is therefore ultimately based on a lie, though a "noble

lie," if you will. The shared customs and religion that give a nation cohesion, when regarded dispassionaely and objectively, cannot be shown to be any better in reality than those of any other nation. But each nation, according to Rousseau, needs emotional loyalty from its citizens, rather than mere approval of its authority on the basis of reason.

It is the same with the family. As Allan Bloom puts it, we would think it monstrous if a man neglected his own children in favor of some others he thought superior.[32] The strong claim is that these loyalties are arbitrary – accidents of history. This is why, according to Rousseau, philosophers make poor kinsmen and citizens.

Particular affective relations in the family are therefore a foundation for particular affective relations to a given state. The relation of mother and child is the prototype of particular attachment, whether considered in relation to the philosophic history Rousseau provides in the Second Discourse, or in relation to the development of the individual within the civil state. It is the human relationship that precedes all others, for the species and for the individual. As we have seen, it provides the link between children and artificial paternity. Without a feminine role grounded on motherhood, the family, viewed from within this model, loses its unique quality of being a human artificial institution which incorporates natural relations. Losing that, it can no longer function as a "natural base" for the development of *amour de la patrie* and hence civic virtue.

In addition to the need for a family as a natural base for the development of *amour de la patrie*, Rousseau needs a mechanism to ensure certainty of paternity for the inheritance of property. In spite of Rousseau's criticism of bourgeois individualism, there is no doubt that from Rousseau's point of view private property is an inviolable requirement of civil life. In *Emile* he writes: "The unfaithful woman . . . dissolves the family and breaks all the bonds of nature. In giving the man children which are not his, she betrays both. She joins perfidy (*perfidie*) to infidelity. I have difficulty seeing what disorders and what crimes do not flow from this one." To the husband, a child not his own represents "the plunderer of his own children's property."[33]

Much of the force of this may be traced to the theme already presented – that the family is not a family unless united in the manner described by the woman's playing a correct feminine role. It is only necessary to establish a link between this and property.

In spite of Rousseau's criticism of economic inequality, as well as other forms of inequality, he never moves toward the view that private property ought to be done away with. Whatever other reasons there may be for Rousseau's repeated insistence that private property is a basic, even a "sacred" right, the male-headed private family has a basic inexorable economic requirement: it requires to have its subsistence in the form of private property in control of the male head of the family. This is necessary because the family is not "private" if the mode of acquisition, use, and disposal of its subsistence and surplus do not meet the basic requirements of the institution of private property; and it is not male-headed unless these rights and duties are centered on the husband and father.

The Transformation of Natural Qualities by Social Relations

The Pure State of Nature	The State of War (There may or may not be a bogus social contract)	Legitimate Civil State
Emotional autonomy	*Amour propre*	Moral liberty
Practical autonomy	Master/slave relations	Equality
Self-preservation	Particular or personal interest	Virtue (conformity of the particular will to the general will)
Female weakness and sexual timidity	Sexual manipulation or pseudo-masculinity	Modesty
Male sexual spontaneity	Compulsive and violent sexuality, domination of unsuccessful female manipulators	Male sexual spontaneity, governed by reason and knowledge
Spontaneous compassion (*pitié*)	(All but destroyed)	Patriotism friendship romantic love

It is clear that Rousseau's ideal family is made up of a male provider and a dependent wife and children, so that the basic requirement of privacy is met. Family privacy, because of the way it particularizes the individual's relations to certain others, is necessary, as we have seen, for the particular attachments so important to the early development of citizens and for the provision of a link between nature and social life. On the other hand, an equal distribution of private property among men is seen as necessary for the autonomy of the male head of the family in relation to other males. The particularlity of his relation to his family would collapse if he did not have unique responsibilities and rights in relation to them.

From Nature to Virtue

In his treatment of the nature of the sexes, Rousseau's principles and method are precisely the same as what he exhibits in connection with all his important claims concerning human nature. The structure of his views can be shown to be parallel to that of his views of the natural man and citizen (see table). A natural quality is transformed by social relations. It may be corrupted by bad social relations, a process which occurs as the "golden age" of savagery degenerates into civilized social relations dominated by particular interests and *amour propre*. This process results in the development of a state of war like that of Hobbes, that is, one in which the interests of each individual are opposed to the interests of every other individual. This state, according to Rousseau, may or may not be characterized by a bogus social contract which primarily serves the interests of the rich.[34] Alternatively, a good civil society ruled by the general will would make possible the development of the uniquely human potential of these natural qualities.

Democratic Feminism

Reading Rousseau helps to provoke thoughts as to what sort of social arrangements would be most conducive to sexual equality. In particular, it challenges the liberal individualist view that women's liberation can be furthered primarily by means of the removal of legal and social obstacles to the advancement of individual women.

In a period when political philosophy was still preoccupied with the new ideal of equality before the law, Rousseau leapt ahead to the insight that where there is objective inequality, virtually any law helps the powerful and harms the less powerful.[35] Therefore, no legal system can morally reform the relations of men and women so long as there is social and economic inequality of the sexes, or general social and economic inequality. So long as women are socially and economically unequal to *each other*, and occupy the society of individualism and *amour propre*, relations between the sexes will be either patriarchal, or competitive and manipulative. In view of the differences in physical strength, this would also undoubtedly include continued male violence against women.

Rousseau's analysis of the particular interest and *amour propre* of social inequality reveals the pitfalls of attempting the integration of women, on the same footing as men, into an unequal, competitive, society. Particular interest and the consciousness of *amour propre* militate against the abandonment of male attempts to dominate women, and also against the abandonment of sexual manipulation of men by women. Reading Rousseau makes it clear that in possessive individualist society, it is imprudent to abandon any potential source of power over others. It is therefore very unlikely that moral improvement can occur without basic social change.

Rousseau contended that women who demand equality with men usually do not abandon the feminine wiles that pressupose inequality. They attempt to play two incompatible roles, and as a result succeed at neither.[36] He wrongly thought that the continued inequality of women despite substantial sentiment in favor of their equality was the result of inferior capacity, but the hampering effects of contradictory role-playing remain as Rousseau perceived them.

Despite some substantial sentiment in favour of the equality of women in the present age, and in spite of some legal and economic reforms, for most women, particularly if they want children, dependence on a particular man remains their best option for a livelihood. Sexual monogamy and other adherence to his wishes remains part of the price they pay. If we were to extend Rousseau's philosophy of moral autonomy to women, it appears that these cannot be truly *moral* choices unless and until women have personal autonomy. The male-dominated family is therefore an immoral institution which corrupts its members and is inimical to the development of a good society. It is clear, for example, that men resist reform of the abuses of sexism to a large extent because they do not want to lose their personal privileges based on power over women. At the same time, women are often afraid to resist sexism because of their dependence on men. It also should not be forgotten that the sexual division of labor between public and private spheres is undemocratic even in the relatively narrow, liberal individualist, sense of "democracy," never mind Rousseau's more thoroughgoing sense of egalitarianism. It prevents women from participating in public discourse as autonomous citizens with the freedom to speak out about social reforms.

But so long as women and men live together with any degree of intimacy and privacy, will even economic equality and legal restraint be enough to prevent masculine violence against women from continuing to be a common occurrence? It is suddenly apparent that the lack of opportunity for sharing housework and childcare is not the only reason why women are worse off the more individualistic a society is. More communal ways of life may give women more security and freedom from personal oppression than the social relations of private property and an atomized private life. From the perspective of feminist criticism, Rousseau's theory shows very clearly the links between private property, individualism, and male domination of women. The male head of the family requires private property in order to have a private sphere within which to control the female.

The present law in Western countries concerning masculine violence against women displays a deepseated ambivalence in the political will of its makers. It is against the law for a man to attack a women with whom he lives, yet enforcement is feeble for a number of reasons. One is the lack of genuine autonomy on the part of women, sufficient to be able to make use of legal remedies for harm. Another is the high value placed on the retention of a private sphere, on personal freedom in intimate relations, and on the use and disposal of private property. To make the injunction against masculine violence unambivalent would represent not only a fundamental change in the social relations of the sexes, but also significant social change in general.

Yet many communal societies have exhibited serious sexual inequality. The potential of more communal ways of life is greater enforcement of *desirable* norms in hitherto private areas of life. So the problem, finally, is still the choice of egalitarian norms of sexual and reproductive behavior.

On account of the unique characteristics of the relations between the sexes, democratic feminism is a force for basic social change. But law is only an aspect of this. Law which opposes the physical force of individual men with yet greater force, and which reaches a long arm into the home even as far as the bedroom, is a necessary, but not a sufficient, condition for material sexual equality.

Reading Rousseau serves two functions. First, because he was a modern thinker, he was and still remains useful to antifeminism. For this reason reading him is an exercise in "knowing the enemy." However, he understands very clearly many aspects of the structure of male dominance, which from the critical perspective of feminism function as effective criticisms of that system, often virtually without revision. The second, and larger, message for feminist thinkers in this study is that they cannot afford to do less than examine the whole of the social structure, for any attempt to examine the relations of men and women in isolation from other questions may be very misleading.

Since the early 1980s, grass roots and socialist feminism in North America have suffered marginalization, while liberal individualist feminism has institutionalized itself, and presented itself as if it *is* feminism. Some individual women have made stellar careers for themselves within institutionalized feminism, but women's condition in general has benefited little from it. Considering Rousseau's epigraph to the First Discourse, from Horace, it may also happen to feminists that: "We are deceived by the appearance of right."

Notes

1 "J'ai écrit sur divers sujets, mais toujours dans les même principes." "Lettre à Beaumont" (1762), in Jean-Jacques Rousseau, *Oeuvres Complètes*, ed. B. Gagnebin and M. Raymond (Paris: Editions de la Pleiade, 1959–), vol. 4, p. 928.
2 Work on this subject includes: Susan Moller Okin, *Women in Western Political*

Thought (Princeton, NJ: Princeton University Press, 1979); Nannerl O. Keohane, "But For Her Sex . . . the Domestication of Sophie", and Lynda Lange, "Women and the General Will", both in *Trent Rousseau Papers*, ed. MacAdam, Neumann, Lafrance (Ottawa: University of Ottawa Press, 1980); and Eva Figes, *Patriarchal Attitudes* (London: Panther, 1972), p. 105.

3 Allan Bloom, introduction to Jean-Jacques Rousseau, *Emile: Or, On Education*, trans. and annotated Allan Bloom (New York: Basic Books, 1979).

4 C. B. MacPherson, *The Political Theory of Possessive Individualism* (London: Oxford University Press, 1962), p. 53.

5 My interpretation of Rousseau substantiates the claim of C. E. Vaughan that Rousseau attacked individualism "in its theoretical stronghold." Vaughan, introduction, *Political Writings of Rousseau* (Cambridge: Cambridge University Press, 1915).

6 *Emile*, trans. Bloom, p. 359.

7 Rousseau, *Oeuvres Complètes*, vol. 4, p. 695.

8 *Emile*, trans. Bloom, p. 358.

9 Ibid., p. 358. Compare Sigmund Freud, "Femininity," in his *New Introductory Lectures on Psychoanalysis*, trans. and ed. James Strachey (New York: W. W. Norton, 1965): "it is our impression that more constraint has been applied to the libido when it is pressed into the service of the feminine function . . . And the reasons for this may lie – thinking once again teleologically – in the fact that the accomplishment of the aim of biology has been entrusted to the aggressiveness of men and has been made to some extent independent of women's consent" (pp. 179–80).

10 *Emile*, trans. Bloom, p. 359.

11 Jean-Jacques Rousseau, *Discourse on the Origin and Foundations of Inequality* (Second Discourse), ed. Roger D. Masters, trans. Roger D. and Judith R. Masters (New York: St Martin's Press, 1964), p. 117.

12 *Emile*, trans. Bloom, p. 358.

13 Ibid., p. 364.

14 Ibid., p. 359.

15 These observations of Rousseau appear to be a remarkable substantiation of the theory of reproduction in Mary O'Brien, *The Politics of Reproduction* (Boston and London: Routledge and Kegan Paul, 1981).

16 Second Discourse, trans. Masters, pp. 146–7.

17 The "naturalness" of a sexual division of labor is widely assumed. Even Marx, who infers no "natural" inequality of the sexes as a result, *assumes* this, rather than concluding it after reflection or investigation. See, for example, *Capital*, vol. I, part 4, ch 14, section 4; and *The German Ideology*, part A.

18 Second Discourse, trans. Masters, p. 121.

19 *Emile*, trans. Bloom, p. 361.

20 Ibid., p. 364.

21 Ibid., p. 365.

22 Jean-Jacques Rousseau, *On the Social Contract*, Book I, ch. 8.

23 Jean-Jacques Rousseau, *Politics and the Arts: Letter to M. d'Alembert on the Theatre*, trans. Allan Bloom (Ithaca, NY: Cornell University Press, 1977), p. 87.

24 *Emile*, trans. Bloom, p. 361.

25 "Forced to combat nature or the social institutions, one must choose between making a man or a citizen, for one cannot make both at the same time." Ibid. On the Legislator, essential to the founding of a good society, he writes: "One who dares to undertake the founding of a people should feel that he is capable of changing human nature, so to speak; of transforming each individual . . ." *On the Social Contract*, Book II, ch. 7.

26 *Letter to M. d'Alembert*, trans. Bloom, p. 103.

27 Ibid., p. 105.

28 It is *la vanité*, and not, as yet, *amour propre*. Rousseau, *Oeuvres Complètes*, vol. 3, p. 170.

29 Second Discourse, trans. Masters, p. 149.

30 See, for example, the first version of *Du Contrat Social* (Geneva manuscript), in *On the Social Contract*, ed. Roger D. Masters, trans. Judith R. Masters (New York: St Martins Press, 1978), p. 158.

31 *Political Economy*, in *On the Social Contract*, ed. Masters, p. 218.

32 Interpretative essay, in Plato, *Republic* (New York: Basic Books, 1968), p. 385.

33 *Emile*, trans. Bloom, p. 361.

34 Second Discourse, ed. Masters, pp. 159–60.

35 "Under bad governments, this equality is only apparent and illusory. It serves merely to maintain the poor man in his misery and the rich in his usurpation. In fact, laws are always useful to those who have possession and harmful to those who have nothing." *On the Social Contract*, trans. Masters, p. 58.

36 *Emile*, trans. Bloom, p. 364.

6

"The Oppressed State of My Sex": Wollstonecraft on Reason, Feeling and Equality

Moira Gatens

Still harping on the same subject you will exclaim – How can I avoid it, when most of the struggles of an eventful life have been occasioned by the oppressed state of my sex: we reason deeply when we forcibly feel.

Mary Wollstonecraft, Letter XIX, in Janet Todd,
A Wollstonecraft Anthology

Reason and feeling is the governing dichotomy and the source of the major conflicts in Mary Wollstonecraft's work and in her life. It is her concentration on this dichotomy and her obvious faith in the power of reason to reform sociopolitical life that places her firmly within the Enlightenment tradition. Yet, because she is concerned to address the specificity of female social and political existence, her treatment of the reason/feeling distinction inevitably conjures up its partners: the nature/culture and private/public distinctions. Enlightenment philosophers were able to treat man's political possibilities without (explicit) reference to sexuality, reproduction, the family and the domestic sphere because these matters were assumed to fall outside the public realm of politics. Certainly, the political body assumes the private sphere, which underpins public life, but this sphere is taken to be the natural base of political life. Any consideration of women's access to or place in the public sphere necessarily raises the question of their role in the private sphere.

Whereas Enlightenment philosophers argued that political authority is artificial and conventional they assumed that relations between the sexes and within the family are based on natural authority. Wollstonecraft argued against this assumption in favour of a conception of reason as the sole authority in all matters and in all spheres. Her insistence on the role of reason, in all areas of human life, created paradoxes in her application of Enlightenment notions of equality that she was unable to resolve. Eighteenth-century notions of equality were articulated specifically in connection with the public sphere. Men, as husbands/fathers, presumably did not want (or need) to assert the principles of equality in the private sphere since this would, in fact, be acting against their interests. One of Wollstonecraft's major aims is to insist that the power and authority that men wielded in the private sphere was as artificial as the authority of royalty and aristocracy in the sphere of politics. She sees clearly that liberating women from political oppression is not simply a matter of political enfranchisement, since they are also subjected in the private sphere. This makes Wollstonecraft's task far more complex than the task that confronted the political philosophers who were concerned only with men's political rights.

Another major aim of Wollstonecraft's writings is to insist that the natural rights of men are human rights. Therefore women, no less than men, are entitled to political equality and representation. It is in her articulation of this claim that Wollstonecraft strikes paradox after paradox. In her attempt to extend liberal principles of equality to women she neglects to note that these principles were developed and formulated with men as their object. Her attempt to stretch these principles to include women results in both practical and conceptual difficulties. These principles were developed with an (implicitly) male person in mind, who is assumed to be a head of a household (a husband/father) and whose domestic needs are catered for (by his wife). Although the citizen is not explicitly male, the assumed characteristics of the citizen coincide with those of a husband/ father. No matter how strong the power of reason, it cannot alter the fact that male and female embodiment, at least as lived in eighteenth-century culture, involved vastly different social and political consequences. Wollstonecraft did not take sufficient account of these consequences in her call for the realization of the rights of women. Women's (traditional) labor is not even visible in the public sphere. It does not count as socially necessary work and is not acknowledged in any system of public exchange. This point is no less relevant in our contemporary context where the equality that women are entitled to, for example in the sphere of employment, is limited to activities which overlap with male activities. Those aspects of women's lives that bear on female specificity were, until very recently, completely ignored: for example, sexual harassment, maternity, childcare, and so on. Wollstonecraft's tendency to treat the role of wife/mother/ domestic worker as one which follows directly from women's biology raises further problems for a feminist analysis of women's social and political status.

The tendency to conceive of women's bodies as complicit in their social and political oppression has certainly been a feature of much contemporary feminist writing. Wollstonecraft was able to tolerate the paradoxes of liberal theory in a way that contemporary feminist theory, at least from the time of Simone de Beauvoir, cannot. This intolerance has caused a marked rift in feminist responses to women's place in contemporary society. On one side are those like Shulamith Firestone[1] who advocate the use of science to effectively "neuter" the female body. Woman can thus truly become a "rational man." On the other, theorists like Carol McMillan[2] see this corporeal denial as anti-woman and argue that difference does not necessarily involve relations of inferiority/superiority. Men and women, she argues, are different and have necessarily different roles, but these roles are of equal value.

The source from which these two responses flow is clearly present in Wollstonecraft's writings. Both views locate the cause of women's social role in her body. This assumption must be challenged on at least two levels. First, feminists must challenge the notion inherited from Cartesian dualism that human beings are separable into two neat bundles: a neutral, universal mind; and a sexed body. Second, we must challenge the imputed "naturalness" of the form and capacities of the female body along with the idea that this form determines the scope of female social being. The converse proposition – that social and political arrangements curtail or impede the form and capacities of the female body – must also be considered. This must be done not simply in order to allot primacy to the social but rather to bring out the complexity of the relationship between the biological and the social.

In this paper these issues are brought to bear on Wollstonecraft's struggle with the reason/feeling distinction. *A Vindication of the Rights of Woman* and *The Wrongs of Women, or Maria* will be examined in the light of Wollstonecraft's attempts to work through the power of both reason and feeling in women's lives. The progressive sophistication with which Wollstonecraft analyzes the complexities of women's social and political position may be linked to the increasing social and political complexity in the progress of her own life. Various commentators have railed against the legitimacy of referring to Wollstonecraft's personal life in the context of appraising her work. Given the close kinship between her life and her politics, the subject matter of much of her writings and her own lived experience, it seems appropriate to at least indicate the links between her intellectual development and her biography. For one thing this approach allows the contemporary reader to ponder the relation between an eighteenth-century feminist's analysis of her social and political context and the exigencies of a life that was lived in that context. Wollstonecraft's life was certainly a struggle and undeniably eventful. She lived through one of the most turbulent and politically unstable times in our recent past. She was vocal in the movement which sought to restore to "men" their natural rights; she was adamant that women also possessed natural rights and natural equality; and she spent some time in France during the revolution. Wollstonecraft also bore two children, had two significant heterosexual relationships, attempted suicide twice, and wrote prolifically. Much of what she wrote is concerned to expose and remedy the social and political injustices experienced by women. However, her work as a whole displays a passionate rejection of oppression in general, regardless of its specific form.

Her first major work of political importance is *A Vindication of the Rights of Men* (1790). This text carries the distinction of being the first published response to Edmund Burke's *Reflections on the Revolution in France* (1790). The dynamics of her response are governed by the dichotomy of reason and sentiment. Burke's lauding of tradition and hereditary rights and his dogmatic insistence on the conservation of existing rigid political relations are all treated by Wollstonecraft as evidence of his lack of reason. Instead of using his rational capacity – which would reveal to him the natural rights and natural equality of all "men" – he allows his sentiments, his passions and his feeling to dominate his political thinking. For Wollstonecraft it is the preponderance of sentiment in political thought that gives rise to nostalgia and social stagnation, which act to impede the dynamic and progressive nature of sociopolitical life. Moreover, the sentiment displayed by Burke and his kind is riddled with hypocrisy. The romanticism of his conception of a hierarchically ordered political system is belied by the profligacy and corruption of the rich, the degradation of the poor and their appalling conditions of life. It is reason and not sentiment that should dictate the terms of political life and what any person's rational capacities will show is that "The birthright of Man . . . is such a degree of liberty, civil and religious, as is compatible with the liberty of every other individual with whom he is united in a social compact, and the continued existence of that compact."[3] Burke is not only guilty of irrationality, hypocrisy and impeding the progress of civilization, he is also complicit in reneging on the terms of the social compact and so represents a threat to its continuing existence. Wollstonecraft thus relocates the responsibility for political unrest with the conservatives.

The social and political status of women is not central to the concerns of *A Vindication of the Rights of Men*. Nevertheless, Wollstonecraft is careful to insist that women, no less than men, are parties to the social compact. Their sociopolitical rights and duties are not, however, identical with those of men. It is the part of the rational woman to "superintend her family and suckle her children, in order to fulfil her part of the social compact."[4] This difference between the sexes in fulfilling the compact will be treated further when we turn to *A Vindication of the Rights of Woman*. At this stage Wollstonecraft seems content to understand women's rights as implicit in the genus of men's rights, appending comments which bear on women's specificity – childbearing, for example – when necessary. Her naiveté is, perhaps, explicable by the context in which she was then living, working and thinking. At the time of the writing of *A Vindication of the Rights of Woman* (1792) Wollstonecraft was single and part of a (predominantly male) intellectual milieu which included William Blake, Thomas Paine, William Godwin and Henry Fuseli. This group was intoxicated with the idea of social reform and exhibited the boundless optimism typical of the Enlightenment. Yet they, no less than the general reading public, were inclined to understand the rights of man as being just that, the rights of men. This is the context in which Wollstonecraft resolves to write specifically on the question of women's rights.

A Vindication of the Rights of Woman presents an argument for an enlightened understanding of human nature which stresses that women, no less than men, share in this nature. The result is a text that is plagued with contradictions and irresolvable tensions. Again, the overriding tension is that between reason and sentiment. The tension between these two terms is present in her treatment of friendship versus sexual passion, the socially responsible family versus the sensual couple; the respectable mother versus the degraded concubine. As Cora Kaplan has observed, it is as if Wollstonecraft sees sexuality and pleasure as special dangers to women, as "narcotic inducements to a life of lubricious slavery."[5] Wollstonecraft's amulet against the temptations of sensuality is, of course, reason.

A Vindication of the Rights of Woman is not so much an appeal to women's reason – which she takes to be obscured by a culture which encourages the exaggerated development of women's sentiment, feeling and passion – as it is an appeal to men's reason. The addressee, as Anca Vlasopolos convincingly argues,[6] is male. It is pertinent to recall that *A Vindication of the Rights of Woman* is dedicated to Charles Talleyrand whose proposal for free national education (for boys) was then before the French National Assembly. By dedicating her treatise to Talleyrand, Wollstonecraft hoped to encourage him to extend his proposal to include girls (needless to say, he did not). The future strength of the New Republic, she argued, will be ensured only when children of both sexes are trained to reason. She challenges Talleyrand:

> if women are to be excluded, without having a voice, from a participation of the natural rights of mankind, prove first, to ward off the charge of injustice and inconsistency, that they want reason – else this flaw in your NEW CONSTITUTION will ever shew that man must, in some shape, act like a tyrant, and tyranny, in whatever part of society it rears its brazen front, will ever undermine morality.[7]

Her own analysis of women's social and political status, she tells him, aims "to prove that the prevailing notion respecting a sexual character was subversive of morality."[8] In fact her target is much wider than morality. She also seeks to show that reason has no sex, knowledge has no sex, in short, that the mind itself is sexless.[9] The distinction between the sexes is entirely bodily and of relevance to one issue only: the reproduction of the species. All other human activity, if it is to deserve the title "human," should be governed by the principles of reason which are "the same in all" and appropriate to any task – even, or especially, childrearing.[10] It is to the shame and detriment of the society she addresses that human activity is so infrequently governed by these principles. Rather, it is passions and prejudices that determine social mores and this is nowhere more evident that in the social expectations surrounding women.

Wollstonecraft's social theory is very much dependent on her conception of human being and what it is capable of becoming. A rational society is one which takes account of and founds itself on the character and needs of human nature. That society is most just and rational that allows human beings to actualize, to the highest possible degree, their potentialities. Her opposition to a society which is governed by royalty and aristocracy, or as she calls them, the "pestiferous purple," is grounded in her belief that this kind of society limits the freedom of human beings to improve themselves, which in turn limits the progress of society. A human life is not worth living, is not truly a human life, unless there is opportunity for growth and self-improvement:

> the perfection of our nature and capability of happiness, must be estimated by the degree of reason, virtue, and knowledge, that distinguish the individual, and direct the laws which bind society: and that from the exercise of reason, knowledge and virtue naturally flow, is equally undeniable, if mankind be viewed collectively.[11]

Just as monarchical rule is an irrational basis for society, so too is patriarchal rule. She chastises the enlightened philosophers for not going far enough in their challenge to illegitimate authority. She argues that "the divine right of husbands," like the "divine right of kings," must be contested. If hereditary power amounts to illegitimate authority and is damaging to society then it is damaging in all its forms.

In the presentation of her case for the rights of women, Wollstonecraft most frequently employs the *reductio ad absurdum* form of argument. She repeatedly undermines her opponents' accounts of women's roles and duties by uncovering the inconsistencies in their arguments. The central example, which appears in several guises throughout the text, is the following: men argue that rights and duties assume one another; men deny women their rights; yet, men expect women to honour their duties. Wollstonecraft's own views on rights and duties are complex. She does not deny that much of what has been written about women is easily verified by experience. Some passages in *A Vindication of the Rights of Woman*, which describe the frivolity, vanity and inconstancy of women, are far from flattering. However, rather than judging that social and political rights should not be granted to such weak creatures, she argues that rights are the only remedy for their weaknesses. Women will not become dutiful or rational until they are treated with the same dignity and allowed to share in the same privileges as men. In this context she asks: "Why do men halt between two opinions, and expect impossibilities? Why do they expect virtue from a slave, from a being whom the constitution of civil society has rendered weak, if not vicious?"[12]

In order to answer this question Wollstonecraft turns to a critical reading of Rousseau's *Emile*, which was presented, and widely used, as a handbook for the education of children. She also considers several "popular" books that were influential in the formation of bourgeois expectations of female behavior and manners. These include writings by Dr Gregory, Dr Fordyce and Lord Chesterfield. These four writers are her main opponents in *Rights of Woman*. It is significant that it is mainly the informal "philosophy of manners and customs" that Wollstonecraft is obliged to engage with in her assessment of the dominant social attitudes toward the formation of women's character. It reveals the extent to which the socialization and control of women was a "private" affair.

Wollstonecraft condemns these texts for encouraging "a sexual character to the mind." Since all human beings naturally possess the capacity for reason, and hence for knowledge and virtue, the fact that women often are not rational or virtuous indicates that art has "smothered nature." And women are, for Wollstonecraft, the most artificial of creatures. This artifice, however, is not the invention of women. Wollstonecraft very firmly locates the source of women's corrupt nature in the passions of men. She writes that "all the causes of female weakness, as well as depravity, which I have already enlarged on, branch out of one grand cause – want of chastity in men."[13] She finds Rousseau, and his "philosophy of lasciviousness," particularly culpable. Wollstonecraft traces the many inconsistencies of Rousseau's philosophy to his poorly controlled sexual passions. Fearful of losing the services of an odalisque, men withhold the means whereby women could become free and rational companions. The iniquitous result of this attitude is that it denies women the opportunity to "unfold their own faculties and acquire the dignity of conscious virtue."[14] This "philosophy of manners" limits the possibilities of female understanding by ensuring that it is "always subordinated to the acquirement of some corporeal accomplishment."[15]

In this argument Wollstonecraft is worrying a sensitive spot in Enlightenment discourses. If certain rights are "human" and "inalienable" then how can one consistently deny these rights to women (or "savages", or children)? At certain points the Enlightenment discourse threatens to fall back on its dark Aristotelian and Thomistic past. Is woman a part of mankind? Is she a "lesser" or inferior type of man?[16] There are two, overlapping notions that save the "modern" philosophers from falling back on their fathers. The first is the notion of human progress: different cultures, and so perhaps different sexes, progress at a differential rate. This form of argument was certainly used by the newly formed French Republic to justify the exclusion of women from political participation. One such argument, offered by Amar who was representing the views of the Committee for General Security, goes as follows:

> If we take into account the fact that the political education of men is still at its very beginnings, that all the principles are not yet developed, and that we still stammer over the word "liberty," then how much less enlightened are women, whose moral education has been practically non-existent. Their presence in the *sociétés populaires*, then, would give an active part in government to persons exposed to error and seduction even more than are men. And, let us add that women by their constitution, are open to an exaltation which would be ominous in public life. The interests of the state would soon be sacrificed to all the kinds of disruption and disorder that hysteria can produce.[17]

Wollstonecraft dispenses with this argument by pointing out that if the female body is hysterical it will infect the political body whether it has "a voice" or not. Women's indirect influence on the public sphere, she argues, is pernicious precisely because of its clandestine character. If marriage and the family are the "cement of society," excluding women from the civic sphere does not remove the foundational threat they pose to that sphere. Second, Cartesian dualism was called upon to provide a justification for women's weaker reason. Descartes thought that the mind had no sex. Nevertheless female consciousness may be inhibited in its operations by its association with the female body and its unruly passions.

Wollstonecraft's strategy here is quite ingenious. She shifts the cause of women's weaker reason from the female body to the social environment, in particular to educational practices. She effects a neat inversion of the philosopher's arguments by locating the ultimate cause of female inferiority in the male body and its lasciviousness and in the masculine body politic which denies women access to reason. This, of course, puts a new slant on Rousseau's stricture that it is reason and not prejudice that dictates that women be educated "to please men."[18]

It is with arguments such as these that Wollstonecraft refutes the notion that women's social status is just, natural or necessary. She argues for the improvement of the female mind both for the sake of women and society. The performance of the "peculiar duties which nature has assigned them" will only be improved by the acquisition of reason. These duties are no less human for being peculiarly female. Wollstonecraft's arguments for the rights of women are not restricted to the right of the individual to realize and improve his or her own nature. Her particular conception of the relation between the individual and society is such that to improve (or inhibit) the possibilities of an individual necessarily improves (or inhibits) society in general. She therefore has an additional argument in favor of the "revolution in female manners" which bears on the quality of the social body.

Virtue is the product of reason, it is not relative to situation or sex. The sham virtue that women are encouraged to practice – notably by Rousseau – has public repercussions since "public virtue is only an aggregate of private."[19] The dire consequence of rendering women weak and irrational is that the progress and strength of the human race is thereby endangered. Wollstonecraft makes this point graphically:

> Make them [women] free, and they will quickly become wise and virtuous, as men become more so; for the improvement must be mutual, or the injustice which one half of the human race are obliged to submit to, retorting on their oppressors, the virtue of men will be worm-eaten by the insect whom he keeps under his feet.[20]

This view of social progress makes Wollstonecraft's stress on the necessity for both sexes to be chaste, seem less prudish. The relation between the sexes lies at the core of the body politic. If this core is bad it will, eventually, infect the political body.

Wollstonecraft's recommendations, in *A Vindication of the Rights of Woman*, concerning the improvement of women's character, and so society in general, range from an abstract appeal to men that they allow their reason to show them the importance of chastity and intersexual friendship, to the provision of practical guidelines for the institution of national coeducation.

She also stresses the necessity for women to be granted "the protection of civil laws"; the freedom to follow careers compatible with their "natural" duties (for instance, physicians, nurses, midwives); and even mentions, though with some embarrassment, that women ought to have representatives in the government. These recommendations do not sit very easily with her attitude towards women's "natural" role as childrearer and domestic worker. The sexual division of labor, and its corollary, the public/private split, remain structurally untouched. This reflects Wollstonecraft's enormous faith in the power of reason to bring about the revolution in manners. If we follow reason, the flourishing of sexual fidelity, virtue, friendship and equality between the sexes will be the automatic result.

The uneasiness we may feel with this resolution only increases when she, unselfconsciously, paints a picture of domestic bliss – complete with a female servant:

> I have then viewed with pleasure a woman nursing her children, and discharging the duties of her station with, perhaps, *merely a servnt maid to take off her hands the servile part of the household business.* I have seen her prepare herself and children, with only the luxury of cleanliness, to receive her husband, who returning weary home in the evening found smiling babes and a clean hearth. My heart has loitered in the midst of this group, and has even throbbed with sympathetic emotion, when the scraping of the well known foot has raised a pleasing tumult.[21]

From our perspective, it is interesting to note the extent to which Wollstonecraft seems utterly oblivious to the contradictions implicit in her view. The sexual division of labor lies at the heart of the difficulty and she does not see this division as socially constituted, but rather as dictated by nature. This passage is worrying also for its apparent blindness to class differences between women. These difficulties flaw the basic argument of *Rights of Woman* making its conclusion inevitably paradoxical: "The conclusion which I wish to draw, is obvious; make women rational creatures, and free *citizens*, and they will quickly become good *wives*, and *mothers*; that is – if men do not neglect the duties of husbands and fathers.[22]

This formulation leaves the asymmetry between the citizen/husband/ father and the citizen/wife/mother unaddressed. In the eighteenth century, public interest is constructed, both conceptually and practically, in direct opposition to the domestic sphere of women and the family. "Women" and "the family" are almost indistinguishable, both in terms of the way their interests are represented and in terms of their relation to civic and public pursuits. Given the character of liberal social organization it is inappropriate to argue that women are as free as men to occupy the public sphere as "disembodied" rational agents. This ignores the asymmetrical consequences of embodiment for man and woman *within that organization.*[23] For men, the actualization of the option of marriage, parenthood and the establishment of a private familial unit does not intrude on their access to the public sphere. Nor does it deplete their power to act in that sphere; on the contrary, it may enhance their power. The same cannot be said of women. The tensions brought about by the sharp division between the public and the private sphere crystallize around the issue of men's rights and duties and women's rights and duties. Several philosophers (unsuccessfully) attempted to resolve the dilemma by insisting on men's civil and political rights by carefully specifying women's private duties. As Wollstonecraft points out, there is a lacuna in this argument. Human rights and duties seem to be sexually divided: men get the rights and women the duties!

A major problem with the argument of *A Vindication of the Rights of Woman* is its uneasy alliance with the suspect notion of the essential sexual neutrality of the rational agent. Wollstonecraft thinks it is sufficient to overcome social prejudice in order to allow woman to realize her rights and hence her "true nature." This approach simply does not take the structural necessity of women's subordination in liberal society seriously. Yet, limitations on what can be demanded from the public sphere are revealed in Wollstonecraft's own writings. Demands concerning the character and quality of women's lives in the private sphere are inevitably addressed to an individual man, whose own involvement in the private sphere is often marginal, or actually oppositional, to his public activities and interest. In this regard women *qua* women lack a "voice" in the body politic. Their lot seems to be circumscribed by natural, familial or personal arrangements which fall outside the scope of public interest or relevance.

The great difficulty confronting Wollstonecraft in her attempt to resolve the moral and political disjunction between the (female) private sphere and the (male) public sphere is worsened by her acceptance of the idea that it is nature rather than social organization that requires women to assume the responsibility for childcare and home maintenance. This sexual division of labor is inherent in the rationalism of the liberal paradigm. That paradigm is necessarily limited when it comes to consider the question of the social status of women. It may well be that it offers an inconsistent argument, as Wollstonecraft herself recognizes. However, she does not, in *A Vindication of the Rights of Woman*, seem to acknowledge that it is a necessary inconsistency that cannot be resolved within the terms of liberal political theory. While feminists continue to accept the liberal emphasis on the essential neutrality of the mind, sexual discrimination will continue to be "justified" by natural bodily difference. Given the high value placed on the neutrality and universality of mind, it will be female corporeality which is conceived as limiting. The female body will appear as the natural site of women's oppression, turning attention from the sociopolitical organization that can then present itself as an *effect*, rather than a cause.

It is an implicit assumption of modern political theory that men are able to dissociate themselves from sexuality, reproduction and natural passions. Male subjectivity and male sexuality are divorceable conceptually and spatially in a way that female subjectivity and female sexuality are not. As Rousseau puts it, "man is only man now and again, but the female is always a female."[24] Since it is she who has been allotted the role of perpetuating and managing the natural base of culture, she cannot be considered independently of these functions, which coincide, in traditional accounts, with her sexuality. The satisfaction of the needs of "natural man" has become the work of woman. She tends to his natural, corporeal needs while he is transforming himself into rational "social man."

Any attempt to introduce women into the body politic necessarily raises the question of how these "natural" human needs are to be satisfied. The social reduction of woman to her function of satisfying these needs makes it conceptually impossible to consider her social possibilities without also considering, as a social problem, the question of the reproduction and management of the natural base of cultural life.

The liberal paradigm, assumed by Wollstonecraft, is not helpful at this point. Its traditional concern with protecting the individual in his private sphere of thought, personal taste and private relations from the intrusions of the state forecloses the possibility of challenging the "private" arrangements between men and women. The labour, effort and "self" of women are contained in the private sphere – "protected" from public scrutiny and legislation – making structural inequalities between its inhabitants socially and politically invisible.

By the time Wollstonecraft begins her next major piece on women, *The Wrongs of Women, or Maria*, she has obviously become painfully aware of this fact. If *A Vindication of the Rights of Woman* was Wollstonecraft's eulogy to the powers of reason, *Maria* is her diatribe against the bondage of passion. Yet in both cases the reason and the passion are peculiarly masculine. The figure of woman stands in an ambiguous relation to the eighteenth-century Enlightenment ideal of man. She may gain from sharing in masculine rationality but can be ruined by masculine passion. And it is here that the source of the tension in this central dichotomy is bared. Reason, which Wollstonecraft saw as the force of progress, is Janus-faced. *How* such reason is lived in eighteenth-century culture is closely associated with the public/private split. This division is a highly sexualized one: the public or civic sphere is conceptualized as the realm of rational and contractual pursuits and the private sphere as the realm of nature, feeling and the family. Wollstonecraft, in *A Vindication of the Rights of Woman*, hoped to neutralize passion in both spheres, going so far as to argue that "a master and mistress of a family ought not to continue to love each other with passion. I mean to say, that they ought not to indulge those emotions which disturb the order of society."[25]

However, from our present context we must question this neutralization. How dependent is Wollstonecraft's conception of (public) reason on the privatization of passion? Does masculine reason, in the sociopolitical sphere, rest on and assume men's access to the corporeal and passionate via their role as "head" of a familiar body corporate? If the response to these questions is affirmative then how can women have an independent relation to either reason or passion? This cluster of questions was not consciously raised by Wollstonecraft. Her historical placement is such that these questions defy clear articulation. Yet, from our perspective, a parallel reading of *Rights of Woman* and *Maria* displays the problem clearly enough. It is just not the case that reason and passion or reason and feeling are the provinces of men and women, respectively. Rather, women's exclusion from the social contract bars them from the civic sphere of reason and their containment in the private sphere of feeling and the "natural" family does not guarantee their access to either passion or feeling since they are the servicers rather than the consumers even in the private sphere.

What motivated the writing of the novel, *Maria?* Within two years of the publication of *Rights of Woman*, Wollstonecraft had a passionate affair with Gilbert Imlay – who, from most accounts, was an opportunist, an entrepreneur, and a womanizer – had borne a child by him and was abandoned by him. This precipitated her first suicide attempt. Many commentators have seen this episode as evidence of a damning inconsistency between Wollstonecraft's rational recommendations for heterosexual relations in *Rights of Woman* and her irrational behavior with Imlay. There is no good reason for accepting this interpretation. Any inconsistency in this episode should be located in the sociopolitical body and its constitution rather than in Wollstonecraft and her (mental and/or physical) constitution. In fact, Wollstonecraft's life becomes an unfortunate illustration or verification of her analysis of society and women's position within it. It is a testimony to the power of social structures to ensnare (and sometimes destroy) even, or perhaps especially, those who have a reflective grasp of their operations. "Free love," mutual respect and an ethical relationship between the sexes all suppose a sociopolitical context suitable to such relations. The sociopolitical context in which Wollstonecraft wrote and lived not only tolerated but actually encouraged "the tyranny of men."[26] One of Wollstonecraft's letters, written while travelling in Scandinavia, captures not only her personal disappointment with Imlay, but also, by her provocative use of metaphor, something of the general feminine tenor of sexual disenchantment:

Uniting myself to you, your tenderness seemed to make me amends for all my former misfortunes. – On this tenderness and affection with what confidence did I rest! – but I leaned on a spear, that has pierced me to the heart. – You have thrown off a faithful friend, to pursue the caprices of the moment.[27]

Read in its context this letter is, among other things, a complaint concerning the difficulty of assigning a value to friendship in heterosexual relations.

It is tempting to see her next liaison, with Godwin, as the inverse of her relation with Imlay. Godwin is a friend, a comrade in political struggle, a rational companion. Their love is certainly no *grande passion* and in her relation to Godwin it seems clear that Wollstonecraft has forfeited passion/sensuality for "a convenient part of the furniture of a house."[28] Were these the choices for women? If the public/private split ensured that, once wedded and bedded, a woman's access to the public sphere of reason is forfeited for the role of wife/mother, how can she maintain a relation to either reason or feeling? The (male) citizen is certainly differently placed. He straddles the dichotomy and enjoys a spatial split between his civic, rational pursuits and his sensual, sentimental ones. How can woman, in early modern liberal society, achieve this dual role? (How this quandary should be assessed in our contemporary context is not considered here.) Perhaps it was the experience of motherhood which presented these paradoxes of female existence to Wollstonecraft in such stark form. The task of deciding how best to socialize a female child must have presented her with great difficulties. As Wollstonecraft laments in a letter concerning her daughter Fanny: "I dread lest she should be forced to sacrifice her heart to her principles, or principles to her heart . . . I dread to unfold her mind, lest it should render her unfit for the world she is to inhabit."[29]

These reflections on Wollstonecraft's life and intellectual development help to explain why she turns, not to the genre of the political treatise but to the novel in order to explore how the sociopolitical context constructs women as victims of (male) passion and feeling. *The Wrongs of Women, or Maria* is the result. The addressee of this work is not the enlightened (male) social reformer. It reads as a novel designed for the edification and chastening of a culture. In the introduction Wollstonecraft writes: "In writing this novel, I have rather endeavoured to pourtray passions than manners . . ." and "my main object, the desire of exhibiting the misery and oppression, peculiar to women, that arise out of the partial laws and customs of society."[30] She certainly achieves her object. *Maria* is set in an insane asylum, yet none of its characters is insane. The three main figures are Maria, Darnford and Jemima. Maria is a middle-class woman whose husband wastes her fortune, offers her person as payment to a debtor and finally separates Maria from her daughter when he exercises his legal right of having her committed. Darnford, a middle-class man, functions mainly as the recipient of Maria's affections. He represents the precarious possibility of intersexual friendship. Jemima is a lower-class woman who was born out of wedlock, the issue of a heartless seduction, who is seduced and abandoned in turn, who became a thief and a prostitute and whose relative social "respectability" is bought at the ironic price of acting as a "keeper of the mad." By acting as madhouse attendant, she colludes with the society that rejects her by guarding those whom, like her, society wishes to exclude from its ranks. *Maria* was never finished. Wollstonecraft died from complications arising from childbirth before it could be completed. The outcome of the web of friendships linking this unlikely trio is thus left open to history, open to our present.

Is there any reason for us to be more optimistic than Wollstonecraft could have been about the possibility of friendship between women of different classes or about friendships between men and women? It is at least possible, in our current context, to raise these questions as meaningful political and ethical issues. But is there, even now, a basis for ethical relations between women? The governing ethic between men and women is still primarily conjugal in that it treats women primarily as wives/ mothers/sexual partners. Perhaps the most important insight we have to gain from Wollstonecraft's novel is that political and economic reforms are necessary but not sufficient for women's genuine access to social, political and ethical life. This inevitably returns us to the "private" arrangements made between men and women in the shadow of the civic sphere.[31] We need to bring that relation out of the shadows and examine it. Claims that it is based on nature, natural desire or necessary reproductive survival have by now worn thin. We also need to ask how this shadowy relation effects relations between men and women, and women and women, in the public sphere. Perhaps it is time to return, with new insight, to Wollstonecraft's early claim that "The most holy band of society is friendship. It has been well said, by a shrewd satirist, 'that rare as true love is, true friendship is even rarer.' "[32] This is an issue that feminists should resist reducing to a question of sexuality or, as is more usual, *heterosexuality*. The logically prior problem is a problem in ethics: the meaning and value of friendship.

If the liberal paradigm posits that sexual equality can only be had at the price of sexual *neutrality* (meaning the "neutering" of women, since men are already "neutral") then there is a serious problem with the relevance of this paradigm to women's situation. Part of the problem is that the liberal notion of "equality" has developed historically with a male bias towards the public sphere. As Wollstonecraft's writings show, this notion has great difficulty extending itself to issues relating to sexual difference. All liberal theory has to offer on the question of sexual equality is that women are entitled to be treated "like men," or "as if they were men." In order to pinpoint what is wrong with this response, we are compelled to return to a morality that takes account of bodily specificity. The demand for political equality thus spills over into the ethical, because the very terms in which the demand for political equality is made misses the ethical point: to treat all beings as "the same" is to deny some beings the most basic ethical principle, that is, acknowledgement of its specific being.[33] It is on this point that Wollstonecraft, and other liberal feminists, are at their weakest. On their paradigm, fair and equal treatment for women will only apply to those activities which simulate the neutral subject. In those aspects of her being that bear on her specificity, she will be offered little or no protection: for example, rape, domestic violence, enforced pregnancy. These infringements on women's autonomy significantly overlap in that they represent the unwanted use or abuse of her bodily capacities. The ultimate irony of the liberal state, in relation to woman, is revealed. The founding principle of liberal theory, the right and freedom to use one's bodily capacities as one sees fit, is denied to women with regard to the specific character of their bodies.

Rights of Woman and *Maria* are fruitful texts to study in attempting to clarify these two issues of embodiment and ethics. This problem, in all its complexity, can be found there. Wollstonecraft shows, albeit unintentionally, that settling the political question will not settle the ethical one. Perhaps this should not surprise us. The liberal tradition itself was ushered in not simply with a political question but also with an *ethical* one. Is monarchical power legitimate? What would constitute an ethical relation between men? Aspects of Wollstonecraft's work can be read as gesturing toward questions that still have not been satisfactorily addressed. What would constitute an ethical life for women *qua* women? What are the possibilities for women and men sharing a co-authored ethical community? Viewed from the standpoint of present feminist concerns, these unanswered questions are perhaps the most important legacy of Mary Wollstonecraft's life and work.

Notes

My thanks to Mary Lyndon Shanley who offered extensive comments and suggestions on an earlier draft of this essay.

1 Shulamith Firestone, *The Dialectic of Sex* (New York: Bantam, 1971).
2 Carol McMillan, *Women, Reason and Nature* (Oxford: Basil Blackwell, 1982).
3 Mary Wollstonecraft, *A Vindication of the Rights of Men* in Janet Todd, *A Wollstonecraft Anthology* (Bloomington: Indiana University Press, 1977; Cambridge: Polity, 1989), p. 65.

4 Ibid., p. 72.

5 Cora Kaplan, "Wild Nights: Pleasure/Sexuality/Feminism," in *Formations of Pleasure* (London: Routledge and Kegan Paul, 1983), p. 18.

6 Anca Vlasopolos, "Mary Wollstonecraft's Mask of Reason in *A Vindication of the Rights of Woman*," *Dalhousie Review*, 60 (3), 1980.

7 Mary Wollstonecraft, *A Vindication of the Rights of Woman*, ed. C. H. Poston (New York: Norton, 1975), p. 5.

8 Ibid., p. 4.

9 Ibid., p. 42.

10 Ibid., p. 53.

11 Ibid., p. 12.

12 Ibid., p. 47.

13 Ibid., p. 138.

14 Ibid., p. 26.

15 Ibid., p. 23.

16 Cf. ibid., p. 35n.

17 Quoted in J. Abray, "Feminism in the French Revolution," *American Historical Review*, 80, 1975, p. 56.

18 See Jean-Jacques Rousseau, *Emile* (London: Dent, 1972), p. 324, and Moira Gatens, "Rousseau and Wollstonecraft: Nature vs. Reason," *Australasian Journal of Philosophy*, 64 supplement, June, 1986.

19 Wollstonecraft, *Rights of Woman*, p. 192.

20 Ibid., p. 175.

21 Ibid., pp. 142–3 (emphasis added).

22 Ibid., p. 178 (emphasis added).

23 For an interesting discussion of this question see M. Tapper, "Can a Feminist be a Liberal?" *Australasian Journal of Philosophy*, 64 supplement, June, 1986.

24 Rousseau, *Emile*, p. 324.

25 Wollstonecraft, *Rights of Woman*, p. 30.

26 That this was Wollstonecraft's view is obvious from Letter XXXI in *Letters Written During a Short Residence in Sweden, Norway and Denmark*, in Todd, *Wollstonecraft Anthology*.

27 Letter LXVII, in ibid.

28 Letter from Wollstonecraft to Godwin, quoted in R. M. Wardle, *Mary Wollstonecraft* (Lawrence: University of Kansas Press, 1951), p. 296.

29 Letter VI, in Todd, *Wollstonecraft Anthology*.

30 *The Wrongs of Women, or Maria*, in Todd, *Wollstonecraft Anthology* p. 195.

31 See Pateman, *The Sexual Contract* (Cambridge: Polity; Stanford: Stanford University Press, 1988).

32 Wollstonecraft, *Rights of Woman*, p. 30.

33 See L. Irigaray, *L'éthique de la différence sexuelle* (Paris: Minuit, 1984).

7

On Hegel, Women and Irony

Seyla Benhabib

Das Bekannte überhaupt ist darum, weil es bekannt ist, nicht erkannt.

(The well-known is unknown, precisely because it is well-known.)

G. W. F. *Hegel*, Phaenomenologie des Geistes

Some Methodological Puzzles of a Feminist Approach to the History of Philosophy

The 1980s have been named "the decade of the humanities" in the USA. In many institutions of higher learning a debate is underway as to what constitutes the "tradition" and the "canon" in literary, artistic and philosophical works worth transmitting to future generations in the last quarter of the twentieth century. At the center of this debate is the question: if what had hitherto been considered the major works of the Western tradition are, almost uniformly, the product of a specific group of individuals, namely propertied, white, European and North American males, how universal and representative is their message, how inclusive is their scope, and how unbiased their vision?

Feminist theory has been at the forefront of this questioning, and under the impact of feminist scholarship the surface of the canon of Western "great works" has been forever fractured, its unity dispersed and its legitimacy challenged. Once the woman's question is raised, once we ask how a thinker conceptualizes the distinction between male and female, we experience a *Gestalt* shift: we begin to see the great thinkers of the past with a new eye, and in the words of Joan Kelly Gadol "each eye sees a different picture."[1] The vision of feminist theory is a "doubled" one: one eye sees what the tradition has trained it to see, the other searches for what the tradition has told her was not even worth looking for. How is a "feminist reading" of the tradition in fact possible? At the present, I see two dominant approaches, each with certain shortcomings.

I describe the first approach as "the teaching of the good father." Mainstream liberal feminist theory treats the tradition's views of women as a series of unfortunate, sometimes embarrassing, but essentially corrigible, misconceptions. Taking their inspiration from the example of a progressive thinker like John Stuart Mill, these theorists seek in the classical texts for those moments of insight into the equality and dignity of women. They are disappointed when their favorite philosopher utters inanities on the subject, but essentially hold that there is no incompatibility between the Enlightenment ideals of freedom, equality and self-realization and women's aspirations.

The second view I would characterize as "the cry of the rebellious daughter." Agreeing with Lacan that language is the symbolic universe which represents the "law of the father," and accepting that all language has been a codification of the power of the father, these rebellious daughters seek for female speech at the margins of the Western logocentric tradition. If it is impossible to think in the Western logocentric tradition without binary oppositions, then the task of feminist reading becomes the articulation not of a new set of categories but of the transcendence of categorical discourse altogether. One searches not for a new language but for a discourse at the margins of language.

Juxtaposed to these approaches, in this essay I would like to outline a "feminist discourse of empowerment." With the second view, I agree that the feminist challenge to the tradition cannot leave its fundamental categories unchanged. Revealing the gender subtext of the ideals of reason and the Enlightenment compromises the assumed universality of these ideals. Nonetheless, they should not be thrown aside altogether. Instead we can ask what these categories have meant for the actual lives of women in certain historical periods, and how, if women are to be thought of as subjects and not just as fulfillers of certain functions, the semantic horizon of these categories is transformed. Once we approach the tradition to recover from it women's subjectivity and their lives and activities, we hear contradictory voices, competing claims, and see that so-called "descriptive" discourses about the sexes are but "legitimizations" of male power. The traditional view of gender differences is the discourse of those who have won out and who have codified history as we know it. But what would the history of ideas look like from the standpoint of the victims? What ideals, aspirations and utopias of the past ran into a dead-end? Can we recapture their memory from the battleground of history? This essay attempts to apply such a "discourse of empowerment" to G. W. F. Hegel's views of women.

Hegel's treatment of women has received increased attention in recent years under the impact of the feminist questioning of the tradition.[2] This feminist challenge has led us to ask, is Hegel's treatment of women merely a consequence of his conservative predilections? Was Hegel unable to see that he made the "dialectic" stop at women and condemned them to an ahistorical mode of existence, outside the realms of struggle, work and diremption which in his eyes are characteristic of human consciousness as such?[3] Is the "woman question" in Hegel's thought one more instance of Hegel's uncritical endorsement of the institutions of his time, or is this issue an indication of a flaw in the very structure of the dialectic itself? Benjamin Barber, for example, siding with the second option has recently written:

> What this paradox reveals is that Hegel's position on women is neither a product of contingency nor an effect of ad hoc prejudice. Rather, it is the necessary consequence of his belief that the "Prejudices" of his age are in fact *the* actuality yielded by history in the epoch of liberation. Hegel does not have to rationalize them: because they *are*, they are already rational. They need only be encompassed and explained by philosophy. Spirit may guide and direct history, but ultimately, history alone can tell us where spirit means it to go.[4]

Judging, however, where "history alone can tell . . . spirit" it means it to go, requires a more complicated and contradictory account of the family and women's position at the end of the eighteenth and the beginning of the nineteenth century in the German states than either Barber or other commentators who have looked at this issue so far have provided us with. I suggest that to judge whether or not the Hegelian dialectic has stopped at women, we must first attempt to define the "discursive horizon" of competing claims and visions within which Hegel articulated his position. To evaluate the historical options concerning gender relations in Hegel's time, we have to move beyond the methodology of traditional text analysis to the "doubled vision" of feminist theory. In practicing this doubled vision we do not remain satisfied with analyzing textual discourses about women, but we ask where the women themselves were at any given period in which a thinker lived. With one eye we see what stands in the text, and with the other, what the text conceals in footnotes and in the margins. What then emerges is a "discursive space" of competing power claims. The discursive horizon of Hegel's views of women and the family are defined on the one hand by the rejection of political patriarchy (which mixes the familial with the political, the private with the public), and on the other by disapproval of and antagonism toward efforts of early female emancipation.

This essay is divided into two parts: by using the traditional method of text analysis in the first part I explore *the logic of oppositions* according to which Hegel develops his views of gender relations and of female subordination. In particular I focus on the complex relationship between reason, nature, gender and history. Second, having outlined Hegel's views of women in his political philosophy, I situate his discourse within the context of historical views on women and the family at the turn of the eighteenth century. I read Hegel against the grain; proceeding from certain footnotes and marginalia in the texts, I move toward recovering the history of those which the dialectic leaves behind.

Women in G. W. F. Hegel's (1770–1831) Political Thought

In many respects Hegel's political philosophy heralds the end of the traditional doctrine of politics, and signals its transformation into social science. *Geist* which emerges from nature, transforms nature into a second world; this "second nature" comprises the human, historical world of tradition, institutions, laws, and practices (*objektiver Geist*), as well as the self-reflection of knowing and acting subjects upon objective spirit, which is embodied in works of art, religion, and philosophy (*absoluter Geist*). *Geist* is a transindividual principle that unfolds in history, and whose goal is to make externality into its "work." *Geist* externalizes itself in history by appropriating, changing, and shaping the given such as to make it correspond to itself, to make it embody its own subjectivity, that is, reason and freedom. The transformation of substance into subject is attained when freedom and rationality are embodied in the world such that "the realm of freedom" is actualized, and "the world of mind [is] brought forth out of itself like a second nature." The social world is *Substance*, that is, it has objective existence for all to see and to comprehend;[5] it is also *subject*, for what the social and ethical world is can only be known by understanding the subjectivity of the individuals who compose it.[6] With Hegel's concept of objective spirit, the object domain of modern social science, that is, individuality and society, make their appearance.

Does his concept of *Geist* permit Hegel to transcend the "naturalistic" basis of gender conceptions in the modern period, such as to place the relation between the sexes in the social, symbolic, historical, and cultural world? Hegel, on the one hand, views the development of subjectivity and individuality within the context of a human community; on the other hand, in assigning men and women to their traditional sex roles, he codifies gender-specific differences as aspects of a rational ontology that is said to reflect the deep structure of *Geist*. Women are viewed as representing the principles of particularity (*Besonderheit*), immediacy (*Unmittelbarkeit*), naturalness (*Natürlichkeit*), and substantiality (*Substanzialität*), while men stand for universality (*Allgemeinheit*), mediacy (*Vermittlung*), freedom (*Freiheit*), and subjectivity (*Subjektivität*). Hegel develops his rational ontology of gender within a logic of oppositions.

The thesis of the "natural inequality" of the sexes

On the basis of Hegel's observations on the family, women, and the rearing of children, scattered throughout the *Lectures on the Philosophy of History*, I conclude that he was well aware that differences among the sexes were culturally, symbolically, and socially constituted. For example, in the section on Egypt, Hegel refers to Herodotus' observatations "that the women urinate standing up, while men sit, that the men wear one dress, and the women two; the women were engaged in outdoor occupations, while the men remained at home to weave. In one part of Egypt polygamy prevailed; in another, monogamy. His general judgment on the matter is that the Egyptians do the exact opposite of all other peoples."[7]

Hegel's own reflections on the significance of the family among the Chinese, the great respect that is shown to women in this culture, and his comment on the Chinese practice of concubinage again indicate an acute awareness that the role of women is not naturally but culturally and socially defined.[8]

These passages show a clear awareness of the cultural, historical, and social variations in family and sexual relations. Nevertheless, although Hegel rejects that differences between "men" and "women" are naturally defined, and instead sees them as part of the spirit of a people (*Volksgeist*), he leaves no doubt that he considers only one set of family relations and one particular division of labor between the sexes as rational and normatively right. This is the monogamic sexual practice of the European nuclear family, in which the woman is confined to the private sphere and the man to the public. To justify this arrangement, Hegel explicitly invokes the superiority of the male to the female while acknowledging their *functional complementarity* in the modern state.

The "superiority" of the male

The most revealing passages in this respect are paragraphs 165 and 166 of the *Philosophy of Right* and the additions to them. In the Lasson edition of the *Rechtsphilosophie*, Hegel writes that "The natural determinacies of both sexes acquire through its reasonableness *intellectual* as well as *ethical* significance."[9] This explicit reference to the "natural determinacies of the sexes" is given an ontological significance in the next paragraph:

> Thus one sex is mind in its self-diremption into explicit self-subsistence and the knowledge and volition of free universality, i.e. the self-consciousness of conceptual thought and the volition of the objective final end. The other sex is mind maintaining itself in unity as knowledge and volition in the form of concrete individuality and feeling. In relation to externality, the former is powerful and active, the latter passive and subjective. It follows that man has his actual substantive life in the state, in learning, and so forth, as well as in labour and struggle with the external world and with himself so that it is only out of his diremption that he fights his way to self-subsistent unity with himself. In the family he has a tranquil intuition of this unity, and there he lives a subjective ethical life on the plane of feeling. Woman, on the other hand, has her substantive destiny in the family, and to be imbued with family piety is her ethical frame of mind.[10]

For Hegel men's lives are concerned with the state, science, and work in the external world. Dividing himself (*sich entzweiend*) from the unity of the family, man objectifies the external world and conquers it through activity and freedom. The woman's "substantial determination," by contrast, is in the family, in the unity and piety (*Pietät*) characteristic of the private sphere. Hegel suggests that woman are not *individuals*, at least, not in the same measure and to the same extent as men are. They are incapable of the spiritual struggle and diremption (*Entzweiung*) which characterize the lives of men. In a passage from the *Phänomenologie* concerned with the tragedy of Antigone, he indicates that for the woman "it is not *this* man, not *this* child, but *a man* and *children in general*" that is significant.[11] The man by contrast, individuates his desires, and "since he possesses as a citizen the self-conscious power of universality, he thereby acquires the right of desire and, at the same time, preserves his freedom in regard to it."[12]

   Most significant is the fact that those respects in which Hegel considers men and women to be spiritually different are precisely those aspects that define women as "lesser" human beings. Like Plato and Aristotle, Hegel not only assigns particularity, intuitiveness, passivity to women, and universality, conceptual thought, and "the powerful and the active" to men, but sees in men the characteristics that define the species as human. Let us remember that *Geist* constitutes second nature by emerging out of its substantial unity into *bifurcation* (*Entzweiung*), where it sets itself over and against the world. The process through which nature is humanized and history constituted is this activity of *Entzweiung*, followed by *external-ization* (*Entäusserung*), namely the *objectification* (*Vergegenständlichung*) of human purposes and institutions in a world such that the world becomes a home for human self-expression. Women, since they cannot overcome unity and emerge out of the life of the family into the world of *universality*, are excluded from history-constituting activity. Their activities in the private realm, namely, reproduction, the rearing of children, and the satisfaction of the emotional and sexual needs of men, place them outside the world of *work*. This means that women have no history, and are condemned to repeat the cycles of life.

The family and political life

By including the family as the first stage of ethical life (*Sittlichkeit*), along-side "civil society" and "the state," Hegel reveals how crucial, in his view, this institution is to the constitution of the modern state. The family is significant in Hegel's political architectonic because it is the sphere in which the right of the modern individual to particularity (*Besonderheit*) and subjectivity (*Subjektivität*) is realized.[13] As Hegel often notes, the recognition of the "subjective moment" of the free individual is the chief strength of the modern state when compared to the ancient *polis*. In the family the right to particularity is exercised in love and in the choice of spouse, whereas the right to subjectivity is exercised in the concern for the welfare and moral well-being of other family members.

The various Additions to the section on the family, particularly in the Griesheim edition of the *Philosophy of Right*,[14] reveal that Hegel is concerned with this institution, not like Aristotle in order to discipline women, nor like Rousseau to prepare the true citizens of the future, but primarily from the standpoint of the freedom of the male subject in the modern state. Already in the *Philosophy of History*, Hegel had observed that the confusion of familial with political authority resulted in *patriarchalism*, and in China as well as in India this had as consequence the suppression of the freedom of the will through the legal regulation of family life and of relations within it. The decline of *political patriarchy* also means a strict separation between the private and the public, between the moral and intimate spheres, and the domain of public law. The legal system stands at the beginning and at the end of family; it circumscribes it but does not control its internal functioning or relations. It recognizes and administers, along with the church, the marriage contract as well as legally guaranteeing rights of inheritance when the family unit is dissolved. In this context, Hegel allows women certain significant legal rights.

He radically criticizes Kant for including women, children, and domestic servants under the category of *jura realiter personalia* or *Personen-Sachen-*

Recht.[15] Women are persons, that is, legal-juridical subjects along with men. They are free to choose their spouse;[16] they can own property, although once married, the man represents the family "as the legal person against others."[17] Nevertheless, women are entitled to property inheritance in the case of death and even in the case of divorce.[18] Hegel is against all Roman and feudal elements of the law that would either revert family property back to the family clan (*die Sippe*), or that would place restrictions on its full inheritance and alienability.[19]

The legal issue besides property rights that most concerns Hegel is that of divorce. Divorce presents a particular problem because, as a phenomenon, it belongs under two categories at once. On the one hand, it is a legal matter just as the marriage contract is; on the other hand, it is an issue that belongs to the "ethical" sphere, and more specifically to the subjectivity of the individuals involved. Hegel admits that because the bodily-sensual as well as spiritual attraction and love of two particular individuals form the basis of the marriage contract, an alienation between them can take place that justifies divorce; but this is only to be determined by an impersonal third-party authority, for instance, a court.[20] Finally, Hegel justifies monogamy as the only form of marriage that is truly compatible with the *individuality* of personality, and the subjectivity of feeling. In an addition to this paragraph in the Griesheim lectures he notes that monogamy is the only marriage form truly compatible with the equality of men and women.[21]

Contrary to parroting the prejudices of his time, or ontologizing them, as Benjamin Barber suggests, with respect to the right of the free choice of spouse, women's property and divorce rights, Hegel is an Enlightenment thinker, who upholds the transformations in the modern world initiated by the French Revolution and the spread of the revolutionary Code Civil. According to the Prussian *Das Allgemeine Landrecht* of 1794, the right of the free choice of spouse and in particular marriage among members of the various *Stände* – the feudal stratas of medieval society – was strictly forbidden. It was legally stipulated "that male persons from the nobility . . . could not enter into marriage . . . with female persons of peasant stock or the lesser bourgeoisie (*geringerem Bürgerstand*)."[22] If such marriages nonetheless occurred, they were declared "null" and the judges "were not empowered to accept their continuation."[23] To avoid social dilemmas, the lawgivers then distinguished between "the lesser" and "the higher bourgeoisie."

Hegel's position on this issue, by contrast, follows the revolutionary proclamations of the French Assembly which, codified as the "Code Civil" in 1804, were also adopted in those parts of Germany conquered by Napoleon.[24] Social strata differences are irrelevant to the choice of spouse and must not be legally regulated: the free will and consent of two adults (as well as of their parents), as long as they are legally entitled to marriage (that is, have not been married before or otherwise have falsified their civil status), is the only relevant point of view.

Yet Hegel inserts an interesting detail in considering this issue, which is wholly characteristic of his general attitude towards modernity. Distinguishing between the extremes of arranged marriages and the wholly free choice of spouse, he argues that: "The more ethical way to matrimony may be taken to be the former extreme or any way at all whereby the decision to marry comes first and the inclination to do so follows, so that in the actual wedding both decision and inclination coalesce."[25] Presumably this decision can also involve such relevant "ethical" considerations as the social background and appropriateness of the spouses involved. Consideration of social origin and wealth are now no longer legal matters to be regulated, as they were in feudal society, but personal and ethical criteria to be kept in view by modern individuals, aware of the significance, as the British Hegelian Bradley named it, of "my station and its duties."

While Hegel certainly was ahead of the Prussian legal practices of his time, and endorsed the general transformations brought about by the French Revolutionary Code Civil, he was, as always, reluctant to follow modernity to its ultimate conclusion and view the choice of spouse as a wholly individual matter of love and inclination between two adults. Hegel's views on love and sexuality, when placed within the larger context of changes taking place at this point in history, in fact reveal him to be a counter-Enlightenment thinker. Hegel surreptitiously criticizes and denigrates attempts at early women's emancipation and seeks to imprison women once more within the confines of the monogamous, nuclear family which they threatened to leave.

The Question of Free Love and Sexuality: The Thorn in Hegel's Side

Hegel's 1797–8 "Fragment on Love" reflects a more romantic conception of love and sexuality than the tame and domesticized view of marriage in the *Rechtsphilosophie*. Here love is given the dialectical structure of spirit; it is unity in unity and separateness; identity in identity and difference. In love, lovers are a "living" as opposed to a "dead" whole; the one aspect of dead matter that disrupts the unity of love is property. Property separates lovers by making them aware of their individuality as well as destroying their reciprocity. "True union or love proper exists only between living beings who are alike in power and thus in one another's eyes living beings from every point of view . . . This genuine love excludes all oppositions."[26]

Yet the discussion of the family in the *Philosophy of Right* is in general more conservative and criticizes the emphasis on free love as leading to libertinage and promiscuity. One of the objects of Hegel's greatest ire is

Friedrich von Schlegel's *Lucinde*, which Hegel names "Die romantische Ab-
wertung der Ehe" ("the romantic denigration of love").[27] To demand free
sexuality as proof of freedom and "inwardness" is in Hegel's eyes sophistry,
serving the exploitation of women. Hegel, in smug bourgeois fashion, observes:

> Friedrich v. Schlegel in his *Lucinde*, and a follower of his in the *Briefe eines
> Ungennanten*, have put forward the view that the wedding ceremony is
> superfluous and a formality which might be discarded. Their reason is that
> love is, so they say, the substance of marriage and that the celebration
> therefore detracts from its worth. Surrender to sensual impulse is here
> represented as necessary to prove the freedom and inwardness of love – an
> argument not unknown to seducers.

And he continues:

> It must be noticed in connexion with sex-relations that a girl in surrendering
> her body loses her honour. With a man, however, the case is otherwise,
> because he has a field for ethical activity outside the family. A girl is
> destined in essence for the marriage tie and for that only; it is therefore
> demanded of her that love shall take the form of marriage and that the
> different moments in love shall attain their true rational relation to each
> other.[28]

Taking my cue from this footnote in the text, I want to ask what this
aside reveals and conceals at once about Hegel's true attitudes toward
female emancipation in this period. The seemingly insignificant reference
to Friedrich Schlegel's *Lucinde* is extremely significant in the context of the
struggles for early women's emancipation at this time.

Remarking on the transformations brought about by the Enlightenment
and the French Revolution, Mary Hargrave has written:

> The close of the eighteenth and the beginning of the nineteenth centuries
> mark a period of Revolution for men and Evolution for women. The ideas of
> the French Revolution, that time of upheaval, of revaluing of values, of
> imperious assertion of the rights of the individual, swept over Europe like a
> quickening wind and everywhere there was talk of Liberty, Equality, Fra-
> ternity, realised (and perhaps only realisable) in that same order of
> precedence. . . .
>
> The minds of intellectual women were stirred, they became more conscious
> of themselves, more philosophic, more independent . . . France produced a
> writer of the calibre of Madame de Staël, England a Mary Sommerville, a
> Jane Austen; and Germany, although the stronghold of the domestic ideal,
> also had her brilliant intellectual women who, outside their own country,
> have perhaps not become as widely known as they deserve.[29]

In this work devoted to *Some German Women and their Salons*, Mary
Hargrave discusses Henriette Herz (1764–1847) and Rahel Varnhagen

(1771–1833), both Jewesses, Bettina von Arnim (1785–1859), and Caroline Schlegel (1763–1809), among others. Of particular importance in this context is also Karoline von Günderode (1780–1806), the most significant woman German poet of the Romantic era, in love with Hegel's high-school friend, Hölderlin. These women, through their lives and friend-ships, salons and contacts, and in some cases through their letters, publica-tions and translations, were not only forerunners of the early women's emancipation, but also represented a new model of gender relations, aspiring to equality, free love and reciprocity.

Definitive for Hegel's own contact with these women and their ideals, was the so-called Jenaer Kreis, the Jena circle, of the German Romantics, Friedrich and August Wilhelm Schlegel, Novalis, Schleiermacher, and Schelling. The journal *Athenäum* (1798–1800) was the literary outlet of this circle, frequented by Goethe as well as Hegel after his arrival in Jena in 1801. The "Jena circle" had grown out of friendship and literary cooperation among men but counted Caroline Schlegel among its most influential members. She had extraordinary impact on the Schlegel brothers, and was the inspiration for many of Friedrich Schlegel's literary characters as well as for his views on women, marriage and free love.[30] It is widely believed that Caroline Schlegel was the model for the heroine in the novel *Lucinde*.

Born as Caroline Albertina Michaelis, in Göttingen, as the daughter of a professor of Old Testament, Caroline was brought up in an intellectual household.[31] Following traditional patterns, in 1784 she married a young country doctor Georg Böhmer and moved from Göttingen to Clausthal, a mining village in the Hartz mountains. Although she suffered from the narrowness of her new surroundings and from the lack of intellectual stimulation, she remained here until suddenly her husband died in 1788. Caroline, who was then mother of three, lost two of her children after her husband's death. With her daughter Auguste Böhmer, she returned to the parental city. At Göttingen she met August Wilhelm Schlegel, six years her junior, who fell in love with her. In 1792 she left Göttingen for Mainz, the home now of her childhood friend Teresa Forster, born Heym. In December 1792 the city fell to the French under General Custine; the aristocrats fled and the republic was proclaimed. Teresa's husband, Forster, who was an ardent republican, was made president of the Jacobin Club. His wife, no longer in sympathy with his views, left him but Caroline stayed on and worked with revolutionary circles. In the spring of the following year, 1793, a German army mustered from Rheinisch principal-ities, retook Mainz. Caroline was arrested and with her little daughter Auguste was imprisoned in a fortress. After some months, her brother petitioned for her release, offering his services as an army surgeon in return, and August Wilhelm Schlegel exercised what influence he could to obtain her freedom.

Caroline was freed, but was banned from the Rheinisch provinces; even Göttingen, her home town, closed its doors to her. She was now pregnant, expecting the child of a French soldier, and August Wilhelm arranged for her to be put under the protection of his brother, Friedrich, then a young student in Leipzig. A lodging outside the city had to be found for her; here a child was born, but it did not live. In 1796, urged by her family and realizing the need for a protector, Caroline agreed to become August Schlegel's wife and settled with him in Jena. She never really loved Schlegel, and with the appearance of the young Schelling on the scene in 1798 a new love started in her life. Caroline's daughter, Auguste, died in July 1800. Schlegel settled in Berlin in 1802, and the increasing estrangement between them was resolved by a divorce in 1803. A few months later, she and Schelling were married by his father, a pastor, and they lived in Jena until her death in 1809.

Hegel lived in the same house with Caroline and Schelling from 1801 to 1803, and certainly the presence of this remarkable woman, an intellectual companion, a revolutionary, a mother, and a lover, provided Hegel with a flesh and blood example of what modernity, the Enlightenment and the French Revolution could mean for women. And Hegel did not like what he saw. Upon her death, he writes to Frau Niethammer: "I kiss a thousand times over the beautiful hands of the best woman. God may and shall preserve her as befits her merit ten times longer than the woman of whose death we recently learned here [Caroline Schelling], and of whom a few here have enunciated the hypothesis that the Devil had fetched her."[32] A damning and unkind remark, if there ever was one!

Whether Hegel should have liked or approved of Caroline, who certainly exercised a caustic and sharp power of judgment over people, making and remaking some reputations in her circle of friends – Schiller's for example – is beside the point. The point is that Caroline's life and person provided an example, and a very close one at that, of the kinds of changes that were taking place in women's lives at the time, of the possibilities opening before them, and also of the transformation of gender relations. In staunchly defending women's place in the family, in arguing against women's education except by way of learning the necessary skills to run a household, Hegel was not just "falling prey to the prejudices of his time." "His time" was a revolutionary one, and in the circles closest to Hegel, that of his Romantic friends, he encountered brilliant, accomplished and nonconformist women who certainly intimated to him what true gender equality might mean in the future. Hegel saw the future, and he did not like it. His eventual critique of Romantic conceptions of free love is also a critique of the early Romantics' aspirations to gender equality or maybe some form of androgyny.

Schlegel's novel *Lucinde* was written as a eulogy to love as a kind of

union to be enjoyed both spiritually and physically. In need of neither
religious sanction – Lucinde is Jewish – nor formal ceremony, such true
love was reciprocal and complete.[33] In the Athäneums-Fragment 34,
Schlegel had defined conventional marriages as "concubinages" to which
a "marriage à quatre" would be preferable.[34] *Lucinde* is a critical text,
juxtaposing to the subordination of women and the duplicitous sexual
conduct of the times a utopian ideal of true love as completion between
two independent beings. Most commentators agree, however, that *Lucinde*,
despite all noble intentions, is not a text of female emancipation: Lucinde's
artistic pursuits, once they have demonstrated the equality of the lovers,
cease to be relevant. The letters document Julius's development as a man,
his *Lehrjahre*, his movement from sexual desire dissociated from respect
and equality to his attainment of the ultimate companionship in a spiritually
and erotically satisfying relationship. Women are idealized journey-mates,
accompanying the men on this spiritual highway. "Seen on the one hand
as the complementary opposites of men, embodying the qualities their
counterparts lack, they are on the other, complete beings idealized to
perfection."[35] Although in a section of the novel called "A dithyrambic
fantasy on the loveliest situation in the world,"[36] there is a brief moment of
reversal of roles in sexual activity which Julius sees as "a wonderful . . .
allegory of the development of male and female to full and complete
humanity,"[37] in general in the *Lucinde*, the spiritual characteristics of the
two genders are clearly distinguished.

In his earlier essays such as "Über die weiblichen Charaktere in den
griechischen Dichtern" and "Über die Diotima" (1793–4), composed
after meeting Caroline Schlegel Schelling, and being enormously influenced
by her person, Friedrich Schlegel had developed the thesis – to be echoed
later by Marx in the *1844 Manuscripts* – that Greek civilization decayed or
flourished in proportion to the degree of equality it accorded to women. In
particular, Schlegel emphasized that inequality between men and women,
and the subordination of women, led to a bifurcation in the human
personality, whereby men came to lack "innocence, grace and love," and
women "independence." As opposed to the crudeness of male–female
relations in Homer, Sophocles in Schlegel's eyes is the poet who conceives
his male and female characters according to the same design and the same
ideal. It is Antigone who combines the male and female personality into
an androgynous ideal: she "desires only the true Good, and accomplishes
it without strain," in contrast to her sister, Ismene, the more traditional
feminine, who "suffers in silence."[38] Antigone transcends these stereotypes and represents a blending of male and female characteristics; she "is
the Divine."

Read against the background of Schlegel's views, Hegel's generally
celebrated discussion of Antigone in the *Phenomenology of Spirit* reveals a

different message. In Hegel's version of Antigone, she and Creon respectively stand for "female" and "male" virtues, and forms of ethical reality. Antigone represents the "hearth," the gods of the family, of kinship and of the "nether world."[39] Creon stands for the law, for the city, human law and the dictates of politics that are of "this world". Their clash is a clash between equal powers; although through her acknowledgement of guilt, Antigone presents that moment in the dialectic of action and fate which Hegel considers necessary, it is eventually through the decline of the family and the "nether world" that Spirit will progress to the Roman realm of law and further to the public light of the Enlightenment. Spiritually, Antigone is a higher figure than Creon, although even the most sympathetic commentators have to admit that what Hegel has accomplished here is "an apologia for Creon."[40]

Ironically, Hegel's discussion of the *Antigone* is more historically accurate in terms of the condition of Greek women, their confinement to the home, and the enormous clash between the newly emerging order of the *polis* and the laws of the extended family on which Greek society until the sixth and seventh centuries had rested than was Schlegel's.[41] But in his version of Antigone, Hegel was not simply being historically more accurate than Schlegel; he was robbing his romantic friends of an ideal, of a utopian vision. If Antigone's greatness derives precisely from the fact that she represents the ties of the "hearth and blood" over and against the *polis*, notwithstanding her grandeur, the dialectic will sweep Antigone in its onward historical march, precisely because the law of the city is public as opposed to private, rational as opposed to corporal, promulgated as opposed to intuited, human as opposed to divine. Hegel's narrative envisages no future synthesis of these pairs of opposites as did Schlegel's; whether on a world-historical scale or on the individual scale, the female principle must eventually be expelled from public life, for "Womankind — the everlasting irony (in the life) of the community — changes by intrigue the universal end of the government into a private end."[42] Spirit may fall into irony for a brief historical moment, but eventually the serious transparency of reason will discipline women and eliminate irony from public life. Already in Hegel's discussion of Antigone, that strain of restorationist thought, which will celebrate the revolution while condemning the revolutionaries for their actions, is present. Hegel's Antigone is one without a future; her tragedy is also the grave of utopian, revolutionary thinking about gender relations. Hegel, it turns out, is women's gravedigger, confining them to a grand but ultimately doomed phase of the dialectic, which "befalls mind in its infancy."

What about the dialectic then, that locomotive of history rushing on its onward march? There is no way to disentangle the march of the dialectic in Hegel's system from the bdoy of the victims on which it treads. Historical necessity requires its victims, and women have always been among the numerous victims of history. What remains of the dialectic is what Hegel precisely thought he could dispense with: irony, tragedy and contingency. He was one of the first to observe the ironic dialectic of modernity: freedom that could become abstract legalism or selfish pursuit of economic satisfaction; wealth that could turn into its opposite and create extremes of poverty; moral choice that would end in a trivial project of self-aggrandizement; and an emancipated subjectivity that could find no fulfillment in its "other." Repeatedly, the Hegelian system expunges the irony of the dialectic: the subject posits its opposite and loses itself in its other, but is always restored to selfhood via the argument that the "other" is but an extension or an exteriorization of oneself. Spirit is infinitely generous, just like a woman; it gives of itself; but unlike women, it has the right to call what it has contributed "mine" and take it back into itself. The vision of Hegelian reconciliation has long ceased to convince: the otherness of the other is that moment of irony, reversal and inversion with which we must live. What women can do today is to restore irony to the dialectic, by deflating the pompous march of historical necessity – a locomotive derailed, as Walter Banjamin observed – and by giving back to the victims of the dialectic like Caroline Schlegel Schelling their otherness, and this means, in true dialectical fashion, their selfhood.

Notes

Some of the material in this essay formerly appeared as Seyla Benhabib and Linda Nicholson, "Politische Philosophie und die Frauenfrage," in Iring Fetscher and Herfried Münkler, eds, *Pipers Handbuch der politischen Ideen*, vol. 5 (Munich/Zurich: Piper Verlag, 1987), pp. 513–62. I would like to thank Linda Nicholson for her agreement to let me use some of this material in the present article.

1 Joan Kelly Gadol, "Some Methodological Implications of the Relations Between the Sexes," *Women, History and Theory* (Chicago: University of Chicago Press, 1984), pp. 1ff.

2 Cf. Genevieve Lloyd, *The Man of Reason: "Male" and "Female" in Western Philosophy* (Minneapolis: University of Minnesota Press, 1984); Patricia J. Mills, *Woman, Nature and Psyche* (New Haven: Yale University Press, 1987); Benjamin Barber, "Spirit's Phoenix and History's Owl," *Political Theory*, 16 (1), 1988, pp. 5–29.

3 Cf. Heidi Ravven, "Has Hegel Anything to Say to Feminists?", *The Owl of Minerva*, 19 (2), 1988, pp. 149–68.

4 Barber, "Spirit's Phoenix and History's Owl," p. 20. Emphasis in the text.

5 Hegel, *Hegel's Philosophy of Right*, trans. and ed. T. M. Knox (Oxford: Oxford University Press, 1973), para. 144, p. 105.

6 Ibid., para. 146, pp. 105–6.

7 G. W. F. Hegel, *Vorlesungen über die Philosophie der Weltgeschichte*, in *Hegels*

Sämtliche Werke, ed. G. Lasson, vol. 8 (Leipzig, 1923), p. 471. English translation by J. Sibree, *The Philosophy of History* (New York: Dover, 1956), p. 205. Since Sibree's translation diverged from the original in this case, I have used my translation of this passage.

8 *Philosophy of History*, trans. Sibree, pp. 121–2.

9 I have revised the Knox translation of this passage in *Hegel's Philosophy of Right*, para. 165, p. 114, in accordance with Hegel, *Grundlinien der Philosophie des Rechts*, ed. Lasson, para. 165, p. 144. Emphasis in the text.

10 *Hegel's Philosophy of Right*, ed. Knox, para. 166, p. 114.

11 G. W. F. Hegel, *Phänomenologie des Geistes*, ed. J. Hoffmeister, Philosophische Bibliothek, vol. 114 (Hamburg, 1952), p. 326. English translation by A. V. Miller, *Hegel's Phenomenology of Spirit* (New York: Oxford University Press, 1977), p. 274. Emphasis in the text.

12 Ibid.

13 *Hegel's Philosophy of Right*, ed. Knox, paras. 152, 154, p. 109.

14 Cf. the excellent edition by K. H. Ilting, prepared from the lecture notes of K. G. v. Griesheim (1824–5), *Philosophie des Rechts* (Stuttgart: Klet-Cotta, 1974), vol. 6.

15 *Hegel's Philosophy of Right*, ed. Knox, para. 40 Addition, p. 39; cf. also Griesheim edition, para. 40 Z, pp. 180–1.

16 *Hegel's Philosophy of Right*, ed. Knox, para. 168, p. 115.

17 Ibid., para. 171, p. 116.

18 Ibid., para. 172, p. 117.

19 The one exception to this rule is the right of primogeniture, that is, that the oldest son among the landed nobility receives the family estate. It has long been observed that here Hegel indeed supported the historical interests of the landed Prussian gentry against the generally bourgeois ideology of free and unencumbered property and commodity transactions, which he defended in the rest of his system. However, on this issue as well Hegel is a modernist insofar as his defense of primogeniture among the members of the landed estate is justified not with reference to some family right but with reference to securing an independent income for the eldest son of the family, who is to function as a political representative of his class. Cf. *Hegel's Philosophy of Right*, ed. Knox, para. 306 and Addition, p. 293.

20 Ibid., para. 176, p. 118.

21 *Philosophie des Rechts*, Griesheim edition, para. 167 Z, p. 446.

22 Hans Ulrich Wehler, *Deutsche Gesellsachftsgeschichte* (Darmstadt: C. H. Verlag, 1987), vol. 1, p. 147.

23 Ibid.

24 Emil Friedberg, *Das Recht der Eheschliessung* (Leipzig: Bernhard Tauchnitz, 1865), pp. 593ff.

25 *Hegel's Philosophy of Right*, ed. Knox, para. 162, p. 111.

26 G. W. F. Hegel, "Love," in his *Early Theological Writings*, trans. T. M. Knox (Philadelphia: University of Pennsylvania Press, 1971, p. 304).

27 *Hegel's Philosophy of Right*, ed. Knox, para. 164 Addition, p. 263; cf. Griesheim edition, p. 436.

28 *Hegel's Philosophy of Right*, ed. Knox, para. 164, p. 263.

29 Mary Hargrave, *Some German Women and their Salons* (New York: Brentano, n.d.), p. viii.

30 Cf. ibid., pp. 259ff; Kurt Lüthi, *Feminismus und Romantik* (Vienna: Harmann Böhlaus Nachf., 1985), pp. 56ff.

31 Cf. ibid., pp. 251ff.

32 G. W. F. Hegel, *The Letters*, trans. Clark Butler and Christiane Seiler (Bloomington: Indiana University Press, 1984), p. 205.

33 Friedrich Schlegel, *Friedrich Schlegel's Lucinde and the Fragments*, trans. and intro. Peter Frichow (Minneapolis: University of Minnesota Press, 1971); cf. Sara Friedrichsmeyer, *The Androgyne in Early German Romanticism*, Stanford German Studies, vol. 18 (New York: Peter Lang, 1983), pp. 151ff.

34 Schlegel, *Lucinde and the Fragments*, p. 165.

35 Friedrichsmeyer, *Androgyne*, p. 160; cf. also, Lüthi, *Feminismus und Romantik*, pp. 95ff.

36 Schlegel, *Lucinde and the Fragments*, pp. 46ff.

37 Ibid., p. 49.

38 Cited in Friedrichsmeyer, *Androgyne*, p. 120.

39 Hegel, *Phenomenology of Spirit*, p. 276.

40 George Steiner, *Antigones* (New York: Oxford University Press, 1984), p. 41.

41 Hegel's reading of Antigone is more inspired by Aeschylus, who in his *Oresteia* exposed the clash between the early and the new orders as a clash between the female power of blood and the male power of the sword and the law. The decision to speak Orestes free of the guilt of matricide is signalled by an astonishingly powerful statement of the clash between the maternal power of birth and the paternal power of the law. Athena speaks on behalf of Orestes: "It is my task to render final judgement: / this vote which I possess / I will give on Orestes' side / For no mother had a part in *my* birth; / I am entirely male, with all my heart, / except in marriage; I am entirely my father's. / I will never give precedence in honor / to a woman who killed her man, the guardian of her house. / So if the votes are but equal, Orestes wins." Aeschylus, *The Oresteia*, trans. David Grene and Wendy O'Flaherty (Chicago: University of Chicago Press, 1989), pp. 161–2.

42 Hegel, *Phenomenology of Spirit*, p. 288.

8

Masculine Marx

Christine Di Stefano

We set out from real, active men, and on the basis of their real-life process we demonstrate the development of the ideological reflexes and echoes of this life process.
Marx and Engels, The German Ideology

A Personal Introduction: Confessions of a Former Marxist

I want to begin on a personal note, a note of appreciation for the theorist scheduled for critical scrutiny in this essay. Like many students who came of age in the United States during the late 1960s and early 1970s, my early attraction to political theory was made possible by the work of Karl Marx and those teachers and writers who gave him a sympathetic and expanded reading. Thanks to Marx, political theory came alive as an intellectual enterprise that might contribute to the minimization of oppression and human misery, to the creation of an improved and far better world. Next to Marx, the figures of Plato, Machiavelli, Hobbes and even Rousseau paled in comparison. Classroom discussions about the *polis* seemed irrelevant; Machiavelli bore a disturbing resemblance to Henry Kissinger; and Rousseau was simply impossible to pin down. Marx held out the possibility of theory that could be simultaneously rigorous, systematic, elegant, passionate, critical, utopian, and revolutionary. Feminist theory followed close on the heels, and sometimes directly in the footprints, of academic Marxism. Marx's youthful call for "a ruthless criticism of everything" was taken to heart by many feminists as they worked to expose the historically contingent dimensions of women's sexually differentiated experience and exploitation. Socialist-feminist theory is a significant testament to the intimate, if unstable and unsettling, alliance between Marxism and Western feminism.

Today, my disillusionment with Marxism, as a theory and as a politics, is profound, as this essay will reveal. But the countervailing strength of my indebtedness to Marx cannot be denied. An important measure of this indebtedness is the fact that Marx himself frequently provides the very tools and insights of his subsequent and often immanent criticism by feminists. I like to imagine that Marx would be pleased with and honored by his feminist fate, although this fantasy may imbibe the very ontology of masculinist transcendence of which he now stands accused. That is, it may demand a suprahistorical form of cognitive and empathetic achievement on the part of an imagined contemporary Marx. On the other hand, this fantasy (including my own complicity in the transcendent ontology that I will be criticizing, as well as my need to imagine the father's approval) conveniently captures the disconcerting sense of relation I have tried to convey here: in a word, ambivalence.

Gender Theory and the Critique of Masculinity

Feminist rereadings and criticisms of Marx now abound. These many and excellent studies focus attention on the explanatory inadequacies of orthodox Marxism.[1] There is general agreement among feminists that the Marxist categories of "production," "reproduction," "labor," "exploitation," and "class" fail to capture important dimensions of women's lives. As such, orthodox Marxism is also found lacking as a strategic theory of social change for women. In this essay, I will take a different approach. My interest lies not with the question of descriptive and explanatory relevance or adequacy, but rather with the background conditions of this now well-documented failure. An appraisal of these background conditions, in turn, underscores and intensifies the judgment that Marxist-feminism is a misguided, if not impossible or self-refuting, hybrid. For Marx's theory, as I will argue, is profoundly embedded within a masculine horizon of meaning and sensibility. As such, it is not merely inadequate; rather, it is part and parcel of a misogynous configuration of values, meanings, and practices to which feminism stands opposed.

The links between masculinity and misogyny are detailed and explored within gender theory, a contemporary offshoot of psychoanalytic theory.[2] "Gender" refers to apparent representations of sexual difference and identity which are in fact imposed on human subjects, and social and natural phenomena. In most cultures, gender is patterned in dualistic, dichotomous, and hierarchical modes which promote male privilege and female subordination. Nevertheless, the actual contents of gendered representations carry enormous cross-cultural variability. The implication is that gender is simultaneously a ubiquitous feature of culture, and that it has no fixed, transcultural or trans-historical contents. In short, it is best understood as a complex convention. Leaving aside the difficult and important issue of just how pervasive gender is in cross-cultural terms, it is now unquestionably the case that modern Western culture is and has been profoundly gendered. Humanistic pretensions of the Enlightenment and liberal political discourse notwithstanding, modern Western peoples inhabit a politicized cultural universe elaborately carved out and apportioned in terms of presumed meaningful sexual differences.[3] The key terms of this difference, which are partly but also significantly constitutive of modern subjectivities, and currently in a process of social change and radical assessment, are "femininity" and "masculinity."

In broad, if not coarse, outline, contemporary gender theory suggests that identity formation for males and females is enacted according to asymmetrical, although sometimes complementary, gender scripts. These scripts are first played out during the early months and years of an individual's life (the pre-oedipal period) and the central characters are two: mother (or female caretaker) and child. The net effect of female caretaking is that the mother figure comes to be heavily invested with the ambivalent feelings of her charges. As Isaac Balbus describes this:

> she is at once the being with whom the child is initially indistinguishably identified and the one who enforces the (never more than partial) dissolution of this identification. Thus it is the mother who becomes the recipient of the unconscious hostility that accumulates in children of both sexes as the result of this inescapably painful separation. This mother who is loved is also necessarily the mother who is hated.[4]

In societies where all mothers are female and where most females face likely destinies as mothers, the initial ambivalence towards the mother is easily and subsequently transferred to women in general.

But the ambivalence itself comes to be further differentiated in gender-specific terms. In effect, it becomes heightened for the boy child in his subsequent struggle for a specifically gendered identity, which is the only kind of identity "offered" to him by the culture at large. This is where aspects of separation and individuation take on special and different significance for boys and girls. Coppélia Kahn summarizes the difference, explicated most extensively by Nancy Chodorow and Dorothy Dinnerstein, this way:

> For though [the girl] follows the same sequence of symbiotic union, separation and individuation, identification, and object love as the boy, her femininity arises in relation to a person of the *same* sex, while his masculinity arises in

relation to a person of the *opposite* sex. Her femininity is reinforced by her original symbiotic union with her mother and by the identification with her that must precede identity, while masculinity is threatened by the same union and the same identification. While the boy's sense of *self* begins in union with the feminine, his sense of *masculinity* arises against it.[5]

This account suggests that the critical threat to masculinity is not castration, as orthodox psychoanalysis suggests, but rather the threat of maternal reengulfment. Masculine identity requires a massive repudiation of identification with that all-satisfying/all-terrifying maternal source. The basic ambivalence of male and female children towards the mother is intensified for boys because of the need to define masculinity in *contrast* to maternal femininity. An important feature of masculine development, as outlined in this psychoanalytic literature, is the *negative* articulation of masculine selfhood *vis à vis* the pre-posited maternal-feminine presence. (As a boy, I am that which is *not*-mother). The rudimentary building blocks of the boy's struggle to understand what it is that makes him a "boy" and a future "man," a masculine subject and agent in a gender-differentiated world, consist of negative counterfactuals garnered through comparison with the all-too-proximate mother. This prototypical process of masculine individuation and identity formation is susceptible to a process of "false differentiation" whereby the (m)other is unrealistically objectified in split versions rather than accommodated as a more complex entity. In effect, false differentiation is implicated in the inability/refusal to tolerate ambivalence and to acknowledge difference.[6] Nancy Chodorow sums up her reconstruction of the origins and ramifications of masculinity in a manner that bears directly on these themes:

> The division of labor in childrearing results in an objectification of women – a treating of women as others, or objects, rather than subjects, or selves – that extends to our culture as a whole. Infantile development of the self is explored in opposition to the mother, as primary caretaker, who becomes the other. Because boys are of opposite gender from their mothers, they especially feel a need to differentiate and yet find differentiation problematic. The boy comes to define his self more in opposition than through a sense of his wholeness or continuity. He becomes the self and experiences his mother as the other. The process also extends to his trying to dominate the other in order to ensure his sense of self. Such domination begins with mother as the object, extends to women, and is then generalized to include the experience of all others as objects rather than subjects. This stance in which people are treated and experienced as things, becomes basic to male Western culture.[7]

The literature on gender formation and acquisition suggests that there are ways in which masculine experience yields certain cognitive proclivities, tendencies which structure perception.[8] Such cognitive proclivities may comprise or contribute to intellectual frameworks implicitly organized around the ontological and epistemological primacy of the masculine subject, and include several among the following elements: a combative brand of dualistic thinking, a persistent and systematic amplification of the primal Self–Other oppositional dynamic; the creation of dichotomized polarities by which to describe and evaluate the events, objects, and processes of the natural and social worlds; the need for and privileging of singular identity and certainty with respect to one's "own" identity and that of other "objects" in the environment; the denial or refusal of related-ness, to fellow human beings and to nature; a fear and repudiation of natural contingency, including those limits imposed by the body and the natural surround; an identification of such contingency with the feminine; versions of a solitary subject immersed in a hostile and dangerous world; detailed expressions and descriptions of radical or heroic individualism; preoccupation with themes of freedom, autonomy and transcendence; accounts of knowledge-as-opposition and knowledge-as-struggle, based on a distanced relation between the subject and object of knowledge; attitudes of fear, denigration and hostility towards whatever is identified as female or feminine; idealization and glorification of the feminine. This last set of seemingly incompatible attitudes would recapitulate the effects of false differentiation from the maternal object, the (m)other.

Marx was, of course, a brilliant and acute analyst of the very objectifying stance that Nancy Chodorow and others have identified as basic to male Western culture. To what extent is he exempt from or implicated in the masculine configuration of sensibility and meaning briefly detailed above? I explore this question in the remainder of this essay, with special reference to Marx's style and selected substantive areas of his theory.

Marx's Style

Students of Marx are well aware of the intimate relationship between the substance and style of his work. Critics and disciples of Marx would agree that his characteristic polemical style was an aggressive one, which involved "marking out his own position by eliminating former or potential colleagues from it."[9] Marx's approach to an issue was invariably one that proceeded over the toppled remains of existing, would-be and sometimes fabricated opponents, some of whom began as friends, teachers, and mentors. "From his student days to the time of *Capital*," writes Jerrold Seigel, "Marx's characteristic mode of defining himself was by opposition, excluding others from the personal space he occupied."[10] It would seem that Marx could only create a discursive space for himself by invading and re-appropriating the territory of displaced and vanquished others. In this sense, Marx evinces a combative, heroic, and hence, masculine style.[11]

In speculating on the possible sources of this aggressive style, Seigel has suggested that Marx's mother may provide a clue. He argues that Marx's style might have been a reaction against Henriette Marx's intrusive and dominating nurture style. This interpretation is problematic on several counts, although it contains an important measure of insight.

First, we simply do not know enough about Henriette Marx or her relationship to Karl to characterize her as an overbearing mother.[12] However, we might well ask, when is maternal nurturance within the bourgeois, nuclear family *not* intrusive and dominating? Seigel slides into the tendency of "blaming the mother," whereas the real issue here is a more structural one. That is, the kind of family in which Karl Marx was reared is precisely that modern, intensely affective, socially isolated nuclear configuration in which children are likely to perceive their mothers as intrusive beings, regardless of the particular activities and attitudes of specific mothers. These perceptions, in turn, are likely to be retained in adulthood, often in unconscious, elaborated and/or disguised forms. Marx's estranged adult relationship with his mother, coupled with his inflated-romantic courtship to Jenny von Westphalen, suggest that he suffered from an unresolved ambivalence toward the primal, pre-oedipal (m)other. This ambivalence, as we will see, carries over into his analysis of women's labor under capitalism. But it has precious little to do with the actual woman who mothered him.

A second problem with Seigel's analysis of Marx's aggressive style is that it proceeds as if this style is simply an individual personality quirk. That is, Seigel pays little attention to the intellectual discursive tradition within which Marx was embedded. An adversarial, aggressive style is a significant feature of the Western philosophical tradition;[13] furthermore, this style may have found in dialectics a particularly hospitable environment, since the dialectical conversational form has assumed combative, as well as dialogic, features. Marx's aggressive intellectual style should be recast in terms which acknowledge a pre-existing legacy for which he was temperamentally suited, if not gifted.

Finally, we can augment Seigel's treatment of Marx's style by noting that the aggressive, adversarial mode partakes of a masculine cognitive structure. This style (which Marx shares with other political theorists of notable rhetorical skill, such as Hobbes) may be understood, in part, to recapitulate, at the level of adult intellectual practice, the prior process of struggle for a location and identity *vis à vis* the pre-oedipal (m)other. The echoes of this earlier struggle ramify in distinctive ways on Marx's polemical style, which flourishes in hostile territory and will brook no contenders. Ironically, the radical theorist of species-being and communism embodied an intellectual stance and style which contradicted his social ontology.[14]

Seigel's analysis is vindicated, then, with the proviso that we substitute the fantasized mother of Marx's primary process memory and early experience for his "real" mother, and that we go on to acknowledge that mothers of the former sort lurk within the stylistic tradition of adversarial intellectual discourse and have "helped" (as projections of the masculine imagination) to shape the style and subtext of that tradition.[15]

A Tale of Post-embeddedness

At first glance, Marx seems to elude, if not overtly contest, the masculine scheme of meaning outlined above and initially detected in Marx's polemical style. Modern dialectics, for example, is a methodological attempt to transcend the dichotomies which Cartesian-inspired epistemologies promote. Initially, it would seem, dialectics is more closely allied with a feminine epistemological orientation, most especially in its relational and dialogic orientation. The materialist aspect of Marx's method also bears some apparent affinity with feminist critiques of idealist or rationalist presumptions which elevate the (male) brain at the expense of the (female) body. Yet, in spite of these potential affinities between Marxism and feminism, the actual rendition and deployment of dialectics and materialism found in Marx's work play into and out of a specifically masculinist frame of reference and meaning.

"Marx's procedure was in fact to set out from men's labor and to ignore the specificity of women's labor," writes Nancy Hartsock.[16] This invisibility of women's labor is implicated in important ways with Marx's account of "human" labor. Given Marx's ontological and materialist stress on the laboring activities of human beings and the preconditions for certain forms of distinctively "human" activity, the invisibility of women (and especially of women as caretakers and as mothers) is notably striking and problematic.

In *The German Ideology* Marx and Engels discuss the history of the division of labor and locate its first primordial instance in the sexual division of labor in the family. They go on to categorize familial relations, including the sexual division of labor, as "natural" relations. Adding insult to injury, they dismiss the significance of the familial sexual division of labor by stating that a "real" division only emerges with the (presumably distinct and subsequent) distinction between manual and mental labor.[17] Given Marx's insistence that social relations be analyzed as historically determined and specific outcomes rather than as eternal verities, this is especially troublesome. What Marx and Engels subsequently miss in their focus on the division between "brain" and "hand" is what Hilary Rose refers to as the "heart":

Women's work is of a particular kind – whether menial or requiring the sophisticated skills involved in child care, it always involves personal service. Perhaps to make the nature of this caring, intimate, emotionally demanding labor clear, we should use the ideologically loaded term "love." For without love, without close interpersonal relationships, human beings, and it would seem especially small human beings, cannot survive. This emotionally demanding labor requires that women give something of themselves to the child, to the man. The production of people is thus qualitatively different from the production of things. It requires caring labor – the labor of love.[18]

It seems more reasonable to locate the first materialist premise of human existence in the phenomenon of birth; to acknowledge that some woman has "labored" to bring me into the world. On this view, the second premise is that we will be cared for during our early years of biological and emotional vulnerability. And this second premise calls on, but is not exhausted by, Marx and Engels's first: the production of the means to satisfy our needs for nourishment, shelter, and protection. To this premise we should also add the human neonate's need for social intercourse.

Strangely enough, reproduction enters the scene for Marx and Engels as the third premise of history: "men, who daily remake their own life, begin to make other men, to propagate their kind: the relationship between man and woman, parents and children, the family."[19] The sense of historical sequence here is strangely, but familiarly, skewed. For the starting point of their analysis of the premises of history-making men is the already born and nurtured human being. Not only do mothers not make an appearance until the third act, but mothers and fathers enter the Marxian historical scene simultaneously. History and common sense suggest, however, that "mothers" predated "fathers." Feminist history also suggests that fathers have gone to extensive lengths to eradicate this threatening knowledge. In this sense, *The German Ideology* is thoroughly complicitous with patriarchal history and ideology.

This fanciful historical account saturates Marx's economic framework of description and explanation, in which women's gender-specific labor vanishes and we are left with "a gender-biased account of social production and an incomplete account of the life-processes of human beings."[20] The issue here is not simply one of nominal exclusion, which could be rectified by including women and their labor in the theory. Marx's failure to acknowledge and theorize reproductive and caring labor directly influences his understanding of "human" labor, most artfully captured in his comparison of the architect and the bee in *Capital*. While this comparison rightly emphasizes the creative and self-conscious aspects of human labor, it errs in postulating an idealized and over-voluntarist image of unalienated labor emancipated from the realm of necessity:

> In fact, the realm of freedom begins *only where labor which is determined by necessity and mundane considerations ceases*; thus in the very nature of things it lies beyond the sphere of actual material production. . . . Freedom in this field can only consist in socialized men, the associated producers, rationally regulating their interchange with Nature, *bringing it under their common control*, instead of being ruled by it as the blind forces of Nature; and achieving this with the least expenditure of energy and under conditions most favorable to, and worthy of, their human nature. (Emphasis added)[21]

Necessity – that ultimately ineradicable foe – must be diminished as much as possible for a truly "human" history to flourish. Nature and humanity are thus, in a significant sense, opposed. On this level, Marx shares a similar orientation towards nature with an unlikely ally, J. S. Mill.[22] This vision of freedom is intimately tied up with Marx's sense of history, especially with his sense of progress as a steadily expanding control over nature. The material and technological conditions for such control are necessary, if not sufficient, guarantors of human self-realization. Marx's youthful anticipated "reconciliation" of humanity and nature in *The Economic and Philosophical Manuscripts* thus takes place at the dialectical expense of nature controlled.

Isaac Balbus argues that Marx's concept of production entails the domination of nature because it requires an "instrumental relationship between humans and their surrounding world."[23] As the substance of "necessity," nature is humanity's adversary in its quest for self-creative, self-sufficient freedom. When we approach nature on these instrumental terms, we must assume that it "has no intrinsic worth, no dignity of its own," and therefore that it makes no normative claims on humanity.[24] William Petty's analogy – quoted approvingly by Marx in *Capital* – that "labour is the father of the material world, the earth is its mother," reinforces the notion that nature provides the inert material substratum for "productive" labor, as it associatively plays on the sexist depiction of women as passive, natural, and therefore less-than-fully human creatures. While the young Marx was obviously groping for some means of reconciliation between humanity and nature, his subsequent vision of communism effectively renders the "humanization" of nature as its sadistic domination by human beings:

> Communism . . . treats *all* natural premises as the creatures of hitherto existing men, *strips* them of their natural character and *subjugates* them to the power of the united individuals . . . . The reality, which communism is creating, is precisely the true basis for rendering it impossible that *anything should exist independently of individuals*, insofar as reality is *only* a product of the preceding intercourse of individuals themselves. (Emphasis added)[25]

The subjugation of natural premises is, in turn, implicated in the act of self-affirmation and self-creation. This agenda for self-creation as the achieved solution to and victory over the threat of uncontrolled natural forces parallels the masculine invention of identity against the (m)other.

If Marx had stopped seriously to consider the labor of female caretakers and mothers, he would have been forced in one of two directions: either to characterize such labor as less than human because it is bound to nature and necessity; or to rethink his account of labor to accommodate reproductive and emotional labor, which is complexly constituted by biology and messy necessity, as well as by culture and history. (If he had done this, he would also have had to recast his historical narrative, which is less obviously "progressive" for women.) Implicitly, the former characterization prevails in his analysis of labor. Explicitly, the laboring mother is conveniently ignored. In short, what we have here is another case of the missing mother in Western political theory.

Mary O'Brien's comparison of the mother and the architect introduces some of the more stubborn and interesting features of maternal labor which Marx avoided. They are worth considering in some detail:

> Biological reproduction . . . is not an act of rational will. No one denies a motherly imagination, which foresees the child in a variety of ways . . . . Female reproductive consciousness knows that a child will be born, knows what a child is, and speculates in general terms about this child's potential. Yet mother and architect are quite different. The woman cannot realize her visions, cannot make them true, by virtue of the reproductive labor in which she involuntarily engages, if at all. Unlike the architect, her will does not influence the shape of her product. Unlike the bee, she knows that her product, like herself, will have a history. Like the architect, she knows what she is doing; like the bee, she cannot help what she is doing.[26]

At issue here are fundamental questions concerning control, the human relationship to nature, and the characterization of identifiably human activities as exclusively rational and self-generative. Stressing the planned, conscious, and purposive dimensions of human labor, Marx counterposes such labor to the realm of Necessity (Nature) and so is constitutionally unable to see women's reproductive labor and its derivatives as human labor. The fact that "productive" labor as such would be impossible without reproductive and caring labor makes this blindspot all the more problematic. Marx has failed to fully specify the preconditions for "human" labor as he defines it. At this point, we could well ask Marx a feminist-inspired version of the question that he put to liberal psychological theories that ignored the history of industry and production in their pronouncements on the psychological life of "man": "What should one think of a science [Marxism] whose preconceptions disregarded this large field of man's [sic] labour [maternal labor] and which is not conscious of its incompleteness . . . ?"[27]

Marx has essentially *denied* and then *reappropriated* the labor of the mother in his historical and labor-based account of self-created man.[28] What is wrong with this familiar account of independence, self-creation and self-sufficiency, within which we can discern a strong dose of modernist sensibility? First, it relies on an overly, but only apparently, "plastic" conception of human nature. That is, plasticity is not the open or un-encumbered account of human nature that it claims to be. Secondly, it is arrogant and in keeping with problematic Enlightenment notions concerning the status of nature. Thirdly, it is implicated in the denial of the mother.

Marx provided a significant and much-needed critique of the presocial individual monad of liberal theory who is constituted as a subject prior to the society in which he lives. However, his substitute notion of the individual as "the ensemble of social relations" creates a good many problems. Robert Heilbroner has been especially acute in describing the hazards of a plastic conception of human nature:

> There is a severe price to be paid for a view of the human being as without any definition other than that created by its social setting. For the individual thereupon becomes the expression of social relations binding him or her together with *other* individuals who are likewise nothing but the creatures of their social existences. We then have a web of social determinations that has no points of anchorage other than in our animal bodies.[29]

And our animal bodies, within the frame of Marx's antinaturalist analysis, can't tell us very much about ourselves. Dennis Wrong's identification of a theoretical partnership between an oversocialized view of man and an over-integrated view of society is substantiated in the fate of politics within Marx's theory and the political history of successful Marxist movements.[30] Marx's collapsed vision of a complementary and trouble-free relationship between the individual and communist society is too seamless to admit political struggle and dialogue over society's means, ends, limits, and possibilities. That the theorist *par excellence* of struggle and contradiction should end up with this kind of static vision is rather incredible. Or is it? Perhaps Marx himself embodies a human-all-too-human limit for living with perpetual conflict. Intense, dichotomously framed, do-or-die conflict engenders its opposite: pure, yet false, reconciliation.

An exaggerated emphasis on man's self-creative abilities is also arrogant. It denies our natural embeddedness and promotes resentment against a nature that (like a mother) has not made us godlike. It pits the "human" essence against the "natural" backdrop of limitations. And it actually anticipates a state of "post-embeddedness," where according to Jeremy Shapiro's favorable commentary: "the individual has ceased to become the object of uncontrolled forces and is instead entirely self-created, ceaselessly going beyond its own limits by means of its creativity, and continuously participating in the movement of its own becoming."[31]

Post-embeddedness is a dangerous and arrogant fiction. It is also masculinist and misogynous. It is dangerous because it elicits the revolt of nature. It is masculine because it issues out of a configuration of perceptions and needs rooted in a gendered identity fashioned out of opposition to the maternal world. It is misogynous because it perpetuates a fear of and consequent need to dominate naturalized, and hence, "dangerous" women. The domination of nature issues in a longing to return to it. This return, as Silvia Bovenschen argues, is negotiated through the female: "The biological-natural moments of human existence only appear to have been fully expunged from masculine everyday life: that relationship to inner [and outer] nature which has not yet been mastered is projected onto women, so that women must pay for the dysfunctionality of man's natural drives."[32]

Marx's systematic and related failures to accommodate nature and women within his grand scheme of explanation may help to explain a central tension at the heart of his theory, that between humanistic voluntarism ("man makes himself") and sociostructural determinism ("life is not determined by consciousness, but consciousness by life"). For while this tension may be artfully combined, as we find in *The Eighteenth Brumaire*, it also threatens to erupt in onesided formulations. Humanity's domination over nature promises a human omnipotence which is eternally threatened. Notice that the capitalist version of this threat, analyzed by Marx under the rubrics of "accumulation" and "reproduction," takes on vitalistic, naturelike, and even female capacities, including dynamically regenerative ones. In effect, the mother banished from the realms of history and labor reappears in Marx's portrayal of a fecund capitalism that reproduces and augments itself, while his own intellectual efforts are cast as the contributions of a midwife helping to shorten the birth pangs of an eventual or incipient revolution.[33]

An exaggerated emphasis on self-creation denies that we were born and nurtured. It denies the biosocial basis for species-continuity and projects it exclusively on to the arena of "labor." And it promotes a view of communism as severing "the umbilical cord [!] of the individual's natural connection with the species."[34] These themes help us to ponder Mary O'Brien's suggestion that "underlying the doctrine that man makes history is the undiscussed reality of why he must."[35]

When we deny our first biosocial relationship we deny our own natural embeddedness as physical, vulnerable, animal creatures. We also deny the origins and ground of our sociability as a species. Philosophers such as Marx who wish to articulate and promote this important aspect of human life without reference to maternal or parental labor are forced to ground it in activities which postdate (by a long shot) our first experience of sociability. Small wonder that the theory comes out sounding "utopian" and unrealistic. When we deny maternal labor and women's labors of caring love, which tend to be more aware of a noninstrumental, cooperative and also difficult relationship with nature, we construct a deficient view of "specifically human labor" and of "species life."[36] Without some retrospective appreciation for our biosocial origins, we are all the more likely to join Marx in viewing the past as a mere and disgusting pile of "muck."

This denial of the mother in Marx's theory – which is also central to the social acquisition, definition, and defense of masculinity – helps to maintain the domination of women and the domination of nature. Hence, Marxist social theory may be perpetuating problems – some of which it would like to solve, others of which it is unaware – that involve not only half of the human species, but our literal survival as a species.

Yet there are intimations in Marx (especially the young Marx) of yearning for a genuine, mutually reciprocal relationship between humanity and nature, men and women.[37] A more generous reading than I have offered here would locate him in the tension between the recognition of nature and its domination, within the complex contrariness of his thinking.[38] Such a reading would take issue with Isaac Balbus's argument that Marx is unredeemable because his conception of production is "the ultimate possible expression of" the " 'hubris of domination.' "[39] It would be more in keeping with Nancy Hartsock's suggestion that Marx needs to be (and can be) transplanted to a new epistemological terrain, one that is gender-sensitive, inclusive of a larger subject of history, and explicitly feminist.

Is Marx's theory the "ultimate" in modernist, Enlightenment-inspired attempts to dominate nature? This is a difficult question, one that I am inclined to answer negatively because of Marx's latent intimations of an alternative dialectical interplay between humanity and nature. If we take Marx's failure to consist of "his inability to [maintain and] extend his splendid insight into the epistemological validity of sensuous experience and the sensuousness of the 'man/nature' relationship expressed in labor,"[40] then the terms of his failure, at least, are preferable to those of others.

On the other hand, we had better think twice before we attempt to transplant Marx to new epistemological ground, as Nancy Hartsock suggests. For Marx's theoretical universe is bound up with an ontological habitat that is profoundly masculine. And the knowledge which issues out of and is produced by this framework is limited and damaging, not simply in its inability to "see" aspects of gender-differentiated experience and knowledge, but also in the very action and substance of its interpretive horizon. Marx's epistemological commitment to the arena of "production" commits him to an ontological reality which is detectably masculine, not merely male. As such, it lacks a reflexive appreciation of its own material and ideological roots which, within the Marxian view, is the prerequisite of a genuinely rigorous critical theory. To a great extent, the "root" that Marx unwittingly grasped was gender-specific modern man.

Conclusion

Marx's "real connections" to his social world reflect, in significant measure, the introjected connections of a masculine subject. We find masculinity at work in Marx's need to clear the ground for his intellectual and polemical endeavors. But more significantly, Marx has "successfully" banished the mother from his overall account of social relations. (In this respect, he is not so different from the majority of modern political theorists.) This enables a number of crucial and distinctive turns in his theory: a view of history as forward-moving progress; a dichotomous account of antagonistic class relations; a cataclysmic theory of historical change; and a view of human labor as ultravoluntarist. The missing mother underwrites the Marxian account of labor by helping to subsume nonvoluntarist dimensions of human laboring practices. The voluntarist account of labor, in turn, is a key component of Marx's objectification of nature, for it conveniently promotes a view of nature as the (feminized) passive substratum of (hu)manly active efforts. The inverse relationship between freedom and necessity informs and issues out of the voluntarist conception of labor, and it parallels the antagonistic relationship between son and (m)other, (hu)manity and nature. Post-embeddedness is the inevitably "utopian" endpoint of such a scheme. What it recapitulates at the level of social and political theory is a yearning and fantasy embedded in the deep psychology of masculine identity: clean and ultimate release from the (m)other.

Notes

For generous comments, criticisms, and editorial help, I would like to thank Susan Hekman, Mary Shanley, Katherine Teghtsoonian, and Diane Wolf.

1 It would be impossible to do full justice to this literature in a single note. What follows is a selective list derived primarily from the socialist-feminist genre. Christine Delphy, *Close to Home: A Materialist Analysis of Women's Oppression* (Amherst: University of Massachusetts Press, 1984); Zillah Eisenstein, ed., *Capitalist Patriarchy and the Case for Socialist Feminism* (New York: Monthly Review Press, 1979); Nancy C. M. Hartsock, *Money, Sex, and Power: Toward a Feminist Historical Materialism* (New York and London: Longman, 1983); Alison Jaggar, *Feminist Politics and Human Nature* (Totowa, NJ: Rowman and Allanheld, 1983; Sussex: The Harvester Press, 1983); Mary O'Brien, *The Politics of Reproduction* (Boston and London: Routledge and Kegan Paul, 1981); Juliet Mitchell,

Woman's Estate (New York: Random House, 1973); Lydia Sargent, ed., *Women and Revolution* (Boston: South End Press, 1981); Hilda Scott, *Does Socialism Liberate Women?* (Boston: Beacon Press, 1974); Eli Zaretsky, *Capitalism, the Family, and Personal Life*, revised and expanded edn (New York: Harper and Row, 1986). An excellent recent contribution to the debate concerning the relationship between feminism and Marxism, which extends into postmodern theoretical territory, is the collection of essays edited and introduced by Seyla Benhabib and Drucilla Cornell, *Feminism as Critique* (Cambridge: Polity; Minneapolis: University of Minnesota Press, 1987).

2 Again, it is impossible to do justice to this literature in one note. A helpful review and summary of object relations theory, which often provides the theoretical starting point for American feminist gender theory, is Jay R. Greenberg and Stephen A. Mitchell, *Object Relations in Psychoanalytic Theory* (Cambridge, Mass., and London: Harvard University Press, 1983). Influential works in this feminist object relations genre are: Nancy Chodorow, *The Reproduction of Mothering* (Berkeley: University of California Press, 1978) and Dorothy Dinnerstein, *The Mermaid and the Minotaur* (New York: Harper and Row, 1976). The more orthodox defense and utilization of psychoanalytic theory for feminist analysis is exemplified in Juliet Mitchell, *Psychoanalysis and Feminism* (New York: Random House, 1975) and "Introduction I," to Juliet Mitchell and Jaqueline Rose, eds, *Feminine Sexuality: Jacques Lacan and the École Freudienne* (New York: Norton, 1982). For an influential feminist criticism of psychoanalytic gender theory, see Luce Irigaray, *This Sex Which Is Not One*, trans. Catherine Porter (Ithaca: Cornell University Press, 1985) and *Speculum of the Other Woman*, trans. Gillian C. Gill (Ithaca: Cornell University Press, 1985). For an influential application of Chodorow and Dinnerstein to models of moral development, see Carol Gilligan, *In a Different Voice* (Cambridge, Mass., and London: Harvard University Press, 1982). A similarly influential application of object relations theory to the history and philosophy of science is Evelyn Keller, *Reflections on Gender and Science* (New York and London: Yale University Press, 1985).

3 For important contemporary discussions of the theoretical and political status of gender differences, see the following edited anthologies: Seyla Benhabib and Drucilla Cornell, eds, *Feminism as Critique*; Hester Eisenstein and Alice Jardine, eds, *The Future of Difference* (Boston: G. K. Hall, 1980); Alice Jardine and Paul Smith, eds, *Men in Feminism* (New York and London: Methuen, 1987); Linda Nicholson, ed., *Feminism/Postmodernism* (New York and London: Routledge, 1990).

4 Isaac Balbus, "Disciplining Women: Michel Foucault and the Power of Feminist Discourse," in Benhabib and Cornell, eds, *Feminism as Critique*, pp. 110–27, especially p. 112.

5 Coppélia Kahn, *Man's Estate: Masculine Identity in Shakespeare* (Berkeley: University of California Press, 1981), p. 10.

6 See Jessica Benjamin, "The Bonds of Love: Rational Violence and Erotic Domination," *Feminist Studies*, 6, spring 1980, pp. 144–74.

7 In Judith Lorber, Rose Laub Coser, Alice S. Rossi and Nancy Chodorow, "On *The Reproduction of Mothering:* A Methodological Debate," *Signs: Journal of Women in Culture and Society*, 6, spring 1981, pp. 482–513, especially pp. 502–3.

8 It may also be said that feminine experience yields distinct cognitive proclivities. However, feminine experience has not, until very recently, been systematically articulated in literate form, nor generalized into universalizing statements and theories about humanity, society and social inquiry. Given the contemporary instability of gender in conceptual as well as phenomenological terms, it is unlikely that "femininity" – or feminism, for that matter – will ever imitate or appropriate masculinity's hegemonic achievement.

9 Jerrold Seigel, *Marx's Fate: The Shape of a Life* (Princeton: Princeton University Press, 1978).

10 Ibid., p. 182.

11 On the links between heroism and masculinity, see the following: Christine Di Stefano, "Masculinity as Ideology in Political Theory: Hobbesian Man Considered," *Women's Studies International Forum*, 6, 1983, pp. 633–44; Hartsock, *Money, Sex and Power*, ch. 8; Marina Warner, *Joan of Arc: The Image of Female Heroism* (New York: Random House, 1981).

12 The little evidence that we do have of Henriette Marx's relationship to her son is one letter (reproduced in Seigel, *Marx's Fate*, p. 49) wherein she is solicitous of her son's health and well-being. We also know that she subsequently became critical of his inability to support himself and his family. The record also suggests that Marx showed little affection for her during his adult years and that he visited her infrequently, and then primarily to request money.

13 See Janice Moulton, "A Paradigm of Philosophy: The Adversary Method," in Sandra Harding and Merrill B. Hintikka, eds, *Discovering Reality* (Dordrecht: D. Reidel, 1983), pp. 149–64.

14 For helpful discussions of Marx's ontology, see the following: Norman Geras, *Marx and Human Nature: Refutation of a Legend* (London: New Left Books, 1983); Carol C. Gould, *Marx's Social Ontology: Individuality and Community in Marx's Theory of Social Reality* (Cambridge, Mass., and London: MIT Press, 1978); Bertell Ollman, *Alienation: Marx's Conception of Man in Capitalist Society* (Cambridge: Cambridge University Press, 1971).

15 For an original and helpful discussion of maternal subtexts, see Coppélia Kahn, "Excavating 'Those Dim Minoan Regions': Maternal Subtexts in Patriarchal Literature," *Diacritics: A Review of Contemporary Criticism*, 12, 1982, pp. 32–41.

16 Hartsock, *Money, Sex, and Power*, p. 146.

17 Karl Marx and Frederick Engels, *The German Ideology*, part I, ed. C. J. Arthur (New York: International Publishers, 1970), pp. 43–4, 51–2.

18 Hilary Rose, "Hand, Brain, and Heart: A Feminist Epistemology for the Natural Sciences," *Signs: Journal of Women in Culture and Society*, 9, autumn 1983, pp. 73–90, especially p. 75.

19 Marx and Engels, *The German Ideology*, p. 57.

20 Hartsock, *Money, Sex and Power*, p. 148.

21 *Capital*, vol. III (New York: International Publishers, 1967), p. 820.

22 See J. S. Mill, "Nature," in Marshall Cohen, ed., *The Philosophy of John Stuart Mill: Ethical, Political and Religious* (New York: Random House, 1961).

23 Isaac Balbus, *Marxism and Domination*, (Princeton: Princeton University Press, 1982), p. 269.

24 Ibid., p. 271.

25 Marx and Engels, *German Ideology*, 86.

26 O'Brien, *Politics of Reproduction*, pp. 37–8.

27 Karl Marx, *Economic and Philosophic Manuscripts*, in *Karl Marx: Selected Writings*, ed. David McLellan (Oxford: Oxford University Press, 1977), p. 93.

28 Consider the following passages from the *Economic and Philosophic Manuscripts*: "For socialist man what is called world history is nothing but the creation of man by human (sic) labor and the development of nature for man . . ." "Socialist man . . . has the observable and irrefutable proof of his self-creation and the process of his origin." "A being only counts itself as independent when it stands on its own two feet and it stands on its own two feet as long as it owes its existence to itself." Ibid., pp. 94, 95.

29 Robert Heilbroner, *Marxism: For and Against* (New York and London: Oxford University Press, 1980), p. 163.

30 Dennis Wrong, "The Oversocialized Conception of Man in Modern Sociology," *American Sociological Review*, 26, April 1961, pp. 183–93.

31 Jeremy Shapiro, "The Slime of History: Embeddedness in Nature and Critical Theory," in *On Critical Theory*, ed. John O'Neill (New York: Seabury Press, 1976), pp. 145–63, especially p. 149.

32 Silvia Bovenschen, "The Contemporary Witch, the Historical Witch, and the Witch Myth," *New German Critique*, 15, fall 1978, pp. 83–119, especially p. 117. The "revolt of nature" was theorized by Theodor Adorno and Max Horkheimer in *Dialectic of Enlightenment*. It has subsequently been reinvoked and extended by feminists seeking to articulate a critical theory of feminist ecology. What Adorno and Horkheimer saw in the trajectory of Enlightenment thought and practice was a steady "progress" in the domination of internal and external nature that was necessarily accompanied by social and affective regression. They were also attuned to the gendered dimensions of this dialectic. Women, as Adorno argued in another essay, were "not yet in the grasp of society" (that is, not in a position of power). Furthermore, they were implicated in the dialectic as beings thought to be more "natural" than men; and "where the mastery of nature is the true goal, biological inferiority remains a glaring stigma, the weakness imprinted by nature as a key stimulus to aggression." In other words, "uncivilized" aggression is unleashed by "civilized" men against "naturalized" women, nature, and other "others." Horkehimer and Adorno, *Dialectic of Enlightenment* (New York: Seabury Press, 1972), p. 248.

33 For explorations of the male appropriation of female reproductive powers, see the following: Azizah al-Hibri, "Reproduction, Mothering and the Origins of Patriarchy," in *Mothering: Essays in Feminist Theory*, ed. Joyce Trebilcot (Totowa, NJ: Rowman and Allanheld, 1983), pp. 81–93; Eva Feder Kittay, "Womb Envy: An Explanatory Concept," in the same collection, pp. 94–128; O'Brien, *Politics of Reproduction*.

34 Marx, *Capital*, quoted in Shapiro, "Slime of History," p. 148.

35 O'Brien, *Politics of Reproduction*, p. 53.

36 See Ulrike Prokop, "Production and the Context of Women's Daily Life," *New German Critique*, 13, winter 1978, pp. 18–33; and Sara Ruddick, "Maternal Thinking," in *Rethinking the Family: Some Feminist Questions*, ed.

Barrie Thorne and Marilyn Yalom (New York and London: Longman, 1982), pp. 76–94.

37 The following passage from the *Economic and Philosophical Manuscripts* is especially provocative in this regard: "The infinite degradation in which man exists for himself is expressed in his relationship to woman. . . . In this natural [sic] relationship of the sexes man's relationship to nature is immediately his relationship to man, and his relationship to man is immediately his relationship to nature . . . Thus, from this relationship the whole cultural level of man can be judged." In *Karl Marx: Selected Writings*, ed. McLellan, p. 62.

38 I want to thank Sara Lennox for this suggestion, even though I do not pursue it.

39 Balbus, *Marxism and Domination*, p. 269.

40 Mary O'Brien, "Between Critique and Community" (review of Nancy Hartsock's *Money, Sex, and Power*), *The Women's Review of Books*, 1, April 1984, p. 9.

9

Marital Slavery and Friendship: John Stuart Mill's *The Subjection of Women*

Mary Lyndon Shanley

John Stuart Mill's essay *The Subjection of Women* was one of the nineteenth century's strongest pleas for opening to women opportunities for suffrage, education, and employment. Although hailed by women's rights activists in its own day, it was rarely treated with much seriousness by Mill scholars and political theorists until feminists, beginning in the 1970s, demonstrated the centrality of its themes for feminist theory and political thought. Many feminists have, however, been ambivalent about the legacy of *The Subjection of Women*, seeing in it a brief for "equal rights," and questioning the efficacy of merely striking down legal barriers against women as the way to establish equality between the sexes. Mill's failure to extend his critique of inequality to the division of labor in the household, and his confidence that most women would choose marriage as a "career," in this view, subverted his otherwise egalitarian impulses.[1]

While fully acknowledging the limitations of "equal rights feminism," I argue in this essay that *The Subjection of Women* was not solely about equal opportunity for women. It was also, and more fundamentally, about the corruption of male–female relationships and the hope of establishing friendship in marriage. Such friendship was not only desirable for emotional satisfaction, it was crucial if marriage were to become, as Mill desired, a "school of genuine moral sentiment."[2] The fundamental assertion of *The Subjection of Women* was not that equal opportunity would ensure the liberation of women, but that male–female equality, however achieved, was essential to marital friendship and to the progression of human society.

Mill's vision of marriage as a locus of sympathy and understanding between autonomous adults not only reforms our understanding of his feminism, but also draws attention to an often submerged or ignored aspect of liberal political thought. Liberal individualism is attacked by Marxists and neo-conservatives alike as wrongly encouraging the disintegration of affective bonds and replacing them with merely self-interested economic and contractual ties. Mill's essay, however, emphasizes the value of noninstrumental relationships in human life. His depictions of both corrupt and well-ordered marriage traces the relationship of family order to right political order. His vision of marriage as a locus of mutual sympathy and understanding between autonomous adults stands as an unrealized goal for those who believe that the liberation of women requires not only formal equality of opportunity but measures which will enable couples to live in genuine equality, mutuality, and reciprocity.

The Perversion of Marriage by the Master–Slave Relationship

Mill's reconstruction of marriage on the basis of friendship was preceded by one of the most devastating critiques of male domination in marriage in the history of Western philosophy. In *The Subjection of Women* Mill repeatedly used the language of "master and slave" or "master and servant" to describe the relationship between husband and wife. In the first pages of the book, Mill called the dependence of women on men "the primitive state of slavery lasting on."[3] Later he said that despite the supposed advances of Christian civilization, "the wife is the actual bond-servant of her husband: no less so, as far as legal obligation goes, than slaves commonly so called."[4] Still later he asserted that "there remain no legal slaves, except the mistress of every house."[5] The theme of women's servitude was not confined to *The Subjection of Women*. In his speech on the Reform Bill of 1867, Mill talked of that "obscure feeling" which members of parliament were "ashamed to express openly" that women had no right to care about anything except "how they may be the most useful and devoted servants of some man."[6] To Auguste Comte he wrote comparing women to "domestic slaves" and noted that women's capacities were spent "seeking happiness not in their own life, but exclusively in the favor and affection of the other sex, which is only given to them on the condition of their dependence."[7]

But what did Mill mean by denouncing the "slavery" of married women? How strongly did he wish to insist on the analogy between married women and chattel slaves? While middle-class Victorian wives were clearly not subject to the suffering of chattel slaves, Mill chose the image quite deliberately to remind his readers that by marriage a husband assumed legal control of his wife's property and her body.[8] The social and economic system gave women little alternative except to marry; once married, the legal personality of the woman was subsumed in that of her husband; and the abuses of human dignity – including rape– permitted by custom and law within marriage were egregious.

In Mill's eyes, women were in a double bind: they were not free within marriage, and they were not truly free not to marry.[9] What could an unmarried woman do? Even if she were of the middle or upper classes, she could not attend any of the English universities, and thus she was barred from a systematic higher education. If somehow she acquired a professional education, the professional associations usually barred her from practicing her trade. "No sooner do women show themselves capable of competing with men in any career, than that career, if it be lucrative or honorable, is closed to them."[10] Mill's depiction of the plight of Elinor Garrett, sister of Millicent Garrett Fawcett, the suffrage leader, is telling:

> A young lady, Miss Garrett, . . . studied the medical profession. Having duly qualified, she . . . knocked successively at all the doors through which, by law, access is obtained into the medical profession. Having found all other doors fast shut, she fortunately discovered one which had accidentally been left ajar. The Society of Apothecaries, it seems, had forgotten to shut out those who they never thought would attempt to come in, and through this narrow entrance this young lady found her way into the profession. But so objectionable did it appear to this learned body that women should be the medical attendants even of women, that the narrow wicket through which Miss Garrett entered has been closed after her.[11]

Working-class women were even worse off. In the *Principles of Political Economy*, Mill argued that their low wages were due to the "prejudice" of society which "making almost every woman, socially speaking, an appendage of some man, enables men to take systematically the lion's share of whatever belongs to both." A second cause of low wages for women was the surplus of female labor for unskilled jobs. Law and custom ordained that a woman has "scarcely any means open to her of gaining a livelihood, except as a wife and mother."[12] Marriage was, as Mill put it, a "Hobson's choice" for women, "that or none."[13]

Worse than the social and economic pressure to marry, however, was women's status within marriage. Mill thoroughly understood the stipulations of the English common law which deprived a married woman of a legal personality independent of that of her husband. The doctrine of coverture or spousal unity, as it was called, was based on the Biblical notion that "a man [shall] leave his father and his mother, and shall cleave to his wife, and they shall be one flesh" (Genesis 2:24). If "one flesh," then, as Blackstone put it, "by marriage, the husband and wife are one person in law." And that "person" was represented by the husband. Again Blackstone was most succinct: "The very being or legal existence of the woman is suspended during the marriage, or at least is incorporated and consolidated into that of the husband."[14] One of the most commonly felt injustices of the doctrine of spousal unity was the married woman's lack of ownership of her own earnings. As the matrimonial couple was "one person," the wife's earnings during marriage were owned and controlled by her husband.[15] During his term as a member of parliament, Mill supported a Married Women's Property Bill, saying that its opponents were men who thought it impossible for "society to exist on a harmonious footing between two persons unless one of them has absolute power over the other," and insisting that England has moved beyond such a "savage stage."[16] In *The Subjection of Women* Mill argued that the "wife's position under the common law of England [with respect to property] is worse than that of slaves in the laws of many countries: by the Roman law, for example, a slave might have his peculium, which to a certain extent the law guaranteed to him for his exclusive use."[17] Similarly, Mill regarded the husband's exclusive guardianship over the married couple's children as a sign of the woman's dependence on her husband's will.[18] She was, in his eyes, denied any role in life except that of being "the personal body-servant of a despot."[19]

The most egregious aspects of both common and statute law, however, were those which sanctioned domestic violence. During the parliamentary debates on the Representation of the People Bill in 1867, Mill argued that women needed suffrage to enable them to lobby for legislation which would punish domestic assault:

> I should like to have a Return laid before this House of the number of women who are annually beaten to death, or trampled to death by their male protectors; and, in an opposite column, the amount of sentence passed.
> . . . I should also like to have, in a third column, the amount of property, the wrongful taking of which was . . . thought worthy of the same punishment. We should then have an arithmetical value set by a male legislature and male tribunals on the murder of a woman.[20]

But the two legal stipulations which to Mill most demonstrated "the assimilation of the wife to the slave" were her inability to refuse her master "the last familiarity" and her inability to obtain a legal separation from her husband unless he added desertion or extreme cruelty to his adultery. Mill was appalled by the notion that no matter how brutal a tyrant a husband might be, and no matter how a woman might loathe him, "he can claim from her and enforce the lowest degradation of a human being," which was to be made the instrument of "an animal function contrary to

her inclination."[21] A man and wife being one body, rape was by definition
a crime which a married man could not commit against his own wife. By
law a wife could not leave her husband on account of this offense without
being guilty of desertion, nor could she prosecute him. The most vicious
form of male domination of women according to Mill was rape within
marriage; it was particularly vicious because it was legal. Mill thus talked
not of individual masters and wives as aberrations, but of a legally
sanctioned system of domestic slavery which shaped the character of
marriage in his day.[22]

Mill's depiction of marriage departed radically from the majority of
Victorian portrayals of home and hearth. John Ruskin's praise of the
home in *Sesame and Lilies* reflected the feelings and aspirations of many:
"This is the true nature of home – it is the place of Peace; the shelter, not
only from all injury, but from all terror, doubt, and division. . . . It is a
sacred place, a vestal temple, a temple of the hearth watched over by
Household Gods."[23] Walter Houghton remarked that the title of Coventry
Patmore's poem, *The Angel in the House*, captured "the essential character
of Victorian love," and reflected "the exaltation of family life and feminine
character" characteristic of the mid-nineteenth century.[24] James Fitzjames
Stephen, who wrote that he disagreed with *The Subjection of Women* "from
the first sentence to the last," found not only Mill's ideas but his very
effort to discuss the dynamics of marriage highly distasteful. "There is
something – I hardly know what to call it; indecent is too strong a word,
but I may say unpleasant in the direction of indecorum – in prolonged and
minute discussions about the relations between men and women, and the
character of women as such."[25]

The Subjection of Women challenged much more than Victorian decorum,
however; it was a radical challenge to one of the most fundamental and
preciously held assumptions about marriage in the modern era, which is
that it was a relationship grounded on the consent of the partners to join
their lives. Mill argued to the contrary that the presumed consent of
women to marry was not, in any real sense, a free promise, but one
socially coerced by the lack of meaningful options. Further, the laws of
marriage deprived a woman of many of the normal powers of autonomous
adults, from controlling her earnings, to entering contracts, to defending
her bodily autonomy by resisting unwanted sexual relations. Indeed, the
whole notion of a woman "consenting" to the marriage "offer" of a man
implied from the outset a hierarchical relationship. Such a one-way offer
did not reflect the relationship which should exist between those who were
truly equal, among beings who should be able to create together by free
discussion and mutual agreement an association to govern their lives
together.

In addition, Mill's view of marriage as slavery suggested a significantly more complicated and skeptical view of what constituted a "free choice" in society than did either his own earlier works or those of his liberal predecessors. Hobbes, for example, regarded men as acting "freely" even when moved by fear for their lives. Locke disagreed, but he in turn talked about the individual's free choice to remain a citizen of his father's country, as if emigration were a readily available option for all. In other of his works Mill himself seemed overly sanguine about the amount of real choice enjoyed, for example, by wage laborers in entering a trade. Yet Mill's analysis of marriage demonstrated the great complexity of establishing that any presumed agreement was the result of free volition, and the fatuousness of presuming that initial consent could create perpetual obligation. By implication, the legitimacy of many other relationships, including supposedly free wage and labor agreements and the political obligation of enfranchised and unenfranchised alike, was thrown into question. *The Subjection of Women* exposed the inherent fragility of traditional conceptualizations of free choice, autonomy, and self-determination so important to liberals, showing that economic and social structures were bound to limit and might coerce any person's choice of companions, employment, or citizenship.

Mill did not despair of the possibility that marriages based on true consent would be possible. He believed that some individuals even in his own day established such associations of reciprocity and mutual support. (He counted his own relationship with Harriet Taylor Mill as an example of a marriage between equals.)[26] But there were systematic impediments to marital equality. To create conditions conducive to a marriage of equals rather than one of master and slave, marriage law itself would have to be altered, women would have to be provided equal educational and employment opportunity, and both men and women would have to become capable of sustaining genuinely equal and reciprocal relationships within marriage. The last of these, in Mill's eyes, posed the greatest challenge.

The Fear of Equality

Establishing legal equality in marriage and equality of opportunity would require, said Mill, that men sacrifice those political, legal, and economic advantages they enjoyed "simply by being born male." Mill therefore supported such measures as women's suffrage, the Married Women's Property Bills, the Divorce Act of 1857, the repeal of the Contagious Diseases Acts, and the opening of higher education and the professions to women. Suffrage, Mill contended, would both develop women's faculties through participation in civic decisions and enable married women to protect themselves from male-imposed injustices such as lack of rights to child custody and to control of their income. Access to education and jobs would give women alternatives to marriage. It would also provide a woman whose marriage turned out badly some means of self-support if separated or divorced. The Divorce Act of 1857, which established England's first civil divorce courts, would enable women and men to escape from intolerable circumstances (although Mill rightly protested the sexual double standard ensconced in the Act by which men might divorce their wives for adultery, but women had to prove their husbands were guilty of incest, bigamy or cruelty as well as adultery). And for those few women with an income of their own, a Married Women's Property Act would recognize their independent personalities and enable them to meet their husbands more nearly as equals.

However, Mill's analysis went further. He insisted that the subjection of women could not be ended by law alone, but only by law and the reformation of education, of opinion, of social inculcation, of habits, and finally of the conduct of family life itself. This was so because the root of much of men's resistance to women's emancipaton was not simply their reluctance to give up their position of material advantage, but many men's fear of living with an equal. It was to retain marriage as "a law of despotism" that men shut all other occupations to women, Mill contended.[27] Men who "have a real antipathy to the equal freedom of women" were at bottom afraid "lest [women] should insist that marriage be on equal conditions."[28] One of Mill's central assertions in *The Subjection of Women* was that "[women's] disabilities [in law] are only clung to in order to maintain their subordination in domestic life: *because the generality of the male sex cannot yet tolerate the idea of living with an equal*" (emphasis added).[29] The public discrimination against women was a manifestation of a disorder rooted in family relationships.

Mill did not offer any single explanation or account of the origin of men's fear of female equality. Elsewhere, he attributed the general human resistance to equality to the fear of the loss of privilege, and to apprehensions concerning the effect of levelling on political order.[30] But these passages on the fear of spousal equality bring to a twentieth-century mind the psycho-analytic works about human neuroses and the male fear of women caused by the infant boy's relationship to the seemingly all-powerful mother, source of both nurturance and love and of deprivation and punishment.[31] Mill's own account of the fear of equality was not psychoanalytic. He did, however, undertake to depict the consequences of marital inequality both for the individual psyche and for social justice. The rhetorical purpose of *The Subjection of Women* was not only to convince men that their treatment of women in law was unjust, but also that their treatment of women in the home was self-defeating, even self-destructive.

Women were those most obviously affected by the denial of association with men on equal footing. Women's confinement to domestic concerns was a wrongful "forced repression."[32] Mill shared Aristotle's view that participation in civic life was an enriching and ennobling activity, but Mill saw that for a woman, no public-spirited dimension to her life was possible. There was no impetus to consider with others the principles which were to govern their common life, no incentive to conform to principles which defined their mutual activity for the common good, no possibility for the self-development which comes from citizen activity.[33] The cost to women was obvious; they were dull or petty, or unprincipled.[34] The cost to men was less apparent but no less real; in seeking a reflection of themselves in the consciousness of these stunted women, men deceived, deluded, and limited themselves.

Mill was convinced that men were corrupted by their dominance over women. The most corrupting element of male domination of women was that men learned to "worship their own will as such a grand thing that it is actually the law for another rational being."[35] Such self-worship arises at a very tender age, and blots out a boy's natural understanding of himself and his relationship to others.

A boy may be "the most frivolous and empty or the most ignorant and stolid of mankind," but "by the mere fact of being born a male" he is encouraged to think that "he is by right the superior of all and every one of an entire half of the human race: including probably some whose real superiority he has daily or hourly occasion to feel."[36] By contrast, women were taught "to live for others" and "to have no life but in their affections," and then further to confine their affections to "the men with whom they are connected, or to the children who constitute an additional indefeasible tie between them and a man."[37] The result of this upbringing was that what women would tell men was not, could not be, wholly true; women's sensibilities were systematically warped by their subjection. Thus the reflections were not accurate and men were deprived of self-knowledge.

The picture which emerged was strikingly similar to that which Hegel described in his passages on the relationship between master and slave in *The Phenomenology of Mind.*[38] The lord who sees himself solely as master, wrote Hegel, cannot obtain an independent self-consciousness. The master thinks he is autonomous, but in fact he relies totally upon his slaves, not only to fulfill his needs and desires, but also for his identity: "Without slaves, he is no master." The master could not acquire the fullest self-consciousness when the "other" in whom he viewed himself was in the reduced human condition of slavery: to be *merely* a master was to fall short of full self-consciousness, and to define himself in terms of the "thing" he owns. So for Mill, men who have propagated the belief that all men are superior to all women have fatally affected the dialectic involved in knowing oneself through the consciousness others have of one. The present relationship between the sexes produced in men that "self-worship" which "all privileged persons, and all privileged classes" have had. That distortion deceives men and other privileged groups as to both their character and their self-worth.

No philosopher prior to Mill had developed such a sustained argument about the corrupting effects on men of their social superiority over and separation from women. Previous philosophers had argued either that the authority of men over women was natural (Aristotle, Grotius), or that while there was no natural dominance of men over women prior to the establishment of families, in any civil society such preeminence was necessary to settle the dispute over who should govern the household (Locke), or the result of women's consent in return for protection (Hobbes), or the consequence of the development of the sentiments of nurturance and love (Rousseau).[39] None had suggested that domestic arrangements might diminish a man's ability to contribute to public debates in the *agora* or to the rational governing of a democratic republic. Yet Mill was determined to show that the development of the species was held in check by that domestic slavery produced by the fear of equality, by spousal hierarchy, and by a lack of the reciprocity and mutuality of true friendship.

The Hope of Friendship

Mill's remedy for the evils generated by the fear of equality was his notion of marital friendship. The topic of the rather visionary fourth chapter of *The Subjection of Women* was friendship, "the ideal of marriage."[40] That ideal was, according to Mill, "a union of thoughts and inclinations" which created a "foundation of solid friendship" between husband and wife.[41]

Mill's praise of marital friendship was almost lyrical, and struck resonances with Aristotle's, Cicero's, and Montaigne's similar exaltations of the pleasures as well as the moral enrichment of this form of human intimacy. Mill wrote:

> When each of two persons, instead of being a nothing, is a something; when they are attached to one another, and are not too much unlike to begin with; the constant partaking of the same things, assisted by their sympathy, draws out the latent capacities of each for being interested in the things . . . by a real enriching of the two natures, each acquiring the tastes and capacities of the other in addition to its own.[42]

This expansion of human capacities did not, however, exhaust the benefits of friendhsip. Most importantly, friendship developed what Montaigne praised as the abolition of selfishness, the capacity to regard another human being as fully as worthy as oneself. Therefore friendship of the highest order could only exist between those equal in excellence.[43] And for precisely this reason, philosophers from Aristotle to Hegel had consistently argued that women could not be men's friends, for women lacked the moral capacity for the highest forms of friendship. Indeed, it was common to distinguish the marital bond from friendship not solely on the basis of sexual and procreative activity, but also because women could not be part of the school of moral virtue which was found in friendship at its best.

Mill therefore made a most significant break with the past in adopting the language of friendship in his discussion of marriage. For Mill, no less than for any of his predecessors, "the true virtue of human beings is the fitness to live together as equals." Such equality required that individuals "[claim] nothing for themselves but what they as freely concede to every one else," that they regard command of any kind as "an exceptional necessity," and that they prefer whenever possible "the society of those with whom leading and following can be alternate and reciprocal."[44] This picture of reciprocity, of the shifting of leadership according to need, was a remarkable characterization of family life. Virtually all of Mill's liberal contemporaries accepted the notion of the natural and inevitable complimentariness of male and female personalities and roles. Mill, however, as early as 1833 had expressed his belief that "the highest masculine and the highest feminine" characters were without any real distinction.[45] That view of the androgynous personality lent support to Mill's brief for equality within the family.

Mill repeatedly insisted that his society had no general experience of "the marriage relationship as it would exist between equals," and that such marriages would be impossible until men rid themselves of the fear of equality and the will to domination.[46] The liberation of women, in other words, required not just legal reform but a reeducation of the passions. Women were to be regarded as equals not only to fulfill the demand for individual rights and in order that they could survive in the public world of work, but also in order that women and men could form ethical relations of the highest order. Men and women alike had to "learn to cultivate their strongest sympathy with an equal in rights and in cultivation."[47] Mill struggled, not always with total success, to talk about the quality of such association. For example, in *On Liberty*, Mill explicitly rejected von Humbolt's characterization of marriage as a contractual relationship which could be ended by "the declared will of either party to dissolve it." That kind of dissolution was appropriate when the benefits of partnership could be reduced to monetary terms. But marriage involved a person's expectations for the fulfillment of a "plan of life," and created "a new series of moral obligations . . . toward that person, which may possibly be overruled, but cannot be ignored."[48] Mill was convinced that difficult though it might be to shape the law to recognize the moral imperatives of such a relationship, there were ethical communities which transcended and were not reducible to their individual components.

At this juncture, however, the critical force of Mill's essay weakened, and a tension developed between his ideal and his prescriptions for his own society. For all his insight into the dynamics of domestic domination and subordination, the only specific means Mill in fact put forward for the fostering of this society of equals was providing equal opportunity to women in areas outside the family. Indeed, in *On Liberty* he wrote that "nothing more is needed for the complete removal of [the almost despotic power of husbands over wives] than that wives should have the same rights and should receive the same protection of law in the same manner, as all other persons."[49] In the same vein, Mill seemed to suggest that nothing more was needed for women to achieve equality than that "the present duties and protective bounties in favour of men should be recalled."[50] Moreover, Mill did not attack the traditional assumption about men's and women's different responsibilities in an ongoing household, although he was usually careful to say that women "chose" their role or that it was the most "expedient" arrangement, not that it was theirs by "nature."

Mill by and large accepted the notion that once they marry, women should be solely responsible for the care of the household and children, men for providing the family income: "When the support of the family depends . . . on earnings, the common arrangement, by which the man earns the income and the wife superintends the domestic expenditure, seems to me in general the most suitable division of labour between the two persons."[51] He did not regard it as "a desirable custom, that the wife should contribute by her labour to the income of the family."[52] Mill indicated that women alone would care for any children of the marriage; repeatedly he called it the "care which . . . nobody else takes," the one vocation in which there is "nobody to compete with them," and the occupation which "cannot be fulfilled by others."[53] Further, Mill seemed to shut the door on combining household duties and a public life: "like a man when he chooses a profession, so, when a woman marries, it may be in general understood that she makes a choice of the management of a household, and the bringing up of a family, as the first call upon her exertions . . . and that she renounces . . . all [other occupations] which are not consistent with the requirements of this."[54]

Mill's acceptance of the traditional gender-based division of labor in the family has led some critics to fault Mill for supposing that legal equality of opportunity would solve the problem of women's subjection, even while leaving the sexual division of labor in the household intact. For example, Julia Annas, after praising Mill's theoretical arguments in support of equality, complains that Mill's suggestions for actual needed changes in sex roles are "timid and reformist at best. He assumes that most women

will in fact want only to be wives and mothers."[55] Leslie Goldstein agrees
that "the restraints which Mill believed should be imposed on married
women constitute a major exception to his argument for equality of
individual liberty between the sexes – an exception so enormous that it
threatens to swallow up the entire argument."[56] But such arguments,
while correctly identifying the limitations of antidiscrimination statutes as
instruments for social change, incorrectly identify Mill's argument for
equal opportunity as the conclusion of his discussion of male–female
equality.[57] On the contrary, Mill's final prescription to end the subjection
of women was not equal opportunity but spousal friendship; equal opportunity was a means whereby such friendship could be encouraged.

The theoretical force of Mill's condemnation of domestic hierarchy has
not yet been sufficiently appreciated. Mill's commitment to equality in
marriage was of a different theoretical order than his acceptance of a
continued sexual division of labor. On the one hand, Mill's belief in the
necessity of equality as a precondition to marital friendship was a profound
theoretical tenet. It rested on the normative assumption that human
relationships between equals were of a higher, more enriching order than
those between unequals. Mill's belief that equality was more suitable to
friendship than inequality was as unalterable as his conviction that democracy was a better system of government than despotism; the human spirit
could not develop its fullest potential when living in absolute subordination
to another human being or to government.[58] On the other hand, Mill's
belief that friendship could be attained and sustained while women bore
nearly exclusive responsibility for the home was a statement which might
be modified or even abandoned if experience proved it to be wrong. In this
sense it was like Mill's view that the question of whether socialism was
preferable to capitalism could not be settled by verbal argument alone but
must "work itself out on an experimental scale, by actual trial."[59] Mill
believed that marital equality was a moral imperative; his view that such
equality might exist where married men and women moved in different
spheres of activity was a proposition subject to demonstration. Had Mill
discovered that managing the household to the exclusion of most other
activity created an impediment to the friendship of married women and
men, *The Subjection of Women* suggests that he would have altered his view
of practicable domestic arrangements, but not his commitment to the
desirability of male–female friendship in marriage.

The most interesting shortcomings of Mill's analysis are thus not found
in his belief in the efficacy of equal opportunity, but rather in his blindness
to what other conditions might hinder or promote marital friendship. In
his discussion of family life, for example, Mill seemed to forget his own
warning that women could be imprisoned not only "by actual law" but
also "by custom equivalent to law."[60] Similarly, he overlooked his own

cautionary observation that in any household "there will naturally be more potential voice on the side, whichever it is, that brings the means of support."[61] And although he had brilliantly depicted the narrowness and petty concerns of contemporary women who were totally excluded from political participation, he implied that the mistresses of most households might content themselves simply with exercising the suffrage (were it to be granted), a view hardly consistent with his arguments in other works for maximizing the level of political discussion and participation whenever possible. More significantly, however, Mill ignored the potential barrier between husband and wife which such different adult life experiences might create, and the contribution of shared experience to building a common sensibility and strengthening the bonds of friendship.

Mill also never considered that men might take any role in the family other than providing the economic means of support. Perhaps Mill's greatest oversight in his paean of marital equality was his failure to entertain the possibilities that nurturing and caring for children might provide men with useful knowledge and experience, and that shared parenting would contribute to the friendship between spouses which he so ardently desired. Similarly, Mill had virtually nothing to say about the positive role which sex might play in marriage. The sharp language with which he condemned undesired sexual relations as the execution of "an animal function" was nowhere supplemented by an appreciation of the possible enhancement which sexuality might add to marital friendship. One of the striking features of Montaigne's lyrical praise of friendship was that it was devoid of sensuality, for Montaigne abhorred "the Grecian license," and he was adamant that women were incapable of the highest forms of friendship. Mill's notion of spousal friendship suggested the possibility of a friendship which partook of both a true union of minds and of a physical expression of the delight in one's companion, a friendship which involved all of the human faculties. It was an opportunity which (undoubtedly to the relief of those such as James Fitzjames Stephen) Mill himself was not disposed to use, but which was nonetheless implicit in his praise of spousal friendship.[62]

One cannot ask Mill or any other theorist to "jump over Rhodes" and address issues not put forward by conditions and concerns of his own society.[63] Nevertheless, even leaving aside an analysis of the oppression inherent in the class structure (an omission which would have to be rectified in a full analysis of liberation), time has made it clear that Mill's prescriptions alone will not destroy the master–slave relationship which he so detested. Women's aspirations for equality will not be met by insuring equal civic rights and equal access to jobs outside the home. To accomplish that end would require a transformation of economic and public structures which would allow wives and husbands to share those domestic tasks which Mill assigned exclusively to women. In their absence it is as foolish to talk about couples choosing the traditional division of labor in marriage as it was in Mill's day to talk about women choosing marriage: both are Hobson's choices, there are no suitable alternatives save at enormous costs to the individuals involved.

Mill's feminist vision, however, transcends his own immediate prescriptions for reform. *The Subjection of Women* is not only one of liberalism's most incisive arguments for equal opportunity, but it embodies as well a belief in the importance of friendship for human development and progress. The recognition of individual rights is important in Mill's view because it provides part of the groundwork for more important human relationships of trust, mutuality and reciprocity. Mill's plea for an end to the subjection of women is not made, as critics such as Gertrude Himmelfarb assert, in the name of "the absolute primacy of the individual," but in the name of the need of both men and women for community. Mill's essay is valuable both for its devastating critique of the corruption of marital inequality, and for its argument, however incomplete, that one of the aims of a liberal polity should be to promote the conditions which will allow friendship, in marriage and elsewhere, to take root and flourish.

Notes

1 Contemporary authors who criticize Mill's analysis of equal opportunity for women as not far-reaching enough are Julia Annas, "Mill and the Subjection of Women," *Philosophy*, 52, 1977, pp. 179–94; Leslie F. Goldstein, "Mill, Marx, and Women's Liberation," *Journal of the History of Philosophy*, 18, 1980, pp. 319–34; Richard Krouse, "Patriarchal Liberalism and Beyond: From John Stuart Mill to Harriet Taylor," in *The Family in Political Thought*, ed. Jean Bethke Elshtain (Amherst: University of Massachusetts Press, 1982), pp. 145–72; Susan Moller Okin, *Women in Western Political Thought* (Princeton: Princeton University Press, 1979). From a different perspective, Gertrude Himmelfarb, *On Liberty and Liberalism: The Case of John Stuart Mill* (New York: Alfred Knopf, 1974) criticizes Mill's doctrine of equality as being too absolute and particularly takes issue with modern feminist applications of his theory.

2 J. S. Mill, *The Subjection of Women* (1869) in *Essays on Sex Equality*, ed. Alice Rossi (Chicago: University of Chicago Press, 1970), ch. 2, p. 173.

3 Ibid., ch. 1, p. 130.

4 Ibid., ch. 2, p. 158.

5 Ibid., ch. 4, p. 217.

6 Hansard, *Parliamentary Debates*, series 3, vol. 187 (May 20, 1867), p. 820.

7 Letter to August Comte, October, 1843, in *The Collected Works of John Stuart Mill*, vol. XIII, *The Earlier Letters*, ed. Francis C. Mineka (Toronto: University of Toronto Press, 1963), p. 609, my translation.

8 For an assessment of black slave women's possession by their masters, see

Jacqueline Jones, *Labor of Love, Labor of Sorrow: Black Women, Work, and the Family from Slavery to the Present* (New York: Basic Books, 1985).

9 Mill's analysis of women's choice of marriage as a state of life reminds one of Hobbes's discussion of some defeated soldier giving his consent to the rule of a conquering sovereign. Women, it is true, could decide which among several men to marry, while Hobbes's defeated yeoman had no choice of master. But what could either do but join the only protective association available to each?

10 Hansard, vol. 187 (May 20, 1867), p. 827.

11 Ibid. In the United States, one well-documented case in which a woman was prohibited from practicing law was *Bradwell v Illinois*, 83 US (16 Wall) 130 (1873).

12 J. S. Mill, *The Principles of Political Economy* (1848) in *Collected Works*, vol. II, p. 394, and vol. III, pp. 765–6.

13 *Subjection of Women*, ch. 1, p. 156. Tobias Hobson, a Cambridge carrier commemorated by Milton in two Epigraphs, would only hire out the horse nearest the door of his stable, even if a client wanted another. *Oxford English Dictionary*, II, p. 369.

14 William Blackstone, *Commentaries on the Laws of England* (4 vols, Oxford: Clarendon Press, 1765–69), Book I, ch. XV, p. 430.

15 The rich found ways around the common law's insistence that the management and use of any income belonged to a woman's husband, by setting up trusts which were governed by the laws and courts of equity. A succinct explanation of the law of property as it affected married women in the nineteenth century is found in Erna Reiss, *Rights and Duties of Englishwomen* (Manchester: Sheratt and Hughes, 1934), pp. 20–34.

16 Hansard, vol. 192 (June 10, 1868), p. 1371. Several Married Women's Property Bills, which would have given married women possession of their earnings, were presented in parliament beginning in 1857, but none was successful until 1870.

17 *Subjection of Women*, ch. 2, pp. 158–9.

18 Ibid., p. 160.

19 Ibid., p. 161.

20 Hansard, vol. 187 (May 20, 1867), p. 826.

21 *Subjection of Women*, ch. 2, pp. 160–1.

22 For a full discussion of the legal disabilities of married women in Mill's day see Mary Lyndon Shanley, *Feminism, Marriage and the Law in Victorian England, 1850–1895* (Princeton: Princeton University Press, 1989).

23 John Ruskin, "Of Queen's Gardens," in *Works*, ed. E. T. Cook and A. D. C. Wedderburn (39 vols. London: G. Allen, 1902–12), vol. XVIII, p. 122.

24 Walter E. Houghton, *The Victorian Frame of Mind* (New Haven: Yale University Press, 1957), p. 344.

25 James Fitzjames Stephen, *Liberty, Equality, Fraternity* (New York: Henry Holt, n.d.), p. 206.

26 On the relationship between John Stuart Mill and Harriet Taylor see F. A. Hayek, *John Stuart Mill and Harriet Taylor; Their Correspondence and Subsequent Marriage* (Chicago: University of Chicago Press, 1951); Michael St. John Packe, *The Life of John Stuart Mill* (New York: Macmillan, 1954); Alice Rossi,

"Sentiment and Intellect," in *Essays on Sex Equality*, ed. Rossi; and Himmelfarb, *On Liberty and Liberalism*, pp. 187–238.

27 *Subjection of Women*, ch. 1, p. 156.

28 Ibid.

29 Ibid., ch. 3, p. 181.

30 For a discussion of Mill's views on equality generally, see Dennis Thompson, *John Stuart Mill and Representative Government* (Princeton: Princeton University Press, 1976), pp. 158–73.

31 For a reading of Mill from this perspective which challenges my own, see Christine Di Stefano, "Rereading J. S. Mill: Interpolations from the (M)Otherworld," in *Discontented Discourses: Feminism/Textual Intervention/Psychoanalysis*, ed. M. Barr and R. Feldstein (Urbana: University of Illinois Press, 1989). See also Linda Zerilli, *"Women" in Political Theory: Agents of Culture and Chaos* (Madison: University of Wisconsin, 1990).

32 *Subjection of Women*, ch. 1, p. 148.

33 See also Mill's *Considerations on Representative Government* (1861), in *Collected Works*, vol. XIX, pp. 399–400, 411. During his speech on the Reform Bill of 1867, Mill argued that giving women the vote would provide "that stimulus to their faculties . . . which the suffrage seldom fails to produce." Hansard, vol. 189 (May 20, 1867), p. 824.

34 *Subjection of Women*, ch. 2, p. 168, and ch. 4, p. 238.

35 Ibid., ch. 2, p. 172.

36 Ibid., ch. 4, p. 218.

37 Ibid., ch. 1, p. 141.

38 G. W. F. Hegel, *The Phenomenology of Mind*, trans. J. B. Baillie (New York: Harper and Row, 1969). This paragraph is indebted to the excellent study of the *Phenomenology* by Judith N. Shklar, *Freedom and Independence* (Cambridge: Cambridge University Press, 1976), from which the quote is taken, p. 61. Mill's analysis also calls to mind Simone de Beauvoir's discussion of "the Other" and its role in human consciousness in *The Second Sex*, trans. H. M. Parshley (New York: Random House, Vintage Books, 1974), pp. xix ff.

39 For studies of the views of each of these authors on women (except for Grotius) see Okin. Grotius' views can be found in his *De Juri Belli et Pacis Libri Tres (On the Law of War and Peace)* (1625), trans. Francis W. Kelsey (Oxford: Clarendon Press, 1925), Book II, ch. 5, section i, p. 231.

40 *Subjection of Women*, ch. 4, pp. 233, 235.

41 Ibid., pp. 231, 233.

42 Ibid., p. 233.

43 Montaigne's essay, "Of Friendship" in *The Complete Works of Montaigne*, trans. Donald M. Frame (Stanford: Stanford University Press, 1948), pp. 135–44.

44 *Subjection of Women*, ch. 4, pp. 174–5.

45 Letter to Thomas Carlyle, October 5, 1833, in *Collected Works*, vol. XII, *Earlier Letters*, p. 184.

46 Letter to John Nichol, August 1869, in *Collected Works*, vol. XVII, *The Later Letters*, ed. Francis C. Mineka and Dwight N. Lindley (Toronto: University of Toronto Press, 1972), p. 1634.

47 *Subjection of Women*, ch. 4, p. 236.

180   *Mary Lyndon Shanley*

48 *Collected Works*, vol. XVIII, p. 300. Elsewhere Mill wrote, "My opinion on Divorce is that . . . nothing ought to be rested in, short of entire freedom on both sides to dissolve this like any other partnership." Letter to an unidentified correspondent, November 1855, *Collected Works*, vol. XIV, *Later Letters*, p. 500. But against this letter was the passage from *On Liberty*, and his letter to Henry Rusden of July 1870 in which he abjured making any final judgments about what a proper divorce law would be "until women have an equal voice in making it." He denied that he advocated that marriage should be dissoluble "at the will of either party," and stated that no well-grounded opinion could be put forward until women first achieved equality under the laws and in married life. *Collected Works*, vol. XVII, *Later Letters*, pp. 1750–1.

49 *Collected Works*, vol. XVIII, p. 301.

50 *Subjection of Women*, ch. 1, p. 154.

52 Ibid., ch. 2, p. 179.

53 Ibid., ch. 2, p. 178; ch. 3, p. 183; ch. 4, p. 241.

54 Ibid., ch. 1, p. 179.

55 Annas, "Mill and the Subjection of Women," p. 189.

56 Goldstein, "Mill, Marx and Women's Liberation," p. 328.

57 Richard Krouse points out that Mill's own "ideal of a reformed family life, based upon a full nonpatriarchal marriage bond," requires "on the logic of his own analysis. . . [the] rejection of the traditional division of labor between the sexes." Krouse, "Patriarchal Liberalism," p. 39.

58 *Considerations on Representative Government*, in *Collected Works*, vol. XIX, pp. 399–403.

59 *Chapters on Socialism* (1879), in *Collected Works*, vol. V, p. 736.

60 *Subjection of Women*, ch. 4, p. 241.

61 Ibid., ch. 2, p. 170.

62 Throughout his writings Mill displayed a tendency to dismiss or deprecate the erotic dimension of life. In his *Autobiography* he wrote approvingly that his father looked forward to an increase in freedom in relations between the sexes, freedom which would be devoid of any sensuality "either of a theoretical or of a practical kind." His own 20-year friendship with Harriet Taylor before their marriage was "one of strong affection and confidential intimacy only." *Autobiography of John Stuart Mill* (New York: Columbia Unviersity Press, 1944), pp. 75, 161. In *The Principles of Political Economy* Mill remarked that in his own day "the animal instinct" occupied a "disproportionate preponderance in human life." *Collected Works*, vol. III, p. 766.

63 G. W. F. Hegel, *The Philosophy of Right*, ed. T. M. Knox (London: Oxford University Press, 1952), p. 11, quoted in Krouse, "Patriarchal Liberalism," p. 40.

10

John Rawls: Justice as Fairness – For Whom?

Susan Moller Okin

Theories of justice are centrally concerned with whether, how, and why persons should be treated differently from each other. Which initial or acquired characteristics or positions in society, they ask, legitimize differential treatment of persons by social institutions, laws and customs? In particular, how should beginnings affect outcomes? Since we live in a society in whose past the innate characteristic of sex has been regarded as one of the clearest legitimizers of different rights and restrictions, both formal and informal, the division of humanity into two sexes would seem to provide an obvious subject for such inquiries. But the deeply entrenched social institutionalization of sexual difference, which I will refer to as "the gender system" or simply "gender," has rarely been subjected to the tests of justice. When we turn to the great tradition of Western political thought with questions about the justice of gender in mind, it is to little avail.[1] Except for rare exceptions, such as John Stuart Mill, those who hold central positions in the tradition almost never questioned the justice of the subordination of women. When we turn to contemporary theories of justice, however, we might expect to find more illuminating and positive contributions to the subject of gender and justice. In this essay, I turn to John Rawls's extremely influential *A Theory of Justice*, to see not only what it says explicitly on the subject but also what undeveloped potential it has as we try to answer the question "How just is gender?"[2]

There is little indication throughout most of *A Theory of Justice* that the modern liberal society to which the principles of justice are to be applied is deeply and pervasively gender structured. Thus an ambiguity runs throughout the work, which is continually noticeable to anyone reading it from a feminist perspective. On the one hand, as I shall argue below, a consistent and wholehearted application of Rawls's liberal principles of justice can lead us to challenge fundamentally the gender system of our society. On the other hand, in his own account of his theory, this challenge is barely hinted at, much less developed. The major reason is that throughout most of the argument, it is assumed (as throughout almost the entire liberal tradition) that the appropriate subjects of political theories are not all adult individuals, but heads of families. As a result, although Rawls indicates on several occasions that a person's sex is a morally arbitrary and contingent characteristic, and although he states initially that the family itself is one of those basic social institutions to which the principles of justice must apply, his theory of justice develops neither of these convictions.

Rawls, like almost all political theorists until very recent years, employs in *A Theory of Justice* supposedly generic male terms of reference.[3] "Men," "mankind," "he" and "his" are interspersed with gender-neutral terms of reference such as "individual" and "moral person." Examples of inter-generational concern are worded in terms of "fathers" and "sons," and the difference principle is said to correspond to "the principle of fraternity."[4] This linguistic usage would perhaps be less significant if it were not for the fact that Rawls is self-consciously a member of a long tradition of moral and political philosophy that has used in its arguments either such sup-posedly generic male terms, or even more inclusive terms of reference ("human beings," "persons," "all rational beings as such"), only to exclude women from the scope of the conclusions reached. Kant is a clear example.[5] But when Rawls refers to the generality and universality of Kant's ethics, and when he compares the principles chosen in his own original position to those regulative of Kant's kingdom of ends, "acting from [which] expresses our nature as free and equal rational persons,"[6] he does not mention the fact that women were not included in that category of "free and equal rational persons" to which Kant meant his moral theory to apply. Again, in a brief discussion of Freud's account of moral develop-ment, Rawls presents Freud's theory of the formation of the male super-ego in largely gender-neutral terms, without mentioning the fact that Freud considered women's moral development to be sadly deficient, on account of their incomplete resolution of the Oedipus complex.[7] Thus there is a certain blindness to the sexism of the tradition in which Rawls is a participant, which tends to render his terms of reference even more ambiguous than they might otherwise be. A feminist reader finds it difficult not to keep asking: "Does this theory of justice apply to women, or not?"

This question is not answered in the important passages listing the characteristics that persons in the original position are not to know about themselves in order to formulate impartial principles of justice. In a subsequent article, Rawls has made it clear that sex *is* one of those morally irrelevant contingencies that are hidden by the veil of ignorance.[8] But throughout *A Theory of Justice*, while the list of things unknown by a person in the original position includes "his place in society, his class position or social status . . . his fortune in the distribution of natural assets and abilities, his intelligence and strength, and the like . . . his conception of the good, the particulars of his rational plan of life, [and] even the special features of his psychology . . ."[9] "his" sex is not mentioned. Since the parties also "know the general facts about human society,"[10] presumably including the fact that it is gender structured both by custom and still in some respects by law, one might think that whether or not they knew their sex might matter enough to be mentioned. Perhaps Rawls means to cover it by his phrase "and the like," but it is also possible that he did not consider it significant.

The ambiguity is exacerbated by the statement that those free and equal moral persons in the original position who formulate the principles of justice are to be thought of not as "single individuals," but as "heads of families" or "representatives of families."[11] Rawls says that it is not necessary to think of the parties as heads of families, but that he will generally do so. The reason he does this, he explains, is to ensure that each person in the original position cares about the well-being of some persons in the next generation. These "ties of sentiment" between generations, which Rawls regards as important in the establishment of his just savings principle, would otherwise constitute a problem, because of the general assumption that the parties in the original position are mutually disinterested.[12] In spite of the ties of sentiment *within* families, then, "as representatives of families their interests are opposed as the circumstances of justice imply."[13]

The head of a family need not necessarily, of course, be a man. Certainly in the US, at least, there has been a striking growth in the proportion of "female-headed households" during the last several decades. But the very fact that, in common usage, the term "female-headed household" is used *only* in reference to households without resident adult males implies the assumption that any present male takes precedence over a female as the household or family head. Rawls does nothing to contest this impression when he says of those in the original position that "imagining themselves to be fathers, say, they are to ascertain how much they should set aside for their sons by noting what they would believe themselves entitled to claim of their fathers."[14] Although the "heads of families" assumption is made in order to address the issue of intergenerational justice, and is presumably not intended to be sexist, Rawls is effectively trapped by it into the traditional mode of thinking that life within the family and relations between the sexes are not properly to be regarded as part of the subject matter of a theory of social justice.

Before I go on to argue this, I must first point out that Rawls, for good reason, states at the outset of his theory that the family *is* part of the subject matter of a theory of social justice. "For us," he says, "the primary subject of justice is the basic structure of society . . . the political constitution and the principle economic and social arrangements." These are basic because "taken together as one scheme, [they] define men's rights and duties and influence their life prospects, what they can expect to be and how well they can hope to do. The basic structure is the primary subject of justice because its effects are so profound and present from the start."[15] Rawls specifies "the monogamous family" as an example of such major social institutions, together with the political constitution, the legal protection of essential freedoms, competitive markets, and private property. This initial inclusion of the family as a basic social institution to which the principles of justice should apply, although a break with earlier liberal thought, seems unavoidable given the stated criteria for inclusion in the basic structure. Different family structures, and different distributions of rights and duties within families, clearly affect men's "life prospects, what they can expect to be and how well they can hope to do," and even more clearly affect the life prospects of women. There is no doubt, then, that in Rawls's initial definition of the sphere of social justice, the family is included. However, it is to a large extent ignored, though assumed, in the rest of the theory.[16]

The two principles of justice that are derived and defended in part 1 – the principle of equal basic liberty, and the difference principle combined with the requirement of fair equality of opportunity – are intended to apply to the basic structure of society. They are "to govern the assignment of rights and duties and to regulate the distribution of social and economic advantages."[17] Whenever in these basic institutions there are differences in authority, in responsibility, in the distribution of resources such as wealth or leisure, these differences must be both to the greatest benefit of the least advantaged, and attached to positions accessible to all under conditions of fair equality of opportunity.

In part 2, Rawls discusses at some length the application of his principles of justice to almost all of the major social institutions listed at the beginniing of the book. The legal protection of liberty of thought and conscience is defended, as are democratic constitutional institutions and procedures; competitive markets feature prominently in the discussion of the just distribution of income; the issue of the private or public ownership of the means of production is explicitly left open, since Rawls argues that his principles of justice might be compatible with certain versions of either.

But throughout all these discussions, he never raises the question of whether the monogamous family, in either its traditional or any other form, is just. When he announces that "the sketch of the system of institutions that satisfy the two principles of justice is now complete,"[18] Rawls has still paid no attention at all to the internal justice of the family. In fact, apart from passing references, the family appears in *A Theory of Justice* in only three contexts: as the link between generations necessary for the just savings principle; as an obstacle to fair equality of opportunity – on account of the inequalities among families; and as the first school of moral development. It is in the third of these contexts that Rawls first specifically mentions the family as a just institution. He mentions it, however, not to *consider* whether the family "in some form" is just, but to *assume* it.[19]

Clearly, however, by Rawls's own reasoning about the social justice of major social institutions, this assumption is unwarranted, and this has serious significance for the theory as a whole. The central tenet of the theory, after all, is that justice as fairness characterizes institutions whose members could hypothetically have agreed to their structure and rules from a position in which they did not know which place in the structure they were to occupy. The argument of the book is designed to show that the two principles of justice are those that individuals in such a hypothetical situation would agree to. But since those in the original position are only the heads or representatives of families, they are *not in a position to determine questions of justice within families*.[20] As far as children are concerned, Rawls makes a convincing argument from paternalism for their temporary inequality. But wives (or whichever adult member[s] of a family are *not* its "head") go completely unrepresented in the original position. If families are just, as is assumed, then they must become just in some different way (unspecified by Rawls) than other institutions, for it is impossible to see how the viewpoint of their less advantaged members ever gets to be heard.

There are two occasions when Rawls seems either to depart from his assumption that those in the original position are "family heads," or to assume that a "head of a family" is equally likely to be a woman as a man. In the assignment of the basic rights of citizenship, he argues, favoring men over women is "justified by the difference principle . . . only if it is to the advantage of women and acceptable from their standpoint."[21] Later, he seems to imply that the injustice and irrationality of racist doctrines are also characteristic of sexist ones.[22] But in spite of these passages, which appear to challenge formal sex discrimination, the discussions of institutions in part 2 implicitly rely, in a number of respects, on the assumption that the parties formulating just institutions are (male) heads of (fairly traditional) families, and are therefore not concerned with issues of just distribution within the family or between the sexes. Thus the "heads of families" assumption, far from being neutral or innocent, has the effect of banishing a large sphere of human life – and a particularly large sphere of most women's lives – from the scope of the theory.

One example of this occurs during the discussion of the distribution of wealth. Here Rawls seems to assume that all the parties in the original position expect, once the veil of ignorance is removed, to be participants in the paid labor market. Distributive shares are discussed in terms of household income, but reference to "individuals" is interspersed into this discussion as if there were no difference between the advantage or welfare of a household and that of an individual.[23] This confusion obscures the fact that wages are paid to employed members of the labor force, but that in societies characterized by gender (all current societies) a much larger proportion of women's than men's labor is unpaid, and is often not even acknowledged to be labor. It obscures the fact that the resulting disparities in the earnings of men and women, and the economic dependence of women on men, are likely to affect power relations within the household, as well as access to leisure, prestige, political power, and so on, among its adult members. Any discussion of justice *within* the family would have to address these issues.

Later, too, in his discussion of the obligations of citizens, Rawls's assumption that justice is agreed on by heads of families in the original position seems to prevent him from considering an issue of crucial importance to women – their exemption from the draft. He concludes that military conscription is justifiable in the case of defense against an unjust attack on liberty, so long as institutions "try to make sure that the risks of suffering from these imposed misfortunes are more or less evenly shared by all members of society over the course of their life, and that there is no avoidable *class* bias in selecting those who are called for duty."[24] However, the issue of the complete exemption of women from this major interference with the basic liberties of equal citizenship is not even mentioned.

In spite of two explicit rejections of the justice of formal sex discrimination in part 1, then, Rawls seems in part 2 to be so heavily influenced by his "family heads" assumption that he fails to consider as part of the basic structure of society the greater economic dependence of women and the sexual division of labor within the typical family, or any of the broader social ramifications of this basic gender structure. Moreover, in part 3, where he *assumes* the justice of the family "in some form" as a given, he does not discuss any alternative forms, but sounds very much as though he is thinking in terms of traditional, gendered family structure and roles. The family, he says, is "a small association, normally characterized by a definite hierarchy, in which each member has certain rights and duties." The family's role as moral teacher is achieved partly through parental expectations of "the virtues of a good son or a good daughter."[25] In the family and in other associations such as schools, neighborhoods, and peer groups, Rawls continues, one learns various moral virtues and ideals, leading to those adopted in the various statuses, occupations, and family positions of later life: "The content of these ideals is given by the various conceptions of a good wife and husband, a good friend and citizen, and so on."[26] Given these unusual departures from the supposedly generic male terms of reference used throughout the rest of the book, it seems likely that Rawls means to imply that the goodness of daughters is distinct from the goodness of sons, and that of wives from that of husbands. A fairly traditional gender system seems to be assumed.

However, despite this, not only does Rawls "assume that the basic structure of a well-ordered society includes the family *in some form*"; he adds to this the comment that "in a broader inquiry the institution of the family might be questioned, and other arrangements might indeed prove to be preferable."[27] But why should it require a broader inquiry than the colossal task engaged in *A Theory of Justice* to raise questions about the institution and the form of the family? Surely Rawls is right at the outset when he names it as one of those basic social institutions that most affects the life chances of individuals. The family is not a private association like a church or a university, which vary considerably in type and in degree of commitment expected, and which one can join and leave voluntarily. For although one has some choice (albeit a highly constrained one) about marrying into a gender-structured family, one has no choice at all about whether to be born into one. Given this, Rawls's failure to subject the structure of the family to his principles of justice is particularly serious in the light of his belief that a theory of justice must take account of "how [individuals] get to be what they are" and "cannot take their final aims and interests, their attitudes to themselves and their life, as given."[28] For the gendered family, and female parenting in particular, are clearly crucial determinants in the different socialization of the two sexes – in how men and women "get to be what they are."

If Rawls were to assume throughout the construction of his theory that all human adults are participants in what goes on behind the veil of ignorance, he would have no option but to require that the family, as a major social institution affecting the life chances of individuals, be constructed in accordance with the two principles of justice. I shall develop this positive potential of Rawls's theory in the final section of this essay. But first I shall turn to a major problem for the theory that results from its failure to address the issue of justice within the family – its placing in jeopardy Rawls's account of how one develops a sense of justice.

Gender, the Family, and the Development of a Sense of Justice

Apart from being briefly mentioned as the link between generations necessary for Rawls's "savings principle," and as an obstacle to fair equality of opportunity, the family appears in Rawls' theory in only one context – albeit one of considerable importance – as the earliest school of moral development. Rawls argues, in a much neglected section of part 3 of *A Theory of Justice*, that a just, well-ordered society will be stable only if its members continue to develop a sense of justice – "a strong and normally effective desire to act as the principles of justice require."[29] He specifically turns his attention to the question of childhood moral development, aiming to indicate the major steps by which a sense of justice is acquired.

It is in the context of early moral development, in which families play a fundamental role, that Rawls *assumes* that they are just. In these supposedly just families, the love of parents for their children, coming to be reciprocated in turn by the child, is important in the development of a sense of self-worth. By loving the child and being "worthy objects of his admiration . . . they arouse in him a sense of his own value and the desire to become the sort of person that they are."[30] Next, Rawls argues that healthy moral development in early life depends on love, trust, affection, example and guidance.[31]

Later in moral development, at the stage he calls "the morality of association," Rawls perceives the family, which he describes in gendered and hierarchical terms, as the first of many associations in which, by moving through a sequence of roles and positions, our moral understanding increases. The crucial aspect of the sense of fairness that is learned during this stage is the capacity to take up the points of view of others and to see things from their perspectives. We learn to perceive from what they say and do what other people's ends, plans and motives are. Without this experience, Rawls says, "we cannot put ourselves into another's place and find out what we would do in his position," which we need to be able to do in order "to regulate our own conduct in an appropriate way by reference to it."[32] Participation in different roles in the various associations of society leads to the development of a person's "capacity for fellow feeling" and to "ties of friendship and mutual trust."[33] Rawls says that, just as in the first stage certain natural attitudes develop towards the parents, "so here ties of friendship and confidence grow up among associates. In each case certain natural attitudes underlie the corresponding moral feelings: a lack of these feelings would manifest the absence of these attitudes."[34]

This whole account of moral development is strikingly unlike that of Kant, whose ideas are so influential in other respects on Rawls's thinking about justice. For Kant, any feelings that did not follow from independently established moral principles were morally suspect.[35] But Rawls clearly acknowledges the importance of feelings, first nurtured within supposedly just families, in the development of the capacity for moral thinking. In accounting for his third and final stage of moral development, where persons are supposed to become attached to the principles of justice themselves, Rawls says that "the sense of justice is continuous with the love of mankind."[36] At the same time, he allows for the fact that we have particularly strong feelings about those to whom we are closely attached, and says that this is rightly reflected in our moral judgements: even though "our moral sentiments display an independence from the accidental circumstances of our world . . . our natural attachments to particular persons and groups still have an appropriate place."[37] He indicates clearly that empathy, or imagining oneself into the place of others, plays a major role in moral development, and he turns from Kant to other philosophers – such as Adam Smith and Elizabeth Anscombe – who have paid more attention to such aspects of moral learning, in developing his ideas about the moral emotions or sentiments.[38]

Rawls believes that three psychological laws of moral development help account for the development of a sense of justice. The three laws, Rawls says, are: "not merely principles of association or of reinforcement . . . [but] assert that the active sentiments of love and friendship, and even the sense of justice, arise from the manifest intention of other persons to act for our good. Because we recognize that they wish us well, we care for their well-being in return. . ."[39] Each of the laws of moral development, as set out by Rawls, depends on the one before it, and the first assumption of the first law is: "given that family institutions are just. . ." Thus Rawls frankly admits that the whole of moral development rests at base on the loving ministrations of those who raise small children from the earliest stages, and on the moral character – in particular the *justice* – of the environment in which this takes place. At the foundation of the development of the sense of justice, then, are an activity and a sphere of life that – though by no means necessarily so – have throughout history been predominantly the activity and the sphere of women.

Rawls does not explain the basis of his assumption that family institutions are just. If gendered family institutions are *not* just, but are, rather, a relic of caste or feudal societies in which roles, responsibilities and resources are distributed not in accordance with the two principles of justice, but in accordance with innate differences that are imbued with enormous social significance, then Rawls's whole structure of moral development seems to be built on uncertain ground. Unless the households in which children are first nurtured and see their first examples of human interaction are based on equality and reciprocity rather than on dependence and domination, how can whatever love they receive from their parents make up for the

injustice they see before their eyes in the relationship between these same
parents? How, in hierarchical families in which sex roles are rigidly
assigned, are we to learn to "put ourselves into another's place and find
out what we would do in his position"? Unless they are parented equally
by adults of both sexes, how will children of both sexes come to develop a
sufficiently similar and well-rounded moral psychology to enable them to
engage in the kind of deliberation about justice that is exemplified in the
original position? Rawls's neglect of justice within the family is clearly in
tension with his own theory of moral development, which *requires* that
families be just.

What Can Rawls's Theory of Justice Contribute to Feminism?

The significance of Rawls's central, brilliant idea, the original position, is
that it forces one to question and consider traditions, customs, and institutions from all points of view, and ensures that the principles of justice
are acceptable to everyone, regardless of what position "he" ends up in.
The critical force of the original position is clear from the fact that some of
the most creative critiques of Rawls's theory have resulted from others
interpreting the original position more radically or broadly than he did.[40]
For feminist readers, the problem of the theory as stated by Rawls himself
is encapsulated in that ambiguous "he." While Rawls briefly rules out
formal, legal discrimination on the grounds of sex, he fails entirely to
address the justice of the gender system, which, with its roots in the sex
roles of the family, is one of the fundamental structures of our society. If,
however, we read Rawls in such a way as to take seriously both the notion
that those behind the veil of ignorance are sexless persons, and the
requirement that the family and the gender system, as basic social institutions, are to be subject to scrutiny, then constructive feminist criticism of
these contemporary institutions follows. So also, however, do hidden
difficulties for the application of a Rawlsian theory of justice in a gendered
society.

   Both the critical perspective and the incipient problems of a feminist
reading of Rawls can be illuminated by a description of a cartoon I saw a
few years ago. Three elderly, robed male justices are depicted looking
down with astonishment at their very pregnant bellies. One says to the
others, without further elaboration: "Perhaps we'd better reconsider that
decision." This illustration points to several things. First, it graphically
demonstrates the importance, in thinking about justice, of a concept like
Rawls's original position, which makes us adopt the positions of others –
especially positions that we ourselves could never be in. Second, it suggests

that those thinking in such a way might well conclude that more than formal legal equality of the sexes is required if justice is to be done. As we have seen in recent years, it is quite possible to institutionalize the formal legal equality of the sexes and at the same time to enact laws concerning pregnancy, abortion, maternity leave, and so on, that in effect discriminate against women, not as women *per se*, but as "pregnant persons."[41] One of the virtues of the cartoon is its suggestion that one's thinking on such matters is likely to be affected by the knowledge that one might become "a pregnant person." Finally, however, the illustration suggests the limits of our abilities to think ourselves into the original position as long as we live in a gender-structured society. While the elderly male justices can, in a sense, imagine *themselves* pregnant, what is much more difficult is whether, in constructing principles of justice, they can imagine themselves *women*. This raises the question whether, in a society structured by gender, sex *is* a morally irrelevant and contingent characteristic.

Let us first assume that sex is contingent in this way, though I shall later question this assumption. Let us suppose that it is possible, as Rawls clearly considers that it is, to hypothesize the moral thinking of representative human beings who are ignorant of their sex. Although Rawls does not do so, we must consistently take the relevant positions of both sexes into account in formulating and applying principles of justice. In particular, those in the original position must take special account of the perspective of women, since their knowledge of "the general facts about human society" must include the knowledge that women have been and continue to be the less advantaged sex in a great number of respects. In considering the basic institutions of society, they are more likely to pay special attention to the family than virtually to ignore it, since its customary unequal assignment of responsibilities and privileges to the two sexes and its socialization of children into sex roles make it, in its current form, a crucial institution for the perpetuation of sex inequality.

In innumerable ways, the principles of justice that Rawls arrives at are inconsistent with a gender-structured society and with traditional family roles. The critical impact of a feminist application of Rawls's theory comes chiefly from his second principle, which requires that inequalities be both "to the greatest benefit of the least advantaged" and "attached to offices and positions open to all."[42] This means that if any roles or positions analogous to our current sex roles, including those of husband and wife, mother and father, were to survive the demands of the first requirement, the second requirement would prohibit any linkage between these roles and sex. Gender, with its ascriptive designation of positions and expectations of behavior in accordance with the inborn characteristic of sex, could no longer form a legitimate part of the social structure, whether inside or outside the family. Three illustrations will help to link this conclusion with specific major requirements that Rawls makes of a just or well-ordered society.

First, after the basic political liberties, one of the most essential liberties is "the important liberty of free choice of occupation."[43] This liberty is obviously compromised by the customary expectation, central to our gender system, that women take far greater responsibility for housework and childcare, whether or not they also work for wages outside the home. In fact, both the assignment of these responsibilities to women – resulting in their economic dependence on men – and also the related responsibility of husbands to support their wives, compromise the liberty of choice of occupation of both sexes. But the current roles of the two sexes inhibit women's choices over the courses of a lifetime far more severely than those of men; it is much easier to switch from being a wageworker to a domestic role than to do the reverse. While Rawls has no objection to some aspects of the division of labor, he asserts that in a well-ordered society, "no one need be servilely dependent on others and made to choose between mono-tonous and routine occupations which are deadening to human thought and sensibility"; work can and should be "meaningful for all."[44] These conditions are far more likely to be met in a society that does not assign family responsibilities in a way that makes women into a marginal sector of the paid workforce and renders likely their economic dependence on men.

Second, the abolition of gender seems essential for the fulfillment of Rawls's criterion for political justice. For he argues that not only would equal formal political liberties be espoused by those in the original position, but that any inequalities in the *worth* of these liberties (for example, the effects on them of factors like poverty and ignorance) must be justified by the difference principle. Indeed, "the constitutional process should pre-serve the equal representation of the original position to the degree that this is practicable."[45] While Rawls discusses this requirement in the context of *class* differences, stating that those who devote themselves to politics should be "drawn more or less equally from all sectors of society,"[46] it is just as clearly and importantly applicable to sex differences. The equal political representation of women and men, especially if they are parents, is clearly inconsistent with our gender system.[47]

Finally, Rawls argues that the rational moral persons in the original position would place a great deal of emphasis on the securing of self-respect or self-esteem. They "would wish to avoid at almost any cost the social conditions that undermine self-respect," which is "perhaps the most important" of all the primary goods.[48] In the interests of this primary value, if those in the original position did not know whether they were to be men or women, they would surely be concerned to establish a thorough-going social and economic equality between the sexes that would preserve either from the need to pander to or servilely provide for the pleasures of the other. They would be highly motivated, for example, to find a means of regulating pornography that did not seriously compromise freedom of speech, and would be unlikely to tolerate basic social institutions that asymmetrically either forced or gave strong incentives to members of one sex to serve as sex objects for the other.

There is, then, implicit in Rawls's theory of justice a potential critique of gender-structured social institutions which can be developed by taking seriously the fact that those formulating the principles of justice do not know their sex. At the beginning of my brief account of this feminist critique, however, I made an assumption that I said would later be questioned – that a person's sex is, as Rawls at times indicates, a contingent and morally irrelevant characteristic, such that human beings really can hypothesize ignorance of this fact about them. First, I shall explain why, unless this assumption is a reasonable one, there are likely to be further feminist ramifications for a Rawlsian theory of justice in addition to those I have just sketched out. I shall then argue that the assumption is very probably not plausible in any society that is structured along the lines of gender. The conclusion I reach is that not only is gender incompatible with the attainment of social justice, in practice, for members of both sexes, but that the disappearance of gender is a prerequisite for the *complete* development of a nonsexist, fully human *theory* of justice.

Although Rawls is clearly aware of the effects on individuals of their different places in the social system, he regards it as possible to hypothesize free and rational moral persons in the original position who, temporarily freed from the contingencies of actual characteristics and social circumstances, will adopt the viewpoint of the "representative human being." He is under no illusions about the difficulty of this task, which requires a great shift in perspective from the way we think about fairness in everyday life. But with the help of the veil of ignorance, he believes that we can "take up a point of view that everyone can adopt on an equal footing," so that "we share a common standpoint along with others and do not make our judgments from a personal slant."[49] The result of this rational impartiality or objectivity, Rawls argues, is that – all being convinced by the same arguments – agreement about the basic principles of justice will be unanimous.[50] He does not mean that those in the original position will agree about *all* moral or social issues – "ethical differences are bound to remain" – but that complete agreement will be reached on all basic principles, or "essential understandings."[51] However, it is a crucial assumption of this argument for unanimity that all the parties have similar motivations and psychologies (for example, he assumes mutually disinterested rationality and an absence of envy), and that they have experienced similar patterns of moral development, and are thus presumed capable of a shared sense of justice. Rawls regards these assumptions as the kind of "weak stipulations" on which a general theory can safely be founded.[52]

The coherence of Rawls's hypothetical original position, with its unanimity of representative human beings, however, is placed in doubt if the kinds of human beings we actually become in society not only differ in respect of interests, superficial opinions, prejudices, and points of view that we can discard for the purpose of formulating principles of justice, but also differ in our basic psychologies, conceptions of the self in relation to others, and experiences of moral development. A number of feminist theorists have argued in recent years that in a gender-structured society the different life experiences of females and males from the start in fact affect their respective psychologies, modes of thinking, and patterns of moral development in significant ways.[53] Special attention has been paid to the effects on the psychological and moral development of both sexes of the fact that children of both sexes are primarily reared by women. It has been argued that the experience of individuation – of separating oneself from the nurturer with whom one is originally psychologically fused – is a very different experience for girls than for boys, leaving the members of each sex with a different perception of themselves and of their relations with others. In addition, it has been argued that the experience of *being* primary nurturers (and of growing up with this expectation) also affects the psychological and moral perspective of women, as does the experience of growing up in a society in which members of one's sex are in many ways subordinate to the other. Feminist theorists' scrutiny and analysis of the different experiences that we encounter as we develop, from our actual lived lives to our absorption of their ideological underpinnings, have in valuable ways filled out de Beauvoir's claim that "one is not born, but rather becomes, a woman."[54]

What is already clearly indicated by these studies, despite their incompleteness so far, is that *in a gender-structured society* there is such a thing as the distinct standpoint of women, and that this standpoint cannot be adequately taken into account by male philosophers doing the theoretical equivalent of the elderly male justices in the cartoon. The very early formative influence on children of female parenting, especially, seems to suggest that sex different in a gendered society is more likely to affect one's thinking about justice than, for example, racial difference in a society in which race has social significance, or class difference in a class society. The notion of the standpoint of women (while not without its own problems) suggests, first, that a fully human moral or political theory can be developed only with the full participation of both sexes. At the very least, this will require that women take their place with men in the dialogue in approximately equal numbers and in positions of comparable influence. In a society structured along the lines of gender, this cannot happen.

In itself, moreover, this is insufficient for the complete development of a fully human theory of justice. For if principles of justice are to be adopted unanimously by representative human beings ignorant of their particular characteristics and positions in society, they must be persons whose psychological and moral development is in all essentials identical. This means that the social factors influencing the differences presently found between the sexes – from female parenting to all the manifestations of female subordination and dependence – would have to be replaced by genderless institutions and customs. Only when men participate equally in what have been principally women's realms of meeting the daily material and psychological needs of those close to them, and when women participate equally in what have been principally men's realms of larger scale production, government, and intellectual and creative life, will members of both sexes be able to develop a more complete *human* personality than has hitherto been possible. Whereas Rawls and most other philosophers have assumed that human psychology, rationality, moral development and so on are completely represented by the males of the species, this assumption itself has now been exposed as part of the male-dominated ideology of our gendered society.

It is not feasible to consider here at any length what effect the consideration of women's standpoint might have on Rawls's theory of justice. I would suggest, however, that it might place in doubt some assumptions and conclusions, while reinforcing others. For example, the discussion of rational plans of life and primary goods might be focussed more on relationships and less exclusively on complex activities if it were to encompass the traditionally more female parts of life.[55] On the other hand, those aspects of Rawls's theory, such as the difference principle, that require a far greater capacity to identify with others than is normally characteristic of liberal theory might well be strengthened by reference to conceptions of relations between self and others that seem in gendered society to be more predominantly female, but that would in a gender-free society be more or less evenly shared by members of both sexes.[56]

The arguments of this essay, while critical of some aspects of Rawls's theory of justice, suggest the potential usefulness of the theory from a feminist viewpoint. Rawls himself neglects gender and, despite his initial inclusion of the family in the basic structure, he does not consider issues having to do with justice *within* the family. In recent work, moreover, he suggests that the family belongs with those "private" and therefore non-political associations for which the principles of justice are not appropriate. He does this, moreover, despite the fact that his own theory of moral development rests centrally on the early experience of persons within a family environment that is both loving and just. Thus the theory as it stands contains an internal paradox. Because of his assumptions about gender, he has not applied the principles of justice to the realm of human nurturance which is so crucial for the achievement and the maintenance of justice.

On the other hand, I have argued that the feminist *potential* of Rawls's method of thinking and his conclusions is considerable. The original position, with the veil of ignorance hiding from its participants their sex as well as their other particular characteristics, their talents, circumstances and aims, is a powerful concept for challenging the gender structure. In particular – notwithstanding the difficulties for those socialized in a gendered society of thinking in the original position – it provides a viewpoint from which we can think about how to achieve justice within the family.

Notes

1 I have analyzed some of the ways in which theorists in the tradition have avoided considering the justice of gender, in "Are Our Theories of Justice Gender Neutral?" in *The Moral Foundations of Civil Rights*, ed. Robert Fullinwider and Claudia Mills (Totowa, NJ: Rowman and Littlefield, 1986), pp. 125–43).

2 John Rawls, *A Theory of Justice* (Cambridge, Mass.: Harvard University Press, 1971).

3 This is no longer the case in his most recent writings. See for example "Justice as Fairness: Political not Metaphysical," *Philosophy and Public Affairs*, 14(3), summer 1985, pp. 223–51.

4 Rawls, *Theory*, pp. 105–6, 208–9, 288–9.

5 See my "Women and the Making of the Sentimental Family," *Philosophy and Public Affairs*, 11(1), winter 1982, pp. 65–88, at pp. 78–82; Carole Pateman, *The Sexual Contract* (Stanford: Stanford University Press, 1988), pp. 168–73.

6 Rawls, *Theory*, pp. 251, 256. See also "Kantian Constructivism in Moral Theory," *The Journal of Philosophy*, 77(9), September 1980, pp. 515–72.

7 *Theory*, p. 459.

8 John Rawls, "Fairness to Goodness," *Philosophical Review*, 84, 1975, p. 537.

9 *Theory*, p. 137; see also p. 12.

10 Ibid. Numerous commentators on *Theory* have pointed out how controversial some of these "facts" are.

11 Ibid., pp. 128, 146.

12 As I have argued elsewhere, this assumption has frequently been misinterpreted by those of Rawls's critics who consider it in isolation from other crucial components of the original position, especially the veil of ignorance. See my "Reason and Feeling in Thinking about Justice," *Ethics*, 99(2), January 1989, pp. 229–49.

13 *Theory*, p. 128; see also p. 292.

14 Ibid., p. 289.

15 Ibid., p. 7.

16 It is noteworthy that in a subsequent paper on the subject of why the basic structure is the primary subject of justice, Rawls does *not* mention the family as part of the basic structure. See "The Basic Structure as Subject," *American Philosophical Quarterly*, 14(2), April 1977, p. 159. More significantly, whereas at the beginning of *Theory* he explicitly distinguishes the institutions of the basic structure from other "private associations," "less comprehensive social groups," and "various informal conventions and customs of everyday life" (p. 8), for which he suggests the principles of justice might be less appropriate or relevant, in two recent papers he classifies the family as belonging *with* such private, nonpolitical associations. See "Justice as Fairness," at p. 245; "The Priority of Right and Ideas of the Good," *Philosophy and Public Affairs*, 17(4), fall 1988, pp. 251–76, at p. 263.

17 *Theory*, p. 61.

18 Ibid., p. 303.

19 Ibid., pp. 463, 490. See Deborah Kearns, "A Theory of Justice – and Love; Rawls on the Family," *Politics (Australasian Political Studies Association Journal)*, 18(2), November 1983, pp. 36–42, at pp. 39–40, for an interesting discussion of the significance for Rawls's theory of moral development of his failure to address the justice of the family.

20 As Jane English says, "By making the parties in the original position heads of families rather than individuals, Rawls makes the family opaque to claims of justice." "Justice between Generations," *Philosophical Studies*, 31(2), 1977, pp. 91–104, at p. 95.

21 *Theory*, p. 99.

22 Ibid., p. 149.

23 Ibid., pp. 270–4, 304–9.

24 Ibid., pp. 380–1 (emphasis added).

25 Ibid., p. 467.

26 Ibid., p. 468.

27 Ibid., p. 463 (emphasis added).

28 Rawls, "Basic Structure as Subject," p. 160.

29 *Theory*, p. 454.

30 Ibid., p. 465.

31 Ibid., p. 466.

32 Ibid., p. 469.

33 Ibid., p. 470.

34 Ibid., p. 471.

35 See Okin, "Reason and Feeling."

36 *Theory*, p. 476.

37 Ibid., p. 475.

38 Ibid., pp. 479ff.

39 Ibid., p. 494; see also pp. 490–1.

40 Charles Beitz, for example, argues that there is no justification for not extending its application to the population of the entire world, which would lead to challenging virtually everything that is currently assumed in the dominant

"statist" conception of international relations. *Political Theory and International Relations* (Princeton: Princeton University Press, 1979).

41 The US Supreme Court decided in 1976, for example, that "an exclusion of pregnancy from a disability benefits plan . . . providing general coverage is not a gender-based discrimination at all." *General Electric v. Gilbert*, 429 US 125 (1976).

42 *Theory*, p. 302.

43 Ibid., p. 274.

44 Ibid., p. 529.

45 Ibid., p. 222; see also pp. 202–5, 221–8.

46 Ibid., p. 228.

47 The paltry numbers of women in high political office is an obvious indication of this. As of 1987, 41 out of the 630 members of the British House of Commons were women. Since 1789, over 10,000 men have served in the US House of Representatives, but only 107 women; some 1,140 men have been senators, compared with 15 women.

48 *Theory*, pp. 440, 396; see also pp. 178–9.

49 Ibid., pp. 516–17.

50 Ibid., pp. 139–41.

51 Ibid., p. 517.

52 Ibid., p. 149.

53 Major works contributing to this thesis are Jean Baker Miller, *Toward a New Psychology of Women* (Boston: Beacon Press, 1976); Dorothy Dinnerstein, *The Mermaid and the Minotaur* (New York: Harper and Row, 1977); Nancy Chodorow, *The Reproduction of Mothering* (Berkeley: University of California Press, 1978): Carol Gilligan, *In a Different Voice* (Cambridge, Mass.: Harvard University Press, 1982); Nancy Hartsock, *Money, Sex, and Power* (New York: Longmans, 1983). Important individual papers are Jane Flax, "The Conflict between Nurturance and Autonomy in Mother–Daughter Relationships and within Feminism," *Feminist Studies*, 4(2), summer 1978; Sara Ruddick, "Maternal Thinking," *Feminist Studies*, 6(2), summer 1980. Summaries and/or analyses are presented in Alison Jaggar, *Feminist Politics and Human Nature* (Totowa, NJ: Rowman and Allenheld, 1983), ch. 11; Jean Grimshaw, *Philosophy and Feminist Thinking* (Minneapolis: University of Minnesota Press, 1986), chs 5–8; Susan Moller Okin, "Thinking Like a Woman," in Deborah Rhode, ed., *Theoretical Perspectives on Sexual Difference* (New Haven: Yale University Press, 1990); Joan Tronto, "Women's Morality: Beyond Gender Difference to a Theory of Care," *Signs*, 12(4), summer 1987, pp. 644–63.

54 Simone de Beauvoir, *The Second Sex*, trans. H. M. Parshley (New York: Vintage Books, 1952), p. 301.

55 Brian Barry has made a similar, though more general, criticism of Rawls's focus on complex and challenging practices – the "Aristotelian Principle" – in *The Liberal Theory of Justice* (Oxford: Oxford University Press, 1973), pp. 27–30.

56 I have developed this argument in "Reason and Feeling."

11

Simone de Beauvoir and Women: Just Who Does She Think "We" Is?

Elizabeth V. Spelman

The critics often repeat in new contexts versions of the old assumptions they set out to contest.

Martha Minow

In *The Second Sex*, Simone de Beauvoir explores the many ways in which men have depicted women as ruled by forces in human nature that men can neither fully accept nor fully deny.[1] *The Second Sex* is a landmark work in contemporary feminist thought (even though for many years de Beauvoir apparently resisted being identified as a feminist).[2] She attempted to give an account of the situation of women in general and to include proposals for the conditions that would have to change if women were to become free. Although not all feminists subsequent to de Beauvoir referred to her work, or even necessarily knew about it, there is hardly any issue that feminists have come to deal with that she did not address. Indeed, she touched on issues such as attitudes towards lesbianism that some later feminists didn't dare to think about.[3]

De Beauvoir explicitly recognized that we live in a world in which there are a number of forms of oppression, and she tried to locate sexism in that context. In her work, we have all the essential ingredients of a feminist account of "women's lives" that would not conflate "woman" with a small group of women – namely, white middle-class heterosexual Christian women in Western countries. Yet de Beauvoir ends up producing an account which does just that. Here I shall explore how both de Beauvoir's theoretical perspective and her empirical observations lend themselves to a far richer account of "women's nature" than she herself ends up giving. (I am not going to argue about the strengths or weaknesses of her theory or the accuracy of her observations, but rather raise some questions about why she took them to lead in one direction rather than another.) Then I want to suggest reasons for the serious discrepancy between the potential broad scope of her views and the actual narrow focus of her position. De Beauvoir is a thinker of great perspicacity, so to explain the discrepancy simply in terms of a kind of race and class privilege that makes it easy for her to think of her own experience as representative of the experience of others is not enough. We need to ask what it might be in the language or methodology or theory employed by de Beauvoir that enables her to disguise from herself the assertion of privilege she so keenly saw in women of her own position.

I

Human beings aren't satisfied merely to live, de Beauvoir insists: we aspire to a meaningful existence.[4] But much about our constitution conspires against the possibility of such an existence: our being creatures of the flesh entails the ever-present possibility that our grand projects will be mocked. It is not only the facts of our birth and death that give the lie to our being pure, unembodied, immortal spirit. Our bodies need tending to each day, and there is nothing meaningful in the many activities involved in this tending. The feeding and cleaning of bodies, the maintenance of shelter against the powerful vagaries of the natural world, are necessary if we are to live. But if that is all we did, or all we thought we could do, we wouldn't find anything valuable about human life. As de Beauvoir says, unless we can engage in activities that "transcend [our] animal nature," we might as well be brute animals: "On the biological level a species is maintained only by creating itself anew; but this creation results only in repeating the same Life in more individuals. But man assures the repetition of Life while transcending Life through Existence; by this transcendence he creates values that deprive pure repetition of all value."[5]

"Existing," as opposed to merely "living," is best expressed in those aspects of life that are the function of "the loftiest human attitudes: heroism, revolt, disinterestedness, imagination, creation."[6] Only "existing" gives any reason for life; mere living "does not carry within itself its reasons for being, reasons that are more important than life itself."[7] To exist is to be a creative subject, not a passive object of the forces of nature; it is to be molding a new future through the power of one's intelligence, rather than being at the play of the repetitive rhythms of one's animal nature. Existing is as different from living as consciousness is from matter, will from passivity, transcendence from immanence, spirit from flesh.[8]

But life is necessary for existence, and we must preserve life even while we struggle against its demands. Descent into life is possible because of the never fully eradicated allure of dumbness and unfreedom, the ever-present possibility of forgoing (or seeming to forgo) the responsibilities, uncertainties, and risks of intelligence and freedom. Men, de Beauvoir says, make women the repository of the multiform threats to a life of transcendence, agency, freedom, spirit; woman remains "in bondage to life's mysterious processes," "doomed to immanence."[9] Her life "is not directed towards ends: she is absorbed in producing or caring for things that are never more than means, such as food, clothing, and shelter. These things are inessential intermediaries between animal life and free exist-ence."[10] Though woman is no less capable of real "existence" than man, it is in her corporeality rather than his own that man sees palpable and undeniable reminders of his own animal nature, of his own deeply regret-table and undignified contingency. Desirous of seeing no part of himself in her, he regards her as thoroughly Other, or as thoroughly Other as he can, given that he nevertheless needs her as a companion who is neither merely an animal nor merely a thing: "Man knows that to satisfy his desires, to perpetuate his race, woman is indispensable."[11]

Although women are constitutionally no less desirous or capable than men of "existing" rather than merely "living," historically most women have not resisted men's definition of them as embodying mysterious, dumb forces of nature. They have done little to try to undermine the economic, social, and political institutions that reinforce and are reinforced by such attitudes. In this, de Beauvoir says, women are unlike other oppressed groups – for example, Blacks, Jews, workers.

There are two reasons for this. First, women are spread throughout the population, across racial, class, ethnic, national, and religious lines, and this presents huge obstacles to their working together politically. They don't share the same economic and social position, nor do they have a shared consciousness. Moreover, "the division of the sexes is a biological fact, not an event in human history."[12] In all other cases of oppression, she claims, both the oppressors and the oppressed have taken their relative positions to be the result of historical events or social change and hence in principle capable of alteration: "A condition brought about at a certain time can be abolished at some other time, as the Negroes of Haiti and others have proved." Similarly, "proletarians have not always existed, whereas there have always been women."[13]

De Beauvoir's point here presumably is not that whites never have taken racial differences to be biological; rather she seems to be pointing out that the idea that biological differences entitle whites to dominate

Blacks has been undermined in theory (to the extent that differences between Black and white are held to be less significant than their similarities as human beings) and nullified in political struggles (through which Blacks make clear their capacity to regard themselves as "subjects" and whites as "others").[14] De Beauvoir seems to be saying here that owing to a deep and apparently unbridgeable biological divide, women constitute for men the Other, whereas Blacks or the proletariat, for example, have not always constituted an Other for those by whom they may be dominated.

At the same time, despite these differences among women and between women and other oppressed groups, women do share something in common – but what they share paradoxically works against any possible solidarity. They "identify with each other" but do not communicate, as men do, "through ideas and projects of personal interest," and are only "bound together by a kind of immanent complicity."[15] By this de Beauvoir means that women are aware of inhabiting a special domain separate from men – in which they discuss recipes, frigidity, children, clothing – but nevertheless they regard each other as rivals for the attention of the masculine world. They are capable of ceasing to be Other. Despite what men find it convenient to believe, the difference between men and women is no more a biological given and historical necessity than the difference between bourgeoisie and proletariat. There is, however, a difference between the biological condition of being female and the social condition of being woman. So despite the differences among women, their different social and political locations, they could join in resisting the domination of men. But they haven't.[16]

And why haven't they? Sometimes de Beauvoir suggests that it is because being a "true woman" is inseparable from being the Other, so that it is logically impossible both to be a real woman and to be a subject, while there is no definitional problem, whatever other problems there are, in being a Black, or a worker, or a Jew, and also a subject. But this does not explain why women don't refuse to be "true women." And indeed sometimes de Beauvoir suggests that women simply choose to take the less arduous path: "No doubt it is more comfortable to submit to a blind enslavement than to work for liberation"; to "decline to be the Other, to refuse to be a party to the deal – this would be for women to renounce all the advantages conferred upon them by their alliance with the superior caste."[17]

Hence sometimes when she says that economic independence is the necessary condition of women's liberation, there is the suggestion that only if women are forced by circumstance to provide for themselves will they embrace their transcendence rather than fall into their immanence, see themselves as subjects rather than objects, as Self rather than Other. Women recognize the imporance and value of transcendence, but only enough to search for men whose creative and productive flights will rub off on them, metaphysically speaking. Women want what men have, but only in wanting the men who have it. What we need, de Beauvoir is saying, is a world in which if women are to get it at all, they must do it on their own.

In short, de Beauvoir argues that there are at least three things that help to explain the fact of women's domination by men:

1 Men's having the attitudes they do toward women;
2 the existence of economic, social, and political institutions through which such attitudes are expressed, enforced and perpetuated;
3 women's failure to resist such attitudes and institutions.

II

Differences among women

As noted above, de Beauvoir more than once remarks on class, racial, and national differences among women and how such differences bear on the economic, social, and political positions of women thus variously situated. Her comments on the lack of a sense of shared concerns among women are quite arresting: "If [women] belong to the bourgeoisie, they feel solidarity with men of that class, not with proletarian women; if they are white, their allegiance is to white men, not to Negro women."[18] The housewife is hostile toward her "servant [and toward] the teachers, governesses, nurses and nursemaids who attend to her children."[19] "Freed from the male, [the middle-class woman] would have to work for a living; she felt no solidarity with workingwomen, and she believed that the emancipation of bourgeois women would mean the ruin of her class."[20] De Beauvoir, then, is saying that the women least prepared to have their status changed have been white middle-class women, who are willing to keep the sexual status quo in return for the privileges of their class and race.

In all such examples, she cites the unwillingness of women with race or class privileges to give them up as the main obstacle to women's all doing something together to resist the domination of men. That is, what prevents a white middle-class woman from attacking sexism is her awareness that if she undermines sexism she will thereby undermine her race and class privilege. This ties in with de Beauvoir's point about the difference class makes to privilege based on sex. She argues that the less class privilege men and women enjoy, the less sexual privilege men of that class have; the more extreme class oppression is, the less extreme sex oppression is. So according to de Beauvoir sexism and classism are deeply intertwined. An important way in which class distinctions can be made is in terms of male–female relationships: we can't describe the sexism women are subject to without specifying their class; nor can we understand how sexism works without looking at its relation to class privilege. What makes middle-class women dependent on men of their class is the same as what distinguishes them from working-class women.[21]

But de Beauvoir does not heed her own insights here. On the contrary, she almost always describes relations between men and women as if the class or race or ethnic identity of the men and women made no difference to the truth of statements about "men and women." This poses some very serious difficulties for her attempt to give a general account of "woman." On her own terms it ought to be misleading to say, as she does, that we live "in a world that belongs to men,"[22] as if all differences between princes and paupers, masters and slaves, can be canceled out by the fact that they are all male.[23] In describing the psychological development of girls, she remarks on the ways in which everything in a girl's life "confirms her in her belief in masculine superiority."[24] And yet she later makes clear that a white girl growing up in the United States hardly believes that Black men are superior to her: "During the War of Secession no Southerners were more passionate in upholding slavery than the women." She describes ways in which girls of the upper classes are taught to believe in their superiority to working-class men: "In the upper classes women are eager accomplices of their masters because they stand to profit from the benefits provided. . . . The women of the upper middle classes and the aristocracy have always defended their class interests even more obstinately than have their husbands."[25] Whether or not de Beauvoir is entirely accurate in her descriptions of some women's passionate insistence on preserving privilege – were they really more fierce about it than the men of their race and class?[26] – the point is that these descriptions undermine her claims elsewhere about the common position of women.

De Beauvoir's perceptiveness about class and race inequality should make us wonder about her account of the "man" as "citizen" and "producer" with "economic independence" and all "the advantages attached to masculinity" in contrast to the "woman," who is "before all, and often exclusively, a wife," "shut up in the home," enjoying "vast leisure," and entertaining at tables "laden with fine food and precious wines."[27]

> Since the husband is the productive worker, he is the one who goes beyond family interest to that of society, opening up a future for himself through cooperation in the building of the future: he incarnates transcendence. Woman is doomed to the continuation of the species and the care of the home – that is, to immanence.[28]

Here de Beauvoir, despite evidence she provides to the contrary, makes it look as if racism, for example, had never existed and never affected the conditions under which a man can "incarnate transcendence." Here and elsewhere when she points to the role women play in reproducing family and species – "the oppression of woman has its cause in the will to perpetuate the family and to keep the patrimony intact"[29] – she chooses to ignore questions about legitimacy even while alluding to them elsewhere. She quotes Demosthenes: "We have hetairas for the pleasures of the spirit, concubines for sensual pleasure, and wives to give us sons";[30] and her argument implies among other things that human beings typically do not "continue the species" randomly or without regard to what kinds of beings will populate the future. Both Plato and Aristotle were concerned about joining the right kind of men with the right kind of women to produce philosopher-rulers and citizens of the *polis*. De Beauvoir surely was aware of the extent to which racial, class, and religious conventions dictate what comprises appropriate sexual behavior and "legitimate" reproduction. Indeed, as we shall see below, she explicitly points out but does not consider the implications of the fact that everything she says about sexual privilege only works when the man and woman belong to the same race and class.[31]

De Beauvoir sabotages her insights about the political consequences of the multiple locations of women in another way: she frequently compares women to other groups – in her language, "Jews, the Black, the Yellow, the proletariat, slaves, servants, the common people." For example, she asks us to think about the differences between the situation of women, on the one hand, and, on the other "the scattering of the Jews, the introduction of slavery into America, the conquests of imperialism." She discusses with considerable appreciation Bebel's comparison of "women and the proletariat." She remarks that some of what Hegel says about "master and slave" better applies to "man and woman." In reflecting on slavery in the United States, she says that there was a "great difference" between the case of American Blacks and that of women: "the Negroes submit with a feeling of revolt, no privileges compensating for their hard lot, whereas woman is offered inducements to complicity." She speaks of the role of religion in offering "women" and "the common people" the hope of moving out of immanence: "When a sex or a class is condemned to immanence, it is necessary to offer it the mirage of some form of transcendence." She compares the talk of women about their husbands to conversations "of domestics talking about their employers critically in the servants' quarters."[32]

I bring up these comparisons not in order to assess their historical accuracy but to note that in making them de Beauvoir obscures the fact that half of the populations to whom she compares women consists of women. This is particularly puzzling in light of her recognition of the ways in which women are distributed across race, class, religious, and ethnic lines. She sometimes contrasts "women" to "slaves," sometimes describes women as "slaves,"[33] but she never really talks about those women who according to her own categories belonged to slave populations – for example, Black female slaves in the United States. She does say at one point that "there were women among the slaves, to be sure, but there have always been free women"[34] and then she proceeds to make clear that it is free women whom she will examine. She also says that in "classes in which women enjoyed some economic independence and took part in production . . . women workers were enslaved even more than the male workers."[35] But in contrasting "women" to a number of other groups, and in choosing not to pay attention to the women in those other groups, she expresses her determination to use "woman" only in reference to those females not subject to racism, anti-Semitism, classism, imperialism.

Perhaps she is aware at some level that this is the price she must pay for consistency: for where she does describe briefly the situation of females who belong to the groups she contrasts to "women," what she says does not follow from her account of "women." For example, she claims that in the Middle Ages peasant men and women lived on a "footing of equality," and that "in the working classes economic oppression nullified the inequality of the sexes."[36] If she believes this, then of course she has to restrict her use of the word "woman" to those females not subject to the other forms of oppression she refers to; otherwise her large claims about the subordination of women to men would be undermined by her own account. And yet at the same time, she subjects them to question, which we see as we turn to a third way in which de Beauvoir fails to pay attention to her own significant insights.

Toward the end of *The Second Sex*, de Beauvoir acknowledges that the differences in privilege and power between men and women she has been referring to are "in play" only when men and women are of the same class and race.[37] This is a logical conclusion for someone who holds, as we have seen she does, that the wives of white slaveowners in the United States fought even harder than their husbands to preserve the privileges of race; since she thought of "slaves" as male, she could hardly maintain that men who were slaves dominated women who were not. But there is a problem even in the way she signals here that claims about privilege based on sex apply only within the same class or race. For that suggests that sexism within one class or race is just like that within any other class or race. If so, her claims do have a kind of generality after all – for example, what characterizes relations between white men and white women would also characterize those between Black men and Black women. But we've seen that de Beauvoir also holds that sexual oppression is essentially nullified when men and women are subject to other forms of oppression. In that case, her claim is not really that the sexism she describes operates only when class and race are constant, but rather that she is talking about the sexism in effect only when the men and women involved are not subject to class or racial oppression. She herself leads us to the conclusion that the sexism she is concerned with in *The Second Sex* is that experienced by white middle-class women in Western countries.

The creation of women

"One is not born, but rather becomes, a woman". This opening sentence from Book 2 of *The Second Sex* has come to be the most often cited and perhaps most powerful of de Beauvoir's insights. Among other things it offers a starting point for the distinction between sex and gender. It is one thing to be biologically female, quite another to be shaped by one's culture into a "woman" – a female with feminine qualities, someone who does the kinds of things "women," not "men," do, someone who has the kinds of thoughts and feelings that make doing these things seem an easy expression of one's feminine nature.

If being a woman is something one can become, then it also is something one can fail to become. De Beauvoir insists that while being or not being female is a biological matter, becoming or not becoming a woman is not. "Civilization as a whole" produces women. In the absence of other humans, no female would become a woman; particular human "intervention in her destiny is fundamental" to who and what she becomes: "Woman is determined not by her hormones or by mysterious instincts, but by the manner in which her body and her relation to the world are modified through the action of others than herself." In particular, "in men's eyes – and for the legion of women who see it through men's eyes – it is not enough to have a woman's body nor to assume the female function as mistress or mother in order to be "true woman."[38] What she has to do to become a "true woman" is to be seen and to see herself as Other in contrast to the Self of the male, as inessential in contrast to the essential, as object in contrast to the subject. Females of the species don't come created in this way; they are made this way by the concerted efforts of men and women.

Moreover, de Beauvoir insists that humans create whatever significance is attached to having a body and more particularly to having a male or female body. She directs us to thinking about "the body as lived in by the subject" as opposed to the body as described by the biologist. The consciousness one has of one's body in this way is acquired "under circumstances dependent upon the society of which [one] is a member" or indeed even upon the class one belongs to. De Beauvour suggests, for example, that the physical event of having an abortion is experienced differently by conventional middle-class women and by those "schooled by poverty and misery to disdain bourgeois morality." Along similar lines, she claims that the biological changes that take place during menopause are experienced differently by those "true women" who have "staked everything on their femininity" and by "the peasant woman, the work man's wife," who, "constantly under the threat of new pregnancies, are happy when, at long last, they no longer run this risk."[39]

Biology is not destiny in at least two senses, according to de Beauvoir. First, being female is not the same thing as being a "woman"; nor does it determine whether and how one will become a "woman." Second, different women experience biological events associated with being female differently, depending on how their bodies are otherwise employed and their beliefs about what are the proper things to do with or to their bodies. But de Beauvoir doesn't take this insight as far as she might in the directions to which her own comments lead. She seems to be saying that there is no particular significance that must be given to biological facts about our bodies, that whether or how a female becomes a "woman" depends upon human consciousness and human action. But she is well aware of the fact that in many ways human consciousness and human action take quite different forms in different societies. We get a hint of this in her comment quoted above about how a woman's consciousness of femininity is dependent on the society in which she lives, as well as in her reminder that the intervention of others is so crucial a factor in the creation of a "woman" out of a female that "if this action took a different direction, it would produce a quite different result."[40]

This surely points to the variability in the creation of "women" across and within cultures. Here is where de Beauvoir's lack of attention to females belonging to the populations she contrasts to "women" is particularly disappointing. She doesn't reflect on what her own theoretical perspective strongly suggests and what her own language mirrors: namely, that different females are constructed into different kinds of "women"; that under some conditions certain females count as "women," others don't.

Moreover, de Beauvoir's analysis of racial oppression, cursory as it is, tells us that she believes people have attached different significance to racial differences at different times. She counts as successful social change those economic and political reversals in which a people once regarded as Other no longer are regarded as such by those who formerly dominated them. When she comments, early in the book, on the change of status of Blacks in Haiti after the revolution,[41] and much later on how Black suffrage helped to lead to the perception of Blacks as worthy of having the vote,[42] she is alluding to changes in the significance attached by whites to what they take to be biological differences between whites and Blacks. If we follow up her insistence that we pay attention to "the body as lived in by the subject," we might begin to ask not only about living in a male or female body in the context of sexism but also about living in a black or white or brown or yellow or red body in the context of racism. Though de Beauvoir refers to the variability in ideals of feminine beauty[43] and, as we've seen, is certainly aware of racial oppression, she does not speak at length about women subject to racism and so does not talk about the ways in which notions of beauty are racially coded. While she certainly is aware of the significance attached to skin color, she does not join that to her point about the distinction between other physical differences among human bodies (i.e., sexual differences) and what humans make of those differences.

The real and the ideal woman

A third promising ingredient of de Beauvoir's analysis is her attack on the discrepancy between the reality of actual women and a static ideal of "woman." The latter is not an empirical generalization based on observations of specific women but a male myth about the nature of femininity:

> As against the dispersed, contingent, and multiple existences of actual women, mythical thought opposes the Eternal Feminine, unique and changeless. If the definition provided for this concept is contradicted by the behavior of flesh-and-blood women, it is the latter who are wrong; we are told not that Femininity is a false entity, but that the women concerned are not feminine.[44]

De Beauvoir believes that this mythical ideal reaches deep into the idea of woman as Other, and as we've seen, she sometimes speaks as if men's treatment of women as Other is inevitable. But on the other hand, it is clear that she thinks that if political and economic conditions change in the right direction, women will be seen in their historical specificity – that is, women might come to be truly known by men rather than being the occasion for men's projection of a mythic ideal of femininity.

> It is noteworthy that the feminine comrade, colleague, and associate are without mystery [being "mysterious" is one version of the mythic ideal]; on the other hand, if the vassal is male, if, in the eyes of a man or a woman who is older, or richer, a young fellow, for example, plays the role of the inessential object, then he too becomes shrouded in mystery. And this uncovers for us a substructure under the feminine mystery which is economic in nature.[45]
>
> The more relationships are concretely lived, the less they are idealized. The fellah of ancient Egypt, the Bedouin peasant, the artisan of the Middle Ages, the worker of today has in the requirements of work and poverty relations with his particular woman companion which are too definite for her to be embellished with an aura either auspicious or inauspicious.[46]

De Beauvoir seems to be making a brief here for establishing a set of conditions under which people can see each other as they actually are. The liberation of women depends upon establishing economic and political conditions under which men won't simply project their notion of "woman" onto women but will look at who women in fact are, observing "the behavior of flesh-and blood women." De Beauvoir has high regard for what she refers to as "knowledge," "empirical law," "laws of nature," "scientific explanation."[47] Though she does not explain exactly what she means by these terms, it is clear that she accuses men of not being very scientific in their claims about women. Men are right to look for universally true statements about women, but they don't realize that the only solid grounds for such claims are empirical óbservations. Clear thinking about women would lead to universally true statements about them.

De Beauvoir has not of course laid out a full-blown epistemology here, but the hints of one point to the potential richness of her account of women. As we have noted on several occasions, de Beauvoir at one level is quite aware of the diverse historical, economic, and political situations of women, of the differences class and race make to women's relationships with men and to their relationships with other women. She likens the notion of the "Eternal Feminine" to a Platonic "Idea, timeless, unchangeable." As an existentialist, she has no truck with the idea of an "essence" of anything – of humanity, of man, of woman. We are not who or what we by by virtue of being particular instances of some transcendental entity; rather, "an existent *is* nothing other than what he does . . . he is to be measured by his acts."[48]

De Beauvoir suggests that a search for some essence of "woman" is deeply misplaced: we would look in vain for some metaphysical nugget of pure womanhood that defines all women as women. We have to look at what women do to find out who they are. This means that we cannot decide prior to actual investigation of women's lives what they do or do not have in common; and this means that we cannot assume that what we find to be true about the lives of women of one class or race or nationality or historical period will be true about the lives of other women. De Beauvoir warns us against any inclination to assume that the lives of women of one race or class are representative of the lives of all other women. Both existentialism and "scientific thinking" tell us we have to look and see what women are really like.

But at the same time, de Beauvoir also warns, neither existentialism nor "scientific reasoning" will lead us to the viewpoint of "woman," who "lacks the sense of the universal" and takes the world to be "a confused conglomeration of special cases." So while we can't assume, ahead of time, that any particular universal truth about "humanity" or "men" or "women" will be true, we can assume that investigation of women's lives will lead to such a truth or truths about women. Women's isolation from one another – the very isolation that de Beauvoir cites as one reason for their not constituting a likely political class – accounts in large part for their lacking "the sense of the universal": "She feels she is a special case because she is isolated in her home and hence does not come into active contact with other women."[49] If she had the opportunity to know about other women's lives, she might come to see the grounds for universal truths in the similarities in cases she earlier had taken to be special, unique, *sui generis*.

De Beauvoir has a lively concern that views about women be based neither on the assumption that women necessarily share some metaphysical essence nor on the assumption that women share nothing at all. Yet the universal truths she claims to be noting about "women" do not follow from the observations she makes about differences among women.

III

What might explain the contradictory pulls in de Beauvoir's account of women? The point of asking this is not to exonerate her from the charge of inconsistency or of misrepresenting the situation of white middle-class women as that of "women in general." The point, rather, is to see where white middle-class privilege has to lodge in order to make itself resistant to observations and theoretical perspectives that tell against it.

Certain strands of de Beauvoir's thought lead inexorably in the direction of a central focus on white middle-class women to illuminate the condition of "woman." As we've seen, at least some of the time she holds the following conditions to be true:

1 If one is not a "man," one is either a woman or a Black, a woman or Jewish, a woman or a poor person, etc.
2 Sexism is different from racism and other forms of oppression: sexism is the oppression women suffer as women, racism the oppression Blacks, for example, suffer as Blacks.
3 Sexism is most obvious in the case of women not otherwise subject to oppression (i.e., not subject to racism, classism, anti-Semitism, etc.).

Now insofar as de Beauvoir takes these conditions to be true, it is quite logical for her to take the examination of white middle-class women to be the examination of all women. Indeed, anyone who assumes the truth of these three conditions will take it to be the most logical thing in the world for feminists to focus on white middle-class women. De Beauvoir certainly is not alone in this position. To the degree that conditions 1, 2, and 3 seem logical, we ought to think of the white middle-class privilege her work expresses, not as a personal quirk in de Beauvoir, but as part of the intellectual and political air she and many of us breathe.

There are two important features of what we might call the 1–2–3 punch. First, it has the status of near truism: points 1 and 2 may appear to be true by definition (de Beauvoir, as we saw it, at times took them utterly for granted), and 3 may seem just to be a matter of common sense, something not even needing the confirmation of historical inquiry (aren't the effects of sexism on women more distinct and hence easier to investigate when other forms of oppression don't affect the women in question?). Second, it leads to the focus on white middle-class women *without mentioning white middle-class women*.

These two features are crucial to the way in which white middle-class privilege works in feminist theory and hence crucial to understanding why we would miss a golden opportunity if we simply dismissed de Beauvoir's focus as an individual expression of her privilege and left it at that. (Indeed, it would also be an expression of that privilege to mention its presence but not bother to explore and expose its depth and pervasiveness.) Privilege cannot work if it has to be noted and argued for. For someone to have privilege is precisely *not* to have to beg for attention to one's case. For feminist theory to express white middle-class privilege is for it to ensure that white midle-class women will automatically receive attention. How can it ensure this without making explicit what it is doing? Conditions 1–3 do the trick, by making the default position of feminist inquiry an examination of white middle-class women: unless otherwise noted, that's who we are going to be talking about.

De Beauvoir was very attuned to the expression of privilege in women's behavior: as we saw, she took note of the desire of white slaveowners' wives to preserve the racial status quo; she talked about the hostile treatment of female domestic workers by their middle- and upper-class female employers. But privilege, we well know, can lodge almost anywhere, and since it works best when it is least obvious, it is not surprising that we should find it reflected in what appear to be axioms of her inquiry into the condition of "women."

Insofar as any of us agree to points 1–3 (and the agreement is likely to be implicit, not explicit), we are not likely to give much weight to those strands in de Beauvoir's thought that might give us reason to question their status. For example, we aren't likely to be struck by the fact that if, as de Beauvoir claims, one of the reasons women don't seem to form a natural political class is that we are found in every population, then, contra 1, it is very odd to contrast women with Blacks, Jews, the poor. Nor are we likely to notice the force of de Beauvoir's saying that we ought always to ask about the race and class of any men and women we are talking about, since claims about sexual hierarchy hold only when race and class are kept constant: if this is so, the sexism women are subject to will vary in accordance with their race and class privilege. But in that case, contra 2, there is no simple form of sexism the same for all women as women. Thus even if, as condition 3 claims, sexism is easier to track in the case of women not otherwise subject to oppression, it doesn't mean the sexism one finds is just like the sexism one would find in the case of women who are subject to other forms of oppression. We have to be very careful: the oppression white middle-class women are subject to is not the oppression women face "as women" but the oppression white middle-class women face. Their race and class are not irrelevant to the oppression they face even though they are not oppressed on account of their race and class.

IV

We have been trying to see what might explain the discrepancy between the implicit complexity of de Beauvoir's assessment of the lives of women and the oversimplification in her explicit rendering of "woman's situation" and of gender relations. We've suggested that while it is true that such oversimplification expresses the privileged tunnel vision of someone of de Beauvoir's race and class, we must also take the task of unmasking privilege seriously by trying to locate the places it finds a home, rather than simply noting that it must be at work. Since de Beauvoir herself was highly attuned to and bothered by the presence of such privilege, we honor her work by asking how such privilege functions in her own thinking.

There's no doubt that the case de Beauvoir makes about "woman" would be less compelling, at least to many of her readers, if she were to wonder aloud whether there is any difficulty posed for her account by the fact that there are women among the populations she contrasts to "woman"; if she were to say, "Notice, by the way, that the account I give of relations between middle-class men and women is not the same one I give of relations between working-class men and women"; if she did not hide away on page 605 of a 689-page book the reminder that any time we speak of male–female relations we must make sure that the men and women are of the same race and class.[50]

Such explicit musings would produce a less forceful argument for anyone who thinks that if we cannot talk about "woman" or about "women in general," then no case can be made about the injustice done to women, no strategy devised for the liberation of women. According to this line of thinking, a coherent feminist political analysis and agenda requires that we be able to talk about the history of the treatment of all women, as women. In order to be taken seriously, feminists have to make a case that they are speaking about more than a small group of people and that those referred to have been mistreated. So, for example, a group of white middle-class women would not claim that harm has come to them for being white or middle-class, but for being women. And they might well believe that not only would it be irrelevant to refer to being white and middle-class, but it would suggest that the group is not as representative as it otherwise would appear. So were de Beauvoir to make more explicit than she does who "woman" refers to in her analysis, she would defuse its potential impact: the case would not be that of "woman" but of particular women.

Furthermore, as we've seen, de Beauvoir thinks women lack a "sense of the universal." This has been a crucial part of their failure to resist the domination of men: not caring to notice the similarities in their experiences, each one given to "overestimat[ing] the value of her smile" because "no one has told her that all women smile." They fail to "sum . . . up in a valid conclusion" the many instances that ground claims about the conditions of "woman's" existence. Until women see beyond their own individual cases, they will not "succeed in building up a solid counter-universe whence they can challenge the males."[51] De Beauvoir may well regard it as a kind of weakness on her part were she to resist generalizing from the case of a woman like herself.

But it is one thing to urge women to look beyond their own cases; it is quite another to assume that if one does one will find a common condition or a common hope shared by all women. Perhaps there is a common condition or hope, but de Beauvoir's own work speaks against it. Given her insistence on the different social and economic positions occupied by women, she suggests not that similarities among women's various conditions are there to be found, but rather that they need to be created.

Notes

1 Simone de Beauvoir, *The Second Sex*, trans. and ed. H. M. Parshley (New York: Knopf, 1953).

2 See, for example, Judith Okely, *Simone de Beauvoir* (London: Virago, 1986).

3 This is not to say that feminists have not found reason to disagree with her. For a recent extended critique, see Mary Evans, *Simone de Beauvoir: A Feminist Mandarin* (London and New York: Tavistock, 1985).

4 Though de Beauvoir's terminology is certainly different from Aristotle's, there are echoes here of his distinction between a group of cattle grazing and a vibrant human *polis*.

5 *Second Sex*, pp. 58, 59.

6 Ibid., p. 588.

7 Ibid., p. 59. The translator here renders *l'existence* as "existing" and *la vie* as

"living." "Living" carries more weight for contemporary English speakers than mere "existing."

8   Ibid., p. 134.
9   Ibid., pp. 72, 68.
10 Ibid., p. 569.
11 Ibid., p. 74.
12 Ibid., p. xix.
13 Ibid., p. xviii.
14 Ibid.
15 Ibid., pp. 513, 511.
16 De Beauvoir does say quickly in passing that only feminists have done this. Ibid., pp. xviii–xix.
17 Ibid., pp. 246, xx. But she also insists for example, that "woman's 'character' [is] to be explained by her situation" (p. 588).
18 Ibid., p. xix; cf. pp. 103, 566, 590.
19 Ibid., p. 513.
20 Ibid., p. 103.
21 The idea that white middle-class women might be more reluctant than other women to battle sexism – if doing so is to cost them the privileges they have over white working-class women and all women of color – appears to conflict with what has become a historical truism: that the nineteenth- and twentieth-century women's movements in England, Europe, and the United States were founded and maintained by white middle-class women. Two questions immediately arise. Did they perceive their activity to be something that would involve giving up race or class privilege? Was what they were fighting for in fact something that would lead to loss of privilege whether or not they so perceived it? Were white female abolitionists actually fighting to end race privilege? Did they think it could be ended without ending sex privilege in the white population? In any event, if middle-class women were as reluctant as de Beauvoir says, what might this tell us about those middle-class women who were not reluctant?
22 *Second Sex*, pp. xx, 512, 563.
23 Contemporary feminists now stick in the qualifying adjective "white," as if that took care of the problem. But if it matters whether a man is white, it surely also matters – even if not in the same way – that a woman is white.
24 *Second Sex*, p. 38.
25 Ibid., pp. 566, 590.
26 On this see Ann Firor Scott, *The Southern lady: From Pedestal to Politics* (Chicago: University of Chicago Press, 1971).
27 *Second Sex*, pp. 430, 443, 497, 508, 663.
28 Ibid., p. 404.
29 Ibid., p. 82.
30 Ibid., p. 81.
31 Ibid., p. 605.
32 Ibid., pp. xviii, 49, 59, 278, 585, 579.
33 For instance, ibid., pp. 454, 569.
34 Ibid., p. 131.

35 Ibid., pp. 119–20.
36 Ibid., pp. 94, 96.
37 Ibid., p. 605.
38 Ibid., pp. 249, 682, 245.
39 Ibid., pp. 33, 44, 461, 542.
40 Ibid., p. 682.
41 Ibid., pp. xviii–xix.
42 Ibid., p. 686.
43 Ibid., p. 146.
44 Ibid., p. 237.
45 Ibid., pp. 241–2.
46 Ibid., p. 244.
47 Ibid., pp. 237, 580.
48 Ibid., pp. 237, 241.
49 Ibid., p. 580.
50 As Margaret Simons has pointed out, the English translation of *The Second Sex* does not include all of the original French version. See "The Silencing of Simone de Beauvoir: Guess What's Missing from *The Second Sex*," *Women's Studies International Forum*, 6, 1983, pp. 559–64.
51 *Second Sex*, pp. 580–1.

12

Foucault and Feminism: Toward a Politics of Difference

Jana Sawicki

The beginning of wisdom is in the discovery that there exist contradictions of permanent tension with which it is necessary to live and that it is above all not necessary to seek to resolve.

André Gorz, Farewell to the Proletariat

It is not difference which immobilizes us, but silence. And there are so many silences to be broken.

Audre Lorde, Sister Outsider, p. 44

The question of difference is at the forefront of discussions among feminists today.[1] Of course, theories of difference are certainly not new to the women's movement. There has been much discussion concerning the nature and status of women's differences from men (for instance, biological, psychological, cultural). Theories of sexual difference have emphasized the shared experiences of women across the divisions of race, class, age or culture. In such theories the diversity of women's experiences is often lumped into the category "women's experience," or women's caste, presumably in an effort to provide the basis for a collective feminist subject.

More recently, however, as a result of experiencing conflicts at the level of practice, it is the differences among women (for instance, differences of race, class, sexual practice) that are becoming the focus of theoretical discussion. To be sure, Marxist feminists have consistently recognized the significance of class differences among women, but other important differences cry out for recognition. The question arises: do the differences and potential separations between women pose a serious threat to effective political action and to the possibility of theory?

Perhaps the most influential and provocative ideas on the issue of difference in feminism are to be found in the writings of black, lesbian feminist poet and essayist Audre Lorde. In her work, Lorde describes the ways in which the differences among women have been "misnamed and misused in the service of separation and confusion."[2] As a lesbian mother and partner in an inter-racial couple, she has a unique insight into the conflicts and divided allegiances which put into question the possibility of a unified women's movement. She has experienced the way in which power utilizes difference to fragment opposition. Indeed this fragmentation can occur not only within groups but also within the individual. Hence, Lorde remarks: "I find I am constantly being encouraged to pluck out some one aspect of myself and present this as the meaningful whole, eclipsing or denying the other parts of self."[3]

Lorde claims that it is not the differences among women which are the source of separation but rather our "refusal to recognize those differences, and to examine the distortions which result from our misnaming them and their effects upon human behavior and expectation."[4] Thus, she appears to be saying that difference is not necessarily counter-revolutionary. She suggests that feminists devise ways of discovering and utilizing their differences as a source for creative change. Learning to live and struggle with many of our differences may be one of the keys to disarming the power of the white, male, middle-class norm which we have all internalized to varying degrees.

In what follows I shall elaborate on the notion of difference as resource and offer a sketch of some of the implications that what I call a "politics of difference" might have for "revolutionary" femininist theory.[5] In order to elucidate these implications I shall turn to the writings of the social philosopher and historian Michel Foucault. It is my contention that despite the androcentrism in his own writings he too has recognized the ambiguous power of difference in modern society; that is, he recognizes that difference can be the source of fragmentation and disunity as well as a creative source of resistance and change.

My aim in this paper is two-fold: (1) to turn to Foucault's work and method in order to lay out the basic features of a politics of difference; and (2) to show how such a politics might be applied in the feminist debate concerning sexuality. In order to accomplish these aims I shall begin by contrasting Foucault's politics with two existing versions of revolutionary feminism, namely, Marxist and radical feminism. I have selected these two feminist frameworks because they contain the elements of traditional revolutionary theory which Foucault is rejecting.[6] Other Foucauldian feminisms are developed by Morris and Martin.[7]

Foucault's Critique of Revolutionary Theory

It will be helpful to contrast Foucault's approach with Marxism, on the one hand, and radical feminism, on the other. Both Marxism and radical feminism conceive of historical process as a dialectical struggle for human liberation. Both have turned to history to locate the origins of oppression, and to identify a revolutionary subject. Yet radical feminists have criticized Marxism for its inability to give an adequate account of the persistence of male domination. They identify patriarchy as the origin of all forms of oppression. Hence, they view the struggles of women as a sex/class as the key to human liberation.

The recent intensification of feminist attention to the differences among women might be understood as a reaction to the emergence of a body of feminist theory which attempts to represent women as a whole on the basis of little information about the diversity of women's experiences, to develop universal categories for analyzing women's oppression, and, on the basis of such analysis, to identify the most important struggles. When Audre Lorde and others speak of the importance of preserving and re-defining difference, of discovering more inclusive strategies for building theory, and of the need for a broad based, diverse struggle, they are calling for an alternative to a traditional revolutionary theory in which forms of oppression are either overlooked or ranked and the divisions separating women exacerbated. The question is: are there radical alternatives to traditional revolutionary theory? As I have indicated, it is in the writings of Foucault that we find an attempt to articulate an alternative approach to understanding radical social transformation.

Foucault's is a radical philosophy without a theory of history. He does not utilize history as a means of locating a single revolutionary subject, nor does he locate power in a single material base. Nevertheless, historical research is the central component of his politics and struggle a key concept for understanding change. Accordingly, in order to evaluate the usefulness of Foucault's methods for feminism we must first understand the historical basis for his critique of traditional revolutionary theory.

Foucault's rejection of traditional revolutionary theory is rooted in his critique of the "juridico-discursive" model of power on which it is based. This model of power underpins both liberal theories of sovereignty (that is, legitimate authority often codified in law and accompanied by a theory of rights) and Marxist theories which locate power in the economy and the state as an arm of the bourgeoisie. The juridico-discursive model of power involves three basic assumptions:

1 power is possessed (for instance, by individuals in the state of nature, by a class, by the people);
2 power flows from a centralized source from top to bottom (for instance, law, the economy, the state); and
3 power is primarily repressive in its exercise (a prohibition backed by sanctions).

Foucault proposes that we think of power outside the confines of state, law or class. This enables him to locate forms of power which are obscured in traditional theories. Thus, he frees power from the political domain in much the same way as radical feminists did. Rather than engage in theoretical debate with political theorists, Foucault gives historical descriptions of the different forms of power operating in the modern West. He does not deny that the juridico-discursive model of power describes one form of power. He merely thinks that it does not capture those forms of power which make centralized, repressive forms of power possible, namely, the myriad of power relations at the microlevel of society.

Foucault's own model of power differs from the traditional model in three basic ways:

1 power is exercised rather than possessed;
2 power is not primarily repressive, but productive; and
3 power is analyzed as coming from the bottom up.

In what follows I will give Foucault's reasons for substituting his own view of power for the traditional one.

1 Foucault claims that thinking of power as a possession has led to a preoccupation with questions of legitimacy, consent and rights. (Who should possess power? When has power overstepped its limits?) Marxists have problematized consent by introducing a theory of ideology, but Foucault thinks this theory must ultimately rest on a humanistic notion of authentic consciousness as the legitimate basis of consent. Furthermore, the Marxist emphasis on power as a possession has resulted in an effort to locate those subjects in the historical field whose standpoint is potentially authentic, namely, the proletariat. Foucault wants to suspend any reference to humanistic assumptions in his own account of power because he believes that humanism has served more as an ideology of domination than liberation.

For the notion that power is a possession Foucault substitutes a relational model of power as exercised. By focusing on the power relations themselves, rather than on the subjects related (sovereign–subject, bourgeois-proletarian), he can give an account of how subjects are constituted by power relations.

2   This brings us to the productive nature of power. Foucault rejects the repressive model of power for two reasons. First, he thinks that if power were merely repressive, then it would be difficult to explain how it has gotten such a grip on us. Why would we continue to obey a purely repressive and coercive form of power? Indeed, repressive power represents power in its most frustrated and extreme form. The need to resort to a show of force is more often evidence of a lack of power. Second, as I have indicated, Foucault thinks that the most effective mechanisms of power are productive. So, rather than develop a theory of history and power based on the humanistic assumpton of a presocial individual endowed with inalienable rights (the liberal's state of nature) or based on the identification of an authentic human interest (Marx's species being), he gives accounts of the ways in which certain institutional and cultural practices have produced individuals. These are the practices of a disciplinary power which he associates with the rise of the human sciences in the nineteenth century.

Disciplinary power is exercised on the body and soul of individuals. It increases the power of individuals at the same time as it renders them more docile (for instance, basic training in the military). In modern society disciplinary power has spread through the production of certain forms of knowledge (the positivistic and hermeneutic human sciences) and through the emergence of disciplinary techniques which facilitate the process of obtaining knowledge about individuals (techniques of surveillance, examination, discipline). Thus, ways of knowing are equated with ways of exercising power over individuals. Foucault also isolates techniques of individualization such as the dividing practices found in medicine, psychiatry, criminology and their corresponding institutions, the hospital, asylum and prison. Disciplinary practices create the divisions healthy/ill, sane/mad, and legal/delinquent, which, by virtue of their authoritative status, can be used as effective means of normalization and social control. They may involve the literal dividing off of segments of the population through incarceration or institutionalization. Usually the divisions are experienced in the society at large in more subtle ways, such as in the practice of labeling one another or ourselves as different or abnormal.

For example, in *The History of Sexuality* Foucault gives an historical account of the process through which the modern individual has come to see herself as a sexual subject. Discourses such as psychoanalysis view sexuality as the key to self-understanding and lead us to believe that in order to liberate ourselves from personality "disorders," we must uncover the truth of our sexuality. In this way dimensions of personal life are psychologized, and thus become a target for the intervention of experts. Again, Foucault attempts to show how these discourses, and the practices based on them, have played more of a role in the normalization of the modern individual than they have in any liberatory processes. He calls for a liberation from this "government of individualization," for the discovery of new ways of understanding ourselves, new forms of subjectivity.

3   Finally, Foucault thinks that focusing on power as a possession has led to the location of power in a centralized source. For example, the Marxist location of power in a class has obscured an entire network of power relations "that invests the body, sexuality, family, kinship, know-ledge, technology. . ."[8] His alternative is designed to facilitate the des-cription of the many forms of power found outside these centralized loci. He does not deny the phenomenon of class (or state) power, he simply denies that understanding it is more important for resistance. As I have indicated, Foucault expands the domain of the political to include a heterogeneous ensemble of power relations operating at the microlevel of society. The practical implication of his model is that resistance must be carried out in local struggles against the many forms of power exercised at the everyday level of social relations.

Foucault's "bottom-up" analysis of power is an attempt to show how power relations at the microlevel of society make possible certain global effects of domination (such as class power, patriarchy). He avoids using universals as explanatory concepts at the start of historical inquiry in order to prevent theoretical overreach. He states:

> One must rather conduct an ascending analysis of power starting, that is, from its infinitesimal mechanisms, which each have their own history, their own trajectory, their own tactics, and then see how these mechanisms of power have been – and continue to be – invested, colonized, utilized, involuted, transformed, displaced, extended, etc., by even more general mechanisms and by forms of global domination. It is not that this global domination extends itself right to the base in a plurality of repercussions. . . .[9]

In other words, by utilizing an ascending analysis Foucault shows how mechanisms of power at the microlevel of society have become part of dominant networks of power relations. Disciplinary power was not invented by the dominant class and then extended down into the microlevel of society. It originated outside this class and was appropriated by it once it revealed its utility. Foucault is suggesting that the connection between power and the economy must be determined on the basis of specific historical analyses. It cannot be deduced from a general theory. He rejects both reductionism and functionalism insofar as the latter involves locating forms of power within a structure or institution which is self-regulating. He does not offer causal or functional explanations but rather historical descriptions of the conditions which make certain forms of domination possible. He identifies the necessary but not sufficient conditions for domination.

In short, Foucault's histories put into question the idea of a universal binary division of struggle. To be sure, such divisions do exist, but as particular and not universal historical phenomena. Of course, the corollary of his rejection of the binary model is that the notion of a subject of history, a single locus of resistance, is put into question.

Resistance

Despite Foucault's neglect of resistance in *Discipline and Punish*, in *The History of Sexuality* he defines power as dependent on resistance.[10] Moreover, emphasis on resistance is particularly evident in his more recent discussions of power and sexuality.[11]

In recent writings Foucault speaks of power and resistance in the following terms:

> Where there is power, there is resistance, and yet, or rather consequently, this resistance is never in a position of exteriority in relation to power.[12]

> I'm not positing a substance of resistance facing a substance of power. I'm simply saying: as soon as there's a relation of power there's a possibility of resistance. We're never trapped by power; it's always possible to modify its hold, in determined conditions and following a precise strategy.[13]

There are two claims in the above remarks. The first is the weaker claim that power relations are only implemented in cases where there is resistance. In other words, power relations only arise in cases where there is conflict, where one individual or group wants to affect the action of another individual or group. In addition, sometimes power enlists the resistant forces into its own service. One of the ways it does this is by labeling them, by establishing norms and defining differences.

The second claim implied in Foucault's description of power is the stronger claim that wherever there is a relation of power it is possible to modify its hold. He states: "Power is exercised only over free subjects and only insofar as they are free."[14] Free subjects are subjects who face a field of possibilities. Their action is structured but not forced. Thus, he does not define power as the overcoming of resistance. When resistant forces are overcome, power relations collapse into force relations. The limits of power have been reached.

So, while Foucault has been accused of describing a totalitarian power from which there is no escape, he denies that "there is a primary and fundamental principle of power which dominates society down to the smallest detail.[15] At the same time he claims that power is everywhere. He describes the social field as a myriad of unstable and heterogeneous relations of power. It is an open system which contains possibilities of domination as well as resistance.

Foucault describes the social and historical field as a battlefield, a field of struggle. Power circulates in this field and is exercised on and by individuals over others as well as themselves. When speaking of struggle, he refuses to identify the subjects of struggle. When asked the question: "Who is struggling against whom?" he responds:

> This is just a hypothesis, but I would say it's all against all. There aren't immediately given subjects of the struggle, one the proletariat, the other the bourgeoisie. Who fights against whom? We all fight against each other. And there is always within each of us something that fights something else."[16]

Depending on where one is and in what role (for instance, mother, lover, teacher, anti-racist, anti-sexist) one's allegiances and interests will shift. There are no privileged or fundamental coalitions in history, but rather a series of unstable and shifting ones.

In his theory of resistant subjectivity Foucault opens up the possibility of something more than a history of constructions or of victimization. That is, he opens the way for a historical knowledge of struggles. His genealogical method is designed to facilitate an "insurrection of subjugated knowledges." These are forms of knowledge or experience which "have been disqualified as inadequate to their task, or insufficiently elaborated: naive knowledges, located low down in the hierarchy, beneath the required level of cognition or scientificity."[17] They include the low-ranking knowledge ("popular knowledge") of the psychiatric patient, the hysteric, the imprisoned criminal, the housewife, the indigent. Popular knowledge is not shared by all people, "but it is, on the contrary, a particular, local, regional knowledge, a *differential* knowledge incapable of unanimity."[18]

The question whether some forms of resistance are more effective than others is a matter of social and historical investigation and not of a priori theoretical pronouncement. The basis for determining which alliances are politically viable ought not to be an abstract principle of unity, but rather historical and contextual analysis of the field of struggle. Thus feminism can mobilize individuals from diverse sites in the social field and thereby use differences as a resource.[19]

Genealogy as a form of resistance

Foucault introduces genealogical critique as his alternative to traditional revolutionary theory. He attempts to liberate us from the oppressive effects of prevailing modes of self-understanding inherited through the humanist tradition. As one commentator suggests, for Foucault, "Freedom does not basically lie in discovering or being able to determine who we are, but in rebelling against those ways in which we are already defined, categorized and classified."[20] Moreover, the view that the purpose of a theory of history is to enable us to control history, is part of the Enlightenment legacy from which Foucault is attempting to "free" us. For him, there is no theory of global transformation to formulate, no revolutionary subject whose interest the intellectual or theoretician can represent. He recommends an alternative to the traditional role for the intellectual in modern political struggles. He speaks of the "specific intellectual" in contrast to the "universal intellectual," that is, the "bearer of universal values" who is the enlightened consciousness of a revolutionary subject.

The specific intellectual operates with a different conception of the relation between theory and practice: "Intellectuals have gotten used to working, not in the modality of the 'universal,' the 'exemplary,' the 'just-and-true-for all,' but within specific sectors, at the precise points where their own conditions of life or work situate them (housing, the hospital, the asylum, the laboratory, the university, family and social relations).[21] Focusing attention on specific situations may lead to more concrete analyses of particular struggles and thus to a better understanding of social change. For example, Foucault was involved in certain conflicts within medicine, psychiatry and the penal system. He facilitated ways for prisoners to participate in discussions of prison reform and wrote a history of punishment in order to alter our perspectives on the assumptions which inform penal practices.

In part, Foucault's refusal to make any universal political, or moral, judgments is based on the historical evidence that what looks like a change for the better may have undesirable consequences. Since struggle is continual and the idea of a power-free society is an abstraction, those who struggle must never grow complacent. Victories are often overturned; changes may take on different faces over time. Discourses and institutions are ambiguous and may be utilized for different ends.

So Foucault is in fact pessimistic about the possibility of controlling history. But this pessimism need not lead to despair. Only a disappointed traditional revolutionary would lapse into fatalism at the thought that much of history is out of our control. Foucault's emphasis on resistance is evidence that he is not fatalistic himself, but merely skeptical about the possibilities of global transformation. He has no particular utopian vision. Yet, one need not have an idea of utopia in order to take seriously the injustices in the present. Furthermore, the past has provided enough examples of theoretical inadequacy to make Foucault's emphasis on provisional theoretical reflection reasonable.

In short, genealogy as resistance involves using history to give voice to the marginal and submerged voices which lie "a little beneath history," that is, the mad, the delinquent, the abnormal, the disempowered. It locates may discontinuous and regional struggles against power both in the past and present. These voices are the sources of resistance, the creative subjects of history.[22]

Foucault and Feminism: Toward a Politics of Difference

What are the implications of Foucault's critique of traditional revolutionary theory, his use of history and his analysis of power for feminism? I have called Foucault's politics a politics of difference because it does not assume that all differences can be bridged. Neither does it assume that difference must be an obstacle to effective resistance. Indeed, in a politics of difference, difference can be a resource insofar as it enables us to multiply the sources of resistance to particular forms of domination and to discover distortions in our understandings of each other and the world. In a politics of difference, as Audre Lorde suggests, redefining our differences, learning from them, becomes the central task.

Of course, it may be that Lorde does envision the possibility of some underlying commonality, some universal humanity, which will provide the foundation for an ultimate reconciliation of our differences. Her own use of the concept of the "erotic" might be understood as an implicit appeal to humanism.[23] As we have seen, Foucault's method requires a suspension of humanistic assumptions. Indeed, feminists have recognized the dangers of what Adrienne Rich refers to as "the urge to leap across feminism to 'human liberation.' "[24] What Foucault offers to feminism is not a humanist theory, but rather a critical method which is thoroughly historical and a set of recommendations about how to look at our theories. The motivation for a politics of difference is the desire to avoid dogmatism in our categories as well as the elision of difference to which such dogmatism can lead.

In conclusion, I want to illustrate the value and limitations of Foucault's politics of difference by bringing it to bear on a recent discussion of difference within feminism, namely, the sexuality debate. This debate has polarized American feminists into two groups, radical and libertarian feminists.[25] The differences being discussed threaten to destroy communications between them. Hence, an understanding of their differences is crucial at this conjuncture in American feminism.

Radical feminists condemn any sexual practices involving the "male" ideology of sexual objectification which, in their view, underlies both male sexual violence and the institutionalization of masculine and feminine roles in the patriarchal family. They call for an elimination of all patriarchal institutions in which sexual objectification occurs, such as pornography, prostitution, compulsory heterosexuality, sadomasochism, cruising, adult/child and butch/femme relations. They substitute an emphasis on intimacy and affection for the "male" preoccupation with sexual pleasure.

In contrast, libertarian feminists attack radicals for having succumbed to sexual repression. Since radicals believe that sex as we know it is male, they are suspicious of any sexual relations whatsoever. Libertarians stress the dangers of censoring any sexual practices between consenting partners and recommend the transgression of socially acceptable sexual norms as a strategy of liberation.

What is remarkable about these debates from the perspective of a politics of difference is the extent to which the two camps share similar views of power and freedom. In both camps, power is represented as centralized in key institutions which dictate the acceptable terms of sexual expression, namely, male-dominated heterosexual institutions whose elements are crystallized in the phenomenon of pornography on the one hand, and all discourses and institutions which distinguish legitimate from illegitimate sexual practice (including radical feminism) thereby creating a hierarchy of sexual expression, on the other. Moreover, both seem to regard sexuality as a key arena in the struggle for human liberation. Thus, for both, understanding the truth about sexuality is central for liberation.

In addition, both operate with repressive models of power. Radical feminists are in fact suspicious of all sexual practices insofar as they view sexual desire as a male construct. They think male sexuality has completely repressed female sexuality and that we must eliminate the source of this repression, namely, all heterosexual male institutions, before we can begin to construct our own. Libertarians explicitly operate with a repressive model of power borrowed from the Freudo-Marxist discourses of Wilhelm Reich and Herbert Marcuse. They recognize that women's sexual expression has been particularly repressed in our society and advocate women's right to experiment with their sexuality. They resist drawing any lines between safe and dangerous, politically correct and politically incorrect, sex. Radical feminists accuse libertarians of being male identified because they have not problematized sexual desire; libertarians accuse radicals of being traditional female sex-prudes.

There are other similarities between the two camps. In the first place, as Ann Ferguson has pointed out, both involve universalist theories of sexuality, that is, they both reify "male" and "female" sexuality and thus fail to appreciate that sexuality is a historically and culturally specific construct.[26] This is problematic insofar as it assumes that there is some essential connection between gender and sexual practice. An historical

understanding of sexuality would attempt to disarticulate gender and
sexuality and thereby reveal the diversity of sexual experiences across
gender as well as other divisions. For example, Rennie Simpson suggests,
Afro-American women's sexuality has been constructed differently from
white women's.[27] They have a strong tradition of self-reliance and sexual
self-determination. Thus, for American black women, the significance of
the sexuality debates may be different. Indeed, the relationship between
violence and sexuality takes on another dimension when viewed in the
light of past uses of lynching to control black male sexuality. And consider
the significance of black women's emphasis on issues such as forced
sterilization or dumping Depo Provera on third world countries over that
of white American feminists on abortion on demand.[28] Yet radical feminists
still tend to focus on dominant culture and the victimization of women.
Ann Snitow and Carol Vance clearly identify the problem with this
approach when they remark:

> To ignore the potential for variations (in women's sexual expression) is
> inadvertently to place women outside the culture except as passive recipients
> of official systems of symbols. It continues to deny what mainstream culture
> has always tried to make invisible – the complex struggles of disenfranchised
> groups to grapple with oppression using symbolic as well as economic and
> political resistance.[29]

Rather than generalize on the basis of the stereotypes provided by "dominant culture," feminists must explore the meaning of the diversity of
sexual practices to those who practice them, to resurrect the "subjugated
knowledge" of sexuality elided within dominant culture.

Secondly, both radicals and libertarians tend to isolate sexuality as the
key cause of women's oppression. Therefore, they locate power in a
central source and identify a universal strategy for seizing control of
sexuality (for instance, eliminate pornography, transgress sexual taboos
by giving expression to sexual desire). Both of these analyses are simplistic
and reductionist. While it is important, sexuality is simply one of the
many areas of everyday life in which power operates.

In sum, the critique of the sexuality debates developed out of a politics
of difference amounts to (1) a call for more detailed research into the
diverse range of women's sexual experiences, and (2) avoiding analyses
which invoke universal explanatory categories or a binary model of oppression and thereby overlook the many differences in women's experience
of sexuality. Although a politics of difference does not offer feminists a
morality derived from a universal theory of oppression, it need not lapse
into a form of pluralism in which anything goes. On the basis of specific
theoretical analyses of particular struggles, one can make generalizations,
identify patterns in relations of power and thereby identify the relative

effectiveness or ineffectiveness, safety or danger of particular practices. For example, a series of links have been established between the radical feminist strategy of antipornography legislation and the New Right's efforts to censor any sexual practices which pose a threat to the family. This is not to suggest that the antipornography movement is essentially reactionary, but rather that at this time it may be dangerous. Similarly, one ought not to assume that there is any necessary connection between transgression of sexual taboos and human liberation. Denying that censorship is the answer is not tantamount to endorsing any particular form of transgression as liberatory.

In a feminist politics of difference, theory and moral judgements would be geared to specific contexts. This need not preclude systematic analysis of the present, but would require that our categories be provisional. As Snitow and Vance point out: "We need to live with the uncertainties that arise along with the change we desire."[30] What is certain is that our differences are ambiguous; they may be used either to divide us or to enrich our politics. If we are not the ones to give voice to them, then history suggests that they will continue to be either misnamed and distorted, or simply reduced to silence.

Notes

1 See Cherrie Moraga and Gloria Anzaldúa, eds, *This Bridge Called My Back: Writings of Radical Women of Color* (Boston: Persephone Press, 1981); Bonnie Thornton Dill, "Race, Class, and Gender: Prospects for an all inclusive Sisterhood," *Feminist Studies*, 9(1), 1983, pp. 131–50; Floya Anthias and Nira Yuval-Davis, "Contextualizing Feminism – Gender, Ethnic, and Class Divisions," *Feminist Studies*, 15, 1983, pp. 62–74.
2 Audre Lorde, *Sister Outsider*, (New York: Crossing Press, 1984).
3 Ibid., p. 120.
4 Ibid., p. 115.
5 "Revolutionary" feminisms are those which appeal to the notion of a "subject of history" and to the category of a "social totality" in their analyses of the theory and practice of social transformation.
6 Socialist feminism is an obvious alternative to the ones that I have chosen. It represents a theoretical development in feminism which is closest to embodying the basic insights of a politics of difference. See for example the work of Linda Nicholson, *Gender and History: The Limits of Social Theory in the Age of the Family* (New York: Columbia University Press, 1986).
7 Meaghan Morris and Paul Patton, eds, *The Pirate's Fiancée: Michel Foucault: Power, Truth, and Strategy* (Sydney: Feral, 1979) and Biddy Martin, "Feminism, Criticism and Foucault," *New German Critique*, 27, 1982, pp. 3–30.
8 Michel Foucault, introduction to *Herculin Barbarin: Being the Recently Discovered*

Memoirs of a Nineteenth Century French Hermaphrodite (New York: Pantheon, 1980), p. 122.

9 Ibid., p. 99.

10 One feminist critic charges that Foucault's institutionalist theory of sexuality results in a picture of the "one-dimensional" containment of sexuality by objective forces beyond our control. She claims that it obscures the "continuous struggles of women against . . . patriarchy. . ." Yet her criticism begs the question since it assumes that an emancipatory theory must rest on the notion of a continuous revolutionary subject. Foucault, after all, is attempting to displace the problem of the subject altogether. See Jacqueline Zita, "Historical Amnesia and the Lesbian Continuum," in *Feminist Theory: A Critique of Ideology*, ed. Nannerl Keohane, Michèlle Z. Rosaldo, and Barbara C. Gelpi (Chicago: Chicago University Press, 1982), p. 173.

11 See Foucault's reproduction of the memoirs of a hermaphrodite for an example of his effort to resurrect a knowledge of resistance. This memoir is an account of the despair experienced by Herculine (formerly Alexina) once a male sexual identity is imposed upon her in her "happy limbo of non-identity." This occurs at a time when the legal and medical profession has become interested in the question of sexual identity and has decided that every individual must be either male or female. Foucault, *Herculin Barbarin*.

12 Michel Foucault, *The History of Sexuality, 1: An Introduction* (New York: Pantheon, 1978), p. 95.

13 Michel Foucault, "The History of Sexuality: An Interview," trans. Geoff Bennington, *Oxford Literary Review*, 4(2), 1980, p. 13.

14 Michel Foucault, "The Subject and Power," afterword, in Hubert Dreyfus and Paul Rabinow, *Michel Foucault: Beyond Structuralism and Hermeneytics*, (Chicago: University of Chicago Press, 1982–3), p. 221.

15 Ibid., p. 224.

16 Foucault, *Herculin Barbarin*, p. 208.

17 Ibid., p. 82.

18 Ibid., emphasis added.

19 For a similar argument against ahistorical criteria of effective resistance see Kathryn Pyne Addelson, "Words and Lives," in *Feminist Theory*, ed. Keohane et al.

20 John Rajchman, "The Story of Foucault's History," *Social Text*, 8, 1984, p. 15.

21 Foucault, *Herculin Barbarin*, p. 126.

22 Linda Nicholson describes an explicitly historical feminism in which the search for origins (genealogy) involves an attempt to deconstruct (give an account of the process of construction of) our present categories (e.g. "personal," "public") and thereby free us from a rigid adherence to them. Foucault's genealogies serve the same function. See Nicholson, *Gender and History*.

23 Lorde, *Sister Outsider*, pp. 53–9.

24 Adrienne Rich, "Toward a Woman-centered University," in *On Lies, Secrets and Silence: Selected Prose 1966–1978*, (New York: W. W. Norton, 1979), p. 134.

25 Ann Ferguson, "Sex War: The Debate between Radical and Libertarian Feminists," *Signs*, 10(1), 1984, pp. 106–12.

26 Ibid., p. 110.

27 Rennie Simpson, "The Afro-American Male," in *The Powers of Desire: The Politics of Sexuality*, ed. Ann Snitow, Christine Stansell, and Sharon Thompson (New York: Monthly Review Press, 1983), pp. 229–35.

28 Valerie Amos and Pratibha Parmer, "Challenging Imperial Feminism," *Feminist Review*, 17, 1984, pp. 1–19.

29 Ann Snitow and Carol Vance, "Towards a Conversation about Sex in Feminism: A Modest Proposal," *Signs*, 10(1), 1984, p. 132.

30 Ibid., p. 133.

13

Hannah Arendt and Feminist Politics

Mary G. Dietz

Hannah Arendt, perhaps the most influential female political philosopher of the twentieth century, continuously championed the *bios politikos* – the realm of citizenship – as the domain of human freedom. In her major work, *The Human Condition*, Arendt appropriated the Aristotelian distinction between "mere life" and "the good life" in order to characterize the crisis of the contemporary age in the West. What we are witnessing, she argued, is the eclipse of the public realm of participatory politics and the emergence of an atomized society bent on sheer survival. Arendt's political vision was decisively Hellenic: the classical Greek *polis* of male citizens was her model of the public; Pericles, the Athenian statesman, was her exemplary citizen-hero; and the quest for freedom as glory was her political ideal.

A political theory so indebted to a culture of masculinity and hero worship was bound to meet with resistance in the feminist writings of the 1970s and 1980s, as feminists began to pursue a woman-centered theory of knowledge, and debunk the patriarchal assumptions of "male-stream" Western political thought. Thus Arendt was not spared the critical, anti-canonical gaze of feminist theory. For Adrienne Rich and Mary O'Brien, *The Human Condition* was simply another attempt to discredit "women's work," to deny the value of reproductive labor, and to reassert the superiority of masculinity. Pulling few punches, Rich argued that Arendt's work "embodies the tragedy of a female mind nourished on male ideologies"; and O'Brien called Arendt "a woman who accepts the normality and even the necessity of male supremacy."[1] For both Rich and O'Brien, Arendt's sins were not simply those of omission. By elevating politics and "the common world of men," they contended, she reinforced the legitimacy of "paterfamilias on his way to the freedom of the political realm," and denied the truly liberatory potential of the female realm of reproduction and mothering.[2]

Other scholars, however, drew some distinctively feminist dimensions from Arendt's political thought. In *Money, Sex, and Power*, Nancy Hartsock noted the significance of Arendt's concept of power as collective action, and her appreciation of "natality" or beginning anew, as promising elements for a feminist theory "grounded at the epistemological level of reproduction."[3] Hanna Pitkin observed that *The Human Condition* is located within "a framework of solicitude for the body of our Earth, the Mother of all living creatures"; so Arendt could hardly be described as hostile in principle to women's concerns.[4] More recently, Terry Winant found in Arendt's work, "the missing element in recent attempts to address the problem of grounding the feminist standpoint."[5]

These differing feminist interpretations of Arendt's political theory serve as the organizational framework of this essay. With the critical attacks of Rich and O'Brien in mind, I argue that *The Human Condition* does, in fact, exhibit a gender blindness that renders it a far less powerful account of politics and human freedom than it otherwise might have been had Arendt been attentive to women's place in the human condition. Unlike Rich and O'Brien, however, I am not ready to dismiss *The Human Condition* as hopelessly "male-stream"; nor do I think "the necessity of male supremacy" follows from Arendt's theoretical presuppositions. This essay also contends, then – in line with Hartsock and others – that Arendt's work has much to offer feminist thought, especially in its attempts to articulate a vision of politics and political life. Unlike Hartsock, however, I argue that an "Arendtian feminism" must continue to maintain an analytical distinction between political life on the one hand, and reproduction on the other, and also recognize the problematical nature of a feminist politics grounded in reproductive processes. Before proceeding to these arguments, it is necessary to outline in brief Arendt's understanding of the *vita activa* – labor, work, and action – which is the core of her theory in *The Human Condition* and the subject of so much feminist debate.

Labor, Work, and Action

Arendt begins *The Human Condition* by distinguishing among three "general human capacities which grow out of the human condition and are permanent, that is, which cannot be irretrievably lost so long as the human condition itself is not changed."[6] The three capacities and their "corresponding conditions" are labor and life, work and worldliness, and action and plurality; together they constitute the *vita activa*.[7] Arendt envisions labor, work, and action not as empirical or sociological generalizations about what people actually do, but rather as existential categories intended to distinguish the *vita activa* and reveal what it means to be human and "in the presence of other human beings" in the world.[8] These "existentials," however, do more than disclose that human beings cultivate, fabricate, and organize the world. In an expressly normative way, Arendt wants to judge the human condition, and to get us, in turn, "to think what we are doing" when we articulate and live out the conditions of our existence in particular ways.[9] Underlying *The Human Condition* is the notion that human history has been a story of continuously shifting "reversals" within the *vita activa* itself. In different historical moments from the classical to the contemporary age, labor, work, and action have been accorded higher or lower status within the hierarchy. Arendt argues that some moments of human experience – namely those in which "action" has been understood as the most meaningful human activity – are more glorious and free than those in which either "the labor of our body or the work of our hands" is elevated within the *vita activa*.[10] Hence her reverence for the age of Socrates and the public realm of the Greek *polis*, and her dismay over the ensuing events within Western culture and political thought (including liberalism and Marxism), as citizen-politics is increasingly lost and the world of action is displaced by the primacy of labor and work. The critique of the modern world that *The Human Condition* advances rests on the claim that we are now witnessing an unprecedented era in which the process-driven activity of labor dominates our understanding of human achievement. As a result, we live in and celebrate a world of automatically functioning jobholders, having lost all sense of what constitutes true freedom and collective public life.

When Arendt calls "life" the condition of labor, "worldliness" the condition of work, and "plurality" the condition of action, she means to associate a corresponding set of characteristics with each. Labor (*animal laborans*) corresponds to the biological process of the human body and hence to the process of growth and decay in nature itself. Necessity defines labor, insofar as laboring is concentrated exclusively on life and the demands of its maintenance. Labor takes place primarily in the private realm, the realm of the household, family, and intimate relations. The objects of labor – the most natural and ephemeral of tangible things – are the most consumed and, therefore, the least worldly. They are the products of the cyclical, biological, life process itself, "where no beginning and no end exist and where all natural things swing in changeless, deathless, repetition."[11] *Animal laborans* is also distinguished by a particular mentality or mode of thinking-in-the-world. It cannot conceive of the possibility of breaking free or beginning anew; "sheer inevitability" and privatization dominate it. Hence, Arendt refers to the "essential worldly futility" of the life process and the activity of *animal laborans*.[12]

In contrast to labor, work (*homo faber*) is the activity that corresponds to the "unnaturalness" of human existence. If "life" and the private realm locate the activity of *animal laborans*, then "the world" locates *homo faber*. Work is, literally, the working up of the world, the production of things-in-the-world. If *animal laborans* is caught up in nature and in the cyclical movement of the body's life processes, then *homo faber* is, as Arendt puts it, "free to produce and free to destroy."[13] The fabrication process, with its definite beginning and predictable end, governs *homo faber* activity. Repetition, the hallmark of labor, may or may not characterize work; at least it is not inherent in the activity itself. The objects of this activity, unlike those of labor, are relatively durable, permanent endproducts. They are not consumed, but rather used or enjoyed. The "fabrications" of *homo faber* have the function of "stabilizing" human life and they bear testimony to human productivity.[14]

Insofar as they are all *homo faber*, human beings think in terms of gaining mastery over nature, and approach the world itself as a controllable object, the "measure of man." This tendency to objectify things and persons in the world is a foreboding of, in Arendt's words, "a growing meaninglessness, where every end is transformed into a means," and even those things not constructed by human hands lose their value and are treated as instruments at the behest of the "lord and master of all things."[15] The corresponding mentality of *homo faber*, then, is a rational-instrumental attitude concerned with the usefulness of things and with the "sheer worldly existence" made possible through human artifice. Understood as an existential "type," *homo faber* is that aspect of human beingness that places its confidence in the belief that "every issue can be solved and every human motivation reduced to the principle of utility."[16]

What Arendt calls "action" stands in sharp contrast with, but is not unrelated to the activities of labor and work. In order to act, human beings must first have satisfied the demands of life, have a private realm for solitude, and also have a stable world within which they can achieve "solidity" and "retrieve their sameness . . . their identity."[17] At the same time, human beings possess extraordinary capabilities that neither labor nor work encompass. They can disclose themselves in speech and deed, and undertake new beginnings, thereby denying the bonds of nature and moving beyond the means–end confines of *homo faber*.[18] Without action to bring new beginnings (natality) into the play of the world, Arendt writes, there is nothing new under the sun; without speech, there is no memorialization, no remembrance.[19] Unlike either labor or work, action bears no corresponding singular Latin synonym, perhaps because Arendt means for it to capture an aspect of human life that is essentially collective, rather than solitary or distinguished by the "separateness" of persons. This collective condition, where speech and action materialize, Arendt calls "the human condition of plurality."[20]

Plurality is perhaps the key concept in Arendt's understanding of action. She uses it to explore the situation humans achieve when they "gather together and act in concert," thus finding themselves enmeshed within a "web of relationships."[21] In general terms, plurality is the simultaneous realization of shared equality and distinctive, individual differences. Arendt calls it "the basic condition of both action and speech."[22] Without equality, individuals would not be able to comprehend each other or communicate, and without distinctiveness, they would have no need or reason to communicate, no impetus to interject themselves as *unique* selves into the shared world. Plurality, then, is the common condition in which human beings reveal their "unique distinctiveness." Arendt presents this in terms of a paradox: "Plurality is the condition of human action because we are all the same, that is, human, in such a way that nobody is ever the same as anyone else who ever lived, lives, or will live."[23] Thus, plurality promotes the notion of a politics of shared differences.

Because Arendt introduces plurality as a political and not a metaphysical concept, she also locates this common condition in a discernible space which she calls "the public" or "the space of appearances."[24] The public exists in stark contrast to the private realm; it is where the revelation of individuality amidst collectivity takes place. The barest existence of a public realm "bestowed upon politics a dignity," Arendt writes, "that even today has not altogether disappeared."[25]

Arendt's concept of plurality as the basic condition of action and speech allows her to reconceptualize politics and power in significant ways. Put simply, politics at its most dignified is the realization of human plurality – the activity that simply *is* the sharing of the world and exemplary of the human capacity for "beginning anew" through mutual speech and deed.[26] Power, which Arendt understands as "acting together," maintains the space of appearances; as long as it persists, the public realm is preserved.[27] Politics is the activity that renders us something more than just the *animal laborans*, subject to the cyclicality of human biological processes, or the *homo faber*, artificer of the world. When Arendt characterizes action as the only activity entirely dependent on "being together" and "the existence of other people," she intends to posit the existential difference between politics on the one hand, and labor and work on the other. She also wants to use action as a way of getting us to consider yet one other dispositional capacity we possess – something she variously calls common sense, judging insight, or "representative thinking."[28] Representative thinking can be distinguished from both the process logic of *animal laborans* and the instrumentalism of *homo faber* insofar as it is guided by a respect for persons as distinctive agents, as "speakers of words and doers of deeds." In order to flourish, the public realm requires this way of thinking; it proceeds from the notion that we can put ourselves in the place of others, in a manner that is open, communicative, and aware of individual differences, opinions, and concerns.

Without question, Arendt understands politics as existentially superior to both labor and work. Thus she has often been interpreted as devaluing the latter, or worse, as having contempt for the lives of the poor and working classes – in her own words, "the vast majority of humankind."[29] Here it is worth repeating that Arendt presents labor, work, and action *not* as constructs of class or social relations, but rather as properties of the human condition which are within the range of every human being. Likewise, our "world alienation" is not a matter of rising masses or threatened aristocracies, but has to do with the fact that, as *humans*, we are rapidly losing our collective capacity for exercising power through shared word and deed, and succumbing ever more steadily to an existence governed by the instrumental calculations of *homo faber* and the process mentality of *animal laborans*. Freedom is fast disappearing in the face of the sheer survivalism and automatic functioning that is the condition of the modern world.

Women and the Human Condition

The feminist critic who approaches *The Human Condition* for the first time is likely to conclude that Arendt's *magnum opus*, with its generic male terms of reference, its homage to the canon of Western political thought, and its silences about women, reads like another contribution to a long line of political works in the tradition. Inconceivable as it may sound to contemporary feminists, Arendt mentions women only twice (aside from a few footnotes) in her lengthy discussion of the classical conception of labor and work, public and private. She observes, without comment, that in the sphere of the Greek household, men and women performed different tasks, and she acknowledges, briefly, that women and slaves "belonged to the same category and were hidden away" because their lives were devoted to bodily functions.[30] Her scholarly development of a conceptual history of labor and work is remarkably silent on the sexual division of labor in the family and on the way in which gender informed traditional understandings of labor and work in both classical and modern thought. Also missing from *The Human Condition* is any sustained discussion of women's systematic exclusion from the public realm throughout occidental history. Not only does Arendt seem to be trading in abstract, ahistorical categories; she also seems to have little awareness of the gender assumptions that underlie and complicate them.

Nevertheless, the feminist critic is well advised to give *The Human Condition* a second look. For, not unlike many other supposedly "male-stream" texts in political thought, Arendt's work is an enriching, not simply a frustrating, site for feminist criticism. Partly this is because of its scope and complexity; as the various feminist accounts mentioned earlier reveal, *The Human Condition* admits of no definitive interpretive conclusions. Moreover, Arendt herself offers some promising directions for feminist speculation concerning labor, work, and action. In this sense, although a feminist analysis never emerges in *The Human Condition*, the materials for one are always threatening to break out. What these materials are, and how they might enrich a feminist political theory despite Arendt's neglect of women and gender, is what I explore below. What I want to argue is that, from one possible feminist perspective, *The Human Condition* is *both* flawed and illuminating.

Although Arendt has been accused of romanticizing the public realm and ignoring the brutality and patriarchalism that attends politics, she is, in fact, not wholly inattentive to the historically grounded relationships that have structured the activities she posits as fundamental to the human condition.[31] From the beginning, she argues, some have sought ways to ease the burden of life by forcibly assigning to others the toil of *animal laborans*. Those who have been regularly reduced to the status of "world-less specimens of the species mankind," have made it possible for others to transcend "the toil and trouble of life" by standing on the backs of those they subordinate.[32] In the modern age, this subordination is most vividly revealed within the working class. The activity of *homo faber* has lost its worldly character and is now performed by a mass of workers who are bent upon sheer survival and reduced to little more than servants of mechanized processes. (Work of this kind brings *homo faber* ever closer to *animal laborans*.) Arendt is also aware that the freedom of the "man of action" – the speaker of words and doer of deeds in the public realm – is made possible because of others who labor, fabricate, and produce. The man of action, as citizen, thus "remains in dependence upon his fellow men."[33] She does not press the sociological analysis of labor, work, and action along the lines of master and slave, elite and mass, privileged and oppressed, nearly as far as she could. But she is not completely unconcerned with the coercive and oppressive aspects of human experience that have allowed the privileged alone to enjoy the benefits of action in the public realm.

Likewise, Arendt cannot be accused of completely overlooking the manifestations of patriarchal power within the historical development of the public and private realm. Although she literally renders the discussion as footnotes, she provides in small print some illuminating insights into various dimensions of our patriarchal history. She tells us, for instance, that the terms *dominus* and *paterfamilias* were synonymous throughout "the whole of occidental antiquity."[34] The realm of the ancient household was, literally, a miniature *patria* – a sphere of absolute, uncontested rule exercised by the father over women, children, and slaves. Only in the public realm did the *paterfamilias* shed his status as ruler, and become one among equals, simultaneously ruling and ruled. Only he was able to move between public and private as both citizen among citizens, and ruler over those not fit for admission to the public realm.

In her subtext discussion of the Greek distinction between labor and work (*ponos* and *ergon*), Arendt notes that Hesiod considered labor an evil that came out of Pandora's box. Work, however, was the gift of Eris, the goddess of good strife.[35] Earlier she also tells us that, for Aristotle, "the life of woman" is called *ponetikos* – that is, women's lives are "laborious, driven by necessity, and devoted, by nature, to bodily functions.[36] Following the poet and the philosopher, our patriarchal history begins by counting painful labor (*ponon alginoenta*) as "the first of the evils plaguing man," and by assigning to women and slaves the inevitable and ineliminable task of carrying out this labor, according to their respectively less rational and irrational natures.[37] These are the tasks that, for the Greeks, occupied and defined the private realm and were forced into hiding within the interior (*megaron*) of the house. Here Arendt observes that the Greek *megaron* and the Latin *atrium* have a strong connotation of darkness and blackness.[38] Thus the realm of women and slaves is, for the ancients, a realm of necessity, painful labor, and blackness. In its toil and trouble, the private realm symbolizes the denial of freedom and equality, and the deprivation of being heard and seen by others. In its material reality, it makes possible the Greek male's escape from the "first evil" into the life of the public.

As Arendt implies, then, for the realm of freedom and politics to exist and take on meaning, it needed an "other" – a realm of necessity and privacy against which it could define and assert itself.[39] That this realm of the other and the human practices that distinguish it came to be conceptualized in terms of the female and made the domain of women's lives is something feminist theorists have brought to light in powerful detail. In *The Human Condition*, Arendt presents even more evidence for this argument, but it is evidence she does not utilize in her own theorizing of the human condition. Indeed, despite numerous instances in which she comes close to something like a nascent "gender insight" in her analysis of the public and private realm, and the activity of labor and work, Arendt never fully develops this insight or incorporates it systematically into her theory of the human condition.

Nowhere, perhaps, is Arendt's failure to develop her evidence about gender more striking than in her discussion of the character and conditions of *animal laborans*. It is the most illuminating example of how the materials for a feminist analysis are present in *The Human Condition*, but in the end are left unplumbed by Arendt herself. Consider again some of the characteristics that distinguish the life of *animal laborans*, as Arendt presents them: enslavement by necessity and the burden of biological life, a primary concern with reproduction, absorption with the production of life and its regeneration, and a focus on the body, nature, and natural life processes. Labor assures "not only individual survival, but the life of the species," and, finally, there is the elemental happiness that is tied to laboring, to the predictable repetition of the cycle of life and from just "being alive."[40] As Arendt writes:

> The blessing or joy of labor is the human way to experience the sheer bliss of being alive which we share with all living creatures, and it is even the only way men, too, can remain and swing contentedly in nature's prescribed cycle . . . with the same happy and purposeless regularity with which day and night and life and death follow each other.[41]

The reference to "men" in this last passage sounds especially odd because the laboring Arendt has captured so vividly is more readily recognizable for the feminist reader as that associated with women's traditional activities as childbearers, preservers, and caretakers within the household and family.[42] Yet the activity of "world-protection, world-preservation, world-repair" that Arendt encompasses in her category "labor" is not acknowledged in *The Human Condition* as indicative of women's practices and activities.[43] But surely being "submerged in the over-all life process of the species," and identified with nature has been *women's* lot; being tied to biological processes has been women's destiny; facing the "essential worldly futility" of the lifecycle, within the darkness of the private realm, has been women's challenge. The cyclical, endlessly repetitive processes of household labor – cleaning, washing, mending, cooking, feeding, sweeping, rocking, tending – have been time-honored female ministrations, and also conceived of and justified as appropriate to women. Since the Greeks, the cyclical, biological processes of reproduction and labor have been associated with the female, and replicated in a multitude of historical institutions and practices. It is indeed curious that Arendt never makes this central feature of the human condition an integral part of her political analysis. Let us speculate nonetheless: what if *The Human Condition* had explored the category *animal laborans* as a social construction of "femaleness"? What else might we learn? A number of lessons emerge.

First, an Arendtian analysis enlightened by gender reveals that the "permanent capacities" of labor, work, and action are neither antiseptic analytical categories, nor "generic" human activities but rather social practices that have been arranged according to socially constituted and deeply entrenched sex differences. From Aristotle on, women have been systematically constructed as *animal laborans*, and deemed neither capable nor worthy of location with in the "space of appearances" that is action. Moreover, even when they are in the guise of *homo faber* – in the workplace of the "artificer" – women have carried out the routinized tasks of stoop labor on assembly lines, and as cleaners, cooks, and clericals. The mechanisms of institutionalized sexism have assigned to women unpaid, devalued, monotonous work, both within the private realm and within the world outside. Nominally *homo faber*, they are really *animal laborans*, transported from life into worldliness. It seems, then, that the fundamental existentials Arendt designates have actually been lived out as either male or female *identities*. *Animal laborans*, the "reproducer," has been structured and experienced as if it were natural to the female, and *homo faber* the "fabricator," has been constructed as if it were natural to the male. Once we see this, we can no longer understand the *vita activa* as a neutral stage on which male and female players appear in modes of laboring, working, or acting. These activities have, from the start, been "cordoned off" according to sex, and women have been consistently relegated – both materially and symbolically – to the lowest dimension of the *vita activa*, to the life or world of labor.

Second, and following from the above, an Arendtian analysis informed by gender allows us to see that the disappearance of the public world, and the loss of freedom, has been a reality for only one small part of humanity. Just as "citizen" is an identity until recently granted to (some) men alone, so the "lost treasure" of political freedom, as Arendt calls it, has in fact been the historical possession of only (some) men. The feminist reader who shares Arendt's regret over the disappearance of freedom in the modern world is also aware that the treasure was never women's to lose.[44] The most emancipatory aspect of human experience as Arendt presents it -- the collective determination of human community through shared speech and deliberation in the public sphere – is not a central aspect of female experience. Thus the human condition must be assessed not only for what it has lost, but for what it has done – for how it has systematically subordinated a portion of the human race, and refused them, on Arendt's telling, the most meaningful experience of human freedom.

Finally, an Arendtian analysis informed by gender, and the recognition of women's exclusion from the public, amplifies our conception of the relationship between public and private, and of freedom itself. Even if we were to recover the public realm Arendt so vididly imagines, no society could count itself free so long as women were refused admittance to the space of appearances or confined to gendered institutions within the private realm. But the admission of women into the public raises other questions, not the least of which is "who will tend to the private?" Or, as a graduate student I know puts it wryly, "Every citizen needs a wife."[45]

Thus, if we are to have a truly emancipated *human* condition, we must inquire after both the arrangements that constitute the public, and the conditions of the realm of necessity, without which the public world of citizens cannot flourish. Susan Okin acknowledges this when she writes:

> Only when men participate equally in what have been principally women's realms of meeting the daily material and psychological needs of those close to them, and when women participate equally in what have been principally men's realms of larger scale production, government, and intellectual and creative life, will members of both sexes develop a more complete *human* personality than has hitherto been possible.[46]

Notice that this formulation does not require the abandonment of a conception of public and private, or a refusal of the distinction between labor, work, and action. But it does require us, in both theory and practice, to disconnect gender from these conceptions and reconceptualize them accordingly, as genderless realms and genderless activities. By "genderless" I do not mean "androcentric," but rather relations and realms unfettered by roles assigned according to perceived "natural" differences between the sexes. As Hanna Pitkin writes: "Women should be as free as men to act publicly; men should be as free as women to nurture . . . A life confined entirely to personal and household concerns seems . . . stunted and impoverished, and so does a life so public or abstracted that it has lost all touch with the practical, everyday activities that sustain it."[47]

Arendt's failure to recognize, much less develop, the issues that surround the constitution of women as *animal laborans* is readily apparent. Her failure to integrate these issues into *The Human Condition* is particularly serious given her belief that we must "think what we are doing," lest we lose forever our understanding of those "higher and more meaningful activities" for the sake of which our release from the bonds of necessity deserves to be won."[48] Had she recognized that "thinking what we are doing" entails not just a reconsideration of the *vita activa*, but also an account of how gender is implicated in the *vita activa* itself, *The Human Condition* would have been a far more emancipatory project. For all her attentiveness to the relationship between public and private, however, Arendt's gender blindness prevents her from seeing these realms as domains that have historically enforced women's subordination. For all her concern for freedom, she seems not to consider the exclusion of women from the public world at all informative of her analysis of the alienation of the contemporary age. In these respects, the androcentrism of Arendt's political theory diminishes her account of the very human condition she wishes us to comprehend.

Feminist Theory and the Public Realm

To the extent that *The Human Condition* fails to acknowledge the problem of women's subordination and (in bell hooks' terms) "the sexism perpetuated by institutions and social structures," it does not contribute to what we might call the "world-disclosing" aspect of a feminist theory.[49] It does not help us understand the ways in which the symbolic construction of gender has organized existing social practices and legitimized relations of domination.

Nevertheless, despite its inattention to issues related to sex and gender, *The Human Condition* has much to offer a feminist political theory. Accordingly, in the final section, I want to turn the tables and argue that Arendt's understanding of action and plurality as meaningful experiences of human freedom is something feminist theory should heed. In this respect, *The Human Condition* provides an orienting role for political self-understanding, and it encourages us to reconsider the way we think about the relationship between human practices and human identities.

Part of Arendt's critique of contemporary society involves her argument that politics as public life, as a space of appearances where citizens engage one another, deliberate, and debate, has nearly disappeared. As her emphasis on plurality indicates, Arendt means more by "participation in the space of appearances" than casting a ballot every four years or engaging in interest group activities. Indeed, the fact that we need to clarify the difference between voting and the active, public self-revelation of equals and peers as citizens is proof to Arendt that we have ceased to think of ourselves as, potentially, something more than just reproducers, producers, laborers, role-players, or fragile psyches. As the *vita activa* steadily becomes the province of *animal laborans*, so too, it seems, do our self-understandings. Our conceptualizations of who we are and what we are capable of doing are driven by the imperatives of "the last stage of laboring society"; hence we are less and less capable of imagining ourselves as mutually engaged citizens, or of thinking in terms of a political "we" rather than just an isolated "me." Our access to an understanding of politics as a public happiness has diminished; "mere" life overrules other considerations, the body supercedes the body politic, and the sheer survival of the individual as a "self" predominates over sensitivity to human plurality.

Athough it is not easy to say precisely what Arendt means by the notion that we have come to think what we are doing as *animal laborans*, she surely is getting at something more than just a cliché about the "me generation." Perhaps her argument is best summed up in terms of her own concepts: the modern age operates under the assumption that life, and not the world, is the highest good; the *immortality* of life – the possibility of achieving glory through speech and deed as public-spirited citizens – is a fading ideal. We are turned inward, and thrown back upon ourselves and our endlessly analyzed psyches. We are obsessed with society, wealth, and entertainment, but at a loss to comprehend the human condition as a being-in-the-presence-of-others in the *political* world. Remarking on the modern age, Arendt writes (in gendered language): "none of the higher capacities of man was any longer necessary to connect individual life with the life of the species; individual life became part of the life process, and to labor, to assure the continuity of one's own life and the life of the family, was all that was needed."[50]

Arendt intends for this indictment to cover philosophers of the modern age as well as ordinary agents. She numbers Marx, Kierkegaard, Nietzsche, and Bergson among those for whom political freedom and the worldliness of action have lost their meaning, or at least been radically transfigured. Hence the ultimate point of reference in their writings is not politics, action or plurality, but rather "life and life's fertility."[51] At least in the case of Kierkegaard and Nietzsche, the alternately agitated or aesthetic "I" replaces the politically engaged "we."

In the late twentieth century, a similar reluctance to theorize in political terms, by grounding the identity of human agents in the condition of plurality and in the capacity for speech and deed, seems to characterize certain forms of feminist theory. Nowhere perhaps is the temptation to theorize in the terms of *animal laborans* – with heightened attention to nature, reproduction, birth, the body, and the rhythmic processes of life itself – more prevalent than among those feminists who are concerned to argue that a privileged epistemological perspective emerges from specifically female practices and a generalizable women's condition. Consider, as examples, Mary O'Brien's emphasis on birth and reproduction as a starting point for a feminist theory of material relations, Nancy Hartsock's attention to the body's "desires, needs, and mortality" as a primary element in feminist epistemology, Adrienne Rich's concentration on "housework, childcare, and the repair of daily life" as the distinctive feature of women's community, Sara Ruddick's claim that daily nurturance and maternal work give women special insights into peace, and Julia Kristeva's case for the subversive potential of gestation, childbirth, and motherhood.[52] Although these theories are variously materialist, maternalist, and poststructuralist, they have in common an emancipatory vision that defends the moral (or subversive) possibilities of women's role as reproducer, nurturer, and preserver of vulnerable human life. O'Brien, for one, envisions a feminist theory "which celebrates once more the unity of cyclical time with historical time in the conscious and rational reproduction of the species. It will be a theory of the celebration of life in life rather than death in life."[53] Within this presumably celebratory vision an Arendtian might notice a tribute to *animal laborans*.

The temptation to theorize from the standpoint of women's bodies, and with an emphasis on reproduction, childbirth and mothering, bears a compelling logic. Women have been construed in terms of bodily processes and the so-called imperative of nature, and feminist theory, in its "world-disclosing" or critical aspects, confronts these putatively natural attributes and demystifies them. Feminist theory has revealed that, in O'Brien's words, "the private realm is where the new action is," insofar as the unmasking of structures of female subordination is concerend.[54] However, in the process of unmasking the manifold faces of power, many feminist theorists have, in effect, elevated the activities of *animal laborans* as the central features of women's identity and feminist politics. Guided by a reading of *The Human Condition* and Arendt's categories of the *vita activa*, we might consider why this feminist maneuver poses problems for a feminist theory of politics.

Unavoidably, when feminist theorists locate emancipatory or interventionist possibilities in "female reproductive consciousness" or within traditional female activities, they grant some warrant to the very patriarchal arrangements that have historically structured the *vita activa*. Of course, feminists appropriate these arrangements for purposes of emancipatory consciousness, but the subordination of women to *animal laborans* remains intact nonetheless. Accordingly, these feminist arguments – despite their transvaluation of women's work and bodily processes – legitimize a minimalist conception of women without considering a more expansive set of possibilities about what it means to be "in the presence of other human beings in the world." The celebration of *animal laborans* plays to a reduced, uniform conception of women's range of capabilities and their human identity within the *vita activa*. As Arendt's discussion of labor, work, and action invites us to see, however, being human involves more than just what Kristeva (appreciatively) calls "cycles, gestation, [and] the eternal recurrence of a biological rhythm which conforms to that of nature."[55] If female subjectivity has been traditionally linked to this latter form of temporality, then the goal of a feminist political theory should be to disengage female subjectivity from the straitjacket rather than to reinforce so restrictive a view of existential possibility and human potentiality.

Moreover, for an Arendtian, this disengagement from a theory of subjectivity rooted in *animal laborans* must be undertaken with a specifically political goal in mind. Whatever else we might wish to make of women as reproducers, mothers, or "celebrators of life in life," we should not confuse gender identification – or theories of subjectivity – with *political* emancipation. A feminist theory of political emancipation needs more than a focus on reproduction, birth, and childcare to sustain it. For, as much as we need to be reminded of the centrality of these experiences in the human condition, they do not and cannot serve as the focal point of a liberatory political theory. This is not only because, historically, reproduction, birth, and childcare have been practices as conducive to political oppression as to liberation. In addition, and perhaps more importantly, the language of birth and reproduction – constrained by its emphasis on a singular female physiology (or orientation) and the uniformity of women – simply does not provide feminism with the linguistic or conceptual context necessary for a theory of politics and political action. A theory of emancipatory politics must pay attention to diversity, solidarity, action-coordination, conflict, plurality, and the political equality (not the sameness) of women as citizens. None of these conceptual categories are forthcoming in theories grounded on singularity, physiology, necessity, uniformity, subjectivity, and the identity of women as reproducers.

Here, I think is where *The Human Condition* has the most to offer a feminist political theory. By articulating a conception of politics and political equality as collective action and the mutual engagement of peers in a public realm Arendt has us focus on what it means to be "speakers of words and doers of deeds" whose particular and distinctive identities deserve revelation in the public space of citizen politics. As a result, we shift our focus on human practices away from sheer biological, bodily processes on the one hand, and economic productivity on the other, and toward the constitution of public, political life. In this sense, Arendt forces theory to become expressly political, because she directs us toward the *public* aspect of human life and toward the human activity that determines all other human relations and arrangements in demonstrable ways. Moreover, she argues that the only polity that truly advances the freedom and plurality human beings are capable of experiencing, not to mention the conditions of existence they value and defend, is the polity that exhibits widespread participation in the public realm. To return to the notion of plurality, freedom is advanced when politics unfolds as the communicative interaction of diverse equals acting together as citizens.

Few feminist theorists have confronted the question of what constitutes a feminist politics in any systematic fashion, and fewer still have attempted to outline the contours of a feminist public realm.[56] In part, perhaps, this is because feminist theory has long had an ambivalence about matters public and political, and theoretical difficulties in distinguishing "politics" from "the patriarchal state." What has been historically constituted as the province of masculinity is often ceded to the male-stream, as feminists turn their attention toward the private domain of women's lives, thereby perpetuating the binary oppositions of "private woman, public man." As Arendt's existential analysis of the *vita activa* suggests, however, there is nothing intrinsically or essentially masculine about the public realm, just as there is nothing intrinsically or essentially feminine about laboring in the realm of necessity. The point is not to accept these gendered realms as fixed and immutable, but rather to undermine the gendering of public and private and move on to a more visionary and liberating conception of human practices, including those that constitute politics.

For feminists, Arendt's conception of plurality as politics may provide a promising place to begin. Plurality reinforces the notion of what Iris Young calls a "politics of difference," and emphasizes the heterogeneity of citizens. The unity Arendt imagines in the public realm is not mere uniformity, but rather a kind of solidarity engendered by the engagement of diversely constituted, unique individuals. Although Arendt did not pursue the concrete manifestations of plurality in any depth, she laid the groundwork for a political theory of action and difference, and a conception of civic "publics" as spaces where plurality can manifest itself. Without question, a feminist turn to plurality and politics would require the abandonment of some of the epistemological longings that underlie some current feminist theories – particularly the quest for univocality, certainty, and a fixed "standpoint" on reality. A feminist theory of politics as plurality needs to acknowledge multivocality, conflict, and the constantly shifting and ambiguous nature of politics itself. Given their appreciation of "otherness," however, and a growing attention to cultural diversity and heterogeneity, feminist theorists are also particularly well-situated for the task of developing our understanding of politics as plurality. Feminist theory also provides a powerful critique of the masculine virtue of "glory" that plays such an important role in Arendt's vision of action in the public realm. A feminist ethic of care, for example, might encourage us to imagine other dimensions of freedom, beyond glory, as vital to the public realm.

Equally significantly, Arendt's conception of politics places emphasis on a human capacity that has been central to much feminist theorizing – speech or "voice." Her case for political equality is informed by two basic insights concerning the human condition: that it is within the range of all human beings to insert themselves into the public realm through speech; and that the communicative interaction in which shared speakers engage as self-determining agents and representative thinkers is the essence of freedom. These insights raise other interesting questions for feminists that Arendt herself did not pursue, among them: what constitutes an ethic of communicative interaction among citizens? How can the diversity of speech and speakers be maintained and allowed to flourish? Do women bring a "different voice" or a "female consciousness" into the public realm? If so, how have these been manifested in practical, historical experience?[57] What should a feminist politics make of this voice and consciousness, if they indeed exist? All of these questions invite feminist attention, and encourage us to theorize both about who women are as citizens and about citizenship itself as a nongendered activity.

I have argued that Arendt's concepts of action and plurality provide an orienting role for a feminist theory of politics. Implicit in my argument is also an acceptance of the general distinctions she draws between labor, work, and action as general and permanent human capacities. In accepting the general framework of Arendt's theory, however, I do not mean to suggest that the distinctions she draws between these three modes of the *vita activa* are completely unproblematic. Nor are they exhaustive. Maternalist theorists, for instance, could rightly argue that mothering is as vital and perennial a human activity as labor, work, and action, and rightly insist that it does not fit easily under the parameters Arendt establishes for the *vita activa*. But neither are Arendt's analytical categories marked by the "artificiality" and "literal thoughtlessness" that O'Brien attributes to them. In some respects, of course, all analytical constructions are "artificial"; the issue is whether or not the theorist makes them a convincing and illuminating source for political reflection, as I think Arendt does.

In closing, then, I want briefly to reassert my case for *The Human Condition* as a source of political reflection, and with the hope of deflecting some possible responses to my appropriation of Arendt for a feminist theory of politics. Perhaps the most predictable response to this case for Arendt is that her theory not only privileges male "logocentric" reason but also continues in a tradition of disparaging the female body – or a "politics of the body" – and women's work. Rich comes close to the latter when she alludes to the "contempt and indifference" for the efforts of "women in labor" that typify theories like Arendt's.[58] But Rich misunderstands Arendt's characterization of labor. Nowhere does Arendt suggest that labor is a contemptible or insignificant activity. Her refusal to romanticize it should not be taken as offhand dismissal. To the contrary, Arendt writes that, "From the viewpoint of the life of the species, all activities indeed find their common denominator in laboring," and she says that the "blessing of life as a whole" is inherent in labor.[59] What Rich rightly wants to have philosophers acknowledge is not, however, in Arendt's view, the highest expression of human *freedom*. That comes only with collective action in the public realm. In fact, the glorification of *animal laborans* that Rich, like O'Brien, comes very close to exhibiting is precisely what Arendt thinks characterizes alienation and the loss of our capacity to think coherently about freedom in the contemporary world.

As for a "politics of the body," there is nothing in Arendt's discussion of plurality that posits "reason" over "passion" or condemns the literal body (or issues concerning life or the social control of the body) to the sphere of the private realm. In fact, Arendt's account of politics in the public realm brings courage, the spontaneity of passion, and "appearance" to the foreground, as crucial elements in the revelation of self that is part of collective speech and action. What she rejects, then, is not the presence of the body or a bodily politics but rather a political theory that locates the identity of persons only in a collective, singular, physiology – or in practices tied to the rhythmic cycles of nature. Arendt realizes human beings are ineliminably bound to nature, but we are also able to act in ways that at least temporarily defy the unremitting play of natural forces. Our bodies, in other words, are not merely the vessels of generative forces; they are also, along with our voices, integral to our appearance in the public world. This is one thing Arendt's discussion of plurality and individuals attempts to have us recognize. It is the *distinction* between the processes of reproduction on the one hand, where the body is conceived in a singularly narrow way, and action on the other, the collective power of embodied persons made political, that Arendt wants to preserve. Thus, Nancy Hartsock's attempt to return Arendt's theory of power to the body at "the epistemological level of reproduction" misses a fundamental point. In Arendt's theory, a "bodily politics" exists and exhibits itself in the life of action within the public realm. To ground politics in reproduction, as Hartsock wants to do, and thereby make *animal laborans* the source of power, is apples and oranges – Arendt's theory simply cannot be transformed this way and remain coherent.[60]

Finally, the problem of "reason." Although Arendt obviously considers thinking and rational argumentation essential to the interaction of citizens in the public realm, she distinguishes between the communicative rationality indicative of plurality, and the instrumental rationality of *homo faber*, who thinks in terms of ends and means. In short, Arendt is rightly aware that there are many different forms of reason, some of which are appropriate to the realm of politics and not antithetical to the recognition of otherness, some of which are not. Representative thinking, the mentality that distinguishes action in the public realm, is a good example of a form of reason that defies characterization in terms that would have us drive a wedge between reason and passion. It encompasses and incorporates both. Those who would dismiss her conception of public life as "too rational" or lacking in passion misapprehend the complexity of rationality in general and Arendt's "communications theory" of power more specifically.[61] We need only remember Tiananmen Square, a perfect example of the boundless and unpredictable "space of appearances" as Arendt envisions it, to understand that her vision of public life admits of passion and spontaneity as well as rational discourse, and the drama of visual, bodily appearances as well as "*logos*" and reason.

My defense of *The Human Condition* as a possible starting place for a feminist theory of politics is not an endorsement of Arendt's theory *tout court*. As I hope I have shown, a feminist analysis reveals much about the inadequacies of Arendt's major work as a commentary on both the classical and the contemporary age. Still, feminism – at least in its academic guise – needs a calling back to politics. In this respect, *The Human Condition* gives feminist thought ground on which to stand and develop an action-co-ordinating theory of political emancipation. Because she articulates such a powerful defense of public, participatory citizenship and of empowerment as speech and action in plurality, Arendt provides feminist thinkers with a way to proceed toward politics. For a movement such as feminism, which has so vividly illuminated the inequalities and injustices of existing gender relations, but has not yet advanced a transformative vision of politics, *The Human Condition* offers a place to begin anew, as we try to imagine better political worlds.

Notes

1 Adrienne Rich, *On Lies, Secrets, and Silence: Selected Prose 1966–1978* (New York: W. W. Norton, 1979), p. 212; and Mary O'Brien, *The Politics of Reproduction* (London: Routledge and Kegan Paul, 1981), pp. 99–100.
2 O'Brien, *Politics of Reproduction*, p. 101.
3 Nancy Hartsock, *Money, Sex, and Power* (Boston: Northeastern University Press, 1985), p. 259.
4 Hanna Fenichel Pitkin, "Justice: On Relating Private and Public," *Political Theory*, 9, 1981, pp. 303–26.
5 Terry Winant, "The Feminist Standpoint: A Matter of Language," *Hypatia*, 2, 1987, p. 124.
6 Hanna Arendt, *The Human Condition* (Chicago: University of Chicago Press, 1958), p. 6.
7 Ibid., p. 7.
8 Ibid., p. 22.
9 Ibid., p. 5.
10 Arendt takes the phrase in quotes from Locke, and uses it to set off her discussion of labor and work as the human activities elevated in both liberal and Marxist thought.
11 Arendt, *Human Condition*, p. 96.
12 Ibid., p. 131. For a helpful clarification of the relationship between labor, work, and action and the mentalities Arendt associates with them, see Pitkin, "Justice."
13 Arendt, *Human Condition*, p. 144. Or, as she also puts it, *homo faber*, the creator of human artifice, is also a "destroyer of nature" (p. 139).
14 Ibid., pp. 136–7.
15 Ibid., p. 157.
16 Ibid., p. 305.
17 Ibid., p. 137.
18 Ibid., p. 190.
19 Ibid., p. 204.

20 Ibid., p. 7.
21 Ibid., p. 244.
22 Ibid., p. 175. The spontaneous political uprising of the Chinese people in Tiananmen Square was one of the most dramatic examples of what Arendt means by "action" and "plurality." What arose there was a community of equals, "where everybody has the same capacity to act . . . and the impossibility of remaining unique masters of what they do, of knowing its consequences and relying upon the future" (p. 244). Arendt calls this the "price paid for plurality" – for the joy of inhabiting together with others a world whose reality is guaranteed for each by the presence of all. Hence her emphasis on the "unpredictability" and the "boundlessness" of action, as well as its inherent glory and irreducible collectivity.
23 Ibid., p.8.
24 Ibid., pp. 52, 204.
25 Ibid., p. 205.
26 Ibid., p. 9.
27 Ibid., p. 204.
28 Arendt develops the dimensions of this mentality more fully in her essay, "The Crisis in Culture," in her *Between Past and Future* (New York: Viking Press, 1961), pp. 220–4. In contemporary terminology, the capacity to judge is communicative, not rational-instrumental.
29 Arendt is well aware that, throughout history, vast numbers of people have been prevented from realizing their existentially highest human activities. See *Human Condition*, p. 199.
30 Ibid., p. 72.
31 See O'Brien, *Politics of Reproduction*, pp. 103–7.
32 Arendt, *Human Condition*, pp. 118–19.
33 Ibid., p. 144.
34 Ibid., p. 28.
35 Ibid., p. 83.
36 Ibid., p. 72.
37 Ibid., p. 48.
38 Ibid., p. 71.
39 Arendt notes that the private "was like the other, the dark and hidden side of the public realm." Ibid., p. 64.
40 Ibid., pp. 8, 88, 111, 119.
41 Ibid., p. 106.
42 By putting this point in this way I do not mean to imply that the activity of labor has been everywhere the same for all women or that we can understand women's laboring in some universal, transhistorical fashion. For my purposes, what is significant is that Arendt leaves out of her discussion any acknowledgement that it is *women* who have in fact been assigned this activity she describes as the "lowest" in the human condition.
43 The phrase in quotes is from Rich, *On Lies, Secrets, and Silence*, p. 205. As far as I can tell, she was the first to make this prescient observation about Arendt's *animal laborans*.
44 I am not suggesting that women have never participated in political life, only

that, historically, they have not been accorded formal recognition as the equals and peers of men as citizens in the public realm. For a stimulating account of the ways in which women in the United States have found ways of participating in public life despite the denial of political equality, see Sara Evans, *Born for Liberty: A History of Women in America* (New York: Free Press, 1989).

45 Thanks to Ron Steiner.

46 See p. 195 above.

47 Hanna Fenichel Pitkin, "Food and Freedom in *The Founder*," *Political Theory*, 12, 1984, p. 481.

48 Arendt, *Human Condition*, p. 5.

49 bell hooks, *Feminist Theory from Margin to Center* (Boston: South End Press, 1984), p. 43. For a lucid discussion of the difference between "world-disclosing" and "action-coordinating" theories, see Stephen White, "Poststructuralism and Political Reflection," *Political Theory*, 16, 1988, pp. 186–208.

50 Arendt, *Human Condition*, p. 321.

51 Ibid., p. 313.

52 See O'Brien, *Politics of Reproduction*; Hartsock, *Money, Sex and Power*; Rich, *On Lies, Secrets, and Silence*; Sara Ruddick, *Maternal Thinking: Toward a Politics of Peace* (Boston: Beacon Press, 1989); and Ann Rosalind Jones, "Julia Kristeva on Femininity: The Limits of a Semiotic Politics," *Feminist Review*, 18, 1984, pp. 56–73.

53 O'Brien, *Politics of Reproduction*, p. 209.

54 Ibid., p. 208.

55 Julia Kristeva, "Women's Time," in *Feminist Theory: A Critique of Ideology*, ed. Nannerl O. Keohane, Michelle Z. Rosaldo, and Barbara C. Gelpi (Chicago: University of Chicago Press, 1981), pp. 31–54.

56 One exception is Iris Marion Young, whose work has expressly addressed the nature of a feminist politics and civic public. See "Impartiality and the Civic Public: Some Implications of Feminist Critiques of Moral and Political Theory," in *Feminism as Critique*, ed. Seyla Benhabib and Drucilla Cornell (Cambridge: Polity; Minneapolis: University of Minnesota Press, 1987), pp. 56–76; "The Ideal of Community and the Politics of Difference," *Social Theory and Practice*, 12, 1986, pp. 1–26; and "Polity and Group Difference: A Critique of the Ideal of Universal Citizenship," *Ethics*, 99, 1989, pp. 250–74. Also see Nancy Fraser, "Toward a Discourse Ethic of Solidarity," *Praxis International*, 5, 1986, pp. 425–9.

57 On the significance of a "female consciousness" in politics, see Temma Kaplan, "Female Consciousness and Collective Action: The Case of Barcelona, 1910–1915," in *Feminist Theory*, ed. Keohane et al., pp. 55–76.

58 Rich, *On Lies, Secrets and Silence*, p. 206.

59 Arendt, *Human Condition*, pp. 107–8.

60 Hartsock, *Money, Sex, and Power*, pp. 258–9.

61 For a cogent critique of how some feminists misapprehend rationality and reason, see Mary Hawkesworth, "Knowers, Knowing, and Known: Feminist Theory and Claims of Truth," *Signs: Journal of Women in Culture and Society*, 14, 1989, pp. 533–57.

14

What's Critical about Critical Theory? The Case of Habermas and Gender

Nancy Fraser

To my mind, no one has yet improved on Marx's 1843 definition of Critical Theory as "the self-clarification of the struggles and wishes of the age."[1] What is so appealing about this definition is its straightforwardly political character. A critical theory, it says, frames its research in the light of the contemporary social movements with which it has a partisan though not uncritical identification. For example, if struggles contesting the subordination of women figured among the most significant of a given age, then a critical social theory for that time would seek to shed light on the character and bases of such subordination. It would employ categories and explanatory models that revealed rather than occluded relations of male dominance and female subordination. And it would demystify as ideological rival approaches that obfuscated or rationalized those relations. In this situation, then, one of the standards for assessing a critical theory, once it had been subjected to all the usual tests of empirical adequacy, would be: how well does it theorize the situation and prospects of the feminist movement? To what extent does it serve the self-clarification of the struggles and wishes of contemporary women?

In what follows, I am going to presuppose the conception of critical theory that I have just outlined. In addition, I am going to take as the actual situation of our age the scenario I just sketched as hypothetical. On this basis, I shall examine the critical social theory of Jürgen Habermas as elaborated in *The Theory of Communicative Action* and related recent writings.[2] I shall ask: In what proportions does Habermas's theory clarify and/or mystify the bases of male dominance and female subordination in modern societies? In what respects does it challenge and/or replicate prevalent ideological rationalizations of such dominance and subordination? To what extent does it serve the self-clarification of the struggles and wishes of contemporary women's movements? In short, with respect to gender, what is critical and what is not in Habermas's social theory?

I shall proceed as follows. In the first section, I examine some elements of Habermas's social-theoretical framework in order to see how it casts childrearing and the male-headed, modern, restricted, nuclear family. In the second section, I look at his account of the relations between public and private spheres of life in classical capitalist societies and I reconstruct the unthematized gender subtext. Finally, in the third section, I consider Habermas's account of the dynamics, crisis tendencies, and conflict potentials specific to contemporary, Western, welfare state capitalism, so as to see in what light it casts contemporary feminist struggles.

The Social-theoretical Framework: A Feminist Interrogation

Let me begin by considering two distinctions that are central to Habermas's framework. The first is the distinction between the symbolic reproduction and the material reproduction of societies. On the one hand, claims Habermas, societies must reproduce themselves materially; they must successfully regulate the metabolic exchange of groups of biological individuals with a nonhuman, physical environment and with other social systems. On the other hand, societies must reproduce themselves symbolically; they must maintain and transmit to new members the linguistically elaborated norms and patterns of interpretation that are constitutive of social identities. Habermas claims that material reproduction transpires via "social labor." Symbolic reproduction, on the other hand, involves the socialization of the young, the cementing of group solidarity, and the transmission and extension of cultural traditions.[3] Finally, according to Habermas, in capitalist societies, the activities comprising the sphere of paid work count as material reproduction activities, since they are "social labor" and serve the function of material reproduction. In contrast, the childrearing practices performed without pay by women in the domestic sphere – let us call them "women's unpaid childrearing work" – count as symbolic reproduction activities, since, in his view, they serve socialization and the function of symbolic reproduction.[4]

It is worth noting, I think, that Habermas's distinction between symbolic and material reproduction is susceptible to two different interpretations. The first takes it to demarcate two objectively distinct "natural kinds," implying that childrearing, for example, simply *is* in itself a symbolic reproduction activity. The second interpretation, by contrast, treats the distinction pragmatically and contextually, implying only that it could be useful for certain purposes to consider childrearing practices from the standpoint of symbolic reproduction.

Now I want to argue that the natural kinds interpretation is conceptually inadequate and potentially ideological. I claim that it is not the case that childrearing practices serve symbolic as opposed to material reproduction. Granted, they comprise language-teaching and initiation into social mores, but also feeding, bathing, and protection from physical harm. Granted, they regulate children's interactions with other people, but also their interactions with physical nature. In short, not just the construction of children's social identities but also their biological survival is at stake. And so, therefore, is the biological survival of the societies they belong to. Thus, childrearing is not *per se* symbolic reproduction activity; it is equally and at the same time material reproduction activity. It is a "dual-aspect" activity.[5]

But the same is true of the activities institutionalized in modern capitalist paid work. Granted, the production of food and objects contributes to the biological survival of members of society. But it also and at the same time reproduces social identities. Not just nourishment and shelter *simpliciter* are produced, but culturally elaborated forms of nourishment and shelter. Moreover, such production occurs via symbolically mediated, norm-governed social practices. These serve to form, maintain, and modify the social identities of persons directly involved and indirectly affected. One need only think of an activity like computer programming for a wage in the US pharmaceutical industry to appreciate the thoroughly symbolic character of "social labor." Thus, such labor, like unpaid childrearing work, is a "dual-aspect" activity.

Thus, the distinction between women's unpaid childrearing work and other forms of work cannot be a distinction of natural kinds. Indeed, the classification of childrearing as symbolic reproduction and of other work as material reproduction is potentially ideological. It could be used, for example, to legitimate the institutional separation of childrearing from paid work, a separation that many feminists, including myself, consider a linchpin of modern forms of women's subordination. Whether Habermas uses the distinction in this way will be considered shortly.

The second component of Habermas's framework that I want to examine is his distinction between "socially integrated action contexts" and "system integrated action contexts." Socially integrated action contexts are those in which different agents coordinate their actions with one another by means of an explicit or implicit intersubjective consensus about norms, values, and ends. System-integrated action contexts, on the other hand, are those in which the actions of different agents are coordinated by the functional interlacing of unintended consequences, while each individual action is determined by self-interested, utility-maximizing calculations in the "media" of money and power.[6] Habermas considers the capitalist economic system to be the paradigm case of a system-integrated action context. By contrast, he takes the modern nuclear family to be a socially integrated action context.[7]

Once again, I think it useful to distinguish two possible interpretations of Habermas's position. The first takes the contrast between the two kinds of action contexts as registering an absolute difference. It implies that system-integrated contexts involve absolutely no consensuality or reference to moral norms and values, whereas socially integrated contexts involve absolutely no strategic calculations in the media of money and power. This "absolute differences" interpretation is at odds with a second possibility that takes the contrast, rather, to register a difference in degree.

Now I contend that the absolute differences interpretation is too extreme to be useful for social theory and that, in addition, it is potentially ideological. In few if any human action contexts are actions coordinated absolutely nonconsensually and nonnormatively. In the capitalist marketplace, for example, strategic, utility-maximizing exchanges occur against a horizon of intersubjectively shared meanings and norms; agents normally subscribe to some commonly held notions of reciprocity and to some shared conceptions of the social meanings of objects, including what sorts of things are exchangeable. Similarly, in the capitalist workplace, managers and subordinates, as well as coworkers, normally coordinate their actions to some extent consensually and with some reference to normative assumptions, though the consensus be arrived at unfairly and the norms be incapable of withstanding critical scrutiny. Thus, the capitalist economic system has a moral-cultural dimension.

Similarly, few if any human action contexts are wholly devoid of strategic calculation. Gift rituals in noncapitalist societies, for example, once seen as veritable crucibles of solidarity, are now known to have a significant strategic, calculative dimension, one enacted in the medium of power, if not in that of money.[8] And, as I shall argue in more detail later, the modern nuclear family is not devoid of individual, self-interested, strategic calculations in either medium. These action contexts, then, while not officially counted as economic, have a strategic, economic dimension.

Thus, the absolute differences interpretation is not of much use in social theory. It fails to distinguish the capitalist economy – let us call it "the official economy" – from the modern nuclear family. For both of these institutions are mélanges of consensuality, normativity, and strategicality. But if this is so, then the classification of the official economy as a system-integrated action context and of the modern family as a socially integrated action context is potentially ideological. It could be used to exaggerate their differences and occlude their similarities, for example, by casting the family as the "negative," the complementary "other," of the (official) economic sphere, a "haven in a heartless world."

Now which of these possible interpretations of the two distinctions are the operative ones in Habermas's social theory? What use does he make of these distinctions? Habermas maps the distinction between action contexts onto the distinction between reproduction functions in order to model the institutional structure of modern societies. He holds that modern societies differ from premodern societies in that they split off some material reproduction functions from symbolic ones and hand over the former to two specialized institutions – the (official) economy and the state – which are system integrated. Modern societies also develop two "lifeworld" institutions, which specialize in symbolic reproduction and are socially integrated: the nuclear family, or "private sphere" and the space of political deliberation, or "public sphere." Thus, modern societies "uncouple," or separate, two distinct but previously undifferentiated aspects of society: "lifeworld" and "system."[9]

Now what are the critical insights and blindspots of this model? Consider, first, that Habermas's categorial divide between the "private sphere of the lifeworld" and the "private economic system" faithfully mirrors the institutional separation of family and official economy, household and paid workplace, in male-dominated, capitalist societies. It thus has some prima facie purchase on empirical social reality. But consider, too, that the characterization of the family as a socially integrated, symbolic reproduction domain and of the paid workplace, on the other hand, as a system-integrated material reproduction domain tends to exaggerate the differences and occlude the similarities between them. It directs attention away from the fact that the household, like the paid workplace, is a site of labor, albeit of unremunerated and often unrecognized labor. It obscures the fact that in the paid workplace, as in the household, women are assigned distinctively feminine, service-oriented and often sexualized occupations. And it fails to focalize the fact that in both spheres women are subordinated to men.

Moreover, this characterization casts the male-headed, nuclear family as having only an extrinsic and incidental relation to money and power. These "media" are taken as definitive of interactions in the official economy and the state but as only incidental to intrafamilial ones. But this assumption is counterfactual. Feminists have shown via analyses of contemporary familial decision-making, handling of finances, and wife-battering that families are thoroughly permeated with money and power. They are sites of egocentric, strategic, and instrumental calcuation as well as sites of usually exploitative exchanges of services, labor, cash, and sex, not to mention sites, frequently, of coercion and violence.[10] But Habermas's way of contrasting the modern family with the official capitalist economy occludes all this. It overstates the differences between these institutions and blocks the possibility of analyzing families as economic systems – as sites of labor, exchange, calculation, distribution, and exploitation.

Thus, Habermas's model has some empirical deficiencies. It is not easily able to capture some dimensions of male dominance in modern societies. Yet his framework does offer a conceptual resource suitable for understanding *other* aspects of modern male dominance. He subdivides the category of socially integrated action contexts into two subcategories. On the one hand, there are "normatively secured" forms of socially integrated action. These are actions coordinated on the basis of a conventional, prereflective, taken-for-granted consensus about values and ends, consensus rooted in the precritical internalization of cultural tradition. On the other hand, there are "communicatively achieved" forms of socially integrated action. These involve actions coordinated by explicit, reflectively achieved consensus, consensus reached by unconstrained discussion under conditions of freedom, equality, and fairness.[11]

This distinction constitutes a critical resource for analyzing the modern male-headed nuclear family. Such families can be understood as normatively secured rather than communicatively achieved action contexts, as contexts where actions are (sometimes) mediated by consensus and shared values, but where such consensus is suspect because prereflective or because achieved through dialogue vitiated by unfairness, coercion or inequality. This fits nicely with recent research on patterns of communication between husbands and wives. This research shows that men tend to control conversations, determining what topics are pursued, while women do more "interaction work" like asking questions and providing verbal support.[12]

Thus, Habermas's distinction enables us to capture something important about intrafamilial dynamics. What is insufficiently stressed, however, is that actions coordinated by normatively secured consensus are actions regulated by power. It is a grave mistake to restrict the use of the term "power" to bureaucratic contexts. Habermas would do better to distinguish different kinds of power, for example, domestic-patriarchal power, on the one hand, and bureaucratic-patriarchal power, on the other, not to mention other kinds as well.

Let me turn now to the normative political implications of Habermas's model. What sorts of social arrangements does it legitimate and what sorts of social transformations does it rule out? The view of modernization as the uncoupling of system and lifeworld tends to legitimate the modern institutional separation of family and official economy, childrearing and paid work. For Habermas claims that symbolic reproduction activities cannot be turned over to specialized systems set apart from the lifeworld; their inherently symbolic character requires that they be socially integrated.[13] It follows that women's unpaid childrearing work could not be incorporated into the (official) economic system without "pathological" results. Yet Habermas also holds that it is a mark of societal rationalization that systems be differentiated to handle material reproduction functions; the separation of a specialized (official) economic system enhances a society's capacity to deal with its natural and social environment. "System complexity," then, constitutes a "developmental advance." It follows that the (official) economic system of paid work could not be dedifferentiated with respect to childrearing without societal "regression." But if child-rearing could not be nonpathologically incorporated into the (official) economic system, and if the (official) economic system could not be nonregressively dedifferentiated, then the continued separation of child-rearing from paid work would be unavoidable.

This amounts to a defense of an arrangement that is widely held to be a linchpin of modern women's subordination, namely, the separation of the official economic sphere from the domestic sphere and the enclaving of childrearing from the rest of social labor. The fact that Habermas is a socialist does not alter the matter. For the (undeniably desirable) elimination of private ownership, profit orientation and hierarchical command in paid work would not of itself alter the official-economic/domestic separation.

Now I want to challenge several premises of the reasoning I have just reconstructed. First, this reasoning assumes the natural kinds inter-pretation of the symbolic reproduction versus material reproduction dis-tinction. But since childrearing is a dual-aspect activity, and since it is not categorially different in this respect from other work, there is no warrant for assuming that the system-integrated organization of childrearing would be any more (or less) pathological than that of other work. Second, this reasoning assumes the absolute differences interpretation of the social integration versus system integration distinction. But since the modern male-headed nuclear family is a mélange of (normatively secured) con-sensuality, normativity and strategicality, and since it is in this respect not categorially different from the paid workplace, then privatized childrearing is already permeated by money and power. Third, the reasoning just sketched permits system complexity to trump proposed social transform-ations aimed at overcoming women's subordination. But this is at odds with Habermas's professions that system complexity is only one measure of "progress" among others. More importantly, it is at odds with any reasonable standard of justice.

What, then, should we conclude about the normative, political implica-tions of Habermas's model? If the conception of modernization as the uncoupling of system and lifeworld institutions does indeed have the implications I have just drawn from it, then it is in important respects androcentric and ideological.

Public and Private in Classical Capitalism: Thematizing the Gender Subtext

The foregoing difficulties notwithstanding, Habermas offers an account of arenas of public and private life in classical capitalism that has some genuine critical potential. But in order to realize this potential fully, we need to reconstruct the unthematized gender subtext.

Consider Habermas's account of the ways in which the (official) economic and state systems are linked to the lifeworld. The "private sphere," or family, is linked to the (official) economy by means of a series of exchanges conducted in the medium of money; it supplies the (official) economy with appropriately socialized labor power in exchange for wages; and it provides monetarily measured demand for commodified goods and services. Exchanges between the family and the (official) economy, then, are channeled through the "roles" of worker and consumer. In contrast, the "public sphere," or space of political participation, is linked to the state-administrative system by exchanges in the "medium of power"; loyalty, obedience, and tax revenues are exchanged for "organizational results" and "political decisions." Exchanges between the public sphere and the state, then, are channeled through the "role" of citizen and, in late welfare state capitalism, that of client.[14]

This account has a number of important advantages. By modelling a relation among four terms – family, (official) economy, state, and "public sphere" – Habermas corrects standard dualistic approaches to the separation of public and private. His view suggests that in classical capitalism there are actually two distinct but interrelated public/private separations. There is one public/private separation at the level of "systems," namely, the separation of the state, or public system, from the (official) capitalist economy, or private system. There is another public/private separation at the level of the "lifeworld," namely, the separation of the family, or private sphere, from the space of political participation, or public sphere. Moreover, each of these public/private separations is coordinated with the other. One link runs between private system and private lifeworld sphere, that is, between (official) capitalist economy and nuclear family. Another runs between public system and public lifeworld sphere, or between state administration and arenas of political participation. In each case, the link consists in the institutionalization of specific roles: worker and consumer, citizen and (later) client.

Thus, Habermas provides a sophisticated account of the relations between public and private institutions in classical capitalist societies. Yet there are also some significant weaknesses. These are due to his failure to thematize the gender subtext of the material.

Take the role of the worker. In male-dominated, classical capitalist societies, this role is a masculine role. Masculinity here is in large part a matter of leaving home each day for a place of paid work and returning with a wage that provides for one's dependents. This internal relation between being a man and being a provider explains why in capitalist societies unemployment can be so psychologically as well as economically devastating for men. It also explains the centrality of the struggle for a "family wage" in the history of the workers' and trade union movements of the nineteenth and twentieth centuries. This was a struggle for a wage conceived not as a payment to a genderless individual for the use of labor power but, rather, as a payment to a man for the support of his economically dependent wife and children; and it rationalized the practice of paying women less for equal or comparable work.[15]

The masculine subtext of the worker role is confirmed by the vexed character of women's relation to paid work in male-dominated classical capitalism. As Carole Pateman puts it, it is not that women are absent from the paid workplace; it's rather that they are present differently[16] – for example, as feminized and sometimes sexualized "service" workers; as members of the "helping professions" utilizing mothering skills; as targets of sexual harassment; as low-waged, low-skilled, low-status workers in sex-segregated occupations; as part-time workers; as "working wives," "working mothers" and "supplemental earners." These differences in the quality of women's presence in the paid workplace testify to the conceptual dissonance between femininity and the worker role in classical capitalism and, so, to the masculine subtext of that role.

Conversely, the consumer, the other role linking the official economy and the family in Habermas's scheme, has a feminine subtext. For the sexual division of labor assigns to women the work – and it is indeed work, though unpaid and usually unrecognized work – of purchasing and preparing goods and services for domestic consumption. You can confirm this even today by visiting any supermarket or department store. Or by looking at the history of consumer goods advertising. Such advertising has nearly always addressed the consumer as feminine. It is only relatively recently, and with some difficulty, that advertisers have devised ways of interpellating a masculine subject of consumption. The difficulty and lateness of that development confirm the gendered character of the consumer role in classical capitalism. Men occupy it with conceptual strain and cognitive dissonance, much as women occupy the role of worker.

Moreover, Habermas's account of the roles linking family and (official) economy contains a significant omission. There is no mention in his schema of any childrearer role, although the material clearly requires one. For who else is performing the unpaid work of overseeing the production of the "appropriately socialized labor power" that the family exchanges for wages? Of course, the childrearer role in classical capitalism (as elsewhere) is patently a feminine role. Its omission here is a mark of androcentrism.

What, then, of the other set of roles and linkages identified by Habermas? What of the citizen role that connects the public system of the administrative state with the public lifeworld sphere of political participation? This role, too, is a gendered role in classical capitalism, indeed, a masculine role. And not simply in the sense that women did not win the vote in, for example, the US and Britain until the twentieth century. Rather, the lateness and difficulty of that victory are symptomatic of deeper strains. In Habermas's view, citizenship means participation in political debate and public opinion formation. It depends crucially on the capacities for consent and speech, the ability to participate on a par with others in dialogue. But these are capacities that are connected with masculinity in male-dominated, classical capitalism; they are often denied to women and deemed at odds with femininity. I have already cited studies about the effects of male dominance and female subordination on the dynamics of dialogue. Now consider that even today in most jurisdictions there is no such thing as marital rape. A wife is legally subject to her husband; she is not an individual who can give or withhold consent to his demands for sexual access. Consider also that even outside of marriage the legal test of rape is whether a "reasonable man" would have assumed that the woman had consented. Consider what that means when both popular and legal opinion widely holds that when a woman says "no" she means "yes." It means, says Carole Pateman, that "women find their speech . . . persistently and systematically invalidated in the crucial matter of consent, a matter that is fundamental to democracy. [But] if women's words about consent are consistently reinterpreted, how can they participate in the debate among citizens?"[17]

Thus, there is conceptual dissonance between femininity and the dialogical capacities central to Habermas's conception of citizenship. And there is another aspect of citizenship not discussed by him that is even more obviously bound up with masculinity. I mean the soldiering aspect of citizenship, the conception of the citizen as the defender of the polity and protector of those – women, children, the elderly – who allegedly cannot protect themselves. As Judith Stiehm has argued, this division between male protectors and female protected introduces further dissonance into women's relation to citizenship.[18] It confirms the gender subtext of the citizen role that links the state and the public sphere in male-dominated classical capitalism.

Thus, there are some major lacunae in Habermas's model. The gender-blindness of the model occludes important features of the arrangements he wants to understand. By omitting any mention of the childrearer role, and by failing to thematize the gender subtext underlying the roles of worker and consumer, Habermas fails to understand precisely how the capitalist workplace is linked to the modern male-headed, nuclear family. Similarly, by failing to thematize the masculine subtext of the citizen role, he misses the full meaning of the way the state is linked to the public sphere of political speech. Moreover, Habermas misses important cross-connections among the four elements of his model. He misses, for example, the way the masculine citizen-soldier-protector role links the state and public sphere not only to one another but also to the family and to the paid workplace, that is, the way the assumptions of man's capacity to protect and woman's need of man's protection run through all of them. He misses, too, the way the masculine citizen-speaker role links the state and public sphere not only to one another but also to the family and official economy, that is, the way the assumptions of man's capacity to speak and consent and woman's comparative incapacity run through all of them. He misses, also, the way the masculine worker-breadwinner role links the family and official economy not only to one another but also to the state and the political public sphere, that is, the way the assumptions of man's provider status and of woman's dependent status run through all of them. And he misses, finally, the way the feminine childrearer role links all four institutions to one another by overseeing the construction of the masculine and feminine gendered subjects needed to fill *every* role in classical capitalism.

Once the gender-blindness of Habermas's model is overcome, however, all these connections come into view. It then becomes clear that gender norms run like pink and blue threads through paid work, state administration, and citizenship as well as through familial and sexual relations. Moreover, a gender-sensitive reading of these connections has some important theoretical and conceptual implications. It reveals that male dominance is intrinsic rather than accidental to classical capitalism, since the institutional structure of this social formation is actualized by means of gendered roles. It follows that the forms of male dominance at issue here are not properly understood as lingering forms of premodern status inequality. They are, rather, intrinsically modern in Habermas's sense, since they are premised on the separation of waged labor and the state from female childrearing and the household. It also follows that a critical social theory of capitalist societies needs gender-sensitive categories. The preceding analysis shows that, contrary to the usual androcentric understanding, the relevant concepts of worker, consumer, and wage are not, in fact, strictly economic concepts. Rather, they have an implicit gender subtext and thus are "gender-economic" concepts. Likewise, the relevant concept of citizenship is not strictly a political concept; it has an implicit gender subtext and so, rather, is a "gender-political" concept. Thus, this analysis reveals the inadequacy of those critical theories that treat gender as incidental to politics and political economy. It highlights the need for a critical-theoretical categorial framework in which gender, politics, and political economy are internally integrated.

In addition, a gender-sensitive reading of these arrangements reveals the thoroughly multidirectional character of social motion in classical capitalism. It gives the lie to the orthodox Marxist assumption that all or most significant causal influence runs from the (official) economy to the family and not vice versa. It shows that gender norms structure paid work, state administration and political participation. Thus, it vindicates Habermas's claim that in classical capitalism the (official) economy is not all-powerful but is, rather, inscribed within and subject to the norms and meanings of everyday life. Of course, Habermas assumed that in making this claim he was saying something more or less positive. The norms and meanings he had in mind were not the ones I have been discussing. Still, the point is a valid one. It remains to be seen, though, whether it holds also for late, welfare state capitalism, as I believe, or whether it ceases to hold, as Habermas claims.

Finally, this reconstruction of the gender subtext of Habermas's model has some normative political implications. It suggests that an emancipatory transformation of male-dominated capitalist societies requires a transformation of these gendered roles and of the institutions they mediate. As long as the worker and childrearer roles are fundamentally incompatible with one another, it will not be possible to universalize either of them to include both genders. Thus, some form of dedifferentiation of unpaid childrearing and other work is required. Similarly, as long as the citizen role is defined to encompass death-dealing soldiering but not life-fostering childrearing, as long as it is tied to male-dominated modes of dialogue, then it, too, will remain incapable of including women fully. Thus, changes in the very concepts of citizenship, childrearing, and paid work are necessary, as are changes in the relationships among the domestic, official economic, state, and political public spheres.

The Dynamics of Welfare State Capitalism: A Feminist Critique

Let me turn, then, to Habermas's account of late, welfare state capitalism. Unlike his account of classical capitalism, its critical potential cannot be released simply by reconstructing the gender subtext. Here, the problematical features of his framework inflect the analysis as a whole and diminish its capacity to illuminate the struggles and wishes of contemporary women. In order to show how this is the case, I shall present Habermas's view in the form of six theses.

1 Welfare state capitalism emerges in response to instabilities inherent in classical capitalism. It realigns the relations between the (official) economy and state, rendering them more deeply intertwined with one another as the state actively engages in "crisis management." It tries to avert or manage economic crises by Keynesian "market replacing" strategies which create a "public sector." And it tries to avert or manage social and political crises by "market compensating" measures, including welfare concessions to trade unions and social movements. Thus welfare state capitalism partially overcomes the separation of public and private at the level of systems.[19]

2 The realignment of the (official) economy and the state brings changes in the roles linking those systems to the lifeworld. First, there is a major increase in the importance of the consumer role as dissatisfactions related to paid work are compensated by enhanced commodity consumption. Second, there is a major decline in the importance of the citizen role as journalism becomes mass media, political parties are bureaucratized, and participation is reduced to occasional voting. Finally, the relation to the state is increasingly channeled through a new role, the social welfare client.[20]

3 These developments are "ambivalent." On the one hand, there are gains in freedom with the institution of new social rights limiting the power of capital in the (paid) workplace and of the paterfamilias in the bourgeois family; and social insurance programs represent a clear advance over the paternalism of poor relief. On the other hand, the bureaucratic and monetary means employed to realize these new social rights tend perversely to endanger freedom. As these media structure the entitlements, benefits, and social services of the welfare system, they disempower clients, rendering them dependent on bureaucracies and therapeutocracies, and preempting their capacities to interpret their own needs, experiences and life problems.[21]

4 The most ambivalent welfare measures are those concerned with things like health care, care of the elderly, education, and family law, for when bureaucratic and monetary media structure these things, they intrude upon "core domains" of the lifeworld. They turn over symbolic reproduction functions like socialization and solidarity formation to modes of system integration. But given the inherently symbolic character of these functions, the results, *necessarily* are "pathological." Thus, these measures are more ambivalent than, say, reforms of the paid workplace. The latter bear on a domain that is already system integrated and that serves material as opposed to symbolic reproduction functions. So paid workplace reforms, unlike, say, family law reforms, do not necessarily generate "pathological" side-effects.[22]

5 Welfare state capitalism thus gives rise to an "inner colonization of

the lifeworld." Money and power cease to be mere media of exchange *between* system and lifeworld. Instead, they tend increasingly to penetrate the lifeworld's *internal* dynamics. The private and public spheres cease to subordinate (official) economic and administrative systems to the norms, values, and interpretations of everyday life. Rather, the latter are increasingly subordinated to the imperatives of the (official) economy and the administration. The roles of worker and citizen cease to channel the influence of the lifeworld to the systems. Instead, the newly inflated roles of consumer and client channel the influence of the system to the lifeworld. Moreover, the intrusion of system-integration mechanisms into domains inherently requiring social integration gives rise to "reification phenomena." The affected domains are detached not merely from traditional, normatively-secured consensus but from "value-orientations *per se*." The result is the "desiccation of communicative contexts" and the "depletion of the non-renewable cultural resources" needed to maintain personal and collective identity. Thus, symbolic reproduction is destabilized, identities are threatened, and social crisis tendencies develop.[23]

6 The colonization of the lifeworld sparks new forms of social conflict specific to welfare state capitalism. "New social movements" emerge in a "new conflict zone" at the "seam of system and lifeworld." They respond to system-induced identity threats by contesting the roles that transmit these. They contest the instrumentalization of professional labor transmitted via the worker role, the commodification of lifestyles transmitted via the inflated consumer role, the bureaucratization of life problems transmitted via the client role, and the rules and routines of interest politics transmitted via the impoverished citizen role. Thus, the conflicts at the cutting edge of developments in welfare state capitalism differ both from class struggles and from bourgeois liberation struggles. They respond to crisis tendencies in symbolic, as opposed to material, reproduction; and they contest reification and "the grammar of forms of life" as opposed to distribution or status inequality.[24]

The various new social movements can be classified with respect to their emancipatory potential. The criterion is the extent to which they advance the "decolonization of the lifeworld." Decolonization encompasses three things: first, the removal of system-integration mechanisms from symbolic reproduction spheres; second, the replacement of (some) normatively secured contexts by communicatively achieved ones; and third, the development of new, democratic institutions capable of asserting lifeworld control over state and (official) economic systems. Thus, those movements like religious fundamentalism which seek to defend traditional lifeworld norms against system intrusions are not genuinely emancipatory; they actively oppose the second element of decolonization and do not take up the third. Movements advocating peace and ecology are better; they aim both to resist system intrusions and also to instate new, reformed, communicatively achieved zones of interaction. But even these are "ambiguous" inasmuch as they tend to "retreat" into alternative communities and "particularistic" identities, thereby effectively renouncing the third element of decolonization and leaving the (official) economic and state systems unchecked. The feminist movement, on the other hand, represents something of an anomaly. It alone is "offensive," aiming to "conquer new territory," and it alone retains links to historic liberation movements. In principle, then, feminism remains rooted in "universalist morality." Yet it is linked to resistance movements by an element of "particularism." And it tends, at times, to "retreat" into identities and communities organized around the natural category of biological sex.[25]

Now what are the critical insights and blind spots of this account of the dynamics of welfare state capitalism? To what extent does it serve the self-clarification of the struggles and wishes of contemporary women? I shall take up the six theses one by one.

1 Habermas's first thesis is straightforward and unobjectionable. Clearly, the welfare state does engage in crisis management and does partially overcome the separation of public and private at the level of systems.

2 Habermas's second thesis contains some important insights. Clearly, welfare state capitalism does inflate the consumer role and deflate the citizen role, reducing the latter essentially to voting – and, we should add, also to soldiering. Moreover, the welfare state does increasingly position its subjects as clients. On the other hand, Habermas again fails to see the gender subtext of these developments. He overlooks that it is overwhelmingly women who are the clients of the welfare state: especially older women, poor women, single women with children. He overlooks, in addition, that many welfare systems are internally gendered. They include two basic kinds of programs: "masculine" ones tied to primary labor-force participation and designed to benefit principal breadwinners; and "feminine" ones oriented to "defective" households, that is, to families without a male breadwinner. Clients of feminine programs, virtually exclusively women and their children, are positioned in a distinctive, feminizing fashion as the "negatives of possessive individuals"; they are largely excluded from the market both as workers and as consumers and are often stigmatized, denied rights, subjected to surveillance and administrative harassment.[26] But this means that the rise of the client role in welfare state capitalism has a more complex meaning than Habermas allows. It is not only a change in the link between system and lifeworld institutions. It is also a change in the character of male dominance, a shift, in Carol Brown's phrase, "from private patriarchy to public patriarchy."[27]

3 This gives a rather different twist to the meaning of Habermas's

third thesis. It suggests that he is right about the "ambivalence" of welfare state capitalism, but not quite in the way he thought. Welfare measures do have a positive side insofar as they reduce women's dependence on an individual male breadwinner. But they also have a negative side insofar as they substitute dependence on a patriarchal and androcentric state bureaucracy. The benefits provided are, as Habermas says, "system-conforming" ones. But the system they conform to is not simply the system of the official, state-regulated capitalist economy. It is also the system of male dominance, which extends even to the lifeworld. The ambivalence, then, does not only stem, as Habermas implies, from the fact that the role of client carries effects of "reification." It stems also from the fact that this role perpetuates in a new "modernized" form women's subordination. Or so Habermas's third thesis might be rewritten in a feminist critical theory – without, of course, abandoning his insights into the ways in which welfare bureaucracies and therapeutocracies disempower clients by pre-empting their capacities to interpret their own needs, experiences, and life problems.

4 Habermas's fourth thesis, by contrast, is not so easily rewritten. This thesis states that welfare reforms of, for example, the domestic sphere are more ambivalent than reforms of the paid workplace. This is true empiric-ally in the sense I have just described. But it is due to the patriarchal character of welfare systems, not to the inherently symbolic character of lifeworld institutions, as Habermas claims. His claim depends on two assumptions I have already challenged. First, it depends on the natural kinds interpretation of the distinction between symbolic reproduction activities and material reproduction activities, on the false assumption that childrearing is inherently more symbolic and less material than other work. Second, it depends on the absolute differences interpretation of the system-integrated versus socially integrated contexts distinction, on the false assumption that money and power are not already entrenched in the internal dynamics of the family. But once we repudiate these assumptions, then there is no categorial, as opposed to empirical, basis for differentially evaluating the two kinds of reforms. If it is basically progressive that paid workers acquire the means to confront their employers strategically and match power against power, right against right, then it must be just as progressive *in principle* that women acquire similar means to similar ends in the politics of familial and personal life. Likewise, if it is "pathological" that, in the course of achieving a better balance of power in familial and personal life, women become clients of state bureaucracies, then it must be just as "pathological" *in principle* that paid workers, too, become clients – which does not alter the fact that *in actuality* they become two different sorts of clients. But of course the real point is that the term "pathological"

is misused here insofar as it supposes that childrearing differs categorially from other work.

5 This sheds new light as well on Habermas's fifth thesis concerning the "inner colonization of the lifeworld." This thesis depends on three assumptions, two of which have just been rejected: the natural kinds interpretation of the distinction between symbolic and material reproduction activities, and the assumed virginity of the domestic sphere with respect to money and power. The third assumption is that the basic vector of motion in late capitalist society is from state-regulated economy to lifeworld and not vice versa. But the feminine gender subtext of the client role contradicts this assumption. It suggests that even in late capitalism gender norms continue to channel the influence of the lifeworld on to systems. These norms continue to structure the state-regulated economy, as the persistence, indeed exacerbation, of labor-force segmentation according to sex shows.[28] And they also structure state administration, as the gender segmentation of US and European social welfare systems shows.[29] Thus, it is not the case that in late capitalism "system intrusions" detach life contexts from "value-orientations *per se*." On the contrary, welfare capitalism simply uses other means to uphold the familiar "normatively secured consensus" concerning male dominance and female subordination. But Habermas's theory overlooks this and so it posits the evil of welfare state capitalism as the evil of a general and indiscriminate reification. It fails to account for the fact that it is disproportionately women who suffer the effects of bureaucratization and monetarization and for the fact that bureaucratization and monetarization are instruments of women's subordination.

6 This entails the revision, as well, of Habermas's sixth thesis concerning new social movements in late capitalist societies. He explains these movements as responses to colonization, that is, to the intrusion of system-integration mechanisms into symbolic reproduction spheres and to the consequent erosion and desiccation of contexts of interpretation and communication. But given the multidirectionality of causal influence in welfare state capitalism, the terms "colonization," "intrusion," "erosion," and "desiccation" are too negative and onesided to account for the identity shifts manifest in social movements. Let me attempt an alternative explanation, at least for women, by invoking the experience of millions of women, especially married women and women with children, who have in the postwar period become paid workers and/or social welfare clients. Granted, this has been an experience of new, acute forms of domination. But it has also been an experience in which many women could, often for the first time, taste the possibility of a measure of relative economic independence, an identity outside the domestic sphere, and expanded

political participation. Above all, it has been an experience of conflict and contradiction as women try to juggle the mutually incompatible roles of childrearer and worker, client and citizen. This experience of role conflict has been painful and identity-threatening, but not simply negative. Interpellated simultaneously in contradictory ways, women have become split subjects; and, as a result, the roles themselves, previously shielded in their separate spheres, have suddenly been opened to contestation. Should we, like Habermas, speak here of a "crisis in symbolic reproduction"? Surely not, if this means the desiccation of meaning and values wrought by the intrusion of money and organizational power into women's lives. Emphatically yes, if it means, rather, an opening on to new possibilities that cannot be realized within the established framework of gendered roles and institutions.

If colonization is not an adequate explanation of contemporary feminism, then decolonization cannot be an adequate conception of an emancipatory solution. The first element of decolonization, the removal of system-integration mechanisms from symbolic reproduction spheres, is conceptually and empirically askew of the real issues. If the real point is the moral superiority of cooperative and egalitarian interactions over strategic and hierarchical ones, then it mystifies matters to single out lifeworld institutions – the point should hold for paid work and political administration as well as for domestic life. Similarly, the third element of decolonization, namely, the reversal of the direction of influence and control from system to lifeworld, needs modification. Since the social meanings of gender still structure late-capitalist official economic and state systems, the question is not *whether* lifeworld norms will be decisive but, rather, *which* lifeworld norms will.

What, then, of the remaining element of decolonization, the replacement of normatively secured contexts of interaction by communicatively achieved ones? Something like this is occurring now as feminists criticize traditional gender norms embedded in legal, government, and corporate policy. It is also occurring as feminists and antifeminists clash over the social meanings of "femininity" and "masculinity," the interpretation of women's needs, and the social construction of women's bodies. In these cases, the political stake is hegemony over what I call the "means of interpretation and communication." Feminists are struggling to redistribute access to and control over these sociocultural discursive resources. We are, therefore, struggling for women's autonomy in the following special sense: a measure of collective control over the means of interpretation and communication sufficient to permit us to participate on a par with men in all types of social interaction, including political deliberation and decision-making.[30]

This suggests that a caution is in order concerning the use of the terms "particularism" and "universalism." Recall that Habermas emphasized feminism's links to historic liberation movements and its roots in universalist morality. Recall that he was critical of those tendencies within feminism, and in resistance movements in general, that retreat from political struggle into particularistic countercommunities defined, for example, by biological sex. Now I want to suggest that there are really three issues here and that they need to be disentangled from one another. One is the issue of political engagement versus apolitical countercultural activity. Insofar as Habermas's point is a criticism of separatist cultural feminism, it is well taken in principle, although it needs the following qualifications: cultural separatism, while inadequate as long-term political strategy, is in many cases a shorter-term necessity for women's physical, psychological, and moral survival; and separatist communities have been the source of many politically fruitful reinterpretations of women's experience. The second issue is the status of women's biology in the elaboration of new social identities. Insofar as Habermas's point is a criticism of reductive biologism, it is well taken. But this does not mean that one can ignore the fact that women's biology has nearly always been interpreted by men; and that women's struggle for autonomy necessarily and properly involves, among other things, the reinterpretation of the social meanings of our bodies. The third issue is the difficult and complex one of universalism versus particularism. Insofar as Habermas's endorsement of universalism pertains to the metalevel of access to and control over the means of interpretation and communication, it is well taken. At this level, women's struggle for autonomy can be understood in terms of a universalist conception of distributive justice. But it does not follow that the substantive content that is the fruit of this struggle, namely, the new social meanings we give our needs and our bodies, our new social identities and conceptions of femininity, can be dismissed as particularistic lapses from universalism. These, certainly, are no more particular than the sexist and androcentric meanings and norms they are meant to replace. More generally, at the level of substantive content, as opposed to dialogical form, the contrast between universalism and particularism is out of place. Substantive social meanings and norms are always necessarily culturally and historically specific; they always express distinctive shared but nonuniversal forms of life. Feminist meanings and norms will be no exception, but they will not, on that account, be particularistic in any pejorative sense. Let us simply say that they will be different.

Now what is the relation between feminist struggles over the means of interpretation and communication and institutional change? Such struggles, I claim, are implicitly and explicitly raising the following questions. Should the roles of worker, childrearer, citizen, and client be fully degendered? Can they be? Or do we, rather, require arrangements that permit women to be workers and citizens *as women*, just as men have always been workers and citizens *as men*? And what might that mean? In any case, how should the character and position of paid work, childrearing, and citizenship be defined *vis-à-vis* one another? Should democratic, socialist-feminist, self-managed paid work encompass childrearing? Or should childrearing, rather, replace soldiering as a component of transformed, democratic, socialist-feminist, participatory citizenship? What other possibilities are conceivable?

Let me conclude this discussion of the six theses by restating the most important critical points. First, Habermas's account fails to theorize the patriarchal, norm-mediated character of late-capitalist official-economic and administrative systems. Likewise, it fails to theorize the systemic, money- and power-mediated character of male dominance in the domestic sphere of the late-capitalist lifeworld. Consequently, his colonization thesis fails to grasp that the channels of influence between these institutions are multidirectional. And it tends to replicate, rather than to problematize, a major institutional support of women's subordination in late capitalism, namely, the gender-based separation of both the masculine public sphere and the state-regulated economy of sex-segmented paid work and social welfare from privatized female childrearing. Thus, while Habermas wants to be critical of male dominance, his diagnostic categories deflect attention elsewhere, to the allegedly overriding problem of gender-neutral reification. Finally, Habermas's categories tend to misrepresent the causes and underestimate the scope of the feminist challenge to welfare state capitalism. In short, the struggles and wishes of contemporary women are not adequately clarified by a theory that draws the basic battle line between system and lifeworld institutions. From a feminist perspective, there is a more basic battle line between the forms of male dominance linking "system" to "lifeworld" *and us*.

Conclusion

In general, then, the principal blindspots of Habermas's theory with respect to gender are traceable to his categorial opposition between system and lifeworld institutions. And to the two more elementary oppositions from which it is compounded, the reproduction one and the action contexts one. Or, rather, the blindspots are traceable to the way in which these oppositions, ideologically and androcentrically interpreted, tend to override and eclipse other, potentially more critical elements of Habermas's framework – elements like the distinction between normatively secured and communicatively achieved action contexts, and like the four-term model of public/private relations.

Habermas's blindspots are instructive, I think. They permit us to conclude something about what the categorial framework of a socialist-feminist critical theory of welfare state capitalism should look like. One crucial requirement is that this framework not be such as to put the male-headed nuclear family and the state-regulated official economy on two opposite sides of the major categorial divide. We require, rather, a framework sensitive to the similarities between them, since both appropriate our labor, short-circuit our participation in the interpretation of our needs, and shield normatively secured need interpretations from political contestation. A second crucial requirement is that this framework contain no a priori assumptions about the unidirectionality of social motion and causal influence, that it be sensitive to the ways in which allegedly disappearing institutions and norms persist in structuring social reality. A third crucial requirement, and the last I shall mention here, is that this framework not be such as to posit the evil of welfare state capitalism exclusively or primarily as the evil of reification. It must, rather, be capable of foregrounding the evil of dominance and subordination.[31]

Notes

I am grateful to John Brenkman, Thomas McCarthy, Carole Pateman and Martin Schwab for helpful comments and criticism; to Dee Marquez and Marina Rosiene for crackerjack word processing; and to the Stanford Humanities Center for financial support.

1 Karl Marx, "Letter to A. Ruge, September 1843" in *Karl Marx: Early Writings*, trans. Rodney Livingstone and Gregor Benton (New York: Vintage, 1975), p. 209.

2 Jürgen Habermas, *The Theory of Communicative Action*, vol. I, *Reason and the Rationalization of Society*, trans. Thomas McCarthy (Boston: Beacon Press, 1984). Hereafter, TCA I. Jürgen Habermas, *Theorie des kommunikativen Handelns*, vol. II, *Zur Kritik der funktionalistischen Vernunft* (Frankfurt am Main: Surhkamp Verlag, 1981). Hereafter TCA II. Both are also published in English by Polity Press.

3 TCA II, pp. 214, 217, 348–9; Habermas, *Legitimation Crisis*, trans. Thomas McCarthy (Boston: Beacon Press, 1975), pp. 8–9; Habermas, "A Reply to My Critics," in David Held and John B. Thompson, eds, *Habermas: Critical Debates* (Cambridge, Mass.: MIT Press, 1982), pp. 268, 278–9; Thomas McCarthy, "Translator's Introduction," TCA I, pp. xxv–xxvii; John B. Thompson, "Rationality and Social Rationalisation: An Assessment of Habermas's Theory of Communicative Action," *Sociology*, 17(2), 1983, pp. 278–94.

4 TCA II, p. 208; "A Reply to My Critics," pp. 223–5; McCarthy, "Translator's Introduction," pp. xxiv–xxv.

5 I am indebted to Martin Schwab for the expression "dual-aspect activity."

6 TCA I, pp. 85, 87–8, 101, 342, 357–60; TCA II, p. 179; *Legitimation Crisis*, pp. 4–5; "A Reply to My Critics," pp. 234, 237, 264–5; McCarthy, "Translator's Introduction", pp. ix, xxix–xxx.

7 TCA I, pp. 341, 357–9; TCA II, pp. 256, 266; McCarthy, "Translator's Introduction," p. xxx.

8 See Pierre Bourdieu, *Outline of a Theory of Practice*, trans. Richard Nice (New York: Cambridge University Press, 1977), and Arjun Appadurai, "Commodities and the Politics of Value," in *The Social Life of Things: Commodities in Cultural Perspective* ed. Arjun Appadurai (New York: Cambridge University Press, 1986).

9 TCA I, pp. 72, 341–2, 359–60; TCA II, p. 179; "A Reply to My Critics," pp. 268, 279–80; *Legitimation Crisis*, pp. 20–1; McCarthy, "Translator's Introduction," pp. xxviii–xxix; Thompson, "Rationality," pp. 285, 287. It should be noted that in TCA Habermas draws the contrast between system and lifeworld in two distinct senses. On the one hand, he contrasts them as two different methodological perspectives on the study of societies. The system perspective is objectivating and "externalist," while the lifeworld perspective is hermeneutical and "internalist." In principle, either can be applied to the study of any given set of societal phenomena. Habermas argues that neither alone is adequate. So he seeks to develop a methodology that combines both. On the other hand, Habermas also contrasts system and lifeworld in another way, namely, as two different kinds of institutions. It is this second system/lifeworld contrast that I am concerned with here. I do not explicitly treat the first one in this essay. I am sympathetic to Habermas's general methodological intention of combining or linking structural (in the sense of objectivating) and interpretive approaches to the study of societies. I do not, however, believe that this can be done by assigning structural properties to one set of institutions (the official economy and the state) and interpretive ones to another set (the family and the "public sphere"). I maintain, rather, that all of these institutions have both structural and interpretive dimensions and that all should be studied both structurally and hermeneutically. I have tried to develop an approch that meets these aims in "Women, Welfare and the Politics of Need Interpretation," and "Struggle over Needs: Outline of a Socialist-Feminist Critical Theory of Late Capitalist Political Culture," both in Nancy Fraser, *Unruly Practices: Power, Discourse and Gender in Contemporary Social Theory* (Minneapolis: University of Minnesota Press; Cambridge: Polity, 1989).

10 See, for example, the essays in Barrie Thorne and Marilyn Yalom, eds, *Rethinking the Family: Some Feminist Questions* (New York and London: Longman, 1982). Also, Michele Barrett and Mary McIntosh, *The Anti-Social Family* (London: Verso, 1982).

11 TCA I, pp. 85–6, 88–90, 101, 104–5; TCA II, p. 179; McCarthy, "Translator's Introduction," pp. ix, xxx.

12 Pamela Fishman, "Interaction: The Work Women Do," *Social Problems*, 25(4), 1978, pp. 397–406.

13 TCA II, pp. 523–4, 547; "A Reply to My Critics," p. 237; Thompson, "Rationality," pp. 288, 292.

14 TCA I, pp. 341–2, 359–60; TCA II, pp. 256, 473; "A Reply to My Critics,"

p. 280; McCarthy, "Translator's Introduction," p. xxxii; Thompson, "Rationality," pp. 286–8.

15 Carole Pateman, "The Personal and the Political: Can Citizenship be Democratic?", lecture 3 of her "Women and Democratic Citizenship," The Jefferson Memorial Lectures, delivered at the University of California, Berkeley, February 1985, unpublished typescript.

16 Ibid., p. 5.

17 Ibid., p. 8.

18 Judith Hicks Stiehm, "The Protected, the Protector, the Defender," in *Women and Men's Wars*, ed. Judith Hicks Stiehm (New York: Pergamon, 1983). This is not to say, however, that I accept Stiehm's conclusions about the desirability of integrating women fully into the US military as presently structured and deployed.

19 TCA II, pp. 505ff; *Legitimation Crisis*, pp. 33–6, 53–5; McCarthy, "Translator's Introduction," p. xxxiii.

20 TCA II, pp. 522–4; *Legitimation Crisis*, pp. 36–7, McCarthy, "Translator's Introduction," p. xxxiii.

21 TCA II, pp. 530–40; McCarthy, "Translator's Introduction," pp. xxxiii–xxxiv.

22 TCA II, pp. 540–7; McCarthy, "Translator's Introduction," p. xxxi.

23 TCA II, pp. 275–7, 452, 480, 522–4; "A Reply to My Critics," pp. 226, 280–1; Habermas, introduction to *Observations on "The Spiritual Situation of the Age": Contemporary German Perspectives*, ed. Jürgen Habermas, trans. Andrew Buchwalter (Cambridge, Mass.: MIT Press, 1984), pp. 11–12, 16–20; McCarthy, "Translator's Introduction," pp. xxxi–xxxii; Thompson, "Rationality," pp. 286, 288.

24 TCA II, pp. 581–3; *Observations*, pp. 18–19, 27–8.

25 TCA II, pp. 581–3; *Observations*, pp. 16–17, 27–8.

26 For the US social welfare system, see the analysis of male versus female participation rates, and the account of the gendered character of the two subsystems in Fraser, "Women, Welfare and the Politics of Need Interpretation"; Barbara J. Nelson, "Women's Poverty and Women's Citizenship: Some Political Consequences of Economic Marginality," *Signs: Journal of Women in Culture and Society*, 10(2), 1985; Steven P. Erie, Martin Rein and Barbara Wiget, "Women and the Reagan Revolution: Thermidor for the Social Welfare Economy," in *Families, Politics and Public Policies: A Feminist Dialogue on Women and the State*, ed. Irene Diamond (New York: Longman, 1983); Diana Pearce, "Women, Work and Welfare: The Feminization of Poverty", in *Working Women and Families* ed. Karen Wolk Feinstein (Beverly Hills: Sage, 1979), and "Toil and Trouble: Women Workers and Unemployment Compensation," *Signs*, 10(3), 1985, pp. 439–59; Barbara Ehrenreich and Frances Fox Piven, "The Feminization of Poverty," *Dissent*, spring 1984, pp. 162–70. For an analysis of the gendered character of the British social welfare system, see Hilary Land, "Who Cares for the Family?" *Journal of Social Policy*, 7(3), 1978, pp. 257–84. For Norway, see the essays in Harriet Holter, ed., *Patriarchy in a Welfare Society* (Oslo: Universitetsforlaget, 1984). See also two comparative studies: Mary Ruggie, *The State and Working Women: A Comparative Study of Britain and Sweden* (Princeton, NJ: Princeton University Press, 1984); and Birte Siim "Women and the Welfare State:

Between Private and Public Dependence," unpublished typescript circulated at Stanford University, 1985.

27 Carol Brown, "Mothers, Fathers and Children: From Private to Public Patriarchy," in *Women and Revolution*, ed. Lydia Sargent (Boston: South End Press, 1981). Actually, I believe Brown's formulation is theoretically inadequate, since it presupposes a simple dualistic conception of public and private. Nonetheless, the phrase "from private to public patriarchy" evokes in a rough but suggestive way the phenomena a socialist-feminist critical theory of the welfare state would need to account for.

28 The most recent available data for the US indicate that sex segmentation in paid work is increasing, not decreasing. See Drew Christie, "Comparable Worth and Distributive Justice," paper read at meeting of the American Philosophical Association, Western Division, April 1985.

29 See note 26 above.

30 I develop this notion of the "sociocultural means of interpretation and communication" and the associated conception of autonomy in "Toward a Discourse Ethic of Solidarity," *Praxis International*, 5(4), January 1986, pp. 425–9, and in "Struggle over Needs." Both notions are extensions and modifications of Habermas's conception of "communicative ethics."

31 My own recent work attempts to construct a conceptual framework for a socialist-feminist critical theory of the welfare state which meets these requirements. See "Women, Welfare and the Politics of Need Interpretation," "Toward a Discourse Ethic of Solidarity" and "Struggle over Needs." Each of these essays draws on those aspects of Habermas's thought that I take to be unambiguously positive and useful, especially his conception of the irreducibly sociocultural, interpretive character of human needs, and his contrast between dialogical and monological processes of need interpretation. The present paper, on the other hand, focuses mainly on those aspects of Habermas's thought that I find problematical or unhelpful, and so does not convey the full range either of his work or of my views about it. Readers are warned, therefore, against drawing the conclusion that Habermas has little or nothing positive to contribute to a socialist-feminist critical theory of the welfare state. They are urged, rather, to consult the essays cited above for the other side of the story.

Index

action
  plurality and, 243–4, 246–50
  work and labor, 6, 233–42
adultery, 167, 170
ambivalence
  gender theory, 147–9, 151
  of welfare state capitalism, 265,
    268
androcentrism, 218, 242, 262, 268
androgyny, 27, 140, 141, 173
animal nature, 200, 201
Arendt, Hannah, 2, 6, 8, 232
  feminist theory, 243–50
  The Human Condition, 232–4,
    237–42, 245–50
  work, labor and action, 233–42
Aristotle, 3, 4, 134, 171, 172, 205,
    232, 239
  Ethics, 49
  family and political stability,
    40–50
  The Generation of Animals, 34
  hierarchy and limits of observa-
    tion, 35–40
  Politics, 35–7, 40, 45, 47, 49
  Rhetoric, 42
  teleology and nature, 32–5
authority, 38–9, 40

conjugal, 89
illegitimate, 117–18
military, 42
monarchical, 74, 75–8, 80, 82, 83
patriarchal, *see* patriarchy
political, 41–2
private sphere, 112–13
autonomy, 106, 270, 271
  moral, 101, 108, 127

biblical history, 75–7, 81–3, 88
biological approach, 98, 101, 207–8
biological differences, 201–2
biological process, 234, 236, 240
biological survival, 255
biosocial relationship, 157, 158
Blackstone, Sir William, 67, 167
body
  Aristotelian tradition, 35, 40, 43,
    50
  consciousness and, 119–20, 127,
    207–9, 245
  contract theory, 68–9
  politics of, 248–9
  sexual neutrality, 8–9, 114,
    121–4, 126–7
  soul and, 12, 35, 50

bourgeois individualism, 105
bureaucratization, 269

capitalism, 96, 151, 157, 175
    classical, 260–4
    welfare state, 264–72
Cartesian dualism, 114, 119
censorship, 229
childrearing, 254–5, 258–9, 261–4,
    268–9, 270, 271–2
children
    moral development, 188–90
    –mother relationship, 54, 105
    ownership of, 21, 22, 23
    –parent relationship, 84, 88,
        99–100
choice, 33–4, 38–9, 53, 169
citizenship, 2, 4–7, 10, 19, 249, 250
    freedom of, 232, 238–9, 241–4,
        246–8
    gender subtext, 260, 262–4
    justice and, 185, 186
    political stability, 45, 47, 50
    second-class, 9, 12, 13, 23, 25–6
    welfare state capitalism, 265–7,
        272
civic loyalty, 16, 18
civil freedom, 59
civil laws, 66–8, 121
civil society
    Lockean, 86–7
    patriarchy and, 56, 59, 61–2,
        66–7, 69–70
    Rousseau's critical analysis, 96,
        99, 100, 102–3, 104–6, 107
civil state, legitimate, 104–6
Clarke, Lorenne, 2
class
    difference, 121, 192, 194, 203–7
    relations, 159
    structure, 176
    struggle, 266
    see also middle class; working class

client role, 260, 267, 269–72
Code Civil (France), 136, 137
coercion, 60, 168, 169, 257, 258
cognitive structure, 151
colonization thesis, 265–6, 269–70,
    272
communal ownership, 12, 13–14,
    15, 23
communal societies, 108, 109
'communication theory' of power,
    249
communism, 151, 154, 156, 157
    of property, 23, 43, 46
concubinages, 141
conjugal rights, 55–8, 66–7, 69, 70,
    84–90
conjugal society, 84–6
consensus, 256, 258, 259
consent theory, 74, 79, 86–8,
    168–9, 172
consumer role, 260, 261, 265–7,
    270–2
Contagious Diseases Acts, 169
contract theorists, 55, 59
    Filmer and, 77–81
contract theory, 85, 104
    state of nature and, 59–62,
        66–70
coverture, law of, 24, 67–8, 166–7
crisis management, 265, 267
critical theory (Habermas), 2, 253
    classical capitalism, 260–4
    social-theoretical framework,
        254–9
    welfare state capitalism, 264–72
cultural separatism, 271
culture, 147–8
    natural base, 123, 133
custom, 105, 183, 190, 195

de Beauvoir, Simone, 9, 114
    creation of women, 194, 207–9
    differences among women, 203–7

living/existing, 199, 200–2
privilege, 211–13
real and ideal woman, 209–11
The Second Sex, 2, 199, 206–7
woman's situation, 213–14
democratic feminism, 97, 107–9
dialectics, 151, 152, 154, 158
dialogic orientation, 152
difference, poitics of, 9, 217–18,
    226–9
disciplinary power, 221, 222
discourse of empowerment, 130–1
division of labor
    household, 164, 174, 177, 192
    political, 8
    sexual,100, 108, 121–2, 133, 152,
        174–5, 186, 237, 261
divorce, 75, 85, 136, 169, 170
domination, 158,172, 203, 253–4,
    258
    in marriage, 36–7, 40, 64, 165–9,
        171, 174–5
'doubled vision' of feminist theory,
    130, 131
duties,16, 121
    justice and, 184, 186
    rights and, 116, 118, 120, 122

education, 116–17
    Locke's thoughts, 90–2
    of women, 7, 21–3, 26, 27, 42,
        166
emotion, 18, 38–9
Enlightenment, 7, 112–13, 116,
    119, 123, 130, 138, 140, 142,
    148, 156
epistemology, 150, 152, 158, 233,
    244, 247, 249
    materialist, 104
equal opportunities, 18–19, 24–6,
    164–5, 169, 174–5, 177
    justice and, 184, 185
equality

in community of women, 42–5
fear of, 169–72
female in the polity, 45–50
legal, 169–70, 174, 191
marital friendship and, 173–5
political, 113–14, 126–7
political society, 89–90
ethics, 126, 127, 173–4, 182
existence, living and, 199, 200–2
existentialism, 210, 236

fabrication process, 6, 235
'false differentiation', 149, 150
family
    abolition, 14–24 *passim*, 27
    Hobbesian, 5, 62–6
    justice in, 185–90, 195
    nuclear, 151, 254, 256–9, 260,
        263, 273
    patriarchal, *see* patriarchy
    political life and, 135–7
    political stability and, 40–50
    women and (Plato), 4, 11–28
    see also children; marriage
family wage, 261
father-right, 54–5, 56, 57–9
fatherhood, 56, 57, 59–61, 153
feelings, 188–9
    –reason dichotomy, 112, 114–16,
        124–5
female
    consciousness, 119–20
    in the polity, 45–50
    power (problem of), 102–3
feminism
    democratic, 97, 107–9
    Foucault and, 226–9
    liberal roots, *see* Locke, John
    political theory and, 1–10
    radical, 218–19, 226–8, 229
    Rawls's theory of justice, 190–6
feminism, modern (Rousseau),
    95–6

feminism, modern (Rousseau)
(*cont.*):
democratic feminism, 107–9
good society, 103–6
nature of the sexes, 106–7
problem of female power, 102–3
sexual inequality, 97–101
feminist approach to history of
philosophy, 129–32
feminist critique (welfare state
capitalism), 264–72
feminist debates on patriarchy,
53–4
feminist discourse of empowerment,
130–1
feminist interrogation, 254–9
feminist politics, Arendt and,
232–50
feminist theory (and public realm),
243–50
femininity, 3, 262
ideal woman, 209–11
Marxist gender theory, 148–9
maternal, 149, 150, 151
social meaning of, 270, 271
feudalism, 136, 137
Filmer, Sir Robert
classic patriarchy, 53, 56–9, 69
contract theorists and, 77–81
statement of patriarchy, 74–7
Foucault, Michel, 2, 9
critique of revolutionary theory,
219–26
Discipline and Punish, 223
feminism and, 226–9
The History of Sexuality, 221, 223
theories of difference, 217–18
fraternity, 182
free choice, 169
free love, 124
sexuality and, 137–43
freedom, 133, 154, 159
of citizenship, 232, 238–9,

241–4, 246–8
of mankind, 59
for women (Sparta), 41–2
see also civil freedom; natural
freedom
French Revolution, 7, 136, 137,
138, 140
friendship, 116, 125, 126, 188
in marriage, 6, 45–6, 164–5,
172–7
functionalism, 38, 222

Geist, 132–3, 134
gender
blindness, 233, 242, 262, 263
critical theory and, 253–73
identity, 148–50, 157
justice and, 181–3, 186–96
neutrality, 8–9, 114, 121–4,
126–7, 182, 272
subtext, 6, 260–4, 267, 269
theory (Marx), 147–50
gender relations
de Beauvoir, 213
Hegel, 131, 132, 139, 140, 142
genealogy (form of resistance),
224–6
general will, 103, 104
Genesis, Book of, 57–8, 75–7, 81–
3, 88, 90, 166–7
Gestalt, 130
God, 82, 85, 97
good society, 101, 102, 108
foundation of, 103–6

Habermas, Jürgen, 2, 253, 273
classical capitalism, 260–4
social-theoretical framework,
254–9
The Theory of Communicative Action,
253
welfare state capitalism, 264–72
happines, 12, 50

Hartsock, Nancy, 152, 158, 233, 244, 249
Hegel, G. W. F., 7, 205
  feminist approach to history of philosophy, 129–32
  free love and sexuality, 137–43
  Phenomenology of Mind, 171
  Phenomenology of Spirit, 141–3
  Philosophy of History, 135
  Philosophy of Right, 133–5, 137
  women (in political thought), 132–7
hierarchy, 35–40
Hobbes, Thomas, 5, 107
  contract theory, 66–9
  De Cive, 63
  Elements of Law, 63
  family, 62–6
  Filmer's classic patriarchy, 56–9
  Leviathan, 63–4, 68, 69–70
  modern patriarchy, 69–70
  patriarchy theory, 53–6
  state of nature, 59–62
household
  division of labor, 164, 174, 177, 192
  head of, 183, 185–6
  income, 186
Human Condition, The (Arendt), 232–4, 237–42, 245–50
human nature, 5–6, 12, 17–18, 22, 74, 78, 107, 116, 156
humanism, 220, 226
humanity, nature and, 154–5, 158, 159
humanization of nature, 154

ideal city, 12–14, 19, 49–50
ideal state, 11, 12, 13, 14, 16–19
identity formation, 148–50
individualism, 59, 81, 83, 97, 107, 150
  bourgeois, 105

liberal, 6, 165
radical, 53, 70
individuality, 132, 136, 236
individualization, 221–2
individuation, 148, 149, 194
inequality, sexual, 95, 97–101
inferiority, 34–7, 82–3, 108, 120
inheritance, 23, 24, 85, 105, 136
instrumentalism, 236, 237
intergenerational links, 182–5, 188
irony/ironic dialectic, 7, 142–3

Jacobin Club, 139
'Jena circle', 139
just savings principle, 183, 185, 188
justice
  in families, 185–7, 188–90, 195
  moral development, 188–90
  Rawls's principles, 184–5
  Rawls's theories, 181–4, 190–6

Kant, Immanuel, 135, 182, 188–9
kinship, 18, 59
knowledge, 150, 224

labor
  action and work, 6, 233–42, 248
  post-embeddedness, 152–8, 159
legal equality, 169–70, 174, 191
legal personality, 166–7
legal system/rights, 135–6
leisure, 4, 39–40, 48–9, 184
liberal individualism, 6, 165
liberal paradigm, 122, 123, 126–7
liberalism, 6, 74, 81, 91, 177
libertarian feminism, 226–7, 228
life process, 234–5, 236, 237, 240, 244
lifeworld, 257, 260
  colonization of, 265–6, 269–70, 272
  decolonization of, 266–7, 270

Locke, John, 2, 5–6, 74
    Filmer and contract theorists,
        77–81
    First Treatise, 81–2, 84
    patriarchy attacked, 77, 81–4
    rational woman, 90–2
    Second Treatise, 84–90
    social relations, 84–90
    statement of patriarchy (Filmer),
        75–7
    Thoughts on Education, 90
logic of oppositions, 132, 133
logocentric reason, 248
logos, 33, 38, 48, 249
Lorde, Audre, 218, 219, 226
love, 16, 46
    female power (problem of),
        102–3
    free, 124, 137–43
    justice and, 188, 189
    labor of, 153, 158
    patriotic, 104–5
    of self, 12, 43, 44

mainstream theory, 1, 3, 130
male
    domination, 253–4, 258
    domination in marriage, 36–7,
        40, 64, 165–9, 171
    superiority, 4, 133–5, 171–2,
        204, 232
    see also father-right; fatherhood;
        manhood; masculinity;
        paternity; patriarchy
'male-stream' theories, 232, 233,
    238, 246
manhood, 3, 5
marriage, 14, 16–17, 49
    conjugal rights, 55–8, 66–7,
        84–90
    contract, 136
    domination, 36–7, 40, 64, 165–9,
        171

fear of equality, 169–72
free choice of spouse, 136–7
friendship in, 45–6, 164–5,
    172–7
laws, 23–4, 60, 66–8
master–slave relationship, 36–7,
    40, 64, 165–9, 171, 176
rape in, 167–8, 262
in state of nature, 60
Married Women's Property Act,
    170
Married Women's Property Bills,
    167, 169
Marx, Karl, 8, 141
    Capital, 150, 153, 154
    *The Economic and Philosophical
        Manuscripts*, 154
    gender theory, 147–50
    The German Ideology, 152–3
    Marx's style, 150–52
    post-embeddedness, 152–9
Marxism, 146–7, 218–22, 264
masculine right, 54
masculinity
    critical theory, 261, 262, 270
    critique of, 147–50
    post-embeddedness, 157–9
master–servant relationship, 64–5
master–slave relationship, 39
    in marriage, 36–7, 40, 64, 165–9,
        171, 176
material reproduction, 254–5, 259,
    268, 269
materialism, 152, 153
materialist epistemology, 104
maternal
    femininity, 149, 150, 151
    labor, 155–6, 157–8, 159
    power, 59
    right, 66
matriarchy, 61
matrimonial law, 23–4, 60,
    66–8

men
  rights of, 4–5, 115–16
  see also father-right; fatherhood;
    male; manhood; masculinity;
    paternal *entries*; paternity;
    patriarchy
middle class, 165–6, 199, 203–4,
  211–13, 214
military service, 26–7, 41–2
Mill, John Stuart, 2, 3, 6, 154
  fear of equality, 169–72
  friendship in marriage, 172–7
  master–slave, 165–9
  On Liberty, 173–4
  Principles of Political Economy, 166
  The Subjection of Women, 164–5,
    167, 168–70, 172, 175, 177
misogyny, 2, 8, 50, 147, 157
modernization, 258, 259
monarchy, 74, 75–7, 78, 80, 82, 83
money, 12
  power and, 268, 269, 272
monogamy, 24, 27, 85, 101, 133,
  136, 137, 184, 185
Montaigne, 172, 176
moral autonomy, 101, 108, 127
moral development, 182, 185,
  188–90, 193–4, 195
moral goodness, 12
moral virtue, 173
morality, 117, 127
morality of association, 188
mother–child relationship, 54, 105
motherhood, 7–8, 19–22, 26, 61–2,
  105, 125, 153, 244, 248
mother-right, 54, 56, 59, 61–3, 65,
  68, 70
mutuality, 169, 172, 177

natality, 233, 235
natural compassion, 98, 99, 106
natural condition, 59–62
  contract theory and, 66–9

family in, 62–6
state of nature, 59–62
natural freedom, 56–7, 59, 65, 77,
  79–81, 88, 90
natural inequality, 133
natural man, 77, 123
natural power, 87
natural rights, 113–16
nature
  domination of, 157, 158
  hierarchy and, 35–9
  humanity and, 154–5, 158, 159
  necessity and, 154, 155, 159
  of the sexes, 106–7
  teleology and, 32–5
  of women, 11, 28, 95, 200
necessity, nature and, 154, 155, 159
nuclear family, 151, 254, 256–9,
  260, 263, 273
nurture, 56, 80, 151, 153, 194, 196,
  244

obligation theory, 57, 80
O'Brien, Mary, 155, 157, 232–3,
  244–5, 248
Oedipus complex, 182
oligarchy, 36, 47
oppression, 115, 123, 125, 146, 176,
  205, 228
  political, 113, 114, 246
  privilege and, 211–13
  racial, 201–2, 206–7, 208–9
  sexist, 199, 203, 206–7
  social, 114
other/otherness, 7, 143, 150, 202,
  207, 209, 247, 249

parent–child relationship, 84, 88,
  99–100
particularism, 14, 43, 133, 134, 135,
  267, 271
passion, 8, 118–20, 126–7
  –reason dichotomy, 116, 117,
    123–5, 249

paternal power, 53–4, 57, 69, 85–7, 89

paternal right, 54, 56, 57, 59, 66

paternal rule, 56–7

paternalism, justice and, 185

paternity, 100
  certainty of, 104, 105–6

pathological approach, 259, 268–9

patriarchal household, 47

patriarchal power, 238–9

patriarchal rule, 5

patriarchal state, 246

patriarchal world view, 74

patriarchy, 4, 135, 153, 238
  classic, 56–9, 69
  contract theory, 66–9
  family and, 62–6
  Hobbesian theory, 53–6
  Locke's attack, 81–4
  modern, 59, 66, 69–70
  state of nature and, 59–62
  statement of (Filmer), 74–7

'patrimonial kingdom', 63

patriotism, 104–5

philosophy, history of, 129–32

physis, 32, 36

Plato, 104, 134, 205
  Euthyphro, 16
  family (abolition), 15–21, 23–4
  Laws, 4, 11–12, 13–14, 16, 21–8
  property rights, 12–16, 20, 22, 23, 27–8
  Republic, 4, 11–16, 18–23, 25–8, 41, 42–5, 51
  women (role), 18–28

plurality, 233, 236
  action and, 243–4, 246–50

polis, 11, 16, 33, 40, 41, 135, 142
  female in the polity, 45–50

political emancipation, 245–6

political justice, 192

political life, family and, 135–7

political oppression, 113, 114, 246

political patriarchy, 135

political right, 54, 55, 56–9, 61–2, 64, 66–7

political society, 56, 88–90

political stability, family and, 40–50

political status, 112–18, 121–6

political thought, Hegel's, 132–7

polygamy, 133

pornography, 227, 229

post-embeddedness, 152–9

power, 258
  as collective action, 233, 236
  deliberative, 38–9
  disciplinary, 221, 222
  female (problem of), 102–3
  Foucault's model, 220–4, 227, 228
  juridico-discursive model, 219–20
  Lockean state of nature, 85–7, 89
  maternal, 59
  monarchical, 74–8, 80, 83
  money and, 268, 269, 272
  paternal, 53–4, 57, 69, 85–6, 87, 89
  patriarchal, 238–9
  in private sphere, 113
  resistance and, 223

private property, *see* property

private sphere, 3–4
  in classical capitalism, 260–4
  political status and, 112–13, 121–6
  see also family

private women, 14–15, 23, 26–8

privilege, middle-class, 211–13

process logic, 234–5, 236, 237

production, 154, 158

property, 108, 109, 136
  in conjugal society, 85, 86
  paternity and, 104, 105–6

Plato's view, 12–16, 20, 22–4, 27–8
protection/protective state, 68, 70, 127, 172, 262–3
protective confederations, 64–5, 66
public sphere, 3–4, 119, 171
  classical capitalism, 260–4
  feminist theory and, 241–50
  political status and, 112–13, 121–3, 125–6

quality of life, 122

race/racism, 201–2, 203, 204–7, 208–9
radical democracy, 6
radical feminism, 218–19, 226–8, 229
radical individualism, 53, 70
rape, marital, 167–8, 262
rational agent, 8–9, 114, 121–2
rational choice, 38, 53
rational egoism, 97, 98–9, 102–3, 104, 106, 107
rational women, 90–2
rationalism, 83
rationality, 249
Rawls, John, 2, 8
  justice in families, 185–90, 195
  moral development, 188–90
  principles of justice, 184–5
  theories of justice, 181–4, 190–6
  A Theory of Justice, 181–7, 188
reason, 113, 120, 121
  –feeling dichotomy, 112, 114–16, 124–5
  –passion dichotomy, 116, 117, 123–5, 249
  –speech, 33, 48–9
reciprocity, 189
  in marriage, 169, 172–3, 177
reductive biologism, 271
Reform Bill (1867), 165

reification, 266,268, 272, 273
religion, 105
  see also biblical history
Representation of the People Bill (1867), 167
representative thinking, 236, 249
reproduction, 6, 19–20, 84–5, 98, 117, 135
  Aristotelian tradition, 40, 46, 48–9
  epistemological level, 233, 244, 249
  generation, 34–5, 58–9, 61
  material, 254–5, 259, 268–9
  post-embeddedness, 153, 155
  procreative power, 58, 69
  symbolic, 254–5, 257–9, 265–6, 268–70
resistance
  Foucault's theory, 222, 223–4
  genealogy as form of, 224–6
revolutionary theory, 218, 219–26
Rich, Adrienne, 226, 232–3, 244, 248
rights
  conjugal, 55–8, 66–7, 69–70, 84–90
  duties and, 116, 118, 120, 122
  father-, 54–5, 56, 57–9
  maternal, 66
  of men, 4–5, 115–16
  mother-, 54, 56, 59, 61–3, 65, 68, 70
  natural, 113–14, 115, 116
  paternal, 54, 56–7, 59, 66
  property, *see* property
  sex-, 56, 57–8
  of women, 5, 116–23
Romantics, 140
Rousseau, Jean-Jacques, 2, 6–7
  Emile, 18–19, 96–8, 101, 103–4, 105, 118–19, 120, 123
  First Discourse, 95, 109

Rousseau, Jean-Jacques (*cont.*):
  Julie ou la nouvelle Héloise, 95, 103
  *Lettre à M. D'Alembert sur les spec-
    tacles*, 95–6, 101, 102
  On the Social Contract, 96
  Second Discourse, 95, 97, 99, 103
  see also feminism, modern
    (Rousseau)
ruling and ruled, 12, 15, 16, 18, 20,
  35–9, 46–7, 239

savings principle, 183, 185, 188
Schlegel, Caroline, 139–41, 143
scientific reasoning, 210
second-best cities, 12, 13, 21–6
second-class citizenship, 9, 12, 13,
  23, 25–6
self-conciousness, 134, 171
self-creation, 154–5, 156–7
self-development, 171
self-esteem, 192
self-expression, 135
self-interest, 36, 47, 60, 99, 104,
  165, 256
self-knowledge, 171
self-love, 12, 43, 44
self–other dynamic, 150
self-preservation, 97, 98, 106
self-realization, 130, 154
self-reflection, 132
self-respect, 192
self-worship, 171, 172
self-worth, 188
selfhood, 143, 149
selfishness, 13, 15, 172
sensuality, 116, 176
separation, 34, 86, 148, 172, 194
sex-right, 56, 57–8
sexes
  natural inequality, 133
  nature of, 106–7
  see also gender
sexism, 108, 182, 185, 199, 203,
  206–7
  institutionalized, 241, 243
sexual
  difference, 3–4, 5, 9, 217–18,
    226–9
  division of labour, *see main entry*
  neutrality, 8–9, 114, 121–4,
    126–7, 182, 272
  objectification, 227
  passion, *see* passion
sexual equality, 5
  democratic feminism, 107–9
  liberal paradigm, 126–7
sexual inequality, 95
  origins/foundations, 97–101
sexuality
  between men, 16–17
  between women, 199, 218
  Foucault's theory, 221, 223,
    226–9
  free love and, 137–43
  male, violence and, 98–9
  in marital friendship, 176
  subjectivity, 123
  Wollstonecraft and, 116, 124–6
slavery, 39, 205–6
  see also master–slave relationship
social change, 147–8, 175, 201, 208
social contract, 67, 70, 79, 124
  bogus, 106, 107
social control, 221
social inequality, 107
social institutionalization of sexual
  difference, 181–3, 186–96
social justice, 184, 185, 193
social labor, 254, 255, 259
social movements, 269–70
social relations, 107, 108, 109
  Marx on, 152, 156, 159
  rational egoism in, 97, 98–9
social rights, 265
social status, 112, 114–18, 120,
  122–3

socialism, 175
socialization, 28, 100, 104, 118, 125, 187, 191, 196, 254, 265
socially integrated action contexts, 255–9 *passim*, 269
sociopolitical context, 124, 125
Sophocles, 37, 141
soul, 12, 35, 39, 50
sovereignty, 63–4, 69
Sparta, 41–2
speech, 33, 48–9
spousal unity, 24, 67–8, 166–7
state, modern, 7, 133, 135
state of nature, 5, 54, 55
  contract theory, 59–62, 66–70
  family in, 62–6
  Lockean, 86–7
  Rousseau's, 98, 99–100, 106
Subjection of Women, The (Mill), 164–5, 167–70, 172, 175, 177
subjectivity, 132–3, 135, 136, 245
subordination (of women), 4, 38, 141, 147, 181, 206
  critical theory, 253–4, 259, 268, 269, 272
  human condition and, 238, 242–3, 245
  in marriage, 170, 174
substantiality, 133
suffrage, women's, 7, 164, 167, 169, 176
superiority (male), 4, 133–5, 171, 172, 204, 232
symbolic reproduction, 254–5, 257–9, 265–6, 268–70
sympathy, 165
system-integrated action contexts, 255–9, 265–6, 269, 270, 272

tacit consent, 79
teleology, nature and, 32–5
trade unions, 261, 265

'true women', 202, 207, 208
trust, 177, 188

unemployment, 261
unity, 14, 15, 20, 28, 46, 69, 134–5
  of love, 137
  spousal, 24, 67–8, 166–7
universalism, 271
universality, 133, 134, 135

violence, 98–9, 107–9 *passim*, 167
virtue, 12, 37, 39, 45, 100–1, 106–7
  justice and, 186–7
  passion and, 118–19, 120

wages, 166, 167, 186
war, 12, 50, 106, 107
wealth, 41, 50, 97, 184, 186
welfare state capitalism, 264–72, 273
Wollstonecraft, Mary, 7–8
  Enlightenment philosophers, 112–13
  equality, 113–14, 126–7
  Maria, 114, 123–7
  personal life, 114–15, 124–6
  reason–feeling dichotomy, 112, 114
  reason–passion dichotomy, 123–5
  rights of men, 115–16
  rights of women, 116–23
  A Vindication of the Rights of Men, 115–16
  A Vindication of the Rights of Woman, 2, 114, 116–18, 120–4, 127
women
  community of, 42–5
  creation of, 207–9
  differences among, 203–7
  domination of, *see* domination
  employment, 261, 263, 264
  family and, 4, 11–28

women (*cont.*):
  freedom for (Sparta), 41–2
  The Human Condition, 232–4,
    237–42, 245–50
  ideal, 209–11
  inferiority, 34–7, 82–3, 108, 120
  irony and, *see* Hegel, G. W. F.
  middle-class, 9, 211–13
  nature of, 11, 28, 95, 200
  and the problem of political
    stability, 40–50
  rational, 90–2
  real, 209–11
  role (Plato), 18–28
  role (Rousseau), 95
  subordination of, *see* subordina-
    tion (of women)
  see also female; feminism; mater-
    nal; mother-right; motherhood
work, 192
  labor and action, 6, 233–42,
    248
  see also labor
worker (role), 260–1, 265–6,
  268–72
working class, 166, 204, 206, 213,
  238